Texte und Studien zum Antiken Judentum

herausgegeben von
Martin Hengel und Peter Schäfer

16

The Faces of the Chariot

Early Jewish Responses to
Ezekiel's Vision

by

David J. Halperin

J. C. B. Mohr (Paul Siebeck) Tübingen 1988

CIP- Kurztitelaufnahme der Deutschen Bibliothek

Halperin, David J.:
The faces of the Chariot / by David J. Halperin. –
Tübingen: Mohr, 1988.
  (Texte und Studien zum antiken Judentum; 16)
  ISBN 3-16-145115-5
  ISSN 0721-8753

NE: GT

© 1988 by J. C. B. Mohr (Paul Siebeck), P.O. Box 2040, D-7400 Tübingen.

Typeset by Sam Boyd Enterprise in Singapore; printed by Gulde-Druck GmbH in Tübingen; bound by Heinrich Koch KG in Tübingen.

Printed in Germany.

To my Rose
whom I love so very much

Preface

This book has been a long time growing. The seed was first sown one spring afternoon in 1967, in a conversation I had with my teacher and undergraduate advisor at Cornell University, Isaac Rabinowitz. We had been discussing a theory advanced by an article in the campus newspaper, that a tragic recent incident of fire had been the result of a deranged arsonist's brooding on the fiery vision described in the first chapter of the Book of Ezekiel. Rabinowitz pointed out that, if the writer's theory were indeed correct, the arsonist would have to have considerably misinterpreted the text of Ezekiel. I agreed, but remarked that such a false exegesis of Ezekiel, and its effect on the person who so interpreted it, would itself interest me. "Halperin," he said, "I'll study the true exegeses of Ezekiel; you study the false ones." Thus began *The Faces of the Chariot*.

I have stayed more or less faithful to this division of labor. I have not been altogether indifferent to the question of what Ezekiel meant when he described his vision of the *merkabah* ("chariot"), as the rabbis were later to call it. But Ezekiel's real intentions have interested me far less than the question of why certain rabbis, living anywhere from seven to eleven centuries afterward, reacted to it with a peculiar mixture of excitement and fear; or why the authors of bizarre texts called the *Hekhalot* seem to have been bent on re-experiencing the *merkabah* vision, apparently in the context of a heavenly ascent. All of these people must have had their understandings of what Ezekiel was trying to say, which may or may not have been accurate in terms of the prophet's own intentions.

What these understandings were, and why they had the powerful effects they did on those who held them, seems to me a problem of the greatest interest and importance. It touches on many diverse issues relating to the history, psychology, and even philosophy of religion. These include the role of Scripture in a Scripture-following community; the roots and meaning of religious dread; the significance of ecstatic experience, or of the belief in the possibility of ecstatic experience; and, as we will see, the problem of evil and its relation to the divine.

I assume, therefore, that others beside scholars of Judaica may want to read this book; and I have tried to write it so that my arguments will be accessible to them. I do not pretend that what follows is a "popular" book. But Samuel Sandmel once distinguished "popular" writings from "non-

technical" ones [73a]¹, and I think I can reasonably claim this book for
the latter category. I assume no knowledge of Hebrew or any other foreign
language on the reader's part, avoid the use of terms from other languages
(and technical terms in general) wherever I can, and fully explain such
terms wherever I cannot avoid them. I do not assume any but the most
general knowledge of Jewish or world history, or of the teachings of Judaism or any other religion. Although the body of the book presupposes a
certain basic acquaintance with the rabbinic literature, readers lacking this
acquaintance can make up for it by reading Appendix I, "Orientation to
Rabbinic Sources." My arguments are usually detailed and often intricate.
But I have tried to write so that the non-specialist can, with a certain
amount of patience, follow their intricacies.

As much as possible, I have tried to lay out my arguments fully and
clearly in the body of the text, with the least possible use of footnotes and
the allusive reasoning characteristic of footnotes. The footnotes I do include (marked with raised numbers, and printed at the bottom of the page)
are often intended to provide bits of clarifying background for non-special-
ists. Otherwise, they are parenthetical remarks that I judge indispensable.

In addition to footnotes, I have made use of endnotes. These are marked
with raised letters, and gathered at the end of the book. They contain technical discussions, often on matters of text and translation, which I judge
useful only for specialists. (Occasionally I use them to offer suggestions
which I do not want to omit altogether, but which I do not consider
necessary to include on the same page as the text.) The specialist may turn
to the endnotes to discover why I have preferred this or that reading of a
difficult text, this or that rendering of a puzzling word. The non-specialist
may ignore them without loss.

For the purpose of citing secondary sources, and editions of primary
sources, I have used neither footnotes *nor* endnotes. Instead, I have followed the practice recommended in Mary-Claire van Leunen's *Handbook
for Scholars* [860], of attaching to the end of the book a reference list
(replacing, and to a great extent corresponding to, the bibliography that
would normally be found in a book of this sort), its items numbered
sequentially. These "items" include not only the books and articles I cite,
but, where appropriate, individual pages and clusters of pages. A bracketed
number in the text directs the reader to the appropriate item in the reference list. Thus, by looking up "860" in the reference list, the reader will
find bibliographical information for *Handbook for Scholars*; and, by looking up "73a," information on where to find the remarks of Sandmel cited
above. I deviate from van Leunen's method in one important particular,

---

1 I will presently explain the meaning of the bracketed number.

that I find it essential to pinpoint within the text the pages of modern editions of primary sources. Thus, for example, my citation (at the beginning of chapter VII) of "*Gen. R.* 27:1" is followed by "(ed. 255—256 [188])." This means that the passage is to be found on pages 255—256 of the standard modern edition of midrash *Genesis Rabbah*; which, as the reader will discover by looking up "188" in the reference list, is the edition of Theodor and Albeck.

As I have said, Isaac Rabinowitz first inspired me with the idea for this study in the spring of 1967. I was able to pursue various aspects of it in courses I took at Cornell with Rabinowitz (1969), and at the University of California at Berkeley with David Winston, Mordechai A. Friedman, and Hamid Algar (1971—73). Much of the material contained in chapters I—VIII originally formed part of an early draft of my Ph.D. dissertation, which I wrote in Jerusalem in 1975. I later expanded, under the guidance of Baruch M. Bokser, a portion of this draft into my actual Ph.D. dissertation, which I submitted to Berkeley in 1977 and published (under the title *The Merkabah in Rabbinic Literature* [552]) in 1980. I wrote this book, in its present form, in 1981—84.

These last years have seen a remarkable blossoming of studies on the *merkabah* and the *Hekhalot*. Before 1980, Gershom Scholem stood practically alone, a solitary pioneer exploring these strange and alien realms [589,605]. In 1980, Ithamar Gruenwald's *Apocalyptic and Merkavah Mysticism* appeared [535]; in 1982, Ira Chernus's *Mysticism in Rabbinic Judaism* [512]; in these years, a string of important articles by Yosef Dan [517,518,520,521,522] and Peter Schäfer [579,580,582a,583,586]. Schäfer's synoptic publication of seven *Hekhalot* manuscripts under the title *Synopse zur Hekhalot-Literatur*, which appeared late in 1981, made these texts fully accessible to scholars for the first time [495]. I am convinced that it is the single most important work on the *Hekhalot* ever to appear, and that future historians of the scholarship on the *Hekhalot* will speak of "pre-*Synopse*" and "post-*Synopse*" eras. Chapter IX, and many other parts of this book, could not have been written without it[2].

I owe an enormous debt to all of these researchers, and particularly Schäfer. That I have been deeply influenced by Scholem's writings, even where I disagree with them, goes almost without saying; it is hard to imagine anyone in the second part of the twentieth century writing on any subject remotely connected with Jewish mysticism without being under Scholem's influence. But I must acknowledge another influence that does

---

2 I received Schäfer's sequel to the *Synopse, Geniza-Fragmente zur Hekhalot-Literatur* [494a], too late to take account of it in this book.

not belong to the realm of Judaic studies, narrowly defined. This is the work of Sigmund Freud, and particularly his *Interpretation of Dreams*, which I read with excitement and wonder at a particularly crucial stage of the writing of this book. Only seldom have I offered suggestions that are what most of us are accustomed to think of as "Freudian"; that is, having to do with sex. But anyone who has read Freud will appreciate how much his genius has shaped my approach to the problems with which I deal.

I cannot possibly list here all those people who helped me at various stages of my eighteen-year research. My special appreciation goes to the teachers whom I have mentioned, who started me off on it; and, particularly, to Baruch Bokser, who carefully read and meticulously annotated my 1975 draft. Among those teachers who inspired and helped me in Israel were Moshe Greenberg, M. J. Kister, Yaakov Zussman, Moshe Herr, and Joseph Dan. All of these men took time from their crowded schedules to listen to my ideas and read drafts of my work, and to give me sound advice and warm encouragement. Of my fellow-students and fellow-researchers, I must single out Marc Bregman, whose conversation (mostly over coffee in the Hebrew University cafeteria) taught me much of what I know about midrash; Ithamar Gruenwald, Herbert W. Basser, Peter Schäfer, and Alan F. Segal, all of whom shared with me, in person and in writing, the results of their investigations of the *merkabah* and *Hekhalot*. Ira Chernus kindly sent me a copy of several chapters of the manuscript of his book, before it was published.

Abraham Katsh, of Dropsie University, Philadelphia, allowed me in the fall of 1974 to consult pertinent Genizah manuscripts in the university's possession. His successor, David Goldenberg, sent me a photocopy of one of these manuscripts. John Strugnell allowed me to examine photographs of the Qumran materials discussed in chapter II; Michael Sokoloff discussed with me linguistic aspects of the *Visions of Ezekiel*; Thorkild Jacobsen answered my query about the "Bull of Heaven" (chapter V); and Daniel Sheerin sent me valuable material on the development of Christian exegesis of Psalm 24. In the spring of 1982, Eric Ormsby, then curator of Near East Collections at the Princeton University Library, took time to guide me through Princeton's Arabic holdings, and patiently answered my subsequent queries. My friend and colleague Gordon D. Newby (North Carolina State University, Raleigh) put his private Arabic library at my disposal; and, with great patience, helped me make my way to what I needed. Edmund Meltzer helped me locate translations of the Egyptian tales of Setne Khamwas, and discussed with me the significance of these documents.

"The mind," George Orwell wrote, "will not work to any purpose when it is quite alone" [848a]. I cannot begin to state my debt to my colleagues in the Department of Religious Studies, University of North Carolina,

Chapel Hill, for having provided me with rich intellectual companionship over the past ten years. In general, they have given and continue to give me a post-doctoral education; in particular, they have listened to two presentations of ideas contained in this book, and given me valuable responses. I am proud to belong, also, to the "Society for the Culture and Religion of the Ancient Mediterranean," a society of Southeastern scholars which heard a presentation of, and helped me think through, many of the ideas I present in chapter IX. Robert C. Gregg, of Duke University, has been particularly helpful. My friendship with Gordon Newby has given me access, not only to his Arabic learning, but to the wealth of his lively and creative mind.

At one stage or another of the research and writing of this book, I have received financial assistance from the American Schools of Oriental Research, the Marsden Foundation (New York City), the National Foundation for Jewish Culture (New York City), the Mabelle McLeod Lewis Memorial Fund (Stanford, California), the University Research Council (University of North Carolina), and the Arts and Sciences Foundation (UNC). The University Research Council, the Duke-UNC Cooperative Program in Judaic Studies, the UNC College of Arts and Sciences Endowment Committee for Scholarly Publications, Artistic Exhibitions, and Performances, and the UNC Department of Religious Studies, all contributed to the cost of publication. John Van Seters, chairman of the Department of Religious Studies, has given the work sympathetic attention, and has provided me with funds for research assistance. I was fortunate to have been able to engage in this capacity my student and friend Robert B. Spencer, a talented and conscientious scholar- and teacher-to-be whose fine and diligent work lightened the load of preparing the manuscript.

To the good offices of William H. Friedman and Julie Daniel, and to the latter's skill with a word processor, I owe the manuscript itself. June Williams, Teresa Weaver, and Yuming Hu helped me check the proofs. Ms. Weaver, Carol Selkin, and my students Darcy Baird, Samuel Kaplan, Mary Pat Karmel, and Janelle Mason helped me prepare the index.

Most important of all have been the dear friends and family who cheered my life through the years of research and writing. My father, Elias W. Halperin (whose departure I now mourn), and my aunt, Sara Garb, have sustained me with encouragement and love. My father's wife, Klida McLaughlin-Halperin, has been a good friend through easy times and through hard. The Mazar family (Esther, Talli, Eilat, and Adi) made a home for me in Israel. My wife's parents, Sol and Dora Shalom, her sister Rebeca, and her brother Ralph, have given me their friendship. And I have found joy, delight, and comfort with my wife, my beloved bride Rose Shalom; who, like the *merkabah* in the time of Johanan b. Zakkai, has filled my days with rainbows.

Chapel Hill, North Carolina   David J. Halperin
February, 1988

Contents

Abbreviations

^cA.Z. = ^cAbodah Zarah

b.   = ben; bar; ibn ("son of," in Hebrew, Aramaic, and Arabic, respectively)

B.B.   = Baba Batra

Ber.   = Berakhot

B.M.   = Baba Meṣi^ca

B.Q.   = Baba Qamma

BT   = Babylonian Talmud

^cEd.   = ^cEduyot

^cEr.   = ^cErubin

Gen. R., Ex. R., Lev. R., etc.
       = *Genesis Rabbah, Exodus Rabbah, Leviticus Rabbah,* etc.

Gitt. = Giṭṭin

Hag.   = Ḥagigah

Ket.   = Ketubbot

LXX   = Septuagint

M.   = Mishnah

Meg.   = Megillah

Midd. = Middot

M.Q.   = Mo^ced Qaṭan

MT   = Masoretic Text

Naz.   = Nazir

Pes.   = Pesaḥim

Pes. R. = *Pesiqta Rabbati*

PT   = Palestinian Talmud

Qidd. = Qiddushin

R.   = Rabbi

R.H.   = Rosh Hashanah

RSV   = Revised Standard Version

Sanh. = Sanhedrin

Shabb. = Shabbat

Sheb. = Shebu^cot

Sheq. = Sheqalim

Sot.   = Soṭah

Sukk. = Sukkah

T.   = Tosefta

Tem.   = Temurah   I do not abbreviate titles of books or journals.

Introduction

This book is about *merkabah* midrash. That is, it is about the ways in which Jews in antiquity interpreted the cryptic and bizarre vision described at the beginning of the Book of Ezekiel, which came early to be designated as the vision of the *merkabah*. (The Hebrew word means "chariot"; in this case, the chariot of God.)

Most moderns know about the *merkabah* vision only that

Ezekiel saw the wheel, 'way in the middle of the air
...
And the little wheel run by faith,
And the big wheel run by the grace of God ... [852a]

But the pertinent passages of Ezekiel describe much more than "the wheel." Beginning with a stormy wind and a fiery cloud which approach from the north, the vision unfolds as a description of four fantastic beings, each with four different faces. Four wheels, each one like "a wheel within a wheel," accompany these beings. A platform, like crystal, is over their heads. A human-like manifestation of the Deity sits above the platform, on a lapis-lazuli throne. All of this is set forth in the first chapter of Ezekiel. Chapter 10 repeats it, with important variations. Ezekiel 43:1–4 refers back to it.

It is not easy to make sense of these details, and still less easy to determine what the totality of the vision is supposed to convey. Generations of Bible-readers, from the ancient Jewish interpreters whose expositions we shall examine, down to space-age fantasists like Erich von Däniken [846, 848, 859], have applied themselves to the *merkabah*'s riddles.

I do not propose here to join their company. I cannot, to be sure, entirely ignore the question of what Ezekiel was talking about; and, from time to time, I will touch on the problem of the original meaning of the *merkabah* vision. But my real concern is with the Jewish interpretations themselves, and with the light they can shed, not on the text they purport to interpret, but on the religious perceptions of the culture that created them.

For early Judaism, like its sister Christianity, was a Scripture religion, and thus lived in symbiosis with the library of ancient texts that its adherents

accepted as the word of God [729c]. Within this collection the diligent inquirer could, at least in theory, discover all knowledge worth having.

   "Turn it this way, turn it that way," said one rabbi of the Torah, "everything is in it" (M. Abot 5:22, in Goldin's translation [244a])[1]. Early in
the third century, a Jew told the Christian scholar Origen[2] that the Scriptures are like a great house whose rooms are all closed, with a key beside
each locked door. Only, the key does not fit the door it is placed beside,
and the inquirer must know how to find the right key for the door he
wants to open [668a]. The ancient Jewish study of Scripture was less a
matter of interpreting a text, as we are apt to conceive this process, than of
exploring a vast storehouse of sacred treasure. These explorations could
vary tremendously in their sophistication. The Jewish philosopher Philo of
Alexandria (ca. 20 B.C.–40 A.D.) made elaborate efforts to find the truths
of Platonism hiding behind the stories and laws of the Pentateuch [729d] ;
while one rabbinic midrash pressed the language of Genesis 3:14 for details
on the gestation period of snakes (*Gen. R.* 20:4; ed. 185–186 [188])[3].

   Normally, the explorer found in the storehouse of Scripture what he had
himself brought into it, whether Platonic philosophy or (to choose an example from rabbinic Judaism) the detailed rules of Sabbath observance that
had become traditional in second-century A.D. Palestine. If he interpreted
two Scriptural passages in the light of each other, and thus discovered a
new meaning which neither passage had in its own context – in Origen's
image, if he fit the key into the lock and opened the door – this was because he already had a predisposition to correlate precisely those two texts.
And yet the interpreter's ideas were transformed in the process of reading
them into Scripture and then out again. The shape of the Bible's language
modified and redirected his intentions, at the same time that his intentions
reshaped his perception of the Bible and its message. Jews in antiquity
came to Scripture to learn its wisdom; they in fact recreated it in their
own image. Yet this image was itself born of Scripture, and refashioned
under the influence of Scripture.

   This complex and paradoxical process, which I have in mind when I
speak of a symbiosis of Jews (and Christians) with their Bible, will be ex-
emplified many times in the following pages. It is near the heart of Jewish

---

1 For an explanation of this reference, see Appendix I, section 1.
2 Origen was by all odds the most profound scholar and extraordinary thinker of the early church.
   He was born about 185, and lived and worked in Alexandria until about 232. Driven out by his
   bishop's hostility, he settled in the Palestinian coastal city of Caesarea, where he remained until
   his death between 251 and 255 [686,700,708]. Caesarea was at that time a major center of
   rabbinic Judaism, and there is ample evidence that Origen had extensive contact with the local
   Jewish scholars – a topic to which we will return, at length, in chapter VIII [421,664].
3 See Appendix I, section 6.

religious development in antiquity. If we want to grasp the essence of any one of the multiple forms of early Judaism, we cannot avoid asking how it understood the substance of its sacred writings, and what it did with that understanding.

A community founded on Scripture may regard all parts of its Bible as equally inspired. It is unlikely to regard them all as equally interesting. A Bible-belt fundamentalist will have an interest in the prophecies of the Book of Revelation that most Catholics or Episcopalians are not likely to share. Orthodox Jews, whose sacred history finds its point of central importance in the Sinai revelation, will not be apt to share the passionate concern with the opening chapters of Genesis that has made the truth of the Creation story a political issue of the 1980's.

So in antiquity. Let us use the number of times the literature of a community quotes a passage of Scripture as a rough indicator of the importance that the community attaches to it. We find that the fifty-third chapter of Isaiah occupies a disproportionately large place in the *Biblia Patristica* (an index of Biblical quotations or allusions in the Christian literature of the first three centuries [800]), because the church saw in this chapter a particularly important prophecy of the sacrificial death of its Messiah. In the counterpart to the *Biblia Patristica* that deals with the rabbinic literature [804], the place occupied by Isaiah 53 is remarkably small, presumably for the same reason. Early Judaism, like Christianity, reshaped Scripture not only by interpreting it. It reshaped it by deciding what portions of it were worth interpreting.

This brings us back to the *merkabah*. Christians, though they might sometimes pay homage to the awesome obscurity of this vision (for example, Jerome's *Epistle 53*, to Paulinus [621]), do not seem on the whole to have found it of outstanding interest [695]. We are not well enough informed about the varieties of Judaism that flourished before the destruction of the Second Temple in 70 A.D. [729a] to judge the role it played in their perceptions. But, when we turn to the form of Judaism that became dominant after 70, the Judaism that is usually called "rabbinic" after the title ("rabbi") given to the men who shaped and directed it, we find explicit evidence that the *merkabah* aroused not only excitement, but also a nervous suspicion that often seems to cross the border into fear. Both responses are strangely, and perhaps uniquely, intense.

Consider, for example, the anonymous regulation preserved in the Mishnah, Hagigah 2:1[4]:

---

4 See Appendix I, section 1.

The laws of forbidden sexual relations [Leviticus 18 and 20] may not be expounded by three persons, nor the account of creation [Genesis 1:1–2:3] by two, nor the *merkabah* by one, unless he is a scholar and has understood on his own. He who contemplates four things – what is above and what below, what is before and what after – would have been better off if he had never been born. He who has no concern for the honor of his creator would be better off if he had never been born.

Several details of this passage are obscure, but its thrust is unmistakable. The *merkabah* is to be treated as the most arcane of the Scriptures. Expounding it brings one dangerously close to those studies whose prosecution is an affront to the glory of God, whose devotee would be better off if he had not been born.

The *merkabah* is physically dangerous, too. Rabbi Judah the Patriarch (early third century A.D.), "had a distinguished student who expounded a segment of *ma^caseh merkabah*[5]. Rabbi [Judah] did not agree, and [the student] became a leper." So, at least, the Palestinian Talmud (Hagigah 2:1, 77a). The Babylonian Talmud (Hagigah 13a)[6] tells an even more frightening story. "It once happened that a certain child was reading the Book of Ezekiel in his teacher's house, and he contemplated *hashmal* [or, perhaps, "he understood what *hashmal* was"][7]. Fire came forth from *hashmal* and burned him up."

But, if expounded well, the *merkabah* could bring dramatic tokens of divine favor to the lucky expositor. A cycle of stories about the *merkabah* expositions of R. Johanan b. Zakkai's disciples (late first century A.D.) well conveys this point. When R. Eleazar b. Arakh, for example, expounded *ma^caseh merkabah* in R. Johanan's presence, "fire descended from heaven and surrounded them. Angels came leaping before them, like a wedding party rejoicing before a bridegroom. An angel spoke from the midst of the fire: 'As you have expounded, Eleazar b. Arakh, thus is *ma^caseh merkabah*' " (PT Hagigah 2:1, 77a).

Evidently, the rabbis saw something in Ezekiel's vision that was vitally important, yet so fearful that the ordinary person must be warned away from it. I know of no other case where the very act of studying a Biblical

---

5 Rabbinic sources sometimes use the phrase *ma^caseh merkabah* in place of *merkabah*, when it is treated, as here, as an object of exposition, study, or teaching. It is not clear how we are to translate the expression. The customary "work of the chariot" is vague, the alternative "account of the chariot" unlikely; "structure of the chariot" (so Ezekiel 1:16 uses the word *ma^caseh*) is possible. There seems to be some slight difference in nuance between *merkabah* and *ma^caseh merkabah*, but it is hard to say just what it is [552].

6 See Appendix I, section 3.

7 *Hashmal* is the mysterious Hebrew word, translated "gleaming bronze" in the Revised Standard Version of the Bible (RSV), which Ezekiel uses to describe the fiery manifestation at the beginning of the *merkabah* vision (1:4), and the luminous splendor at its climax (1:27, cf. 8:3). In modern Hebrew, the word is used for electricity. No one is yet quite sure what Ezekiel meant by it [1a,6,19].

text is the object of extensive discussion, prescription, and restriction — as we find with the *merkabah*.

What was the *merkabah*'s power and danger? Its power, no doubt, had something to do with the obscurity of the *merkabah* vision. In the more intelligible parts of Scripture, the rabbis may have sensed, the divine mysteries hidden behind the veil of the Bible's simple language were kept so far back that the veil hung smoothly before them. Here they thrust themselves forward, their bulges distorting the veil's contours. Otherwise, how explain the difficulties of the prophet's language? The pious expositor could hardly suppose, like the modern interpreter, corruption of the text; still less, some confusion in Ezekiel's own mind. The difficulties, he might well reason, must point to the shape of the secrets behind them. Resolve those difficulties, and the secrets will become plain.

But the fear the vision aroused is still mysterious. We understand it no better when we are told that contemplation of the divine is inherently dangerous, because we do not grasp why this should be so. We may, indeed, look to Rudolf Otto's conception of the *mysterium tremendum* as an essential element of religious experience [849], and infer that the mixture of excitement and nervousness with which the rabbis approached the *merkabah* is far from being an isolated phenomenon. But this still does not give us an answer clear and definite enough to satisfy us. We must ask precisely what there was about the act of interpreting this Scriptural text, that called forth these responses from the rabbis. Otherwise, we miss our chance to understand an important if unconventional aspect of rabbinic Judaism, and perhaps of the phenomenon of the *tremendum* in general.

In his monumental books on Jewish mysticism, the late Gershom G. Scholem has proposed what might be at least a partial solution to our problem [589, 605].

Scholem's position — to simplify to the verge of distortion — is that the rabbis' discussions and restrictions on the *merkabah* point to something well beyond the interpretation of the Book of Ezekiel. They allude to a mystical practice which involved ascent to the divine realms and direct contemplation of the *merkabah* and its attendant beings. A group of strange and at times barely intelligible texts called the *Hekhalot* ("palaces," referring to the heavenly structures) preserve, sometimes in overlaid or distorted form, the experiences of these mystics. M. Hag. 2:1, and the anecdotes that the Palestinian and Babylonian Talmuds gather around it, view this ecstatic mysticism from the outside. To see it from the inside, we must make use of the *Hekhalot*.

In making his case, Scholem followed a path that had first been cut by the eleventh-century scholar Hai Gaon. Hai used the *Hekhalot* to elucidate a puzzling Talmudic account, which occupied Scholem and will presently

occupy us, of four rabbis who entered a mysterious "garden" (BT Hagigah
14b; below, chapters I and VI). Said Hai:

> You may be aware that many of the sages were of the opinion that an individual possessing certain explicitly defined qualities, who wishes to look at the *merkabah* and to peer into the palaces [*hekhalot*] of the celestial angels, has ways to achieve this. He must sit fasting for a specified number of days, place his head between his knees, and whisper to the earth many prescribed songs and hymns. He thus peers into the inner rooms and chambers as if he were seeing the seven palaces with his own eyes, and he observes as if he were going from palace to palace and seeing what is in them. There are two *mishnayot* that the Tannaim have taught on this subject; they are called *Hekhalot Rabbati* and *Hekhalot Zuṭarti*[8]. This much is widely known. [241]

Scholem did not follow Hai Gaon in his uncritical belief that the *Hekhalot* were authored by Tannaim. But, against such nineteenth-century scholars as Heinrich Grätz and Philipp Bloch [528,509], he argued that their central ideas were ancient, going back to the beginning of the Christian Era. The ecstatic journey to the *merkabah* was no medieval import from Islam (so Grätz), but an essential and authentic expression of rabbinic Judaism, which had been part of it from its beginning. The rabbis had been praised as sober rationalists, or condemned as pedantic legalists. Neither stereotype had allowed them a spark of mystical passion. And now, Scholem proclaimed, the "*merkabah* mysticism" of the *Hekhalot* proved that both stereotypes were fantastically wrong.

This same "*merkabah* mysticism," Scholem thought, yielded the key to the stories of heavenly ascension that filled the Jewish and Christian apocalypses of the last two centuries B.C. and first two centuries A.D. It explained particularly well a strange passage in Paul's Second Letter to the Corinthians (12:2—4), where Paul described himself as

> a man in Christ who fourteen years ago was caught up to the third heaven — whether in the body or out of the body I do not know, God knows. And I know that this man was caught up into Paradise — whether in the body or out of the body I do not know, God knows — and he heard things that cannot be taught, which man may not utter.

Paul was "caught up into Paradise." The four rabbis whose story Hai Gaon undertook to explain had entered a "garden"; and the Hebrew word for "garden," *pardes*, might well be understood as "Paradise"[9]. The parallel seemed compelling. Following Hai, Scholem had interpreted the Talmudic story as testimony to mystical ecstasy. So understood, it would now illuminate the Jewish background of Paul's experience.

---

8 Hai uses *mishnayot* to mean "Tannaitic teachings." For a fuller explanation of this word, see Appendix I, section 1; on the "Tannaim," see section 2. In chapter IX, I extensively discuss the *Hekhalot* in general, and the "texts" that have come to be called *Hekhalot Rabbati* and *Hekhalot Zuṭarti* (the "Greater Treatise on the Palaces," the "Lesser Treatise on the Palaces").

9 The Hebrew and English words are in fact related etymologically. Unfortunately for Scholem's argument, rabbinic Hebrew does not seem actually to use *pardes* to mean "Paradise." We will return to this point in chapter I.

It followed that, in whatever ways Paul had broken with his Pharisaic past, in his penchant for mystical experience (II Corinthians 12:7) he remained faithful to it. As for the rabbis, they were far from stifling apocalyptic ecstasy with their "legalism." On the contrary, they treasured and nourished it. The *Hekhalot* texts became its manuals. And the *merkabah* remained, as it had been for centuries, its focus and its goal.

This marvellously attractive synthesis is flawed in several ways. The parallels on which Scholem rested much of his case, such as that between II Corinthians 12 and the rabbinic *pardes* story, are often equivocal [583]. Although it is hard to defend the nineteenth-century consensus that the *Hekhalot* were written after the end of the Talmudic period (that is, early in the Middle Ages), Scholem's early dating is just as doubtful. Scholem's stress on the reality of the *merkabah* mystics' ecstatic experiences can be misleading. He did not, of course, mean that they "really" ascended to heaven, but that they "really" believed they had done so. But it is easy to slip from this into the illusion that we can explain the ascension materials in the apocalypses and the *Hekhalot* by pointing to the supposed reality of the experience underlying them; whereas, of course, this hallucinatory "experience" itself cries out for explanation. This fallacy seems to me to dog much of Scholem's presentation.

I will develop these criticisms at several points in the chapters that follow. (It is a mark of the power of Scholem's synthesis that I am obliged to devote so much space to criticizing it.) For now, I will stress yet another difficulty I have with Scholem's position, which I find the crucial one; namely, that Scholem does not even try to solve the problem of the *merkabah* as I have defined it above, and as rabbinic texts like M. Hagigah 2:1 persuade me it ought to be defined. These texts, as we will see in chapter I, barely refer to ecstatic journeys. Instead, they show clearly that there was *something in the text of Ezekiel itself* that frightened the rabbis. They represent the *merkabah* as an extraordinary case – extraordinarily promising, extraordinarily dangerous – of the rabbis' symbiosis with Scripture. Scholem does not help us understand how this was so.

Yet we cannot dismiss Scholem's work and start from scratch. The links Scholem propounds – particularly the three-way connection of the apocalyptic ascensions, the rabbinic allusions to the *merkabah*, and the *Hekhalot* materials – seem real. If, as I believe, Scholem has not defined them properly, this will not justify our ignoring them. We must find a better way to state and to explain them. And we do best to start where the rabbinic sources suggest we ought, with the exegetical traditions on the *merkabah* visions of Ezekiel.

Sigmund Freud, in his "From the History of an Infantile Neurosis"

(better known as the case history of the "Wolf Man"), records a puzzling
memory fragment of his patient's. "He was chasing a beautiful big butterfly
with yellow stripes and large wings which ended in pointed projections – a
swallow-tail, in fact. Suddenly, when the butterfly had settled on a flower,
he was seized with a dreadful fear of the creature, and ran away screaming"
[837b].

Freud, naturally, believed he had discovered what there was about the
butterfly that so terrified his "Wolf Man." It would not be to our purpose
to go into the details. What concerns us is that Freud believed, I think correctly, that the butterfly was bound into the "Wolf Man's" mental world
by an elaborate network of associations which allowed it to become a tangible emblem of what he desired and what he dreaded. The "Wolf Man" was
of course disturbed. But Freud has taught us that similar processes of association operate in all of us. Any object, however harmless, may become
linked with what we wish and fear, and draw into itself the force of our
wish and our fear.

Midrash, like Freudian psychoanalysis, involves a process of linking. The
midrashic expositor associates one Scriptural passage with another, apparently from a totally different context. To take up again Origen's image, he
fits the key that is beside one door into the lock of another. Midrash thus
constructs from the Scriptures a network of conducting wires, which runs
beneath the skin of the religious perception of reality. Points where particularly powerful wires intersect may take on a tremendous charge. To
understand why a point is so charged, we must trace the wires that lead
from it.

It is my argument in this book that ancient sources, rabbinic and other,
give us the information we need to trace the associative wires that gave the
merkabah its extraordinary charge of excitement and fear.

I do not mean to suggest by this that the rabbis feared the *merkabah*
vision because it seemed to have overtones of some alien religious system
(Christianity, Gnosticism, or the like). Explanations of this sort seldom
appeal to me, because they do not take into account Judaism's ability –
which, I believe, it shares with all or almost all other religions – to absorb
aspects of other religions which seem compatible with its basic structure
[729b]. Alienness *per se*, then, is no ground for rejection, much less terror.
Rather, the *merkabah* must have set the rabbis' minds moving toward something which they found inherently thrilling or appalling. I see no reason
to doubt that this "something" could have been generated within the rabbis' Judaism itself, without any influence from the outside.

What this "something" was, we must now seek.

My plan of investigation is as follows: We shall begin by mining those
rabbinic sources that describe or regulate the process of expounding the

merkabah, for clues as to what direction we are to look for the crucial connections (chapter I). We will then pick out the main lines of *merkabah* exegesis, in extra-rabbinic Jewish literature (chapters II—III) and rabbinic (chapters IV—VIII), and seek to discover how they relate to each other and where they lead. Along our way, we will look at the ascension materials in the apocalypses (chapter III). With our exegetical investigation behind us, we will be ready to find a place for the *Hekhalot* and its ascensions in the *merkabah* tradition (chapter IX).

Chapter I

Shadows of the Merkabah

We begin our search in a state of bewilderment. We are looking for a "something" that somehow has to do with the visions of Ezekiel, that somehow had the power to stir up fear, excitement, and perhaps even ecstasy. But so far we have no inkling of what shape this "something" will take on, or in what direction we are to turn to look for it.

Rabbinic texts, speaking of *merkabah* and *ma^caseh merkabah*, can help us out of our bewilderment. These texts do not actually interpret the first chapter of Ezekiel. Rather, they talk about, and often pass judgment on, the process itself of interpreting this chapter. They do not tell us what the rabbis said about Ezekiel's visions, far less what there was about the encounters of Scripture and believer that could generate excitement and terror. But, like shadows cast by bodies we do not yet see, they point to where we are to look for these encounters; and they hint at what we must expect to see when we find them.

I explored these passages at length in my book, *The Merkabah in Rabbinic Literature* [552]. In this chapter, I summarize my results. Wherever I can, I will indicate the reasoning that underlies these results. But at times I must offer a flat statement in place of a complicated argument, and invite the interested reader to find the details of that argument in my earlier study.

1. "Many expounded the *merkabah*"

We find our first clue in a brief legal discussion, the main point of which does not concern the *merkabah*. In the course of a discussion of the synagogue functions that may be performed by a minor, a man dressed in tatters, and a blind man, the Mishnah (Meg. 4:6) rules:

> A blind man may *pores 'et shema^c*[1] and translate [the Torah reading, for the benefit of the congregation].

---

1 I cannot translate this phrase. To explain it, I must first explain that the word *shema^c* refers pri-

R. Judah says: Anyone who has never seen the luminaries should not *pores 'et shema^c*.

Tosefta[2], expanding and annotating the Mishnah at this point, quotes these two sentences and adds a third:

They said to him: Many expounded the *merkabah* and never saw it. [T. Meg. 3(4):28]

What does this discussion mean? R. Judah b. Ilai, a Tanna of the middle or latter part of the second century, dissents from an anonymous (and therefore, according to the convention of the rabbinic writings, general) view, which permits a blind man to perform a specified liturgical function in connection with the *shema^c*. We do not know the reason for his objection. We may assume that it has something to do with the blessing, preliminary to the recitation of the *shema^c*, that praises God as "fashioner of light"[a]. The man born blind should not publicly praise God for wonders he has never seen. So far the Mishnah.

To this, the anonymous authorities respond: "Many expounded the *merkabah* and never saw it" (Tosefta). In context, this reply must mean: You, R. Judah, hold that it is objectionable for a person to speak before the congregation about phenomena he has never seen. How then do we find that many people expound the *merkabah* without ever having seen it — and no one raises an objection to that!

Only if we interpret the reply this way can we understand its bearing on the argument. Taken in isolation, indeed, it might bear a second interpretation: many people undertook mystical exercises in the hopes of obtaining a vision of the *merkabah*, but failed. But we would be at a loss to understand why R. Judah's opponents use this as a rebuttal. Why should they expect that this information will lead R. Judah to drop his objection to the blind man's being involved in the recitation of the *shema^c*?

It is true that the Babylonian Talmud quotes the anonymous reply with an alteration that points clearly to the second interpretation (Meg. 24b): "Did not many hope to expound the *merkabah*, and yet they never saw it?" That is, when the "many" failed to see the *merkabah*, their hopes of expounding it were disappointed. But we shall see that this change in wording accords with a prejudice of the Babylonian rabbis that *ma^caseh mer-*

---

marily to the verse Deuteronomy 6:4 ("hear O Israel, the Lord is our God, the Lord is one"; in Hebrew, the verse begins with the word *shema^c*), which became Judaism's central credo. It then comes to refer to a sequence of three Biblical passages beginning with this verse (Deuteronomy 6:4–9, 11:13–21, Numbers 15:37–41), which occupies a key position in the synagogue service. The phrase used here, *pores 'et shema^c*, evidently refers to some liturgical action connected with the recitation of the *shema^c*. Unfortunately, despite scholars' efforts [280], we are not sure just what that action was. Fortunately, it does not now matter to us.

2 See Appendix I, section 4.

a)(Endnotes see page 523ff.)

kabah involves some sort of visionary experience. We may regard it as a Babylonian reinterpretation of the older Palestinian source.

Take this older source by itself; what do we learn from it? First, that "expounding the *merkabah*" is a common activity. Next, that it normally does not presuppose or involve any direct experience of the *merkabah*. Third, that R. Judah's interlocutors see nothing wrong with it and assume that he will see nothing wrong with it; otherwise they would not have used it for their counterexample. Finally, if we press the implied parallel with *pores 'et shema[c]*, we can infer that it has some connection with synagogue worship.

A casual allusion of the sort we have here is perhaps the closest thing to unimpeachable evidence the rabbinic literature can offer. A story may be fabricated for tendentious motives we can only guess at. Even legislation need not always accurately reflect the situation at which it is supposed to be directed. But when a writer or speaker mentions something that he assumes to be common knowledge, which does not interest him for itself but for the support it gives to some other point he is making, we have, if not reality itself, at least what the writer's contemporaries think of as reality. In the anonymous reply to R. Judah, we glimpse *merkabah* exposition in Tannaitic Palestine only briefly, but through clear atmosphere and an accurate lens.

2. Johanan b. Zakkai and the *merkabah*

The source we have just examined thus contrasts sharply with the stories to which we now turn, of how R. Johanan b. Zakkai's disciples expounded the *merkabah*. Here whatever reality there may be is so shrouded in a haze of miraculous legend that we do best to forget about the reality and concentrate on the legend.

We have the stories in four versions: T. Hag. 2:1; PT Hag. 2:1 (77a); BT Hag. 14b; and a broken text that occurs at the beginning of a Genizah fragment of a lost "Tannaitic" midrash to Exodus, known as the *Mekhilta of R. Simeon b. Yohai* (ed. 158–159 [196])[3].

The Genizah fragment opens in the middle of the narrative.

> " ... If not, give me permission that I may speak before you." R. Eleazar b. Arakh expounded until fire burned all around him. When R. Johanan b. Zakkai saw that fire was burning all around him, he descended from his ass, kissed him, and said to him: "R. Eleazar b. Arakh, happy is she who bore you! Happy are you, Abraham our father, that this man emerged from your loins!"

The part of the story that would have told us what is going on is of course missing. But we can guess it from the parallels: R. Eleazar b. Arakh

---

3 See Appendix I, section 5c.

has asked his teacher, R. Johanan b. Zakkai, with whom he is travelling, to instruct him concerning *ma*^c*aśeh merkabah*; and Johanan has refused. (In the parallels, Johanan quotes the regulation, familiar to us from M. Hag. 2:1, that "the *merkabah* may not be expounded by an individual unless he is a scholar who understands on his own". We do not know whether *Mek. Simeon* also quoted this passage.) Eleazar has then undertaken to expound *ma*^c*aśeh merkabah* himself, which he does, with dazzling results.

In the two Talmuds, the effects are yet more spectacular:

> Fire descended from heaven and surrounded them. Angels came leaping before them, like a wedding party rejoicing before a bridegroom. An angel spoke from the midst of the fire: "As you have expounded, Eleazar b. Arakh, thus is *ma*^c*aśeh merkabah*!" Thereupon all the trees burst into song: *Then all the trees of the forest shall shout for joy* [Psalm 96:12]. [PT]

> Fire descended from heaven and surrounded all the trees that were in the field. They all began to sing. What was their song? *Praise the Lord from the earth, dragons and all abysses, fruit trees and all cedars! Hallelujah* [Psalm 148:7, 9, 14]. An angel spoke from the fire: "This is indeed *ma*^c*aśeh merkabah*." [BT]

Other disciples of R. Johanan[4] are encouraged to expound *ma*^c*aśeh merkabah*:

> When R. Joseph [= Jose] ha-Kohen and R. Simeon b. Nethaneel heard about this, they too began to expound *ma*^c*aśeh merkabah*. ... Although it was a summer day, the earth shook, and a rainbow was seen in the cloud[5]. A heavenly voice proclaimed: "The place is cleared for you and the couch is spread for you! You and your disciples are designated for the third set"[6]! [PT]

> When word of this reached R. Joshua, he and R. Jose ha-Kohen were walking together. They said: "Let us also expound *ma*^c*aśeh merkabah*"b). ... Although it was a summer day, the skies clouded over, and a sort of rainbow was seen in the cloud. The angels assembled to hear *ma*^c*aśeh merkabah*, like people assembling to see the entertainments of groom and bride.
> R. Jose ha-Kohen went and told R. Johanan b. Zakkai. [Johanan] said: "Happy are you [plural]! Happy your mother! Happy my eyes which thus saw! In my dream, moreover, you [plural] and I were sitting at table on Mount Sinai when a heavenly voice proclaimed from the skies: 'Come up here! Come up here! Large couches are prepared for you, large cushions are spread for you. You, and your disciples, and your disciples' disciples, are designated for the third set.' " [BT]

Tosefta's version, which I have left for last, is entirely bare of miraculous detail. Eleazar asks Johanan for instruction in *ma*^c*aśeh merkabah*. Johanan refuses, quoting either M. Hag. 2:1 or some related source. Eleazar discourses on the subject himself. Johanan then kisses him on the head and delivers a series of encomia, which occurs also in PT and BT, after the miraculous effects. In Tosefta, there is nothing in between. Nor does Tosefta

---

4 "R. Johanan b. Zakkai had five disciples: R. Eliezer b. Hyrcanus, R. Joshua b. Hananiah, R. Jose ha-Kohen, R. Simeon b. Nethaneel, and R. Eleazar b. Arakh" (M. Abot 2:8). Of these five, only R. Eliezer b. Hyrcanus does not appear in any of the *merkabah* stories.

5 Rain during the summer is rare in Palestine.

6 I do not know what "the third set" means.

mention any of Johanan's other disciples. None of the four sources gives us any clue to what Eleazar or the other disciples said about the *merkabah*.

It is natural to assume that Tosefta's version is the oldest of the four and the closest to the historical facts, and that the other three sources have fancifully embellished Tosefta's sober narrative [615]. My own analysis of the sources [552] suggests to me that the development was considerably more complex and proceeded in a different direction. The miracles are the oldest elements of the tradition, which at no stage had anything much to do with historical fact. Tosefta deliberately suppressed them, for reasons we have yet to consider. The authors of the PT and BT versions, drawing on sources that continued to circulate beside the official version of Tosefta, reintroduced them.

The earliest stage of tradition, I believe, consisted of a pool of brief and extremely simple stories [527]. In these stories, one or another of Johanan's disciples expounded the *merkabah*; the powers above gave dramatic signs of their approval; Johanan added his own praise. The stories were extremely fluid — they may never have been written down in their original form — and the storytellers had no qualms about attributing the same miracle now to one disciple, now to another. This explains the ease with which certain details in our sources cross from one episode to another: PT, for example, invokes the image of angels behaving like wedding guests in connection with Eleazar b. Arakh; BT associates it with R. Joshua and R. Jose ha-Kohen[7].

But why do the narrators fail to tell us what Johanan's disciples actually said about the *merkabah*? Because it was not their purpose to tell us any such thing. What they wanted was to show the wondrous greatness of the ancient sages. They did this by describing the vivid tokens by which God and the angels showed their regard for the way these men expounded Scripture. We find the same spirit in an anecdote BT tells of R. Johanan's older contemporary Jonathan b. Uzziel: "When he was sitting engaged in Torah study, any bird that flew over him was immediately burned up" (Sukk. 28a). We miss the point of this story if we ask what part of the Torah Jonathan b. Uzziel was studying or what he thought about it. The point is the effect, emanating from his personal greatness, that the very act of his studying had on his surroundings. So with the *merkabah* stories.

And yet the *merkabah* cannot have been entirely incidental to these stories. The storytellers, after all, could have spoken of how Eleazar b. Arakh and the rest expounded Torah in their master's presence. Instead, they chose to specify the *merkabah* as the object of the disciples' exposition. Why?

---

7 PT describes the angels as "leaping" (*meqappeṣin*), BT as "assembling" (*mitqabbeṣin*). The two are obviously oral variants [406a].

The answer to this question is tied up with another problem: what led the storytellers to their choice of miracles? Fire surrounding the expositors or the neighboring trees; an angel speaking from the fire; trees bursting into song; angels behaving like wedding guests; the earth shaking; a rainbow in summertime; a voice from heaven trumpeting an invitation — why are these wonders, and not others, appropriate responses to a *merkabah* exposition? The earthquake perhaps reflects Ezekiel 3:12—13; the summertime rainbow almost certainly reflects Ezekiel 1:28[8]. But what about the rest?

Ephraim E. Urbach [615] was, as far as I know, the first to notice that most of the miraculous details in the *merkabah* stories have their home in the events surrounding the Sinai revelation. God descends on Mount Sinai in fire (Exodus 19:18), and Deuteronomy stresses the fiery character of the revelation (especially in chapters 4—5). God at Sinai, like the·angel in the *merkabah* stories, speaks "from the midst of the fire" (Deuteronomy 4—5). R. Johanan dreams that he and his disciples are sitting at table on Sinai when the heavenly voice calls; Moses eats on Sinai with his companions before God summons him (Exodus 24:11, 15—18) [525]. The rabbinic elaborations of the Biblical story, some of which we will discuss in more detail later on, have an earthquake accompany the revelation; they picture the Sinai event as a wedding of God and his people, and lovingly describe how myriads of angels were in attendance. The rainbow, I must admit, belongs only to Ezekiel's vision, and I have not been able to find any parallel to the singing of the trees in connection with either Sinai or the *merkabah*. But five out of seven is not a bad score, and gives the impression that the miracles of the *merkabah* stories are intended to be faint reflections of the wonders that accompanied the giving of the Torah. When R. Johanan's disciples expound the *merkabah*, Sinai happens again.

Two stories which the Palestinian Amoraim told about their Tannaitic predecessors confirm this impression. In one story, R. Akiba sees Ben Azzai surrounded by fire as he expounds. Akiba thinks he is exploring "the chambers of the *merkabah*," but it turns out he is joining together verses from the three divisions of Scripture[9], "and the words of Torah were as joyful as the day they were given from Sinai ... in fire" (*Lev. R.* 16:4, ed. 354—355)

---

8 "Like the appearance of the bow that is·seen in a cloud on a rainy day, so was the appearance of the surrounding splendor. This was the appearance of the likeness of the glory of the Lord." The "fourth month" of Ezekiel 1:1 is the "Tammuz" of the Jewish lunar year, corresponding to our June-July. (Targum translates "the fourth month" as "Tammuz"; PT and BT place the events in "summer," *tequfat tammuz*, literally "the season of Tammuz.")

9 That is, the Torah (the Pentateuch, the so-called Five Books of Moses); the Prophets (in which category Jews include the "historical books" from Joshua to II Kings as well as Isaiah, Jeremiah, Ezekiel, and the Twelve); and the Writings (all the other books of the Hebrew Bible).

[191][10]. The second story (PT Hag. 2:1, 77b) is about R. Eliezer and R. Joshua, and it does not mention the *merkabah*, but the point is the same: enveloping fire is a sign that the Sinai event is being replicated.

This assumption explains the details of the New Testament story of Pentecost. Pentecost is the Greek name for the Jewish festival of Shabuᶜot, the day in early summer on which the rabbis believed God had appeared to his people on Sinai. (This belief was older than the rabbis; we find it suggested in the Book of Jubilees, 1:1, 6:17 [431,433,684].) Appropriately, the apostles enter the new covenant, are "baptized with the Holy Spirit" (Acts 1:5), on the very day that their ancestors entered the old. Also appropriately, certain features of the Sinai event are repeated: "There appeared to them tongues as of fire, distributed and resting on each one of them. And they were all filled with the Holy Spirit and began to speak in other tongues, as the Spirit gave them utterance" (Acts 2:3–4). The apostles' speaking in tongues presumably reflects the rabbinic tradition that God gave the Ten Commandments in the seventy languages of humankind (BT Shabb. 88b [394,449]). Similarly, the fire resting upon them is a token of a new Sinai. We can extend the parallelism between the Pentecost phenomena in Acts and the wonders recorded in the *merkabah* stories if we accept the view of some New Testament scholars [71a] that Acts 4:31 was originally a variant of the Pentecost story: "the place in which they had gathered together was shaken, and they were all filled with the Holy Spirit and spoke the word of God with boldness." The Christian writer used for his own purposes Jewish motifs connected with the Sinai event and the annual feast believed to commemorate it. These motifs underlie the stories of Johanan b. Zakkai and his disciples.

Our question now becomes: why are expositions of Ezekiel's *merkabah* answered by miracles associated with the Sinai revelation? What connection is there between these two Biblical episodes? The Book of Acts points us to the answer: the festival of Shabuᶜot.

From at least as far back as the beginning of the Christian Era, Jews read aloud in the synagogue on each Sabbath and festival a section of the Pentateuch, followed by a thematically related passage from the Prophets (Acts 13:15). It was centuries before this practice became a prescribed cycle of fixed readings: the rabbinic literature and the evidence from the Genizah[11] point to considerable local variation even in the Pentateuchal readings, and, as far as we can tell, the choice of Prophetic lection (*haftarah*, plural *haftarot*) was often left to the judgment of the individual preacher. We find in the rabbinic sources only the beginnings of an effort to regulate

---

10 See Appendix I, section 6.
11 See Appendix I, section 5.

the lectionary cycle, extending (M. Meg. 3:4–6, T. Meg. 3[4]:1–9, BT Meg. 30a–31b) to festivals and certain other special occasions [259,263, 306,313,336]. In this, as in other matters relating to synagogue worship, the rabbis do not seem to have invented rules and then tried to get people to follow them, but rather to have regularized what they found people already doing [410a]. When, therefore, the rabbis tell us that a certain passage is to be read on such and such a festival, we may assume that was the practice in the synagogues they knew. When they are not sure which of two passages is to be read, it follows that some synagogues read one passage and some the other.

Thus, to take the case in which we are now interested, M. Meg. 3:5 prescribes that the passage beginning with Deuteronomy 16:9 is to be read on Shabu^cot, while T. Meg. 3(4):5 gives the passage beginning with Exodus 19:1 as an alternative. We may deduce that some synagogue leaders in Tannaitic Palestine thought it appropriate that the people hear a Pentateuchal prescription for Shabu^cot (Deuteronomy 16:9–12) on the occasion of the festival, while others preferred the story of the event that Shabu^cot was supposed to commemorate. Mishnah and Tosefta do not try to fix the *haftarah* for the occasion. But a purportedly Tannaitic passage in BT Meg. 31a tells us that "Habakkuk" (presumably chapter 3, in which the rabbis found references to the Sinai revelation) is the *haftarah* associated with Deuteronomy 16:9ff. [48], while "the *merkabah*" is the *haftarah* to Exodus 19:1ff[12].

We cannot be sure how old the Talmudic passage is that combines the Sinai story and the *merkabah* vision, as, respectively, the Torah reading and the *haftarah* for Shabu^cot. The Gemara's claim that it is Tannaitic is open to some question. But, as we proceed, we will see much circumstantial evidence that the synagogue practice it records was very early and very widespread. Once the preachers noticed that Psalm 68:18[13] has God's "chariotry" (*rekheb*, from the same root as *merkabah*) present at Sinai, Sinai and the *merkabah* were paired, and it became natural to interpret the one passage in the light of the other. We will have plenty of opportunity to examine the midrashic results of this coupling. What is important for us now is that it appears to be behind the combination of *merkabah* expositions and Sinai-like wonders in the stories of Johanan b. Zakkai's disciples.

If this is so, we can make a good guess about the origin of the *merkabah*

---

12 When Shabu^cot was extended to two days, all four passages found a place in its liturgy. Modern synagogues thus read them all.

13 68:17, in most Bible translations. Throughout this book, I use the verse divisions of the Hebrew Bible text, which, especially in the Psalms, sometimes differ slightly from those of most English versions. I cite the English verse number beside the Hebrew, only where I have reason to think that the reader will have difficulty finding the reference.

stories. Their home was the synagogue. The occasion with which they were particularly associated was Shabuᶜot. The prototypes of their heroes were the preachers who expounded the *merkabah* as Shabuᶜot *haftarah*. We recall that T. Meg. 3(4):28 tells us that "many expounded the *merkabah*" in Tannaitic Palestine, and gives us a hint that their expositions had something to do with synagogue worship. We now perhaps get a glimpse of who these men were and the context in which their expositions took place. We will later see that the preachers used the *merkabah* vision in order to give the people a particularly vivid and exciting picture of the glory and power of the God who proclaimed his Torah from Mount Sinai. The people were excited, and wanted more. Contemporary preachers could do no more than bring the spectacle of Sinai before the mind's eye. How great were the holy men of former generations, whose *merkabah* expositions were climaxed by real glimmerings of Sinai's glory! Happy their eyes, which thus saw! All of this was at the level of wistful fantasy. It had not yet occurred to the people that they might indeed find ways to see the things that their preachers told them about. We will later see what happened when it did (chapter IX).

The miracle stories that constitute the oldest stratum of the *merkabah* traditions involving Johanan b. Zakkai give us some sense of what the *merkabah* looked like to the crowds who came to hear the synagogue preachers. They have an atmosphere of thrilled and delighted wonder. All is bathed in the sunshine of divine approval. The skies cloud over, but only to show the rainbow. Fire descends, but does no one any harm. Angels dance. Heavenly voices trumpet invitations to bliss. We are far away from the dour prohibitions of M. Hag. 2:1, from the unfortunate child burned by fire from the *hashmal* (BT Hag. 13a).

Where does this other, grimmer picture of the *merkabah* come from? Who imported it into the Johanan b. Zakkai traditions, in the form of Johanan's quoting the regulation that "the *merkabah* may not be expounded by an individual unless he is a scholar and understands on his own"? How does it come, in Tosefta's version, entirely to choke the miraculous element?

The key to these questions, too, lies in the synagogue.

3. The Mishnah: Megillah 4:10, and parallels

Given the fact that Jews have used the *merkabah* vision at least since Talmudic times as *haftarah* for an important festival, it is a little surprising to find that the Mishnah forbids it to be used as *haftarah* on any occasion whatever. "The *merkabah* may not be used as *haftarah*. R. Judah [however] permits it" (M. Meg. 4:10).

A conflict between accepted practice and Mishnaic dictate is not by itself extraordinary. The collective judgment of the Jewish people on where the authoritative *halakhah* lies has not always been the same as that of the Mishnah's editors, and, in this case, advocates of the synagogue practice could and did appeal to the dissenting opinion of R. Judah b. Ilai[14]. But the opposition between ruling and practice is here so extreme that it gives the impression of going beyond disagreement into confrontation. We must take a closer look at it.

Let us begin with the full text of the passage that contains the restriction on the *merkabah*:

> The story of Reuben [Genesis 35:22] may be read [to the congregation in the synagogue] but may not be translated [into the Aramaic vernacular]. The story of Tamar [Genesis 38] may be both read and translated. The first story of the [golden] calf [Exodus 32:1–6] may be both read and translated, while the second [Exodus 32:21–24] may be read but may not be translated. The blessing of the priests [Numbers 6:24–26] and the story of David and Amnon [? perhaps II Samuel 11–13] may neither be read nor translated.
> The *merkabah* may not be used as *haftarah*. R. Judah permits it.
> R. Eliezer says: *Declare to Jerusalem* [Ezekiel 16] may not be used as *haftarah*.

In order to understand what is going on here, we must briefly leave the *merkabah* for the more general subject of forbidden Scriptures.

Tosefta and BT preserve a baraita that is clearly related to M. Meg. 4:10, but is considerably longer and arranged differently (T. Meg. 3[4]:31–38, BT Meg. 25a–b) [253]. The baraita classifies more than a dozen Biblical passages under three headings:

1. Those that may be both read and translated;
2. those that may be read but may not be translated;
3. those that may be neither read nor translated.

The first list, of those passages "that may be both read and translated," is by far the longest of the three. The use of these texts in the synagogue is not restricted in any way. Obviously, however, some people must have questioned whether the passages listed were suitable for reading in the synagogue. Otherwise the baraita would not have needed specifically to affirm that they are.

What sort of Biblical passages does the baraita treat? More than half of them involve sex — usually, with a heavy touch of brutality or perversion. They include stories that have embarrassed pious readers of the Bible for

---

14 The Mishnah itself (ᶜEd. 1:5–6) offers two alternative explanations of why its editors permit dissenting voices to be heard alongside the authoritative opinion of the majority: so that later courts that vote to overturn the consensus of their predecessors will have some traditional authority to appeal to; or, so that a minority opinion can be clearly identified as such and permanently rejected. Whichever explanation we prefer, there is no doubt that the Mishnah's editors represent the anonymous dictum as majority opinion, and thus place their authority behind it.

generations. Lot's daughters get him drunk and seduce him (Genesis 19: 30–38). Reuben sleeps with his father's concubine (Genesis 35:22). Judah gets his daughter-in-law Tamar pregnant (Genesis 38). Thugs gang-rape a Levite's concubine until she is dead; her master cuts her into twelve pieces "and sent her throughout all the territory of Israel" (Judges 19). David's son Amnon rapes his own half-sister (II Samuel 13). We need not be surprised that some people wondered how hearing these episodes read in synagogue would affect the congregation. Nor is it surprising that they recoiled from the sixteenth chapter of Ezekiel, an obscenely graphic representation of Jerusalem as a promiscuous wife[15].

In one case, which will turn out to be important for our argument, I believe that the baraita conceals an erotic passage behind the discreet title "warnings and punishments" [552]. In rabbinic terminology, a "warning" (*'azharah*) is the Torah's categorical prohibition of a certain action, while a "punishment" (*conesh*) is the Torah's prescription of the penalty you must pay if you do this action. The Pentateuch is full of "warnings" and "punishments"; but the only place I know of where they are concentrated in such a way that they can be used to designate a specific passage is Leviticus 18 and 20, where the subject is forbidden sex, mostly incest. The purpose of these chapters is of course to warn people away from the forbidden relations. But some may reasonably have wondered if the cumulative effect of all the "nakedness" that is being "uncovered" in Leviticus 18 might not be to stir up a yen for exactly what is forbidden[16].

The baraita also lists a few passages whose propriety seems to have been questioned for reasons that had nothing to do with eroticism. The objections to the priestly blessing of Numbers 6:24–26 and to Deuteronomy's "blessings and curses" seem to be connected with the circumstances of their use in the synagogue rather than with their content [302,552]. There remain Genesis's account of creation (*macaśeh bereshit*), which we will meet again when we examine M. Hag. 2:1; and two stories of the golden calf, of which the second is enrolled in the list of those passages "that may be read but may not be translated."

Tannaitic sources quoted in T. Meg. 3(4):36 and BT Meg. 25b, and Amoraic statements collected in PT Meg. 4:11 (75c), make pretty clear that the

---

15 "It once happened that someone read [in synagogue the passage beginning] *declare to Jerusalem her abominations* [Ezekiel 16:2] when R. Eliezer was present. He said to him: 'Why don't you go declare the abominations of your mother?'" (T. Meg. 3[4]:34; parallels in PT Meg. 4:12, 75c, and BT Meg. 25b). R. Eliezer, it should be said, was not famous for his courtesy or tact.

16 Paul seems to have had experiences of this sort. "If it had not been for the law, I should not have known sin. I should not have known what it is to covet if the law had not said, 'You shall not covet.' But sin, finding opportunity in the commandment, wrought in me all kinds of covetousness. Apart from the law sin lies dead. I was once alive apart from the law, but when the commandment came, sin revived and I died" (Romans 7:7–9).

nucleus of the "second story of the calf" is Exodus 32:22–24, where Aaron explains to a furious Moses why and how he has made the golden calf. We may infer from this that the Bible's own account of the calf's construction (Exodus 32:1–6) is the "first story." A statement quoted in the name of R. Simeon b. Eleazar (ca. 200 A.D.) gives us a hint as to why the rabbis thought that the "second story" should be kept under wraps: "From the reply that Aaron gave to Moses, the heretics went astray" (T. Meg. 3[4]:37). BT's version of this statement adds a quotation from Exodus 32: 24: *And I cast it into the fire, and out came this calf* (BT Meg. 25b). The eleventh-century French Talmud commentator Rashi, commenting on this passage, tells us that the heretics "dared to assert that there is reality in idol-worship." We will return to these cryptic remarks in chapter V, where we will see that they provide a key bit of evidence for our investigation.

But what of the *merkabah*? BT's version of our baraita does not mention it at all. Tosefta's version — and this is the only significant point, apart from the textually uncertain ending, on which the two versions differ — tacks a reference to the *merkabah* on to the end of list number one: "The *merkabah* may be read to the public." The formulation of this sentence is entirely different from that of all the preceding rulings, each of which says that the passage in question "may be both read and translated." It is obviously an addition to the first list.

In other words, the author of the original baraita took so for granted that the *merkabah* was appropriate for synagogue use that he did not bother to say so explicitly. It was left for a later writer to affirm that the *merkabah* may be read in public, presumably because some people were questioning the practice.

How does M. Meg. 4:10 fit into this? The Mishnah, as a complete work, is certainly older than BT and almost certainly older than Tosefta. This, together with the general assumption of scholars that the shorter of two sources is likely to be the older, would naturally prejudice us in favor of the view that the author of the baraita has expanded the briefer text of M. Meg. 4:10 [203,390]. My own comparison of the sources has convinced me that the reverse is true [552]. The Mishnaic passage is a digest of the baraita. Its author worked from the version of the baraita that Tosefta preserves, the version that mentioned the *merkabah*. This author's purpose — or, at least, one of his purposes — was to keep the *merkabah*, and perhaps the entire Book of Ezekiel, as far away from public view as possible. To this end, he reversed two of the baraita's rulings. According to the baraita, Ezekiel 16 might be both read and translated; M. Meg. 4:10 ignored this ruling, and recorded only R. Eliezer's opposition to the passage. (We have already seen what R. Eliezer thought of people who read from Ezekiel 16.) According to the baraita, the *merkabah* might be read to the public; M. Meg. 4:10 banished it entirely from the synagogue.

The Mishnaic passage associates the older, more lenient view of the *merkabah* with R. Judah b. Ilai. R. Judah belonged to what is conventionally called the third generation of Tannaim, who worked in the middle and later part of the second century A.D. We may thus place the hardening hostility toward the *merkabah* in the last decades before Judah the Patriarch and his associates edited the Mishnah. In Judah b. Ilai's time, as we have seen, "many expounded the *merkabah*." To judge from the stories of Johanan b. Zakkai's disciples, the crowds in the synagogue saw the *merkabah* as God's own gingerbread house, filled with the wonders of his good pleasure. The author of the baraita in BT Meg. 25a−b, who worried about whether people should be exposed to "the second story of the calf" and the steamy tales of life in David's palace, could not imagine any objection to the *merkabah*. Now someone had seen a witch in the gingerbread house. The people must be kept away. R. Judah the Patriarch and the other scholars who edited the Mishnah evidently shared this alarming vision. As we have just seen, they included in their compilation a tendentious digest of an older source which, if its rulings had been followed, would have kept the *merkabah* out of the synagogue and therefore out of the average Jew's awareness. And, in the middle of a tractate that is supposed to deal with a type of pilgrimage sacrifice called *hagigah*, they included an ominous warning against "expounding the *merkabah*" and otherwise probing what ought not to be probed.

4. The Mishnah: Hagigah 2:1

I have translated the passage in question, M. Hag. 2:1, in the Introduction (pp. 3−4). It is a remarkably difficult text, whose problems grow more complex the more one studies them. As it now stands, this mishnah restricts the exposition of three Biblical passages, each one of which is guarded more stringently than the one before: the laws of forbidden sexual relations (*carayot*, referring to Leviticus 18 and 20), the account of creation (*macaseh bereshit*), and the *merkabah*. It sets, beside the study of these passages, the investigation of the realms that lie outside the visible structure of the world ("what is above and what below, what is before and what after" [573]), and thus hints at the condemnation of both. Anyone who busies himself with such things has no care for God's honor, would be better off if he had not been born. This effect is the work of an editor or series of editors who artfully combined what appear to have been originally discrete elements, each with its own history. Everything in the mishnah, however, is anonymous, and we can trace the development and the assembling of its components only in the most hypothetical and doubtful way [552].

Nothing in M. Hag. 2:1 has anything to do with the *hagigah* sacrifice. The passage stands where it does because of a tenuous chain of word associations: the central link is the immediately preceding mishnah (Hag. 1: 8), which mentions both the laws of the *hagigah* and those of forbidden sexual relations. It is true that the Mishnah often includes material on the basis of what seem to us superficial or fortuitous associations. But I have the impression that here the editors are making the fullest possible use of their liberal conceptions of relevance, and I infer that they were eager indeed to find a place for a hair-raising warning against the sort of studies in which they included the *merkabah*.

I suspect, then, that we may find a consistent ideology behind the inclusion of both Meg. 4:10 and Hag. 2:1 in the Mishnah of Judah the Patriarch. It is perhaps the same ideology that led to the Mishnah's avoidance of angels, the next world, and apocalyptic or theosophic speculations [385, 606].

But, beyond this, there is evidence that the two *mishnayot* share a common background.

Look again at the three Biblical texts Hag. 2:1 restricts. If I am right in thinking that "warnings and punishments," mentioned in the baraita we have earlier examined, refer specifically to the "warnings" of Leviticus 18 and the "punishments" of Leviticus 20, it follows that all three texts mentioned in Hag. 2:1 are part of the larger pool of Biblical passages whose suitability for synagogue use had been questioned. But, if I am again right in thinking that Leviticus 18 and 20 belong among those passages which people objected to because of their possible effect on the sexual imagination, I am at a loss to understand why Hag. 2:1 groups them with the creation story and the *merkabah* — which, whatever else one may say about them, are not very sexy. What common denominator unites the three passages of Hag. 2:1 [202,262,717]?

The answer is that they are all three found, not only in the lists of "suspected" synagogue readings, but also in another list of lections: those prescribed for festivals and other special occasions (M. Meg. 3:4–6, T. Meg. 3[4]:1–9, BT Meg. 30a–31b). We have seen that the *merkabah* was to be read as Shabu^cot *haftarah* (BT Meg. 31a). The creation story was read, a few verses at a time, at prayer gatherings called *ma^camadot*, which were supposed to be lay people's way of participating in the sacrificial cult [413, 452]. The laws of forbidden relations were prescribed, for reasons no one is very sure of, as the afternoon Torah reading for the Day of Atonement (BT Meg. 31a) [264]. *Megillah*'s two lists of Scripture passages — those prescribed, and those that some wanted to forbid — have four texts in common. One of these four is the "blessings and curses" of Deuteronomy (M. Meg. 3:6). The others are *^carayot*, *ma^caseh bereshit*, and the *merkabah*.

What I am suggesting is that the Mishnah's editors knew that earlier generations of Tannaim had drawn up a list of Biblical passages that made people uneasy. The earlier Tannaim had, for the most part, refused to ban these passages from the synagogue; and, except where the Book of Ezekiel was concerned, their successors went along. But Judah the Patriarch and his colleagues also knew that several of the suspected passages occupied highly visible positions within the synagogue lectionary cycle, and therefore could threaten the spiritual welfare of the public. In the case of "blessings and curses," this did not matter, since the objection was in any case to the synagogue recitation of the passage (God forbid, the curses might light on members of the congregation!) rather than to its contents. But, in the other three passages, the contents were the issue, and people must be discouraged from paying too much attention to them. Hence, the restrictions of Hag. 2:1.

Meg. 4:10 and Hag. 2:1, then, both represent the reactions of Judah the Patriarch and his circle to the Scripture readings in the Palestinian synagogues. The main focus of their concern was the *merkabah*. It is unlikely that this was some ecstatic "*merkabah* mysticism." If you want to discourage people from going on psychic journeys, you do not have to go to the length of keeping them from hearing the first chapter of Ezekiel read in the synagogue on Shabu^cot. It seems to have been the Biblical text itself that, for reasons we have not yet cleared up, disturbed the Mishnah's editors. They would rather the people not hear it read at all. But, if the enthusiasm of the preachers should prove too strong to legislate against — and the fact that the *merkabah* is still read in synagogue on Shabu^cot shows that it was — they could be discouraged from pondering what they heard. This is what M. Hag. 2:1 is about. If the gingerbread house must be left where people can get to it, let them at least beware of nibbling.

5. The traditions of concealment

In the preceding sections I have tried to distinguish two responses to Ezekiel's *merkabah* within the world of rabbinic Judaism: one of pious enthusiasm and delight, the other of chilly and apprehensive reserve. I have associated the first with the synagogue, and especially with the Shabu^cot festival; I have located the second within the circle of scholars responsible for editing the Mishnah, and understood it as at least partly a reaction to the first. (I have still not tried to explain what it was that aroused these scholars' apprehensions; that will come later.)

This new, fearful response to the *merkabah*, which at times led to something resembling hostility to the Book of Ezekiel, seems to have reached its full strength toward the end of the second century A.D. and maintained it for the next several decades — that is, during the years whose focal point was the editing of the Mishnah. We do not know how great its impact was on the Jewish public; which is to say, on that segment of the Jewish public that was disposed to listen to the rabbis. The *merkabah* continued to be read in the synagogues, and there is some evidence that the later Amoraim did not take M. Hag. 2:1 entirely seriously [555]. But terrifying stories of the physical dangers of *merkabah* study, which give the impression of being popular in origin, seem then to have begun to circulate [561]. Supernatural fire answers the *merkabah* exposition of the child who studies *hashmal*, as it once answered the exposition of R. Eleazar b. Arakh. But this time it burns.

Several different pieces of evidence combine to suggest that the first half of the third century was the heyday of those who wanted to suppress the *merkabah*.

1. Origen writes in the prologue to his *Commentary on the Song of Songs* that "it is a practice among the Hebrews that no one is permitted so much as to hold [the Song of Songs] in his hands, unless he has reached a full and mature age." The Jewish sages, he continues, teach all the Scriptures to the young, but keep four passages to the end: "the beginning of Genesis, in which the creation of the world is described; the beginnings of Ezekiel the prophet, which tell of the cherubim; the end [of Ezekiel], which deals with the building of the Temple; and this book of the Song of Songs" (ed. 62; cf. tr. 23 [641,645]). If Nautin's chronology of Origen's writings is correct, this testimony will date from about the year 245 [692].

Origen's "Hebrews," like M. Hag. 2:1, treat both *ma^caseh bereshit* and the *merkabah* as texts whose study must be restricted, but the criterion for access to them is entirely different. As usual, Origen seems to have been well informed about what his Jewish neighbors were doing. Fifty years or so later, BT Hag. 13a tells us, R. Eleazar b. Pedath declined R. Johanan b. Nappaha's offer to teach him *ma^caseh merkabah* by saying, "I am not old enough" [555][17]. We will presently see that Origen was also right in thinking that his contemporaries had problems with the end as well as the beginning of the Book of Ezekiel.

---

17 Jerome (d. 420) copies Origen's information in the prologue to his *Commentary on Ezekiel* (ed. 3–4 [622]), but, since he thinks he knows from Numbers 4:3 that "a full and mature age" means thirty (*Commentary* to Ezek. 1:1; ed. 5), he confidently tells us that Jews cannot read the four passages before they are thirty. He makes the same claim in his letter to Paulinus (*Epistle 53*; ed. 460–461 [621]). Gregory Nazianzen (d. 389), using the same logic but a different text of Numbers 4:3 (the Septuagint), gives the age as twenty-five (*Orationes*, II, 48; *PG* 35, 456–457). But Origen was right not to specify an age; there is no evidence from Jewish sources that there was a fixed age before which one could not study *ma^caseh bereshit* or the *merkabah*. (The Jewish prohibition of studying philosophy or kabbalah before age forty does not appear before the later Middle Ages [565].)

There is thus no reason to doubt Origen's testimony that third-century Jews also tried to limit the reading of the Song of Songs, even though there is no rabbinic evidence for such a restriction. (Saul Lieberman has found some trace of it in a medieval Yemenite midrash [322].) We cannot be sure what they objected to about this book. Scholem has proposed that the Song of Songs was the source and focus of speculations on the dimensions of God's bodily organs, later called *Shicur Qomah* (below, chapter IX), and that the rabbis insisted on keeping these secret [597]. He may be right; but there is another explanation more in keeping with the context in Origen, as well as with the character of those passages that some Jews did not want to have read in the synagogues (above, section 3). If a person does not have the maturity to realize that the Song of Songs is a spiritual allegory, he might get the impression that it is a very sexy book.

2. The traditions that Jewish authorities once tried to suppress the entire Book of Ezekiel also seem to date from the first half of the third century.

> Rab Judah said in the name of Rab[18]: Let us remember for good that man, Hananiah b. Hezekiah, without whom the Book of Ezekiel would have been concealed [*nignaz*] on the ground that it contradicted the Pentateuch. What did he do? He had three hundred measures of oil brought to him in his upper chamber, and he sat there and expounded it [until he had explained away the contradictions]. [BT Hag. 13a, Shabb. 13b, Men. 45a]

> It once happened that a certain child was reading the Book of Ezekiel in his teacher's house, and he contemplated *hashmal*, whereupon fire came forth from *hashmal* and burned him up. [The rabbis] therefore tried to conceal the Book of Ezekiel. R. Joshua b. Gamala[c] said to them: "If this one is a scholar [and thus permitted by M. Hag. 2:1 to study the *merkabah*], all are scholars!" [BT Hag. 13a]

The heroes of these stories, Hananiah b. Hezekiah and Joshua b. Gamala, are figures from the prehistory of the rabbinic movement; they lived in the first century A.D., before the destruction of the Temple [427]. But the reality the stories reflect is that of the late second and early third century, when the problems the Book of Ezekiel posed seemed particularly troubling. The book begins with the *merkabah*; it ends with legislation for a restored temple (chapters 40–48), which more than once contradicts the ritual laws of the Torah (BT Men. 45a; *Sifre Deut., Ki Tese'* #294, ed. 313 [220])[19]; in between is a brutally obscene denunciation of the holy city (chapter 16). The Mishnah's editors, in response, tried to exclude parts of the book from the synagogue. From this it was only a step to Ezekiel's total exclusion from the religious life of Judaism[20]. But this last step, our

---

18 Rab was a Babylonian Amora active about 220–250. The man transmitting his statement, *Rab* Judah (b. Ezekiel), is a very different person from *Rabbi* Judah (b. Ilai). ("Rab" was a title given to some Babylonian Amoraim.)

19 See Appendix I, section 5.

20 It is not quite clear what "concealment" implies. The verb *ganaz* is often used for sacred objects which are "concealed" to protect them from being profaned (hence the name *genizah* for a

stories told their third-century audience, would be needlessly drastic. After all, they argued, those parts of Ezekiel that now trouble us also troubled the greater men who came before us, and their leaders were able to resolve the difficulties.

Third-century Jews told similar stories about how their authorities once came near to suppressing Ecclesiastes. I have argued that these accounts respond to their audience's concerns about the apparent hedonism and skepticism of Ecclesiastes. They soothe these concerns by reflecting that King Hezekiah and his colleagues had weighed Solomon's writings and decided that Ecclesiastes was worth preserving after all [403]. I would interpret the stories of the near-concealment of Ezekiel in the same way[d]. Their setting is ancient, but their subject is the anxieties of the third century. Their message is that the problems that caused these anxieties were settled long ago.

3. But the most important relic of the *merkabah* scare of the early third century is a remarkable literary creation which I have reconstructed on the basis of Tosefta and the two Talmuds, and called, for want of a more traditional title, "the mystical collection" [552].

The mystical collection is a series of seven stories, parables, and other items that appear all to treat *ma‘aseh merkabah* and other aspects of Judaism's supposed secret doctrine. All of the components of the collection are older than the collection itself; the compiler wrote none of it on his own. But, like the authors of the Synoptic Gospels, he was a master of creative editing, of the art of gathering and arranging older sources in such a way that they take on the new meaning he wants them to have. (We will see that many of the men who fashioned the rabbinic literature were richly gifted with this talent.) The result was a shudderingly effective pamphlet about the dangers of probing too deeply into the secrets of divinity, filled with vague hints of menace which let the imagination do the work of frightening itself.

The collection begins with the story of Johanan b. Zakkai and Eleazar b. Arakh. But the warm and dreamy atmosphere of celestial approval, which had characterized the old miracle stories, has now turned cold. The compiler — who, I believe, gave the story the form it now has in Tosefta — has

---

synagogue storeroom). "Concealing" the Book of Ezekiel would then affirm its divine origin. On the other hand, rabbinic references to the proposed "concealment" of Solomon's writings seem to be talking about exclusion from the Biblical canon [352,403,404,420,457]. The rabbis themselves seem to have been unsure of the nuance of the verb: T. Shabb. 13 (14):2–3 assumes that the "concealment" of a Targum of Job shows that it is sacred, while BT Shabb. 115a thinks it proves the opposite. But, whether or not the "concealment" of the Book of Ezekiel meant decanonization in theory, the practical result would certainly have been to remove it from the Bible used by the Jewish people.

cut out the miracles. The accent of the story has shifted to the opening dialogue between R. Johanan and his pupil. "Rabbi," Eleazar b. Arakh requests, "teach me one segment of *ma^caseh merkabah*." The master's response is cold and angry: "Did I not say to you from the beginning that 'the *merkabah* may not be expounded by an individual unless he is a scholar and understands on his own'?" To be sure, R. Johanan warms when R. Eleazar shows him how well he indeed "understands on his own." But his praise of Eleazar emphasizes that this is a rare accomplishment: "There are those who expound properly but do not practice properly, those who practice properly but do not expound properly; Eleazar b. Arakh expounds properly and practices properly." Ordinary people, this implies, must keep clear of *ma^caseh merkabah*.

I do not think that the compiler of the mystical collection invented either the opening discouragement of R. Eleazar (it seems also to have been part of *Mek. Simeon*'s version, which is independent of the mystical collection) or the concluding encomia. But, by deleting the miraculous element, he moved them to center stage. They deliver the message that the reader is to carry away with him. R. Johanan b. Zakkai now stands like a grim-faced prophet in a Byzantine painting, holding an open book in one hand and, with the other, pointing to its text: "The *merkabah* may not be expounded ..."

The compiler reinforced the message with the other material at his disposal. R. Johanan b. Zakkai transmitted his doctrine to R. Joshua b. Hananiah, Joshua to R. Akiba, Akiba to Hananiah b. Hakhinai (T. Hag. 2:2 and parallels). Akiba alone, of the four rabbis who entered the mystic "garden" (*pardes*), came out unharmed (T. Hag. 2:3–4 and parallels). Only he, as one of the few privy to the secret teaching, knew how to look upon the "garden" without harming himself, to thread the narrow path between the terrifying dangers that beset the seeker of mysteries (T. Hag. 2:5 and parallels). Akiba's less lucky or less gifted colleague, Ben Zoma, went mad from what he saw in the "garden." Thus it was that Joshua b. Hananiah found Ben Zoma one day walking in a trance, at first seeing and hearing nothing. When R. Joshua finally got his attention, Ben Zoma

said to him: "I was contemplating *ma^caseh bereshit*; and only the space of an open hand divides the upper waters from the lower waters. Scripture speaks of 'hovering' here [in Genesis 1:2, where *the spirit of God was hovering over the waters*] and also [in Deuteronomy 32:11]: *As an eagle stirs up its nest, hovering over its young.* As [in Deuteronomy] 'hovering' means simultaneously touching and not touching, so [in Genesis] 'hovering' means simultaneously touching and not touching."

R. Joshua said to his disciples: "Ben Zoma is outside."

A few days later Ben Zoma was dead. [PT Hag. 77a–b; cf. T. Hag. 2:6, BT Hag. 15a]

"Ben Zoma is outside" — mysterious words, all the more ominous for their obscurity! After reading what happened to Ben Zoma, we hardly need the midrash that concludes the mystical collection — a midrash warning against asking about what happened before the six days of creation (T. Hag. 2:7 and parallels) — to convince us that we ought not think too deeply about the first verses of Genesis. The story seems to hint at unspeakable mysteries whose depths can swallow up all but the most expert inquirers. This solemn impression is so strong that it is at first hard to take seriously Henry A. Fischel's view that the story was originally a variant of a joke that went the rounds of the Hellenistic world, about the dreamy intellectual who is so busy staring at the stars that he forgets to look where he is going and so breaks his neck [386]. Yet I find Fischel's argument, and his use of Hellenistic parallels, persuasive. The compiler of the mystical collection has brilliantly used his editorial techniques to conjure up an atmosphere of mystery and menace.

The compiler did not reinterpret all of his sources so drastically. At least one of them, the midrash with which he concluded his collection, seems originally to have said exactly what he represented it as saying. Yet his skill in teaching his assembled witnesses to sing a new song, a chorus to the Mishnah's restrictions on the *merkabah*, is very impressive. He forced the restraint of M. Hag. 2:1 upon the enthusiasm of the old *merkabah* miracle stories, and introduced R. Johanan b. Zakkai himself as the advocate and possibly even the author of the Mishnah's ruling. He reinforced this message of warning and reserve with a series of parables and anecdotes, most of which seem originally to have had nothing to do with the *merkabah*. Totally anonymous, an editor rather than an original writer, he perhaps made the most important contribution to the picture of *maᶜaseh merkabah* that dominates both *Gemarot* to Hag. 2:1.

This *maᶜaseh merkabah* emerges as a secret doctrine about the divinity, based on a mysterious exegesis of Ezekiel which was known only to a few initiated rabbis. This image can hardly fail to impress anyone who works with the Talmudic materials on the *merkabah*. Yet the secret doctrine remains so elusive — even some of the Palestinian Amoraim admitted they did not know where to find it, and assumed that it had died out after Hananiah b. Hakhinai (PT Hag. 2:1, 77b) — that I suspect it never existed.

We can, I think, understand how the belief in the esoteric *maᶜaseh merkabah* arose: read Johanan b. Zakkai's warning against expounding the *merkabah* and his subsequent praise of Eleazar b. Arakh's exposition, without the miracles in between, and you will hardly escape the impression that Eleazar knew something ordinary folk did not. We can understand more easily why the rabbis cultivated it once it had arisen: if you claim religious authority, it is to your advantage that people believe that some of those with whom you are associated have inside knowledge of the supernatural.

Thus the belief became, as beliefs will, a powerful reality in its own right. But it does not point us toward the ways Jews in fact interpreted Ezekiel's *merkabah* in Tannaitic and Amoraic times, or what these interpretations meant to them. For this, we must look in the two directions that have begun to trace themselves before us: toward the popular synagogue expositions that charged the *merkabah* miracle stories with their excitement; and toward the dark suspicions that moved Judah the Patriarch and his colleagues to try to drive Ezekiel's vision from the synagogue.

Where, in all of this, are the ecstatic journeys to the realms of the *merkabah*? We will see nothing of them as long as we stay with the Palestinian rabbinic sources. When we turn to Babylonia, we will find the situation changed. To understand how, we must turn back to the mystical collection and look at the most mysterious of its stories: the episode of the four rabbis who entered *pardes*.

6. The *pardes* episode: the Palestinian versions

Tosefta (Hag. 2:3—4) relates the following:

> Four men entered a garden (*pardes*): Ben Azzai, Ben Zoma, Aher[21], and R. Akiba. One of them looked and died; one looked and went mad; one looked and cut the young plants; one ascended safely and descended safely.
>
> Ben Azzai looked and died. Of him Scripture says, *Precious in the eyes of the Lord is the death of his saints* [Psalm 116:15].
>
> Ben Zoma looked and went mad. Of him Scripture says, *If you find honey, eat only your fill* [Proverbs 25:16; the Biblical text concludes: *lest you become stuffed with it and vomit it*].
>
> Elisha looked and cut the young plants. Of him Scripture says, *Do not let your mouth bring your flesh into sin* [Ecclesiastes 5:5].
>
> R. Akiba ascended safely and descended safely. Of him Scripture says, *Draw me, we will run after you* [Song 1:4].

PT (Hag. 2:1, 77b) repeats this passage with a few variations. It omits the four names from the very beginning. It has Ben Zoma die and Ben Azzai go mad, and not the other way around; this is, I think, a late alteration of no importance to us [552]. It has Akiba *enter* safely and *go out* safely rather than *ascend* and *descend* safely; one manuscript (Erfurt) of Tosefta shares this reading, which I believe to be the original one.

BT (Hag. 14b, concluded on 15a and 15b) agrees with Tosefta against PT on all three points. (Only one manuscript, Göttingen 3, has Akiba *enter* and *go out*.) But it differs crucially from both Tosefta and PT in another

---

21 Aher, "other one," is a nickname for the heretic rabbi Elisha b. Abuyah. It is normally used in BT, the Palestinian sources preferring to call him simply "Elisha." We do not know why Elisha was called "other one," nor do we have any clear idea what he did or what his heresy consisted of. Gedaliahu G. Stroumsa's suggestion that he was a Sethian Gnostic is the most recent of a long line of challenging but unproven proposals which stretches back more than a century; Stroumsa gives references to other hypotheses [451]. The rabbinic stories about Elisha — many of them hauntingly beautiful — are concentrated in PT Hag. 2:1 (77b—c) and BT Hag. 15a—b. *Ruth R.* 6:13 and *Eccl. R.* 7:8 substantially repeat much of PT's material.

way. The sentence that follows the opening list of names ("one of them looked and died," etc.) is missing from BT. In its place we read: "R. Akiba said to them: 'When you draw near the stones of pure marble, do not say, "Water, water." For it is written, *He who speaks lies shall not be establish-ed in my* [God's] *sight* [Psalm 101:7].'"

If the reader is by this time entirely confused, he will sympathize with the puzzlement of one Jewish community in the eleventh century, who wrote to ask Hai Gaon: "What was that 'garden'? What did [Ben Zoma] look at when he went mad? ... What does it mean that [Elisha] 'cut the young plants'? ... When R. Akiba 'entered,' what place did he enter? Why did he 'enter safely and go out safely'[22]? ... Will our master please explain ... ?" [241].

We have already glanced at Hai Gaon's answer: the "garden" is a meta-phor for the celestial "palaces," entry to the garden a metaphor for heaven-ly ascensions of the sort prescribed in the *Hekhalot*.

It would be pointless to try to survey all the efforts made from Hai Gaon's time to our own to unravel the meaning of the *pardes*. Scholem's interpretation is now the one most commonly accepted. Following Hai Gaon's lead, but taking *pardes* yet more literally, Scholem identified it with the "paradise" into which Paul was caught up (II Corinthians 12:2–4), and suggested that the *pardes* story describes an ecstatic experience essentially the same as Paul's [583,593]. The main problem with this view is that, although *pardes* sounds very much like "paradise" and the two words are in fact linguistically related, rabbinic Hebrew does not seem to use *pardes* with this meaning. Admittedly, the Qumran fragments of the original Aramaic text of the Book of Enoch do use *pardes qushṭa*, "Garden of Righteousness," for paradise (32:3, 77:3; we will have more to say about the Book of Enoch in chapter III) [130,143]. But the relevance of this to rabbinic usage is very doubtful. The rabbinic *pardes* is a pleasure garden or a park.

Following Urbach's suggestions [616], I have tried to show from the structure of the older Palestinian versions (Tosefta, PT) that the first paragraph of Tosefta's account is a metaphor whose application is explain-ed in the following paragraphs [552]. The *pardes* is not a real location which we are to hunt for in heaven or on earth, but an image the author uses to convey something about the lives and actions of his four characters.

---

22 Notice that Hai Gaon's questioners are quoting a text that had Akiba *enter* and *go out* instead of *ascend* and *descend*. Other features of their questions, notably the odd fact that it does not occur to them to ask about the "stones of pure marble," suggest to me that they are reading, not BT, but a source akin to the Erfurt manuscript of the Tosefta. Hai Gaon's reply, however, clearly presupposes the BT version.

Considered this way, the *pardes* passage is no longer as bizarre or as isolated as it seems at first sight. It falls into the category of rabbinic parables that use the image of the pleasure garden or park — once, indeed, to represent "the future paradise[23]," but also the world, the holy land, the people of Israel, and the precepts of the Torah [279,552]. It was the compiler of the mystical collection who, by placing the *pardes* story in its present context, gave it its eerie and other-worldly quality. As we will see, the men who rewrote the passage for BT carried this process of "mystification" a large step further.

To what, then, did the *pardes* metaphor originally apply? I can give only a partial and tentative answer. One parable, in *Deut. R.* 7:4 [327][24], contains a suggestive parallel to Elisha's cutting the young plants: a person who learns Torah and does not practice it is like someone who plants trees in a king's *pardes* and then cuts them down. This would fit the learned libertine Elisha b. Abuyah very well. But it does not much help us understand what happened to his three companions.

We may perhaps explain the reference to Akiba in a different way, by concentrating on the Biblical proof text that the *pardes* passage applies to him. These words are drawn from the beginning of the Song of Songs, from the following context:

> Therefore young girls [*ᶜalamot*] have loved you. Draw me; we will run after you. The king has brought me into his chambers. Let us rejoice and be glad with you [Song 1:3–4].

Both *Mekhilta* and *Sifre Deut.*[25] quote a midrash that explains the first sentence as referring to Judaism's martyrs. The expositor reads the Hebrew consonants of *ᶜalamot*, "young girls," as if they spelled the two words *ᶜal mawet*, "unto death." The text then comes to mean, "unto death have they loved you," that is, God. *Sifre* does not name the author of the midrash, but *Mekhilta* attributes it to R. Akiba. Akiba died for Torah at the hands of the Romans [439a], and it looks very much as if *Mekhilta*'s editor assumed that this exemplary martyr must be the expositor who so eloquently praises martyrdom.

Akiba "went out safely" from the *pardes*. Tosefta elsewhere (Hull. 2:23) applies the expression "went out safely" to a man who departs this life free of the taint of heresy. How did Akiba depart his life? According to the tradition recorded in BT Ber. 61b, he was reciting the *shemaᶜ*'s attes-

---

23 *Gan ᶜeden leᶜatid labo'.*
24 See Appendix I, section 7.
25 *Mekhilta, Shirah* ch. 3, ed./tr. 2:26–27; Sifre, *We-Zot ha-Berakhah* #343, ed. 398–399 [195, 220] (see Appendix I, section 5). *Song R.* 7:1, section 2, contains a parallel (cf. also 5:9). I suspect that Revelation 12:11, which says that the faithful "loved not their lives even unto death," presupposes this midrash. If so, it must be at least as old as Akiba, and very likely older. (Shmuel Safrai attributes a similar conjecture to David Flusser [338a,434a].)

tation that "the Lord is one" while the Romans tortured him to death, "until his soul went forth[26] on the word 'one.' A heavenly voice proclaimed: 'Happy are you, R. Akiba, that your soul went forth on the word 'one'!" Akiba was then presumably transported into celestial bliss. I suggest that the author of the *pardes* passage used Akiba's safe departure from the *pardes* to describe his soul's blessed departure. He applied to it the Scriptural text that, as we have seen from *Mekhilta*, had come to be associated with Akiba. I imagine he understood this text somewhat as follows:

> Therefore unto death [the martyrs] have loved you [God]. Draw me, [Akiba said to God;] we [faithful ones] will run after you. The King has brought me into his chambers [of bliss in the next world]. We will rejoice and be glad with you.

Only after the mystical collection had provided the *pardes* passage with a new context, and therefore a new frame of interpretation, did the King's chambers come to be understood as "the chambers of the *merkabah*" [519].

I offer these solutions to the riddles of the *pardes* passage only tentatively. I am fairly sure, though, that Scholem was essentially wrong as far as its original meaning is concerned. Whatever it is, it is not a literal description of an ecstatic journey to a *pardes*-paradise in heaven or anywhere else. But I am equally sure that, as far as the revised version of the passage that we find in BT is concerned, Scholem was essentially right.

7. The *pardes* episode: the Babylonian version

We recall that BT's version of the *pardes* passage omits the opening statement that "one of them looked and died, one looked and went mad," and so forth. This omission is easily explained. The opening summary is only appropriate within the structure of the metaphor; once the passage is no longer understood as a metaphor, it comes to seem pointless. The author of the BT version, who understood the passage as a literal narrative, deleted it.

In its place he put a cryptic warning which has baffled generations of interpreters. "R. Akiba said to them: 'When you draw near the stones of pure marble, do not say, "Water, water." For it is written, *He who speaks lies shall not be established in my sight* [Psalm 101:7].'"

What can this possibly mean? Where and what are the "stones of pure marble"? How do Akiba's companions "draw near" to them? What might

---

26 The verb used here, *yaṣa'*, is the same as that used in the *pardes* passage to say that Akiba "went out safely." The parallel in PT Ber. 9:5 (14b), however, which differs from BT on several important details, uses a different verb (*pareḥah nishmato*).

induce them to say, "Water, water"; and why should they not say it? How would this seemingly banal utterance mark them as liars in God's eyes?

We will probe these questions in some detail in chapter VI, and weigh Scholem's theory that the warning refers to a test which, according to the *Hekhalot*, the ecstatic traveller will meet at the gate of the sixth palace [593,609]. In the meantime, let us grant Scholem's essential point, that Akiba and his companions are conceived as travelling through some very strange places that do not seem to be on this earth. This is, I repeat, the conception found in the version that is unique to BT.

We meet this conception again in BT's stories of Elisha b. Abuyah. One of these stories is particularly valuable in that, as in the *pardes* passage itself, we can compare it with the Palestinian tradition on which it is based and see how the Babylonian storytellers have shifted the meaning.

In PT Hag. 2:1 (77b) we find Elisha performing the forbidden act of riding his horse on a Sabbath. His student R. Meir, who remains faithful to him to the end, walks after him, learning Torah from him. At one point, Elisha tells Meir to turn back, for he has calculated from his horse's paces that they have gone the distance that an observant Jew is permitted to walk on the Sabbath. Meir calls on Elisha to "turn back" himself — that is, repent.

> He said to him: "You have all this wisdom, and yet you do not repent?"
> "I cannot," he said.
> "Why not?"
> He said to him: "Once I was passing in front of the Holy of Holies mounted on my horse, on a Day of Atonement that happened to fall on a Sabbath. I heard a heavenly voice coming forth from the Holy of Holies: *'Return, backsliding children!* [Jeremiah 3:14] — except for Elisha b. Abuyah, who knew my power and rebelled against me.'"

Now let us hear the same dialogue, as reported in BT Hag. 15a:

> He said to him: "Why don't you turn back, yourself?"
> He replied: "I already heard from behind the *pargod*: *'Return, backsliding children!* — except for Aher.'"

In the Babylonian Talmud, the *pargod* is the celestial curtain that separates God from his attendants. The Babylonian narrator has transferred the scene from the Holy of Holies in Jerusalem to the corresponding Holy of Holies in heaven [365,379,456]. The curtain that separates the earthly Holy of Holies from the rest of the Temple is transformed into the *pargod*[27].

In another story, quoted earlier in BT Hag. 15a, this conception blossoms into a weirdly baroque account of Elisha's damnation. Aher "saw

---

27 I do not mean, of course, to suggest that the older Palestinian version is any more reliable historically than its Babylonian adaptation. The Temple was destroyed at least seventy years before Elisha can have had this conversation with R. Meir.

Metatron, to whom permission had been given to sit one hour each day to record the merits of Israel." He is astonished to find seated any heavenly being but God. "Perhaps," he reasons, "there are two divine powers!" Thereupon:

> They brought out Metatron and flogged him with sixty fiery lashes. "Why," they said, "did you not rise before him when you saw him?" He received permission to erase Aher's merits. A heavenly voice proclaimed: *"Return, backsliding children!* − except for Aher."

We need not here discuss the meaning of Aher's fatal deduction that "there are two divine powers" [445], or the role that the angel Metatron − a very important figure in the *Hekhalot*, to whom we will turn our attention in chapter IX − plays in the story. What is important for us is that BT assumes that Elisha has visited heaven, seen Metatron, heard his doom proclaimed from behind the *pargod*. It is hard to imagine an occasion when all this could have happened apart from the visit to the *pardes*.

We may guess that it was the Babylonian transmitters of the *pardes* story who first changed "R. Akiba entered safely and went out safely" to "R. Akiba ascended safely and descended safely." Medieval scribes "corrected" most Tosefta manuscripts in accord with the Babylonian Talmud, which they thought authoritative.

When are we to date the Babylonian reinterpretation of the *pardes* episode? The stories in BT offer us one clue: the strange punishment of "sixty fiery lashes" that is inflicted on Metatron. We find this image elsewhere in BT, in passages that can be traced to fourth-century Babylonia [552].

Have we seen traces of this reinterpretation in any other materials? Indeed we have. In the very first section of this chapter, we saw how BT Meg. 24b makes a small but crucial alteration in the reply that the anonymous sages give to R. Judah b. Ilai. Tosefta had reported it as:

> Many expounded the *merkabah* and never saw it.

In BT this became:

> Did not many hope to expound the *merkabah*, and yet they never saw it?

The Babylonian transmitter could not believe that the sages would so calmly have taken for granted that people who expound the *merkabah* do not actually see it. As far as the transmitter was concerned, the very essence of "expounding the *merkabah*" was experiencing a vision of this entity. What the sages meant, he reasoned, was that many *hoped* to expound the *merkabah* but, since they never managed to see it, obviously did not succeed.

It is only a guess, but a fair guess, that the same cluster of ideas, cultivated in fourth-century Babylonia, was responsible for the revisions in both BT Hag. 15a and Meg. 24b. R. Akiba and his companions made their way to *pardes* by expounding the *merkabah*. They indeed saw the *merkabah*, but the sight proved more than they had bargained for. Ben Azzai looked and died. Ben Zoma looked and went mad. Elisha b. Abuyah looked and saw his own damnation.

In other words, the Babylonians held beliefs that we can recognize from the *Hekhalot*.

8. Conclusions

The rabbinic testimonies about exposition of the *merkabah* have pointed us in three main directions:

First, toward the synagogues of second-century Palestine. "Many expounded the *merkabah*" to the crowds, particularly on the feast of Sha-·buᶜot. The story of the Sinai revelation was read from the Torah, Ezekiel's vision was read from the Prophets. Working from these two Scriptures, the preachers fed their people's hungry imaginations on the glories of the God who had given them his Torah.

Second, toward R. Judah the Patriarch and his colleagues. They saw danger. If there was food for the imagination in the *merkabah*, this food might be poisoned. It must be kept under lock and key. This they tried to do, but with only moderate success. Their suspicions gave an ominous tinge to the Talmudic traditions about the *merkabah*. But in the synagogues, which were the focus of their concern, the *merkabah* continued to be read and preached.

Third, toward Babylonia in the Amoraic period, particularly the fourth century. Here, expounding the *merkabah* stopped being a matter of Bible study alone. It took on overtones of ecstatic experience, of journeys to realms filled with strange and dangerous sights.

These are the shadows that *merkabah* exegesis cast upon the rabbinic literature. They raise a throng of questions which we have not yet begun to explore. How, for example, did the preachers use the *merkabah* vision to fasten the people's attention on the God of Sinai? Why did the Mishnah's editors find this frightening? How did the idea of the heavenly ascension step into this arena of enthusiasm and fear? How did it beget the *Hekhalot*?

We are ready to look for the entities that projected the shadows.

Chapter II

The Beginnings of Merkabah Interpretation

We are not, however, yet ready to deal with rabbinic *merkabah* exegesis.

Rabbinic Judaism, innovative as it was, was hardly a novel creation of the years after 70 A.D. Judaism had been a Scripture religion for centuries before the birth of the rabbinic movement. When the rabbis took up and read their Bible, they did so equipped with a rich inheritance of exegetical tradition; and this was as true of the *merkabah* vision as of any other part of Scripture.

We know far less than we would like to about the Scripture exegesis of pre-rabbinic Judaism. Yet the sources that survive allow us to trace something of the early development of the lines of *merkabah* interpretation that the rabbis were later to follow. With their aid, we can have a perspective on rabbinic *merkabah* exegesis that the rabbinic texts themselves would not permit us.

In this and the following chapter, I have not tried for a chronological arrangement of the materials to be discussed. The Septuagint Greek translation of Ezekiel, which I discuss in section 3 of this chapter, is probably some decades at least earlier than the Qumran texts treated in section 2. The apocalypses, which require a chapter to themselves, include sources both earlier and later than the Septuagint and the Qumran writings. Rather, I have aimed at an arrangement that will allow the exegetical themes, and the issues that I see developing in them, intelligibly to emerge.

The first source of *merkabah* exegesis we will examine, however, is also the oldest. It is the Book of Ezekiel itself. Ezekiel the book interprets the visions attributed to Ezekiel the prophet; and it is the task of our first section to examine how.

1. The Book of Ezekiel

a) Introduction. At first sight, the proposal that we treat the Book of Ezekiel as a commentary on its own contents is bound to seem paradoxical, not to say eccentric. The book sets forth a series of visions and messages within the framework of a unified narrative, written from beginning to end in the first person. The "I" who speaks is Ezekiel the son of Buzi the priest, a Jewish exile in the land of Babylonia by the river Chebar. It is clear enough, we might think, that this Ezekiel wrote the book himself. Yet, on closer reading, this turns out not to be clear at all. Tensions, disguised at first by the book's appearance of unity and structure, rapidly begin to appear. Some of them are perhaps the creations of hyper-critical modern scholars. But others cannot be dismissed so easily; they suggest that some process of editing, rewriting, and annotation lies between the earliest materials preserved in the Book of Ezekiel, and the book as we now have it.

What was this process, and how large a role did Ezekiel himself play in it? Scholars have not settled on any consensus. The "radicals" of the early twentieth century begrudged Ezekiel more than a few scattered verses of the book named after him; while the more "moderate" scholars of the past few decades have declared the book substantially Ezekiel's, although arranged and expanded by faceless editors [12,14]. Of the three major commentaries published in this century, Cooke's (1936) notes what are supposed to be secondary accretions to the text, but takes little interest in who added them or why; Zimmerli's (1969) boldly dissects the alleged strata of the book and tries to explain the significance of secondary as well as original materials; while Greenberg's (1983, to chapters 1—20 only) sees the Book of Ezekiel as a skillfully crafted composition which may derive, in its entirety, from Ezekiel himself [1,19,6].

Greenberg sharply and effectively criticizes the approach of Zimmerli and his confreres. Their operations, he argues, rest on subjective and arbitrary prejudices about what the prophet must have been trying to say; they prove their assumptions by excising whatever does not conform to them. Significantly, though, Greenberg himself occasionally speaks of editorial activity in the Book of Ezekiel (on pages 125—126, 199, for example). Ezekiel, indeed, may have been his own editor. But, once we are prepared to see the creation of the Book of Ezekiel as a complex process involving more than a single act of composition, we have opened the door to the possibility that the process may have extended beyond Ezekiel's lifetime. I thus find myself, for reasons that will become clearer as we go on, in agreement with Zimmerli's basic position that much editorial labor, involving many years and many contributors, lies between Ezekiel and his book. Even if we cannot hope to reconstruct the details of this labor (and here I disagree with Zimmerli and the rest), we cannot ignore it when we come to consider the visions of the divine entourage and their relation to the book that contains them.

b) Hayyot and cherubim. How this affects us will become clear in connection with the *hayyot* (sing. *hayyah*)[1], the beings whose description

---

1 The word is usually translated, in accord with the basic meaning of the Hebrew root *hay*, "living

occupies the first part of chapter 1. The *hayyot* emerge from the great fiery cloud that Ezekiel sees approaching from the north. There are four of them. This is what they look like:

> Their likeness was human. Each of them had four faces, each four wings. Their legs were straight; the soles of their feet were like the sole of a calf's foot; they sparkled [?] like polished brass. On their four sides they had human hands underneath their wings. ... This was the likeness of their faces: a human face, a lion's face on the right for all four of them, an ox's face on the left for all four of them, and an eagle's face for all four of them. ... This was the likeness of the *hayyot*: their appearance was like blazing coals of fire, like the appearance of torches, going [?] up and down among the *hayyot*. The fire was splendid, and lightning shot out of the fire. The *hayyot* ran and returned [?] like the appearance of lightning [?]. [Ezekiel 1:5–14]

We later learn something about the function of the *hayyot*: they are the bearers of a crystalline "firmament," which itself supports a throne on which God sits (Ezekiel 1:22–28). But we do not understand very well what they are, or why God, who normally appears to his prophets without such elaborate fanfare, chooses to have such creatures in attendance when he reveals himself to Ezekiel.

Where the opening vision leaves us in the lurch, however, the sequel comes – or seems to come – to our rescue. In chapters 8–11, Ezekiel is transported in a vision from the place of his exile in Babylonia to Jerusalem, where he sees how the people of Jerusalem have polluted the Temple and hears how they have filled their city with sin. He then sees what seem like the very same creatures, with their attendant "wheels," that he saw in his first vision in Babylonia by the river Chebar; and he describes the ensemble all over again (ch. 10). Only here the creatures are no longer called *hayyot*, but cherubim; and the writer takes pains to emphasize that the two are the same:

> The cherubim lifted themselves up – this was the *hayyah* that I saw at the river Chebar. ... The glory of the Lord went forth from the threshold of the Temple and stood over the cherubim. The cherubim lifted their wings and rose from the earth while I was watching ... with the glory of the God of Israel resting above them. This was the *hayyah* that I saw beneath the God of Israel at the river Chebar, and [now] I realized that they were cherubim. [10:15, 18–20]

And now we know what is going on; for, while we have never heard of the *hayyot* before Ezekiel 1 describes them, we know very well what cherubim are. They are winged beings on which God sits enthroned (I Samuel 4:4) or rides through the air (II Samuel 22:11). Moses sculpted two of them in gold for the desert Tabernacle, facing each other from opposite ends of the ark-cover, sheltering the ark with their spread wings (Exodus

---

creatures." But *hayyah* more commonly means "beast." I cannot guess which nuance was foremost in the author's own mind; and, since both played a role in Jewish interpretation of the *hayyot* and their significance, I prefer to keep the ambiguous Hebrew word rather than to decide between the two. (We find a similar ambiguity – intentional, I think – in Exodus 1:19, where *hayot* may mean that the Hebrew women are "lively, vigorous"; or, that they are "beasts.")

25:18–22, 37:7–9); God spoke to Moses from a spot above the ark and between the cherubim (Exodus 25:22, Numbers 7:89). Similar creatures, of monstrous size, made of gold-plated olive wood, perched in the Holy of Holies of Solomon's Temple, filling the room with their wings (I Kings 6: 23–28, 8:6–7); it was no doubt there that Ezekiel saw them on his visionary trip to Jerusalem. We get a better idea of what cherubim look like from parallels outside Israel. As winged monsters with animal bodies – usually a lion's or a bull's – and human faces, they guard the entrance to Babylonian temples. The Egyptian sphinx, with its lion body, is perhaps the best known cherub of the ancient world [4,18,20,32].

Ezekiel's *hayyot* do not look very much like cherubim. The *hayyot* have basically human bodies (Ezekiel 1:6) and animal faces; cherubim have the reverse. The four faces of the *hayyot* are, as far as I know, unheard of outside Ezekiel [7,18]; and Exodus 25:20 makes clear that Moses' cherubim had only one face each. To accept the equation proposed in Ezekiel 10, we have to overlook a good deal. But, if we are nonetheless prepared to accept it, we gain one apparent advantage: we understand, or think we understand, what the *hayyot* are doing in Ezekiel 1. God travels to Babylonia enthroned, as Israelite tradition depicts him, on his cherubim. Ezekiel does not understand this until, more than a year later (8:1), he has a chance to compare the real cherubim with the models set up in the Holy of Holies, and realizes that the two are the same. The *hayyot* of the river Chebar and the Temple cherubim merge; the latter become mobile; and, carrying the glory of the God of Israel, they abandon the polluted Temple (10:18–19) and the sinful city (11:22–23). The lesson of this solemn withdrawal appears to be that God is not bound to the Temple of Jerusalem. When he pleases, he can abandon it to its destruction, taking the cultic apparatus that expresses his holiness and his power with him to his people in Babylonia (11:15–16). But there is more. Chapters 40–48 describe in meticulous detail the rebuilt and purified Temple of the future. To this Temple it will someday please God to return, reversing the procession with which he once departed:

> Then he [the angelic being who, in Ezekiel's vision, gives him a guided tour of the future Temple] brought me to the gate facing eastward. The glory of the God of Israel was approaching from the east; his voice [or, "its sound"] was like the sound of many waters [cf. 1:24], and the earth shone from his glory. The vision that I [then] saw was like the vision I had seen when I [?] came to destroy the city, and like the vision I had seen at the river Chebar; I fell on my face[2]. The glory of the Lord entered the house through the gate that faced eastward ... and the house was filled with the glory of the Lord. ... And he said to me: "Son of man, [this is] the place of my throne, the place where my feet will rest. I will dwell here among the children of Israel forever. ..." [43:1–7]

---

2 The Hebrew text of 43:3 seems to be corrupt; the word "vision" is mentioned too often. I translate rather freely, as I understand the writer's drift.

The destroyed Temple is rebuilt, the departed glory has returned; the sin of the Israelites is purged, the wounds of their punishment healed. The action of the Book of Ezekiel, which began at the river Chebar, is concluded on the mountain of the Temple to come (40:2), and its rhythms are marked by the comings and goings of God's glory and the *hayyot*-cherubim that carry it [12b,13]. The initial vision of God and his entourage, which once seemed so purposeless, now appears as a foreshadowing of the grand cycle that underlies the rest of the book.

To put it another way, the Book of Ezekiel has provided a context for the vision of chapter 1, and has thereby proposed an interpretation for it. Were we to assume that the prophet Ezekiel wrote the Book of Ezekiel as we now have it, we could have little hesitation about accepting this interpretation. But, since I am not prepared so to assume, I find matters rather more complicated. I must ask whether it was Ezekiel himself — or, at any rate, the author of chapter 1[3] — who provided this interpretation of the initial vision. If not, is the interpretation nevertheless correct? And, given the scope of our study, I must ask a third question: to what extent did this interpretation influence later expositors of chapter 1?

I think the answer to the first question is probably no. As I have already indicated, I consider the Book of Ezekiel the creation of multiple authors, all of whom wrote under the "I" of Ezekiel. In chapters 8–11, and particularly chapter 10, the original text appears to have been so overlaid by repeated interpretations and expansions that it is almost impossible to distinguish the original, or to separate the several layers that were later added [10]. Ezekiel 10:9–17, I believe, is secondary in its entirety, and consists mostly of a brief commentary on 1:15–21 which was deposited in chapter 10 at some point in that chapter's formation [9]. (We will soon have to look more closely at this important passage.) Beyond this, I am not prepared to go into the very difficult question of who wrote what in chapter 10, let alone the rest of the Book of Ezekiel; especially since, once we reach the point when Jews have come to regard both the primary and the secondary

---

3 For the purpose of this study, I see no need to decide whether or not it was a prophet of the Babylonian captivity who wrote the first chapter of Ezekiel. If I call the author "Ezekiel" in what follows, it is a matter of convenience only, and not a judgment on this question. – It may perhaps seem more urgent for us to decide whether the chapter had in fact a single author, or whether it consists of a series of additions to an original nucleus [11,12]. But I think we can sidestep this issue as well. Our concern is with the impact of the *merkabah* vision on later writers, and with their ways of understanding it. Now, as far back as we can trace the impact of Ezekiel 1 on other sources (including secondary material in the Book of Ezekiel itself), it had this impact as a unified piece of work, evidently not much different from the text that we now have. Of secondary interpretation of chapter 1 preserved in chapter 1 itself, I can find no trace (below). The developmental history of Ezekiel 1 is, as far as we are concerned, its prehistory. I therefore leave it aside, and treat the chapter as if it were a single source by a single writer.

material as the words of Ezekiel and therefore the object of exegetical attention, the issue loses its importance for us.

I do not, however, believe that it was the author of chapter 1 who announces, in chapter 10, that his bizarre *hayyot* are none other than the familiar cherubim. It is true that the *hayyot*, like the cherubim, carry the deity and mark the place where he gives revelation; it is true that the language of chapter 1 occasionally suggests the language describing the Tabernacle or Temple[a]. But the *hayyot* are so unlike the cherubim that I cannot imagine that anyone who knows, on whatever subconscious level, that the two are identical, would describe them with all the idiosyncrasies of Ezekiel 1. Given that so much of chapter 10 was written to interpret chapter 1, it seems to me more likely that the *hayyot* = cherubim equation was made by someone who was baffled by the *hayyot* and needed a context in which he could make sense of them. He found this context in the Jerusalem Temple. He, or some later editor, used this perception as one of the principles around which he organized the Book of Ezekiel.

After this discussion, it should come as no surprise that my answer to the second question is also no. Whatever the *hayyot* were originally supposed to be, I do not think they were the cherubim familiar from Israelite tradition and cult.

But to the third question — about the influence of the *hayyot* = cherubim identification on later Jewish expositors — we would expect a somewhat more positive answer. After all, the whole organization of the Book of Ezekiel seems to vouch for this equation's being the key to the meaning of the *merkabah* vision. The later interpreters who dealt with Ezekiel could hardly be expected to ignore this clear message.

Surprisingly, they do. Not absolutely: the idea that Ezekiel's *hayyot* are the guardians of the ark and the denizens of the Holy of Holies has indeed left its traces on *merkabah* exegesis, particularly outside the rabbinic literature[b]. Most Jewish interpreters take their identity as cherubim seriously enough that it is not until the *Hekhalot* literature that we find *hayyot* and cherubim mentioned side by side, as distinct classes of angels. But, all in all, the impact of this conception on later *merkabah* interpretation is surprisingly slight. We frequently find the *merkabah* placed in a ritual context, sometimes of the Temple, more often of the synagogue. But the presence of the *hayyot* in the role of the Biblical cherubim is rarely more than a minor detail.

Our first foray into history of exegesis has thus reached what is by and large a dead end. Not because it does not lead us back to what the *hayyot* meant to the man who first described them — that is not the question we want to answer here — but because it does not lead us forward into any of the main roads of *merkabah* exegesis in post-Biblical Judaism.

Yet we have not wasted our time. We have touched on the important issue of context and its role in ancient Bible interpretation. The people who first added their interpretations to Ezekiel's visions and organized them into the book that bears Ezekiel's name dealt with a baffling and idiosyncratic image by fitting it into a context where it seemed to make sense: the central shrine of the Temple whose destruction Ezekiel prophesied. The expositors who came after them found this context far less meaningful. Unlike the modern commentator, they felt few qualms about ignoring it and looking for the meaningful context elsewhere in Scripture. In Origen's image of the house of locked rooms, the key will not be found next to the door it opens. One must look for it elsewhere in the Bible.

c) "Blessed be the glory of the Lord from his place." We find evidence of one such extended search for context in the form of a significant scribal error in Ezekiel 3:12–13 — truly a Freudian slip of the pen. The mistake is in one letter only of the Hebrew text; and yet for centuries it had the deepest influence on the way Jews perceived the *merkabah*.

If we reconstruct the text of verse 12 the way nearly all critical commentators agree it must be reconstructed [19], we can translate the passage as follows:

> A spirit [or, "wind"] lifted me. I heard behind me the sound of a great quaking as the glory of the Lord arose from its place [*berum kebod YHWH mimmeqomo*], and the sound of the wings of the *hayyot* rustling against each other, and the sound of the wheels [*'ofannim*] opposite them, and the sound of a great quaking.

Clear enough. But our extant Hebrew text (known as the Masoretic Text, commonly abbreviated "MT") has the graphically similar *barukh* in place of *berum*, with the following result:

> A spirit lifted me. I heard behind me the voice[4] of a great quaking: "Blessed be the glory of the Lord from his place!" [*barukh kebod YHWH mimmeqomo*]. And [I heard] the voice of the wings of the *hayyot* rustling against each other, and the voice of the *'ofannim* opposite them, and the voice of a great quaking.

We cannot be sure just when *berum* was changed to *barukh*. But the error is certainly an early one, for it was already in the Hebrew text that the Jews of Alexandria used when they translated Ezekiel into Greek, probably in the second century B.C. (see below).

What caused the error? Any hand-copied text, sacred or profane, is bound to have its share of random blunders made by overworked or distracted scribes. But I do not think this is one of them. I believe that the copyist had found a context for the *merkabah* vision in another dramatic vision, this time described by Isaiah. Perhaps unconsciously, he altered Ezekiel's text in accord with this context:

---

4 *Qol* can mean both "sound" and "voice." It will soon become clear why I translate it "voice" this time round, and why I leave the *'ofannim* in Hebrew.

In the year that King Uzziah died I saw the Lord sitting on a high and exalted throne, his train filling the Temple. Seraphim were standing over him. Each of them had six wings: with two he would cover his face, with two he would cover his feet, and with two he would fly. And one would cry out to the other: "Holy, holy, holy, is the Lord of hosts! The whole earth is full of his glory." The bases of the thresholds then shook at the voice of the one crying out, and the house [that is, the Temple] would be filled with smoke. [Isaiah 6:1−4]

Once *barukh* has replaced *berum*, the resemblance of Ezekiel 3:12−13 to this passage in Isaiah is almost eerie. Ezekiel's "great quaking" corresponds to the shaking of the bases of the thresholds in Isaiah. Isaiah ties this shaking to a great cry of praise uttered by the Lord's winged attendants[5]. Ezekiel now has a corresponding doxology, nearly meaningless and therefore profoundly evocative: "Blessed be the glory of the Lord from his place[6]." And, just as Isaiah suggests that the attendant beings cry out their formula antiphonally, so the altered text of Ezekiel: the "voice of the *'ofannim*" answers the "wings of the *hayyot*." The wings of the *hayyot* thus give the impression of being their organs of song − a remarkable idea that we will meet again and again − and the *'ofannim*, "wheels," no longer appear as the mechanical objects we might have imagined, but as active supernatural beings who correspond to the *hayyot*.

d) The wheels. We do not know how deliberately our unknown scribe changed *berum* to *barukh*, or whether he was aware how much that tiny alteration had brought Ezekiel's vision into line with Isaiah's. Perhaps he would have been astonished to see, as we will, how later generations dealt with the text he had created. But the change he made is not isolated. One aspect of his new text, the new role hinted at for the *'ofannim*, seems to link it to the treatment of the *'ofannim* in Ezekiel 10:9−17, and to suggest that these two passages belong to the same exegetical process.

Ezekiel 10:9−17, I have argued [9], paraphrases and interprets the description of the "wheels" in the original *merkabah* vision (1:15−21). Although its author assumes and supports the equation of the *hayyot* with the cherubim, made throughout chapter 10, his real interest is in the *'ofannim*. He turns these "wheels" from machines into angels, almost literally fleshing them out. In verse 11, he equips them with heads; in verse 12, with flesh, arms, and wings. (It is clear both from the context of these

---

5 We know very little about the seraphim. The root of their name suggests the idea of burning (cf. Isaiah 6:6). The Bible elsewhere uses "seraph" for snakes, perhaps mythological (Numbers 21:6 Deuteronomy 8:15), who are sometimes supposed to be able to fly (Isaiah 14:29, 30:6). But the seraphim of Isaiah 6, who have to cover their feet, do not sound like flying snakes.

6 "I have seen him [the Israeli scholar David Flusser] disconcert other scholars by insisting that the errors in sacred texts and the ignorant misreadings of them were really the constructive element in the history of civilization, since the religious ideas that have had most success have mainly been founded upon them." − Edmund Wilson [79].

verses and from their relationship to 1:17–18 that their subject is the *'ofannim* – not, as commentators normally assume, the *ḥayyot*-cherubim.) While he does not go so far as to specify what the heads of the *'ofannim* look like, a later author made up for his reticence by inserting verse 14 into his text (in MT only: the Alexandrian translators did not know this passage):

> Each one had four faces: first, a cherub's face; second, a human face; third, a lion's face; and, fourth, an eagle's face.

When I originally discussed 10:14, I tried to show that its author had taken his cue from a corrupt reading at the end of Ezekiel 1:15 (according to MT), which suggested that the *'ofannim* have the same four faces as do the *ḥayyot*. (He does not, however, give them precisely the same four faces; we will return to this point.) But this suggestion only went so far, because I could not think of any real reason why either the author of 10:14 or the earlier author of the rest of 10:9–17 should want to turn the *'ofannim* into a second order of angels, differing from the *ḥayyot*-cherubim only in their names and perhaps a few of their features. But now I think the alteration in Ezekiel 3:12–13 provides the clue. Influenced either by the altered text itself, or by the exegetical tradition that gave rise to the alteration, the writers of 10:9–17 wanted to affirm that the *'ofannim* stand over against the *ḥayyot* as a second angelic choir. The two groups can now cry aloud to each other, as 3:12–13 suggests they do: "Blessed be the glory of the Lord from its place!"

The process we are seeing here is a bit paradoxical. Ezekiel 10:9–17, by reinforcing the equation of the *ḥayyot* and the cherubim, confirms that the *merkabah* belongs in the context of the Jerusalem Temple, and that its importance is to mark the changes in God's attitude toward this Temple. But the Temple setting suggests something else: that Ezekiel's vision should be coupled with Isaiah's, which also takes place both around God's throne and in his Temple. Once this happens, Ezekiel's *merkabah* begins to vibrate to rhythms set by Isaiah. The *ḥayyot* and the *'ofannim*, for all their idiosyncrasies, absorb some of the energy of the seraphim and begin to act like them. Later on, we will find all three groups of angels calling out their doxologies from everlasting to everlasting, in realms considerably more exalted than the Jerusalem Temple; the historical context that the editors of the Book of Ezekiel gave to the *merkabah* is left far below.

I do not know how far this midrashic process had gone when Ezekiel 10: 9–17 was written, or when someone made the change that turned *berum* into *barukh*. It seems clear, however, that we have at least its beginning in the text of the Book of Ezekiel itself. We will presently see that it develops into a tradition of *merkabah* exegesis so distinct that it will be useful to give it a name. We will call it, for the time being, the *hymnic tradition*.

In the meantime, why does the writer of 10:14 change the four faces of the *ḥayyot* when he transfers them to the *'ofannim*? Why does he delete the ox's face of 1:10, and replace it with a not very informative "cherub's face"? Here, too, we seem to be at the beginning of a tradition. We will see, again and again, that the bovine features of the *merkabah* (1:7 and 10) particularly engage expositors' attention. They must therefore engage ours. Let us file this question away, until we can do more with it.

e) Expansions of Ezekiel 1? In describing the *merkabah* exegesis preserved within the Book of Ezekiel, I have said nothing about exegetical expansions of chapter 1 itself. This is because, with one trivial exception to be noted below, I do not think there were any. If the text of Ezekiel 1 were in fact open to such expansions, as many modern scholars think it was, it is very strange that it occurred to none of the busy glossators to insert into it some hint that the *ḥayyot* are in fact cherubim. More likely, chapter 1 was a fixed text from relatively early times. The later editors and commentators, who filled chapter 10 with their exegetical suggestions, considered chapter 1 too sacred to meddle with.

It is true that MT's text of Ezekiel 1 contains words and even sentences that we do not find in the Alexandrian Greek translation (the Septuagint; abbreviated "LXX"), and that modern scholars often regard these as interpolations which were added too late to find their way into the text that the Alexandrians translated. This is a plausible hypothesis; as I have said, I think it is true for 10:14. But, in chapter 1, it is normally possible to show either that MT's "pluses" derive from mechanical scribal error — from which even chapter 1 was never immune — rather than deliberate alteration (as in 1:27); or else that MT's reading is in fact older and better than the shorter LXX text (as in 1:14, 24, 25–26) [34]. We will see shortly that the Alexandrian translators had their own exegetical axes to grind.

There is only one place in chapter 1 where I would say that MT contains an exegetical addition missing from LXX: verse 22, where MT adds a single word that characterizes the crystalline firmament as "terrible" or "awesome." To this, I would add 8:2, where, in the brief gloss "like the appearance of splendor," an annotator of MT makes the earliest attempt we know of to explain the mysterious word *ḥashmal*. Add also 10:14, and we have the only three MT "pluses" I can think of in the *merkabah* materials that seem to represent deliberate exegesis.

f) The merkabah as Scripture. We do not know when the Book of Ezekiel came to be essentially the document we now have, or when it was enrolled among the Prophetic books of the Hebrew canon. The second development need not have followed directly upon the first. An ingenious suggestion of Robert H. Pfeiffer (following A. B. Ehrlich) would, if correct, imply that not all of the book's early readers approached it in a spirit of reverence. Three Hebrew words that break the context of Ezekiel 45:20, Pfeiffer thinks, were originally a marginal gloss, a reader's disgusted comment on Ezekiel's eccentric Temple legislation: "From [the pen of] a man mistaken and foolish" [43].

This unknown critic, if he indeed existed, did not prevail. The Book of Ezekiel could hardly have been preserved if it had not come to be regarded as a true oracle of God, deserving its place among the words of the prophets. We can be fairly sure that this happened before about 200 B.C. Early in the second century, a Palestinian scribe named Joshua b. Sira listed Ezekiel in his catalog of ancient pious men, placing him between Jeremiah and "the twelve prophets"; this order reflects the sequence of books in the Jewish canon (Sira 49:6–10 [45])[7]. As far as Ben Sira was concerned, Ezekiel's main claim to attention was that he had seen the *merkabah*: "Ezekiel saw a vision, and told about varieties of chariot [*zene merkabah*]." We do not know what Ben Sira meant by "varieties of chariot." We may take comfort from the fact that Ben Sira's grandson evidently did not know either; in his translation, Ezekiel "saw a vision of glory, which [God] showed him upon a chariot of cherubim."

This is the first time this chapter that we have seen the word *merkabah* inside quotation marks. The Hebrew text of the Book of Ezekiel never uses "chariot" to designate the totality of what Ezekiel saw; and Sira 49:8 is, with the possible exception of I Chronicles 28:18[8], the first surviving Hebrew source to do so. (LXX Ezekiel 43:3, which we will look at below, may be nearly as early, but it is in Greek.) The choice of this title reflects a natural enough interpretation of Ezekiel's vision. But it is worth noting that it is an interpretation; for, thanks to this name, the *merkabah* vision can and will find new Biblical contexts which extend its implications far beyond what we have seen so far.

With the beginning of the second century B.C., our study of the *merkabah* exegesis in the Book of Ezekiel is over. Our study of the exegesis of the Book of Ezekiel must begin.

---

7 The Greek translation of Ben Sira's book, made by his grandson late in the second century, was included in the Apocrypha under the title of "Ecclesiasticus," or "The Wisdom of Jesus son of Sirach" (the Greek form of Ben Sira's name). Substantial portions of the Hebrew original, including the passage that now concerns us, were found in the Cairo Genizah [45].

8 The detailed instructions that David gives Solomon for building the Temple include a plan for "the model of the chariot [*merkabah*], the cherubim, in gold, for those who spread their wings and shelter the ark of the covenant of the Lord." This may or may not refer to Ezekiel's vision. (The Greek translation of this verse, incidentally, seems to have influenced the translation of Sira 49:8.)

2. Qumran

a) Introduction. Khirbet Qumran is the name the Arabs gave to a small ruin on the eastern shores of the Dead Sea. Until 1947, when an Arab shepherd discovered seven Hebrew scrolls in a jar in one of the nearby caves, no one cared much to know what it was. In the early 1950's, the ruin was excavated, and turned out to be a building complex that had evidently been occupied from the late second century B.C. to about 68 A.D. (with a gap of a few decades at the end of the first century B.C.). The Romans had apparently destroyed it while suppressing the Jewish revolt of 66—70, which ended with the destruction of the Temple.

We are not absolutely certain who lived at Qumran. But the scholarly consensus is that it was a monastery of the Jewish sect known as the Essenes, who hid their extensive library in the surrounding caves when they fled before the Roman armies in 68. The remains of this library are what we now call the "Dead Sea Scrolls." They include not only the seven original scrolls from what is now called Cave I, but several other scrolls from nearby caves; and, from the so-called Cave IV, tens of thousands of fragments of what had once been scrolls. The Roman soldiers had perhaps found Cave IV centuries before the archaeologists did, and hacked the better part of the Essenes' library to pieces [71b] [9].

The Essenes, like the early Christians to whom they have often been compared, believed that they and their times were the focus and fulfillment of Biblical prophecy. Few of the prophets interested and influenced them more than Ezekiel [55,66]. Because, for example, Ezekiel prophesied that the Zadokite priests would be God's chosen ministers in the future era (44: 15), they called their priests "the sons of Zadok" (*Damascus Rule*, iii, 20 — iv, 3; tr. 100 [77]). Because Ezekiel suggested that the punishment of the Israelites is to last 390 years (4:4—5), they dated the beginning of their sect "three hundred and ninety years after [God] had given [Israel] into the hand of king Nebuchadnezzar of Babylon" (*Damascus Document*, i, 16; tr. 97 [77]) [72]. What, we may wonder, did these devoted students of Ezekiel do with his *merkabah*?

b) The "Angelic Liturgy." In 1960, John Strugnell published two fragments from Cave IV which seemed to bear on this question [75]. Both are

---

9 As a first introduction to the Dead Sea Scrolls, Edmund Wilson's *Dead Sea Scrolls 1947—1969* is a fine and appealing book. Wilson was of course no specialist; and the books of Millar Burrows, Frank Moore Cross, Jr., and Geza Vermes provide a more scholarly orientation [78,57,58,61, 77a]. Vermes has translated most of the Dead Sea material that has so far been published (most of the Cave IV fragments have not yet appeared) [77]. Fitzmyer's bibliography extends through the early 1970's [65].

parts of a much longer work — we do not know how long it was — which Strugnell called "the Angelic Liturgy." Strugnell found fragments of what he thought were four manuscripts of this composition among the Cave IV materials. (One fragment has also turned up at Masada [80,81].) He dated his four manuscripts on the basis of their script, and assigned the oldest of them to about 50 B.C., which thus becomes the latest possible date for the composition of the "Angelic Liturgy."

Strugnell published, with the text of his two fragments, translations and commentaries. In the following years, Carmignac proposed improvements on Strugnell's readings and translations; Yadin, Baumgarten, Fujita, and Rowland discussed different aspects of the material Strugnell had publish-ed; Dupont-Sommer, Gaster, and Vermes incorporated the Angelic Liturgy into their translations of the Scrolls [59,80,53a,67,160,63,68,77]. In 1982, Lawrence H. Schiffman again published Strugnell's fragments, with new translations and very extensive notes [74]. Carol Newsom's masterful publication of all the surviving fragments — *Songs of the Sabbath Sacrifice: A Critical Edition* (Scholars Press, 1985) — appeared too recently for me to take account of it here.

Strugnell referred also to a Cave IV fragment, not part of the Angelic Liturgy, which contained a paraphrase of the *merkabah* vision [76]. He never published this text, but he kindly allowed me to examine it in 1975. After I discuss the Angelic Liturgy, I will report on what I saw.

As I have said, we do not know how long the Angelic Liturgy was. We also do not know why it was written. Sections of its text begin with rub-rics which specify what follows as "the song of the burnt-offering" of this or that Sabbath, described with an ordinal number and a date. We do not know just who is singing the songs or offering the sacrifices. The actors in these compositions, if not the speakers, are celestial beings with titles like "priests of the exalted heights"; the realms in which they move are des-cribed in language drawn from the Temple (*hekhal, 'ulam, parokhet, debir*). One unpublished passage, which Strugnell permitted me to examine, seems humbly to contrast "our" earthly priesthood and praise with that of the celestial beings. Some of the Qumran hymns found in other sources express an aching desire to join the heavenly company (*Hymns* [1QH] iii, 19–23, vi, 12–13, xi, 10–14; *Blessings* [1QSb] iii, 26–27, iv, 23–26; tr. 158–159, 169–170, 186, 208), and the Angelic Liturgy may perhaps have been intended as a bridge[10].

Most people who have studied the Angelic Liturgy, Scholem among them

---

10 In Newsom's edition, the "unpublished passage" appears as 4Q400 2, lines 6–7; the passages Strugnell published are 4Q403 1 i, lines 16–26, and 4Q405 20 ii–21–22, lines 7–14. — Newsom has perhaps solved the problem of the text's extent and structure.

[604], have found it strongly reminiscent of the *Hekhalot*. I share this impression, although I do not find it easy to put my finger on just what it is that creates it. Strugnell's second fragment, like much of the *Hekhalot*, is saturated with language drawn from Ezekiel's *merkabah*; both fragments, but especially the second, use terminology that resembles that of the *Hekhalot*[c]. But there are also less tangible resemblances. As Schiffman remarks, both the Angelic Liturgy and the *Hekhalot* are remarkably difficult to punctuate. Phrases and sentences run into each other, and the reader often does not know where one thought ends and another begins. The result is that one comes away from these texts, even if one has understood most of the words, with only the vaguest idea of what has been said. Some sort of poetic structure, usually involving parallelism, often breaks the surface; but, in both the *Hekhalot* and Strugnell's second fragment, the structure is sporadic and inconsistent.

The first of Strugnell's fragments consists of the latter part of a series of poetic stanzas describing blessings pronounced by seven "chief princes," apparently angels[11]. I cannot identify any reference to Ezekiel's *merkabah* in this fragment, and therefore do not think that it advances our inquiry.

The second fragment is much different. It is a description of the heavenly hymnody, obviously inspired by the *merkabah* vision. Although it is not exegetical in form, it presupposes a considerable development of *merkabah* midrash in what I have called the hymnic tradition, often hidden behind innocent-seeming poetic expressions. Unlike most of the texts belonging to the hymnic tradition which we will examine, it makes no use at all of Isaiah 6. Its two poles are, on the one hand, the tumultuous noise that Ezekiel associates with his vision (1:24–25, 3:12–13); and, on the other, the Lord's coming to Elijah in "a sound of delicate silence" (I Kings 19:12). The author of the Angelic Liturgy develops this paradox, which is already implicit in the latter Biblical text.

The difficulty of deciding where sentences and phrases begin and end makes it almost impossible to translate this passage with any confidence. I attack this problem by focusing on what I see as traces of poetic structure – or, better, of several poetic structures – and using them to indicate units of content.

---

11 To give some idea of the texture of the passage, I quote Schiffman's translation of one stanza:
> The fifth of the chief princes
> Shall invoke blessing in the name of His wonders
> Upon all who know the secrets of the most pure
> With seven words of His true exaltation.
> And bless all who hasten to do His will
> With seven wondrous words,
> And bless all who acknowledge Him
> With seven majestic words for those who acknowledge (His) wondrousness.

The fragment begins with nine words that are broken and hard to read. Schiffman translates them: " ... those who serve before the glory in the tabernacle of the angels of knowledge. The *keruvim* [cherubim] fall before him ..." I propose the following translation of the rest:

> They give blessing as they raise themselves;
>> A sound of divine silence.
> [   ] and tumultuous chant as they lift their wings;
>> A sound of divine silence.
> They bless the image of the *merkabah*-throne   5
>> Above the firmament of the cherubim,
> And they hymn the splendor of the firmament of light
>> Beneath the seat of his glory.
> When the *'ofannim* go, the angels of the holy place return;
> The spirits of the Holy of Holies go forth, like appearances of fire, from   10
>> beneath his glorious wheels [*galgalle kebodo*].
>
> All around are appearances of fiery grain-ears [? perhaps "rivers" or
>> "paths"] in the likeness of *hashmal*;
> Constructions of brightness, gloriously interwoven;
> Wondrous colors, mixed in purity —
>> The spirits of the living God that travel about perpetually
>> with the glory of the wondrous chariots.
>
> There is a silent sound of blessing in the tumult of their movement,   15
> And they praise the holy place when they turn back.
> When they raise themselves, they raise wondrously;
> And when they return [?] they stand still.
> The joyful sound of hymning becomes quiet
> And the silent blessing of God.   20
> In all the camps of God ... d)

At this point, the text becomes too broken to translate.

It is not easy to summarize what is being described here. The tension between sound and silence in the divine realm is clearly a major theme. We get a strong impression of endless circular motion, accompanied by the reverent hum of the sound-silence and by a glow of prismatic color (the rainbow image of Ezekiel 1:28?). The "glorious wheels" (*galgallim*, from Ezekiel 10:2, 6, 13) are perhaps the model for this movement.

The author, as I show in endnote *d*, draws upon Ezekiel even more extensively than appears at first sight. He seems to assume certain features of the hymnic tradition of interpretation, which are becoming familiar to us. The parallelism of the *'ofannim* and the "angels of the holy place" in line 9 suggests that the *'ofannim* have been detached from the chariot and become angelic beings in their own right [160]. Line 3 associates the lifting of angels' wings with "tumultuous chant"; we may suspect that the author, like the later Jewish sources we will examine, has taken from Ezekiel 3:12– 13 the hint that the *hayyot* use their wings as organs of song. (The Hebrew of line 3 is marvelously assonant: *hamon rinnah barim kanfehem.*)

But there is more. The fragment, near its end, refers to "the camps of

God" (*maḥane 'elohim*). This of course points to Ezekiel 1:24: "I heard
the sound of their wings ... like the sound of a camp [*maḥaneh*]" [67,74,
75]. But it also points to another Biblical text:

> While Jacob was travelling on his way, angels of God met him. When he saw them, Jacob said:
> "This is the camp of God [*maḥaneh 'elohim*]." And he called the name of that place Mahanayim
> ["two camps"]. [Genesis 32:1–2]

Which passage was our author using, Genesis 32:1–2 or Ezekiel 1:24?
To pose the question like this is to miss the point. He used both; or, more
correctly, he used Genesis to interpret Ezekiel, and then incorporated the
result of this exegesis. What kind of "camp" do the wings of the *hayyot*
sound like? Hardly an ordinary military camp, whose noises would probably not be the most pious or edifying. Surely Ezekiel meant the "camp of
God" that Jacob saw; surely it was the praises of these angelic soldiers that
the *hayyot* pronounced with their wings. The author has ranged as far as
Genesis to construct a context for the *merkabah*.

Line 14 introduces us to a more complicated case of context-building,
this time involving the Book of Zechariah. Here we read of "the spirits
[*ruḥot*] of the living God that travel about [*mithallekhim*] perpetually
with the glory of the wondrous chariots [*markebot*]." The plural "chariots" warns us that there is more going on here than meets the eye. Ezekiel,
after all, sees only one *merkabah*; why does the Angelic Liturgy use the
plural [67,74,75,160]?

For the answer, we must turn to Zechariah 6:1–7:

> I again lifted up my eyes, and I saw four chariots [*markabot*] going forth from between the two
> mountains, which were mountains of brass. The first chariot had red horses; the second chariot
> had black horses; the third chariot had white horses; the fourth chariot had spotted [?], powerful
> [?] horses[12].
>
> I said to the angel who was speaking with me: "What are these, my lord?"
>
> He replied: "These are the four winds [or "spirits"; *ruḥot* can mean both] of the heavens,
> who go forth from attending upon the Lord of all the earth. The one with black horses goes forth
> to the north country; the white horses went forth after them; the spotted [?] horses went forth
> to the south country. The powerful [?] horses went forth, and wanted to go travel about [*lehit-
> hallekh*] the earth. He [God?] said, 'Go, travel about [*hithallekhu*] the earth.' So they travelled
> about [*wattithallakhnah*]."

We thus find three of line 14's key words – "spirits/winds," "travel
about," and plural "chariots" – in Zechariah 6:1–7. I have no doubt that
the author of the Angelic Liturgy (or the tradition that he followed), wanting to know more about Ezekiel's chariot, turned to Zechariah's description
of angelic chariots for information. One passage of the *merkabah* vision, in
particular, seemed to suggest that this was the right direction to go:

---

12 The translation of *beruddim 'amuṣṣim* is uncertain, and the text evidently corrupt. Verses 6–7
seem to forget about the red horses, and to treat the "spotted" and the "powerful" ones as two
different groups. This problem has no bearing on the point I am making.

This was the likeness of the *hayyot*: their appearance was like blazing coals of fire, like the appearance of torches, travelling about [*mithallekhot*] [13] among the *hayyot*. [Ezekiel 1:13]

The author superimposed Zechariah's vision, like a transparency, over Ezekiel's, using the verb *hithallekh* as his fixed point of orientation. The result:

Ezekiel:	Coals/torches		travel about	as part of	*merkabah*.
Zechariah:	Spirits	attend God,	travel about	as	*markabot*.
Ang. Lit.:	Spirits	of living God	travel about	with	*markabot*.

When we look at the first column, we see that Zechariah's "spirits" occupies the same slot as Ezekiel's "coals of fire ... torches." We may guess that the Angelic Liturgy's description of the "spirits" as "fiery grain-ears" (*shibbole 'esh*) results from a combination of the two, and that the expression is a poetic variation of Ezekiel's "coals of fire" (*gahale 'esh*).

Line 10 also refers to "spirits": "The spirits of the Holy of Holies *go forth*, like appearances of fire, from between his glorious wheels." Here, too, the author combines Ezekiel 1:13 with Zechariah 6:1–7. "Appearances of fire" reflects Ezekiel's "appearance of torches"; in Zechariah, "the spirits [= "winds"] of the heavens *go forth* from attending upon the Lord of all the earth"; and the rest of Ezekiel 1:13–14 suggests that the *hayyot go forth* and return like lightning[14]. The Angelic Liturgy does not tell us where the spirits "go forth" to, or why they "travel about perpetually with the glory of the wondrous chariots." But the context in Zechariah would lead us to expect that they act as God's messengers, patrolling the earth on his behalf (cf. Zechariah 1:7–15).

If we assume that this last conception was indeed part of the hymnic tradition as the author of the Angelic Liturgy knew it, we begin to understand some of the details of the Book of Revelation. "Before the throne [of God]," the seer tells us in Revelation 4:5, "burn seven torches of fire, which are the seven spirits of God"; and, in 5:6, "the seven spirits of God" are "sent out into all the earth." We will see in the next chapter that the author of the Book of Revelation drew from the same stream of *merkabah* tradition as did the Angelic Liturgy, and therefore might be expected to combine Scriptural passages in a similar way and draw similar conclusions.

---

13 MT has here *hi' mithallekhet*. But the Hebrew text that LXX translated seems to have had *mithallekhot* [19], and the use of Ezekiel 1:13 in the Angelic Liturgy and the Book of Revelation (chapter III, below) best makes sense if we assume the latter reading. I have slightly altered the translation of this verse that I gave in section 1, in order to make my present point clearer.

14 Verse 13 concludes: "The fire was splendid, and from the fire lightning *went forth*" (*yose'*, the verb I have consistently translated "go forth" throughout this discussion). Verse 14 is difficult, and is usually – incorrectly, in my opinion [34] – taken to be a late addition to the text [1,19]. We will look at its problems more closely when we consider the Targum (chapter IV). For now, let us translate it: "The *hayyot went forth* and returned like the appearance of lightning."

The Angelic Liturgy itself represents this tradition somewhat as follows: The *merkabah* beings — who include cherubim, *'ofannim*, angels, and spirits — hymn their Lord in a tumult of praise that is, paradoxically, "a sound of delicate silence." They use their wings (if I have interpreted line 3 correctly) as their organs of song. Jacob saw them, as God's soldiers, in their camps. Zechariah saw them, as God's messengers, going forth to patrol the earth.

c) The merkabah paraphrase. The Cave IV fragment paraphrasing the *merkabah* vision, which I mentioned at the beginning of this section, will give us a brief rest from all of this midrashic entanglement. It seems simple enough, if only because too little of the text is preserved for us to guess how complicated it is.

The fragment is only fourteen lines long and is badly damaged. We have no idea of its context, although Strugnell has correlated it with several other fragments of a pseudo-Ezekiel, sometimes paraphrasing the canonical Ezekiel. Unlike some of the other fragments, this text speaks of Ezekiel in the third person; oddly, however, the few remaining words of the lines that precede the description of the *merkabah* include a first-person suffix. These opening words seem to depend on Daniel 10:7.

The account of the *merkabah* is much shorter than Ezekiel 1, and does not strictly follow the order of the Biblical account. The word *merkabah* (which, we recall, Ezekiel does not use) appears near the beginning. There follow the four *ḥayyot* and their four faces, then the *'ofannim*, then the "coals of fire" of Ezekiel 1:13. The last line, which is badly broken, contains four letters which I think are the beginning of *hannora'*, "the terrible", this is the adjective that MT applies to the crystalline "firmament" of 1:22[e]. There is no reference to "cherubim" (as opposed to *ḥayyot*), or any other trace I can detect of Ezekiel 10.

There is an odd detail in the enumeration of the faces of the *ḥayyot*. Instead of the "face of an ox [*shor*]" that we find in Ezekiel 1:10, the author of the paraphrase speaks of a "calf" (*'egel*). I do not know if this makes any real difference. But we have seen that the author of Ezekiel 10:14 was also for some reason unhappy with the ox's face, and I have suggested we keep an eye on the way expositors treat the *merkabah*'s bovine elements. Here is a second datum for our file.

3. The Septuagint

a) Introduction. The Septuagint (LXX) is the oldest translation of the Bible into Greek, made at Alexandria before the beginning of the Christian Era. Although it later became the standard Old Testament of the Christian

Church, LXX was translated by Jews and, as far as we can tell, for Jews. We may therefore hope that it has something to tell us about how Greek-speaking Jews outside Palestine perceived the *merkabah*. We will not be disappointed.

We do not know when the Greek translation of Ezekiel that we now have was made. The Alexandrian Jews did not translate all their sacred Hebrew books into Greek at the same time. To make things more complicated, there is evidence that they and their Palestinian cousins continued to revise and improve upon their translations for centuries, and it is hard to be sure what edition of a given book our LXX manuscripts represent [22,37]. According to the tradition of the Alexandrian Jews, the Pentateuch was the first part of the Bible to be translated, and the translation was made during the reign of Ptolemy II Philadelphus (285–247 B.C.) by seventy Palestinian scholars (hence its name Septuagint, "seventy," LXX). We may safely believe that the translation of the Pentateuch indeed came first; and, although we must take the rest of the tradition with a grain of salt, it is more likely to exaggerate than to understate the antiquity of the translation. It follows that the Greek Ezekiel cannot be any older than about the middle of the third century B.C. As for its latest possible date, Ben Sira's grandson evidently knew a Greek Ezekiel when he translated his grandfather's book toward the end of the second century B.C., for he mentions in his prologue translations of "the law itself, the prophecies, and the rest of the books." But this does not give us an airtight dating, for we do not know for sure that his Greek Ezekiel was our Greek Ezekiel.

H. St. John Thackeray argued in 1903 that more than one individual took part in the translation of Ezekiel, and Nigel Turner has since developed his suggestions [47,49]. My own study of the *merkabah* chapters of LXX [34], which I will be summarizing in the next few pages, has suggested to me that Thackeray and Turner were on the right track. The translator of Ezekiel 43 seems to have had before him a Hebrew text of Ezekiel 1:24 that was fuller, and closer to our MT, than that which lay before the translator of Ezekiel 1. Further, he inserted into his translation of 43:2 a midrash that properly belongs in 1:24. This suggests that some distance, probably of time but possibly also geography, separated the two translators. It also implies that the translator of chapter 43 was the later of the two, and that an accepted translation of chapter 1 already existed when the translator of chapter 43 set to work; otherwise, why would the latter translator have had to find room in his own work for a midrash that belongs in chapter 1? If chapter 1 was read in the synagogues in Alexandria on special occasions (Shabu{c}ot, for example), as we have seen that it was in Babylonia and probably Palestine at a later time, we can understand that it might have been translated into Greek long before the rest of the book.

This still does not give us a date for the passages in which we are interested. I have found only one feeble clue that might help us. The noun *qalal* occurs in the Hebrew Bible only in Ezekiel 1:7 and Daniel 10:6, and in both places LXX translates it "flashing like lightning" (*exastraptōn*). This rendering has the support of the context in Daniel 10:6, but seems baseless in Ezekiel 1:7. We might infer from this that the translator of Ezekiel 1:7 drew on the translation of Daniel 10:6. No conclusion of Bible scholarship is more certain than that chapters 10–12 of Daniel were written in 166–164 B.C. (below, chapter III); add a few years for Daniel to be translated into Greek, and we have about 150 B.C. as the earliest possible date for the translation of Ezekiel 1. The translation of Ezekiel 43 must be even later. If this argument is right, its upshot is that the evidence we are about to consider is probably earlier than the Qumran Angelic Liturgy, but by less than a hundred years.

b) Ezekiel 43:2. Let us begin with Ezekiel 43. The most obvious modification of the *merkabah* material in this chapter is that the translation of verse 3 actually calls the object of Ezekiel's vision "the chariot"; it is one of the earliest sources in any language to do so. But a variation in verse 2 is nearly as striking and a good deal more instructive. MT's Hebrew text, describing the glory of God that approached from the east, says:

His voice[15] was like the sound of many waters.

But LXX translates:

The voice of the camp was like the voice of many repeaters [*diplasiazontōn*].

In a situation like this, the text critic's first suspicion is that LXX is translating a Hebrew text that is different from MT's. But this is only a plausible explanation when — as is often the case — the Hebrew words that LXX seems to be translating are graphically similar to those in MT, so that we can imagine how a scribal error would get us from one text to the other. That is not the case here.

The first part of the simile is plainly drawn from Ezekiel 1:24:

I heard the sound of their wings like the sound of many waters, like the voice of Shaddai[16], when they went; a sound of tumult [?] like the sound of a camp. When they stood, they let down their wings.

---

15 Hebrew *qol* means both "voice" and "sound"; so does Greek *phōnē*. I translate "voice" or "sound" according to context.

16 "Shaddai," or "El Shaddai," is a Biblical name for God, used frequently in the Book of Job. It is conventionally translated "the Almighty," although nobody knows what it means. The author of Ezekiel 10:5 explains "the voice of Shaddai" as "the voice of El Shaddai when he speaks." Despite James Barr's criticism, I am attracted to G. R. Driver's suggestion that 1:24 originally read *keqol shedi*, "like the sound of a downpour" [21,2]. But this has nothing to do with the use of the verse by later Jewish expositors, who took for granted that the Scripture intended the divine name Shaddai.

Like the author of the Angelic Liturgy, the translator of Ezekiel 43:2 evidently understands the "camp" of 1:24 as the camp of God's angels that Jacob saw (Genesis 32:1–2). The "many repeaters," then, must be those angels who ceaselessly praise God (as in the Angelic Liturgy), repeating phrases like *Holy, holy, holy is the Lord of hosts* and *Blessed be the glory of the Lord from his place.* (The author of the Book of Revelation, too, applies Ezekiel's "sound of many waters" to the voice of the multitudes singing hymns before God; 14:1–3, 19:6.)

Even the rather odd term "repeaters," which the author applies to them, has its source in the Hebrew Bible:

God's chariotry is two myriads, thousands of *shin'an*;
The Lord is among them [at?] Sinai in holiness. [Psalm 68:18]

We do not know what *shin'an* are. The rabbis applied their midrashic ingenuity to the puzzling word[17]; less imaginatively, RSV translates the phrase, "thousands upon thousands." The root of the word seems to be *shanah*, "to double" or "repeat." The translator of Ezekiel 43:2 – or, more likely, the tradition that he followed – deduced from this etymology that the *shin'an* are the "repeaters" of God's praises, who were present with God's chariotry (*rekheb*) at Sinai, and who therefore were part of Ezekiel's chariot vision. He aptly translated their title into Greek as *diplasiazontōn* (Greek *diplos*, "double," corresponds to Hebrew *shanah*).

Apart from my philological observations, practically everything I have said about LXX Ezekiel 43:2 was already said nearly 1600 years ago. Jerome wrote, in his commentary on this verse (ed. 623 [622]):

Like the voice of camps and like the voice of many doublers[18], [says Scripture,] in order that one may grasp the mysteries of God's army. Jacob, understanding this, *called the name of that place "Camps"* [Genesis 32:2]; and it is elsewhere written concerning these [camps] that *God's chariot is myriads multiplied, thousands of those who rejoice* [Psalm 68:18]. The camps and the multitude are said to have one *voice* because of their common agreement in the praise of God. And the voice of those hymning the Father, Son and Holy Spirit is *doubled: Holy, holy, holy is the Lord God Sabaoth; the earth is filled with his Glory* [Isaiah 6:3].

The translator's allusion to Psalm 68:18, which Jerome seems instinctively to have grasped, establishes a link between Ezekiel's *merkabah* and the chariots that came to Sinai. We have already seen that the later synagogue practice of reading about both Sinai and the *merkabah* on Shabu^cot attests a belief that the two are connected. Now we find a trace of this belief in

---

17 *Pesiqta de-Rab Kahana, Ba-Ḥodesh* #22 (ed. 219–221 [206]); see below, chapter IV.
18 Jerome quotes LXX Ezekiel 43:2 rather freely, and translates *diplasiazontōn* as "doublers" (*geminantium*) rather than "repeaters." His subsequent translation of Psalm 68:18 is based on LXX, which translates *shin'an* as if it were *sha'anan*, "at ease." (So one of the rabbis quoted in *Pesiqta de-Rab Kahana.* The translator of Ezekiel 43 obviously understood the word differently from the translator of Psalms.)

pre-Christian Alexandria. The Sinai event has entered the hymnic tradition of *merkabah* exegesis, as part of the context in which Ezekiel's vision must be understood.

c) Ezekiel 1:23. We find another trace of the hymnic tradition in the translation of Ezekiel 1 itself, which we have seen to be older than that of Ezekiel 43.

1:23 says about the *hayyot*, according to MT:

> Beneath the firmament their wings were straight, each to the other.

But LXX translates:

> Beneath the firmament their wings were stretched out, fluttering to each other.

"Stretched out" seems a reasonably straightforward translation of "straight." But where does the wings' "fluttering" come from?

The word that I translate "fluttering," *pteryssomenai*, occurs in only two other places in LXX. One of them is Ezekiel 3:13:

> And I saw [!] the voice of the wings of the living creatures[19] fluttering to each other [MT: "rustling against each other"], and the voice of the wheels opposite them, and the voice of the quaking.

The other is Ezekiel 1:24, where fourteen manuscripts read *pteryssesthai*, "fluttered," in place of *poreuesthai*, "went":

> I heard the sound of their wings when they fluttered like the sound of much water ...

The use of "fluttering" in all three passages only makes sense if we assume that, in the dialect of Greek used by the LXX translator, the word could indicate the creation of a musical sound. (I must admit that I have no other evidence of the word's having this nuance.) We have already seen a hint in Ezekiel 3:12–13 that the *hayyot*'s wings are their organs of song, and have perhaps detected a trace of this notion in the Angelic Liturgy. When we examine the Targum in chapter IV, we will see this belief developed in the context of Ezekiel 1:24–25. The LXX translator reads it into 1:23, in a particularly ingenious way: instead of *yesharot*, "straight," he reads midrashically *sharot*, "singing." "Their wings were singing, each to the other."[20]

d) Ezekiel 1:7. We have so far been able to use the Greek translation of Ezekiel as evidence that certain features of the hymnic tradition were

---

19 *Zōa*, the word LXX uses to translate *hayyot*, is unambiguous.

20 Another Greek source – admittedly, much later than LXX – attests this belief. The Paris Magical Papyrus preserves an exorcism, written (according to Deissmann) about 300 A.D. and saturated with Jewish ideas, that refers to the Jewish God as the one "to whom the wings of Cheroubin [*sic*] sing praises" (line 3061) [707].

known, even outside Palestine, as far back as the second century B.C. (The most important of these features, for our purposes, is the use of Psalm 68: 18 and the consequent linking of the *merkabah* to Sinai.) But there is one more peculiarity[f] of LXX Ezekiel 1 that does not fit in with the hymnic tradition, but with another line of thought which we have begun to trace. It appears in the translation of verse 7:

[MT:] Their legs were straight, and the soles of their feet were like the sole of a calf's foot, and they sparkled like polished [?] brass.

[LXX:] Their legs were straight, and their feet were winged, and [were?] sparks like flashing brass; and their wings were swift.

LXX's concluding "and their wings were swift" is apparently a midrashic expansion of the unusual word *qalal* (which I have hesitantly translated "polished"), whose root can mean "to be swift." We will meet this rendering again in an unexpected context in chapter VIII. For now, I am more interested in the first appearance of the wings in this verse; when they sprout, so to speak, in place of the missing "calf's foot" of MT.

We can explain their appearance, if we want, as the result of two scribal errors in the Hebrew text that lay before the translator: the concluding *ᶜegel* ("calf") was omitted because of its resemblance to the preceding *regel*; and *kekhaf* was accidentally written *kenaf* (the two words look almost alike in Hebrew). The best the translator could do with the resulting *wekhaf raglehem kenaf regel* was "their feet were winged." This is plausible enough. Yet we have seen that a scribal error can serve a purpose, and we must ask if the disappearance of the calf's foot could have been a goal important enough to justify some manipulation of the text, either during the process of translation or earlier.

It is at least an odd coincidence that two later translations, both associated with rabbinic Judaism — the Aramaic Targum and the Greek Aquila — also apply a vanishing cream to the calf's foot: they vocalize *ᶜegel* as *ᶜagol* and thus translate, ungrammatically, "a round foot" in place of "a calf's foot" [389]. We recall that the ox's face disappears from Ezekiel 10:14. This item, too, must be filed away.

4. Conclusions

The earliest Jewish *merkabah* expositors whose work we have were the unknown persons who built the *merkabah* vision into the structure of the Book of Ezekiel. They did not allow the apparition at the river Chebar to stand solitary and baffling; they proposed for it a context which gave it a meaning within the concerns of the prophet whom they supposed to have seen it. The cornerstone of their proposal was their equation of the bizarre *ḥayyot* of Ezekiel 1 with the familiar cherubim of Israelite tradition. So identified, the *ḥayyot* appear to Ezekiel at Chebar in order to foreshadow God's leaving his earthly home in Jerusalem, and his eventual return to it. They and their *merkabah* become part of Ezekiel's prophecy of the exile and restoration of God's people.

We need not debate the correctness of these editors' understanding of the *merkabah* vision. What is important for us is that later expositors by and large ignored it. Of course, they did not literally dismember the Book of Ezekiel; the book had become part of the Holy Scriptures, inspired and untouchable. But they dissolved the context that the book's editors had created, and built a new one for it, drawing their material in bits and pieces from other Scriptures. Isaiah saw God surrounded by seraphim chanting his holiness; Zechariah saw his chariots on patrol. Jacob saw a "camp of God"; Elijah heard a "sound of delicate silence." The hymnic tradition of *merkabah* exegesis brought these elements together, to form a new setting for Ezekiel's vision.

In this company, the *merkabah* appears to have little to do with Nebuchadnezzar's destruction of Jerusalem or with the Babylonian exile. It has risen into an ethereal realm, where its only contacts are with other celestial entities. The seraphim, *'ofannim*, and *ḥayyot* everlastingly sing *Holy holy holy* and *Blessed be the glory of the Lord* to each other. They do not have much to say to human beings.

This last sentence, of course, cannot be true. The *merkabah* and its attendants can hardly have interested anyone unless they seemed to communicate something important to earthly folk. The hymnic tradition must convey a message of this sort, which it is our task to decipher.

Besides, we have already seen a hint that the hymnic tradition is not quite as indifferent to history as appears at first sight. If it carries the *merkabah* up and away from Ezekiel's Babylonia, it brings it down to earth again at Mount Sinai. The myriads of God's chariotry, the author of Psalm 68 had written, made their appearance at Sinai. Now the hymnic tradition wove this passage into its net of Scriptures, and thereby made the Sinai revelation part of the setting of the *merkabah*.

We now seem for the first time to be moving toward a solution to some of the questions we raised at the end of chapter I. We have not yet gone very far. We have seen the earliest evidence of Sinai and the *merkabah* brought together, but do not know what this combination meant to the people who proposed it. We have begun to trace the contours of the hymnic tradition, but have not yet grasped why its bearers or their audiences found it important and exciting. Nor have we seen grounds for aversion to the *merkabah*. A few odd ripples, indeed, have appeared around the details of the calf's foot and the ox's face; and they may hint at something sinister moving beneath the surface. But we do not know what it is.

Of heavenly ascensions, too, we have so far seen nothing. We do not have long to wait, however, before we must face this issue and its swarm of attendant difficulties. The apocalyptic texts that occupy our next chapter drop the whole cluster of problems squarely in our path, and we cannot go further without making our way through them. We must also deal with a number of related questions, less obvious but not less important, of what it means when the *merkabah* turns up in the visions of apocalyptic seers. It is these questions, and our responses to them, that will guide our approach to the more sensational issue of the heavenly ascent.

Chapter III

The Merkabah and the Apocalypses

Many, although by no means all, of the ancient Jewish visionary writings that we call *apocalypses* describe how their heroes ascended to the heavenly realms and there received revelations[1]. Some — but, again, not all — of these apocalyptic ascensions involve visions of Ezekiel's *merkabah*.

The apocalyptic literature thus bears on our investigation in two ways. First, the ascensions that the apocalyptic writers attribute to their heroes practically demand to be compared with the heavenly journeys hinted at in the Babylonian Talmud and set forth in the *Hekhalot*. Second, the apocalyptic visions of the *merkabah*, like the poetic imagery of the Angelic Liturgy, presuppose certain understandings of Ezekiel's text, and thus can guide us in tracing the earliest development of *merkabah* exegesis.

These two issues may be closely related. It is at least an arguable position that the apocalyptic ascensions, for all their fanciful settings in Biblical antiquity, reflect actual mystical practices which the writers knew from their own experience. If we can show this, and if we can show also that the vision of the *merkabah* was the goal of these mystical practices, we can make a good case that "*merkabah* mysticism" is far older than the extant

---

1 It is not easy to devise a universally valid definition of "apocalypse." We will not be much misled if we think of an apocalypse as a composition, often written in what seems a very bizarre and fanciful style, which claims to be supernatural revelation of otherwise inaccessible knowledge. This knowledge often, but by no means always, concerns the coming end of days [150]. Normally, the apocalyptist will not write under his own name, but will assume the personality of some hero of the Bible (Enoch, Abraham, Ezra, or the like). Both Jews and Christians wrote apocalypses; the ancient Jewish apocalypses, with which we are mainly concerned here, survive almost entirely in translations made and preserved by Christians. – For nearly seventy years, the standard collection in English of early Jewish apocalypses has been the second volume of R. H. Charles' *Apocrypha and Pseudepigrapha of the Old Testament* [98]. The first volume of a new and more complete set of translations, edited by James H. Charlesworth, appeared in 1983 [104]. (Charlesworth's second volume appeared too late for me to make use of it, as did the very handy collection by H. F. D. Sparks [168a].) I have found it convenient normally to quote the older translations in Charles; I make reference also to Charlesworth where appropriate. – D. S. Russell's *Method and Message of Jewish Apocalyptic* [165] remains the best general introduction to the apocalyptic literature and its problems. Charlesworth has compiled an exhaustive bibliography of recent work on the surviving apocalypses and related texts [105].

Hekhalot literature, and stretches back to well before the beginning of the
Christian Era. We would then have to rethink the conclusions we drew in
chapter I, and ask why the Palestinian rabbis seem not to have envisioned
any such practices when they spoke about "expounding the *merkabah*" –
or, perhaps, re-examine the arguments by which we concluded that they
did not.

As we examine this question, we will see that the connection between
the two issues is less direct than this, and that it is the second of them –
the *merkabah* exegesis of the apocalypses – that is primary. But this does
not give us license to neglect the heavenly ascensions. We cannot avoid
asking what these journeys meant to the apocalyptic writers who claimed
them; and what bearing, if any, the idea of ascension had on their perceptions of the *merkabah*.

1. Preliminary: apocalypses, ascensions, and the *merkabah*

a) Ascension and ecstasy. The "Book of Watchers," an early section of
the *Ethiopic Book of Enoch* that goes back at least to the early part of the
second century B.C. (I Enoch chapters 1–36; tr. 2:188–208 [98]), describes how clouds, stars, lightnings, and winds carry Enoch upward for an
audience before God in the throne room of his heavenly Temple (chapter
14). The "Testament of Levi," in its original form a Jewish writing probably of the second century B.C. [111,129a,165] (tr. 2:304–315 [98]),
has Levi receive an invitation in a dream to enter the opened heavens; he
rises through a series of heavens and finally, in the heavenly Temple, is
declared God's priest (chapters 2–5). Adam, according to a brief apocalypse of the first century A.D., "saw a chariot like the wind and ... was
caught up into the Paradise of righteousness," where the Lord sits in judgment on him (tr. 2:139–141 [98]; see below). John of Patmos, a first-
century Christian who evidently identified himself with Judaism and whose
Book of Revelation is a Jewish apocalypse in the name of Jesus[2], sees an
open door in heaven and instantly finds himself before God's throne (Revelation 4:1–2). The *Book of the Secrets of Enoch* (II Enoch, tr. 2:431–
469 [98]), which some scholars regard as a Jewish work of the first century

---

2 We will have more to say below about Revelation and its Jewish character. I infer John's self-
identification from 2:9: "I know your tribulation ... and the slander of those who say that they
are Jews and are not, but are a synagogue of Satan." And, again, 3:9: "Behold, I will make those
of the synagogue of Satan who say that they are Jews and are not, but lie – behold, I will make
them come and bow down before your feet, and learn that I have loved you." The writer's
emphatic denial of the right of certain people to call themselves Jews implies that he reserves the
title for himself and his audience; it is they who are the true "orthodox Jews," as opposed to the
"synagogue of Satan," who are perhaps the rabbis and their followers.

A.D. [530] but others as a medieval Christian composition [140], describes how two gigantic angels carry Enoch on their wings through seven heavens to God's throne (chapters 1−22). The *Greek Apocalypse of Baruch* (III Baruch, tr. 2:533−541 [98]; first or second century A.D.?) has an angel lead Baruch up to the fifth − perhaps originally the seventh [113] − heaven. In the *Apocalypse of Abraham* [90,160a] (perhaps early second century A.D.?), Abraham and his angelic guide ride to heaven on the backs of a sacrificial pigeon and turtle-dove (chapter 15).

This summary list, several items of which will occupy us later in this chapter, is perhaps not exhaustive, but does give a fairly complete enumeration of the heavenly journeys described in the Jewish apocalyptic literature. At first glance, we are inclined to dismiss them as purely fantastic relations, whose authors had no more shared the experiences of their heroes than Jack's creator had climbed the beanstalk.

But there is one more heavenly journey that suggests we should look again. It is contained in a Christian text, probably of the second century A.D., called the *Ascension of Isaiah* [98a,649]. Apart from its antique setting and a few fanciful details, the scene described sounds very much as if it could have happened:

> In the twentieth year of the reign of Hezekiah, king of Judah, Isaiah the son of Amoz and Jasub the son of Isaiah came from Gilgal to Jerusalem to Hezekiah. And ⟨after he (Isaiah) had entered⟩ he sat down on the king's couch and (although) they brought him a chair, he refused to sit on it. So Isaiah began to speak words of faith and righteousness with Hezekiah, while all the princes of Israel sat (around) with the eunuchs and the king's councillors. And there were there forty prophets and sons of the prophets who had come ... to greet him and to hear his words, and that he might lay his hands upon them and that they might prophesy and that he might hear their prophecy; and they were all before Isaiah. When Isaiah was speaking to Hezekiah the words of truth and faith, they all heard [the door which someone had opened, and] the voice of the spirit. Then the king called all the prophets and the entire people who were found there, and they came (in), and Micaiah and the aged Ananias, and Joel and Jasub sat on his right hand ⟨and on his left⟩. ... And while he was speaking by the Holy Spirit in the hearing of all, he (suddenly) became silent and his consciousness was taken from him and he saw no (more) the men who were standing before him: his eyes were open, but his mouth was silent and the consciousness in his body was taken from him; but his breath was (still) in him, for he saw a vision. And the angel who was sent to make him behold it belonged neither to this firmament nor to the angels of the glory of this world, but had come from the seventh heaven. And the people who were standing around, with the exception of the circle of prophets, did ⟨not⟩ think that the holy Isaiah had been taken up. And the vision which he saw was not of this world, but from the world which is hidden from ⟨all⟩ flesh. And after Isaiah had beheld this vision, he imparted it to Hezekiah, his son Jasub, and the remaining prophets. But the leaders, the eunuchs and the people did not hear, with the exception of Sebna the scribe, Joachim and Asaph the chronicler, for they were doers of righteousness and the sweet fragrance of the spirit was upon them. But the people did not hear, for Micaiah and Jasub his son had caused them to go forth, when the knowledge of this world was taken from him and he became as a dead man. [Ascension of Isaiah, chapter 6; tr. 651−652 [649]][3]

---

[3] The parentheses and brackets are the translators'.

The vision that follows — Isaiah's ascent through seven heavens, his successive transformations in each heaven, and his prophecy of the corresponding descent that Jesus is to make — interests me now far less than does the vivid and realistic-sounding account of a shamanistic trance that we have just read. The visionary loses consciousness, though his eyes remain wide and staring; his soul seems to leave his inert body and travel through distant realms; only when he comes to himself again can he tell his audience what he has seen.

I know of nothing in the Jewish apocalyptic literature that is comparable, in that it gives a circumstantial account of a trance which creates the impression that the author experienced or witnessed something of the kind. We do have a parallel in another early Christian source which, like the *Ascension of Isaiah* [127], has strong Gnostic overtones. This is the *Acts of Thomas* [648], which describes how the apostle Thomas anoints parts of his head and body and places a crown on his head. Then, holding "a branch of reed in his hand" and staring at the ground (we think of Hai Gaon's description of the practices of the *Hekhalot* mystics), he chants a Gnostic hymn to the accompaniment of music by a "Hebrew" flute girl. "They saw also his appearance changed, but they did not understand what he said, since he was a Hebrew and what he said was spoken in the Hebrew tongue" (chapters 5–8, tr. 444–447 [648]).

We may compare with both of these Christian sources a story found in the text conventionally called *Hekhalot Rabbati*. At R. Nehuniah b. ha-Qanah's direction, R. Ishmael assembles the scholars in the Temple. R. Nehuniah sits on "a stool of pure marble ... and we sat before him while the multitude of the colleagues stood." Fiery globes and torches separate the inner from the outer circle of auditors. R. Nehuniah explains the details of how one descends to the *merkabah* and comes back up from it[4]. He is evidently in a trance; for, at one point, he uses an expression that the scholars do not understand, and they ask R. Ishmael to "bring him back to us from the vision that he sees of the *merkabah*, that he may explain [it] to us." R. Ishmael uses a complicated magical procedure to bring R. Nehuniah back from before the throne of glory — that is, to bring his spirit back, for the narrative makes clear that his body was always present [568,587, 588,591]. R. Nehuniah then explains that he had been referring to the practice of "those who descend to the *merkabah*" to take certain people, "cause them to stand over them [?] or seat them before them, and say to them: 'Watch and look and listen, and write down everything that we say and everything that we hear from before the throne of glory.'" Trance

---

4 We would, of course, expect the "descent" and "ascent" to be reversed, since the world of the *merkabah* should be above us rather than below. We will return in chapter VI to this strange usage, which is characteristic of *Hekhalot Rabbati*.

states akin to R. Nehuniah's are apparently habitual (##201–228; ed. 1:91 –98; cf. tr. 59–71 [495,500,463]).

Very few people would claim that the historical prophet Isaiah, apostle Thomas, and R. Nehuniah b. ha-Qanah actually had the experiences attributed to them in these stories. But it would be very plausible to say that the authors of the stories were familiar with such experiences, and, indeed, knew ways to induce them; they projected the realities that they knew into the lives of their heroes [155]. If we accept this much, we might go further and deduce, from the Old Testament setting of one Christian account and the importance given to the Hebrew language in the other, that the Christians got their knowledge of trance experiences from the Jews who cultivated them. Yet another step would take us to the conclusion that the awareness of these experiences passed from Jewish apocalyptic into Christian, and that it was some kind of ecstatic mysticism actually practiced in pre-Christian apocalyptic circles that underlies the heavenly journeys of Enoch, Levi, and the rest.

Appealing as this argument is, I am not willing to take the last few steps. I find it very odd, to begin with, that the trance accounts that sound the most real occur precisely in the latest sources, two of them Christian. Further, while the *Hekhalot* source indicates that trance states are all in a day's work for those so inclined, the *Ascension of Isaiah* suggests that Isaiah's experience is unique: "But I say to thee, Isaiah, that no one who has to return to a body in the world has ascended or seen or perceived what thou hast perceived and what thou shalt (yet) see" (8:11; tr. 655 [649]). I detect here an echo of a much older apocalyptist's boast: "And I, Enoch, saw the vision, the ends of all things: and no man shall see as I have seen" (I Enoch 19:3; tr. 201 [98]).

The chronology of the sources suggests that the apocalyptic writers believed in the supernatural journeys of their heroes long before they were able to give any plausible account of the mechanics of these journeys. They knew that Enoch had "walked with God, and he was not, for God took him" (Genesis 5:24). *Wayyithallekh*, which I here translate "walked," is the same Hebrew verb that I translated "travel about" in Zechariah 6:1–7 (above, chapter II). The apocalyptists naturally supposed that, like the chariots that Zechariah saw, Enoch had travelled about heaven and earth under God's auspices, visiting places barred to ordinary humans and seeing things that no one else could have seen. Other ancient saints, they imagined, had done the same. Only later did they try to describe the method of travel. The Jewish author of the *Apocalypse of Abraham* made use of a fantastic and obviously supernatural mode of travel (riding on the sacrificial birds of Genesis 15:9–10); while his younger Christian contemporary who wrote the *Ascension of Isaiah* preferred the more naturalistic medium of an ecstatic trance.

The realistic-sounding description of Isaiah's trance is deceptive. Isaiah's journey, like Enoch's and Abraham's, is an event of the past, which cannot be replicated at the convenience of the modern would-be mystic. The authors of the latest sources, the *Hekhalot*, may perhaps have proposed that technique might take the place of inspiration, and ordinary folk replicate what had been the treasured experiences of a few ancient sages. But, as we will see in chapter IX, the *Hekhalot* evidence is far more equivocal than Gershom Scholem and his followers have supposed. We will need to sift it carefully before deciding on its implications.

The view that the visions recorded in apocalyptic literature reflect the real mystical experiences of their authors in fact explains far less about these visions than we might at first suppose. The key word here is "real." When we say that the apocalyptists "really" went on ecstatic journeys to heaven or that their writings were shaped by their "real" experiences on these journeys, we do not mean to imply that they penetrated the heavens like a modern astronaut, or that they visited the environs of God's throne the way you or I might visit Australia. What we are saying is that they entered a psychological state in which their fantasies felt so real that they could not distinguish them from experience; in other words, fantasy had become hallucination. It is an interesting and occasionally important question whether the visions of the apocalypses were bona fide hallucinations, or whether they were conscious fantasies which the authors set down in full awareness that they had not seen what they described. But this question does not affect the source of the material in the vision, which in either case must be the author's normally acquired experience (including religious tradition and study of the Scriptures), filtered through his own psyche. If he is hallucinating, we would expect his unconscious to play a larger role in the shaping of the vision than if he is daydreaming, and this may affect our interpretation of the vision's details (below, chapter IX). But we cannot in any event explain what he sees the way we would explain a traveller's report of a hopping pouched animal in Australia: it was really there, he really saw it. The contents of the visions always emanate from the visionary, must always be explained in terms of the visionary's own experiences and needs. Much recent scholarship has lost sight of this point. We will need to recall it again and again as we proceed.

In the meantime, we must confront the question of how the apocalyptic writers knew (that is, thought they knew) what Enoch and the rest had seen on their travels; and we must do so without taking refuge in the pseudo-answer, which answers nothing, that they learned it from their own ecstatic experiences[5]. We cannot, it seems to me, deal with this question

---

5 The distinct, and far more important, question of what the heavenly ascensions of Enoch and the

in isolation. It is part of the broader problem of apocalyptic pseudepigraphy.

The issue is this: Anonymous writers, living in the last two centuries B.C. or the first two centuries A.D., wrote in the names of Enoch, Abraham, Baruch and Ezra, calling themselves by the "I" of Enoch, Abraham, Baruch and Ezra. If they were cynical forgers, trying to get greater authority for their writings by passing them off as the work of an ancient sage, we could easily understand the practice; but the religious passion evident in the apocalypses seems to rule out the idea of cynicism. There seems to have been something in the psychology of the apocalyptic writers that allowed them to believe that in some way they were the ancient sages in whose names they wrote, that the imagined experiences of the ancients were indeed theirs. What was it?

Modern scholars have not made a great deal of progress in unraveling this problem, which is obviously basic to the understanding of apocalyptic [151,166]. I cannot pretend to offer a solution. But I think that it is in the apocalyptists' role as inspired interpreters of Scripture [536] that we must look for the keys to many of the problems surrounding the apocalyptic experience in general and the apocalyptic ascensions in particular.

This will bring us back to the *merkabah* exegesis of the apocalypses.

b) Exegesis and experience. A eulogy of Origen, traditionally but probably falsely attributed to Saint Gregory Thaumaturgus [687], credits the great exegete with having understood the mysterious sayings of the prophets "by the communication of the divine Spirit; for those who prophesy and those who understand the prophets need the same power, and no one can understand a prophet unless the same Spirit who has prophesied give him the understanding of his discourse" [685]. The author of this eulogy would have well understood the Essene writer who, in a much-discussed passage of the Dead Sea *Habakkuk Commentary*, applied Habakkuk 2:2 to the sect's Teacher of Righteousness:

> ... God told Habakkuk to write down that which would happen to the final generation, but He did not make known to him when time would come to an end. And as for that which He said, *That he who reads may read it speedily* [Habakkuk 2:2], interpreted this concerns the Teacher of Righteousness, to whom God has made known all the mysteries of the words of His servants the Prophets. [1QpHab vii 1–5; tr. 239 [77]]

To the basic conception that God's inspiration is necessary for the understanding of God's word, the Essene author adds a more startling idea: the prophets themselves were not inspired as fully as the Teacher of Righteousness, who can understand Habakkuk's prophecy better than Habakkuk did.

---

others meant to the apocalyptists – what needs of theirs did fantasies about these ascensions answer to? – will take us the rest of this book to solve.

God speaks to the prophet's interpreter more openly than he spoke to the prophet.

This idea lies at the root of the apocalyptists' conception of their own inspiration.

Thus, the apocalyptic "Daniel," who writes about 165 B.C., ponders Jeremiah's unfulfilled prophecy that salvation will come at the end of a seventy-year period (Jeremiah 25:11−14, 29:10−14). An angel reveals to him that the seventy years are really seventy *weeks* of years, and that this new period of 490 years is due to expire shortly after the apocalyptist writes (Daniel 9:1−2, 20−27). Daniel thus rescues Jeremiah's prophecy from the disproof of history. But history soon catches up with Daniel himself: Daniel's fourth (Seleucid) kingdom indeed passes away, but it is the Romans and not the saints who succeed it. This is why, more than 250 years after the Book of Daniel was written, the apocalyptic "Ezra" must do for Daniel what Daniel did for Jeremiah [155]:

> The eagle which you saw coming up from the sea [says an angel to Ezra] is the fourth kingdom which appeared in a vision to your brother Daniel. But it was not explained to him as I now explain or have explained it to you. [The fourth kingdom turns out "really" to have been Rome; IV Ezra 12:10−30 (RSV).]

The apocalyptist not only interprets the prophet, he knows more than the prophet. He thus becomes what the prophet ought to have been, and sees and hears what the prophet ought to have seen and heard.

The author of the Book of Revelation gives us a good example of this, which brings us close to our concern with the *merkabah*.

> Then the voice which I had heard from heaven spoke to me again, saying, "Go, take the scroll which is open in the hand of the angel who is standing on the sea and on the land." So I went to the angel and told him to give me the little scroll; and he said to me, "Take it and eat; it will be bitter to your stomach, but sweet as honey in your mouth." And I took the little scroll from the hand of the angel and ate it; it was sweet as honey in my mouth, but when I had eaten it my stomach was made bitter. And I was told, "You must again prophesy about many peoples and nations and tongues and kings." [Revelation 10:8−11]

The inspiration for this account is unquestionably Ezekiel 2:8−3:3, where God says to Ezekiel:

> "But you, son of man, hear what I say to you; be not rebellious like the rebellious house; open your mouth, and eat what I give you." And when I looked, behold, a hand was stretched out to me, and, lo, a written scroll was in it; and he spread it before me; and it had writing on the front and on the back, and there were written on it words of lamentation and mourning and woe. And he said to me, "Son of man, eat what is offered to you; eat this scroll, and go, speak to the house of Israel." So I opened my mouth, and he gave me the scroll to eat. And he said to me, "Son of man, eat this scroll that I give you and fill your stomach with it." Then I ate it; and it was in my mouth as sweet as honey. [RSV]

We now understand why the seer of Revelation finds the scroll sweet as honey in his mouth. But why is it bitter in his stomach? This detail, too, turns out to be from Ezekiel: "A spirit lifted me up and took me away, and I went, bitter in the heat of my spirit, God's hand being mightily upon me"

(3:14). The apocalyptist, who reads his Scripture carefully, learns that the sweetness Ezekiel experienced was only his immediate perception of the scroll; bitterness was the more lasting sensation [99][6]. By thus interpreting Ezekiel 3:3 in the light of 3:14, he understands why the text does not simply say, as it might have: "it was sweet as honey." Scripture adds the apparently superfluous words "in my mouth" in order to convey that somewhere else it was *not* sweet as honey.

Who, then, is the "I" who ate the sweet and bitter scroll, and who speaks in Revelation? It is, of course, the putative author, John of Patmos. But it is also Ezekiel. Better: it is Ezekiel as he would have spoken had he fully understood the implications of what had been revealed to him.

But even this is not enough. Ezekiel normally does not stand alone in the Book of Revelation, as he does in this passage, as the author's sole source of inspiration. As may be seen from any good commentary on Revelation, much of the rest of the Hebrew Bible, and especially the books of Zechariah and Daniel, also deeply influenced the author's thought and expression; many passages of Revelation weave together materials drawn from different Old Testament sources. This is entirely characteristic of midrash. But midrash, unlike apocalypse, does not say "I saw." The "I" who sees must not only be super-Ezekiel, super-Zechariah, super-Daniel, but a composite prophetic personality who sees what each would have seen had he understood what he in fact saw. The average apocalyptist selects out of the welter of Biblical figures who go into his composite perception one cardinal figure who will represent the perception, who will give a name to the "I" who perceives. Revelation, practically unique among the surviving apocalypses, does not do this; we cannot be sure why not. But the reshaping of midrash into vision is, if anything, clearer in Revelation than in its pseudonymous cousins.

When an apocalyptic visionary "sees" something that looks like Ezekiel's *merkabah*, we may assume that he is seeing the *merkabah* vision as he has persuaded himself it really was, as Ezekiel would have seen it had he been inspired wholly and not in part.

c) Method in apocalyptic exegesis. How, then, does the apocalyptist learn what the *merkabah* really was, what Enoch saw on his travels, or any of the hundred and one other things that he tells his reader? When I speak of midrash transformed into vision, I offer only a very general and programmatic answer to this question. We must derive specific answers from examining individual cases.

---

6 So the twelfth-century French-Jewish commentator on Ezekiel, Eliezer of Beaugency [5].

We will not always succeed. The process by which the apocalyptist derives his information is not always as straightforward and easily traceable as it is in Revelation 10:8—11. His midrash may seem entirely arbitrary to the reader who does not share his divine inspiration. Its contents may turn out to come from some alien and disreputable source such as Greek mythology. (This is why much of what Enoch sees when he "travels about with God" reminds us of myths that we read in Plato [118a].) Yet we occasionally find traces of discipline and system in the apocalyptic writers' use of motifs, as if what they were able to "see" was bounded not only by what their sources contained, but also by certain principles of how these sources could legitimately be used.

As we saw at the beginning of section 1a, several apocalyptic ascension narratives describe a series of heavens, often seven, through which the visionary passes. We do not know where the idea of plural heavens comes from. Although we find it frequently in rabbinic sources, there are only the vaguest and most doubtful traces of it in the Hebrew Bible (Deuteronomy 10:14, for example). Writing in 1901, Wilhelm Bousset supposed that the Jews had learned the idea from Babylonians or Iranians [704], and I know of no one who has since bettered Bousset's guess. Apocalyptic writers domesticated the concept. Yet, strikingly, they did not combine it with the *merkabah*. The visionary progresses through several heavens, or sees the *merkabah*, but not both.

Thus, the *Testament of Levi* describes Levi's ascent through the several heavens without reference to the *merkabah* or any of its features. The heavens of *II Enoch* are nearly bare of anything that might suggest Ezekiel's vision. Enoch sees composite animal forms in the fourth heaven; but these are not the *ḥayyot*, but the "Phoenixes and Chalkydri, marvellous and wonderful, with feet and tails in the form of a lion, and a crocodile's head" (12:1; tr. 436 [98]). Only in the names of certain angels, "Cherubim" and "Ophannim" (29:3) and "many-eyed ones" (20:1, 21:1), do we find traces of Ezekiel's vision. (We must even perhaps delete the "many-eyed ones," for these occur only in the longer, Christian recension of the text, and may be drawn from Revelation 4:6 rather than Ezekiel.) *III Baruch* provides chariots for the sun and the moon in the third heaven (6:1—2, 9:1—3), but no *merkabah* like Ezekiel's; it describes oxen and lambs which are "also angels" (9:4), and composite animal forms which turn out to be the builders of the Tower of Babel (2:3, 3:3), but nothing like Ezekiel's *ḥayyot*. None of the sights that Isaiah sees in the seven heavens, in the Christian *Ascension*, reminds us of Ezekiel.

By contrast, Enoch in *I Enoch*, Adam in *Vita Adae*, John in Revelation, all see something like Ezekiel's *merkabah*. But none of them visits more than one heaven.

The Apocalypse of Abraham seems at first sight to contradict this rule. Abraham, at the climax of his ascent, sees what is plainly a vision of the *merkabah* (chapter 18). God then tells him to look down, and, peering down from the seventh firmament, he sees the heavens opened beneath him (chapter 19; similarly in chapter 21, and cf. the textually uncertain reference to "the seventh expanse upon the firmament" in chapter 10). But it is very odd that, although Abraham obviously must have passed through six heavens to get to the seventh, the previous account of his ascent does not breathe a word about them. We must conclude that the author of the apocalypse has combined two originally independent traditions, one of them describing an ascent to the *merkabah* without reference to the seven heavens (chapters 15–18), the other describing a cosmic vision which we will presently see to have been based on a midrash of Genesis 15:5 (chapters 19–21). The writer's fidelity to his sources forced him to the incongruity that Abraham can look down on the seven heavens without first having travelled through them.

When, in chapter VIII, we examine the Genizah midrash known as the *Visions of Ezekiel*, we will see the themes of *merkabah* and seven heavens integrated in a more thoroughgoing and skillful manner. But, aside from the Apocalypse of Abraham, the only source I know of with any affinity to the apocalypses that tries to combine them is a Greek version of the "Life of Adam and Eve" (below). And this text, which does not describe a visionary ascension, is only doubtfully apocalyptic.

If the apocalyptic writers take care to keep the *merkabah* and the seven heavens apart, they take even greater care not to let *ḥayyot* and cherubim appear side by side. I Enoch 14, like the Angelic Liturgy, knows cherubim but not *ḥayyot*. The reverse is true in the Book of Revelation and, with an exception to be noted, the Apocalypse of Abraham. Daniel 7 knows four "beasts," who seem to be the *ḥayyot* in a new and frightening form, but says nothing of cherubim. It is, of course, clear from Ezekiel 10 that *ḥayyot* and cherubim are the same and therefore cannot logically appear together. But this does not keep the authors of the *Hekhalot* from using both to swell the heavenly ranks[7]. It need not have kept the apocalyptic authors from doing the same, if they had not been restrained by a sense of exegetical discipline and responsibility.

We may, then, imagine the apocalyptic writers as disciplined craftsmen who use their resources in accordance with obscure but consistent patterns dictated by the traditions of their art. We will not be chasing phantoms when we trace the exegetical patterns underlying the apocalyptic visions of

---

7 *3 Enoch*, chapters 20–22 (in Odeberg's edition; Schäfer, ##31–34 [490,495]) is one example out of many. (I discuss *3 Enoch*, with the rest of the *Hekhalot*, in chapter IX.)

the *merkabah*. For all the bewildering freedom they permit the expositor, who may range all over the Bible to construct a context for the *merkabah* — which then becomes what he perceives as the real and total *merkabah* vision, the one that Ezekiel ought to have had — we will find them to be intelligible, governed by associations similar to those we have examined in the last chapter.

It is first and foremost through their patterns of treating Scripture that the apocalyptic books contribute to our investigation of the problem of the *merkabah*. The technology of their heavenly ascents, which I consider just as imaginary as the Biblical landscapes in which they are set, is far less central. Yet we will find ourselves paying attention to these ascents as well. For they too presuppose a network of Scriptural associations, not limited to the reference to Enoch in Genesis 5:24, which we will see to bear on *merkabah* exegesis in an unexpected way.

Five apocalyptic sources principally concern us: the Book of Daniel, the Ethiopic Book of Enoch, the Book of Revelation, a brief apocalypse preserved in the Latin version of the "Life of Adam and Eve," and the Apocalypse of Abraham.

I am not the first modern writer on the *merkabah* to treat these texts as a group. In *Apocalyptic and Merkavah Mysticism*, Ithamar Gruenwald examined Enoch, Revelation, and the Apocalypse of Abraham. So did Christopher Rowland — first in an article; then, in more detail and with the inclusion of Daniel, in *The Open Heaven* [537,159,150]. The questions that Gruenwald and Rowland ask of the material are similar to the ones that I am posing, and our discussions overlap to some extent. But my way of responding to these questions is different enough from either of theirs that I cannot simply quote and build upon their conclusions. We must examine the texts afresh.

2. The Book of Daniel

a) Introduction. The Book of Daniel is the only full-blown, full-length apocalypse to make its way into the canon of the Hebrew Bible. It is not the earliest apocalypse that will demand our attention in connection with Ezekiel's *merkabah* — the Enochian "Book of Watchers," which we will consider in the next section, is almost certainly older. But, since Daniel is the more familiar of the two, I prefer to begin with it[8].

---

8 Elias Bickerman's *Four Strange Books of the Bible* [85] includes a good introduction to the Book of Daniel and its problems. In working with Daniel, I have made much use of the commentary (Anchor Bible) by Louis F. Hartman and Alexander A. Di Lella [126].

The second half of Daniel consists of a series of four apocalyptic visions: chapters 7, 8, 9, and 10–12. For reasons no one really understands, the first of these is written in Aramaic and the rest in Hebrew. We do not know if all four were written by the same individual or at exactly the same date. But they are obviously closely related to each other, and all respond to Antiochus IV's persecution of Judaism in 167–164 B.C. If there is a book of the Hebrew Bible or the Jewish apocryphal literature that can be more precisely dated by its historical allusions than Daniel, I do not know what it is.

There is little question that the author(s) of Daniel made heavy use of Ezekiel's *merkabah* vision. A. Feuillet extensively documented and discussed Daniel's borrowings from Ezekiel 1, which he considered crucial for the understanding of the "one like a son of man" in Daniel 7:13. John Bowman, M. Delcor, Matthew Black, and Christopher Rowland have similarly observed the links between the two sources [116,89,109,87,150]. All of these scholars are primarily interested, as we also will be, in Daniel 7. Since, however, the strongest evidence for Daniel's use of Ezekiel is in the Hebrew visions, we do best to start there.

b) Daniel 8 and 10. Daniel, like Ezekiel (1:1), receives his visions while he is beside a river (8:2, 10:4)[9]. Like Ezekiel (1:28–2:2), he reacts by falling on his face, and a supernatural agency must set him on his feet (8: 17–18, 10:9–11). His delayed reaction, like Ezekiel's (3:15), is to fall into a stupor (8:27). In 10:18–19, he describes how an angel "strengthens" him, using the root *ḥzq* five times in two verses; this repetition seems to me rather excessive, and leads me to suspect that the author is subtly alluding to Ezekiel's name, *Yeḥezqel*, "God strengthens"[10].

Daniel's description of the terrifying being that appears to him at the beginning of his last vision (10:5–6) is practically a pastiche of phrases from Ezekiel:

I lifted up my eyes, and saw a man clothed in linen, his loins girded with pure gold[11] [cf. Ezekiel 9:2–3, 11, 10:2, 6–7]. His body was like *tarshish* [whatever that means [33, 655]; cf. Ezekiel 1:16, 10:9]; his face was like lightning and his eyes like fiery torches [cf. Ezekiel 1:13]; his arms and legs were like the color of polished [?] bronze [cf. Ezekiel 1:7, 40:3]; and the sound of his words was like the sound of a multitude [cf. Ezekiel 1:24, 10:5, 43:2].

It is easy to establish Daniel's use of Ezekiel in this passage [153]. It is far less easy to explain what the author was trying to convey by collecting

---

9 Certain rabbis observed this parallel, but naturally did not draw from it the same conclusions that I do (*Mekhilta, Pisḥa* ch. 1; ed./tr. 1:6 [195]). The name of Ezekiel's "river Chebar" means, in Akkadian, "the great river" [1]; it is perhaps more than coincidence that Daniel 10:4 uses this phrase of the Tigris.

10 Greenberg makes a similar suggestion concerning Ezekiel 3:8–9 [8].

11 Emending with Hartman and Di Lella [126].

several features of the *merkabah* into this single figure. Perhaps the "likeness of a human being" who subsequently touches and comforts Daniel
·(10:16—19) gives us the clue. On the one hand, he seems to correspond to
the human-like being who appears at the climax of the *merkabah* vision
(Ezekiel 1:26—28). On the other hand, comparison of verse 13 with verses
20—21 shows that he is none other than the monstrosity who so terrified
Daniel to begin with, but who now appears in a less intimidating form. The
whole complex apparatus of Ezekiel's *merkabah*, the author seems to be
saying, was essentially a manifestation of the same being who appeared to
Ezekiel at the end in human form. After overwhelming Ezekiel with his
terrifying multiplicity, this being finally spoke to him in a form that the
prophet's humanity could deal with. (We think of Elijah's experience in I
Kings 19:11—13.) As usual, the apocalyptic author expresses his understanding of Ezekiel's vision by "seeing" it anew, in its truer form.

Even if my explanation of Daniel 10 is correct — and I am not confident
that it is — it does not get us very far. Let us turn to chapter 7.

c) Daniel 7. Daniel has a strange dream. He sees "the four winds of
heaven stir up the great sea," and "four great beasts, different from one
another," emerge (verses 2—3). It is clear from the rest of the dream, and
from the interpretation of it that Daniel receives, that the four great
beasts symbolize four worldly powers, inimical to God, and ultimately to
be destroyed. After the fourth beast's reign of terror, thrones are established, an "ancient of days" takes his seat, and he sits in judgment over all four
beasts (verses 11—12). "One like a human being" — literally, "son of man"
— comes with the clouds of heaven, appears before the ancient of days, and
receives from him universal and eternal power (verses 13—14). We later
discover that this human figure represents "the people of the saints of the
most high" (verse 27).

Daniel describes the ancient of days as follows:

> His clothing was white as snow, the hair of his head like pure wool. His throne was flames of fire,
> its wheels blazing fire. A river of fire flowed forth from before him. Thousands of thousands
> served him, and myriads of myriads stood before him. [Daniel 7:9—10]

We will see a very similar description of a throne and its occupant when
we turn to the vision of Enoch, which seems to be at least a few decades
older than Daniel 7.

Not all of Daniel's details can be derived from the *merkabah*. But the
throne's fieriness suggests Ezekiel 1:27, and the prominence given to its
"wheels"[12] seems to reflect Ezekiel's extended description of the *'ofannim*.
The "one like a human being" clearly points to the enthroned human form

---

12 *Galgillohi* in Aramaic. Targum regularly translates *'ofannim* in Ezekiel 1 and 10 with *galgalayya*.

of Ezekiel 1:26 [116]; only, Daniel's use of this figure to represent the Jewish people forces him to distinguish it from the occupant of the throne.

At its climax, then, Daniel 7 converges with Ezekiel 1. What about its earlier events? Daniel's vision, like Ezekiel's (1:4), begins with the coming of wind (7:2). Ezekiel sees four *hayyot*. Daniel sees four *hewan* [153], an Aramaic word that is etymologically related to *hayyot* but, unlike its ambiguous Hebrew cognate, clearly means "beasts." Daniel's beasts do not physically resemble Ezekiel's *hayyot* except in scattered details. Like the *hayyot*, however, their appearance is a prelude to that of the divine throne; and, at the climax of Daniel 7, they are in subjection to it.

No sooner do I say this than the obvious objections to equating Ezekiel's vision with Daniel's present themselves. In the first place, the value given the *hayyot* in Ezekiel is entirely different from that given the *hewan* in Daniel: God's loyal servants and thronebearers in the one case, his menacing enemies in the other. Secondly, the progression in Ezekiel is spatial — we follow the prophet's eye from the *hayyot* to the *'ofannim* to the throne — while, in Daniel, it is temporal. But I am suggesting, not that the author of Daniel 7 simply copied from Ezekiel's *merkabah*, but that he interpreted it. As he understood it, the sequence of Ezekiel's description hinted at a historical sequence in which a human-like entity emerges supreme over four bestial ones. Ezekiel himself, of course, may not have understood the deeper meaning of his own vision; but that was neither here nor there.

As to the docility and benevolence of the *hayyot*, is that really clear from Ezekiel? We have, indeed, come from examining several products of the hymnic tradition of *merkabah* exegesis, where the *hayyot* appear as God's effusively loyal servants. But that is not the only way to read the text. The author of Daniel, following an entirely different tradition, saw the *hayyot* as inimical forces, subjected against their will to the figure on the throne. (The influence of Ezekiel's description explains the curious fact that each of Daniel's first three beasts is not destroyed when its successor comes; all are subjected together to the throne and its occupant.) Of the two nuances of *hayyot*, the author of Daniel discarded "living creatures" and focused on "beasts," with all the word's implications of wildness and inhumanity.

Daniel's beasts emerge from the sea. We do not find, at least at first examination, any sea in Ezekiel's *merkabah*. The detail seems to have come to Daniel from an archaic Near Eastern myth that haunted Jewish fantasy for centuries. The sea, in this myth, is the primordial home of chaos and enemy of God; the monsters it spawns emerge to challenge the order that God imposed on the world [27,49a,107,109,122,417]. We will discover that later *merkabah* interpreters who took up Daniel's tradition found a place for the sea in Ezekiel's vision by identifying it with the crystalline firmament of 1:22 — which then became, as the MT gloss has it, truly "terrible." But this identification does not seem to have occurred to Daniel. He took the sea from the ancient myths that he drew upon, and added it as a new element to his reworking of Ezekiel's *merkabah*.

The most vulnerable point of my analysis of Daniel 7 is its description of the four beasts. Why does Daniel abandon Ezekiel at this point, and give his beasts a new set of characteristics whose origin and meaning are still a mystery [109]? I cannot answer this question. But, if the reader is prepared to credit that something of Ezekiel's original four *ḥayyot* may survive underneath Daniel's new details, I would point out that one of the four beasts is singled out for special horror and a special destruction (verses 11–12), and that this is the only one of the four who possesses horns. This perhaps reflects, once again, some peculiarity of the ox's face.

3. The Book of Enoch

a) Introduction. We must preface our study of the Book of Enoch with two observations. First, it is five books and not one. Second, it exists complete only in a translation of a translation; only the tiniest fragments of the original survive.

In 1773, the explorer James Bruce brought back from Ethiopia three manuscripts of the Book of Enoch, in an Ethiopic translation which had apparently been made from a lost Greek text. A long Greek fragment containing the first thirty-two chapters of Enoch came to light in Egypt late in the nineteenth century; bits of another Greek version had long been known through quotations by the Byzantine chronographer Syncellus [86, 98b]. But the Greek was itself a translation. It was not until the 1950's that scholars sifting through the manuscript fragments from Qumran Cave IV discovered small pieces of several different manuscripts of the Aramaic original. It was not until 1976 that J. T. Milik published them [138].

The Book of Enoch is a loose compilation of five shorter books which, although they belong to the same stream of tradition, are plainly independent works written at different times. Milik has argued that we should call them "the Book of Watchers," "the Book of Parables," "the Astronomical Book," "the Book of Dreams," and "the Epistle of Enoch." We will be primarily interested in the Book of Watchers, which is perhaps the oldest of the five. We must also glance at the Book of Parables, which may be the latest.

The "Watchers" of the book's title are the fallen angels of Genesis 6:1–4, the "sons of God" who mated with the "daughters of men" and begot giants. Chapters 6–11 describe their descent, the havoc they work on the earth, and their punishment. The angels implore Enoch to present God with their petition for forgiveness. He ascends, in a dream, into the divine presence (chapters 13–14). God flatly rejects the angels' petition (chapters 15–16). Thereupon, for reasons that are not very clear, Enoch receives a guided tour of remote and fantastic regions of the earth (chapters 17–36). He reports his bad news to the angels when he wakes; we are told about this, however, back in chapter 13, before the beginning of the description of the dream journey.

The inconsistencies, duplications, and incoherences within chapters 1–36 make it pretty certain that the Book of Watchers is itself composite. We cannot be sure how its elements should be separated; but our best guess is that the myth of the fallen angels in chapters 6–11 [125,145,171] is the oldest part, the account of Enoch's ascent in chapters 12–16 an addition to it, and the rest of the book a series of additions made around this nucleus. If Milik has correctly dated the script of the Qumran fragments, it would appear that manuscripts of the Book of Watchers as a whole already existed in the early or middle second century B.C. Since it must have taken years, and probably decades, for the Book of Watchers to develop from its' earliest materials into its present form, it is virtually certain that Enoch's ascension vision is older, and perhaps much older, than the Book of Daniel.

b) I Enoch 14: the text. Let us look more closely at this vision and its relation to the *merkabah* [146,155,159,537]. Enoch, the author tells us (speaking in first person), writes out the angels' petition, "and I went off and sat down at the waters of Dan, in the land of Dan, to the south of the west of Hermon: I read their petition till I fell asleep" (13:7–8 [98]). It is not clear just what happens next. An Aramaic fragment has here the words "my eyelids to the gates of" something, presumably heaven; the translations omit this entire passage. The upshot is that Enoch receives "a vision of wrath," which he communicates, when he wakes, to the unfortunate angels.

Chapter 14 gives the details of Enoch's dream journey to the divine presence[13]:

> [8]Behold, in the vision clouds invited me and a mist summoned me, and the course of the stars and the lightnings sped and hastened me, and the winds in the vision caused me to fly and lifted me upward, and bore me into heaven.
>
> [9]And I went in till I drew nigh to a wall which is built of crystals [that is, hailstones] and surrounded by tongues of fire: and it began to affright me.

---

13 I quote Charles' translation [98], breaking it into paragraphs for the sake of clarity. (Words in parentheses are Charles'; words in brackets are mine.) Charles' translation is eclectic, using both the Greek and Ethiopic versions. Michael A. Knibb translates his own critical edition of the Ethiopic text, referring to the Greek and Qumran Aramaic readings in his footnotes. E. Isaac's translation is similarly based on the Ethiopic. Nickelsburg provides a fresh eclectic translation of 14:8–22, using the Aramaic fragments as well as the Greek and Ethiopic [130,128a,146].

[10]And I went into the tongues of fire and drew nigh to a large house which was built of crystals: and the walls of the house were like a tesselated floor (made) of crystals, and its groundwork was of crystal[14]. [11]Its ceiling was like the path of the stars and the lightnings, and between them were fiery cherubim, and their heaven was (clear as) water. [12]A flaming fire surrounded the walls, and its portals blazed with fire. [13]And I entered into that house, and it was hot as fire and cold as ice: there were no delights of life therein: fear covered me, and trembling gat hold upon me. [14]And as I quaked and trembled, I fell upon my face.

And I beheld a vision, [15]And lo! there was a second house, greater than the former, and the entire portal stood open before me, and it was built of flames [literally, "tongues"] of fire. [16]And in every respect it so excelled in splendour and magnificence and extent that I cannot describe to you its splendour and its extent. [17]And its floor was of fire, and above it were lightnings and the path of the stars, and its ceiling also was flaming fire.

[18]And I looked and saw therein a lofty throne: its appearance was as crystal, and the wheels thereof as the shining sun, and there was the vision of cherubim[15]. [19]And from underneath the throne came streams of flaming fire so that I could not look thereon.

[20]And the Great Glory sat thereon, and His raiment shone more brightly than the sun and was whiter than any snow. [21]None of the angels could enter [Greek adds: "into that house"] and could behold his face by reason of the magnificence and glory, and no flesh could behold Him[16]. [22]The flaming fire was round about Him, and a great fire stood before Him, and none around could draw nigh Him: ten thousand times ten thousand (stood) before Him, yet He needed no counsellor. [23]And the most holy ones who were nigh to him did not leave by night [Knibb adds: "or day"] nor depart from Him.

[24]And until then I had been prostrate on my face, trembling: and the Lord called me with His own mouth, and said to me: 'Come hither, Enoch, and hear my word.' [25]And one of the holy ones came to me and waked me, and He made me rise up and approach the door: and I bowed my face downwards.

c) The merkabah in the heavenly Temple. What are we to make of this narrative?

Let us begin with the climactic scene in which Enoch sees God enthroned (verses 18–23). This passage has so many features in common with Daniel

---

14 So the Ethiopic; which other translators render: "and the wall of that house (was) like a mosaic (made) of hailstones, and its floor (was) snow" (Knibb); "and the inner wall(s) were like mosaics of white marble, the floor of crystal" (Isaac). Nickelsburg translates the Greek: "and the walls of this house were like stone slabs; and they were all of snow, and the floor was of snow." Milik discusses the word *lithoplakes*, "stone slabs" (which apparently does not occur anywhere else in Greek literature) in connection with Revelation 4:6 [142].

15 The translation of this sentence is doubtful. Knibb and Nickelsburg translate "ice" instead of "crystal"; Greek *krystallinon* can refer to either, but the fact that it has not been used earlier for hailstones, snow, or ice, suggests that here it describes a new phenomenon (see below). The next phrase, in Greek, is literally "and a wheel like the shining sun" (Milik emends to "and its wheels like the wheel of the shining sun" [142]); Ethiopic, "and its surrounds like the shining sun" (Knibb). "There was the vision of cherubim" is Charles' emendation of the difficult Greek text. Nickelsburg, following Milik, tries to translate the Greek "and its sides were cherubim"; Knibb gives the Ethiopic as "and the sound of Cherubim"; Isaac, "and (I heard?) the voice of the cherubim."

16 Knibb translates: "And no angel could enter, and at the appearance of the face of him who is honoured and praised no (creature of) flesh could look." I believe that the words "into that house," which imply that the angels could not enter the celestial Holy of Holies, are original. The Ethiopic translator deleted them in order to soften the contradiction with verses 22–23, which have the angels continually in attendance on God. See below.

7:9–10 (quoted in the preceding section) that it is impossible to doubt that the two are somehow connected [119,156]. In both, God's clothing is snowy white. In both, he sits on a fiery throne with brilliantly shining wheels. In both, fiery streams flow from his presence. In both, myriads of angels surround him. There are also differences. Daniel does not mention the cherubim that Enoch associates somehow − because of the textual difficulties, we do not know just how − with the vision of the throne. The author of Enoch entangles himself in a peculiar contradiction of which there is no trace in Daniel: he tells us in one breath that the angels cannot enter the structure where God sits (verse 21); and, in the next, he has throngs of angels perpetually in attendance (verses 22–23).

How are we to explain these resemblances, the presence of the cherubim in one vision but not in the other, Enoch's self-contradiction? How are we to explain the fact that cherubim not only appear in connection with the throne, but seem also to be embedded in the ceiling of the first house?

Our first clue is the obvious fact [575] that the building complex through which Enoch passes is the Temple of Jerusalem, transferred to heaven [365,379,456] and constructed of fantastic materials. He enters first the walled Temple court (verse 9), then the Temple structure itself (verses 10–14), and finally the Holy of Holies (verses 15–17). The enthronement scene in Enoch is thus part of a cultic setting that is missing from Daniel 7, at least in its present form. (There is some very slight evidence that Daniel 7:9–18 may have been set in the heavenly Temple[a].)

As in Daniel, the fire that surrounds the enthroned deity and the emphasis on the wheels both seem to point back to Ezekiel's vision. In one respect, Enoch's dependence is perhaps clearer than Daniel's. The Greek text of verse 18, without the improvement of modern scholars, has Enoch see only one "wheel like the shining sun," whose relation to the throne is unclear. This may reflect the "one wheel on the earth beside the *ḥayyot*" that Ezekiel sees in 1:15. Enoch's crystalline throne, too, may go back to the crystalline firmament of Ezekiel 1:22. (It is perhaps no coincidence that LXX renders *krystallou* in 1:22, while the Greek translator of Enoch uses *krystallinon* in 14:18.)

Given all this, it would be surprising indeed if Enoch's cherubim were not Ezekiel's *ḥayyot*, identified (as in Ezekiel 10) with the cherubim of the Holy of Holies, who are thus raised from the earthly Temple to the heavenly. The author of Daniel 7, who did not care to depict heaven as a Temple, had other ideas about the *ḥayyot*. The fact that they do not appear in his enthronement vision as cherubim confirms our impression that they have already appeared in another shape, as the four beasts from the sea.

Enoch's placing God's throne in the Holy of Holies also explains the tension between verse 21 and the following sentences. Daniel and Enoch share an image, perhaps drawn from the hymnic tradition of *merkabah* exegesis (think of the Angelic Liturgy), of God surrounded by multitudes of angels. But, in the Holy of Holies, God sits alone. Even the priests, as Josephus stresses (*Antiquities*, III, 123, 181), may not enter this inner shrine. Only once a year, on the Day of Atonement, the high priest enters to burn incense and to "make atonement for the holy place" which must dwell among the Israelites' impurities (Leviticus 16:11–19). The angels, barred from the inner house, are the priests of Enoch's heavenly Temple. The high priest must be Enoch himself, who appears in the celestial Holy of Holies to procure forgiveness for holy beings – perhaps this is how the author of Enoch understands *qodesh* in Leviticus 16:16 – who have defiled themselves by living among humans (I Enoch 12:4, 15:3–4)[17]. We cannot miss the implication that the human Enoch is superior even to those angels who are still in good standing. This point, to which we will return presently, was so important to the author that he emphasized it in verse 21, even at the price of consistency.

I am reminded of a midrash quoted three times in the Palestinian Talmud:

> They asked R. Abbahu [ca. 300 A.D.]: "It is written, *No human being shall be in the tent of meeting when he* [the high priest] *enters to make atonement in the holy place, until he goes out* [Leviticus 16:17]. Even those of whom it is written, *The likeness of their faces was a human face* [Ezekiel 1:10], must not be in the tent of meeting." [PT Yoma 1:5 (39a), 5:2 (42c), Sukkah 4:6 (54d)][b)

This midrash [419] does not appear to have been originally formulated for the situations in connection with which PT quotes it. We do not know how old it is or how it was originally used. But its point, that the high priest on the Day of Atonement goes where angels cannot, is very similar to the idea underlying I Enoch 14.

d) Psalm 104 and the merkabah. The strong cultic interest of Enoch's author thus explains why he differs from Daniel in representing what appears to be a shared exegetical tradition[18]. But it only complicates the question of why the cherubim, who ought to be only in the Holy of Holies, turn up also in the roof of the outer sanctuary (verse 11). To explain this

---

17 My view that Enoch's angels are heavenly priests accords well with David Suter's argument that the fallen angels are priests who have married outside approved circles [171]. Enoch is not usually treated as a priest; but, in the Book of Jubilees (4:25), we find him burning "the incense of the sanctuary, (even) sweet spices acceptable before the Lord on the Mount" [147,172]. This suggests the high priest's incense offering on the Day of Atonement.

18 I have not yet accounted for two features of this tradition: God's snowy white clothing, and the river (or streams) of fire that flow from God's throne. We will deal with God's clothing very shortly. As for the river of fire, if it is a celestial projection of the river that flows from the restored Temple in Ezekiel 47:1–12 (as seems likely), we must assume that the shared tradition already had some orientation toward the Temple. Enoch emphasized this orientation, while Daniel all but eliminated it.

incongruity, we must assume that the author of Enoch drew, not only on the cultic exegesis of the *merkabah* that generated the *hayyot*-cherubim equation, but on another line of interpretation that was not fully compatible with it. This second line was concerned with the relation of the *merkabah* to the opening verses of Psalm 104.

We cannot doubt that the author of I Enoch 14 drew on Psalm 104. The peculiar statement at the end of verse 11, that "their heaven was water" (so both the Greek and the Ethiopic; Charles' insertion of "clear as" has no basis in the texts), is only intelligible if it is based on Psalm 104:3: God "roofs his upper chambers with water." This encourages us to look for other reflections of the beginning of this psalm:

[1]O Lord my God, you are very great.
You have clothed yourself in glory and splendor.
[2][You are] he who robes himself in light like a garment,
Arches the sky like a tent,
[3]Roofs his upper chambers with water,
Makes clouds his vehicle,
Goes about on wings of wind,
[4]Makes his angels spirits[19],
His servitors flaming fire. [Psalm 104:1–4]

Reading these lines, we immediately understand why Enoch's God wears clothing that "shone more brightly than the sun and was whiter than any snow."

The last line gives us the clue to why, in verse 11, "fiery cherubim" mingle with the watery heaven; and, more generally, why the celestial structures are compounded of fire and ice. The author of Enoch has identified the "servitors" of "flaming fire" with the *hayyot*, whose "appearance was like blazing coals of fire, like the appearance of torches" (MT Ezekiel 1:13). We can begin to grasp how he used this identification when we compare a midrash found in a relatively late rabbinic source called *Midrash Tanhuma*[20]:

> God said to Moses: ... Contemplate the angels, who are flaming fire [Psalm 104:4]; and contemplate how many treasuries of snow and hail I have. Thus it is written, *Have you come to the treasuries of snow? Have you seen the treasuries of hail?* [Job 38:22]. Scripture similarly says, *Who roofs his upper chambers with water* [Psalm 104:3]. Yet the water does not quench the fire, nor does the fire burn up the water. Similarly, the *hayyot* are of fire, and the firmament that rests upon their heads is of water. So it is written, *This was the likeness of the hayyot: their appearance was like blazing coals of fire, like the appearance of torches, going up and down among the hayyot* [Ezekiel 1:13]. It is also written, *There was a likeness upon the heads of the hayyot, a firmament the color of the terrible ice* [or, "crystal"], *arching over their heads* [Ezekiel 1:22].

---

19 RSV, "who makest the winds thy messengers," translates the passage the way its author doubtless intended it. I translate it the way I believe Jewish expositors, like the author of the midrash quoted in *Ex. R.* 25:2, would have understood it. (*Mal'akhim* can mean both "angels" and "messengers"; *ruhot* can mean both "spirits" and "winds.")

20 See Appendix I, section 8; and chapter IV, section 5a.

They stand bearing that immense burden of water ...c) yet the fire does not burn up the water and the water does not quench the fire. Why? *He makes peace in his high places* [Job 25:2]. [*Tanḥuma, Terumah* #11]

The evolution of this midrash can be traced in a number of rabbinic sources. Its germ appears to have been the observation that the stars, which are obviously fiery, can exist in a firmament that consists of water (PT R.H. 2:4, 58a). Under the influence of Psalm 104:4, fiery angels replaced the stars (*Pesiqta de-Rab Kahana, Wa-Yehi be-Yom Kallot Mosheh* #3, ed. 5–6 [206]; Tanh. *Wa-Yiggash* #6). A new pair of Biblical texts then made its appearance: Ezekiel 1:13 reinforced Psalm 104:4, and Ezekiel 1:22 confirmed Psalm 104:3 (Tanh. *Terumah* #11). Eventually, the newcomers replaced the first pair of Scriptures; and, under the influence of Ezekiel 1: 22, the watery firmament became ice (*Song R.* to 3:11, *Numb. R.* 12:8)[21].

These developments of the rabbinic midrash, of course, took place centuries after the Book of Watchers was written. But, as we will observe in other connections, midrashim have a tendency spontaneously to recreate patterns of growth that first made their appearance long before, without any obvious signs of direct dependence. The tradition followed by I Enoch 14, like the much later rabbinic tradition, decided that Ezekiel 1 and Psalm 104 were part of the same context and could be used to interpret each other. The result was that a watery firmament coexists with fiery cherubim in verse 11, and fiery structures mesh with icy ones throughout the rest of the chapter[22].

This exegetical tradition, which occurs side by side in I Enoch 14 with the cultic tradition that we examined in section 3c, makes the following affirmations:

1. There is a large body of water in heaven.
2. In accordance with Ezekiel 1:22, this body of water can manifest itself as ice or snow (note especially the Greek text of verse 10).
3. This water or ice is usually mingled with fiery entities – stars, lightning, cherubim, "tongues of fire."
4. Again in accordance with Ezekiel 1:22 (MT), the reaction that this water or ice produces is terror (verses 9, 13–14).

The conclusion of our discussion of Daniel hints at why these observations are important. Their importance will become clearer when we turn to the Book of Revelation.

---

21 On the rabbinic sources cited here, see Appendix I, sections 6–8.
22 The author of I Enoch 14 seems also to have drawn on Exodus 9:24 ("there was hail, and fire flashing amid the hail") and Psalm 18:14 ("the Lord thunders in heaven, and the Most High raises his voice; hail and coals of fire"). Verbal resemblances to Ezekiel 1 appear to have been responsible for bringing both verses into the author's exegetical web: "coals of fire" (*gaḥale 'esh*) occur in both Psalm 18:14 and Ezekiel 1:13, "fire flashing" (*'esh mitlaqqaḥat*) in both Exodus 9:24 and Ezekiel 1:4 (and, to judge from Targum, *hi' mithallekhet* in 1:13 was considered equivalent to *'esh mitlaqqaḥat* in 1:4).

e) Enoch and the angels. I have already remarked on Enoch's evident superiority to the angels who function as priests in the heavenly Temple. Naturally, he is yet further above the angels who have fallen. The author of the Book of Watchers underlines this point, and the irony of it, when he has God tell Enoch to say to the fallen angels: "You should intercede for men, and not men for you" (15:2).

This remark reminds us that Enoch's ascent is a movement parallel and opposite to the angels' descent. The exaltation of the human being corresponds to the degradation of the heavenly beings. It appears that the ascension is not merely a way of getting the apocalyptic hero in sight of the *merkabah*, but conveys a pointed message about the relative status of humans and angels. This is not the last time we will read this message in the ascension stories. So far, it seems to have no inherent connection with Ezekiel's *merkabah*. But, as we go on, we will see the themes combine.

f) The "Book of Parables" (I Enoch chapters 37−71) is the only one of the five Ethiopic Enoch books of which no fragments have turned up at Qumran. We cannot be sure of its date, and we cannot even be sure that a Jew wrote it. (Milik's theory that it is a third-century Christian work written in Greek [139] has not proved very popular [96a,120,129b,136a, 173,178], but is at least an option. On the other hand, as Greenfield and Stone [120] point out, we do not have any Greek fragments of the Book of Parables either, and cannot prove it ever existed in Greek.) Whatever use we make of it, we must make very cautiously.

David Suter has argued that the author of the Book of Parables drew on traditional sources cognate to those of the Book of Watchers, but not on the Book of Watchers itself [173]. The material in the Book of Parables that concerns our study seems to me to point in the same direction. In its concluding chapter, Enoch sees in "the heaven of heavens ... as it were a structure built of crystals,/And between these crystals tongues of living fire." Streams of fire surround the building; throngs of angels endlessly circle it. A "Head of Days" emerges from the building with the angels, "His head white and pure as wool,/And His raiment indescribable./And I fell on my face. ..." (I Enoch 71:5−11). This sounds very much like I Enoch 14, with some seasoning from Daniel 7:9. But both Daniel 7 and I Enoch 14 leave Ezekiel's *'ofannim* as wheels; while I Enoch 61:10 and 71:7 enroll the "Ophannin" as heavenly beings, beside the "Cherubin" and "Seraphin." In this feature, the Book of Parables is aligned with the hymnic tradition rather than with the Book of Watchers[23].

---

23 The "Book of the Secrets of Enoch" (II Enoch), a writing of very uncertain date [162,165] preserved only in two Slavonic recensions, also mentions "Ophannim" (29:3), as well as "Os-

The sequel to Enoch's falling on his face is very remarkable; and, although it does not bear directly on the issue of *merkabah* exegesis, it will turn out to be important for us in another way. Enoch's body relaxes, his spirit is transfigured, he shouts out praises (71:11). The "Head of Days" approves. Enoch finds himself addressed as "the Son of Man who was born to righteousness, and righteousness remains over you, and the righteousness of the Head of Days will not leave you. ... He proclaims peace to you in the name of the world which is to come. ... And all ... will walk according to your way, inasmuch as righteousness will never leave you; with you will be their dwelling, and with you their lot, and they will not be separated from you, for ever and for ever and ever" (71:14–16, in Knibb's translation)[24].

"Son of man" – Knibb perhaps errs in capitalizing the phrase – is the Book of Parables' designation for a Messianic figure, chosen since the time of creation, who appears with the "Head of Days" and executes judgment on the kings of the earth (46:1–8, 48:2–7, 62:1–16, 63:11, 69:26–29, 70:1). We have little difficulty recognizing Daniel 7:13–14 as the source of both his appellation and the powers attributed to him. But nothing in Daniel, or the Book of Watchers, prepares us to find him equated with the human Enoch. The exaltation of the ascending hero has taken an extraordinary turn [96a,133b]; which we will not fully appreciate until we have examined, in chapter IX, the yet more extreme lengths to which certain *Hekhalot* sources carried it. Meanwhile, it remains for us to note another way in which the Book of Parables accords with what we have seen of the hymnic tradition. Its angels ceaselessly utter formulae of praise. "Holy, holy, holy, is the Lord of Spirits: He filleth the earth with spirits" (39:12). And: "Blessed be Thou, and blessed be the name of the Lord for ever and ever" (39:14, repeated in 61:11, mentioned in 47:2).

This reminds us of what we have missed in the Book of Watchers. The myriads of angels who attend God in I Enoch 14:22–23 do not say a word in his praise. As far as we can tell, they are absolutely silent.

---

tanim" (20:1), which may be a different form of the same name. The longer recension of II Enoch 29:1–2 contains what seems to be a reminiscence of the mingling of fire and ice in I Enoch 14, yet resembles the rabbinic parallels (above) more closely than does the earlier source: "And for all the heavenly troops I [God] imaged the image and essence of fire ... and from the gleam of my eye the lightning received its wonderful nature, which is both fire in water and water in fire, and one does not put out the other, nor does the one dry up the other ..."

24 Charles, disliking the obvious implication that Enoch is the exalted "son of man," arbitarily alters the text.

4. The Book of Revelation

a) Introduction. The last book of the New Testament consists of an elaborate vision purportedly received and described by "John, your brother, who ... was on the island called Patmos on account of the word of God and the testimony of Jesus" (Revelation 1:9). Christian tradition relates that he was exiled there during the reign of the emperor Domitian (81–96 A.D.); and, if the tradition is wrong about the date, it is not likely to be far wrong [115,157].

Since the last century, scholars have argued the presence of a Jewish substratum or Jewish sources in this Christian apocalypse, the criterion for "Christian" or "Jewish" being whether or not the writer recognizes Jesus as Messiah. For our purposes we may treat the entire book as Jewish. The author's viewpoint in 2:9 and 3:9 is that of a Jew who denies certain other Jews the right to this title. He draws the stuff of his visions mainly from the Hebrew Bible, making particularly heavy use of the Book of Ezekiel [134, 175,179]. It is true that he gives the impression of a somewhat bizarre originality in the way he turns Scriptural motifs to new purposes [375]. But, as we will see, his treatment at least of the *merkabah* material is solidly rooted in Jewish exegetical tradition. The rabbis may not have approved of John of Patmos' idea of Judaism, any more than they would have approved of that of the Essenes. This does not prevent us from using the Book of Revelation, as we have used the Angelic Liturgy, as a source for early developments in Jewish *merkabah* exegesis.

The Book of Revelation has not exactly suffered from want of exegetical attention, and the passages that deal with *merkabah* themes (chapters 4–5, in particular) have received their share. The standard commentaries, of which I find G. B. Caird's the most useful, naturally discuss them. So do Rowland's and Gruenwald's studies of the *merkabah* in apocalyptic literature [93,152,155,158,159,537].

Two books, in particular, demand our attention. Pierre Prigent finds in chapters 4–5 crucial evidence for his view that the background of the Book of Revelation is an early Christian liturgy still very close to its Jewish roots [148][d]. Martin McNamara treats these passages in the course of an argument that the Book of Revelation is the most closely tied of all New Testament sources to the tradition of the Palestinian Targums [331]. As McNamara realizes, his argument complements Prigent's, for the Targums originated in the synagogue and preserve for us the Scripture exegesis that accompanied synagogue worship (below, chapter IV). We can, I think, confirm the views of both scholars. Revelation's *merkabah* exegesis often runs parallel to that of the Targum of Ezekiel. Both are connected to the line of interpretation that I have called the hymnic tradition, whose development we can now begin to trace to the synagogue.

b) Revelation 4: the text. Like Enoch, John ascends to heaven. Unlike Enoch, he does not give us any details about his ascent. Again unlike Enoch, he does not proceed from outer to inner spheres of holiness. He sees an open door in heaven and hears a voice invite him to ascend. He is then "in the spirit" (cf. Ezekiel 3:14, 8:3, 37:1), and instantly finds himself at the very center and focus of the celestial spheres, where

> a throne stood in heaven, with one seated upon the throne! [3]And he who sat there appeared like jasper and carnelian, and round the throne was a rainbow that looked like an emerald. [4]Round the throne were twenty-four thrones, and seated on the thrones were twenty-four elders, clad in white garments, with golden crowns upon their heads. [5]From the throne issue flashes of lightning, and voices and peals of thunder, and before the throne burn seven torches of fire, which are the seven spirits of God; [6]and before the throne there is as it were a sea of glass, like crystal.
>
> And round the throne, on each side of the throne [literally, "in the middle of the throne and around the throne"], are four living creatures, full of eyes in front and behind: [7]the first living creature like a lion, the second living creature like an ox, the third living creature with the face of a man, and the fourth living creature like a flying eagle. [8]And the four living creatures, each of them with six wings, are full of eyes all round and within, and day and night they never cease to sing,
>
> "Holy, holy, holy, is the Lord God Almighty,
>
> who was and is and is to come!"
>
> [9]And whenever the living creatures give glory and honor and thanks to him who is seated on the throne, who lives for ever and ever, [10]the twenty-four elders fall down before him who is seated on the throne and worship him who lives for ever and ever; they cast their crowns before the throne, singing,
>
> [11]"Worthy art thou, our Lord and God,
>
> to receive glory and honor and power,
>
> for thou didst create all things,
>
> and by thy will they existed and were created."
>
> [Revelation 4:2–11]

The throngs of featureless angels whom Daniel and Enoch saw are also present in John's heaven. But John does not notice them until 5:8–14, when the Lamb[25] receives the homage first of the living creatures and the elders, then of "myriads of myriads and thousands of thousands" of angels, and finally of "every creature in heaven and on earth and under the earth and in the sea." The angels clearly constitute the outer circle of heaven. In the inner circle are the throne and its occupant, twenty-four elders, seven torches, four "living creatures," and – oddest of all – "a sea of glass, like crystal." All but the elders belong to Ezekiel's *merkabah*.

c) The elders. The identity of these elders has generated an extended and mostly inconclusive controversy [84,117,148]. I myself am inclined

---

25 Jesus usually appears in the Book of Revelation (first in 5:6) as a lamb who has obviously been slaughtered. This image is based on the idea, which Paul expresses in I Corinthians 5:7, that Jesus has died as the Passover sacrifice of the new community, his death foreshadowed in the Biblical command to slaughter the paschal lamb (Exodus 12). From this, it is only a step to actually representing him as that lamb.

to the view that they are representatives of the twenty-four courses of priests and Temple singers (I Chronicles, chapters 24—25), if only because they would then conform to the hieratic imagery that is so marked in Revelation: the spiritual incense offering (5:8, 8:3—5), the altar under which lie the souls of the martyrs (6:9—11; cf. 14:18, 16:7), the golden altar (8:3, 9:13); the heavenly Temple, ark of the covenant, and tent of witness (11: 19, 15:5—16:1, 16:17). A Qumran fragment, which seems to describe a ritual in an eschatological or heavenly "temple" (2Q24, fragment 4 [52]; see endnote *a*), includes a broken reference to "the elders [*šabayya*] that are among them and fourteen priests," and perhaps these "elders" are somehow connected to those of Revelation. Since identifying the elders would not advance our understanding of John's *merkabah* exegesis, we need not resolve this issue. Only, let us remember how "they cast their crowns [that is, garlands] before the throne." We may be able to shed some light on this gesture in the next chapter.

d) The throne itself, and the one sitting upon it, are drawn from Ezekiel 1:26—28; the surrounding rainbow shows this clearly enough. But John turns the human-like shape of Ezekiel's God into a blur of color. The Targum to Ezekiel 1:27 accomplishes the same end with a fog of euphemisms. This resemblance does not, at first sight, seem remarkable; we would, after all, imagine it natural that Jewish expositors would want to tone down the anthropomorphism of the Bible. But this does not seem to have been the case. At least in rabbinic Judaism, it is only the Targums that show any real aversion to anthropomorphism [266]; we will see in chapter VII that rabbinic expositors actually play up the anthropomorphism of Ezekiel 1:26—. 28. Targum and Revelation are here in the same camp.

In 5:1, this inhibition is relaxed to the extent that John can see (following Ezekiel 2:9—10) "in the right hand of him who was seated on the throne a scroll written within and on the back, sealed with seven seals." So also the Targum to Ezekiel 2:9—10, which only softens Ezekiel's "hand" into "the likeness of a hand"[e]. Taking its cue from Ezekiel's statement that the scroll was written *panim we'aḥor*, and understanding these words to mean "before and after" rather than "on the front and on the back" (RSV), Targ. Ezekiel 2:10 explains that the scroll contained "what had been from the beginning and what is going to be in the end. And there was written in it that, if the house of Israel transgresses the Torah, the nations will rule over them; but, if they observe the Torah, lamentation and mourning and woe will cease from among them." The sequel to Revelation 5 suggests that the scroll sealed with the seven seals had similar contents [96, 107a].

e) The torches. The "seven torches of fire, which are the seven spirits of God" (4:5) are not entirely strange to us; we have already met them in our discussion of the Angelic Liturgy (chapter II). 1:4 mentions them as "the seven spirits who are before [God's] throne." They perhaps reappear in 8:2 as "the seven angels who stand before God" (cf. 15:6–7). We certainly find them mentioned in 5:6, where the Lamb has "seven eyes, which are the seven spirits of God sent out into all the earth."

This identification of the spirits with the eyes of the Lamb points us back to Zechariah 4, where the prophet sees in a vision a gold candelabrum with seven lamps, and is told that "these seven are the eyes of the Lord, which range through the whole earth" (verse 10). Zechariah's candelabrum in turn encourages us to connect the seven torches with the seven golden lampstands of Revelation 1:12–20, and the seven stars that seem to belong to them. This perhaps brings us into the territory of the Hellenistic Jewish speculations that made the seven-branched *menorah* of Moses' tabernacle (Exodus 25:31–40) a symbol of the God of the seven planetary spheres, the "image of the God who sees" [332,734].

Revelation 4:5 thus appears to be one edge of a complex web of Biblical allusions. But the main inspiration of this verse itself was certainly Ezekiel 1:13. Hence the image of the torches, and the lightning that goes forth from the throne. The identification of the torches as spirits presupposes the midrash of Ezekiel 1:13 and Zechariah 6:1–7 that we have detected behind the Angelic Liturgy. Revelation 5:6 reflects the consequent understanding of the torches' "travelling about" as the spirits' journeys in God's service[26]. Targum similarly understands Ezekiel 1:14 as describing how "the living creatures are sent forth to do the will of their Lord ... they go about and circle the world and return ... swift as the appearance of lightning."

The Angelic Liturgy, Revelation, and Targum all reflect the same approach to the interpretation of Ezekiel 1:13–14, which I have associated with the hymnic tradition. The author of Revelation extends his *merkabah* exegesis with speculations about the *menorah*. We do not know if he was the first to combine these two related circles of ideas.

f) The living creatures. Revelation's "living creatures" (*zōa*) are obviously Ezekiel's *hayyot*. Like the LXX translator, who also uses *zōa* for the *hayyot*, the author stresses the "living" rather than the bestial nuance of

---

26 The text of Ezekiel 1:13 that lay before the Septuagint translator seems to have had, at the beginning of the verse, *ubenot hahayyot mar'eh* ("in the midst of the *hayyot* was an appearance ...") in place of MT's *udemut hahayyot mar'ehem* ("this was the likeness of the *hayyot*: their appearance ..."). This reading may perhaps have influenced Revelation 5:6, where the Lamb — and hence its seven eyes — stands "in the middle of the throne and the four living creatures" (my translation).

their name[27]. His treatment of them is essentially within the hymnic tradition, as the ceaseless chant he attributes to them indicates (4:8; cf. 5:8—14, 7:11—12, 19:14)[28]. We have seen that the combination of Ezekiel's vision with Isaiah's lies at the very infancy of the hymnic tradition. Now the author of Revelation carries this process so far that he actually combines the *hayyot* with Isaiah's seraphim, giving his living creatures six wings apiece and a cry of "Holy, holy, holy!" He also gives them the multiple eyes that properly belong to the *'ofannim* (Ezekiel 1:18, 10:12) — which appear nowhere in his vision. We recall that the author of the Enochian Book of Parables, who stands in this respect within the hymnic tradition, attributes a threefold "holy" to his angelic triad of "Cherubin, Seraphin and Ophannin," as well as a second formula ("blessed be Thou, and blessed be the name of the Lord for ever and ever") reminiscent of the doxology in Revelation 7:12. Revelation's living creatures are composites of all three orders.

There is another important way in which the living creatures differ from the original *hayyot*. Ezekiel sees four identical, basically human-like beings, each with four animal faces; John sees four distinct animal forms. (The comparison of the fourth creature to a *flying* eagle suggests that the writer is describing its entire body, not just its face.) Only the third creature is different. It is not "like a man," but "with the face of a man"; we do not know what the body looks like. We seem to be closer to the "cherubim" of the ancient Near East — winged animal forms with human heads — than we were in Ezekiel. We will see (chapter V) that much later rabbinic sources agree with Revelation in rearranging the *hayyot* as four different animals.

Within the inner circle of heaven, the living creatures seem to be closer to the center than do the elders. They chant their praises first (4:9—11), and are normally mentioned first (5:6—14, 14:3; against 4:4—8, 7:11). They are bound especially closely to the throne. 4:6 describes them as being "in the middle [*en mesō*] of the throne and around the throne." This self-contradictory statement, which has been the source of endless

---

27 I assume, following Vanhoye [180], that the author of Revelation used a Hebrew text of Ezekiel. This would not rule out the possibility that LXX's choice of words had some influence on him. The language of Revelation 4:5 is very similar to that of LXX Ezekiel 1:13 (cf. the preceding footnote); and, as we will see, the use of *krystallō* in 4:6 may be linked to LXX's choice of this word in Ezekiel 1:22.

28 Not, however, quite ceaseless. "When the Lamb opened the seventh seal, there was silence in heaven for about half an hour" (8:1). In its context, I assume that this silence is an eschatological counterpart to God's rest on the seventh day of Creation (Genesis 2:1—3), perhaps related to the seven days of silence that precede the final judgment in IV Ezra 7:30. But it is worth noting that both Targum (Ezekiel 1:25) and Talmud [101] have the praises of the *hayyot* periodically silenced, for reasons that we will examine in chapter IV.

headache for translators [92], seems to reflect a tension between the hymnic tradition on the one hand, and Ezekiel 10's identification of the *hayyot* with the cherubim on the other. As cherubim, the *hayyot* ought to be part of God's seat (Exodus 25:18−19); as angels in the hymnic tradition, they ought to surround it, singing praises. In 5:6, literally translated, the Lamb stands "in the middle [*en mesō*] of the throne and the four living creatures and in the middle [*en mesō*] of the elders," just as 7:17 locates the Lamb "in the middle [*ana meson*] of the throne." The former passage apparently considers the throne and the *hayyot*-cherubim as one block, ringed by the elders. If the elders are priestly figures, it is natural that they should not be quite as close to the center of holiness as are the cherubim.

Up to the end of chapter 5, the living creatures seem amiable enough. But their behavior soon becomes disturbing. When the Lamb opens each of the first four of the scroll's seals, "I heard one of the four living creatures say, as with a voice of thunder, 'Come!' " − and one of the famed "four horsemen of the apocalypse" emerges, to do his share in devastating the earth (6:1−8). It is again one of the living creatures who instigates the seven plagues of chapters 15−16, when he gives to "the seven angels seven golden bowls full of the wrath of God who lives for ever and ever," to pour out on the earth (15:7). The latter episode is surely based on Ezekiel 10:7, where "the cherub" gives "the man clothed in linen" (cf. Revelation 15:6) coals of fire to scatter on Jerusalem. The Targum to Ezekiel 1:8 generalizes this image in a way similar to Revelation: the living creatures "take coals of fire ... and give them to the seraphim, that they may cast them upon the place of sinners, and destroy the guilty ones who transgress [God's] word" [434]. The hymnic tradition has its darker, or at least its harsher, side.

The Book of Revelation is throughout full of the wrath of God who lives for ever and ever, and perhaps we should not blame the living creatures for being its executors. But this role of theirs − which is not essential for the action of either 6:1−8 or chapters 15−16 − does give them a rather sinister aura, like the traditional executioner with his black mask and bloody axe. Two hymns quoted in the roughly contemporary Syriac Apocalypse of Baruch confirm and perhaps illuminate this image. "Thou ... rulest with great thought the hosts that stand before Thee; also the countless holy [living] beings[29], which Thou didst make from the beginning of flame and fire, which stand around Thy throne Thou rulest with indignation" (II Baruch 21:6). And again: " ... there shall be shown to them the beauty of

---

29 Syriac *hayyata qaddishata*, corresponding to *hayyot haqqodesh* in some rabbinic sources (*Sifre Numb.* #103, ed. 101 [221]; BT Hag. 12b, 13a, R.H. 24b = [C]A.Z. 43b); in the following passage, simply *hayyata*. I insert the word "living" into Charles' translation.

the majesty of the living creatures which are beneath the throne, and all the armies of the angels who [are now held fast [*'ahidin*] by My word, lest they should appear, and][30] are held fast by a command, that they may stand in their places till their advent comes" (51:11)[f]. The living creatures, their beauty and majesty aside, give the impression of being savage dogs, subjected and kept on leash by dint of harsh discipline, but never tamed. The Book of Revelation seems to share this picture of the living creatures, and we are left to ponder what sort of beings they are.

g) The glass sea. This question leads us straight to the most problematic feature of John's heaven.

It appears in 4:6, "as it were a sea of glass, like crystal," located before God's throne. It reappears at the beginning of the episode of seven plagues in chapters 15—16 (in which, we recall, one of the living creatures plays an important role):

> And I saw what appeared to be a sea of glass mingled with fire, and those who had conquered the beast[31] and its image and the number of its name, standing beside the sea of glass with harps of God in their hands. And they sing the song of Moses, the servant of God, and the song of the Lamb ... [15:2—3]

Three explanations of this glass sea suggest themselves.

1. We have already seen that I Enoch 14 implies the presence of a large body of water, often frozen, in heaven; and that this icy sea seems to have been identified with the "firmament the color of the terrible ice" of Ezekiel 1:22. Revelation draws on the same interpretation of Ezekiel 1:22 that underlies Enoch's vision. While Enoch's God plates the walls of his heavenly palace with slabs of ice (*lithoplakes*, in the Greek text of 14:10), Revelation's God uses the entire frozen sea as pavement for his throne room [142]. We may support this suggestion by pointing to the fact that Revelation 4:6 compares the glass sea to *krystallos*, the same word that LXX uses to translate Ezekiel's "ice." But the clinching argument is the fire that is mingled with the sea of glass, which Revelation mentions (15:2) but never explains. Assume as background Enoch's tradition, in which the water or ice normally mingles with fiery entities such as stars, and Revelation's mixture becomes perfectly intelligible [133].

2. The picture drawn in Revelation 15:2—3 — people who have triumphed over mortal peril stand beside a sea and sing the song of Moses — is ob-

---

30 Charles brackets these words as a supposed gloss or a dittograph of what follows.

31 This "beast" is one of a trio of archenemies of the faith in the Book of Revelation (16:13, for example), the others being the "dragon" (or "devil") and the "false prophet" (evidently the same as the beast from the earth of 13:11). Revelation 13 details the beast's misdeeds, and explains the allusions made here. Wilhelm Bousset's *The Antichrist Legend* [88] remains the classic study of the subject.

viously modeled after the crossing of the Red Sea [333]. "Israel saw the Egyptians dead upon the seashore ... and they believed in the Lord and in his servant Moses. Then Moses and the people of Israel sang this song to the Lord ..." (Exodus 14:30—15:1). The fact that Revelation's sea is solid, which we have just explained with reference to the Enoch traditions, can also be explained from Exodus 15:8, which tells us that "the deeps congealed in the heart of the sea" [136]. (We will see this suggestion confirmed in the next section.) The sea is thus symbolic of the dangers that the faithful have escaped, and points both to their salvation and to the destruction of those who have not kept the faith[32]. That is why it is mingled with fire: to indicate the "lake of fire" which is the eternal home of those who succumb to the beast rather than conquering it (14:9—11, 19:20, 20:14—15, 21:8, vs. 20:4). The glass sea seems mainly a sinister symbol, and it appears at first rather mysterious that Revelation 4 gives it a central place in heaven.

3. Behind these ominous implications of the Red Sea we may detect a yet more ominous body of water: the primeval ocean of ancient Near Eastern mythology, embodiment of chaos and home of monsters [27,49a,107, 122,417]. Other references to the sea in the Book of Revelation point in this direction. The beast that casts its shadow over the second half of the book rises out of the sea (13:1). In the renewed heaven and earth, purged of all evil, "the sea was no more" (21:1) [95].

The beginning of Daniel 7, the beginning of Revelation 13, and Revelation 4:6, if we read them one after the other, evoke images that overlap like intersecting circles. In Daniel, four malignant monsters emerge from the sea. In Revelation 13, one malignant monster, a composite of Daniel's four, emerges from the sea. In Revelation 4, four beings stand by the sea — monstrous enough in their forms; and, if not exactly malignant, with enough violence and brutality in their makeup that it is only the fact that they work for the right side that saves them from this adjective[33]. All of these creatures descend from Ezekiel's *ḥayyot*: the *zōa* of Revelation 4

---

32 "For at the command of God the sea became a source of salvation to one party and of perdition to the other." — Philo, *De vita contemplativa*, #86 [727].

33 When I read the Book of Revelation with my students, I often have them write papers that focus on the theme of combat between good and evil, and that list and describe the major characters on each side. I find that many students are at a loss how to classify some of the angels in Revelation. Are "the four angels who are bound at the great river Euphrates ... held ready ... to kill a third of mankind" (9:14—15) to be considered good or evil? Their savagery, and the fact that they have to be restrained, seem to suggest the latter. These students perhaps have not read that "it is a fearful thing to fall into the hands of the living God" (Hebrews 10:31); or, as one of Flannery O'Connor's characters puts it, "even the mercy of the Lord burns" [847]. But they have, I think, perceived a real moral ambiguity in the Book of Revelation. We will see that the rabbis were sensitive to similar ambiguities in their own conception of God.

directly, the "beast" (*thērion*) of Revelation 13 through Daniel's *ḥewan*. It is true that the writer seems deliberately to distinguish the *zōa* from the *thērion* by using different Greek words, which express the different connotations of Hebrew *ḥayyot*. But, in the Hebrew or Aramaic substrate that many scholars detect behind the bizarre Greek of Revelation [64,100, 174a], I cannot imagine how the two would be distinguished[34].

Each of the three hypotheses I have sketched explains some aspect of the data so effectively that we can hardly afford to dispense with it. None of them explains all the data. I see no reason why we cannot keep them all and assume that the glass sea conveys several different but complementary messages.

The combination of these messages takes us away from the well-travelled path of the hymnic tradition, to which the author of Revelation has until now pretty much restricted himself, and introduces us to darker and stranger roads. As I understand it, it runs somewhat as follows:

The sea is the watery chaos from which the evil monsters emerge, and the fiery lake to which they return. Essentially hellish, it manifested itself on earth as the sea that the Israelites crossed. It manifests itself in heaven as a sea that lies before the *merkabah* throne, in which stars and possibly other fiery beings are embedded (following Enoch). God dominates it by making it solid, as he did by the hand of Moses, as he does now in heaven. But it will not be until after the judgment that both heaven and earth will be entirely free of it. Ezekiel saw it when he saw the *merkabah*, and called it, appropriately, "the terrible ice." (The same set of ideas, as we will see in chapters V and VI, underlies the rabbinic notion that the *merkabah* was present at the sea's earthly manifestation at the time that the Israelites crossed it.) The existence of the sea as part of the *merkabah* compromises the moral character of the *ḥayyot*; or, better, calls attention to the fact that their character is compromised in many ways, including some that we have yet to examine. We are not yet ready to say what light this sheds on the character of their Master.

For the first time, we perhaps see a glimmering of a possible reason why one should not say "water, water," when one ascends to the *merkabah*; and why R. Akiba applies to this seemingly harmless remark the stern judgment

---

34 Significantly, the men who translated the Book of Revelation from Greek into the Christian Aramaic dialect known as Syriac either did not try to distinguish *zōon* from *thērion*, and used the word *ḥayyuta* for both; or else resorted to the circumlocution *ḥaywat shenna*, "beast of fang," to translate *thērion* [124a]. — Targum, it is true, distinguishes Ezekiel's *ḥayyot* from ordinary "beasts" by calling them *biryata*, "creatures" (below, chapter IV). But this has no relevance to Revelation's *zōa*. *Biryata* would have been represented in Greek by *ktiseis* (as in Tobit 8:5, 15) or *ktismata* (Revelation 5:1, 8:9; Aquila, Symmachus, and Theodotion use *ktisma* to translate *beri'ah* in Numbers 16:30 [49b]) — certainly not *zōa*.

that *he who speaks lies shall not be established in my sight*[35]. But there is a long distance between the Book of Revelation and the Babylonian Talmud. We can establish a connection between them only in the context of a detailed study of rabbinic traditions about the *merkabah* and the waters. This we will undertake in chapter VI. In the meantime, let us return to the evidence of the apocalypses.

5. The "Life of Adam and Eve"

a) Introduction. R. H. Charles has published, under the title "The Books of Adam and Eve," L. S. A. Wells' translation of a series of ancient Jewish legends about the adventures of Adam and Eve after they were expelled from Eden [98]. These legends survive in a bewildering variety of more or less parallel versions in a number of different languages [112,182]. There is a Latin version, the "Vita Adae et Evae," itself represented by several variant recensions [137,144]. There is a Greek version, mistitled "The Apocalypse of Moses" by the first scholar to publish it [97,167,174]. There are versions in Armenian [108], Slavonic [129], and Georgian. (Wells' translation is mostly restricted to the Greek and the Latin versions, although he includes a section of the Slavonic; Conybeare [108] has translated the Armenian text into English.)

We are not sure how the versions relate to each other, what language or languages they were originally written in, or when they were written or translated. We do not know whether they go back to some parent version, and, if so, how old that parent version is. Even to inquire into these questions would mean getting ourselves into a snarl of problems of hair-raising complexity. We can permit ourselves to stay outside this tangle, especially since, as I will explain presently, the passage of the Adam legends that most interests us can be dated fairly securely to the first century A.D.

b) The ascension of Adam: the text and its date. Wells' use of parallel columns for his translations of the Greek and the Latin makes it easy for us to distinguish a section of the "Vita Adae" (chapters 25–29) which interrupts its context, corresponds to nothing in the Greek version, and, when removed, leaves a smoothly flowing Latin narrative that runs parallel to the Greek. This section is clearly an interpolation, which may be either earlier or later than the legend into which it is inserted. Let us look at it more closely.

---

35 Rowland [155,159] also notes that Akiba's warning seems somehow connected to Revelation's glass sea. But he does not explain the connection in the way I am suggesting here.

[Chapter 25:] And Adam said to Seth, 'Hear, my son Seth, that I may relate to thee what I heard and saw after your mother and I had been driven out of paradise. ²When we were at prayer, there came to me Michael the archangel, a messenger of God. ³And I saw a chariot like the wind and its wheels were fiery and I was caught up into the Paradise of righteousness, and I saw the Lord sitting and his face was flaming fire that could not be endured. And many thousands of angels were on the right and on the left of that chariot.

[Chapter 26:] When I saw this, I was confounded, and terror seized me and I bowed myself down before God with my face to the earth. ²And God said to me, 'Behold thou diest, since thou hast transgressed the commandment of God, for thou didst hearken rather to the voice of thy wife, whom I gave into thy power, that thou mightst hold her to thy will. Yet thou didst listen to her and didst pass by My words.'

[Chapter 27:] And when I had heard these words of God, I fell prone on the earth and worshipped the Lord and said, 'My Lord, All powerful and merciful God, Holy and Righteous One, let not the name that is mindful of Thy majesty be blotted out, but convert my soul, for I die and my breath will go out of my mouth. ²Cast me not out from Thy presence, (me) whom Thou didst form of the clay of the earth. Do not banish from Thy favour him whom Thou didst nourish.'

³And lo! a word concerning thee³⁶ came upon me and the Lord said to me, 'Since thy days †were fashioned† [so Wells indicates an emended text], thou hast been created with a love of knowledge; therefore there shall not be taken from thy seed for ever the (right) to serve Me.'

[Chapter 28:] And when I heard these words, I threw myself on the earth and adored the Lord God and said, 'Thou art the eternal and supreme God; and all creatures give thee honour and praise.

²'Thou art the true Light gleaming above all light(s), the Living Life, infinite mighty Power. To Thee, the spiritual powers give honour and praise. Thou workest on the race of men the abundance of Thy mercy.'

³After I had worshipped the Lord, straightway Michael, God's archangel, seized my hand and cast me out of the paradise †of 'vision'† and of God's command [the text of the last six words is very uncertain]. ⁴And Michael held a rod in his hand, and he touched the waters, which were round about paradise, and they froze hard.

[Chapter 29:] And I went across, and Michael the archangel went across with me, and he led me back to the place whence he had caught me up. ²Hearken, my son Seth, even to the rest of the secrets [and sacraments] ³⁷ that shall be, which were revealed to me when I had eaten of the tree of knowledge, and knew and perceived what will come to pass in this age ...

The group of manuscripts that is usually considered the most reliable ("Class I") breaks off at this point. But the other manuscript groups continue with an apocalyptic prophecy of the lawgiving at Sinai and the building of the First and Second Temples. "In the last time," this passage goes on, "the house of God will be exalted greater than of old. And once more iniquity will exceed righteousness." The "house of God" must be the Temple as rebuilt in grand style by Herod; for if, as some scholars think, it is the Messianic Temple, we cannot understand why "once more iniquity will exceed righteousness" [112]. Only afterward begins the Messianic age,

---

36 So Wells translates *verbum tuum*, evidently understanding "thee" as Seth. "Thy word" seems the more natural translation, although it is odd that God should be referred to in both second and third person in the same sentence. Perhaps we should follow the reading of Mozley's text [144] (recorded in Meyer's apparatus [137]), *ecce uerbum tuum incendit me*, and take "behold thy word inflames me" as the conclusion of Adam's speech.

37 Wells' brackets, indicating a supposed gloss.

when "God will dwell with men on earth in visible form." Then righteousness shines, the house of God is honored, the law is observed, God raises
for himself a faithful people and punishes the wicked. "And in that time,
shall men be purified by water from their sins. But those who are unwilling
to be purified by water shall be condemned."

Some of the references in this apocalypse — God dwells on earth in visible form, people are purified by water from sin — seem to indicate it was
written by a Christian, perhaps either the translator or a copyist of the
"Vita Adae." The fact that the best manuscripts omit it might suggest that
it is a later addition to the passage with which we are concerned. I nevertheless believe that its author was a Jew, that it is the proper conclusion to
Adam's description of his ascension, and that it enables us to fix the date
of this vision.

The text cannot originally have ended where the manuscripts of "Class
I" leave off. To have Adam about to reveal the secrets of what will come
to pass in this age, and then break off with this promise, is to invite an
apoplectic fit in the reader. It is more likely that a Christian scribe omitted
the concluding prophecy because it was not Christian enough. It contains
no hint that God's son will die an atoning death, no hint the Temple will
be destroyed, no hint the law will be abrogated. Instead, the Temple is
honored in the future age, the law cultivated. God dwells with his people
on earth, as Scripture promised he would (Exodus 25:8, Zechariah 2:14–
15, 8:3); only the word *videndus* or *visurus*, "in visible form," which the
various manuscripts give differently and some omit altogether [144], is
likely to be a Christian addition. The reference to purification by water,
although indeed reminiscent of Mark 16:16, could as easily be Jewish as
Christian. "I will spinkle clean water upon you," God promises in Ezekiel
36:25, "and you shall be clean from all your uncleannesses, and from all
your idols I will cleanse you."

The author does not know that Herod's Temple will be destroyed before
God comes to dwell on earth. He must therefore have written while the
Temple stood, between 11 B.C. and 70 A.D.

c) The setting of the ascension. What is the author describing? According
to 25:1, it is what Adam "heard and saw after your mother and I had been
driven out of paradise." But this does not make sense. God's sentence on
Adam in 26:2 is plainly an expansion of Genesis 3:17, and we cannot
understand why God would snatch Adam to his throne to judge him a
second time for the exact same sin he had already punished, only to relent
a moment later. 29:2 tells us (as Kolenkow has pointed out [131]) that
Adam learned what he is about to relate to Seth when he ate of the tree of
knowledge. If so, and if the preceding vision takes place some time after he
has been expelled from paradise, that vision is completely irrelevant to the

revelation of the secrets of the future. Why, then, does Seth have to hear about it?

More likely, chapters 25–28 is a reworking of the Biblical account of God's judgment of Adam: instead of descending to Adam's paradise for this purpose, God carries Adam up to his own. The author's starting point was evidently the question of why Adam does not die when he eats the forbidden fruit, as God threatened he would (Genesis 2:17). Something more must have happened at the judgment of Adam than Genesis 3:8–24 is willing to tell us explicitly, and the author undertakes to explain what it was. God realized that the "love of knowledge" that induced Adam to eat the fruit is really an inborn virtue of his species which, far from effecting Adam's death, should win for his offspring the function of serving God. The originally forbidden knowledge thus became legitimate, with the result that Adam could pass it on to his son. The judgment turned out in Adam's favor[38]. It is a little odd that, despite this divine approval, the author uses "cast me out" to describe Adam's departure from God's presence – odd, that is, until we realize that the author is paraphrasing Genesis 3:24.

The opening words of the story (from "after your mother" to "prayer," in 25:1–2), which transfer Adam's vision to after his expulsion from paradise, must be a mistaken addition, perhaps the work of the editor who inserted the episode into the "Vita Adae." As originally composed, the narrative is a drastic midrash on Genesis 3, which transforms the judgment of Adam into his ascension and election for God's service. The author shows no more interest than does John of Patmos in the mechanics of the ascension, and we may assume that he uses it as a device to express Adam's exaltation. Unlike I Enoch, the "Vita Adae" does not clearly indicate that Adam and his offspring win their success at the angels' expense. Yet we are reminded that God does not choose Adam to serve him because there is no one else around who can do it. "Thousands of angels," who are apparently passed over in Adam's favor, "were on the right and on the left of that chariot."

d) The merkabah, and the waters of paradise. What of the *merkabah* itself? The author tells us little that we have not already learned from Daniel and Enoch: its wheels are fiery, its occupant is fiery, thousands of angels surround it. Unlike the apocalyptic writers we have so far examined, our author actually calls it a "chariot" (*currus*) instead of a throne. When he

---

38 Some of the rabbis, too, seem to have believed that God ruled in Adam's favor. "God said to Adam: 'Let this be a sign for your offspring: just as you came before me for judgment this day and went forth pardoned, so they are going to come before me for judgment this day [Rosh Hashanah] and go forth pardoned' "(*Pesiqta de-Rab Kahana, Rosh ha-Shanah* #1, ed. 334 [206]).

compares it to the wind (25:3), it is just possible he is drawing on Ezekiel 1:4, where a wind is the first thing the prophet notices. One manuscript of I Enoch, which seems to represent an early reading, has Enoch travel by a "chariot of wind" in 52:1 [121,128]. Adam, however, does not ride in the chariot; the very sight of it is enough to carry him upward.

But Adam's most important experience with the *merkabah* – for us, at any rate – happens when he is leaving. "And Michael held a rod in his hand, and he touched the waters, which were round about paradise, and they froze hard [*gelaverunt* or *congelaverunt*, depending on the manuscript; "congealed" would be a better translation]. And I went across, and Michael the archangel went across with me. ..." The "waters" are presumably the rivers that flow from Eden, according to Genesis 2:10–14. But why does it matter whether they are solid or liquid? Given Adam's instantaneous translation into paradise in 25:3, it would be surprising indeed if he and Michael now have to walk home. Michael's gesture only makes sense if we assume it is modelled after that of Moses, who, with his rod, causes "the deeps to congeal in the heart of the sea" (Exodus 14:16, 15:8).

In the Book of Revelation, we saw God's throne surrounded by a sea mirroring the Red Sea, congealed into glass. Now, in a Jewish source that is ten to a hundred years older, we find the *merkabah* surrounded by waters which again mirror the Red Sea, in that they too congeal. The juxtaposition of the *merkabah* and the solidified sea is plainly not an idiosyncrasy of John of Patmos. The evidence of the "Vita Adae" encourages us to think that Revelation has derived its complex of ideas concerning the waters from contemporary traditions of *merkabah* exegesis.

e) The "Apocalypse of Moses." The Greek Adam legends found in the so-called "Apocalypse of Moses" also mention the *merkabah*. Unfortunately, it is almost impossible to date them.

In the passage from the "Vita Adae" we have just studied, God carries Adam up to his *merkabah* in order to judge him. In chapter 22 of the "Apocalypse of Moses," God descends for this purpose with his *merkabah*. "And when God appeared in paradise, mounted on the chariot of his cherubim with the angels proceeding before him and singing hymns of praises, all the plants of paradise, both of your father's lot and mine [Eve's], broke into flowers. And the throne of God was fixed where the Tree of Life was."

The perpetual chant that surrounds the *merkabah* is typical of the hymnic tradition. (Its occurrence here reminds us that the "many thousands of angels" in "Vita Adae" 25:3 seem to be silent.) The plants' blossoming at the approach of the *merkabah* suggests that the author may have been thinking of Psalm 96:12–13: "Let the field exult, and everything in it! Then shall all the trees of the wood sing for joy before the Lord, for he comes, for he comes to judge the earth." If so, this passage offers a remote parallel to the singing of the trees in the Johanan b. Zakkai stories; for, as we saw in chapter I, PT invokes Psalm 96:12 in that connection[g].

The *merkabah* descends once again in the "Apocalypse of Moses," this time at Adam's death (chapter 33). Right after Adam gives up the ghost, Eve looks up to heaven and sees "a chariot of light," preceded by angels, carried by "four bright eagles" who are apparently so dazzling that one cannot look at them. (The Armenian text replaces the eagles with "four fiery beasts," presumably to conform the passage to Ezekiel.) The purpose of the chariot is not to carry away Adam's soul[39] – this is done at a later stage, by "one of the seraphim with six wings" (37:3) – but, as in chapter 22, to convey God to the place of judgment. The *merkabah* halts over the place where Adam's body lies. The attending angels intercede for Adam's soul, burning incense so copiously on the celestial incense-altar[40] (which has apparently descended with the *merkabah*) that "the smoke of the incense veiled the firmaments."

At this point, both Eve and Seth look upward, and see "the seven heavens opened" and the angels and the heavenly luminaries praying on Adam's behalf (chapters 34–36). The writer surely draws the opening of the heavens from Ezekiel 1:1, and he learns that there are several of them from the plural form of the Hebrew word for "heavens" (*shamayim*). The implication, that Eve and Seth see the process of Adam's judgment transpiring beyond the firmaments, does not fit quite comfortably with the context, in which the heavenly court and cult have descended to mid-air. But, in this respect, the story reproduces a tension already present in the original *merkabah* vision. When Ezekiel tells us that "the heavens were opened, and I saw visions of God," we expect him to describe what is happening in the heavenly realms. Instead, he goes on to tell us about the *merkabah*'s appearance on earth. We will see in chapter VIII how later Jewish expositors dealt with this tension; and how they, too, found seven heavens mentioned in Ezekiel 1:1.

This passage of the "Apocalypse of Moses" is the only even marginally apocalyptic text to bring the seven heavens and the *merkabah* into the same picture. The viewpoint from which Eve and Seth observe this picture, however, remains earthbound. They are not transported through the heavens.

Yet there is a heavenly ascension, of a sort, in this episode. Adam's soul is "borne aloft to his Maker," washed three times in God's presence, and finally lifted "into Paradise unto the third heaven" (32:4, 37:3–5). (We

---

39 As in the "Testament of Job," 52:8–9, and in the longer recension of the "Testament of Abraham," chapters 9–15 [104,133a,170].

40 33:4, *thysiastērion*; Wells mistranslates "incense-offering." The celestial incense cult, including the altar, also appears in Revelation 5:8, 8:3–5. The Armenian version of the "Apocalypse of Moses" has "the holy tabernacle" itself on the scene [108].

remember that Paul is "caught up" to the third heaven, into Paradise; II Corinthians 12:2—4.) This is not the sort of visionary ascension we have become used to. But it seems to have a significance similar to the one we have detected in Enoch's ascension, in that it foreshadows Adam's exaltation — and, at the same time, the degradation of certain unnamed beings who are accused of having caused and profited by his woes [168]:

> And God saith to him: 'Adam, what hast thou done [cf. Genesis 3:13]? If thou hadst kept my commandment, there would now be no rejoicing among those who are bringing thee down to this place. Yet, I tell thee that I will turn their joy to grief and thy grief will I turn to joy, and I will transform thee to thy former glory, and set thee on the throne of thy deceiver. But he shall be cast into this place to see thee sitting above him, then he shall be condemned and they that heard him, and he shall be grieved sore when he seeth thee sitting on his honourable throne.' [Chapter 39]

Who are "those who are bringing thee down to this place?" The writer clearly presumes that Adam faces a more complex and imposing phalanx of enemies than the solitary snake in the garden of Eden. We are tempted to suppose that they are the devil and his followers, and this supposition seems to draw support from a passage in the Latin "Vita Adae" (chapters 12—17). The devil here explains to Adam that it was out of spite that he got him expelled from Eden, he himself having been thrown down from his heavenly glory on Adam's account. He had, he says, refused God's command to worship the newly created Adam, and had threatened to "set my seat above the stars of heaven and ... be like the Highest." As a result, "God the Lord was wrath with me and banished me and my angels from our glory; and on thy account were we expelled from our abodes and hurled on the earth. ... And we were grieved when we saw thee in such joy and luxury. And with guile I cheated thy wife and caused thee to be expelled through her (doing) from thy joy and luxury, as I have been driven out of my glory[41]."

This passage indeed seems fairly well to suit the allusion in the "Apocalypse of Moses." But the two do not quite jibe. In the "Vita Adae," the

---

41 The Koran takes up this story, with some variations (Surah 2: 34—36, 7:11, 15:28—38, 20:115—121) [789]. I do not agree with Speyer that it is distinctively Christian [792a]. Rabbinic sources, admittedly, do not explicitly set forth the notion that God ordered the angels to worship Adam; but *Gen. R.* 8:10 (ed. 63—64 [188]) seems to recognize it and to polemicize against it. I would suppose Muhammad to have derived it from a non-rabbinic variety of Judaism, to which we owe some at least of the material in the "Vita Adae," and which survived in one form or another in seventh-century Arabia [773]. — The devil's threat to "set my seat above the stars of heaven and ... be like the Highest" is obviously based on Isaiah 14:13—14: *I will lift up my throne above the stars of God ... I will be like the Most High.* These words are spoken by a mysterious being whom Isaiah calls "Morning-star, son of the Dawn" ("Lucifer," in the Latin translation of the Bible), and whom Christian tradition identified with the devil. Some forms of Judaism, we learn from the "Vita Adae," made the same equation. (This passage from Isaiah will become crucially important to us in chapters VIII and IX.)

devil and his supporters seem themselves to be in a state of exile and disgrace. In the "Apocalypse of Moses," however, we get the strong impression that Adam's enemies are still enthroned in heaven, where they will stay until Adam's future exaltation. We may call their leader Satan, Lucifer, or whatever we want; he and his followers remain heavenly beings, and they will fall only when the human being rises.

This idea does not quite fit our conventional notions of angelology or demonology. But it seems to echo what we have already noticed about Enoch's relation to the angels (above, section 3e). Here, as in Enoch, this theme seems only coincidentally juxtaposed with that of the *merkabah* vision. In the source to which we now turn, we will get our first clue as to how the two may be connected.

6. The Apocalypse of Abraham

a) Introduction. The Apocalypse of Abraham is in some ways the most uncertain and problematic of the texts with which we have to deal. Translated from Greek into Slavonic (at some time in the thirteenth century, according to Turdeanu), it was used for centuries in Russia as one of a series of edifying stories from the Old Testament, and reworked repeatedly into more or less simplified, more or less Christianized versions [176]. We do not possess the smallest portion of the Greek, far less the original Hebrew from which the Greek is sometimes supposed to have been translated [161,162]. We therefore have no way to test how faithfully even the earliest of the Slavonic versions represents the ancient Jewish apocalypse on which it is based, and to what extent it has suffered from the improvements of its Christian translators and transmitters[42].

And yet the Apocalypse of Abraham is so important for any study of the *merkabah* [610] that, having recorded this scruple, we must now proceed to ignore it, and treat the apocalypse as it stands as a product of early Judaism.

How early, we cannot be sure. A bitter reference to the destruction of the Temple (chapter 27) may indicate that this event happened not long before the author wrote. The dialogues in chapters 20–28, in which Abraham questions the workings of God's justice [164], remind us of the more eloquent discussions of this topic found in the Ezra Apocalypse, which we

---

42 The Slavonic text has been translated into English by G. H. Box and J. I. Landsman; and, more recently, by R. Rubinkiewicz and H. G. Lunt [90,160a]. I do not read Slavonic, and have no way to judge the merits of the translations. I use Box's, but note Rubinkiewicz's as well wherever there is a substantive disagreement.

can date fairly securely to about 100 A.D.[43] Using these indications, let us assume that the Apocalypse of Abraham dates from the end of the first century or the early second century [91,160a].

b) Apocalyptic midrash: Genesis 15. The book begins with a series of stories, many of which turn up again in somewhat different form in late rabbinic texts, about Abraham's rejection of idolatry (chapters 1–8). The rest of it is a description of a visionary experience, which can be read as an apocalyptic midrash on the fifteenth chapter of Genesis.

This is unusual for an apocalypse. I have, indeed, argued at length that the apocalyptists saw themselves as inspired interpreters of Scripture, and that we can usually detect midrashic processes at work behind their narratives. But seldom do they stick as faithfully to a single Scriptural home base as does the author of the Apocalypse of Abraham. The visionary section begins with a divine proclamation (chapter 9) obviously based on Genesis 15:1. Its conclusion (chapter 32) is just as obviously drawn from Genesis 15:13–14. Most of the material in between is rooted in this same chapter.

In chapters 19–21 of the apocalypse, God tells Abraham to look down on the firmaments below him from the vantage point of the seventh firmament, and to "consider from above *the stars* which are beneath thee, and *number,* them [for me], and make known [to me] their number" (chapter 20)[44]. The reference to the stars shows us that the source for this whole episode is Genesis 15:5: "And [God] brought [Abraham] outside, and said: 'Look toward the heavens, and count the stars, if you are able to count them.'" Like the rabbis quoted in *Gen. R.* 44:12 (ed. 432–433 [188]) and parallels[45], the apocalyptist understood "outside" to mean "outside the cosmic spheres," and believed that Abraham was told to look downward toward the stars. Like the storyteller in the "Apocalypse of Moses" (above), he understood the plural "heavens" (*shamayim*) to mean the seven firmaments. I have argued in section 1c that he was here following a tradition distinct from the one that he used when he described Abraham's ascent to the *merkabah* in the preceding chapters, for his account of the ascent does not mention the seven firmaments. The tradition underlying the ascent narrative is based primarily, not on Genesis 15:5, but on a different section of the chapter: the vision related in verses 7–21.

---

43 This apocalypse is printed in most editions of the Apocrypha, under the title "II Esdras." Many writers, myself included, refer to it as "IV Ezra."

44 Brackets, italics, and punctuation are Box's. The brackets mean that the manuscript Box considered the most important (Codex Sylvester) omits the enclosed words.

45 Modern editors of rabbinic texts usually provide thorough lists of parallel rabbinic sources in their notes. Whenever I say "and parallels," I am referring to those listed in the note to the text in question.

[9] [God] said to [Abraham] : "Procure for me a three-year-old heifer, a three-year-old she-goat, a three-year-old ram, a turtle dove, and a young pigeon." [10] And he procured for him all those, and divided them down the middle, and set one part over against the other; only the birds he did not divide. [11] The birds of prey[46] descended on the carcasses, but Abram drove them away. [12] As the sun was setting, deep sleep fell on Abram; terror and great darkness fell upon him. ... [17] When the sun set, and there was thick darkness, behold a smoking oven and a torch of fire, which passed between those pieces [of the sacrificial animals].

Some rabbis deduced, from the peculiar and rather eerie details of this vision and its preliminaries, that Abraham foresaw on that occasion the rise of the future world empires, or that he was granted a vision of hell or the World to Come (*Mekhilta, Ba-Hodesh* ch. 9, ed./tr. 2:268–269 [195]; *Gen. R.* 44:15–22, ed. 437–445 [188]; *Lev. R.* 13:5, ed. 284–286 [191]; *Midr. Psalms* 52:8, ed. 143b–144a[199]). Like the author of our text, they saw in Genesis 15:7–21 cryptic references to an apocalyptic experience. Unlike him, they did not describe it in first person.

c) The ascension of Abraham. Abraham's adventure begins when God prescribes for him the sacrifice of Genesis 15:9, promising that "in this sacrifice I will lay before thee the ages (to come), and make known to thee what is reserved, and thou shalt see great things which thou hast not seen (hitherto)." In preparation, Abraham must abstain from meat, wine, and oil (Apocalypse of Abraham, chapter 9). The immediate source of this last detail seems to be Daniel 10:3. But, significantly, it recalls the abstentions of Moses and Elijah (Exodus 34:28, Deuteronomy 9:9, 18, I Kings 19:7–8 [538]); for, like Moses and Elijah, Abraham is to have his experience on "the Mount of God, the glorious Horeb" (chapter 12).

God then sends Abraham an angelic guide, described in language reminiscent of Daniel 8:15–18, 10:5–19. He is called "Jaoel[47]." He introduces himself as "the one who hath been given to restrain, according to His commandment, the threatening attack of the living creatures of the Cherubim against one another, and teach those who carry Him the song of the seventh hour of the night of man. I am ordained to restrain the Leviathan, for unto me are subject the attack and menace of every single reptile." Some manu-

---

46 The Hebrew uses the singular (*ʿayit*) as a collective plural. As we will see, the apocalyptist interprets the singular to refer to one particular "bird of prey" – the rebel angel Azazel.

47 Actually, he is given this name only twice, in chapter 10; afterwards, he is called simply "the angel." Curiously, both uses of the name are vocative ("Go, Jaoel ...") or implied vocative ("I am called Jaoel" [Box]; "I am Iaoel and I was called so" [Rubinkiewicz]). In chapter 17, Abraham addresses God by this name (which is a compound of *yaho* = Yahweh and *'el* = "god"): "Eli, that is, My God ... very glorious El, El, El, El, Jaoel!" In the Greek "Apocalypse of Moses," the angels address God as "Iael" (*yah 'el*; 29:4, 33:5); the Armenian version has "Eliajil" (*'el yah 'el*) in the latter passage [108], and this sounds very like the variant "Eloel" for "Jaoel" in chapter 10 of our apocalypse. It looks as if a formula used to invoke God has been transformed into the name of an angel; Scholem makes some very suggestive remarks that bear on the question of how this might have happened [598,611].

scripts add the sentence: "I am he who hath been commissioned to loosen Hades, to destroy him who stareth at [or, "terrifieth"] the dead[48]." We will later turn our full attention to Jaoel's occupations in the other world. For now, his function is to go with Abraham to the sacrifice, and to help and encourage him (chapters 10—11).

"And we went, the two of us together, forty days and nights, and I ate no bread, and drank no water, because my food was to see the angel who was with me, and his speech — that was my drink." The prescribed sacrificial animals follow them to Horeb. Following the angel's instruction, Abraham slaughters the animals and gives all of them but the birds (which, we recall from Genesis 15:10, he does not divide) to certain other "angels, who had come to us"; we will soon see more of these angels. The "bird of prey" of Genesis 15:11 now appears, in the form of an "unclean bird," Azazel, who tries to frighten Abraham and persuade him not to ascend with the angel. Abraham pays no attention, and the angel sharply rebukes Azazel and encourages Abraham to do the same (chapters 12—14). This dialogue is important to us for several reasons, and we must come back to it.

"And it came to pass *when the sun went down, and lo! a smoke as of a furnace* [cf. Genesis 15:17]. And the angels who had the portions of the sacrifice ascended from the top of the smoking furnace" (chapter 15). This makes sense, in a way. We can imagine that the meat of the sacrificial animals would be burned and thus ascend to heaven in smoke — although Genesis 15 tells us nothing of the sort. But we do not understand why the "smoking oven" of 15:17 is identified with the sacrificial fire; or why these angels, who have no further function in the story, have to be involved in the process. This, too, we will presently clarify.

In the meantime, Abraham and his companion angel mount the pigeon and the turtle dove (which have not been slaughtered) and fly upward "to the borders of the flaming fire." There they find

a strong light, which it was impossible to describe, and lo! in this light a fiercely burning fire for people, many people of male appearance[49], all (constantly) changing in aspect and form, running and being transformed, and worshipping and crying with a sound of words which I knew not.

---

48 Rubinkiewicz's translation of this passage differs in several particulars. It speaks only of "the threats of the living creatures," not their "threatening attack." It renders the last part of the sentence: "I teach those who carry the song through the medium of man's night of the seventh hour" (whatever that may mean). It speaks of plural "Leviathans." It translates the final sentence (which Lunt's note seems to represent as appearing in all manuscripts): "I am ordered to loosen Hades and to destroy those who wondered at the dead." None of these divergences will significantly affect my argument.

49 Rubinkiewicz: "And behold, in this light a fiery Gehenna was enkindled, and a great crowd in the likeness of men." Lunt's note explains that this rendering is based on an emendation of the text translated by Box. Should we prefer to keep the Slavonic text as it is, we may perhaps explain the "fire for people" as going back to an error in the Greek text of Ezekiel 1:13, on which

[Chapter] XVI. And I said to the Angel: "Why hast thou brought me up here now, because I cannot now see, for I am already grown weak, and my spirit departeth from me?" And he said to me: "Remain by me; fear not! And He whom thou seest come straight towards us with great voice of holiness[50] – that is the Eternal One who loveth thee; but Himself thou canst not see. But let not thy spirit grow faint [on account of the loud crying][51], for I am with thee, strengthening thee."

XVII. And while he yet spake (and) lo! fire came against us round about, and a voice was in the fire *like a voice of many waters*[52], like the sound of the sea in its uproar. And the angel bent his head[53] with me and worshipped. And I desired to fall down upon the earth, and the high place, on which we stood, [at one moment rose upright,] but at another rolled downwards.

And he said: "Only worship, Abraham, and utter the song which I have taught thee;" because there was no earth to fall upon. And I worshipped only[54], and uttered the song which he had taught me. And he said: "Recite without ceasing."

Abraham and the angel together recite a hymn, too long to quote here, which invokes God by several of his names (El, Eli, Sabaoth, Jaoel) and his attributes.

Chapter 18 describes the climax of the vision:

And while I still recited the song, the mouth of the fire which was on the surface[55] rose up on high. And I heard a voice like the roaring of the sea; nor did it cease on account of the rich abundance of the fire. And as the fire raised itself up, ascending into the height, I saw under the fire a throne of fire, and, round about it all-seeing ones[56], reciting the song, and under the throne four fiery living creatures singing, and their appearance was one, *each one of them with four faces*. And such was the appearance of their countenances, *of a lion, of a man, of an ox, of an eagle*[57]: four heads [were upon their bodies] [so that the four creatures had sixteen faces]; and each had six wings; from their shoulders, [and their sides] and their loins. And with the (two) wings from their shoulders they covered their faces, and with the (two) wings which (sprang) from their loins they covered their feet, while the (two) middle wings they spread out for flying straightforward[58]. And when they had ended the singing, they looked at one another and threatened one another. And it came to pass when the angel who was with me saw that they were threatening each other, he left me and went running to them and turned the countenance of each living creature from the countenance immediately confronting him, in order that they might not see their countenances threatening each other. And he taught them the song of peace which hath its origin [in the Eternal One].

And as I stood alone and looked, I saw behind the living creatures a chariot with fiery wheels, each wheel full of eyes round about; and over the wheels was a throne; which I saw, and this was

---

this passage seems to be based (see below): a scribe miscopied *anthrakōn*, "of coals," as *anthrō-pōn*, "of people."

50 Rubinkiewicz: "in a great sound of sanctification." This evidently refers to the praises of heavenly beings. Cf. the end of chapter 18.

51 Brackets in this and the following quotations are Box's, and indicate words omitted from Codex Sylvester.

52 Ezekiel 1:24.

53 Rubinkiewicz: "knelt down."

54 Rubinkiewicz punctuates the sentences differently: "Since there was no ground to which I could fall prostrate, I only bowed down ..."

55 Rubinkiewicz: "firmament."

56 Rubinkiewicz: "the many-eyed ones."

57 Ezekiel 1:5, 10.

58 Rubinkiewicz: "erect." But Lunt notes that the word literally means "simple"; and the passage's apparent dependence on Ezekiel 1:12 favors Box's understanding.

covered with fire, and fire encircled it round about, and lo! an indescribable fire environed a fiery host. And I heard its holy voice[59] like the voice of a man.

d) The use of Ezekiel 1. In short, Abraham sees Ezekiel's *merkabah*, with its four living creatures — identified in chapter 10 of the apocalypse with the cherubim[60] — its wheels full of eyes, and the throne that rests upon all of them. The apocalypse goes one step beyond Revelation 4:3 and makes the occupant of the throne entirely invisible [52,158,159]. Ezekiel's phrase, "like the appearance of a man," becomes, in a concluding sentence, that plainly draws on the end of Ezekiel 1:28, "like the voice of a man." Like John of Patmos, the author of the apocalypse surrounds the *merkabah* with angelic chant, and portrays the scene with the help of Isaiah 6. But, unlike the author of Revelation, he adds only a few strokes from Isaiah to a picture that is basically Ezekiel's. He gives the living creatures the six wings of Isaiah's seraphim, but describes the functioning of the middle wings in language drawn from Ezekiel 1:11—12.

After the work we have done with the hymnic tradition, we are not surprised to find that the living creatures spend most of their time singing the praises of the God who sits above them. We *are* surprised, not to say appalled, to find that when they are not singing they are preparing to attack each other. We have been warned of this since chapter 10, when Abraham's companion tells him that one of his jobs is "to restrain ... the threatening attack [Rubinkiewicz: "threats"] of the living creatures of the Cherubim against one another." But this detail does not thereby become any less startling or more intelligible. We must come back to it.

We have seen that the author draws his description of the *merkabah*-throne and its attendants from Ezekiel 1. This encourages us also to trace his account of the oceanic mass of heavenly fire back to the *merkabah* vision. Ezekiel 1:13—14 is its most likely source. Thus, chapter 15's reference to "a fiercely burning fire" suggests 1:13, "blazing coals of fire." The movement of the fire, stressed in chapters 17—18, reminds us of Ezekiel's phrase "going back and forth among the *hayyot*" (1:13), the subject of the verb understood — as it must be, if we accept MT's reading of a feminine singular — as the fire. The phrase "running and being transformed" (chapter 15) suggests Ezekiel 1:14, which can be translated: "The *hayyot* ran and returned like the appearance of lightning" (below, chapter IV). Midrashim of the *Tanḥuma* genre[61] attest that certain rabbis applied Ezekiel 1:13 to the

---

59 Rubinkiewicz: "the voice of their sanctification."
60 Box and Rubinkiewicz both translate "the living creatures of the Cherubim." Turdeanu [176], however, renders "animaux chérubims," and then gives "vivants" as an alternative translation of "animaux." This, and Lunt's note on the passage, suggest that the terms corresponding to *hayyot* and cherubim are set side by side in the text, as two designations of the same beings.
61 See chapter IV, section 4; Appendix I, section 8.

supernal fire, which is the source of the lightning that we see in the sky (Tanh. *Teṣawweh* #6, *Be-Ha^c_alotekha* #5; Tanh. Buber *Be-Ha^c_alotekha* #7, ed. 24b [222]; *Numb. R.* 15:7). We need not be surprised that the author of the Apocalypse of Abraham did the same.

For the writer had excellent reason to believe that Abraham saw the same fire that Ezekiel saw in his *merkabah* vision; namely, Genesis 15:17 told him so. Abraham sees "a torch of fire" (*lappid 'esh*); Ezekiel sees "blazing coals of fire ['*esh*], like the appearance of torches [*lappidim*]." Verbal congruities of this sort may not be enough to convince us of identity. They are enough for midrash. In this case, they were enough to point the apocalyptist toward Ezekiel's *merkabah* as a source for the details of Abraham's vision.

e) The Sinai motif. But they pointed him in another direction as well, and it is most important for us to follow this direction. Abraham sees "a smoking oven [*tannur ^cashan*] and a torch of fire [*lappid 'esh*]." Now, when God descends on Mount Sinai to give the Torah, the mountain is "all in smoke [*^cashan*], because the Lord descended on it in fire ['*esh*], and its smoke rose like the smoke of a furnace" (Exodus 19:18)[62]. The Israelites see "the torches [*lappidim*] ... and the mountain smoking [*^cashen*]" (Exodus 20:15); or, in the parallel Deuteronomy 5:20, "burning with fire" (*bo^cer ba'esh*; Ezekiel's "blazing coals of fire" are *gahale 'esh bo^carot*).

These verbal associations did not escape the rabbis. Comparing Abraham's *tannur ^cashan* with Isaiah 31:9, they deduced that the patriarch received a vision of hell. Comparing his *lappid 'esh* with Exodus 20:15, they deduced he also saw the Sinai revelation (*Mekhilta, Ba-Ḥodesh* ch. 9, ed./tr. 2:268 [195]). In some of the parallels to this midrash[63], we find *lappid 'esh* applied to Sinai, both *tannur ^cashan* and *lappid 'esh* applied to hell (Tanh. *Pequde* #8); or, both terms applied to both Sinai and hell (*Ex. R.* 51:7, quoting Exodus 20:15 in full). The rabbinic sources apparently combine, in different ways, two alternative interpretations of Genesis 15: 17 — Abraham saw the Sinai revelation; or, he saw hell — and these may be much older than the rabbinic texts that manipulate them.

The author of our apocalypse apparently followed the interpretation that applied Genesis 15:17 to Sinai[64], for he gives us several clues that he is modelling Abraham's experience after Moses' at Sinai. The most obvious of these is his locating the experience at Mount Horeb, the name that Deut-

---

62 Unfortunately for my argument, the word used here for "furnace" (*kibshan*) is not the same as that used in Genesis 15:17 for Abraham's oven.

63 They are listed in the apparatus to *Gen. R.* 44:21, ed. 443 [188].

64 But perhaps he knew the alternative explanation as well; for, in chapter 14, he calls hell "the Furnace of the earth."

eronomy regularly uses for Sinai. This, like Abraham's preparatory fast (chapter 9), might point to Elijah (I Kings 19) as well as to Moses. When the angel tells Abraham that he will see God "come straight towards us" (chapter 16), this reminds us that God "passes by" both Moses and Elijah (Exodus 33:22, 34:6, I Kings 19:11−12). But it is only Moses who is told in this connection that "you cannot see my face" and "my face shall not be seen" (33:20, 23), just as the angel goes on to tell Abraham that God "Himself thou shalt not see." Moses, not Elijah, "bowed down upon the earth and prostrated himself" when God passed (34:8) − which explains Abraham's frustrated urge to do the same thing (chapter 17). In the hymn that follows, Abraham addresses God as "self-originated, incorruptible, spotless ... immortal ... unbegotten," and the like, and then praises him as "lover of men, benevolent, bountiful, jealous over me and very compassionate; Eli, that is, My God ..." Compare Exodus 34:6: "When the Lord [YHWH] passed by him, he[65] cried out: 'YHWH! YHWH! Merciful and gracious God ['*el*], slow to anger and full of faithfulness and truth!' " Box points out that the second part of Abraham's hymn (from "lover of men") is based on Exodus 34:6. The first part seems to be a meditation on the twofold proclamation of God's name in this same verse.

Assuming that the author of the apocalypse identified Abraham's "smoking oven" with Sinai, we at last understand why the nameless "angels who had the portions of the sacrifice ascended from the top of the smoking furnace" (chapter 15). They are the angels who, according to Jewish legend (below, chapter VIII), attended the revelation at Sinai. Like cinders, they rise to heaven in Sinai's smoke; for is it not written, *the mountain was burning with fire to the heart of heaven* (Deuteronomy 4:11)? We recall that both angels and fire appear in the Johanan b. Zakkai *merkabah* stories (above, chapter I), as signs that the Sinai event is being repeated.

Further assuming that this interpretation of Abraham's vision was not restricted to our author and certain later rabbis, but was reasonably widespread in Judaism at and before the beginning of the Christian Era, we understand why the author of the Book of Jubilees (whose date is uncertain, but surely pre-Christian) assumes that Abraham had his vision on Shabu^cot (14:8−20; cf. 6:16−21).

f) Abraham and Azazel. More important for our present purpose, we begin to understand what is going on in the conversation between Azazel, Abraham, and the angel (chapter 13):

---

65 The subject could be either God or Moses. The author of the apocalypse plainly took it as Moses; I have translated accordingly.

And the unclean bird [Azazel] spake to me, and said: "What doest thou, Abraham, upon the holy Heights, where no man eateth or drinketh, neither is there upon them (any) food of man, but these consume everything with fire, and (will) burn thee up[66]. Forsake the man, who is with thee, and flee; for if thou ascendest to the Heights they will make an end of thee."

What is Azazel talking about? The rabbinic stories we will examine in chapter VIII, in which Moses must repeatedly ward off the murderous attacks of hostile angels as he climbs to heaven to receive the Torah, show us clearly enough what he means, and prove that his warnings are well grounded. Azazel is right that there is no human food on the "holy Heights," as Moses discovered when he spent forty days on Sinai without eating and drinking (Exodus 34:28, Deuteronomy 9:9). But Moses also discovered that the divine presence is itself nourishment enough. That is why Exodus 24:11 says that Moses and his companions *beheld God, and ate and drank.* This means, one rabbi explained, that the sight of God was food and drink to them; for Scripture also says, *In the light of the King's face there is life* (Proverbs 16:15; interpreted in *Lev. R.* 20:10, ed. 465–466 [191]). We may assume that the author of the Apocalypse of Abraham had such midrashim in mind when he wrote that "my food was to see the angel who was with me, and his speech —that was my drink" (chapter 12).

Azazel, then, is not intimidating Abraham with imaginary terrors. But he is suppressing important information; and his motive in trying to frighten Abraham is far from disinterested. The angel's speech to Azazel gives us a clue to what it is:

"Disgrace upon thee, Azazel! For Abraham's lot is in heaven, but thine upon the earth. Because thou hast chosen and loved this for the dwelling-(place) of thine uncleanness, therefore the eternal mighty Lord made thee a dweller upon the earth. ... For, behold, the vesture which in heaven was formerly thine hath been set aside for him [Abraham] and the mortality which was his hath been transferred to thee."

We see here the theme, which we have already met in the stories of Enoch in the Book of Watchers and of Adam in the "Apocalypse of Moses," of the exaltation of the human and the degradation of the angel corresponding to each other and to some extent depending on each other. If Azazel can persuade Abraham not to make his ascent, he will perhaps be able to keep his own privileged status. What is important about the present passage is that it ties this theme to the Sinai event. It thus comments, indirectly, on the significance of Moses' ascent to receive the Torah. It provides a first clue to a problem that will much occupy us in chapters VIII and IX: why do the angels want to stop him?

---

66 Rubinkiewicz translates Codex Sylvester as follows: "But these all will be consumed by fire and they will burn you up."

g) Synthesis. We may seem, in the past few pages, to have wandered far from the *merkabah*. What we have in fact done is explore the context that the author of the Apocalypse of Abraham constructed for the *merkabah*. We have found a key, though hidden, element of this context to be the revelation at Sinai.

We have learned from rabbinic sources about the practice of reading the Biblical accounts of the Sinai revelation and of the *merkabah* vision together in the synagogue on Shabu^cot. We have seen evidence from LXX that the two episodes were already linked in pre-Christian Alexandria. Now we find the author of our apocalypse using the vision of Genesis 15 as a sort of motion-picture screen on which he can project an image of the Sinai event from one angle, and an image of the *merkabah* from another. We might even go so far as to say that chapters 9–18 of the Apocalypse of Abraham are at least as much concerned with this combined image of Sinai-*merkabah* as they are with Abraham.

What led the apocalyptist to choose Abraham's vision as the setting for his fusion of Sinai and the *merkabah*? Several motives seem to have influenced him. First, he could use the ascent to Sinai-*merkabah* as an apt prelude to the originally independent tradition – based, as we have seen, on Genesis 15:5 – of Abraham's viewing the cosmic spheres from the outside. Second, the reference to the "bird of prey" in 15:11 gave him an opportunity to explain what this ascent meant to those involved in it. Third, and perhaps most important, by transferring the Sinai-*merkabah* experience from Moses and Ezekiel to the ancestor of the whole Jewish people, he was able to emphasize its importance for all Abraham's "seed ... a people, set apart for me in my heritage with Azazel" (chapter 20).

In the Book of Watchers and the "Apocalypse of Moses," the motif of the ascent of the human and the descent of the angel seemed only coincidentally juxtaposed with the vision of the *merkabah*. In the Apocalypse of Abraham, it is an integral part of the Sinai-*merkabah* complex. When, in chapter VIII, we turn our full attention to this complex, we will get a much clearer picture of the role played in it by the ascension. We will then have a background for understanding the *Hekhalot*.

h) The attack of the creatures. One riddle remains untouched. Why are the "living creatures" who carry the throne perpetually on the verge of attacking each other? Why must Abraham's companion restrain them, again and again, by turning their threatening faces around and teaching them God's "song of peace"?

I know of no exegetical basis for this weird conception, nor can it be easily rationalized. I certainly do not think Box goes far enough with his explanation that "the underlying idea of this strange representation seems to be that of emulation and rivalry (in service)." It seems, rather, rooted in the perception, which we have already touched on in connection with Revelation, that there is something fundamentally savage and chaotic about the *hayyot*. They have been bound to God's service, and their role of singing hymns has to some extent tamed them. But their essential savagery has been only suppressed, not uprooted; and Abraham's companion must always be watchful lest it burst forth in a bloody and senseless attack on each other. Compare this with the angel's other tasks: he must restrain the sea-monster Leviathan, turn back "the attack and menace of every single reptile," loosen Hades, destroy an unnamed but apparently demonic being "who stareth at the dead" (chapter 10, following Box's translation). In other words, he must suppress the dark and inimical forces of the cosmos. The holy *hayyot*, who sing hymns beneath God's throne, are among them.

As we have seen, rabbinic midrashim often clarify the details of the Apocalypse of Abraham. It therefore will not surprise us that a *Tanhuma* midrash (Tanh. *Wa-Yiggash* #6) seems to preserve a trace of the *hayyot*'s hostility to each other. Commenting on Genesis 46:28, where Jacob sends Judah before him to Joseph, the midrash remarks: "Judah and Joseph: the one is a lion, the other an ox [Genesis 49:9, Deuteronomy 33:17]. Yesterday they were gouging each other, and now he [Jacob? God?] sends one to the other." The context, which speaks of God's making peace among celestial entities, suggests that the lion and the ox to which the midrash compares Judah and Joseph are heavenly beings rather than ordinary animals. But which ones? A passage in Buber's *Tanhuma* (*Bereshit* #3, ed. 5b [222]) speaks of rivalry among the constellations, singling out Taurus and Gemini; and perhaps Tanh. *Wa-Yiggash* intends the rivalry between Taurus and Leo. But this does not do justice to its strong language. Rather, the author of the midrash seems to imagine the ox and the lion of the *merkabah* as distinct beasts (cf. Revelation) engaged, as in the Apocalypse of Abraham, in ferocious combat.

7. Conclusions

Our study of the *merkabah* in the apocalypses is at an end. Its results are not easy to summarize. We have found ourselves following not one thread but several, which the various apocalyptic writers weave into a bewildering variety of patterns.

Some of these threads end here. For example, the idea that the *hayyot*-cherubim are part of the divine throne (Book of Watchers, Revelation), which goes back to Ezekiel 10's identification of the *hayyot* with the furniture of the Holy of Holies, plays no role in the rabbinic treatments of the *merkabah* that we are going to examine.

But other threads continue into the rabbinic material, and the work that we have done in this and the preceding chapter to identify them will greatly help us understand the rabbinic sources. One of them, particularly important, is the idea that the Sinai event and the *merkabah* vision are two aspects of the same reality, and must be interpreted together (Apocalypse of Abraham). Another is the image of the *hayyot* as the beings who tirelessly sing God's praises (Book of Parables, Revelation, Apocalypse of Abraham), who yet have within them an eerie streak of savagery (Revelation, Apocalypse of Abraham), and who, perhaps for this reason, can be understood as symbols for powers inimical to the divine order (Daniel). Except perhaps for a hint in Daniel, we have seen no trace of the uneasiness about their ox's face or calf's foot that ran through the sources we examined in chapter II. This thread, nearly invisible in the apocalypses, will stand out bright scarlet in the rabbinic sources.

The Book of Revelation is particularly important in that it shows us a sea associated with the *merkabah*, under three interrelated aspects: a frozen yet fiery celestial body (so the Book of Watchers); the Red Sea, also congealed (so the "Vita Adae"); and the home of the forces of supernatural evil (so Daniel). We must remember what we have learned from Revelation when, in chapter VI, we turn to examine the *merkabah* and the waters.

Finally, the Book of Watchers and the Apocalypse of Abraham not only describe ascensions, but, with the support of the "Apocalypse of Moses," hint at the implications of these ascensions for the people who make them — and, through them, for humanity (or the Jewish people) as a whole. The clues these sources provide will help us understand the role of the heavenly ascension in the rabbinic conceptions of the *merkabah*. With them, we can begin to unravel the riddle of the *Hekhalot*.

Chapter IV

The Synagogue Tradition

1. Introduction: the use of rabbinic materials

When we turn to the rabbinic sources, we are obliged to change our strategy.

In dealing with the apocalypses, we are studying literary creations. We may not have any clear idea when a given text was written; we normally have no idea at all who wrote it or for whom. The text may be a composite of several sources, or draw upon older traditions. But, once we have decided that a text is a unit, or we have distinguished its sources, we find ourselves with a composition (or compositions) that did not exist before its author wrote it, and afterwards existed pretty much as we now have it. The question of its dating may be insoluble, but at least we know what we are asking when we pose it, and what the implications will be if it turns out we are able to answer it. We may then choose, if we wish, to pursue the history of the traditions behind the composition. The date we have assigned to the composition itself will then give us a framework in which to pursue our inquiry.

The rabbinic literature provides us with different problems as well as different opportunities. It is usually not very helpful to ask when a rabbinic text was written, because most rabbinic texts were not written, in any normal sense of the word. They were compiled, woven together from older materials that are identified, if at all, by being associated with the names of certain Tannaim or Amoraim. Although we can perhaps talk of source criticism in this connection, the sources we have to deal with are not like the extended and fairly well defined ropes of material that Pentateuch critics are used to, nor again like the blocks and layers of material that we often meet while analyzing the apocalypses. Perhaps the image of a cloth woven .of many threads is less apt than that of a stew prepared of many vegetables, and left to cook for a long time. We know that the stew is a composite entity, but we often cannot determine just what went into it, when it went in, or what it looked like before it went in. And, even if we know when the stew was taken off the stove and thus declared completed, it is not easy to pinpoint when it became the stew "as we know it."

If the rabbinic midrashic collections were simply scrapbooks of older texts pasted together, like the medieval compilations known as *Yalquṭim* (*Yalquṭ Shimᶜoni*, or *Makhiri*), this problem would hardly be so acute. But they are not. The editor, or the generations of editors upon whose work he set the seal, contributed something to the form of the materials as we have them, but we are not sure how much. At the other end, we may assume that the Tannaim and Amoraim whose names are attached to the materials also contributed something to them; again, we are not sure how much. At least, we can usually (not always) date the Tannaim and Amoraim. We seldom can date the editors. Thus, the important body of midrashim that go by the name *Tanḥuma* (below, section 5) are usually relegated to the Never-never-land of "late midrashim," which means that they were compiled in something like their present form some time after the editing of the Palestinian Talmud and the midrashim cognate to it[1] — that is, about the middle of the fifth century A.D. — and some time before the Middle Ages were very far advanced. That is not a very useful determination.

I do not intend the preceding paragraphs as a call to despair, but as a recognition that we are always going to be more or less vague and uncertain when we talk about the dating of rabbinic materials. When we deal with haggadah, as we are now going to do (in contrast to chapter I, where our sources were halakhic), the uncertainty will be more rather than less. While we can never ignore the issue of dating, and must do our best to resolve it in each individual case, our first job must be to pose our questions in such a way that the validity of our answers will not hinge on whether we have dated the source correctly.

It would therefore be a mistake to ask, in the way that we did in the last chapter, what the "classical Palestinian midrashim" have to say about the *merkabah*, or what the *Tanḥuma* midrashim have to say about it; for this question would assume a uniformity of these sources, at least on the redactional level, that we have no right to assume. It would similarly be a mistake to ask what R. Akiba or R. Meir or R. Eliezer had to say about the *merkabah*; for this question would make the equally unwarranted assumption that these scholars actually said everything that the sources attribute to them. Answers to both questions may indeed suggest themselves in the course of our study, but we have no right to approach the material expecting that we are going to find them.

Rather, we must try to sketch the major themes, or streams of tradition, that run through the rabbinic materials dealing with the *merkabah*. The

---

1 *Genesis Rabbah, Leviticus Rabbah, Lamentations Rabbah* and *Pesiqta de-Rab Kahana*; often called the "classical Palestinian midrashim."

broader and the richer the stream, the more likely it is that we are going to be able to trace some evolution in the ideas it represents. If we find the names of specific rabbis attached to some expressions of these ideas, we may be able even to propose a rough chronology for this development. Or we may not. Either way, we will have learned something of the range of rabbinic responses to Ezekiel's vision.

The *merkabah* tradition that is easiest to distinguish is the one that developed in the synagogue, in response to the needs of the synagogue. Our conclusions in chapter I have led us to expect that it will be particularly important. This "synagogue tradition," as I will call it from now on, overlaps to a great extent with what I have called the "hymnic tradition" in the past two chapters, but adds certain important new details. We can trace it in a number of different sources. But we must start out with the source that enables us to identify it to begin with: the product par excellence of the synagogue, the Aramaic Targum.

2. Targum to Ezekiel 1

a) Introduction. There is actually not one Targum but a bewildering variety of Targums[2]. We have a Targum to both the Pentateuch and the Prophets, which evidently originated in Palestine but later acquired something like official status in Babylonia. That portion of the Targum that covers the Pentateuch is called the "Targum of Onkelos," after the man who is supposed to have translated it. Similarly, the portion that covers the Prophets is called "Targum of Jonathan." (Few critical scholars now believe these attributions. They are probably distorted reminiscences of post-LXX Jewish translations of the Bible into Greek [23].) Apart from this "official" Targum, several interrelated Aramaic versions of the Pentateuch were used in the synagogues of Palestine, their texts remaining fluid for centuries. The major surviving representatives of this "Palestinian Targum" tradition are usually called "Targum Pseudo-Jonathan," "Fragment Targum," and "Targum Neofiti."

Some scholars think there was once a Palestinian Targum to the Prophets as well [318,335a,358]. I myself do not; but, since we do not in any case

---

2 Martin McNamara's *Targum and Testament* [335] gives a good general introduction to the Targums. Anthony D. York has a particularly valuable article on the dating of the Targums [354a]; a recent book by Bruce D. Chilton, which I had not yet seen when I wrote the body of the text, deals specifically with Targum Jonathan (*The Glory of Israel: The Theology and Provenience of the Isaiah Targum*; Sheffield, England: JSOT Press, 1982). − Targumic studies have been so popular over the past few decades that it is hard to keep up with them. Roger Le Déaut's survey article, and the bibliographies of Bernard Grossfeld and J. T. Forestell, bring us up to the late 1970's [317,300,281].

have this Targum, it does not matter to us very much whether or not it once existed. Expansions of Targum Jonathan and variant translations of Prophetic passages are often preserved in the margins or even the texts of Targum manuscripts, or in quotations by medieval writers [254,307,310]. These "Targumic Toseftas," as they are called, are sometimes considered fragments of the lost "Palestinian Targum" [271,272,273], but their very heterogeneous character seems to argue against this [307]. We will treat the Toseftas to the Targum of Ezekiel 1 as a series of individual sources, without worrying about how they were transmitted before they found their present homes in the manuscripts.

The Targums to the books of the third division of Scripture, "the Writings," are by and large an unexplored jungle, which we have no reason to enter.

We do not know the date of Targum Jonathan. Because BT often represents the early fourth-century Babylonian Amora Rab Joseph as quoting it, most scholars assume that it existed in Babylonia by about 300 A.D. [265, 316]. Some have pressed for a much earlier date, arguing that Jonathan's exegesis is parallel to that of the Qumran "Habakkuk Commentary" (Weider, Brownlee), or that its Messianic exegesis of Isaiah 53 would have been unthinkable after the rise of Christianity (Koch) [354,261,314,318,339a]. Churgin finds in Jonathan references to events in Palestine at the beginning of the Christian Era, treated as if they were contemporary issues; but also references to Sassanian rule in Babylonia, which began in 226 A.D. [267]. Going to the other extreme, Levey has found what he thinks are allusions to Islam, and dates Targum Jonathan as a whole to the Middle Ages [319]. But Levey's evidence seems to me equivocal, and I have not found anywhere in the Targum to Ezekiel any trace of a reference to Islam. (I have not studied the rest of Jonathan.) Ezekiel 27:21's mention of Arabia would be an ideal place for the translator to refer to the Islamic empire, if he knew it existed. But he makes clear that, when he thinks of the Arabs, he thinks of the Nabatean merchant kingdom.

But, even if we could assign a date to the Targum, it would not help us very much. The haggadic material that Jonathan preserves plainly does not constitute a single source. Thus, the translator of Ezekiel 1:1 knows details about Hilkiah's discovery of the Book of the Torah which we would expect to interest the translator of II Kings 22:8; yet there is not a word about them in the latter passage. Targ. Ezekiel 1:8 tells us that the "man clothed in linen" of Ezekiel 10:7 is one of the seraphim (*sirpayya*); but Targ. Ezekiel 10:7 itself says nothing of this, and Targ. Isaiah 6:2, 6, does not even use the word *sirpayya* to translate "seraphim" (it calls them "holy servants," *shammashin qaddishin*). Given that we are dealing with such heterogeneous stuff, the dating of one passage tells us nothing about the dating of any other passage, nor can we be sure that the date of the Targum as a whole has any bearing on the date of an individual interpretation within it. If we say the Targum is late, we can also say that the passage that concerns us preserves an early tradition. If we say the Targum is early, we can also say that the passage that concerns us is a late revision or interpolation.

As a measure for dating an exegetical tradition, the Targum is therefore practically useless. Its value, which is immense, lies largely in those cases where it spells out the exegetical process that is implicit in another, clearly datable source. If, for example, we can correlate an element of the Book of Revelation with a Targumic exegesis, we learn from Revelation the date of the exegetical tradition (or, at least, the latest possible date for its origin), while the Targum teaches us how it worked. We will see this particularly clearly in Targ. Ezekiel 1:24−25.

But the Targum has yet another contribution to make, which, for our study, is still more important. If we know virtually nothing about the date when Targum Jonathan came into existence, we know a great deal about the setting in which and for which it was created. The Aramaic translations of the Bible may have had more than one function [355], but their primary and essential one was to present and interpret in the vernacular the Scriptures read aloud in the synagogue. True, Jews did not read in the synagogue every word of the Prophets, as they did of the Torah. But they might select as *haftarah* any portion of these books[3], and therefore had use for a translation of them all. Hence, Targum Jonathan.

There is no reason to think that Ezekiel 1 is an exception to the rule that the Targum was made in and for the synagogue. Indeed, we have a specific reason to think it is not an exception. Targ. Ezekiel 1:1 reads: "It happened in the thirtieth year ... in Tammuz, on the fifth day of the month, *the prophet said*, while I was among the captives by the river Chebar, that the heavens were opened," and so forth. Targum inserts the words *the prophet said* in six other places in Ezekiel, half of them the beginnings of first-person accounts (8:1, 14:1, 20:1; cf. 16:23, 19:14, 32:16). We find them also at the openings of Isaiah's and Amos's first-person descriptions of how they "saw the Lord" (Isaiah 6:1, Amos 9:1). They seem entirely pointless; for is it not clear that the prophet is speaking? It is, to someone who reads Amos's or Isaiah's or Ezekiel's vision in private, in its Biblical context. It might not be so clear to an ignorant and perhaps inattentive synagogue goer, who hears the vision read without its context, and who might pos-

---

3 Except, if they followed the ruling of M. Meg. 4:10, "the story of David and Amnon" and the *merkabah* chapter (and, following R. Eliezer, Ezekiel 16). But we have seen that synagogue practice, ignoring M. Meg. 4:10, fixed the *merkabah* as the *haftarah* reading for Shabuᶜot (above, chapter I). If the unusual expansiveness of its Targum is any indication (below), Ezekiel 16:3−13 was also a popular reading.

sibly conceive that the reader is describing his own experience[4]. To be on the safe side, the Targum adds *the prophet said,* and thus betrays that what follows is intended for synagogue use.

Ezekiel 1 — or, more exactly, Ezekiel 1 capped by Ezekiel 3:12, with its doxology — was the customary *haftarah* for Shabu\u1d9cot[a]. This explains why the *merkabah* vision of chapter 1 is swollen with exegetical expansions, while the vision of chapter 10 is bare of them: these expansions are a deposit of generations of preaching on the text of the *haftarah*, year after year. We may assume the same origin for the Targumic Toseftas to Ezekiel 1, the difference being that these expositions were not as popular or as widely used as those that became part of the universally accepted Targum text. This assumption agrees with Rimon Kasher's discovery that Targumic Toseftas tend to occur in those passages of the Prophets that we know to have been used as *haftarot* [309].

The Targum of Ezekiel 1 is thus a particularly important tool for our investigation. It is a sort of touchstone for those interpretations that belong to the popular *merkabah* exegesis of the synagogue. I say "a sort of touchstone," because it is a criterion only of inclusion, not of exclusion. If we find an interpretation in the Targum, we know it is part of the synagogue tradition; we would not expect it to belong to any secret doctrine of "*ma\u1d9caseh merkabah.*" But if the Targum omits a given interpretation, it does not necessarily follow that it was *not* part of the synagogue tradition; we will soon see that this tradition was much broader than that portion of it that left its deposit in the Targum.

What does the Targum do with the *merkabah*[5]? Let us take the themes of its exegesis, one by one.

b) Avoidance of anthropomorphism. It is hardly possible to read anything about the theology of the Targums without learning that one of their main objectives is to soften or eliminate the Bible's anthropomorphic descriptions of God. Targ. Ezekiel 1 is no exception. The Hebrew text of verse 27 twice contains the phrase "from the appearance of his loins." Both times, Targum substitutes for it "an appearance of glory which the eye

---

4 "Once when I was hardly ten I was startled, aroused from my wandering thoughts [during a church sermon], by the awful discovery, the stupendous announcement, that someone had actually *seen* the Lord. This was the prophet Isaiah in the year that King Uzziah died; but, for the moment, so convincing was his voice, I felt sure it was our minister himself — that in his black coat and white linen necktie he, the Reverend Ebenezer Bean, had been before that great throne, high and lifted up, in that train which filled the temple." — Mary Ellen Chase, *A Goodly Heritage* [830].

5 Samson H. Levey has translated the Targum of the entire chapter into English [320]. Jean Potin provides a partial French translation, with commentary [433].

could not look at and which it was impossible to contemplate." Targum uses the same circumlocution in 8:2. Similarly, "the hand of the Lord" in 1:3 becomes "the spirit of prophecy from before the Lord" (so in 3:14, 22, 8:1, 33:22, 37:1, 40:1). For "visions of God" (1:1), Targum has "the vision of the glory of the Shechinah of the Lord"[b]; for "from his place" (3:12), Targum has "from the place of the dwelling of his Shechinah."

All of this is standard Targumic translation technique, without special application to the *merkabah*. But a Targumic Tosefta to Ezekiel 1:26 introduces a striking interpretation of that verse at the same time that it sidesteps its anthropomorphism. According to the Hebrew text, the prophet sees the form of a sapphire throne, "and upon the form of the throne a form like the appearance of a human being, upon it from above." Most Targum manuscripts [226] leave "the appearance of a human being" in Hebrew; Codex Reuchlinianus and the printed editions translate it literally. But one manuscript (Montefiore H.116) records a variant: "the form of Jacob our father upon it from above."

When we read Ezekiel 1:26, we normally assume that "the appearance of a human being" is *sitting* on the throne. But it is just as possible to understand the Hebrew to mean that it is *engraved* on the throne. Both Palestinian and Babylonian rabbinic sources (*Gen. R.* 68:12, ed. 788 [188]; BT Hull. 91b) speak of Jacob's image as being engraved on God's throne [397, 448], but do not give any satisfactory exegetical basis for it. This Tosefta suggests that the idea derives from an anti-anthropomorphic interpretation of Ezekiel 1:26, developed in the synagogue. Of course, we still do not know why the "form" is identified as Jacob's; this is probably connected with the belief that a celestial embodiment of Israel (= Jacob) is perpetually in God's sight [141,398,733].

An Aramaic hymn for Shabu[c]ot, of uncertain date, connects Jacob's image with a heavenly ascension: Moses sees "the image of Jacob rising up opposite him" when he ascends to receive the Torah [305]. Both the language and the apparent liturgical function of this passage suggest that it is connected with the Targumic tradition[6]. The *Hekhalot* literature, too, knows the celestial Israel and the engraving of Jacob, as we will see in chapter IX.

c) The ḥayyot as singers of God's praise. Targ. Ezekiel 1:24—25 sets forth this idea very clearly:

[MT:] [24]I heard the sound of their wings like the sound of many waters, like the voice of Shaddai, when they went; a sound of tumult [?] like the sound of a camp. When they stood, they let down their wings.

---

6 We will have more to say about this hymn, and about another composition of the same type, in chapter VIII (sections B2b, C5d).

[25] And there was a voice from above the firmament that was over their heads. When they stood, they let down their wings.

[Targum] [24] I heard the voice[7] of their wings like the sound of many waters, like a voice *from before* Shaddai, when they went: the sound of *their speech as they praised and blessed their everlasting Lord, ruler of the worlds,* like the sound of the camps *of the exalted angels.* When they stood, they *silenced* their wings.

[25] And *when it was* [God's] *will to communicate revelation to his servants the prophets of Israel,* there was a voice *and it was heard* from above the firmament that was over their heads. When they stood, they *silenced* their wings *before the revelation.* [226]

Targ. Ezekiel 43:2 does not expound its text ("his voice was like the sound of many waters") as fully as this, but does substitute "the voice of those blessing his name" for "his voice."

Targum thus states explicitly the exegesis of Ezekiel 1:24 that I have supposed to underlie the Qumran Angelic Liturgy and LXX Ezekiel 43:2. It compares the "sound of many waters," not to God's voice, but to the voices of those who chant his praise (so Revelation 14:1−3, 19:6). Ezekiel's "camp" becomes the "camps of the exalted angels," as in Genesis 32:1−2. The wings of the "creatures," as Targum calls the *ḥayyot* (see below), have become their organs of song. We have seen evidence that this idea was originally rooted in Ezekiel 3:12−13, interpreted with the aid of Isaiah 6:1−4 (chapter II). Here it is transplanted to 1:24, and fresh support for it discovered: Targum vocalizes the obscure Hebrew word *hamullah* (which I have tentatively translated "tumult") as *hammillah*, "the word[8]," and interprets it as "their speech as they praised and blessed their everlasting Lord." Targum thus helps us understand LXX's peculiarities; at the same time, LXX attests the antiquity of Targum's tradition.

But Targum does something else with 1:24−25, which we have not seen before. It detects a causal connection between the two parts of verse 25[9], and infers from this that the heavenly hymnody is not of supreme importance. God's will to communicate with his people, through prophets like Ezekiel, takes precedence over it. This idea may possibly have left a trace in the "silence in heaven" of Revelation 8:1. We will presently see how the synagogue tradition, preserved in Talmud and midrash, transforms the conception in a way that leads it away from its roots in Ezekiel 1:25, but suits it better to the needs of the synagogue.

---

7 Aramaic *qala*, like Hebrew *qol* and Greek *phōnē*, can mean both "sound" or "voice." I translate according to the context.

8 So the first-century [22] Greek translation of Theodotion, which renders *qol hamullah* with *phōnē tou logou*, "the sound/voice of the word."

9 So Symmachus' second-century Greek translation (preserved in Syriac in the Syro-Hexaplar): "And when there was a sound above the firmament that was over their head, they stood and their wings were slackened." Jerome's Vulgate here follows Symmachus.

Having transferred the singing of the creatures' wings to Ezekiel 1:24–25, Targum is content to translate 3:12–13 almost literally. Between "the voice of a great quaking" and the doxology of verse 12, it adds: "of those who give praise and say ... " (We will soon return to Targum's understanding of the "great quaking.") It translates "rustling against each other" (verse 13), unmusically enough, as "striking against each other."

d) The ḥayyot as God's messengers. Ezekiel 1:14 reads, in Hebrew, *wehaḥayyot raṣo' washob kemar'eh habbazaq.* It is not entirely clear how we are to translate these five words. The first certainly means "and the *ḥayyot.*" The second seems to be a peculiar combined verbal form that mixes the roots *yaṣa',* "to go forth," and *ruṣ,* "to run." The third is a verbal form that, in context, ought to mean "and returned." If, for the sake of argument, we grant that Targum is right in identifying *bazaq* with *baraq,* "lightning" [3], the last words must mean "like the appearance of lightning." The resulting sentence is thus a hybrid of "the *ḥayyot* went forth and returned like the appearance of lightning" (cf. MT Genesis 8:3, 7) and "the *ḥayyot* ran and returned like the appearance of lightning" [1,19]. The Angelic Liturgy may possibly presuppose the former interpretation (above, p. 54); the Apocalypse of Abraham probably reflects the latter. Targum translates the verse:

> When the creatures are sent forth to do the will of their Lord, who established his Shechinah in the heights above them, like the motion of the eye in viewing [?] they go about and circle the world and return, [as if they were] one creature [?] [c]. And they are swift as the appearance of lightning.

The translator evidently analyzes *raṣo'* as a hybrid, not of the roots *yaṣa'* and *ruṣ,* but of *raṣah* ("to desire") and *ruṣ.* That is why he speaks of "the will of their Lord" before he describes the creatures' astounding speed. The same etymology of *raṣo'* is used, in a midrash that *Gen. R.* 50:1 (ed. 515–516 [188]) attributes to the early fourth-century Palestinian Amora R. Aibo, to prove that the *ḥayyot* "desire to fulfill their mission."

I am less interested in the expositors' precise analysis of *raṣo'* than I am in Targum's confirmation that the image of the *ḥayyot* as God's messengers was part of the synagogue tradition. I have argued that the "hymnic tradition," used by the authors of Revelation (4:5, 5:6) and the Angelic Liturgy, read a similar conception into Ezekiel 1:13, identifying the "torches" as spirits sent forth in God's service. Targum shifts the focus of this conception from verse 13 to verse 14, and makes its subject the *ḥayyot* rather than the torches. But the basic idea is the same.

I suspect that Targum's exegesis was influenced by Job 38:35: "Can you dispatch lightnings, so that they go, and say to you, 'Here we are'?"

e) The ḥayyot as executors of God's wrath. I have discussed this conception at some length in connection with the Book of Revelation. Targ. Ezekiel 1:8 develops it, on the basis of Ezekiel 10:7, in a way that is very reminiscent of Revelation 15:7–16:21 [434].

[MT:] They had human hands underneath their wings, on their four sides ...

[Targum:] Hands like human hands were fashioned for them, underneath their wings on their four sides, in order that they might use them to take coals of fire from between the cherubim, under the firmament that is over their heads; and to give [the coals] to the seraphim to throw upon the place of sinners, to destroy the guilty ones who transgress [God's] word.

Notice that the translator has forgotten that the *hayyot* and the cherubim are supposed to be the same. The apocalyptic writers, as we saw in the last chapter, took this equation very seriously. But, in general, it does not seem to have penetrated very deeply into the consciousness of the ancient Jewish expositors. The *Hekhalot*, which develop in this respect the tradition of Targ. Ezekiel 1:8, are so indifferent to it that they regularly enroll *hayyot* and cherubim side by side among their heavenly hosts.

Toward the end of this chapter, we will examine certain rather sinister developments of this grim image of the *hayyot*, cognate to some of the ideas I have detected in Revelation. But the synagogue tradition, as represented by two Targumic Toseftas to Ezekiel 1:8, also tried to soften the image. The creatures, after all, have not one hand but two. Hence, Codex Reuchlinianus adds to the Targum's text, after "to take":

The right hand is extended to receive repentant sinners, that they may be found innocent on the day of judgment and inherit the life of the world [to come]. But the left hand is extended to take coals of fire, etc. [226]

Two other manuscripts (Montefiore H.116, Cincinnati 4/3) and the Antwerp Polyglot follow a textual tradition that adds, after "who transgress [God's] word":

... and to receive with them [their hands] the repentance of all repentant sinners.

I would guess that these Toseftas are independent attempts to reshape the Targum's image, in accord with a midrash quoted in BT Pesahim 119a [320]:

R. Kahana quoted R. Ishmael b. R. Jose – and the rabbis quote R. Simeon b. Laqish as quoting R. Judah [II] the Patriarch [to the same effect][10]: What does *human hands underneath their wings* mean? The *Ketib* reads, *his hand*[11]. This refers to the hand of God, which is extended beneath the wings of the *hayyot* in order to rescue repentant sinners from [God's] attribute of justice.

---

10 The first chain takes us back to Palestine around the beginning of the third century, the second to the middle of the third century. (I insert the reference to "the rabbis" on the basis of the manuscripts that Rabbinowicz quotes [819].)

11 What this remark means is that the consonantal text (*Ketib*) of Ezekiel 1:8 reads *ydw*, which must be pronounced *yado*, "his hand." As often in MT, the vowels written below the line tell us

But the Targumic tradition reshapes the midrash as well. The author of the midrash saw nothing wrong with speaking of God's hand. The authors of the Toseftas, characteristically recoiling from anthropomorphism, preferred to attach the merciful hand(s) to the creatures.

I am not sure whether the Targum's addition to Ezekiel 1:7 also belongs in the "executors of wrath" category. After describing the feet of the *hayyot* (which, in the Targum, are "like the sole of round feet" rather than "like the sole of a calf's foot"; see below), the translator adds: "and they shake [or "terrify"] the world as they travel."

What are the creatures doing [434]? My first impression is that they are performing their role as agents of God's wrath, spreading destruction and terror wherever they go. I think of Revelation's living creatures summoning the horsemen of the apocalypse with their "voice of thunder" (6:1).

But there is another, less grim, explanation. The verb "they shake" is from the same Aramaic root as the noun that the Targum uses for the "great quaking" that results when the creatures, "wheels," and the rest proclaim their doxology (3:12−13). "As they travel" is *bimehakhehon*, the Aramaic word that I translate "when they went" in Targ. Ezekiel 1:24. Perhaps, then, the Targum to 1:7 refers to the literally earth-shaking sound that the creatures make when they set their wings in motion to proclaim their Lord's praises. That, as we will see in chapter IX, is how the *Hekhalot* understood it.

f) Multiplication and magnification. Up to now, the exegetical themes we have treated in the Targum seem more or less comprehensible. But what are we to do with 1:6?

[MT:] Each one had four faces, and each one had four wings.

[Targum:] Each [creature] had four faces, and each [face?] had four faces; each creature thus had sixteen faces. The total number of faces of the four creatures was sixty-four. Each one had four wings, and each [wing?] had four wings; each face thus had sixteen wings; and each creature thus had sixty-four wings. The total number of wings of the four creatures was two hundred and fifty-six.

This exuberant arithmetic seems not only ill grounded in the text, but also pointless. It reminds us faintly of a midrash included in the Passover Haggadah, which multiplies the plagues of Egypt first to fifty, then to two hundred, then to two hundred and fifty [204a]. It reminds us less faintly

---

that we must read a different word (*Qere*): *yede*, "the hands of [a human being]." Like the Targum and every other translator, I have translated the *Qere*, since the *Ketib* makes no sense. But the midrash plays with the implications of the *Ketib*, explaining "his hand" as God's. (Several of Rabbinowicz's textual witnesses omit the words *yado ketib* [819]; original or not, they accurately reflect the midrash's reasoning.)

of the extravagant numbers that the *Hekhalot* texts use to describe the dimensions of the heavenly realms, the multitude of their denizens, and sometimes also the multiplicity of their denizens' features. Thus, looking through Odeberg's translation of the text he calls *3 Enoch,* we find that each of the *ḥayyot* has four faces and four wings, but "the size of their faces is (as the size of) 248 faces, and the size of the wings is (as the size of) 365 wings. And every one is crowned with 2000 crowns on his head" (chapter 21; cf. Schäfer, #32 [490,495]). Or the prince of the Ophannim: "He has sixteen faces, four faces on each side, (also) hundred wings on each side. And he has 8466 eyes, corresponding to the days of the year [sic]. ... His height is (as) the distance of 2500 years' journey" (chapter 25; cf. Schäfer, #39). When we examine the *Hekhalot* materials more carefully, we will find yet closer ties with Targ. Ezekiel 1:6.

In its translations of Ezekiel 1:15 and 18, Targum seems to hint at a magnification of the bodies of the "wheels," which may be parallel to its multiplication of the creatures' faces. Thus:

> [MT Ezekiel 1:15:] ... and behold, one wheel on the earth beside the *ḥayyot* ...

> [Targum:] ... and behold, one wheel *mishtewe kemilra^c lerum shemayya*, beside the creatures ...

> [MT Ezekiel 1:18:] Their [the wheels'] backs [thus literally; RSV "rims"] had height and they had terror ... [9]

> [Targum:] Their backs were *shewan* over against the firmament; they had height and they were terrible ...

The key words in these Targumic passages are so ambiguous that we cannot translate them without discussing their ambiguities. We must clear up two issues: the meaning of the phrase *kemilra^c lerum shemayya*; and the meaning of *mishtewe* and *shewan*, which are two forms of the same root (*šwy*).

Kemilra^c lerum shemayya recurs in Targ. Ezekiel 1:19, 21, 10:16, 19. In all four cases, it translates Hebrew "from the earth" (*me^{c}al ha'areṣ, min ha'areṣ*); in all four cases, it refers to the elevation of the *ḥayyot*/cherubim "from the earth" and to the corresponding elevation of the wheels. Without the prefixed *ke-*, the phrase *milra^c lerum shemayya* would mean "beneath the height of heaven,"[d) and the translation's point would be that the action is not really taking place on earth (as we would think from reading the Hebrew) but on some lower plane of heaven [320]. But the *ke-* is there, and cannot be deleted without challenging all the manuscripts (all those used by Sperber and Silbermann, at any rate [226,225]) in all five passages. It suggests that the phrase describes extent rather than just location: "as from below to the height of heaven"; or even (giving *milra^c* its most literal meaning), "as from the earth to the height of heaven."

This brings us to the problem of *mishtewe*. The word can mean either "placed" (as in Targ. Job 20:4) or "compared, likened." If we choose the first meaning, and ignore the *ke-* of *kemilra^c*, we can translate Targ. Ezekiel 1:15: "one wheel placed beneath the height of heaven." But we have another option, which I prefer: "one wheel, comparable [in size to the distance] from the earth to the height of heaven." At first sight, the latter translation seems a bit strained. But the use of *shewan* in 1:18, to relate the wheels and the sky, supports it. This word must mean "like" or "equivalent" — first, because the dictionaries of Levy and Jastrow [817,818, 808] do not list "placed" as a meaning for this form of the root; second, because it also occurs in Targ. Ezekiel 1:8, where it certainly means "alike"; and, third, because "their backs were placed over against the firmament" does not mean anything. I understand the Targum of 1:18 to say — admittedly, in a very obscure way[e] — that the wheels' "backs" were equal in height to the firmament. This observation will then have been prompted by the following statement that "they had height."

The author of the Targumic Tosefta to Ezekiel 1:1, which I will discuss in chapter VIII, seems to have understood the Aramaic of both 1:15 and 1:18 as I do. He describes the several parts of the bodies of the *hayyot* as "equivalent [in size] to [the distance from] the heights of the earth [?] to the heights of heaven, and corresponding [in size] to the seven firmaments and their thickness [503]." The writer's language suggests that, although he is speaking of the *hayyot*, he is drawing on Targ. Ezekiel 1:15 for the first part of his description and on 1:18 for the second[f]. His interpretation of these passages is of course not sacrosanct. But the fact that it occurred to him to treat them this way shows that my reading of the Aramaic is at least plausible.

Why have I taken all this space to argue the meaning of two doubtful phrases? We are going to meet in the next section a clear and explicit Talmudic statement that the "wheel" of Ezekiel 1:15 is a gigantic angel whose stature links heaven and earth. I will argue that this conception derives from the synagogue tradition, and that its Talmudic formulation strengthens the connection that I am beginning to develop between the synagogue tradition and the *Hekhalot*. It will then be helpful for me to have shown, here, that the Targum also knows Ezekiel's wheel as an entity whose stature spans the distance "from the earth to the height of heaven."

g) Other. The Targum's other amplifications of Ezekiel 1 are of only marginal interest for us.

Targ. Ezekiel 1:3 tells us that revelation first came to Ezekiel in Palestine, and then a second time in Babylonia. The immediate occasion of this idea was obviously the idiomatic repetition of the Hebrew verb in the phrase "the word of the Lord came to Ezekiel." *Hayoh hayah*, says the

Hebrew text of 1:3; and Targum interprets: once (*hayoh*) in Palestine, once (*hayah*) in Babylonia. But what did the translator mean by this? *Mekhilta* invokes this interpretation of Ezekiel 1:3 to clarify the question of how a prophet can receive revelation outside Palestine (*Pisha* ch. 1; ed./ tr. 1:6 [195]); so, perhaps, does BT M.Q. 25a. But the Targum's exegesis does not really resolve this issue, and I suspect it was prompted by a somewhat different concern: how unfair it was that Ezekiel, unlike the other prophets, should never have received the holy spirit in the holy land. We will see in chapter VIII that another product of the synagogue tradition, the Genizah midrash "Visions of Ezekiel," was also concerned with this issue.

Targ. Ezekiel 1:1 explains the mysterious "thirtieth year," with which the book begins, as being counted "from the time that Hilkiah the high priest found the book of the Torah in the Temple, in the court, under the porch, in the middle of the night, after the rising of the moon, in the days of Josiah son of Amon, king of the tribe of the house of Judah." (Jerome mentions this explanation of the "thirtieth year" in his comment to Ezekiel 1:1, ed. 5 [622].) This haggadah is important to us only in that it serves as a starting point for a long Targumic Tosefta [503] to this verse, which will occupy us in chapter VIII in connection with the "Visions of Ezekiel."

One relevant issue, however, remains to be explored. I have supposed throughout this section that the Targum's inclusion of a given interpretation implies that that interpretation was part of the synagogue tradition, an element of what the people at large may and indeed should learn about Ezekiel's vision. But what does it mean if the Targum appears not merely to omit but actually to suppress a certain line of interpretation?

I do not mean the anthropomorphisms of 1:27, which Targum does not treat in an essentially different way from anthropomorphisms anywhere else in the Bible. I am thinking rather of features specific to the *merkabah*. In 1:7, the "sole of a calf's foot" that MT attributes to the *hayyot* becomes "the sole of round feet." The translator has vocalized *ᶜegel*, "calf," as if it were *ᶜagol*, "round," and taken it as an adjective modifying *regel*, "foot." This is grammatically impossible – *regel* is feminine, *ᶜagol* masculine – and suggests that the translator was willing to engage in some manipulation in order to banish the calf from the text. The early second-century Greek translator Aquila, a convert to Judaism who had close ties to R. Eliezer, R. Joshua, and particularly R. Akiba [22,443], did the same thing [389]. In this case, as we will see in chapter V, the translator seems indeed to have been cutting away the basis for objectionable interpretations that he either feared might arise or knew had arisen.

Can we say the same for the Targum's practice of translating *hayyot* with *biryata*, "creatures," throughout the *merkabah* vision? This rendering is remarkable, for several reasons. First, *biryata* conveys neither of the nuances ("living," "beast") of the Hebrew word. Second, outside the *mer-kabah* passages, Targum Jonathan normally renders *ḥayyah* with its Aramaic cognate *ḥayyeta*, except where the translator understands the word to refer to Gentile powers and thus interprets it instead of translating it. Third, the translator of Ezekiel usually prefers, where possible, to translate a Hebrew word with its Aramaic cognate[g]. If, in spite of all this, he chose *biryata* rather than *ḥewata* (plural of *ḥayyeta*) to render *ḥayyot*, it seems fair to assume that there was something about *ḥayyot/ḥewata* that made him uncomfortable and that he wanted to screen out.

We cannot be sure just what the translator's objection was, and we are even less sure about what we would really like to know — was the objection only theoretical, or was it directed against interpretations of the *merkabah* that had actually been proposed? Perhaps the translator disliked the implication that bestiality lies close to the seat of divinity. This might possibly explain why he inserts the word "fashioned" (*ʿabid*) after both the lion's and the ox's face in 1:10, as if to suggest that these faces were mere masks and had nothing to do with the creatures' essence. (He inserts, however, the same word after the "human hands" of 1:8.) Perhaps he had a more specific objection: if he translated *ḥayyot* with *ḥewata*, the word used in Daniel 7, he might encourage the suspicion (which has already occurred to us) that Ezekiel's four *ḥayyot* and Daniel's four beasts were at bottom the same[12].

However this may be, the synagogue tradition seems at some point to have discarded the Targum's inhibition about the use of *ḥewata*. The Targumic Tosefta to Ezekiel 1:1 calls the *ḥayyot* by this name; while the Aramaic hymn for Shabuʿot that I mentioned earlier describes how Moses, during his heavenly ascent, "found himself standing among the *ḥewata*" (or, in another manuscript, *ḥayyata*) [305,337]. We find *ḥayyata* in an Aramaic portion of the *Hekhalot* (below, chapter IX, section B1a).

I must admit, too, that there is another key word that we would expect to occur in the Targumic expansions of the *merkabah* chapter, and yet does not. This word is *merkabah* (or *merkabta*, in Aramaic). Targum Jonathan knows the word in its specialized meaning: Targ. I Kings 7:33, Habakkuk 3:4, 8, speak of the "*merkabah* of glory," *merkebat yeqara*. But in the *merkabah* passages of Ezekiel we do not find it at all[h].

---

12 This suggestion perhaps accords with a similar proposal of Levey's [320]. Throughout the Book of Ezekiel, God addresses the prophet as "son of man," *ben ʾadam*. Levey observes that Targum translates this, not *bar ʾenasha* (as we would expect), but *bar ʾadam*. He plausibly suggests that the translator's purpose was to avoid implying that Ezekiel was the Messianic "son of man" (*bar ʾenash*) of Daniel 7:13.

3. BT Hagigah 13b

a) Introduction. Now that we have begun to get the scent of the synagogue tradition, let us see where else we can find its traces.

One likely place to look is BT Hag. 13b's collection of *merkabah* midrashim.

The story of the child who was fatally burned when he contemplated *hashmal* (above, chapter I, section 5) prompts the Gemara to ask, at the very bottom of Hag. 13a: "What is *hashmal?*" The answer to this question introduces a series of expositions of Ezekiel 1 which goes on until, near the bottom of 13b, the editor's interest shifts from Ezekiel to Daniel 7:9– 10. The ensuing discussion of Daniel, with its fascinating excursuses on the "river of fire," ends abruptly around the middle of 14a.

This passage is certainly not a fragment of any lost midrash on the Book of Ezekiel, for it does not take up the Biblical texts it discusses in their Biblical sequence. Further, I incline to Abraham Weiss's view that the compiler of the Gemara himself created the collection; it was not a preexistent compilation which he simply picked up, as a block, and deposited where he thought appropriate [353]. In other words, the expositions that we find in Hag. 13b may never have been gathered into one spot until the editing of the Babylonian Gemara (to tractate *Hagigah*, at least) had reached a fairly advanced stage, at some time in the sixth or even the seventh century.

Hag. 13b contains almost all of the expositions of Ezekiel 1 that we find in the entire Babylonian Talmud[13]. This suggests that the editor intended to put together as complete an essay as he could on the interpretation of the *merkabah* chapter. But we must make one qualification. It is hardly likely that he intended to reveal any of the esoteric "*maᶜaśeh merkabah*" which the Gemara to M. Hag. 2:1 so effectively wraps in a veil of secrecy and danger [507]. Whatever he lets us know about the *merkabah*, he must have regarded as fit for the public domain. We have no inkling what his criterion was, or whether the third- and fourth-century authorities whom he invoked would have agreed with his judgment.

b) The text. I translate the passage in full. To help me refer back to its component units, I attach a letter (and sometimes also a number) to each.

---

13 Elsewhere only Pes. 119a, M.Q. 25a; I have quoted the former and referred to the latter in the preceding section. Ber. 10b, 59a, Yoma 19b, Hag. 16a, Sot. 17a (= Men. 43b, Hull. 89a) quote verses from Ezekiel 1 but do not explicitly interpret them. We will deal with most of these Talmudic passages in the coming chapters.

[A] What is *hashmal*?

[A1] Rab Judah [var. "R. Jose b. Hanina"] said: Speaking *ḥayyot* of fire [*HAyyot 'eSH meMALlelot*].

[A2] It is taught in a baraita [*matnita*]: At times they are silent [*ḤASHot*], at times they speak [*meMALlelot*]. When revelation goes forth from God's mouth, they are silent. When no revelation goes forth from God's mouth, they speak.

[B] *And the ḥayyot ran and returned like the appearance of bazaq* [Ezekiel 1:14; see above]. What does *ran and returned* mean? Rab Judah said: Like the flame that issues from the mouth of a furnace. What does *like the appearance of bazaq* mean? R. Jose b. Hanina said: Like the flame that issues from between potsherds.

[C] *And I looked, and behold, a storm wind coming from the north: a huge cloud, with fire flashing, and splendor surrounding it, and from its midst like the color of ḥashmal, from the midst of the fire* [Ezekiel 1:4]. Where was it going? Rab Judah quoted Rab: It went to subdue the entire world under the power of wicked Nebuchadnezzar. Why? In order that the Gentiles should not say, "God gave his children into the power of a lowly people."

[C1] God said, "What caused me to become a manservant to idol-worshippers? The sins of Israel."

[D] *As I looked at the ḥayyot, I saw one wheel on the earth beside the ḥayyot* [Ezekiel 1:15].

[D1] R. Eleazar said: There is *one* angel who stands *on the earth* and whose head reaches to *beside the ḥayyot*.

[D2] It is taught in a baraita [*matnita*]: His name is Sandalphon, and he is taller than his companions by the distance of a five-hundred-year journey. He stands behind the *merkabah* and weaves wreaths for his creator.

[D3] Is it really so? It is written, *Blessed be the glory of the Lord from his place* [Ezekiel 3:12], from which it follows that no one knows where *his place* is. [The answer to this objection is that] he [Sandalphon] speaks [God's] name over the wreath, and it goes and sits in its place.

[E] Rava said: Everything that Ezekiel saw Isaiah also saw. What is Ezekiel like? A country fellow who saw the king. What is Isaiah like? A city fellow who saw the king.

[F] Resh Laqish said: What is the meaning of the Scripture, *Sing to the Lord, for he is highly exalted* [Exodus 15:21]? Sing to him who exalts himself over the exalted. The lion is king of beasts, the ox king of animals, the eagle king of birds; humankind exalts itself over them. God exalts himself over them all.

[G] One text says: *This was the appearance of their faces: a human face, a lion's face to the right for the four of them, an ox's face to the left for the four of them*, and so forth [Ezekiel 1:10]. But then it is written: *Each one had four faces: the first was a cherub's face, the second was a human face, the third was a lion's face, and the fourth was an eagle's face* [Ezekiel 10:14] — and the ox's face is not counted. Resh Laqish said: Ezekiel begged for mercy concerning it, and he changed it to a cherub. "Lord of the universe," [Ezekiel] said, "can a prosecuting attorney become an advocate?"

[H] What does "cherub" mean? R. Abbahu derived it from "like a child" [Hebrew *kerub*, from Aramaic *kerabya*], for in Babylonia a child is called *rabya*.

[H1] Rab Papa said to Abaye: But, if this is so, in the passage *the first was a cherub's face, the second was a human face, the third was a lion's face, and the fourth was an eagle's face* [Ezekiel 10:14], the cherub's face and the human face turn out to be the same. [Abaye replied (?)]: Large faces, small faces. [The point is apparently that the human face is larger than the cherub's face (R. Hananel, Rashi).]

[J] One text says, *Each one had six wings* [Isaiah 6:2]. But another says: *Four faces for each, and four wings for each of them* [Ezekiel 1:6]. There is no contradiction: the one passage applied while the Temple was standing, the other when the Temple was no longer standing. The wings of the *ḥayyot* were, if one may say so, reduced[i]).

The compiler, to whom we apparently owe paragraph J, then asks which of the six wings that Isaiah saw disappeared. He answers, with a midrash which he attributes to "Rab Hananel quoting Rab," that it was the pair "with which they uttered song." He then raises an alternative possibility — it was those with which they covered their feet — and proceeds to debate the merits of the two suggestions. We need not follow the progress of his dialectic.

c) Matnita, Targum, Hekhalot. In paragraphs A—H, the compiler quotes four Palestinian Amoraim of the middle or latter part of the third century: Jose b. Hanina, Eleazar b. Pedath, Simeon b. Laqish (= Resh Laqish), and Abbahu. He also quotes five Babylonian Amoraim of the third and fourth centuries: Rab, Judah b. Ezekiel, Abaye, Rava, and Rab Papa. He does not mention a single Tanna by name. But he does quote two anonymous *baraitot*, which he designates (as is common in the Babylonian Talmud) by the term *matnita*. With these anonymous *matnitas*, we are again on the track of the synagogue tradition; for I believe we can trace both to an exegetical tradition closely akin to that of the Targum.

This is very clear in the case of paragraph A2. The *matnita*, which is independent of the Amoraic statement to which it is attached, expresses the same idea that we find in Targ. Ezekiel 1:24—25. Even the language it uses is similar. The word I have translated "revelation" is *dibbera* in the Targum's Aramaic, *dibbur* in the *matnita*'s Hebrew. The Targum learns about the creatures' "speech" (*millulehon*) from Ezekiel's reference to *qol hammillah*, "the sound of the word" (so Targum vocalizes verse 24; MT *qol hamullah*). The *matnita* uses the verb *memallelot*, "they speak," which comes from the same Hebrew-Aramaic root.

But there is also a difference. The *matnita* detaches the haggadah it expresses from its original source in Ezekiel 1:24—25, and roots it instead in a fanciful etymology of *ḥashmal*. The utterance attributed to Judah b. Ezekiel (or Jose b. Hanina) goes yet further: it twists this etymology away from the *matnita*'s conception, and turns it into a rather pointless phrase describing the *ḥayyot*. We can thus trace an evolution of the exegesis from the Targum, through the *matnita*, to Judah b. Ezekiel or Jose b. Hanina, both of whom lived around the middle of the third century. We will see it develop in a different direction before this chapter is over.

The situation in paragraph D2 is more complex. To begin with, the *matnita* as we have it cannot have stood alone. It presupposes an interpretation of Ezekiel 1:15 like the one here attributed to the Amora Eleazar b. Pedath. The "wheel" is *on the earth* and at the same time *beside the ḥayyot* (that is, in the vicinity of the divine throne); and Eleazar b. Pedath resolves the apparent contradiction by making the "wheel" into a gigantic angel who stretches from earth to heaven[14]. I have argued (section 2f) that this conception underlies the obscure language of Targ. Ezekiel 1:15, 18.

---

14 The "five-hundred-year journey" is the conventional measurement of the distance from earth

But this time the *matnita* adds puzzling details that we do not find in the Targum. Why is the angel named Sandalphon? Who are his "companions"? And why does he weave wreaths for his creator? — by which, of course, I am asking what it meant for the author of the *matnita* to imagine him doing so.

Contemporary rabbinic sources do not shed any light on these questions. We do, however, have what amounts to a commentary on the Talmudic passage in a medieval cosmographic text called *Midrash Konen* (ed. 26 [478])[15]:

> On the fifth day ... [God] created *one wheel on the earth*, whose head is opposite the holy *hay-yot*. He is an intermediary between the Jews and their father in heaven. ... His name is Sandalphon; and he weaves wreaths for the Master of glory from *Holy* [*holy holy is the Lord of hosts*] and from *Blessed be he*, and from *Amen may his great name* [*be blessed for ever and ever*], which Jews utter as [liturgical] responses in the synagogue. He then adjures the wreath by the ineffable name, and it ascends by itself to the Lord's head.

I do not see any evidence that the author of *Midrash Konen* drew on any early source other than BT Hag. 13b itself. We therefore are free to accept or reject his interpretation, depending on whether we find it plausible. I am inclined to accept it.

For we have no way to explain the connection between Sandalphon's gigantic size and his occupation of weaving wreaths for God, unless we assume that he is an intermediary figure whose function is to lift the prayers of the Jews across the vast gulf between earth and heaven, into God's presence. Paragraph D3, indeed, blunts this point by claiming that the wreath can travel by its own power. But it is clear from its Aramaic language and its style that paragraph D3 is the work of the compiler, who harmonized the *matnita* with a conventional exegesis of Ezekiel 3:12 (found also in *Sifre Numb.* #103, ed. 101 [221]), at the cost of misrepresenting the tradition he had just quoted. The author of *Midrash Konen*, who understood the older tradition, nevertheless acknowledged with his conclusion the compiler's authority.

A passage in the Palestinian Talmud dramatically expresses the paradox that God, for all the stupendous cosmic distances that separate him from earth, is so close to his worshippers that "none can be closer than he ... one goes into a synagogue, stands behind a pillar, prays in a whisper, and God hears his prayer" (Ber. 9:1, 13a). But one needs a taste for paradox and perhaps a willingness to suspend disbelief in order to appreciate this. The

---

to heaven: PT Ber. 1:1 (2c), 9:1 (13a, misnumbered 12a); BT Hag. 13a, Pes. 94a–b; *Gen. R.* 6:6 (ed. 45–46 [188]); Tanh. *Terumah* #9 (= Tanh. Buber *Terumah* #8, ed. 47a [222]); *Midr. Psalms* 4:3 (ed. 22a [199]); "Visions of Ezekiel" (below, chapter VIII). I note some Islamic parallels in Appendix II.

15 I will say more about *Midrash Konen* in chapter VI, section 8a.

simpler and less imaginative Jew needed a tangible bridge over the physical
distance between synagogue and God. The preacher provided Sandalphon.

The angel's function perhaps explains his name. Poppelauer, followed by
Schwab and then Scholem, derived "Sandalphon" from Greek *synadelphos*,
which we may understand as "brotherly" or "acting as a brother" [432,
444,612]. But brother to whom? To Metatron[16], answer Poppelauer and
Scholem. It would seem odd, though, for the angel's name to describe only
his relation to another angel, without saying anything about his own
characteristics. I suggest that he is the "brother" of the earthbound humans
whose prayers he brings up to God. His size suits him uniquely for this
job; unlike the other angels, his smaller "companions," he can always be
both on the earth and beside God's throne.

We recall that Revelation 4:10 has "the twenty-four elders fall down
before him who is seated on the throne and worship him who lives for ever
and ever," as they "cast their crowns before the throne." The elders seem
to be celestial represenatives of human beings [94,149], and it would be
fitting for the wreaths they offer to be woven of human prayers. The Greek
Apocalypse of Baruch, probably written in the first or second century
A.D., envisions the merits of the righteous as flowers which are to be
thrown into an enormous vessel — "its depth was as great as the distance
from heaven to earth, and its breadth as great as the distance from north
to south" — which the archangel Michael holds (III Baruch, chapters 11—
12). I am a little surprised that there are so many righteous people on earth
that their merits would fill a container of such size, and I suspect that the
underlying idea is that of a channel which conveys these merits from earth
to heaven. (This would explain the Greek text of the end of 11:9, which
ought to be translated: "which are escorted *through it* before the heavenly
God.") III Baruch's vessel would then originally have been a sort of inanimate Sandalphon.

In chapter VIII (section B2c), we will examine in some detail a late passage from the midrash *Pesiqta Rabbati*, obviously dependent on BT Hag.
13b, which coordinates the wreath's progress towards God's head with the
heavenly liturgy, and thus reflects an understanding of the Talmudic passage similar to the one we have seen in *Midrash Konen*. This *Pesiqta* passage
strongly suggests the *Hekhalot* literature; and, when we discuss it, we are
going to have to explain what the resemblance means. But even the *matnita* has a faint whiff of the *Hekhalot* about it, in that it introduces a gigantic angel with a bizarre and alien name, beside or in place of the familiar
Gabriel, Michael, and Raphael.

I now suggest that this *matnita*, like the one in paragraph A2, derives

---

16 On Metatron, see above, chapter I, section 7; below, chapter IX.

from the synagogue and is oriented toward the needs of the synagogue. Its purpose is to assure the worshipper, in the most impressively concrete way, that his prayers are indeed going to reach God. Its essential idea, the stupendous size of the *'ofan*-angel, is reflected in the synagogue translation of Ezekiel 1:15 and 18.

The *matnita*, then, points to the synagogue tradition as one source for the enormous angels that occupy the heavens of the *Hekhalot*. It does not, of course, give us anything like an adequate explanation of what they are doing there. The *Hekhalot* literature's concern with giantism is too strong to be accounted for as an overblown generalization from Sandalphon to the rest of the celestial hosts. As we go on, we must look for new ways to explain what the monstrous size of the angels meant to the people who revelled in describing it. By the time we finish discussing the *Hekhalot* in chapter IX, our explanation should be complete. For now, we must be content with having distinguished one of the roots of this belief, and traced that root back to the synagogue.

It is worth adding that the *matnita*'s conception of the "wheel" may possibly have made its way to the ears of the great Christian exegete St. Jerome, which were usually open to bits of Jewish haggadah [654,659, 671,698]. In his *Commentary* on Ezekiel 1:15–18, he suggests that the wheels may symbolize the Gospels, "whose way and whose stature stretches toward heaven, yet a little bit touches the earth as, ever hastening, it speeds to the heights" (ed. 20 [622]).

d) Other. I am less confident that other materials in BT Hag. 13b originated in the synagogue.

Paragraph C – to which C1 seems to be a later addition – reminds me faintly of Targ. Ezekiel 1:7, where the creatures "shake [or "terrify"] the world as they travel," but the resemblance is too vague to support a connection. This interpretation is the first we have seen, since we left the exegetical work of the Book of Ezekiel itself, that takes the slightest interest in the historical context of the *merkabah* vision. We will see few others that do.

Paragraph F derives, as its attribution to Resh Laqish claims, from a Palestinian haggadah. Several of the later haggadic midrashim preserve slightly different versions of a recension of this haggadah, which circulated in Palestine under the name of R. Abin, an Amora of the early fourth century (*Song R.* to 3:9–10; *Ex. R.* 23:13; Tanh. Buber *Be-Shallaḥ* #14, ed. 31a [222]; *Midr. Psalms* 103:16, ed. 219a–b [199])[j)]. These Palestinian versions open with the statement that "there are four exalted creatures," and end by having them "fixed" or "engraved" in God's throne. There is no reason to believe that the midrashim are drawing on BT; for what would be the point of replacing Resh Laqish's name with R. Abin's? More likely,

R. Abin's Babylonian connections [344] have something to do with the appearance of this originally Palestinian tradition in the Babylonian Talmud.

We do not know the setting in which the haggadah of the four faces originated, or the channels in which it was transmitted. These channels cannot have been very tightly sealed, for we find that Christian writers of the third and fourth centuries, especially in Syria, seem to have been acquainted with it. The third-century Roman bishop Novatian, in a brief but important summary of Ezekiel's vision which will again occupy us before the end of this chapter, says that "those living creatures who hold sovereignty above all others" are placed beneath God's throne (*De Trinitate*, chapter 8; ed. 24 [626]). The *First Homily*, attributed to "Makarios the Egyptian" but now believed to have been composed by fourth-century Syrian pietists [669,681], has the "living creatures" represent the reasoning powers that direct the soul, "just as the eagle rules the birds, the lion the wild beasts, the ox the tame beasts, and humankind the created beings" [625]. Ephraem the Syrian (again, fourth century) says that the faces of the cherubim are those of the "noblest and strongest animals and birds" (*Commentary on Ezekiel*, ed. 166 [619]). Neuss attributes a similar view to Apollinaris, fourth-century bishop of Laodicea in Syria [696]. These Christian witnesses attest that the haggadah of the four faces is at least as old as Resh Laqish, and that it became fairly widely known to Syrian Christians not long after the time of R. Abin.

Was the synagogue the vehicle of its distribution? We have no positive evidence that it was; which is unfortunate, because one *Hekhalot* text takes up the Palestinian recension of the haggadah and develops it into a hymnic composition (below, chapter IX, section B3d) [576].

We find the two "Resh Laqish" haggadot (paragraphs F and G) combined into a single midrash in Tanh. *'Emor* #16 (= Tanh. Buber *'Emor* #23, ed. 49a—b [222]; below, chapter V, section 2c). The *Tanḥuma* editor may have been drawing on BT, but I think it at least as likely that he was using the Palestinian sources that lie behind these two paragraphs. The second of these haggadot presents the issue of the ox's face in a more explicit form than we have seen so far. We must give the passage our full attention in chapter V, when we will be able to place it in a context which will make its importance clear.

I have little to say about paragraphs B, E, and H—H1. The first does not seem to fit with the Targum's assumption that *bazaq* is simply another word for *baraq*, "lightning." The second is extraordinary, and indeed unparalleled, in its cool and rather supercilious view of Ezekiel and his *merkabah*. As for the third, there ought somehow to be a connection between R. Abbahu's etymology (a variation of which occurs in *Gen. R.* 9:5, ed. 70 [188]) and the Renaissance image of a cherub as a chubby little boy [42, 697]. But I cannot imagine what it is.

4. Genesis Rabbah 65:21: the encasing midrash

a) Introduction: the silence of the angels. BT Hag. 12b lists and describes a series of seven heavens. The fifth of these, Maᶜon, is said to be the place where "groups of ministering angels sing hymns by night but are silent [*hashot*] by day, on account of the honor of Israel. As it is written: *By day the Lord commands his kindness, and by night his song is with me* [Psalm 42:9]."

The BT editor seems to imply that Resh Laqish was the author of the whole account of the seven heavens. This may be true for some of the material in the description, but it is almost certainly false for the passage I have just quoted, which is followed immediately by a different interpretation of Psalm 42:9 — itself attributed to Resh Laqish.

Whatever the passage's date, it is clearly related to Targ. Ezekiel 1:24—25 and the associated *matnita* in Hag. 13b (A2). All sources agree that the angels' speech or song is interrupted by periods of silence. Hag. 12b and 13b even use the same word, *hashot*, to refer to this silence. But the reason for the silence in Hag. 12b is a new one. It is no longer God who takes precedence over the heavenly hymnody, but the Jews. Some change has come ver the tradition.

Gen. R. 65:21 (ed. 737—740 [188]) preserves a midrash which shows us this change taking place. The editor of *Gen. R.* ostensibly quotes this midrash as an interpretation of Genesis 27:22, "the voice is the voice of Jacob." The midrash in fact contributes nothing to the understanding of Genesis 27:22, and the hook by which it is attached is nothing but the editor's excuse for incorporating it.

The midrash contains within itself, as in a pouch, a second midrash which originally had nothing to do with the context in which it now appears, and whose purposes were considerably different from those of the midrash that now encases it. The "encased midrash," as I will call it, appears as paragraph A2 of the following translation. We will turn our full attention to it at the end of this chapter. For now, we are interested in it only insofar as the author of the "encasing midrash" used it to advance his own concerns.

b) The text

[A] R. Phinehas quoted R. Reuben: It is written, *When they stood* [understood as "stood up"], *they let down their wings* [Ezekiel 1:24—25].

[A1] Is there indeed sitting in heaven? —

[A2] Did not R. Hanina b. Andrai say in the name of R. Samuel b. Soter: There is no sitting in heaven. *Their feet were straight feet* [Ezekiel 1:7] [means that] they have no knees. [Other Biblical evidence:] *I drew near to one of the standing ones* [Daniel 7:16]. *Seraphim were standing over him* [Isaiah 6:2]. *All the host of heaven was standing to his right and to his left* [1 Kings 22:19].

[A3] — And you say, *When they stood!*

[A4] But what does *when they stood [be^comdam]* mean? [We must read it as] *ba' ^cam dom* ["the people comes, silence"]. Whenever the Jewish people says, *Hear O Israel [the Lord is our God, the Lord is one*; Deuteronomy 6:4, the *Shema^c*], they [the angels] are silent. Only afterward do *they let down their wings.* And what do they [then] say? *Blessed be the name of his glorious kingdom for ever and ever*[17].

[B] R. Phinehas quoted the following from R. Levi, the rabbis from R. Simon: It is written, *When the morning stars sang out together [and all the sons of God shouted for joy*; Job 38:7]. The first to praise God are the offspring of Jacob, who are likened to stars. So Scripture says of them, *And those who justify the many are like stars forever* [Daniel 12:3]. Only afterward do *all the sons of God* — the angels — *shout for joy.* And what do they [then] say? *Blessed be the glory of the Lord from his place* [Ezekiel 3:12].

[C] R. Berechiah quoted R. Samuel: It is written, *I heard after me the voice of a great quaking* [Ezekiel 3:12]. What does *after me* mean? After I, with my companions, had praised God, I heard *the voice of a great quaking.* And what do they say? *Blessed be the glory of the Lord from his place*[k].

c) Analysis of the midrash. The "encasing midrash" combines a series of three expositions of Ezekiel 1:24–25, Job 38:7, and Ezekiel 3:12. Each is purportedly quoted by a late fourth-century Palestinian Amora from a predecessor of the late third century. I see no reason to question these attributions. They do not, however, tell us when the three expositions were combined. We can only assume that this happened some time before the middle of the fifth century, the date to which most scholars assign the editing of *Genesis Rabbah*[18].

Several midrashim of the *Tanḥuma* type, which are usually and plausibly dated later than *Genesis Rabbah* and its congeners, contain different versions of our midrash. So does the still later *Midrash on Psalms (Midr. Psalms)*[l]. But all of these versions seem to be adapted from that of *Genesis Rabbah*, and have no independent claim on our attention.

Paragraph B, the exposition of Job 38:7, gives the impression of being an interloper. It is obvious how the expositor of Ezekiel 3:12 (paragraph C) knows that the angels say *blessed be the glory of the Lord from his place*: the text itself says so. We will soon see why the expositor of Ezekiel 1:24–25 (paragraph A) imagines that the angels give the appropriate liturgical response to the Jewish people's *Shema^c*. But we are at a loss to understand how the interpreter of Job 38:7 can extract from this verse that, when *all*

---

17 This sentence is not from the Bible. It is an early liturgical formula which, according to M. Yoma 3:8, 4:2, 6:2, the "priests and the people" used in Second Temple times as a response to the prayer of the high priest. In the synagogue, the congregation responds with this formula to the recitation of the *Shema^c*; *Deut. R.* Lieberman (ed. 68–69 [186]) and Tanh. *Qedoshim* #6 refer to the practice of pronouncing it in a whisper [380,387,411]. This is the point of the midrash's interpretation of *they let down their wings.* The author understands the Hebrew phrase *(terappenah kanfehen)* to mean "they murmur softly with their wings," in response to the *Shema^c* pronounced by the Jewish people.

18 See Appendix I, section 6.

the sons of God shout for joy, they do so in the language of Ezekiel 3:12; or why it even occurs to him to ask what formula they use. The editor who combined the three midrashim clearly transferred both question and answer from paragraph C, and thus recast the originally independent Job midrash in the image of its two new neighbors. We in fact find this midrash by itself, in a different context, in BT Hull. 91b, which represents it as part of a baraita (cf. *Sifre Deut.* #306, ed. 343 [220])[m].

Setting paragraph B aside, we are left with two expositions of the *merkabah* vision. Both of them develop the synagogue tradition.

The exegesis of Ezekiel 1:24—25 is so strained and farfetched that it could hardly have arisen if the Targum had not first cut a path for it, by discovering in these two verses the information that the chant of the angels' wings is sometimes silenced. The author of our midrash bases himself on the Targum's interpretation, but is eager to find a new reason for the angels' stilling of their wings. He therefore shifts the burden of conveying the angels' silence, from the phrase *they let down their wings,* to the single word *be^comdam.* First, he arbitrarily interprets *be^comdam* as "when they stood *up*." Then, rejecting this interpretation, he chops *be^comdam* into three short words, which give him the reason he wants for the silence. The words *they let down their wings* are now free. Playing on a double meaning of *terappenah,* he finds in them a gentle murmuring of the angels' wings. What could this be, he reasons, if not the whisper in which the docile congregation of angels affirms "the people's" declaration that God is One?

The exposition of 3:12 makes the same point. Ezekiel and his "companions" praise God first; only then may the angels speak. The Biblical context, which represents the prophet in solitary discourse with his God, of course says nothing of any such "companions." But the expositor has no interest in the Biblical context. He projects into the midrash the setting for which he created the midrash — a group of people assembled for prayer. The marks of the synagogue are clear.

d) The purpose of the midrash. In *Gen. R.* 65:21, then, we see the synagogue *merkabah* exegesis take on a shape even better suited to the needs of the synagogue than was the form that the Targum gave it. The preachers constructed the image of Sandalphon out of Ezekiel 1:15 to answer the question, "How can God hear our prayers?" Here, they strain the text of Ezekiel 1:24—25 and 3:12 to answer the question, "Does he want to hear our prayers?" The answer is of course a thunderous yes. God so loves the praise that rises from the synagogues that the angels must silence the praise of their wings to let him hear it.

What needs did these fantasies answer? Their message, the supreme dignity and importance of the synagogue worship, sounds very much like compensation for a reality in which the worshippers felt themselves neither dignified nor important. We can, if we want, look for political or economic reasons why Jews might have needed the encouragement our midrashim provided. We will then have little difficulty finding them.

If we are to trust the attributions of the midrashim, they were composed in the late third century and transmitted during the fourth. Their authors could look back on decades of economic chaos; they themselves suffered under the harsh fiscal reforms that the emperor Diocletian (284—305) imposed to end this chaos. Their transmitters saw the Christian church triumphant, increasingly intolerant, increasingly bent on humiliating the once-chosen people whom God had now rejected [367]. No wonder, in such times, that the preachers' audiences craved to believe that they were so precious to the Lord of the universe that he would silence his magnificent angels in order to hear them. No wonder the preachers hunted for new ways to satisfy their hearers' appetites.

Plausible as this explanation is — and we will see more specific evidence, in chapter VIII, that the synagogue tradition could be used to defend Jewish self-esteem from external challenges — I am not entirely comfortable with it. Its defect is that it cannot be proved wrong, and therefore cannot be proved right. We can date midrashim only within very broad boundaries. Within these boundaries, grim external realities are never lacking. Whenever it pleases us, therefore, we can say that Jews needed the encouragement of this or that midrash, on account of some menace from the outside. Hypotheses of this sort work too easily and too universally to be very useful.

In chapter IX, I will try to explain the function of the *Hekhalot* in terms of tensions within the Jewish community, which led some Jews to build themselves up at the expense of others. This hypothesis may perhaps help explain the fantasies of self-importance reflected in the synagogue *merkabah* tradition, from which I believe the *Hekhalot* to have sprung. For now, it is enough for us to note that these fantasies play a fairly important role in the synagogue's version of what I originally called the "hymnic tradition" of *merkabah* exegesis (chapters II and III). In these dreams of glory, we see for the first time the apparently remote and ethereal speculations of the hymnic tradition touch down on earth; and we begin to understand what they might have given to the people who believed in them.

Perhaps we have here, as well, a clue to the synagogue tradition's motive for magnifying the size of the *merkabah* beings and multiplying their organs (above, section 2f). The grander and more imposing the angels can be made, the greater the importance of the humans whom God prefers over them. Glorifying the *ḥayyot* and the *'ofannim*, the preacher subtly glorified himself and his hearers.

Thus far the purposes and techniques of the "encasing midrash" of *Gen. R.* 65:21. The "encased midrash," with its exegesis of Ezekiel 1:7, so far seems only a minor expedient used to advance them. With its help, the expositor of Ezekiel 1:24—25 can lever *be^{c}omdam* away from its obvious and natural meaning. But he could have made this point without Ezekiel 1:7, and the claim that this verse implies that the *ḥayyot* "have no knees" seems to have a purpose independent of this expositor's aims. We must do our best to plumb this purpose. But first we must look in another direction, toward Sinai.

5. Chariots at Sinai: Pesiqta de-Rab Kahana, Ba-Ḥodesh #22, and parallels [454,513]

a) Introduction: the Tanḥuma midrashim. It is odd that we have seen nothing of Sinai so far this chapter. In chapter I, we found that Sinai-like miracles were God's answer to the *merkabah* expositions of R. Johanan b. Zakkai's disciples. In chapter III, we found a "Sinai-*merkabah*" cluster beneath the visions of the Apocalypse of Abraham. I proposed that we trace both of these phenomena to a synagogue practice, of pairing the *merkabah* vision with the Torah's account of the Sinai revelation. Given all this, we would expect the lectionary coupling of the two episodes to have left a mark on the synagogue tradition of *merkabah* interpretation.

Yet, in this respect, the Targum disappoints us. Perhaps, indeed, we might follow Potin's suggestions and suppose that the "revelation" (*dibbera*) of Targ. Ezekiel 1:25 hints at the Sinai revelation, or that the shaking of the earth that accompanies the creatures' movement (Targ. Ezekiel 1:7) refers to the earthquakes that, in rabbinic tradition, accompanied the Sinai event [434]. But these allusions are so faint that we cannot be sure they are real.

Can we find in the rabbinic literature any trace of a synagogue tradition that combines Sinai and the *merkabah*, and interprets each in the light of the other? In chapter VIII, I will argue that the third-century Palestinian synagogues knew and used an elaborate midrashic cycle that did just that. But this argument will involve a great deal of hypothesis; some of the sources it rests on are uncomfortably late (chapter 20 of *Pesiqta Rabbati*), while others are either on the fringes of the rabbinic literature (the Genizah "Visions of Ezekiel") or definitely outside it (Origen's first homily on Ezekiel). To hold the threads of our argument together, we need something more: a midrash, decently early and clearly among the rabbinic midrashim, that binds the *merkabah* to Sinai and proceeds to expound this connection. When we find this missing link, we can use it as an index to what the synagogue tradition did with the Sinai-*merkabah* connection. If the midrash contains internal evidence pointing to its synagogue origin, this will confirm that we have used it rightly.

This is why the midrash we are about to consider, preserved in several texts of the *Tanḥuma* genre, is so important for us.

What are the "*Tanḥuma* midrashim"? The group takes its name from a haggadic midrash to the entire Pentateuch, first published in 1520 and frequently reprinted since, which is often called "the printed *Tanḥuma*." In 1885, Solomon Buber published, from manuscripts, a second recension of *Tanḥuma* which differed considerably from the printed text, particularly in the portions dealing with Genesis and Exodus [222]. But the linguistic and stylistic features that distinguished the two *Tanḥuma* recensions could also be found in other midrashim, which were therefore accounted members of the same group. These included the familiar printed text of *Deuteronomy Rabbah*; a very different recension of *Deuteronomy Rabbah*, which Saul Lieberman published in 1940 [186]; substantial portions of *Exodus Rabbah* (chapter 15 to the end), *Numbers Rabbah* (again, chapter 15 to the end), and *Pesiqta Rabbati*; and a bewildering multitude of Genizah texts [258].

The use of the *Tanḥuma* midrashim to provide a "decently early" source for *merkabah* exegesis requires some explanation and defence, for the *Tanḥuma* texts are not usually considered early compositions. When we compare the haggadot they contain with parallels in the "classical Palestinian midrashim" (*Genesis Rabbah, Leviticus Rabbah, Lamentations Rabbah, Pesiqta de-Rab Kahana*), the *Tanḥuma* versions usually appear to be derivative. (We saw an example of this in the last section.) Since most scholars date the "classical" texts, on the strength of their resemblance to the Palestinian Talmud, to about the middle of the fifth century, a later dating of the *Tanḥuma* midrashim threatens to remove them altogether from the age of the Amoraim. Late rabbinic texts can indeed preserve early materials — we saw in the last chapter themes found in the Ethiopic Enoch and the Apocalypse of Abraham surviving in *Tanḥuma* midrashim — but to claim that this is true in any given instance without specific evidence will rightly appear to be special pleading.

Let us first examine our midrash, and then see what kind of a case we can make for its date.

b) The texts. We have the midrash in two main recensions. Since the name "Elijah" occurs only in the first and "Yannai" only in the second, I find it convenient to call them the "Elijah Recension" and the "Yannai Recension." The first of these is represented by *Pesiqta de-Rab Kahana, Ba-Ḥodesh* #22 (ed. 219–221 [206]) and by Tanh. Buber *Yitro* #14 (ed. 38b –39b [222]); the second by Tanh. *Ṣaw* #12 and Tanh. Buber *Ṣaw* #15 (ed. 10b [222]).

Pesiqta de-Rab Kahana is of course not a *Tanḥuma* midrash. But much of *Pesiqta's* exposition of the Shabuᶜot Torah reading, Exodus 19–20, is not an authentic part of this midrash (*Ba-Ḥodesh* #12–25, ed. 213–224 [206]). The style of this material is that of *Tanḥuma*. It closely corre-

sponds to Tanh. Buber *Yitro* #7–17 (ed. 37a–40b [222]; there is no parallel in the printed *Tanḥuma*). Most of it, though not all, is found only in
two of the five manuscripts that Mandelbaum used for his edition of *Pesiqta* [208]. It is clearly an extract from a lost recension of *Tanḥuma*, which
an unknown scribe copied into the parent of two of Mandelbaum's *Pesiqta*
manuscripts. Parts of it were later interpolated into the ancestor of the
other three[19].

I translate the Elijah Recension from Mandelbaum's text of *Pesiqta*:

[A] *I am the Lord your God, who brought you out of the land of Egypt* [Exodus 20:2]. This is
what Scripture says: *The divine chariotry is two myriads, thousands of shin'an*[20]*; the Lord is
among them, Sinai, in holiness* [Psalm 68:18].

[B] R. Abdima of Haifa said: I learned in my mishnah [*shaniti bemishnati*; the reference is
to what we would call a baraita] that twenty-two thousand [chariots of] angels[n]) descended
with God to Sinai.

[C] R. Berechiah ha-Kohen be-Rabbi said : [Their number] corresponded to the camp of the
Levites, for God foresaw that none would stand faithful [?] except for the Levites. Therefore
twenty-two thousand descended, corresponding to the Levitic camp[21 o)].

[D] Another explanation: *The divine chariotry is two myriads.* Twenty-two thousand chariots [*markabot*] descended with God, each one like the *merkabah* that Ezekiel saw [emending
with Tanh. Buber].

[E] *The divine chariotry.* They said, on the authority of a band that came up from Babylonia,
that twenty-two thousand chariots descended with God to Sinai. So taught [*shanah*] Elijah of
blessed memory.

Unlike the Yannai Recension, which ends its exposition of Psalm 68:18
with the twenty-two thousand chariots, the Elijah Recension goes on to
offer a series of midrashic etymologies of the word *shin'an*. It then expounds *the Lord is among them* and – in *Pesiqta*, though not in Tanh.
Buber – connects at the end with Exodus 20:2, *I am the Lord your God.*
We thus have in the Elijah Recension a complete *petiḥah* (see below) to
Exodus 20:2; this verse is, in a way typical of the *Tanḥuma* midrashim,
quoted first at the beginning of the *petiḥah*, and again at its end. We will
return to this point.

---

19 We also find parallels to parts of the midrash in Tanh. *Wa-Yishlaḥ* #2, *Ex. R.* 29:2, *Deut. R.* Lieberman ed. 68 [186] (with attribution to Abdimi, or, in *Deut. R.*, to "Ammi of Jaffa"); Tanh.
Be-Midbar #14, Tanh. Buber *Be-Midbar* #15 (ed. 7a–b [222]), *Numb. R.* 2: 3 (without attribution; only the last of these is not a *Tanḥuma* source). The late *Midr. Psalms* 68:10 (ed. 159b–
160a [199]) draws on the Elijah Recension. *Pesiqta Rabbati* 21:8 (ed. 102b–104b [209])
weaves together features of the two recensions, with elements from BT Shabb. 88a; it carries
over from its sources obvious graphic errors as well as important variants.
20 RSV, "thousands upon thousands." I briefly discuss the difficult word *shin'an* in chapter II,
section 3b.
21 The reference is to the Levites' loyalty to God during the episode of the golden calf (Exodus
32:25–29). Numbers 3:39 reckons the total Levite population at twenty-two thousand. The
phrase that I translate "Levitic camp" is *maḥaneh lewiyyah*; the second word may be intended
to suggest *lewayah*, "escort." (We will again touch on this point in chapter VIII.) The titles that
decorate R. Berechiah's name are typical of the style of the *Tanḥuma* midrashim.

I translate the Yannai Recension from the printed *Tanḥuma*:

[A] *The divine chariotry is two myriads, thousands of shin'an.*

[B] R. Abdimi of Haifa said: I learned in my mishnah that, when God revealed himself on Mount Sinai to give the Torah, twenty-two thousand chariots descended with him.

[C] R. Berechiah ha-Kohen said: [This was] because God foresaw that none would stand faithful except for the Levites. Therefore he descended with [those whose number] corresponded to the Levitic camp.

[D] R. Yannai said to him: If so, the words *the divine chariotry is two myriads, thousands of shin'an* must apply to the tribe of Levi! What is meant by *the divine chariotry is two myriads*? Twenty-two thousand chariots descended with God, each one like the chariot that Ezekiel saw [emending with Tanh. Buber].

c) The sources of the midrash. My first impression of this midrash is that of a broken record. Over and over, we are told that Psalm 68:18 implies that twenty-two thousand chariots descended with God to Sinai. It is easy enough to see how this information is extracted. *The divine chariotry* (*rekheb*) of course refers to chariots like Ezekiel's (so paragraph D tells us explicitly). *Two myriads* is twenty thousand; *thousands* adds, by the most conservative assumption, another two thousand. The setting at Sinai is clear from the end of the verse. The exegesis of Psalm 68:18 is thus completely intelligible. But why must the author say it again and again?

In the Yannai Recension, Abdimi of Haifa and Yannai make the same point in slightly different language. In the Elijah Recension, we hear it from Abdimi and from a mysterious Babylonian band who quote the prophet Elijah. It is also reported in paragraph D as "another explanation," which it is not. Only R. Berechiah adds something new.

Paragraph D of the Yannai Recension has problems of its own. Apart from the fact that I do not understand the first sentence of Yannai's argument, Yannai cannot possibly have commented on an utterance of Berechiah's: Yannai was a Palestinian Amora of the early third century, while Berechiah lived more than a hundred years later.

It is not only modern readers who have trouble with the anachronism. In order to eliminate it, the author of the version in Tanh. Buber *Ṣaw* #16 changed the text from "R. Yannai said *to him*" to "R. Yannai said, " and deleted nearly the whole of the following sentence; he left only the tell-tale remnant "if so[p)]". The author of *Pesiqta Rabbati*'s version turned Yannai into his own grandson – "R. Yannai the son of R. Simeon b. Yannai" – and exchanged R. Berechiah for R. Levi, a Palestinian Amora active around 300. The author of the Elijah Recension eliminated Yannai altogether and labeled paragraph D "another explanation." He thereby got himself into even hotter water, since the midrash in paragraph D is no different from that in paragraph B. Transmitters of the text tried to fish him out by deleting "chariots of" from paragraph B (endnote *n*). None of these efforts to resolve the anachronism seems very successful.

The difficulty arose, I suspect, when the author of the midrash that un-

derlies both recensions tried to turn his broken record into a song. He
inherited what were essentially several different versions of the same midrash, and did his best to make a dialogue out of them. Supposing, as I do,
that the attributions were forced upon him by his material, it was clumsy
but understandable for him to have combined them into an impossible conversation. Assume that he devised these attributions on his own, and it becomes incomprehensible. Thus, paradoxically, the anachronism involved
in the exchange between Berechiah and Yannai guarantees that the author
did not arbitrarily attach these names to his material, and the impossibility
of his composition argues for the authenticity of its sources.

To be sure, all I have shown is that the linking of names with utterances
goes back to a time before these utterances were combined as we now have
them. I have not proved that it goes all the way back to the men who bore
these names. I can imagine that someone handing down the tradition that
later became paragraph C might have fathered it upon the famous haggadist
Berechiah. The same is perhaps true of Yannai. But why should the transmitters have made Abdimi of Haifa, a relatively obscure Amora of the late
third century[22], into the most prominent figure in the whole traditon?
Three sources (Tanh. *Wa-Yishlah #2*, *Ex. R.* 29:2, *Deut. R.* Lieberman ed.
68 [186]) mention him and him alone in connection with it. Yet he was
so little known that the last of these passages twists his name into "Ammi
of Jaffa." The simplest explanation is that these utterances were attributed
to Abdimi, Yannai, and Berechiah because they actually said them.

The fact that Abdimi, Yannai, and the group from Babylonia are all
represented as saying the same thing is no argument that at least two out of
the three attributions must be wrong. Neither the Elijah Recension nor the
Yannai Recension represents Abdimi as the original author of this midrash.
He is quoting a traditional teaching, a "mishnah." Similarly, the Babylonians of paragraph E quote a "mishnah" (they indicate this with the verb
shanah, "taught"), which they think goes back to the prophet Elijah. We are
apparently dealing with an anonymous midrash, current in third-century
Palestine, to which both Yannai and Abdimi of Haifa lent their authority.

The "band that came up from Babylonia," and its Elijah traditions, are
a puzzle on which I can shed very little light [571]. The reference is so unconventional that the author of the Elijah Recension is hardly likely to
have invented it. It seems somehow connected with the mysterious literature, called *Seder 'Eliyahu* or *Tanna de-Be 'Eliyahu*, which circulated in
Talmudic times under Elijah's name. Two passages in the extant midrash
known as *Seder 'Eliyahu*, which may or may not have anything to do with

---

22 He appears fourteen times in PT, four times in BT (once under the name "Dimi"; Meg. 29b),
very occasionally in the midrashim [282,806,814,824].

the material that the Talmud refers to by that name, offer an interpretation
of Psalm 68:18 vaguely similar to the one we have been discussing [347].
But the resemblance is too faint to point to a direct relationship[23].

Pesiqta Rabbati 21:8 adopts this reference from the Elijah Recension,
and plainly understands it to mean the Jews who returned from Babylonian
exile in the sixth century B.C. I do not think this interpretation is likely,
for the designation of the returning exiles as a "band" does not seem appropriate. But *Pesiqta Rabbati* also provides a very interesting version of
their tradition: "Two myriads of thousands of *shin'an* of angels descended
with God upon Mount Sinai, to give Torah to Israel." The first part of this
sentence, through "angels," is in Aramaic. I do not understand why the
writer in *Pesiqta Rabbati* would have arbitrarily converted half of a Hebrew
sentence into Aramaic, and am therefore inclined to think he is preserving
a primitive feature. It sounds very much like a bit of Targum to Psalm 68:18.

Pesiqta Rabbati's Aramaic thus seems to me an indication, if only a very
faint one, that the Babylonians' tradition goes back to the synagogue. We
may say the same for Abdimi's reference to "my mishnah," which reminds
us of the *matnita*s of BT Hag. 13b (*matnita* is the Aramaic form of Hebrew
mishnah); like the *matnita*s, this *mishnah* can be understood as the traditional *merkabah* exegesis of the synagogue, which both Yannai and Abdimi
made use of. A third arrow also points to the synagogue. This is the fact,
which we have noticed but not discussed, that the Elijah Recension represents our midrashic composition as the first part of a *petiḥah* leading from
Psalm 68:18 to Exodus 20:2.

d) Openings for lost sermons? The *petiḥah* is a very common midrashic
pattern[24]. It begins, at least in its classic form, with a Biblical verse chosen
by the expositor; it leads from there, often through a complicated series of
twists and turns, to the beginning of the Biblical passage to which the *petiḥah* is attached. This Biblical passage is normally a synagogue lection.
Thus, the midrash *Lamentations Rabbah* opens with a series of thirty-six
petiḥot to the Book of Lamentations, which was read in the synagogue on
the fast of the Ninth of Ab; each *petiḥah* begins with a different Scriptural verse, but all end with Lamentations 1:1.

Although the *petiḥot* as we have them in the midrashic texts are literary
compositions, Joseph Heinemann has persuasively argued that they go back

---

23 *Seder 'Eliyahu Rabbah*, chapter 22; *Zuṭa*, chapter 12 (ed. 119, 193 [211]). Braude, in the introduction to his English translation of *Seder 'Eliyahu*, gives a useful summary and bibliography of
   attempts to unravel the problems that surround this extraordinarily difficult text [248,378a].
   We may perhaps be able to shed a few rays of light on *Seder 'Eliyahu*, below, chapter VIII.
24 To Norman J. Cohen's bibliographical references on the *petiḥah*, we must add the recent studies
   by Arnold Goldberg, Marc Bregman and Richard S. Sarason [268,270,287,260,339].

to actual sermons used in the synagogue to introduce the lections for Sabbaths and holy days [303]. This may not be true of all *petiḥot*; indeed,
some give the impression of being free compositions of midrashic editors
and transmitters. Yet, when we find a midrash cast as a *petiḥah*, we are entitled to suspect, though not to insist, that its material may at one time
have played a role in introducing a synagogue Bible reading.

There are two arguments against making this assumption about our midrashic composition. The first is that it is only the Elijah Recension that
takes the form of a *petiḥah*; the Yannai Recension plays a modest role
within an exposition of Leviticus 8:3. We cannot be sure which preserves
the original context of the composition. We have, however, some evidence
for the priority of the Elijah Recension's setting; namely, that part of the
Yannai Recension's context seems to have developed out of one of the expositions of *shin'an* with which the Elijah Recension concludes[q]. The
second objection is more serious. As we have already seen, our text is not
a free creation which we might expect to hold an audience's interest by
power of its rhetoric, but a repetitious compilation made by an editor with
limited control over his material. We might suggest that the compiler has
taken what was once a one-sentence synagogue *petiḥah*, attributed to several authorities, and repeated it several times in the names of all of these
authorities in order to create the illusion of greater substance. But, while
brevity is part of the art of the *petiḥah*, a one-sentence *petiḥah* seems a bit
extreme.

There is, I think, a way we can resolve these problems and honor the
text's hints at its origins, as well as a prejudice I admit to holding — that
Psalm 68:18, which draws together the Shabu[c]ot Torah reading and *haftarah*, is so perfectly suited to be the starting point of a *petiḥah* for Shabu[c]ot
that it would be astonishing if it were not. This is to suppose that the tune
our midrash keeps playing over and over — "twenty-two thousand chariots
descended with God to Sinai, each one like the *merkabah* that Ezekiel saw"
— was used by Yannai, Abdimi, and perhaps many others as a stereotypic
opening sentence for *petiḥot* leading from Psalm 68:18 to the Sinai revelation.

The ongoing synagogue tradition preserved this opening down to the
time of the compiler of our midrash, whose date I would not care to guess.
It preserved also the memory that Yannai, Abdimi, and others had used
the opening but had not originated it. The compiler learned, further, that
Berechiah had taken a second step based on this opening, a comparison of
God's chariotry to the Levite hosts. What came after this he either could
not discover or did not want to use[25]. Instead, he pieced together a new

---

25 Unless we suppose that the expositions of the word *shin'an* and of the phrase *the Lord is among*

midrash out of the variants of the opening. This new midrash might, as an artificial *petiḥah* to Exodus 20, preserve the memory of the function its materials once had; or, as the Yannai Recension shows, it might serve different purposes altogether.

If we can accept this hypothesis, or some variation of it, we will have found the missing link we are looking for: an early synagogue midrash that expounds Sinai and the *merkabah* as a pair. It is, to be sure, less informative than we might like. We learn from it that the synagogue tradition used Psalm 68:18 as a clip to hold the two episodes together, and little else. But this datum is important. Not only does it support our speculations about the interpretation of LXX Ezekiel 43:2 (above, chapter II), but it can serve as a starting point for the reconstruction of the third-century Shabuᶜot sermons. This we will undertake in chapter VIII.

We can complete this section, and at the same time prepare for our work in chapter VIII, by glancing at some other uses made of Psalm 68:18. Rabbinic sources do not elsewhere connect it with the *merkabah*, but they do apply it to the event at Sinai (*Sifre Numb.* #102, ed. 100 [221]; parallels or derivatives in *Ex. R.* 29:8, *Numb. R.* 11:7, *Midr. Psalms* 18:17, ed. 73b– 74a [199]). They often learn from it that God's heavenly hosts correspond to his earthly ones – specifically, the Israelites in the wilderness (*Sifre Numb.* #84, ed. 83–84 [221]; Tanh. *Be-Midbar* #14, Tanh. Buber *Be-Midbar* #15, ed. 7a–b [222]; *Numb. R.* 2:3). R. Berechiah's haggadah, quoted above, is a variation on this theme.

We have seen that the Targum uses Jacob's "camp of God" (Genesis 32: 1–2) to interpret Ezekiel 1:24. It is therefore worth noting that *Genesis Rabbah* at one point identifies this "camp" with the "chariotry" of Psalm 68:18 (75:10, ed. 888–889 [188]), and at another calculates the number of its angels by analogy with the Israelite camp in the wilderness (74:17, ed. 876–877 [188])[26].

---

them, which the editor of the Elijah Recension appended to the midrash of the twenty-two thousand chariots (above; see also endnote *q*), are also relics of these *petiḥot*. I have no reason to rule out this possibility, although it seems inconvenient that none of the additional expositions bears the name of Yannai, Abdimi, or Berechiah. (The editor credits three alternative explanations of *shinʾan* to the third-century Amora Eleazar b. Pedath. He attributes one statement apiece to the Tannaim Eleazar b. Azariah and Eliezer of Modin, and to the Amoraim Resh Laqish, Tanhum b. Hanilai, Levi, and Judah b. Simon.) But, even if we admit them as fragments of Shabuᶜot *petiḥot*, they do not help us very much. They give us little idea of the contents of the sermons from which they come. They tell us nothing of what we would most like to know: what these sermons did with Ezekiel's *merkabah*.

26 "How many angels were in Jacob's presence when he entered Palestine? R. Huna quoted R. Aibo: Six hundred thousand. It is written, *Jacob said when he saw them, 'This is the camp of God,'* and the Shechinah does not dwell [among] fewer than six hundred thousand. The rabbis say: One million two hundred thousand, [as it is written,] *And he called the name of that place Two-camps.*" Six hundred thousand roughly equals the number of adult male Israelites who left Egypt

Certain Christian sources also deserve mention. The description of the *merkabah* in the eighth chapter of Novatian's *De Trinitate*, which we have already seen to draw on rabbinic haggadah, concludes by applying Psalm 68:18 to the *merkabah*. "This, therefore, is what David calls the chariot of God. *The chariot of God,* he says, *is ten thousand multiplied* by so much; that is, numberless, boundless, immeasurable" [626]. And an early Christian liturgy, apparently of Jewish origin, preserved in the fourth-century *Apostolic Constitutions* (VII, 44), makes Psalm 68:18 the response of "Israel, Thy Congregation on earth," to the heavenly beings' chant of Isaiah 6:3 and Ezekiel 3:12 [680].

6. Genesis Rabbah 65:21: the encased midrash

a) The midrash reconstructed. We can now turn our full attention to paragraph A2 of *Gen. R.* 65:21.

> Did not R. Hanina b. Andrai say in the name of R. Samuel b. Soter: There is no sitting in heaven. *Their feet were straight feet* [Ezekiel 1:7] [means that] they have no knees. *I drew near to one of the standing ones* [Daniel 7:16]. *Seraphim were standing over him* [Isaiah 6:2]. *All the host of heaven was standing to his right and to his left* [I Kings 22:19].

We know nothing at all about the author of this midrash, and very little more about the man who quotes it. PT Meg. 4:5 (75b) represents Hanina b. Andrai as transmitting an utterance of R. Zakkai of Kabul to one "R. Simeon šrh" (I do not know how to pronounce this last word, or what it means), who in turn transmits it to R. Jeremiah. Jeremiah, the only well-known figure of the four, lived in the early fourth century. This would seem to place Hanina b. Andrai in the middle or late third century, and Samuel b. Soter a generation or so earlier.

Aaron Hyman, then, would seem to be wrong in identifying Samuel b. Soter with Samuel b. *ssrty* or *swsrt'* (again, I do not know how these names are pronounced), who transmits statements of R. Abbahu (ca. 300 A.D.) [807]. Wilhelm Bacher identifies Samuel b. Soter with the well-known Amora Samuel b. Nahman [372], but we will soon see that Bacher's evidence — the attribution of a closely related midrash to Samuel b. Nahman — can be more plausibly explained in a different way. As far as I know, Samuel b. Soter appears in rabbinic literature only as the author of this one midrash.

What does the midrash mean? The author of the encasing midrash represents it as saying that no one in heaven, with the unstated but obvious

---

(Exodus 12:37). The parallel in *Song R.* to 7:1, supported by several manuscripts of *Gen. R.* (including the excellent ms Vatican 30 [188] and 60 [187]), represents the angels as dancing before Jacob. This is surely based on Song 7:1, but it is also reminiscent of the way the angels danced at Eleazar b. Arakh's exposition of the *merkabah* (PT Hag. 2:1, 77a; above, chapter I).

exception of God, ever sits down. *Be^comdam* in Ezekiel 1:24 and 25 therefore cannot mean "when they stood up," because the *hayyot* could not have been sitting in the first place. This idea is not new to us. We recall from BT Hag. 15a (above, chapter I) that Elisha b. Abuyah is so stunned to see the angel Metatron sitting down that he falls into dualist heresy. Yet there is one feature of the encased midrash that seems a little suspicious. If I wanted to prove that no heavenly being sits but God, I would take as my main text I Kings 22:19: *I saw the Lord sitting on his throne, all the host of heaven standing to his right and to his left.* I would not rest the weight of my case on the rather weak claim that heavenly beings never sit because Ezekiel can be understood as saying that the *hayyot* have no knees, and then tack on the far more convincing verse from I Kings as an afterthought. Perhaps the author of the encasing midrash has reinterpreted and therefore reworked an older source that originally made a very different point.

A parallel in PT Ber. 1:1 (2c) turns this possibility into a virtual certainty. The Gemara has quoted an unnamed but presumably Tannaitic source as saying that "one who stands and prays must make his feet even." The meaning of this requirement is not self-evident. Two late third-century Amoraim, Levi and Simon, offer differing interpretations: "like the angels" and "like the priests." But these interpretations themselves require clarification, which the Gemara provides in part as follows:

> The [Amora] who says, "like the angels" [is thinking of the passage] *their feet were straight feet* [Ezekiel 1:7].
> R. Hanina b. Andrai said in the name of R. Samuel b. Soter: Angels [*mal'akhim*] have no knees. How do we know? *I drew near to one of the standing ones* [Daniel 7:16][27].

Here we find Samuel b. Soter's midrash, without any reference to the issue of sitting in heaven. It is also without the quotations of Isaiah 6:2 and I Kings 22:19, which were presumably added when the midrash was adapted to suit the needs of *Gen. R.* 65:21.

It does not seem, however, that PT has preserved the midrash in its original form, any more than *Gen. R.* has. PT seems to quote Ezekiel 1:7, not as part of the midrash, but as immediately preceding it; it is from Daniel 7:16 alone that the expositor learns that "angels have no knees." Yet Ezekiel 1:7 is by far the more likely source for this information. *Gen. R.* surely reflects the earliest form of the midrash when it has Samuel b. Soter use Ezekiel 1:7 as his primary text, and afterwards buttress his deduction with Daniel 7:16.

---

27 BT Ber. 10b briefly summarizes the discussion in PT, coming down on the side of the "angels" interpretation: "R. Jose b. Hanina said in the name of R. Eliezer b. Jacob: He who prays must make his feet straight, as it is written, *Their feet were straight feet.*" – On the translation of the quote from Daniel, see endnote *k*.

I imagine that the midrash originally ran somewhat as follows:

Their feet were straight feet. R. Hanina b. Andrai said in the name of R. Samuel b. Soter: [This means that] angels have no knees. And thus Scripture says: *I drew near to one of the standing ones* [28].

We thus have an interpretation of Ezekiel 1:7 that seems clear, straightforward, and basically plausible. It also seems entirely pointless. What can it possibly have meant to Samuel b. Soter to say that "angels have no knees"?

b) The midrash interpreted. A midrash quoted in PT Sheb. 6:5 (37a) and the parallel *Lev. R.* 6:3 (ed. 135—136 [191]), which will ultimately solve our problem, begins by complicating it:

I have sent it [the curse that results from violation of an oath] *forth, says the Lord of hosts, and it will go to the house of the thief and to the house of him who swears falsely by my name,* and so forth [*and it will lodge in his house, and will consume it, its timber, and its stones;* Zechariah 5:4].
R. Samuel b. Nahman said: Angels of destruction [*mal'akhe habbalah*] have no knees. How do we know? *From wandering in the earth and from travelling about in it* [Job 1:7, describing Satan]. But, in this case, [the curse *will lodge in his house*] *and will consume it, its timber, and its stones.* [PT[r)]]

This passage is part of a complex of midrash and folk-tale, focused on Zechariah 5:1—4, that warns against the hazards of swearing oaths[s)]. Its point is clear enough. Demons are in a state of perpetual motion. Satan, after all, comes *from wandering in the earth and from travelling about in it* (Job 1:7). But the result of a false oath *will lodge in* the culprit's *house,* eating away at it and presumably at him as well. A false oath is therefore more dangerous than a demon, who can injure only in passing.

Apart from its curious use of "have no knees" as an idiom for "never stop travelling," this midrash would give us no trouble at all, were it not for the fact that it is obviously derived from the midrash shared by PT Ber. 1:1 and *Gen. R.* 65:21. Both midrashim consist essentially of the unusual statement that angels, or angels of destruction, have no knees. Both are attributed to a "Samuel," although the latter version replaces the unknown Samuel b. Soter with the popular haggadist Samuel b. Nahman (Palestine, late third century). But, between PT Ber. 1:1 and PT Sheb. 6:5, Samuel b. Soter's midrash has undergone a remarkable change. Its "angels" are converted into "angels of destruction" — that is, demons[29] — and Job's descrip-

---

28 This is the text of PT, except that I substitute *wekhen hu' 'omer* ("and thus Scripture says") for *umah ta^cama*.

29 "Angels of destruction" (*mal'akhe habbalah*) may be agents of God's wrath (as in BT Shabb. 55a, referring to the "six men" of Ezekiel 9:2), or out-and-out demons (as in BT Pes. 112b) [549]. The quotation of Job 1:7 suggests that the latter are intended here. As we have observed in connection with the Book of Revelation, it is often hard to tell the two apart. We will return to this point.

tion of Satan replaces Ezekiel's description of the *ḥayyot* as the proof text. How did this happen?

I have twice referred to the summary of Ezekiel's vision in chapter 8 of Novatian's *De Trinitate* (mid-third century; above, sections 3d, 5d), and I have suggested that it makes use of rabbinic *merkabah* midrash. It is therefore not extraordinary that Novatian's text yields the key to understanding the midrash of his contemporary or near-contemporary Samuel b. Soter, and the transformation that befell it.

Ezekiel's wheels, Novatian suggests, represent "the seasons through which all the elements of the world ever revolve, equipped with the sort of feet by which they do not remain always standing still, but are ever in passage[30]." The point is clearly that the wheels are the image of nature's endless cyclic transition through the seasons. But the reference to "feet" is peculiar. Novatian designates their possessors with the neuter pronoun *ista*, which could refer either to the seasons (*tempora*) or to the elements (*membra*). The image seems incongruous in either case. ("Wheels," *rotae*, are feminine in Latin; and Ezekiel does not speak of the wheels as having feet.) But Jerome, in his *Commentary* on Ezekiel 1:6–8, refers to an interpretation which seems to be the same as the one Novatian uses; and, in Jerome's presentation, the wheels symbolize the seasons and the *ḥayyot* the elements (ed. 12–13 [622]). If we suppose that Novatian assumes the second as well as the first of these equations, we will be able to identify *ista* with both the elements and the "living creatures" (neuter *animalia*, in Latin) that stand for them.

It follows that the "feet" are those of Ezekiel 1:7, which Novatian understands to be designed so that their possessors cannot bend them, therefore never pause or rest, but remain in perpetual motion. I propose that Novatian has gotten this idea from Samuel b. Soter's midrash – indirectly, I assume – and that he translates the idiom "have no knees" into its intended meaning. PT Sheb. 6:5 confirms that he has done so correctly.

We now see the point of Samuel b. Soter's midrash. It belongs to that theme of the synagogue tradition that represents the *ḥayyot* as God's messengers. It adds that they are perpetually about their mission; they are so constructed that they have no reason ever to stop.

We have seen that the Targum sets forth this theme in its translation of Ezekiel 1:14, while the Angelic Liturgy and the Book of Revelation develop it in connection with verse 13. The Angelic Liturgy speaks of "the spirits of the living God that travel about [*mithallekhim*] perpetually with the glory of the wondrous chariots." I have suggested that the key word in

---

30 "Nam et rotae subiacent, tempora scilicet quibus omnia semper mundi membra uoluuntur, talibus pedibus adiectis quibus non in perpetuum stant ista, sed transeunt" (ed. 24 [626]).

this passage is the verb *hithallekh*, which occurs in both Ezekiel 1:13 and in Zechariah 6:7, and which thus enabled the author to combine the two passages into one image.

Now, if we are using the presence of *hithallekh* as a criterion for the flowers we are plucking from the field of Scripture, we may find that our bouquet includes a sinister bloom indeed. The verb also occurs in Job 1:7. *The Lord said to Satan, "Whence do you come?" Satan answered the Lord, "From wandering in the earth and from travelling about [hithallekh] in it."* (Compare the end of Zechariah 6:7.)

The use of *hithallekh* in Job 1:7 may have lubricated the *hayyot*'s slide from "angels" into "angels of destruction." It certainly did not cause it. The authors and transmitters of midrash indeed learned from the words of Scripture, but it was they who chose the Scriptural texts that would teach them. They would hardly have allowed Job 1:7 to replace Ezekiel 1:7 in Samuel b. Soter's midrash, unless they perceived it as being in some way appropriate to the *hayyot*.

I believe that its appropriateness lies in the image of the *hayyot* as agents of wrath; which, like the "messenger" theme, we have found in the synagogue tradition. This image is an uneasy one to begin with. When we add that the agents of wrath are designated "beasts," we begin to understand how ancient expositors might have wondered what kind of creatures God is surrounding himself with, and why they might have recalled in this connection that Satan appears in the Book of Job as an honored member of God's entourage.

I suggested in section 2g that the Targum may have translated *hayyot* as "creatures" in order to suppress the implication that they are beasts. In the development of Samuel b. Soter's midrash, the perception that the Targum suppressed bursts forth with such energy that it carries the *hayyot* clear through bestiality into demonism.

c) Divinity and demonism. Is it possible that I am attributing too much to the rabbis in suggesting that the image of God surrounded by agents of his wrath would be likely to disturb them? I think not. Consider a midrash from *Pesiqta de-Rab Kahana*:

R. Levi said: What does *slow to anger* (Joel 2:13)[31] mean? His anger is far away. It is like a king who had brutal troops. He said: "If they are stationed with me in the town, then whenever the townspeople anger me they are going to rise up of their own accord and massacre them. Let me send them far away. Then, if the townspeople anger me, by the time I am able to send for [the troops], they [the townspeople] will already have managed to pacify me." This is what Scripture

---

31 Literally, "long of anger," which the midrash understands to mean that God's anger is a long way off.

says: *They come from a distant land, from the extremity of heaven,* and so forth [*the Lord and the instruments of his wrath, to destroy*[32] *all the earth;* Isaiah 13:5].

R. Isaac said: Not only that, but he bars [the gates] against them. *The Lord opened his treasury and brought forth the instruments of his wrath* [Jeremiah 50:25]. While he is opening and closing [?], his mercies draw near. [*Shubah* #11, ed. 364 [206]]

Or, from *Tanḥuma*:

What does Scripture mean, [*You are not a God who cares for wickedness,*] *evil does not dwell with you* [Psalm 5:5]? ... Only angels of peace and mercy stand before God. Angels of wrath are far away from him; as it is written, *They come from a distant land, from the extremity of heaven, the Lord and the instruments of his wrath, to destroy all the earth.* [Tanh. Buber *Tazria*[c] #11, ed. 20a [222]; Tanh. *Tazria*[c] #9]

In the light of our discussion of Revelation's "glass sea," *Gen. R.* 4:6 (ed. 30 [188]) is particularly interesting. Why, the rabbis ask, does Genesis 1:6–8 not say *God saw that it was good* in regard to the second day, when he created the firmament that separated the waters?

R. Simon quoted R. Joshua b. Levi: It is like a king who had a brutal legion. The king said: "Since this legion is so brutal, I do not want my name inscribed on it." Similarly, God said: "Since these waters were [!] used to punish the generation of Enosh and the generation of the flood and the generation of the tower of Babel, I do not want *it was good* written about them."

In contrast to these passages, Ezekiel's *merkabah* vision tells us that the agents of wrath are as near as can be to the seat of divinity; that evil does indeed dwell with God; that not only his name is upon his brutal legion, but also his throne.

I pursued a similar line of thought in discussing the Book of Revelation, but shrank from asking the question that stands at its end: is God himself tainted by the demonic character of those who carry him? I know of no surviving Jewish (or Christian) source that even considers this idea. But I have found a ninth-century Zoroastrian text which suggests that certain Jews not only posed this question, but answered it in the affirmative.

The text is called *Škand Gumānīk Vičar*. It includes polemic against Judaism, Christianity, Manichaeism, and other views hostile to Zoroastrian orthodoxy. In his attack on Judaism [429], the author denounces the Bible and rabbinic haggadah, as well as some peculiar haggadic material which Gordon Newby and I have identified as the residue of an apocalyptic form of Judaism which survived at least into the seventh century [773]. Among the supposedly abominable Biblical texts that the author quotes we find a passage claiming that God's "voice, like the voice of weeping, is even more like the voice of the demon." Newby and I have proposed that this strange quotation, otherwise untraceable, is based on Ezekiel 1:24: "I heard the sound of their wings like the sound of many waters, like the voice

---

32 *Leḥabbel.* The root recurs in *mal'akhe ḥabbalah,* "angels of destruction."

of Shaddai ... " Only, the consonants *šdy* ("Shaddai") were read as if they were *šd* (*shed*), "a demon."

It is wildly unlikely that the Zoroastrian polemicist mastered Hebrew and then combed the text of the Bible for evidence that the Jewish God is a demon. Far more probably, he drew on a Jewish tradition which pushed the demonic traits of Ezekiel's *merkabah* to their ultimate conclusion.

As I have said, no tradition of this kind has survived in a Jewish source, and we have no way of knowing its context. But the degeneration of *shaddai* into *shed* sounds like an extreme variant of the process we have traced in the past several pages, which transformed the *hayyot* into Satanic "angels of destruction." In the exegetical development that underlies the *Škand*'s quotation, and in the evolution of Samuel b. Soter's midrash from PT Ber. 1:1 to PT Sheb. 6:5, we perhaps have two segments of the same trajectory.

7. Conclusions

We can read *Gen. R.* 65:21 as a paradigm for the synagogue *merkabah* tradition. Its surface, bathed in the sunlight of divine acceptance and approval, shines forth a powerful message of encouragement for any Jew who will contemplate it. But there are shadows beneath the sunny surface. They can be disguised but not eliminated. As we have just seen, it is not certain that God is entirely free of their penumbra.

We might be tempted to envision the *merkabah*'s light as the outer shell of the synagogue tradition, corresponding to the "encasing midrash" of *Gen. R.* 65:21, and the elusive shadows as its hidden core. But this comparison would be misleading, in that it suggests that the light is only a mask for the darkness within — or, at least, is less important than the darkness. To suppose this is to ignore much of the data we have gathered so far.

Our work in chapter I left us with the question of how the *merkabah* kept its place, against the Mishnah's opposition, in the synagogue cycle of festival readings. When we trace the interpretation of Ezekiel 1:24—25, and watch it develop into an ever more inspiring proclamation of God's care for and attention to his children, we begin to understand why the people and their preachers found the *merkabah* too precious to be allowed to slip into concealment. We understand this still better when we look at the images the preachers took from the *merkabah* and used to bridge the distance between God and his worshippers. Jacob, the representative of the people named after him, is engraved on God's throne (Targumic Tosefta to Ezekiel 1:26). The gigantic Sandalphon stands beside the Jews as they pray, lifting their prayers up to God (BT Hag. 13b, interpreted with *Midrash Konen*).

Could not messages of this kind have been drawn from other parts of the

Bible? Undoubtedly. But, taken from the *merkabah* vision, they inherited its drama, force, and mystery. The weight of the most terrifically awesome text of Scripture stood behind their message of comfort.

Indeed, we have already seen indications that some preachers feared that even this weight was not enough; that it had to be multiplied by gigantic dimensions and stupendous numbers, made more impressive with fantastic names. Hence Sandalphon. Hence the twenty-two thousand chariots that descended with God to Sinai. Hence the multiplication of the faces of the *hayyot* in Targ. Ezekiel 1:6. So far, however, we have not seen this tendency cross the border into monstrosity. For that, we will have to wait for the *Hekhalot*.

There is much that we have still to learn about the synagogue tradition. Our discoveries will illuminate the details of the Johanan b. Zakkai stories that we examined in chapter I. This will be particularly true when we turn our attention (in chapter VIII) to the Sinai-*merkabah* theme, which we so far have not glimpsed very clearly. The *merkabah*'s light will appear there at its most dazzling, uniquely appropriate for the Shabu^cot festival. We will discover that, like Sandalphon, the Sinai-*merkabah* theme helps bridge the gap between humans and God, this time through an ascent to heaven. The synagogue tradition will thus lead us into a central concern of the *Hekhalot*.

In the meantime, the shadows await our examination. So far, we have sketched them only very generally. We found in chapter III that the celestial sea has some particularly sinister connotation; and our work in this chapter has reinforced our earlier impression that the *hayyot*, as angels of destruction, ought not to be as close to God as they are. But, with these observations, we have come only to the edge of the darkness. It is now time to probe deeper.

The ox's face and the calf's foot will guide us.

Chapter V

The Merkabah and the Calf

1. Introduction

The shadow of the Sinai revelation is the episode of the golden calf.

Even to a casual reader of the Bible, the incident is perplexing. God has descended on Mount Sinai in the most dramatic way, in full view of the Israelite people. "You have seen for yourselves," he tells them immediately afterwards, "that I have talked with you from heaven. You shall not make gods of silver to be with me, nor shall you make for yourselves gods of gold" (Exodus 20:22—23, RSV). Through Moses, he makes a covenant with the people, who declare that "all that the Lord has spoken we will do and we will hear" (24:7). But no sooner does Moses fail to return from his meeting with God on schedule than the people demand of Aaron that he "make us gods, who will go before us." Aaron complies, and fashions a calf out of the people's gold jewellery. "These are your gods, Israel," the people cry out, "who brought you up from the land of Egypt" (32:1—4).

If the people's sudden faithlessness is puzzling, Aaron's compliance is downright mysterious. Confronted by Moses, he excuses himself by claiming that "you know this people is set on evil. They said to me, 'Make us gods who will go before us ... ,' so I said to them, 'Who has gold? Take it off.' So they gave it to me, and I threw it into the fire, and out came this calf" (32:22—24).

The verbs in Exodus 24:7 seem to be in the wrong order — we would expect "we will hear and we will do[1]." The rabbis were proud of this reversal. So filled with faith and enthusiasm were the Israelites that they promised to obey God's commandments even before they knew what they were (*Mekhilta, Ba-Ḥodesh* chapter 5, ed./tr. 2:234—235 [195]; BT Shabb. 88a, 89b). Or were they? The sequel perhaps suggests the contrary. "They were trying to fool God," a midrash quoted in the Tosefta (B.Q. 7:9) comments sourly; and Buber's *Tanḥuma* elaborates:

---

1 Hence RSV translates "we will be obedient" in place of "we will hear."

Like grapes in the desert I found your fathers [Hosea 9:10, abbreviated]. ... Just as grapes are beautiful on the outside and ugly within, so were the Israelites when they stood before Mount Sinai and said, *We will do and we will hear.* That was [what they said] with their mouths; but their hearts were not right. So David said: *They fooled him with their mouths, and with their tongues they lied to him; their hearts were not right with him* [Psalm 78:36–37]. [Tanh. Buber *Lekh Lekha* #21, ed. 39a [222]]

If this is the way some rabbis described their ancestors, we will not be surprised to find that outsiders used an even harsher tone. Thus, for example, the speech attributed to Stephen in the seventh chapter of Acts:

"This is the Moses ... who was in the congregation in the wilderness with the angel who spoke to him at Mount Sinai, and with our fathers; and he received living oracles to give to us. Our fathers refused to obey him, but thrust him aside, and in their hearts they turned to Egypt, saying to Aaron, 'Make for us gods to go before us; as for this Moses who led us out from the land of Egypt, we do not know what has become of him.' And they made a calf in those days, and offered a sacrifice to the idol and rejoiced in the works of their hands. But God turned and gave them over to worship the host of heaven. ...

"You stiff-necked people, uncircumcised in heart and ears, you always resist the Holy Spirit. As your fathers did, so do you. Which of the prophets did not your fathers persecute? And they killed those who announced beforehand the coming of the Righteous One, whom you have now betrayed and murdered, you who received the law as delivered by angels and did not keep it." [Acts 7:37–42, 51–53]

The polemical writers of the early church were not shy about following this author's lead. When the Jews worshipped the calf, these writers proclaimed, they showed that they were unworthy of God's covenant; from the very beginning, they forfeited God's love. In a classic article published in 1968, Leivy Smolar and Moshe Aberbach have collected Christian accusations on this topic and rabbinic answers to them [447]. The sheer bulk of this material suggests that the rabbis were not far wrong when they imagined themselves surrounded by the hectoring voices of hostile strangers:

Many say to my soul, "He has no salvation with God." Selah [Psalm 3:3]. ... The rabbis apply this verse to the Gentiles. *Many* – these are the Gentiles ... *say to my soul* – they say to the Jews: "How can there be salvation for a people that heard from its God on Mount Sinai, *You shall have no other gods before me* [Exodus 20:3]; and then forty days later it said to the calf, *These are your gods, Israel* [Exodus 32:4]? *He has no salvation with God." Selah.* ... [*But you, Lord, are*] *a shield over me* [Psalm 3:4]. You shielded us with the merits of our ancestors. [*Pesiqta de-Rab Kahana, Ki Tiśśa'* #1, ed. 16–17 [206]]

In the midrash, of course, God takes the Jews' part against their detractors:

Now my head is lifted up over my enemies around me; I will offer sacrifice in [God's] *tent with shouts of joy* [Psalm 27:6]. When Israel performed that act[2], the Gentiles said: "They cannot recover; [God] will never return to them." When the Israelites heard they were to sacrifice an ox [Leviticus 22:27; see below], their heads [which had been bowed] were lifted up; as it is written, *Now my head is lifted up.* They walked with their heads high, and said: "Now we know

---

2 The rabbis find the thought of the calf-worship so unpleasant that they do not even want to name it.

God has forgiven us." So it is written, *I will offer sacrifice in his tent with shouts of joy, I will sing to the Lord.* [Tanh. *'Emor* #16; Tanh. Buber *'Emor* #22, ed. 49a [222]]

I cannot doubt that, as these quotations suggest, the conflict with Christianity stimulated the development of rabbinic haggadah about the calf. But I cannot believe that it was the only, or even the main, stimulus. I cannot imagine that the rabbis would have brooded as obsessively as they did on the implications of the calf episode had they not recognized that the questions they put into the mouths of their enemies were legitimate ones. How *can* there be salvation for a people that saw and heard its God on Mount Sinai, and then forty days later worshipped a molten calf? The rabbis answered over and over that God had indeed forgiven his people, that his mercy and love for them were great enough to swallow up even so enormous a sin. They used any method they could to find this answer; and the fact that they did so again and again suggests that they were never entirely satisfied with any one of their arguments.

Lurking within this question is a second one. How *could* a people that saw and heard its God on Mount Sinai turn around forty days later and worship a molten calf? The question could be asked rhetorically, by the Jews' detractors. To answer such people, one might content oneself with the claim that it was really the "mixed multitude" who left Egypt with the Israelites (Exodus 12:38, Numbers 11:4) who instigated the calf-worship [398a,447]. But, if the question were asked seriously, this answer does not seem adequate, especially in view of Aaron's role in the episode. Nor does the self-laceration expressed in the midrash I quoted, from Tanh. Buber *Lekh Lekha*, at the top of the preceding page. It may have occurred — and we will soon see evidence that it did occur — to some people that the Israelites worshipped the golden calf, not in spite of what they had seen at Sinai, but because of it.

Ezekiel saw the *hayyot* with "an ox's face on the left for all four of them" (1:10), and with feet "like the sole of a calf's foot" (1:7). Exodus 32 describes how the Israelites worshipped a molten calf; and Psalm 106: 20, referring back to this episode, says that "they exchanged their glory for the likeness of an ox that eats grass." By virtue of its ox's face and calf's foot, therefore, the *merkabah* vision could be and was drawn into the circle of ideas that surrounded the calf episode. It seemed to shed light on the first of the two questions we have just looked at, and was thus a welcome addition to the arsenal of evidence that God had forgiven his people for their apostasy. But it also shed light on the second question, of what led the Israelites into apostasy in the first place. As a result, it provoked in the rabbis a discomfort bordering on horror.

Pre-rabbinic sources, as we saw in chapter II, hint obscurely at a recoiling from a real or potential link between the *merkabah* and the calf. Rabbinic texts, we will now see, document this reaction for us. They also give us the details necessary to explain it[3].

2. Leviticus Rabbah 27:3

a) The text. Let us begin with a *petiḥah* preserved in two of the "classical Palestinian midrashim": *Lev. R.* 27:3 (ed. 625—627 [191]) and *Pesiqta de-Rab Kahana, Shor 'o Keśeb* #3 (ed. 151—152 [206])[4].

The *petiḥah* introduces the synagogue lection that begins with Leviticus 22:27 and directs the sacrifice of a newborn *ox, lamb, or goat.* These words, which open the lection, are thus the goal toward which the *petiḥah* moves. Its starting point is Ezekiel 29:16. RSV translates this verse: "And it [Egypt] shall never again be the reliance of the house of Israel, recalling their iniquity ..." But the rabbinic expositor, as usual, tears the passage out of its apparent Biblical context, and understands it to mean: *There shall no more be anything that brings the iniquity of the house of Israel into remembrance*[5]. He can then give it a new set of contexts and a new cluster of meanings. Of the five examples he gives to illustrate these meanings, the first, second, and fifth focus on the golden calf.

I translate *Lev. R.*'s text. *Pesiqta*'s differs from it only in a few trivial details:

[A] R. Jacob b. Zabdi quoted R. Abbahu: *There shall no more be anything that brings the iniquity of the house of Israel into remembrance.* It is written: *Seraphim were standing over him,* and so forth [Isaiah 6:2]. *With two* [wings, the seraph] *would fly,* giving praise. *With two he would cover his face,* so that he might not gaze upon the Shechinah. *With two he would cover his feet,* so that they might not be exposed to the Shechinah[a]. It is written, *The soles of their feet were like the sole of a calf's foot* [Ezekiel 1:7]; and it is written, *They made themselves a molten calf* [Exodus 32:8]. The purpose? *There shall no more be anything that brings the iniquity of the house of Israel into remembrance.*

---

3 After I had completed this manuscript, Lewis M. Barth shared with me his paper "Oxen, Calves and the Heavenly Source of Idolatry" (as yet unpublished), which he discussed at the December 1984 meeting of the Society of Biblical Literature. Stimulated by certain remarks I had made in *The Merkabah in Rabbinic Literature*, Barth closely examined several of the texts discussed here – *Mekhilta* to Exodus 14:29, *Lev. R.* 27:3, Tanh. Buber *'Emor* #23, *Ex. R.* 43:8, BT Hag. 13b – and came to conclusions very similar to my own. Barth's perspective is somewhat different from mine, and he elucidates important issues that I have not dealt with. Yet, given that we proceeded unaware of each other's work, the overall agreement of our deductions from the sources argues powerfully for their correctness.

4 Tanh. *'Emor* #8 = Tanh. Buber *'Emor* #11 (ed. 45b [222]) quotes the *petiḥah* without changing it in any significant way. We will presently see that another passage in *Tanḥuma* makes more creative use of this midrash.

5 I do not know how he understands the word *lemibtaḥ* (RSV, "the reliance"), if he indeed took it into account at all. I leave it out of my translation.

[B] We learned [in the Mishnah] that "the horn of any animal may be used [as the *shofar*, the trumpet blown on New Year's Day], apart from the cow's." Why is the cow's horn excepted? Because it is a calf's horn; and it is written, *They made themselves a molten calf*[6]. The purpose? *There shall no more be anything that brings the iniquity of the house of Israel into remembrance.* ...

[I omit paragraphs C and D, which illustrate the expositor's understanding of Ezekiel 29:16 without reference to the calf.]

[E] So it is in the passage at hand: *When an ox, lamb, or goat is born* [Leviticus 22:27]. Do we speak of an ox being born? Is it not a calf that we speak of as being born? But because it is written, *They made themselves a molten calf*, Scripture chose to call it an ox rather than a calf: *an ox, lamb, or goat.*

The expositor's argument perhaps suffers slightly from overkill. We may well wonder at a taboo on "calf" that is wide enough to encompass "cow" (paragraph B), but not "ox" as well (paragraph E). Besides, Psalm 106:20 calls the golden calf "a grass-eating ox," and we will soon see that this was enough to effect the removal of the ox's face from Ezekiel's *ḥayyot*. We will also see that the author of a *Tanḥuma* midrash, reshaping this *petiḥah*, discarded the untenable distinction between "calf" and "ox" and thus reinterpreted Leviticus 22:27. The midrash at hand, however, is less interested in logical consistency than in rhetorical effectiveness in getting its point across: because the Israelites once *made themselves a molten calf*, the divine mercy takes care to put out of sight anything that might serve, however remotely, to remind God of this atrocity.

b) Third-century parallels. The expositor is identified as Abbahu, a Palestinian Amora active at the end of the third century. I know no reason to doubt this attribution, but also no way to confirm it. There is, however, other evidence that the ideas expressed in the *petiḥah* were circulating in Palestine late in the third century. PT's Gemara to R.H. 3:2 (58d), explaining why the horn of a mountain goat can be used as a *shofar* but not that of a cow, quotes Abbahu's contemporary Levi:

It [the case of the cow's horn] is different: a prosecuting attorney cannot become an advocate.

Similarly, BT R.H. 26a:

ᶜUlla said: The rabbis' reason [for excluding the cow's horn, in M. R.H. 3:2] is the same as that expressed by Rab Hisda. For Rab Hisda said: Why does the high priest not wear his golden robes when he enters the Holy of Holies to perform the rites [of the Day of Atonement]? Because a prosecuting attorney cannot become an advocate.

---

6 I translate rather freely, to bring the point across. The quotation from the Mishnah (R.H. 3:2) runs, more literally: "All *shofarot* [horns] may be used, apart from the cow's, because it is a *qeren* [another word for horn]." The point seems to be that any animal's horn may be considered a *shofar*, except for the cow's, because the Bible calls it *qeren* (or, only *qeren*, to the exclusion of *shofar*). The expositor, after quoting the first part of the mishnah and asking the reason for the exception, answers by quoting the mishnah's conclusion, with an addition of his own: "Because it is a *qeren* – of a calf." The additional words "of a calf," of course, completely change the mishnah's meaning.

Hisda's point is that the gold of the priest's robes would be a reminder of the gold of the calf, and thus would bear witness against the Jewish people on the day of the year when they most need forgiveness. ᶜUlla, who emigrated from Palestine to Babylonia around the end of the third century, doubtless brought with him the ideas circulating in his homeland. He therefore applied the reasoning of his Babylonian contemporary Hisda to the issue of the cow's horn.

We saw in chapter IV that Resh Laqish, a Palestinian of the generation preceding Levi and ᶜUlla, uses the same maxim as theirs to explain why there is no ox's face in Ezekiel 10:14:

> Resh Laqish said: Ezekiel begged for mercy concerning it [the ox's face], and he changed it to a cherub. "Lord of the universe," [Ezekiel] said, "can a prosecuting attorney become an advocate?" [BT Hag. 13b, paragraph G]

Anything that hints at the golden calf is permanently (to change the Talmudic image slightly) a witness for the prosecution, testifying to the defendant's miserable character.

In what setting did these interpretations circulate? The fact that several of them are expressed in a *petiḥah* — which, unlike the *petiḥah* we considered in the previous chapter, is attributed in its entirety to one rabbi, and sounds like it could actually have been used as a sermon — points to the synagogue. So does the fact that paragraph A's exegesis of Isaiah 6:2 seems to build on that found in Targum Jonathan:

> *Each had six wings. With two he would cover his face*, so that he might not see. *With two he would cover* his genitals[b], so that he might not be seen. *With two he would* serve.

Our expositor needs literal "feet" for the seraphim, so of course he cannot follow the Targum in making them into genitals. In accord with the synagogue tradition, he explains how the seraph "serves" God by flying: his wings generate a chant of praise. We have seen that the conflation of seraphim and *ḥayyot* was part of the hymnic tradition, from its very beginnings.

c) Tanḥuma. A midrash quoted in Tanh. *'Emor* #16 and Tanh. Buber *'Emor* #23 (ed. 49a–b [222]), immediately after the passage that I translated above (pp. 158–159), draws together around Leviticus 22:27 what reads like an anthology of third-century Palestinian midrash on the subject of the *merkabah* and the calf. The compiler's sources plainly included part, at least, of the midrash attributed to Abbahu.

I translate Buber's text:

> *An ox, lamb, or goat.* Why did God order them to sacrifice an ox? To make atonement for *the likeness of an ox* [Psalm 106:20]. So it is written: *He forgives all your sins*, and so forth [*heals all your illnesses*; Psalm 103:3].
>
> You may know that this is so from what Scripture says: *Each one had four faces and four wings* [Ezekiel 1:6]. What does the text say there? *Their legs were straight, and the soles of their*

feet were like the soles of a calf's foot [1:7]. For the sake of Israel's atonement, [God] added two more wings; as it is written, [*Each had*] *six wings* [Isaiah 6:2]. For what reason? To cover their feet, which looked like a calf's, so that he should not see them and remember the calf episode: *With two he would cover his feet.* What was the purpose of all this? To make atonement for Israel. *He forgives all your sins.*

There is no bird greater than the eagle. It became a face for the *ḥayyot*; as it is written, *An eagle's face for all four of them* [Ezekiel 1:10]. The greatest of beasts is the lion. It was made a face for the *ḥayyot*; as it is written, *First, a lion's face* [Ezekiel 10:14, misquoted]. The ox is the greatest of animals. [God] made it a face for the *ḥayyot;* as it is written, *An ox's face for all four of them* [1:10]. And *a human face*[7]. For Israel's sake God erased the ox and put a cherub in its place. Hence, later on, we find that Scripture mentions only the cherub, as it is written, *First, a cherub's face* [10:14]. What was the purpose of all this? To make atonement for Israel. Well spoke Scripture: *He forgives all your sins.*

Although the content of this midrash corresponds to some extent with that of BT Ḥag. 13b (paragraphs F–G, J), I see no evidence that the *Tanḥuma* source is dependent on BT. On the contrary: the compiler of Ḥag. 13b may have used a Palestinian collection of *merkabah* midrashim, like the one *Tanḥuma* preserves for us, as both a source and a model for his own more extensive anthology. The *Tanḥuma* passage gives the impression of having once been a *petiḥah* to Leviticus 22:27 from Psalm 103:3, along the lines of the *petiḥah* to this verse attributed to Abbahu. If so, it is possible that BT Ḥag. 13b's debt to the synagogue tradition was considerably greater than the claims I made for it in the preceding chapter.

All of this may seem to argue against any notion that the *merkabah*'s connection with the golden calf was a particularly sore point for the rabbis. If I have correctly interpreted the sources we have just finished examining, certain rabbis expounded this subject from the pulpit for all to hear. We might well have treated the resulting midrashim in chapter IV, with other themes belonging to the synagogue tradition.

But this inference is only partly true. The elements linking the *merkabah* to the calf were a fit topic for public discourse as long as they were brought to bear only on the simpler of the questions raised by the calf episode – has God truly forgiven us for this sin? – which was then, as always, answered with a yes. When the evidence from Ezekiel's *merkabah* was applied to the more profound question of how the sin came to be committed in the first place, silence fell. In the source we are about to consider, we can hear the silence descend.

---

7 These words, quoted from either Ezekiel 1:10 or 10:14, are found both in the printed *Tanḥuma* and in the manuscripts Buber used. They play no role at all in the midrash as it stands, but survive from an older version which represented the human as superior to the three animals (BT Ḥag. 13b, paragraph F, and the parallels cited in chapter IV, section 3d).

3. Mekhilta to Exodus 14:29

a) *Four exegetical dialogues.* The Tannaitic midrash to Exodus (*Mekhilta*) that is conventionally associated with the name of R. Ishmael, and the one called after R. Simeon b. Yohai, both incorporate into their midrash of Exodus 14:29 a series of four brief dialogues between R. Akiba and a "R. Papias." All of these dialogues have the same stereotypic format. Each deals with the interpretation of a different Biblical verse. Akiba's interpretation of one of these verses, Song 1:9, makes reference to Exodus 14:29; the two *Mekhiltas* therefore include the entire series. Of the four dialogues, only the one that deals with Psalm 106:20 directly concerns us. To understand it, however, we must examine its neighbors as well.

Except in the order of the dialogues, the two versions do not materially differ. The progress of the discussion, however, is much easier to follow in the *Mekhilta of R. Ishmael* than in the *Mekhilta of R. Simeon* (ed. 68 [196]), where the speakers often change without explicit notice. I therefore translate the former source, according to Lauterbach's edition (*Be-Shallah* chapter 7, ed./tr. 1:247–249 [195]).

[A1] R. Papias expounded: [*I have likened you, my love,*] *to a mare in Pharaoh's chariotry* [Song 1:9]. Pharaoh rode on a stallion [at the Red Sea]. God appeared to him, if one may say so, on a stallion; as it is written, *You trod the sea with your horses,* and so forth [Habakkuk 3: 15][8]. Pharaoh rode on a mare. God appeared to him, if one may say so, on a mare; as it is written, *To a mare,* and so forth [*in Pharaoh's chariotry*].
R. Akiba said to him: Enough, Papias!
He said to him: How then do you explain the words, *to a mare in Pharaoh's chariotry?*
[A2] He said to him: The *Ketib* reads *Issty*[9]. God said: "Just as I rejoiced to destroy the Egyptians, so I nearly rejoiced to destroy the Israelites." What saved them? [Torah] *to their right and* [phylacteries] *to their left* [Exodus 14:29][10].
[B1] R. Papias expounded: *He is one, who can rebut him?* and so forth. [*What he desires, that he does*; Job 23:13]. He judges by himself all who enter the world, and none can rebut his words.
R. Akiba said to him: Enough, Papias!
He said to him: How then do you explain the words, *he is one, who can rebut him?*

---

8 The Hebrew word for "horses" used in this verse is masculine; hence, the expositor thinks of a stallion. – Mysteriously, *Mekhilta of R. Simeon* replaces this proof text with Psalm 18:11, which does not mention horses, but has God riding a cherub. Perhaps some transmitter of the midrash was influenced by a text like Tanh. *Shofetim* #14, where Pharaoh rides a horse and God a cherub; or like *Song R.* to 1:9 (translated below, chapter VI, section 4).

9 Akiba's point is that the last four consonants can be read *sasti,* "I rejoiced," instead of *susati,* "mare." – I explain the word "*Ketib*" in chapter IV, section 2e.

10 Akiba's reply presupposes another midrash of Exodus 14:29, which *Mekhilta* quotes right before this dialogue. The expositor has detached *to their right and to their left* from the beginning of the verse, and understood these words as referring to the two things that saved the Israelites: Torah, which Deuteronomy 33:2 seems to equate with *to his right*; and phylacteries (reading *tefillin* instead of *tefillah,* "prayer"), which one wears on the *left* arm. This exegesis is, to say the least, very forced.

[B2] He said to him: There is no way one can rebut him who spoke and the world came into being; but [he does] all in truth and all in justice.

[C1] R. Papias expounded: *The man has become like one of us* [Genesis 3:22]: like one of the angels.

R. Akiba said: Enough, Papias!

He said to him: How then do you explain the words, *the man has become like one of us*?

[C2] He said to him: Not like one of the angels; but God set before him two paths, the path of life and the path of death, and he chose the path of death.

[D1] R. Papias expounded: *They exchanged their glory for the likeness of an ox that eats grass* [Psalm 106:20]. I might think that this refers to the celestial ox [*shor shel ma^clah*]. Therefore Scripture says, *that eats grass*.

R. Akiba said to him: Enough, Papias!

He said to him: How then do you explain the words, *they exchanged their glory for the likeness of an ox that eats grass*?

[D2] [Akiba replied:] I might think that this refers to an ox in its normal condition[c]. Therefore Scripture says, *that eats grass*. There is nothing more repulsive and disgusting than an ox when it is eating grass.

This series of exchanges is difficult in a number of respects. The great R. Akiba, who is throughout given the last word, offers a series of Biblical interpretations which are strained to the point of unintelligibility. His comment on Psalm 106:20, in particular, seems meaningless. What is the difference between "an ox in its normal condition" and an ox eating grass? Since when is there "nothing more repulsive and disgusting than an ox when it is eating grass"? Papias's remarks are normally more or less lucid, but his interpretation of Psalm 106:20 leaves us baffled, since we do not know what the "celestial ox" is. And who is R. Papias, anyway?

b) Akiba, Pappus, and the dialogues' author. Let us begin with the last question. The Mishnah mentions a "R. Papias," often with Joshua b. Hananiah, as a figure spanning the times before and after the destruction of the Second Temple[d]. If we accept Lauterbach's reading of the name of Akiba's opponent as "R. Papias," we have little choice but to identify him with the man mentioned in the Mishnah. But it is hard to imagine that the author of *Mekhilta*'s dialogues would represent Akiba as speaking to a senior scholar so rudely and contemptuously.

Moreover, the reading of the name is far from certain. Other witnesses to *Mekhilta*'s text (cited in Horovitz's apparatus [193]) give it as "Pappus"; *Mekhilta of R. Simeon* reads "Papius"; the various manuscripts of *Gen. R.* 21:5 (ed. 200–201 [188]), which draws upon paragraphs C1–2, use all three forms. Further, the manuscripts do not consistently apply to him the title "rabbi." All of this leads us to suspect that we are not dealing with Joshua b. Hananiah's contemporary R. Papias, but with the rather better-known Pappus b. Judah.

Pappus b. Judah appears in rabbinic sources as a slightly comic stock figure. R. Meir is reported to have used him as a proverbial example of an absurdly jealous husband (T. Sot. 5:9, PT Sot. 1:7, 17a, BT Gitt. 90a; but

PT Qidd. 4:4, 65d, and *Numb. R.* 9:12 call him "Judah b. Pappus"). A story quoted twice in the Palestinian Talmud makes "Judah b. Pappus" or "Pappus b. Judah" [286,328,382] a contemporary of Gamaliel II and Joshua b. Hananiah, and represents his extreme strictness as inappropriate and faintly ridiculous (PT Ber. 2:9, 5d, B.B. 5:1, 15a [286]). Most important, a baraita quoted in BT Ber. 61b uses "Pappus b. Judah" as a foil to R. Akiba. Why, Pappus wonders, is Akiba not afraid to teach the Torah in public, in defiance of a Roman edict? Akiba replies with a trenchant fable. When both are put in prison — Akiba for Torah, Pappus for "vain things" — Pappus admits his error. The author of the story can count on his audience's pleasure at hearing Akiba, the hero of Torah, set this timid buffoon straight.

I think that the author of *Mekhilta*'s dialogues is also capitalizing on this image of Pappus. Pappus's opinions are everlastingly wrong, everlastingly in need of correction by Akiba's riper wisdom. Pappus thus becomes a convenient mouthpiece for Biblical interpretations that the author dislikes and wants to see discredited. I cannot insist that the historical Akiba and the historical Pappus (whoever the latter may have been) had nothing to do with the exegeses reported in their names. But I think we best understand *Mekhilta*'s dialogues if we take them as representing first and foremost the attitudes of the anonymous individuals who composed them, and not those of the men whom they name.

When were the dialogues written? I cannot imagine that they are earlier than Akiba's death, about 135 A.D. On the other hand, they cannot be later than the editing of the *Mekhilta*, which the scholarly consensus (recently defended by Günter Stemberger against Ben Zion Wacholder's criticisms [341,350]) places in the third century. As we will see, the use of the expression "celestial ox" points to a relatively early date.

The exegeses that the dialogues attribute to Pappus share two features. They are relatively straightforward interpretations of the passages in question, and they are in one way or another theologically questionable. Akiba's exegeses, by contrast, are very forced and implausible, but yield more acceptable results. Thus, Pappus's natural and reasonable explanation of Genesis 3:22 raises Adam to the rank of the angels, among whom God is, at best, first among equals. Akiba's interpretation is so farfetched that we are not at all sure how the author has managed to torture this meaning out of the text [189]. But it avoids divinizing Adam, and at the same time preaches belief in free will, which the Mishnah (Abot 3:15) attributes to R. Akiba. Pappus's interpretation of Song 1:9 is not only wildly anthropomorphic[11], but represents the miracle at the Red Sea as a mythological

---

11 When Louis Finkelstein argued from this passage that Akiba opposed anthropomorphism, Gedal-

contest between two more or less equal champions; Akiba's emphasizes the saving power of Torah and phylacteries. Commenting on Job 23:13, Akiba softens the arbitrary exercise of power that Pappus attributes to God. In all of these cases, Pappus's explanation is closer to the apparent meaning of the Biblical text.

c) The ox. What about the fourth dialogue? In particular, what about the "celestial ox"?

We might at first think that the author intends the constellation Taurus. Alternatively, we might look beyond Jewish literature and imagine that we have here a dim echo of the "bull of heaven" described in the *Epic of Gilgamesh,* a murderous monster fashioned and sent to earth by the goddess Ishtar, and then dispatched by the epic's heroes [31,35,44]. But neither suggestion explains the force of Pappus's statement, or of Akiba's response. Rabbinic sources point to a better alternative.

Rabbinic texts normally refer to Ezekiel's *hayyot* as *hayyot haqqodesh,* "the holy *hayyot.*" But the Tannaitic midrashim occasionally preserve what appear to be more archaic titles. Thus, *Sifra* to Leviticus 1:1 (*Nedabah, pereq* 1:1), according to ms Assemani 66 [217], calls them *hayyot hannisse'ot,* "the exalted *hayyot.*" The somewhat later parallel in *Sifre Numb.* #103 (ed. 101–102 [221]) replaces this unfamiliar phrase with the more conventional *hayyot haqqodesh*[e]. A baraita, quoted in BT R.H. 24b and ᶜA.Z. 43b, uses the conventional term when it deduces from Exodus 20:20 that one may not "make the image of my [God's] servants who serve before me in the heights, such as Ophannim, seraphim, *hayyot haqqodesh,* and angels." But a passage from the *Mekhilta of R. Simeon* (ed. 147 [196])[f], which derives the same lesson from Exodus 20:4, calls the *hayyot* by a different name:

> When Scripture says, [*You shall not make for yourself ...*] *any likeness,* it bans their [?] likeness. It also bans [with the subsequent words *that is in the water beneath the earth*] the likeness of their reflection. It bans [with the words *that is on the earth beneath*] the likeness of evil beasts [*hayyot raᶜot*]; it bans [with the words *that is in heaven above*] the likeness of celestial *hayyot* [*hayyot shel maᶜlah*].

It seems clear that "celestial *hayyot,*" like *Sifra*'s "exalted *hayyot,*" is an early rabbinic term for the beings that Ezekiel saw. The "celestial ox" (*shor shel maᶜlah*) is the ox-element of the *hayyot,* envisioned, as in Revelation 4:7, as a distinct entity.

---

iahu Alon objected, on the ground that we elsewhere find anthropomorphic haggadot attributed to Akiba [384,364]. Alon's observation supports my opinion that the viewpoint here is not Akiba's, but that of the anonymous author.

We still do not understand how Pappus and Akiba differ. They agree, after all, that the *likeness of an ox* that the Israelites worshipped in the desert was *not* the ox of the *merkabah*. This difficulty led Horovitz [194] to prefer the version of this dialogue given in *Midr. Psalms* 106:6 (ed. 228a –b [199]):

> They exchanged their glory for the likeness of an ox that eats grass. R. Papias said: For the celestial ox. R. Akiba said to him: Enough, Papias! It is written, *that eats grass*, [meaning] in the springtime, when it is filthy.

But we do not have to choose this derivative and confused version over that attested in the older sources. We can explain *Mekhilta*'s text by assuming that the dialogues' author found the notion, that the calf of the desert apostasy was the ox of the *merkabah*, so unbearably hideous that he would not tolerate a midrash that referred to it even as a theoretical possibility. By hook or by crook, he had to find an alternative midrash to give R. Akiba. The one he came up with made no sense at all. But anything was better than the midrash he attributed to Pappus. Anything, that is, but those exegeses that Pappus's was plainly intended to refute, which declared that the ox whose likeness the Israelites worshipped *was* that of the *merkabah*.

d) The dialogues and the later midrashim. Do we have any hope of unearthing these exegeses? There is, to begin with, one encouraging sign. We sometimes find that the editors of later midrashim remove the "Pappus" expositions from the garbage can into which the author of *Mekhilta*'s dialogues had thrown them, dust them off, and put them to use. Of course, these editors cannot declare Pappus right and Akiba wrong. But they can rehabilitate the ideas attributed to Pappus by ignoring or even by switching the attributions. Thus:

> R. Papias expounded: *To a mare in Pharaoh's chariotry*. The *Ketib* reads *lssty*. ... [And so forth, as in paragraph A2, above.]
> R. Akiba said to him: Enough, Papias! ... Rather, Pharaoh rode on a stallion. God appeared to him, if one may say so, on a stallion. ... [*Song R.* to 1:9]

And so on. Under the aegis of R. Akiba, the writer goes on to indulge his and his audience's taste for colorful combat myths by spinning a long baroque account of how God matched each of the tactics that Pharaoh used against him at the Red Sea — while, no doubt, the original author of the dialogue turns over and over in his grave. Other late midrashim treat Song 1:9 similarly: Tanh. *Shofeṭim* #14, *Midr. Psalms* 18:14 (ed. 71b–72b [199])[g].

The writer quoted in *Song R.* manipulates the discussion of Genesis 3:22 in a similar way:

> R. Papias expounded: *The man has become like one of us*: like the Unique One of the universe.
> R. Akiba said to him: Enough, Papias! ... Like one of the angels.

But the sages say: Neither is correct. Rather, Scripture teaches that God set before him [Adam] two paths, the path of life and the path of death, and he chose the path of death, abandoning the path of life.

The writer allows the interpretation given in paragraph C2 of the *Mekhilta* to remain authoritative. But he fobs off on "Papias" an opinion earlier attributed to the Amora R. Judah b. R. Simon (*Gen. R.* 21:5, ed. 200–201 [188]), and thus can attribute the exegesis of paragraph C1 to the more respectable Akiba. His aim was doubtless to justify the popularity of this exegesis, which underlies a whole series of haggadic midrashim[h].

When we add that two later midrashic works (*Numb. R.* 14:6 and *Deut. R.* 1:10) make use of the exegesis of Job 23:13 that *Mekhilta* puts in the mouth of Pappus, we are tempted to conclude that the author's disapproval did not much affect the popularity of the midrashim against which it was directed[i]. But this would be too hasty, and would ignore the fact that the midrashic sources that draw on "Pappus's" exegeses tend to be late. We have found several *Tanḥuma* midrashim that use these exegeses. But, as far as I know, none of them occurs in the Tannaitic midrashim; or, with one exception (*Gen. R.* 21:1), in the "classical Palestinian midrashim."

It looks very much as if the *Mekhilta* author's efforts to suppress the midrashim he found objectionable were indeed successful, but only for a time. As generations passed, his reasons for disapproving of them seemed less and less compelling, the midrashim themselves more and more attractive. The old expositions emerged from eclipse – in *Song R.* to 1:9 we can watch them coming out of the shadow – and entered the later midrashic collections. We thus may reasonably look to these late collections for early midrash, setting forth what the second- or third-century author of *Mekhilta*'s dialogues regarded as the dreadful secret of the *merkabah*.

4. Exodus Rabbah 43:8

a) Introduction. The *Tanḥuma* sources contain one such midrash, which appears in four different versions. Our examination of *Mekhilta*'s dialogues may predispose us to regard this midrash as old. But we are not thereby relieved of the need to demonstrate the midrash's antiquity; and, to this end, we must put some effort into tracing its evolution.

The focus of the midrash is Exodus 3:7. Speaking from the burning bush, God tells Moses: "I have surely seen the affliction of my people ... for I have come to know its sufferings." *I have surely seen* translates a Hebrew idiom in which the verb "see" is used twice (*ra'oh ra'iti*). We might render, more literally: *seeing, I have seen.*

The rabbis, who have a penchant for pressing idiomatic repetitions of this sort (cf. chapter IV, section 2g), deduce from the doubled verb that

God saw two "visions" of his people while they were still in Egypt. These "visions" might be of Israel's present degradation and of its future glory (below). But, more often, they are understood as being of the suffering that Israel presently endures (which naturally awakens God's sympathies), and of the atrocity that it is going to commit.

In support of the second view, the expositor can appeal to the fact that the verb *I have seen* (*ra'iti*) recurs in Exodus 32:9, in reference to the calf-worship: *I have seen this people to be a stiff-necked people*. Even *the affliction of my people* (3:7) turns out to have a double meaning, as we will see.

A *petiḥah* leading from Job 11:11 to Exodus 3:7, preserved in Tanh. *Shemot* #20, briefly and clearly sets forth this understanding of the latter verse:

> He [God] *knew the men of vanity. He saw sin, yet paid no attention* [Job 11:11]. God said to Moses: "I see two visions: *ra'oh* [and] *ra'iti. I have seen* and *I have come to know its* [the Israel-ite people's] *sufferings* [Exodus 3:7], and I will therefore now redeem them[12]. But also *I have seen this people to be a stiff-necked people* [Exodus 32:9], who are going to anger me by making the calf."

Similar understandings of Exodus 3:7 underlie the texts to which we now turn. I arrange these texts in what I consider the order of their development, a view which I will presently defend. To make it easier to refer back to them, I assign a Roman numeral to each.

b) The texts.

[I: *Ex. R.* 43:8.]

[A] [Moses, pleading with God to forgive the people for worshipping the calf, asks: *Why, Lord, should you be angry with your people*,] *whom you brought forth from the land of Egypt* [Exodus 32:11]?

Why did it occur to Moses to mention the Exodus at this point? R. Judah b. Shalom quoted R. Judah b. Simon, quoting R. Levi b. Perata: To what may we compare it? ... [There follows a parable, too long to translate here, about a man who buys a slave with full knowledge of the slave's bad character, and who therefore cannot reasonably punish the slave's bad behavior. The point of the parable follows:]

[B] Thus spoke Moses: "Master of the world, did you not say to me: *Go, that I may send you to Pharaoh* [Exodus 3:10]? And did I not reply: 'By what merit are you redeeming them? They are idol-worshippers.' And did you not answer back: 'You see them now, as idol-worshippers. But I see them as they go forth from Egypt. I will split the sea for them and bring them into the desert, and I will give them my Torah and show them my glory face to face. And they will accept my rulership; and, after forty days, will rebel against me and make the calf.'"

[C] This is what Scripture says: *I have surely seen the affliction* [^coni] *of my people* [Exodus 3:7]. This refers to the sound of the calf: *I hear the sound of affliction* [^cannot; Exodus 32:18][13].

---

12 Other midrashim understand this verse in a similar way, but give a different twist to *its sufferings*: they are not the sufferings that the Israelites endure in Egypt, but those they are going to inflict on God when they make the calf (*Deut. R.* 3:9, followed by *Ex. R.* 3:2).

13 RSV translates *qol* ^c*annot 'anokhi shomea*^c (32:18) as "the sound of singing that I hear," the

[D] "Even before they were redeemed [Moses continued] you told me they were going to make the calf, and now that they have made it you intend to kill them?"

That was why he mentioned the Exodus in his defence.

[E1] R. Phinehas ha-Kohen b. Hama quoted R. Abbahu, quoting R. Jose b. Hanina: [E2] What is the meaning of *I have surely seen* [*ra'oh ra'iti*; Exodus 3:7]? [E3] God said to Moses: [E4] "You see them [as they are] now. [E5] But I see how they are going to contemplate me: I will be going forth in my carriage [*qarukhin*] to give them the Torah (as it is written, *The divine chariotry is two myriads, thousands of shin'an* [Psalm 68:18]); and they will detach one of my team [*tetramulin*] (as it is written, *An ox's face on the left* [Ezekiel 1:10]) [and anger me with it^j)]."

[II: *Ex. R.* 42:5. The context is a discussion of Exodus 32:7, where God says to Moses: *Go, descend, for your people which you brought out of Egypt has behaved corruptly.*]

[A] When Moses realized that matters stood thus, he said [to himself]: "They will never be forgiven." God realized what Moses was thinking, and called to him to comfort him.

[B1] He said: "Did I not tell you, while you [!] were in the bush, what they were going to do?" [B2] So it is written: *The Lord said: I have surely seen* [*ra'oh ra'iti*]. [B3] God said to Moses: [B4] "You see one vision, but I see two. You see them coming to Sinai and receiving my Torah. [B5] But I see that, after I come to Sinai to give them the Torah, while I am returning with my team [*tetramulin*], they will contemplate it and detach one of them and anger me with it. So it is written, *An ox's face on the left for all four of them* [Ezekiel 1:10]. They will anger me with it. So it is written, *They exchanged their glory for the likeness of an ox* [Psalm 106:20]."

[C] Another explanation. *I have surely seen*, and so forth. What is the meaning of *the affliction of my people*? It refers to the sound of the calf[14].

[III. Tanh. *Ki Tissa'* #21. Same context as II.]

[A] When Moses heard this, he said [to himself]: "They will never again be forgiven." God realized what Moses was thinking.

[B1] God said to him: "Did I not say to you in the bush: [B2] '*I have surely seen* [*ra'oh ra'iti*]. [B3 omitted.] [B4] You see one vision, but I see two. [B5] I see them coming to Sinai and receiving my Torah, as I descend on Sinai with my team [*tetramulin*]. [And I see] that they will contemplate it^k), and detach one of them, and anger me with it. So it is written, *An ox's face on the left,* and so forth [Ezekiel 1:10]; and it is written, *They exchanged their glory for the likeness of an ox* [Psalm 106:20].'"

[IV. *Ex. R.* 3:2. The context is a *petihah* leading from Job 11:11 to Exodus 3:7; cf. Tanh. *Shemot* #20, translated above.]

[A1] ...While the Israelites were still in Egypt, God saw what they were going to do. [A2] So it is written: *The Lord said: I have surely seen.* The text does not say, *I have seen* [*ra'iti*], but *I have surely seen* [*ra'oh ra'iti*].

[A3] God said to Moses: [A4] "You see one vision, but I see two. You see them coming to Sinai and receiving my Torah; I, too, see them receiving my Torah. This is what is indicated by

---

reference being to the celebration in the calf's honor. But the root of *^cannot* (*^cny*) looks the same as that of *^coni,* "affliction," and the expositor uses the resemblance to connect Exodus 3:7 with 32:18 and to detect in the former verse a specific reference to the calf-worship. I translate 32:18 the way I think he understood it. (Philologists tell us that two distinct Semitic roots have coalesced into Hebrew *^cny;* but our expositor did not know that, and probably would not have cared if he did.) — *Qol shel ^cegel,* "the sound [or voice] of the calf," might mean the noise made by its worshippers. But, in view of the sources that have the golden calf emit a bovine sound (below), I prefer to take it literally. Later in this chapter, we will try to make sense of the allusion.

14 *Qehal ha^cegel,* "the congregation of the calf," is an obvious error for *qol ha^cegel,* "the sound of the calf." See above, paragraph IC.

ra'oh. [A5] But *ra'iti* refers to a vision of the calf episode [or, "the making of the calf"]. So it is written: *I have seen* [that] *this people* [Exodus 32:9], when I come to Sinai to give them the Torah and descend with my team [*tetramuli*], will contemplate me and detach one of them and anger me with it."

c) How the midrash evolved. The first three of these passages occur in midrashim belonging to the *Tanḥuma* group: the printed *Tanḥuma* and the second part of *Exodus Rabbah.* The fourth text is from the first part of *Exodus Rabbah,* which most regard as a much later source [275a,362]. This does not by itself prove that the fourth passage is later than the first three. But it does justify us in at least provisionally setting text IV aside, and examining the three *Tanḥuma* passages as a group.

All three passages make use of a midrash on Exodus 3:7, which elaborates the opening words (*ra'oh ra'iti*) of God's speech to Moses from the burning bush (IE, IIB, IIIB). All three introduce the midrash into the context of a later, less happy, conversation between God and Moses. All three provide a framework that links the earlier dialogue to the later one (IA, D, IIA, IIIA). The first two passages include within the framework a distinct midrash on the words *the affliction of my people* (IC, IIC). Oddly, the first passage does not place its midrash of *ra'oh ra'iti* inside the framework, but lets it dangle gracelessly afterward. In its place (IB) is another recollection of the burning bush conversation; which turns out, when examined carefully, to be a second midrash on *ra'oh ra'iti.*

Someone has plainly tampered with the text of IB. As the passage stands, God's ability to see the future as well as the present gives him little advantage over Moses. Moses sees the Israelites as idol-worshippers in the present; God sees them as idol-worshippers in the future; we get no explanation of why he thinks they are worth redeeming. The midrash must originally have ended with "face to face," or perhaps with "rulership." It made the point that God rescued the Israelites, not on account of their degraded and idolatrous present, but for the sake of their future glory as his kingdom of priests and holy people. But the editor who inserted the midrash into its present context needed it to prove that God foresaw the making of the calf, and therefore tacked on an ending that spoiled its entire point.

Why did he have to do this? After all, he had another midrash of *ra'oh ra'iti* (IE) which made exactly the point he wanted. Why did he not put IE in the place where IB now stands, instead of leaving it as an awkward postscript to his composition? The only sensible explanation is that the original compiler of the passage had no knowledge of IE. Another, later, editor tacked it on at the end.

When we turn to text II, we find that the editor of this passage has indeed put IE in the place of IB (=IIB). But he has not integrated it very well into its new context. He has, of course, knocked off the opening attribution to "R. Phinehas ha-Kohen b. Hama quoting R. Abbahu, quoting R. Jose b. Hanina," which would not quite suit a discussion between God and Moses, and replaced it with a more appropriate introduction. But, incongruously, he introduces the quotation of Exodus 3:7 with "so it is written" (IIB2), and keeps "God said to Moses" (IIB3). IIB1, "while you were in the bush," suggests that the editor draws also on a source that, like IB, had Moses addressing God; he has forgotten to correct the pronoun.

The editor of text III smooths out all of these roughnesses. He also deletes the brief midrash of *the affliction of my people* (IC), which the editor of text II had retained but made unintelligible by omitting the quotation of Exodus 32:18.

Tracing the midrash of *ra'oh ra'iti* from text I to text III, then, we see a block of material wedged into a structure for which it had not originally been shaped, and the roughnesses resulting from this fit gradually planed and polished away. Alongside this process, we notice a certain degeneration in the internal logic of the midrash. In IE, the contrast between Moses' vision and God's is clear: Moses sees only the present, God sees also the future. But the arithmetic of *ra'oh ra'iti* seduces the editor of text II into thinking that God saw two prophetic visions and that Moses therefore must have seen one. He therefore gratuitously credits Moses with a vision of the Sinai revelation. The editor of text·III, realizing that no issue of Moses' prophetic power is involved, deletes from B4 all reference to what Moses saw, and thus leaves "you see one vision" hanging in the air.

As for text IV, I see no reason to assume that the late editor of the first part of *Exodus Rabbah* has preserved a version of the midrash older than that found in the three *Tanḥuma* passages. We can explain all of the details of this fourth version by supposing that the editor has combined IIB and IIIB, added some clarifications of his own ("the text does not say *ra'iti* but *ra'oh ra'iti*," for example), and used the finished product in a *petiḥah* modelled after that of Tanh. *Shemot* #20.

d) The earliest variant. I have discussed the development of this midrash in such detail largely because one version of it is attributed to the third-century Caesarean scholar Jose b. Hanina, while the other three are reported anonymously. If we had no theory of how the midrash evolved, we might be inclined to think that the *Tanḥuma* editors had either received or formulated an anonymous midrash, and that one of them had added a fictitious chain of authorities in order to create an antique impression. I hope to have shown that this is not so. The chain of authorities is part of the oldest form of the midrash that we have. It fell as an early sacrifice to the process of assimilating the midrash into the context that the *Tanḥuma* editors chose for it.

We cannot, indeed, jump from this to the conclusion that the chain must be authentic. Yet I think I have shifted the burden of proof to the skeptic as effectively as one can in these uncertain matters. If anyone should protest that we cannot grant a third-century date to a source that is not found in any text older than the *Tanḥuma* midrashim, I have shown in the last section why the editors of the "classical Palestinian midrashim" might not have wanted to come within sniffing distance of this haggadah.

We can now assume the priority, not only of the chain of authorities, but also of the other features unique to text I. These are the reference to God's "carriage," and the quotation of Psalm 68:18.

According to text I, God appears at Sinai in a *qarukhin,* apparently drawn by a *tetramulin.* The first of these words is a loan from Greek *karrouchion,* which is itself taken from Latin *carruca,* "carriage." Palestinian rabbinic sources use it frequently to refer to the carriages used by kings or high state officials. *Tetramulin,* also a loan-word, occurs nowhere outside the four versions of this one midrash. It seems clear that it is based on an otherwise unknown Greek form *tetramoulon,* compounded of *tetra* ("four") and *moulos,* a late Greek borrowing from Latin *mula,* "mule" [816]. But the image of God descending to Sinai in a chariot drawn by four mules is fairly silly, and I can only assume that, by Jose b. Hanina's time, *tetramoulon* had become an equivalent in Greek slang for Latin *quadrigae,* "team of four[15]." The use of a colloquial Greek heavily tinged with Latin is about what we would expect of a rabbi living in the Roman administrative center of Caesarea.

It appears that, by the time the editor of text II set to work, the memory of *tetramoulon* had faded. In text I, the word is used as a plural, like *quadrigae,* distinct from the "carriage" that the team draws. Texts II and III omit the "carriage" altogether, and are not sure whether to treat *tetramulin* as a singular ("contemplate it"[16]) or plural ("detach one of them").

In any case, it is very odd that no version of the midrash calls God's vehicle by the name we would most expect: *merkabah.* There is no doubt that the *merkabah* is intended. Even if we did not have the quotations of Psalm 68:18 and Ezekiel 1:10, the idea that the golden calf was once "one of my team" only makes sense as a reference to the ox of the *merkabah.*

---

15 My friend and colleague Gordon Newby has pointed out to me that *caballus,* the Latin ancestor of the words commonly used for "horse" in the Romance languages (French *cheval,* Spanish *caballo,* and so forth), originally meant specifically an inferior horse, a nag. I would guess that its use for horses in general was a bit of late Roman slang that eventually made its way into the language. Once upon a time, I am told, teen-agers referred to their family's car as "the jalopy"; and I imagine that similar affectionate extensions of originally derogatory terms underlie the use of *caballus* for *equus* and *tetramoulon* for *quadrigae.* Like "jalopy" for "family car," *tetramoulon* seems to have quickly passed out of fashion.

16 Unless "it" (*bo*) is simply an error for "me" (*bi*), as in IE5 and IVA5.

Text I's quotation of Psalm 68:18 is important, in that it ties this midrash to the third-century Palestinian synagogue tradition that uses this verse to prove that the Sinai revelation was a greater *merkabah* vision (above, chapter IV, section 5). We perhaps have here an underside of that tradition, reflections on it that occurred to some of the preachers when they were no longer standing before their audiences. Following the synagogue tradition, Jose b. Hanina might have dazzled his congregation with the glory that accumulated on Sinai when God descended with Ezekiel's *merkabah*, and twenty-two thousand more like it. But we can also imagine that, off by himself, he may have pondered the more sinister implications of the *merkabah*'s presence at Sinai, and its link to the event that took place forty days later.

We have no clue to the setting in which Jose b. Hanina propounded the resulting midrash, and we know only a little more about the channels through which it was passed down before it at last reached editors who were willing to make use of it. The chain of authorities in text I names Jose's disciple Abbahu as transmitter of the midrash. We recall from section 2 that Abbahu is also credited with a *petihah* that observes the link between the *merkabah* and the calf, but learns a very different lesson from it. This *petihah* perhaps represents what Abbahu was willing to say on the subject in public. To more limited circles, he revealed the midrash of Jose b. Hanina.

e) Contemplating the calf. This midrash does not say that the Israelites copied the *merkabah*-ox and worshipped its image. Rather, they "detached" it (*shamat*) from God's team. In chapter VI, we will see God "detaching" elements from the *merkabah*. We are not given any explanation of how humans would perform such an operation. But the root of the evil seems to be the Israelites' "contemplation" of the divine vehicle[17].

In chapter I, we saw that Judah the Patriarch, his colleagues, and their third-century successors were afraid of something that might happen if the Jewish people were to contemplate – with their mind's eye, presumably – Ezekiel's *merkabah* vision. Jose b. Hanina's midrash perhaps gives us our first glimpse of what they were afraid of.

The midrash thus implies a warning against contemplating the *merkabah*. But, on another level, it is itself a contemplation, which raises some disturbing questions about the *merkabah* and its role in the calf incident.

The calf, it seems, is no figment of the idolatrous imagination. Nor does it come from any clearly bounded realm of the demonic. Instead, its source

---

17 I am not aware that any other source uses this verb, *hitbonen*, in connection with the *merkabah*.

is God's own chariot. The Israelites, it is true, are blamed for having "detached" it. But what sort of an entity was it before it was detached? Divine? Devilish? What exactly is the distinction between the two categories? (We recall that this is not the first time we have had to ask this question about Ezekiel's *ḥayyot*.) If, as the midrash makes clear, God knew full well before he paraded his "carriage" before the Israelites how they were going to react, why did he do it?

I do not imagine that these questions are likely to have escaped the expositors, concealed in *Mekhilta*'s dialogues behind the name of Pappus, who tried to prove from Psalm 106:20 that the object of the desert idolatry could not have been the "celestial ox." Nor do I imagine they escaped the author of these dialogues, whom this equation so appalled that he tried to suppress even its refutation.

It need not follow, however, that the ideas that horrified the author of *Mekhilta*'s dialogues were precisely the same as those expressed in Jose b. Hanina's midrash. As we are about to learn, there existed in Talmudic times at least one other version of how the *merkabah*-ox became the golden calf, which explained far more clearly the mechanics involved in the transformation. This version placed the fatal vision of the *merkabah*, not at Sinai, but at the Red Sea. We are beginning to move back toward the problems of "water, water," and the Book of Revelation.

5. The calf, the *merkabah*, and the sea

The late Saul Lieberman, whom many have regarded as the greatest contemporary Talmudist, has laid the foundations on which much of this section rests. In his book on Yemenite midrashim and again in his monumental commentary on the Tosefta, Lieberman called attention to the Genizah midrashim that we are about to examine; he showed that their ideas underlie the Koran's story of the making of the golden calf; he proposed that they explain Tannaitic restrictions on the synagogue use of Exodus 32 [323,326]. It remains for us to clarify some of the details and the implications of this material, and to indicate how it bears on the issue of the *merkabah*.

a) Two Genizah texts. In 1928, Louis Ginzberg published a long fragment from the Genizah collection at Cambridge, which he believed to be related to the *Seder 'Eliyahu* midrashim [239][18]. The fragment contains an

---

Perhaps the presence of the same verb in Job 11:11 (which I translated above as "paid attention") has influenced the midrash's usage.

18 See Appendix I, section 9.

assortment of *haggadot*, including one tale (of R. Akiba and a damned soul) that Ginzberg believed to be drawn from Nissim b. Jacob ibn Shahin's *Book of Comfort* — which was written during the first half of the eleventh century. We are obviously dealing with a source that is late indeed.

The fragment includes a haggadah on the four directions, which declares the north to be the source of darkness and evil. In support of this view, the writer invokes Jeremiah 1:14 ("from the north evil shall break forth on all the inhabitants of the earth"), and a midrash of Song 6:12. To convey the expositor's understanding of the latter verse, we must translate it: *Do I not know? It was my* [own] *soul that induced me.* [I brought my] *chariots with me, gracious one* [that I am][19].

> When the Israelites made the calf, the heavenly retinue said: "Master of the world, uproot this people! Only yesterday they were saying, [*All that the Lord has spoken*] *we will do and we will hear* [Exodus 24:7]. But now they say, *These are your gods, Israel* [32:4]."
>
> God replied: "*Do I not know?* It is I who know best. *It was my* [own] *soul that induced me.* It was I who brought this upon myself, in that I showed them my chariots. So it is written: [I brought my] *chariots with me, gracious one* [that I am]. When they crossed the [Red] Sea, I decided to show them my chariots. When they crossed, they saw my chariots carried by the four rulers of the world, human, lion, eagle, and ox: lion over the beasts, ox over the animals, eagle over the birds, and human over all of them[1]). The o⟨x wa⟩s ⟨walking on the left⟩. After they had crossed, they ⟨hurriedly⟩ to⟨ok⟩ dust from under the ⟨feet of the⟩ o⟨x⟩". ... Thus it is ⟨written, *And out came this ca⟩lf* [Exodus 32:24], which shows that ⟨the o⟩x emerged in their presence[20].

At first, we do not see why the writer invokes the midrash in this context. But his point becomes clear when we realize that the Hebrew word *śemol*, which usually means "left," can also mean "north." The midrash's testimony, that the presence of the ox on the *left* of the *merkabah* had the most baleful consequences for the children of Israel, thus confirms the writer's view that the *north* is the source of evil.

But why do the Israelites take dust from under the ox's feet? What has this to do with Exodus 32:24, where Aaron tells Moses that *I threw it* [the people's jewellery] *into the fire, and out came this calf*?

A second Genizah midrash, which Ginzberg had published six years before (in 1922), clarifies these details [240]. The haggadah that interests us

---

19 Vocalizing *ʿimmi*, "with me," instead of MT *ʿammi*, "my people." The American Jewish Version of the Hebrew Bible [36] translates the obscure and difficult MT: "Before I was aware, my soul set me upon the chariots of my princely people." The RSV translators, permitting themselves an emendation of MT, give: "Before I was aware, my fancy set me in a chariot beside my prince."

20 In the last three sentences, I use angular brackets to mark Ginzberg's reconstructions of missing words and letters, which are based partly on the text that we will presently consider. Ginzberg's reconstructions earlier in the text are more nearly certain, and in any case do not affect our argument. I do not judge it worthwhile on their account to clutter the translation with angular brackets. — The ellipsis corresponds to three unintelligible words, *my hw' mynh*. Ginzberg thinks this may be a corruption of *mimino*, "on his right."

is attributed, for reasons we will presently consider, to one "R. Idi." But it gives every sign of being dependent on the passage in the Cambridge fragment. It spells out what the Cambridge text leaves implicit. It weaves the originally independent haggadah on the four directions[m] into the midrash on Song 6:12, while the author of the Cambridge text had been content to juxtapose the two. If the source represented in the Cambridge fragment is late, therefore, the haggadah we are about to examine is later still.

In this second version, it is the demon Sammael who accuses the Israelites of unfaithfulness. God answers with a rebuke for Sammael, and with the confession, drawn from Song 6:12, that he himself had caused the Israelites to make the calf "in that I showed them the likeness of my *merkabah*." He will punish, not his people, but "the place in which they made the calf" — that is, the north. The text explains:

> When God revealed himself at the sea, he came from the west and proceeded toward the east. God's *merkabah* has the likeness of *ḥayyot* carved in it, as it is written, *This was the likeness of their faces: a human face* [and so forth; Ezekiel 1:10]. When the Israelites saw the likeness of an ox travelling on the left [which would be the north side of the *merkabah*], they took dust from under its feet. When they made the calf, they took this dust and threw it in, with the result that it [the calf] stamped. So it is written: *I threw it into the fire, and out came this calf* [Exodus 32: 24]. Scripture does not say *I brought out*, but *out came*, teaching that it came out by its own power. What does *this* mean? That it stood up and ...

The conclusion is broken. On the basis of a similar passage quoted by the sixteenth-century Kabbalist Solomon Alkabetz, Lieberman plausibly restores the word "danced" at the end [326]. But the meaning of the passage is, in any case, clear.

While the sources we examined in the last section have God reveal his *merkabah* at Sinai, the Genizah midrashim place this event at the Red Sea. The Israelites draw the living essence of the *merkabah* ox, through the dust of its footprint, into the molten calf that they make[21]. The writer does not tell us their motive, but gives us to understand that they responded more or less naturally and blamelessly to what they saw. Although he does not quote Ezekiel 1:7, with its reference to the *sole of a calf's foot*, we can hardly doubt that this verse underlies the allusion to the ox's feet.

b) "Micah." Lieberman has discovered yet a third version of this story [323], which adds a new complication. The German Kabbalist Menahem

---

21 A story quoted anonymously (in Babylonian Aramaic) in BT Sanh. 67b similarly reflects the belief that one can get power over another creature by using dust from its footprint. "A woman once hung about R. Hanina, trying to get dust from his footprint. 'Go and do your worst,' he said to her. 'It is written, *There is none beside him.*'" (The quote is from Deuteronomy 4:35; its point here is that no witchcraft can work without God's permission.) Siegmund Fraenkel cites this passage, with parallels from classical, Christian, and Indian sources [763]. R. Campbell Thompson notes still other parallels [859a].

Siyyoni (ca. 1400) claims to have seen, in a now lost midrash on the Song of Songs, a comment on 6:12 which asserted that

> it was Micah who raised up this form. While they [the Israelites] were crossing the sea, he contemplated the vision of the *merkabah* and he kept it in his mind. He took some of the dust that was underneath the ox-element [? *ma^carekhet hashshor*] and kept it with him until the appropriate time.

Who is the "Micah" of this passage? Evidently, we are to identify him with the "man of the hill-country of Ephraim, whose name was Micah," and whose story is told in chapters 17—18 of the Book of Judges. This Micah, the Bible tells us, stole a large amount of silver from his mother. When he returned it to her, she had a portion of it made into "a graven image and a molten image," which Micah kept in his house as an object of worship until a wandering band of Danites took it for themselves.

This rather peculiar story gives us at first the impression that its events belong to an entirely different era from that of the desert wanderings. But, when we look more closely, we find that the young Levite whom Micah installs as priest to the image, and who "became to him like one of his sons" (17:11), turns out to be the grandson of Moses (18:30)[22]. Micah himself is therefore only one generation younger than Moses, and could reasonably be expected to have been present at the crossing of the Red Sea.

An early rabbinic tradition, first attested in Tannaitic midrashim, has Micah's idol cross the sea with the Israelites (*Mekhilta, Pisḥa* chapter 14, ed./tr. 1:114 [195]; other references in Ginzberg and Mandelbaum [395, 207]). It is clear from this, and from other evidence we will consider later in this chapter, that Siyyoni's reference to Micah is hardly isolated. On the contrary, haggadic traditions represent him as having begun his career as idol-maker from the time of the Exodus or even earlier. We do not fully understand the rationale of these traditions, which certainly do not fit comfortably with the apparent sense of Judges 17—18; and we must return to this problem a little later on. But we can already guess that one of their functions is to provide a new villain, who can take some of the blame that would otherwise go to Aaron. It is significant that Siyyoni's quotation represents that villain as "contemplating" (*mistakkel*) the vision of the *merkabah*.

c) Evidence from the midrashim. Given the very late date of the Genizah texts, we may well wonder if either they or Siyyoni's quotation is relevant to the study of rabbinic *merkabah* traditions. Do we find parallels or an-

---

22 The transmitters of the Hebrew text of this verse, embarrassed by the thought of Moses's grandson serving as priest to an idol, inserted the letter *nun* into the name, thus transforming it from "Moses" (*MoSHeH*) into "Manasseh" (*MeNaSHeH*). But, by keeping the *nun* slightly raised, they preserved the memory of the original reading [32a,40b].

ticipations of them in the sources that are conventionally reckoned part of
the rabbinic corpus?

One of the more striking ideas of the Genizah midrashim, that the golden
calf was animate, does occur in three midrashic texts. One of these texts
has the Egyptian magicians bring the calf to life. Another credits this alternatively to the magicians and to Micah. The third lays the blame at the
devil's doorstep.

1. *Song R.* to 1:9. We saw in section 3d how the author of this midrash
reworks *Mekhilta*'s dialogues on Song 1:9 and Genesis 3:22. He leaves the
dialogue concerning Psalm 106:20 intact, but adds to it:

> R. Judan quoted R. Aha: The Egyptian magicians performed sorceries, and it [the calf] appeared
> to leap before them [the Israelites] [n].

2. Tanh. *Ki Tiśśa'* #19. An anonymous haggadah, the purpose of which
seems to be to relieve Aaron of as much responsibility as possible, identifies
the guilty magicians as Moses' archenemies Jannes and Jambres[23]. Aaron
threw the gold into the fire, and "they performed their sorceries." Alternatively:

> Some say that it was Micah. ... He took the plaque on which Moses had drawn an ox, and by
> which he had raised Joseph's coffin. He threw it into the furnace among the jewellery, and the
> calf came out, lowing as it jumped about. They [the Israelites] began to cry, "*These are your
> gods, Israel*[24]."

3. *Pirqe de-Rabbi Eliezer,* chapter 45. Aaron throws into the furnace a
strip of gold with God's name and a picture of a calf incised upon it. "*Out
came this calf* [Exodus 32:24], lowing, and the Israelites saw it. R. Judah
says: Sammael entered into it, and it lowed, in order to deceive the Israelites. So it is written, *The ox knew its master* ... [Isaiah 1:3]." This version
of the haggadah made its way into the Palestinian Targumic tradition,
which appears on other grounds to be related to *Pirqe de-Rabbi Eliezer*
[410]. We find it in Targum Pseudo-Jonathan to Exodus 32:24, from
which it was evidently copied into the margin of Neofiti I.

Do these three passages argue for the antiquity of the tradition found in
the Genizah midrashim? Apparently not. There are some points of contact
— *Pirqe de-Rabbi Eliezer* quotes Exodus 32:24, as do the Genizah texts;
and *Tanhuma*'s statement that "the calf came out" perhaps alludes to this
verse — but in general the picture given by the older midrashic texts is quite

---

23 *Ywnws wywmbrws*; the writer's information evidently goes back to a Greek source. This pair,
who were already known to the pseudo-Pauline author of II Timothy 3:8, have a long and complicated history in Jewish legend and perhaps also Jewish magic [330,712].

24 The midrash refers to a widespread legend about how Moses raised Joseph's coffin from the Nile.
Ginzberg retells the story, Heinemann discusses it [392,407]. – I emend *no^c̣er*, "braying," to
go^c̣eh, "lowing," in accord with *Pirqe de-Rabbi Eliezer* (below). The two words look almost
alike in Hebrew.

different from that in the Genizah sources. The calf indeed comes to life, but not because of any dust from the footprint of the *merkabah*-ox.

Our second Genizah text seems twice to hint at its dependence on the older midrashim. Perhaps taking its cue from *Pirqe de-Rabbi Eliezer*, it brings Sammael into the story. It invokes the name of "R. Idi," which seems to be a variant of *Song R.*'s "R. Judan" and *Pirqe de-Rabbi Eliezer*'s "R. Judah⁰⁾." We might reasonably infer that the Genizah midrashim are medieval adaptations of a rabbinic haggadah which originally made no connection between the *merkabah*-ox and the calf. It would then be medieval Judaism, not rabbinic, for which they speak.

d) The Koran. Lieberman, however, has introduced a new and decisive bit of evidence [323]. This is the strange version of the story of the golden calf found in the twentieth Surah (chapter) of the Koran, verses 80–97.

The outlines of the Koranic narrative are similar to those of Exodus 32. But we find here a new character beside Moses, Aaron, and the people: a mysterious figure called *al-Samiri*, "the Samaritan." Al-Samiri, God tells Moses on the mountain, has led the people astray. The people explain to Moses that al-Samiri induced them to throw their jewellery into the fire, and "he produced for them a calf, of saffron hue, which gave forth a lowing sound[25]." Al-Samiri himself responds to Moses' questioning:

> I perceived what they perceive not, so I seized a handful from the footsteps of the messenger, and then threw it in. Thus my soul commended to me. [Surah 20:96]

This cryptic narration makes sense only if we assume it is a garbled reminiscence of the story preserved in the Genizah midrashim and in Siyyoni's quotation. Lieberman points out that the second sentence reflects Song 6:12, *it was my soul that induced me*; we recall that this verse is the focus of all the medieval Jewish versions. The tale they tell, we now realize, must be older than the Middle Ages. Some Jews in Arabia early in the seventh century were evidently familiar with it, and they passed on what they knew to the prophet Muhammad. At one stage or another, the story lost the details of the *hayyot*. The Koran speaks only of "the messenger" (*al-rasul*, a term often applied to prophets). This designation perhaps echoes the synagogue tradition that represents the *hayyot* as God's messengers (Targ. Ezekiel 1:14, for example).

The Koranic story of the calf is now by and large clear. We still do not understand, however, just who "the Samaritan" is, or what he is doing

---

25 I quote Pickthall's translation [790]. The same expression occurs in Surah 7:148, but without reference to al-Samiri.

there. This problem does not bear directly on the *merkabah*, but it is nevertheless of some importance for us; since, as we will see, its solution clears up the obscurities we earlier noted in connection with the role of Micah. We must therefore turn aside to examine it.

It is an easy guess that the reference to al-Samiri rests upon some Jewish polemic against the Samaritans. The arch-villain of the apostasy, the polemic claimed, was not Aaron or any of the Jews, but a rascally Samaritan who somehow found himself in their company. But this suggestion, while plausible, does not seem quite enough. Scholars have long searched, with moderate success, for some Scriptural warrant for the "Samaritan's" presence.

Thus, Siegmund Fraenkel traced al-Samiri back to Hosea's obscure reference to "the calf of Samaria" (8:5–6); which, he supposed, Jewish expositors understood as pointing to the episode in the desert. A. S. Yahuda, on the other hand, found the key in I Kings 12:28. Here Jeroboam son of Nebat, ruler of the northern Israelite kingdom whose capital later became Samaria (I Kings 16:24), builds two golden calves for Israel to worship. Muhammad's Jewish source, Yahuda thought, told him of the two separate incidents of calf-worship; it was Muhammad himself who conflated them [763,776,789,795].

Both of these suggestions help us understand how Muhammad's source evolved the belief that a "Samaritan" had made the calf, and we cannot afford to discard either of them. But the evidence we have considered so far points to yet a third source for al-Samiri. Micah, according to Judges 17:1, is settled in "the hill country of Ephraim" – the home of the Samaritans. Hosea 8:6 begins with an obscure remark which can easily have been understood: *Someone from Israel, a magician, made it*[26]. The reference seems to be to *the calf of Samaria,* mentioned at the end of the verse. Once Jewish tradition had credited Micah with the uncanny deeds we have read about, it would be natural to identify him with Hosea's *magician,* and to call the Ephraimite magician who had made *the calf of Samaria,* simply, "the Samaritan."

So far we know why the Koran might have called Micah "al-Samiri." We do not know what either Micah or al-Samiri is doing in the calf story in the first place. We find our solution in Muslim traditions quoted by the Koran commentator Tabari, which explain how al-Samiri went about seducing the Israelites into calf-worship[27]. Their details echo Judges' story of Micah, and

---

26 *Ki miyyiśra'el wehu' ḥarash ⁽c⁾aśahu.* The RSV translators, working from the Septuagint text, connect "Israel" with the preceding verse, and understand *ḥarash* as "workman" rather than "magician."

27 Details in Appendix II.

preserve traces of the exegetical process that initially led Jewish expositors to suppose Micah was the maker of the golden calf.

According to one of these traditions, the Israelites felt guilty about the jewellery that they had "borrowed" from the Egyptians and never returned (Exodus 3:21–22, 12:35–36). Another tradition relates how al-Samiri exploits their guilt, convincing them that Moses' delay in returning from the mountain is their punishment for keeping the jewellery. What they must do is give him the jewellery. He then fashions it into the shape of an ox, and brings it to life with "a handful of dust from the footprint of Gabriel's horse." The Israelites, in other words, have stolen the Egyptians' jewellery, and they must make restitution by allowing it to be shaped into a sacred image.

Now, the Book of Exodus knows both the theft of jewellery from the Egyptians (above), and the fashioning of jewellery into the golden calf (32: 2–4). But it does not connect them, nor does it introduce the motif of guilt and restitution. It is precisely this connection and this motif, however, that appear in the Biblical story of Micah. According to Judges 17:1–5, Micah has stolen silver pieces from his mother. She has cursed the thief; and Micah, moved either by conscience or by fear of her curse, confesses and returns the silver. She gives him her blessing, and dedicates "this silver to the Lord on my son's account, to make a graven image and a molten image[28]."

Evidently, certain Jewish expositors understood the story in Judges 17 as a replication of the calf episode, with Micah in the role of the Israelites and his mother in the role of the Egyptians. On the basis of this equation, they filled in the missing links of the calf story. The Israelites, they supposed, stole jewellery from their "mother," Egypt, and made symbolic restitution by building an image of the sacred bull, "the abomination of the Egyptians" (Exodus 8:22). From here it was only a step to transferring Micah bodily into the calf incident, identifying him with the *magician* of Hosea 8:6, and then calling him "the Samaritan." That is why he appears as maker of the calf in both the midrash and the Koran, and why the Koran knows him as "al-Samiri." We will see in our next section that Micah is linked to Jeroboam (above) as well.

One problem, less obvious but ultimately more important than the question of Micah/al-Samiri, remains for us. The Koran twice says that the calf "gave forth a lowing sound" (7:148, 20:88). *Tanḥuma* and *Pirqe de-Rabbi Eliezer* say the same. The source of this detail is surely the *sound of affliction* of Exodus 32:18, understood as the noise made by a suffering animal.

---

28 *Massekhah*, which could easily have suggested to a Jewish interpreter the ᶜ*egel massekhah* ("molten calf") of Exodus 32:8.

A brief midrash preserved in *Ex. R.* 43:8, which we noted in section 4 but did not discuss, attests that some rabbis interpreted the verse in this way:

> This is what Scripture says: *I have surely seen the affliction of my people* [Exodus 3:7]. This refers to the sound of the calf: *I hear the sound of affliction* [Exodus 32:18].

Certain Jewish expositors evidently imagined that the calf was not only animate, but actually in pain. This eerie and rather haunting notion — one does not quite expect an object of idolatry to be suffering even as it is worshipped — does not easily yield itself to rational explanation. We must return to it, in section 7b.

e) "The second story of the calf." If Lieberman's use of Koranic evidence has shown that the midrashic connection of the *merkabah* with the animation of the calf is older than the seventh century, another observation of his allows us to push it back to Tannaitic times [326].

We saw in chapter I (section 3) that Tannaitic sources impose certain restrictions on the lectionary use of Exodus 32. "The first story of the calf," M. Meg. 4:10 rules, "may be both read and translated [in the synagogue], while the second may be read but may not be translated." Both of these rulings are found in the baraita preserved in T. Meg. 3(4):32—38 and BT Meg. 25a—b, which I have shown to be earlier than the Mishnaic passage [552]. Both Tosefta and BT insert into the baraita additional Tannaitic material, which explains that the "second story" is Aaron's own account of why and how he made the calf (Exodus 32:22—24). We find among this material a clue to why the rabbis did not want this specific portion of the calf episode translated into the vernacular:

> ... R. Simeon b. Eleazar said: One is not permitted to answer concerning corruption [?], for, from the answer that Aaron gave Moses, the heretics went astray. [T. Meg. 3(4):37]

> R. Simeon b. Eleazar says: One should always be careful with his answers, for, from the answer that Aaron gave Moses, the heretics broke loose. So it is written, *I threw it into the fire, and out came this calf* [Exodus 32:24]. [BT Meg. 25b]

Rashi comments, on the latter passage, that the heretics "dared to assert that there is reality in idols."

If we are to understand why the Tannaim wanted to keep the "second story of the calf" from being translated, but had no objection to the "first" (Exodus 32:1—6, presumably), we must find some feature unique to the "second story." It is not enough to say that they were embarrassed by the calf incident, or that they feared the Christians' abuse, for these answers do not explain why they allowed the translation of other, equally incriminating, parts of the chapter[29]. BT's version of Simeon b. Eleazar's state-

---

29 I do not deny that some Jewish authorities tried to suppress all or part of Exodus 32 in order to

ment surely points to the sore spot. Second-century rabbis did not want the people to hear Aaron say: *Out came this calf.* They did not want anyone to deduce, as our second Genizah text does, that "Scripture does not say *I brought out,* but *out came,* teaching that it came out by its own power."

Why not? It is hard to believe that they would be concerned to prevent the emergence of stories like those found in *Song R.* to 1:9, Tanh. *Ki Tissa'* #19, or *Pirqe de-Rabbi Eliezer.* After all, if either magicians or Satan made the calf moan and dance, one could hardly blame the Israelites for assuming it was some sort of god. The rabbis would then have both an exciting story and a new reason for God to forgive Israel its lapse. The calf's being alive becomes frightening only if one assumes that the source of its life is in the *merkabah.*

Once that assumption is made, the wall between God and idols collapses. The emblem of evil lives and moves because its roots are in divinity. The calf turns out to have been divine before it became demonic; or, perhaps, it had always been both. The Israelites, who had seen it crossing the Red Sea with God, were entirely right when they declared: *These are your gods, Israel, who brought you up from the land of Egypt.*

f) Reflections. The essence of midrash, as we have often seen, is the combination of verses from different parts of Scripture. Together, they yield a meaning that could not have been imagined for any one of them alone. *Out came this calf* might be harmless, by itself. Combined with *the soles of their feet were like the soles of a calf's foot,* and again with *an ox's face on the left for all four of them,* it became explosive, a bomb for a moral anarchist to plant in the world of divinity.

At least as far back as the second century, the rabbis tried to hide the ingredients that might go into this bomb. They could easily suppress *out came this calf* and the rest of the "second story of the calf," since the entire calf episode was unpopular for other reasons. But, when Judah the Patriarch and his colleagues tried still more stringently to restrict public exposure to the *merkabah* (above, chapter I), they were less successful. The synagogue expositors would not permit the *merkabah* to be taken away from them. However much they might dislike this one implication of Ezekiel's vision, there were others that were too important to be hidden away.

This is not to say that the hints of the calf's link to the *merkabah* did not seriously disturb the preachers. Some of them, as we have seen, responded

---

conceal the shame of the ancient apostasy. Hence, Targum Neofiti I leaves several verses throughout the chapter wholly or partly untranslated [556]. But this does not help us explain the specific objection to Exodus 32:22–24.

to it by deleting the calf's foot from 1:7 (Targum). Others drew attention
to the calf's foot, but explained it in a way that distracted people from its
deeper implications (R. Abbahu's *petiḥah*; above, section 2).

Rabbinic expositors were not the first to censor the text in this way. We
saw in chapter II that some sort of uneasiness about the bovine features of
the *ḥayyot* is one of the earliest traceable elements of *merkabah* exegesis.
Thus, the author of Ezekiel 10:14 replaced the ox's face with a cherub's[30].
The Alexandrian translator of 1:7, like Abbahu's seraphim, used wings to
veil the calf's foot. Evidently, the dark tradition that connects the golden
calf with the *merkabah* goes back very far.

The sources we have examined in this chapter preserve this tradition in
two versions. One of them has the Israelites see the *merkabah* at Sinai[p)],
the other at the Red Sea. It is not easy to decide which is primary. On the
one hand, the "Sinai" version is the more securely grounded exegetically.
We know from Psalm 68:18 that the *merkabah* appeared at Sinai; it is nowhere near so obvious why anyone should have believed it was present at
the Red Sea. (We will return to this problem in the next chapter.) On the
other hand, only the "Red Sea" version is able to give an explanation of
how the Israelites went about detaching the ox-element from the *merkabah*. Further, this version shares with the Book of Revelation a juxtaposition of the *ḥayyot* and the Red Sea (below); which argues, if not for
its primacy, at least for its antiquity. On balance, I suspect that the "Red
Sea" version is the older, and that the setting later shifted to Sinai under
the influence of the synagogue tradition's interpretation of Psalm 68:18.

But, if so, why do we not find the "Red Sea" version in any text written
earlier than the Middle Ages? For reasons that I will presently explain, I
believe that this version was the more threatening of the two, and was therefore suppressed more ruthlessly and for a longer time. In Tanh. *Ki Tiśśa'*
#19, it tries to force its way to the surface. Except in the detail that Micah
throws into the furnace Moses' plaque instead of the dust from the ox's
footprint, *Tanḥuma*'s account is very much like Siyyoni's quotation. I
believe that the author has made a deliberate substitution. He knew that
the "Red Sea" version of the *merkabah*-calf tradition offered a compelling
explanation of the calf episode. He therefore tried to make use of its energies while omitting, and indeed contradicting, its central point. *Song R.* to
1:9 and *Pirqe de-Rabbi Eliezer* make weaker efforts to do the same thing.

I admitted in the last section that we know little of how the "Sinai" version was transmitted before it reached the *Tanḥuma* midrashim. About the
transmission of the "Red Sea" version we have not a clue. For a long time,

---

30 I am not at all sure how to explain the fact that the Qumran Ezekiel fragment replaces it with a
   calf's face (above, chapter II, section 2c).

it may have been expressed only very vaguely, as a sort of shadow clinging to other *merkabah* traditions. It may have taken the form of a cluster of doubts and suspicions that the expositor conceived and then could not forget, however loudly *Mekhilta*'s dialogues told him that such thoughts ought not even to occur to him.

The picture that the "Red Sea" version conveys is oddly similar to that of the fourth chapter of Revelation (above, chapter III). Four *hayyot* are present at a body of water identified as the Red Sea. The ox is not merely a face for the *hayyot*, but actually one of the *hayyot* themselves. The contexts in which this image appears are entirely different, although there may be subtle connections between them[31]; but the image itself is very much the same.

If the parallel is significant, what are we to make of it? Perhaps only that the *merkabah*'s presence at the Red Sea was part of the stock of images that both the author of Revelation and our tradition had available for use. But I think there is a deeper resemblance in the way they use the image. I have tried to show that Revelation uses its "glass sea" to point to some monstrous evil near the seat of divinity. Our tradition, by tracing the golden calf back to the ox of the *merkabah*, does much the same.

This resemblance perhaps suggests that the sea at which the *merkabah* appears is not a neutral entity, but carries a load of sinister associations akin to the ones it has in Revelation. If so, the *merkabah*-calf tradition has chosen a setting that complements and intensifies its message. Its exposure of the demonic within the divine becomes clearer and more frightening. We can understand why it was suppressed longer than the version that described a similar event, but set its scene at Sinai.

So far, this is only a suspicion. To confirm it or to undermine it, we must probe more deeply the meaning of the link between the *merkabah* and the sea. This we will undertake in chapter VI.

6. Midrash to Psalms, 5:8

A passage from the late *Midrash to Psalms* (5:8; ed. 28a [199]) helps clinch our argument.

The author expounds Job 11:11 (*he saw sin, yet paid no attention*) in a way that roughly resembles *Ex. R.* 3:2. But, where *Ex. R.* speaks of the Israelites in the wilderness, *Midr. Psalms* describes another calf-maker. This is

---

31 Thus, the beast that emerges from the sea, and receives the worship properly due to God (Revelation 13), functions very much like the golden calf. The "false prophet" (= the beast from the earth) is able, like Micah, to bring its statue to life (verse 15).

Jeroboam son of Nebat, who led the ten northern tribes of Israel in their revolt against the house of David, and then "made two calves of gold, and said ... 'These are your gods, Israel, who brought you up from the land of Egypt'" (I Kings 12:28).

The focus of the midrash is the Biblical passage that describes Jeroboam's interview with the prophet Ahijah the Shilonite, which takes place before his rebellion and his apostasy (I Kings 11:29—39):

> He saw sin, yet paid no attention. ... R. Hanina b. Papa applied this verse to Jeroboam. [Scripture says:] The two of them [Jeroboam and Ahijah] were alone in the field [I Kings 11:29]. This means that he was the equal of Ahijah the Shilonite. So it is written, The two of them sat down together[32], which means that they sat down to interpret ma^{c}aseh merkabah. The angels came before God and said to him: "Master of the world, do you intend to reveal ma^{c}aseh merkabah to a man who is going someday to set up two calves?" He said to them: "What is he now, righteous or wicked?" "Righteous," they replied. He said to them: "I judge a man solely on the basis of his present conduct."

The midrash emphasizes the apparent incongruity that the future idolmaker should have been permitted to learn the secrets of the merkabah. This much is obvious. What is not obvious is how the expositor knows in the first place that Jeroboam and Ahijah studied ma^{c}aseh merkabah. I Kings 11:29—39 hardly gives the impression that this is what they were doing. I am not aware that rabbinic sources describe any other Biblical character, least of all the wicked kings of Judah and Israel, as having studied ma^{c}aseh merkabah. (We must make an exception for Solomon, if we assume that a midrash to this effect quoted by a medieval Yemenite writer [561] actually goes back to rabbinic times.)

The puzzling "Biblical" quotation, the two of them sat down together, points us toward a possible solution. The passage is not in fact from the Bible[33]. One of the manuscripts that Buber consulted for his edition of Midr. Psalms omits the opening formula "so it is written" — and thus the claim that what follows is Biblical — as well as the word together. If we follow this manuscript, we find ourselves with a quotation from Tosefta's version of the story of how Eleazar b. Arakh expounded ma^{c}aseh merkabah before Johanan b. Zakkai. "R. Johanan b. Zakkai descended from his ass and wrapped himself in his cloak, and the two of them sat down on a rock under an olive tree, and he [Eleazar] lectured before him" (T. Hag. 2:1, ed. Lieberman; above, chapter I, section 2). If together belongs in the text of the midrash, it is perhaps the author's addition, perhaps a variant text of Tosefta.

The author of the midrash, then, pictured the encounter of Ahijah and Jeroboam as having been like that of Johanan b. Zakkai and Eleazar b.

---

32 This quotation is not from the Bible. We will presently trace its source.

33 Judges 19:6 is similar but not quite the same. It has, in any case, nothing to do with Jeroboam and Ahijah.

Arakh. His starting point may have been a passage in the Babylonian Talmud (Sanh. 102a) that expounds I Kings 11:29 in praise of the marvellous scholarship of Ahijah and Jeroboam. Significantly, BT attributes the first of its series of expositions to Hanina b. Papa. A little later on, we read:

> They [Ahijah and Jeroboam] brought forth new interpretations that no one had ever heard before. What does *the two of them were alone in the field* mean? Rab Judah quoted Rab: It means that all the scholars were like the grass of the field compared to them. Some say: All the meanings of Torah were wide open to them, like a field.

The author of the *Midr. Psalms* passage learned from this that I Kings 11: 29—39 describes the extraordinary exegetical activity of Ahijah and Jeroboam. But the Talmud's generalities did not satisfy him. He noticed that I Kings 11:29 describes the two men as being *on the road,* like Johanan and Eleazar; and that, like Johanan, Ahijah is wrapped in a cloak[q]. He deduced from these parallels that, like Johanan and Eleazar, Ahijah and Jeroboam were engaged in expounding *ma^{c}aśeh merkabah.*

All of this is plausible, but, by itself, not entirely satisfying. It sounds like the sort of argument that a person devises to convince himself of something that he is already inclined to believe. We must ask what might have predisposed the author of the midrash to think that Jeroboam had studied *ma^{c}aśeh merkabah.*

I propose that he deduced Jeroboam's involvement with the *merkabah* from the very fact that Jeroboam set up golden calves. In other words, he perceived calf-worship as a routine hazard of "contemplating the *merkabah.*" The Israelites at Sinai fell into it when they saw the *merkabah.* Jeroboam fell into it when he studied the *merkabah.* So might any expositor. The texts we have studied in this chapter have shown us why.

We now understand the reasoning behind a baraita, quoted in BT Sanh. 101b, which claims that Jeroboam's father Nebat was none other than our old acquaintance Micah. Like father, like son.

7. Conclusions

a) Summing up. In this chapter, we have penetrated to the heart of the *merkabah*'s darkness.

I earlier suggested, in more general terms, that certain early Jewish expositors found in Ezekiel's imagery hints of a moral ambiguity lying near the center of God's being, and that at least some of them did not like what they found. Jews might admit God to be the creator of evil; "thou ... formest light and createst darkness," the daily liturgy confesses [216c]. But the notion that he is himself partly evil is more than Judaism has normally been able to swallow.

We have now seen emerge from Ezekiel's vision a clear and specific expression of the unsettling paradox of evil within God. The golden calf, the object of the first and most shameful of Israel's apostasies, the emblem of what God most hates, came from God himself. The Israelites worshipped it because of what they had seen when God exposed himself to them as he was.

Unsettling – to ancient rabbis, or only squeamish moderns whose crotchets I am projecting backwards? I believe we have found evidence in the *Mekhilta* that some at least of the rabbis were deeply disturbed by the idea that the Israelites were worshipping the "celestial ox" when they made the calf. *Mekhilta*'s dialogues reflect an urge to repress some of the implications of the *merkabah*. I think it plausible that this same urge motivated the Mishnah's effort to keep the *merkabah* out of the synagogue, and that it underlies the third-century sources that warn darkly of the fate that befalls those who expound the *merkabah* unprepared (above, chapter I, section 5).

Even if we were to stop here, therefore, I believe that we would have a solution to the problem that I raised in the first chapter, of the shape of the witch that Judah the Patriarch and his colleagues saw in Ezekiel's gingerbread house.

We cannot, however, afford to be content with this solution. Important aspects of the dark side of the *merkabah* have yet to be cleared up. One of them, which now lies before us, is the uneasiness that seems to attend the linking of the *merkabah* to the waters.

But we must first take a short excursion in another direction. Our probe of the *merkabah*'s darkness hints at implications that go well beyond the *merkabah* itself, and well beyond the study of ancient Judaism. We have no way here to follow up these implications. But we can at least look at them, and ponder where they might lead.

b) A step farther: merkabah and quaternity. I cannot claim any great familiarity with the psychological theories of Carl Gustav Jung, or with his views on the history and nature of religion. I certainly do not think I come to the data with any prejudice in their favor. Yet the midrash we examined in section 4 strikes me as a textbook illustration of Jung's speculations about "quaternity," and I believe that this resemblance demands an explanation.

If I have understood Jung correctly, he perceives the number four as an archetype[34] representing wholeness. God is, properly, a four-ness. The

---

34 In Jungian psychology, an "archetype" is an emblem that recurs independently in the dreams of different individuals and the imagery of different cultures. It therefore comes from a common reservoir of the unconscious, on which all humans draw.

Christian Trinity is a mutilated version of an original divine quaternity. Jung himself seems to have remained vague on just what the missing fourth member was. Sometimes he identified it as the female principle of divinity, which appears in Catholicism as the Virgin Mary. But he also thought of it as the devil, the evil within God that Christianity tried to purge from its deity, at the cost of leaving him incomplete [831,839,840,841].

Jung knew the Old Testament well, and leaned heavily on Ezekiel 1 in support of his views on the quaternity. His knowledge of post-Biblical Jewish literature, however, seems to have been very sparse. If he had any knowledge of *Ex. R.* 43:8 and its parallels when he developed his theories, it has left no mark on his writings[35]. This midrash, which describes how one member of a quaternity is separated from the other three and becomes the exemplar of idolatry, therefore seems to be an independent parallel to Jung's conception that one member of a quaternity was separated from the other three and became the devil.

I cannot rule out the possibility that the resemblance is coincidental, and have no way to debate the issue with anyone who finds it less striking than I do. If we grant that it is significant, I am at a loss to explain what it means. It would certainly imply, to put the matter very vaguely, that Jung was "on to something." More specifically, it would suggest that the association of the golden calf with the *merkabah*-ox stems from something far more profound than midrashic play with Ezekiel 1:7 and 10. The authors of the midrashim that make this association did not start out, like Jung, with a Christian trinity to set beside Ezekiel's quaternity. Yet they seem intuitively to have been aware of a process of separation akin to the one that Jung conjectured. If this process involves the tearing apart of a fourfold whole (which I am for the moment assuming, with Jung, to be some sort of psychic entity), we may imagine that it would involve pain for the members being separated. This is perhaps why some midrashim say that the calf *lowed*, which I assume to be an expression of anguish (*the sound of affliction*, Exodus 32:18).

While we are pondering the notion that the midrashim in *Ex. R.* 43:8 and its parallels may be symbolic expressions of a process that really did or does take place in some hazily defined psychic realm, let us also consider a related and in some ways even more controversial proposal. Can it be that these midrashim express what is in fact implicit in Ezekiel 1?

---

35 I base this generalization on the index of his twenty-volume *Collected Works* [838]. My colleague William Peck, who kindly shared with me his knowledge of Jungian psychology, refers me to Heinz Westman's *Springs of Creativity* [861], which approaches midrashic themes from a Jungian perspective. But, although Westman discusses both the Biblical and the rabbinic stories of the golden calf, he does not make the connection with *Ex. R.* 43:8 that I am here proposing.

This suggestion runs directly counter to an assumption that we have made throughout this study, that conceptions developed in midrashic exposition of Scripture are actually the creations of the midrashic expositor himself. The expositor detects threads tying two separate Biblical passages into a new unity. He combines them, and learns from this combination something that he could never have found in either passage taken separately. He thinks he has thus deciphered a hidden meaning that God had long ago coded into his Scriptures. But (we assume) he is wrong; he has underplayed his own originality; the "hidden meaning" is his own and not that of the texts he expounds. Ezekiel would be baffled or outraged, or both, if he could see what the midrashim have done with his *merkabah* vision.

I do not propose we jettison this assumption. Without it, it would be impossible to write an intellectual history of Judaism. If we allowed ourselves to accept the claims of Jewish thinkers from pre-Christian times through the Middle Ages that all they are doing is unfolding the truths hidden in the Hebrew Bible, we could not point out innovations or define changes; and without innovation and change there is no history. But an assumption may be useful and even essential without being absolutely or invariably true. In some situations, it may be worthwhile for us momentarily to disregard our own principles – just to see what happens.

The *merkabah* vision is perhaps one of these situations. It is, as it stands, barely intelligible. Yet its unintelligibility has a provocative quality that suggests it is due to something other than a mechanical piling up of corruptions and glosses. (In chapter II, I have sketched my reasons for believing that secondary accretions have played a much smaller part in the formation of Ezekiel 1 than most scholars have assumed.) The richness of its detail leads us to expect that it will convey something beyond the rather banal message that God is capable of leaving the Temple at Jerusalem and travelling to Babylonia. It had the power to attract the rabbis, and to stir up their fantasies and fears, as no other Biblical vision did.

Can we imagine that it had this power because the rabbis' fantasies and fears drew out what was already lurking within the obscurities of the vision? That the threads running from Ezekiel 1:7 and 10 to Exodus 32 and Psalm 106:20 were, though hidden, as much a part of the *merkabah* vision as verses 7 and 10 themselves[36]? That, in this and other respects, the rabbis correctly intuited that Ezekiel 1 had things to tell them about realms beyond their conscious perceptions, which they could learn nowhere else in the Bible?

---

36 We recall the evidence that the link of the *merkabah* to the golden calf is one of the very oldest elements of *merkabah* exegesis, going back to the secondary material in Ezekiel 10 (above, chapter II).

In short, will the *merkabah* vision yield its secrets more readily if we treat it as coming from some normally inaccessible part of the prophet's psyche, conveying messages that neither he nor his contemporaries could consciously have understood; and which we, following the lead of the midrash, can now only start to grasp?

I am very far from sure that I want to say yes to these questions, and go along with the rather fantastic notions that they express. Still less do I want to turn Jung into the authoritative expositor of the *merkabah*. But I believe that there are times when history and philology will carry us only so far in making sense of Ezekiel's vision and the exegetical traditions founded on it. If the psychologists can take us the rest of the way, we must let them. Where Jung cannot help us, perhaps Freud can. So, at least, we will find reason to believe when we come to examine the *Hekhalot*.

For now, we cannot go further into these waters without being well over our heads. We must turn to waters of a very different sort, which we will perhaps find more negotiable. These are the waters that appear with the *merkabah*.

7 Conclusions

Chapter VI

The Merkabah and the Waters

1. Introduction

Our task now is to confront a question which we left unresolved in chapter I. What is the meaning of the mysterious warning against saying "water, water," that we find in the Babylonian Talmud's version of the *pardes* story?

Four men entered a garden [*pardes*]: Ben Azzai, Ben Zoma, Aher, and R. Akiba. R. Akiba said to them: "When you draw near the stones of pure marble [*'abne shayish tahor*], do not say, 'Water, water.' For it is written, *He who speaks lies shall not be established in my sight* [Psalm 101:7]."

Ben Azzai looked and died. ...[1] Ben Zoma looked and went mad. ... Aher cut the young plants. ... R. Akiba ascended safely and descended safely. ... [BT Hag. 14b]

Although I will refer to the warning as Akiba's, I think it immensely unlikely that the historical Akiba ever spoke it. It certainly was not an original part of the *pardes* story. Tosefta's version of this story (Hag. 2:3—4), which I think preserves the account in its most nearly original form, knows nothing of it. Neither does PT (Hag. 2:1, 77b), or a version preserved in *Song R.* to 1:4, which seems to be based on PT [552]. It seems to be the creation of an anonymous Babylonian transmitter of the story, who reinterpreted the entry into *pardes* as a visit to the heavenly realms, the goal of which was presumably the *merkabah* (above, chapter I, section 7).

This suggestion explains the context of "Akiba's" warning, but leaves its details entirely obscure. What exactly were the "stones of pure marble"? Why would it occur to Akiba's companions to say "water, water," when they saw them? Most important, why would it be terrible if they did say "water, water"? Why would this banal utterance brand them as *speakers of lies*, unfit to *be established in* God's *sight*?

---

1 The ellipses correspond to the Biblical texts that the story applies to each of the four. I give a full translation of Tosefta's version of the story, with these proof texts, in chapter I, section 6.

a) Scholem used this problem as a key argument for the antiquity of the *Hekhalot* traditions of heavenly ascension. Suppose the *Hekhalot* to be the background of the Talmudic passage, Scholem's argument ran, and the questions I have raised practically answer themselves. But, if we leave the *Hekhalot* out of the equation (as Scholem's predecessors would have liked to do), they remain riddles to which we can offer no plausible solution.

Modern interpretations of this famous passage [wrote Scholem], which clearly enough refers to a *real* danger in the process of ascending to 'Paradise,' are extremely far-fetched and not a little irrational in their determination at all costs to preserve the characteristic essentials of rationalism. We are told that the passages [sic] refers to cosmological speculations about the *materia prima*, an explanation which lacks all plausibility and finds no support in the context or in the subject-matter itself. The fact is that the later Merkabah mystics [he means the authors of the *Hekhalot*] showed a perfectly correct understanding of the meaning of this passage, and their interpretation offers striking proof that the tradition of Tannaitic mysticism and theosophy was really alive among them, although certain details may have originated at a later period. The following quotation is taken from the Munich manuscript of the Hekhaloth texts [see text II, in the following section]: "But if one was unworthy to see the King in his beauty, the angels at the gates disturbed his senses and confused him. And when they said to him: 'Come in,' he entered, and instantly they pressed him and threw him into the fiery lava stream. And at the gate of the sixth palace it seemed as though hundreds of thousands and millions of waves of water stormed against him, and yet there was not a drop of water, only the ethereal glitter of the marble plates with which the palace was tesselated. But he was standing in front of the angels and when he asked: 'What is the meaning of these waters,' they began to stone him and said: 'Wretch, do you not see it with your own eyes? Are you perhaps a descendant of those who kissed the Golden Calf, and are you unworthy to see the King in his beauty?' ... And he does not go until they strike his head with iron bars and wound him. And this shall be a sign for all times that no one shall err at the gate of the sixth palace and see the ethereal glitter of the plates and ask about them and take them for water, that he may not endanger himself."

Thus the text. The authenticity of the story's core, the ecstatic's vision of water, hardly requires proof. Nothing could be more far-fetched than to treat it as a *post festum* interpretation of the Talmudic passage; there is no reason whatsoever to doubt that the mystical experience of the dangers of the ascent is really the subject of the anecdote. Similar dangers are described in the so-called "Liturgy of Mithras" contained in the great magical papyrus of Paris, where the description of the mystical ascent shows many parallels of detail and atmosphere with the account given in the "Greater Hekhaloth." [609]

This is indeed a powerful argument. But is it entirely compelling? When we look at it closely, doubts begin to occur to us. For one thing, Scholem seems a bit too confident and dogmatic in ruling out the possibility that the *Hekhalot* passage may be a secondary elaboration of the text from BT Hag. 14b. If we should decide to accept this alternative, Scholem's argument would collapse and we would be back where we started. But, even if we grant the priority of the *Hekhalot* passage, we still have not solved the problem of the significance of "water, water," but only pushed it from the Talmud into the *Hekhalot*. If we at first did not understand why saying "water, water" brands one a liar, we now do not understand why seeing water where there is none brands one a descendant of those who kissed the golden calf.

This problem would be somewhat less acute if the "water" test were one of a series of trials that the *Hekhalot* texts have the angels impose on the would-be mystic. We might then imagine that the Babylonians who rewrote the *pardes* story chose this test, more or less arbitrarily, as an example of the entire series; and we would not need so urgently to find a reason why it is terrible to imagine that there is water in the realms of the divine. Scholem's general reference to "the dangers of the ascent," and his invocation of parallels from the "Liturgy of Mithras," do perhaps give the impression that the *Hekhalot* record such a series of tests. If so, the impression is misleading. In the *Hekhalot* texts that Schäfer published, I have found only two trials imposed on the celestial traveller. One is the "water" test itself. The other is the exercise in heavenly etiquette — one must not enter on the first invitation — that immediately precedes it (see the next section for more details)[a]. The "water" trial stands practically alone.

b) Neher, Maier, Goldberg. Even if Scholem is right in claiming that the warning against saying "water, water" presupposes the *Hekhalot* tradition of the "water" test, he has not gotten us very far toward understanding the rationale either of the warning or the test. More recently, André Neher, Johann Maier, and Arnold Goldberg have explored this problem, but without entirely satisfying results [577,574,526].

The focus of Neher's argument is the rabbinic belief that there exists in heaven a Temple corresponding to the one that once stood in Jerusalem [365,379,456]. The rabbis conceive the celestial Temple as the prototype and model of the earthly one. Secular scholars, naturally, reverse this relationship, and assume that the rabbis have projected the Jerusalem Temple and its furniture into the sky. The *Hekhalot* writers perhaps do the same when they take the word *hekhal* ("palace" or "temple"), which rabbinic sources often apply to the Jerusalem Temple, and use it as a designation for God's seven heavenly palaces (*hekhalot*). (When Scholem, in the passage quoted above, speaks of "the gate of the sixth palace," the Hebrew word translated "palace" is *hekhal*.) Neher therefore supposes, plausibly enough, that the journey of the four took them to the heavenly Temple.

Now, Neher argues, the rabbis believed that the Jerusalem Temple was made of "stones of marble" (*'abne shayish*)[2], and they transferred this detail to its heavenly counterpart. The seven *hekhalot* correspond to the seven areas of the Temple mount described or implied in Mishnaic sources, which were arranged in more or less concentric circles. The "gate of the sixth palace" thus corresponds to the "water gate" of the earthly Temple,

---

2 Neher claims to deduce this detail from M. Sotah 2:2, but it in fact occurs only in Rashi's comment on this passage (in BT Sotah 15b). We will presently see, however, that Neher's assertion has better support than he himself provides for it.

through which water was brought for libation on the Feast of Tabernacles, and from which (according to a haggadah quoted in T. Sukkah 3:3—10) the eschatological waters prophesied in Ezekiel 47:1—12 will someday flow. When Akiba speaks of "water, water," it is these waters that he intends.

So far, Neher's case is more or less reasonable, at least in its broad outlines. But it breaks down when it confronts the essential question of why Akiba should warn so strictly against saying that one sees those waters. Neher supposes that seeing the waters issuing from the Temple is tantamount to believing that the eschatological future predicted by Ezekiel is now upon us, and suggests that Akiba's warning is intended to restrain Messianic enthusiasm. We cannot refute this view by pointing out that Akiba is about the last person we would suspect of wanting to restrain Messianic enthusiasm (PT Ta^{c}anit 4:8, 68d, and *Lam. R.* 2:4 represent him as declaring Bar Kokhba the Messiah [456a]), since the historical Akiba is in any case hardly likely to have spoken the warning. But, on other grounds, Neher's explanation seems lame and inadequate. It does not make clear why the sight of water issuing from the heavenly Temple — the ideal Temple of Ezekiel's vision — should imply that God's kingdom has already arrived on earth. Ezekiel, too, saw the waters flowing from the Temple, in his vision. Did the author of BT's *pardes* story imagine that Ezekiel believed the Messianic age had arrived? Was Ezekiel therefore a liar, unfit to be established in God's sight?

Maier begins with the observation that, in the ancient Near Eastern myths that lie behind the Biblical creation story, the primordial chaos-waters constitute the supreme threat to the cosmos. But he soon leaves this point — which we will presently follow up on our own — and turns his attention to the issue that occupied Neher, of the parallelism between the earthly and the heavenly Temples. In this connection, he finds the key to both Akiba's warning and the related *Hekhalot* passages in another text from the Babylonian Talmud, which Neher overlooked.

The text in question occurs in both BT Sukk. 51b and B.B. 4a. It attributes to the fourth-century Babylonian Amora Rabbah (or Rava, who lived a generation later; the text is uncertain) the claim that Herod built the Jerusalem Temple of "stones of marble ... with alternate layers protruding ... [so that] it looked like the waves of the sea." Here we have "stones of marble" (*'abne shaysha umarmara*)[3] which create the illusion of water, as the "stones of pure marble" (*'abne shayish ṭahor*) of Hag. 14b seem to do. When we recall that this description of the Temple, like the warning against saying "water, water," comes from Babylonia, it begins to seem very plausi-

---

3 I am not sure of the distinction between the two words, *shaysha* and *marmara*, that the passage uses for "marble." The Talmud glosses the former as *shaysha kohala*, "black marble."

ble that the two Talmudic passages are linked, and that Maier is right in
supposing that the transmitters of the *pardes* story have shifted a feature
of the earthly Temple to the celestial one[4].

But Maier's argument disappoints us in the same way that Neher's does.
We still do not understand why it should be a damnable error to mistake
marble stones for water. Why should a person die because he looks at a
wall that has the appearance of waves? Maier asks. His suggestion, of a
series of misunderstandings in the transmission of the *pardes* story, is not
a satisfactory answer.

Goldberg approaches the problem from a different angle. He observes
that the heaven of the *Hekhalot* is a world filled with fire, not water. Anyone who speaks of water in these realms must be mistaken. But why does
this mistake amount to a lie, as BT's quotation of Psalm 101:7 suggests?
Goldberg replies that the error is not itself a lie, but reveals the man who
commits it to have been antecedently a liar. His failure correctly to
recognize the glitter of the marble plates points to a failure correctly to
recognize the God to whom he ascends. He therefore resembles the people
who kissed the calf, in that he worships a false image of his own construction.

Goldberg's proposal, once again, leaves the essential problem unsolved.
We come away with the impression that the use of water or the illusion of
water to reveal the mystic's misapprehension of the divine is basically arbitrary.

Can we do better? Our observations on the "glass sea" of the Book of
Revelation (chapter III) and the appearance of the *merkabah* at the Red
Sea in certain Genizah texts (chapter V) suggest that we can. We have
learned from these sources that the idea of a body of water in the vicinity
of the *merkabah* is not unique to BT Hag. 14b and the relevant *Hekhalot*
material. We have also seen a few hints that there is something sinister
about this water's being near the *merkabah*, which may set us on the way
to explaining why there is something inherently bad in the celestial traveller's saying "water, water."

It is now time for us to follow up these clues with an examination of the
rabbinic and *Hekhalot* sources that combine the *merkabah* and the waters.
We may hope that these texts will help us establish a line of thought connecting the Book of Revelation, BT Hag. 14b, and the Genizah midrashim.

We must keep the definition of our task fairly narrow. Both apocalyptic
and rabbinic sources often speak of a body of water in heaven, the "waters

---

4 Maier's point would be even stronger if Sukk. 51b and B.B. 4a actually used the word *hekhal* for
    Herod's Temple. Unfortunately, they do not.

which were above the firmament" of Genesis 1:7. If we were to take it upon ourselves to analyze all of these references, we would have enough material for another book[5]. We would also be in danger of losing all our focus. We must stay with those texts that bring the waters together with the *merkabah*, leaving this narrow path only when, as will sometimes happen, there seems particularly good reason to do so. On the other hand, the waters need not actually be in heaven in order to attract our interest. As we will see, our most important trail of clues leads us first to, and then through, the Red Sea.

The first stage of our investigation will be the material from the *Hekhalot* on which Scholem rested his case; and we must pause there for a rather long time. I dismissed this evidence in a rather cavalier way when I discussed the *pardes* episode in my earlier book on the *merkabah* [522]. In opposition to Scholem, I thought that it was indeed "a *post festum* interpretation of the Talmudic passage," of no more value than any other commentary on BT Hag. 14b. I now believe that, if Scholem was wrong, I was too. The *Hekhalot* preserve several different sources. All but one of these seem fairly clearly to be dependent on the surviving rabbinic versions of the *pardes* story. But that one exception has the marks of an independent witness, which, no less than the midrashim to be considered later in this chapter, can help us mark out the web of ideas that ancient Judaism spun around the *merkabah* and the waters.

2. *Hekhalot*: the *pardes* episode and the "water" test

a) The texts. As far as I know, no one has yet collected the pertinent *Hekhalot* sources and presented them in such a way that the reader can clearly grasp what they say and how they relate to each other. This must be our first task. Like every other enterprise connected with the *Hekhalot*, it has become immeasurably easier since Peter Schäfer published his synoptic edition of the *Hekhalot* manuscripts [495].

More than a dozen passages of the *Hekhalot* refer to one aspect or another of the *pardes* episode, or contain verbal reminiscences of the rabbinic *pardes* materials[b]. Seven of them bear directly or indirectly on the role of the waters, and therefore demand our close attention here. The first two of these seven belong, respectively, to the clusters of material conventionally dubbed *Hekhalot Rabbati* and *Hekhalot Zutarti*; each is represented by several manuscripts. Each of the remaining five is found

---

5 I do not know any good survey of these sources. David Neiman's article "The Supercaelian Sea" [41] deals only with the Biblical and ancient Near Eastern background of Genesis 1:6–7.

only in a single manuscript. These five are very closely related; as we will see, they represent different stages in the development of the same passage. But there are important differences among them, and I think it best to translate each by itself — with apologies to the reader for the often tiresome repetitions that this will entail.

I. Schäfer, ##258–259; published in Wertheimer's edition of *Hekhalot Rabbati* [500] as chapter 26:1–2. Schäfer prints the texts of mss New York (Jewish Theological Seminary) 8128, Oxford 1531, Munich 22 and 40, Dropsie (University, Philadelphia) 436, Vatican 228, and Budapest 238. I translate ms Oxford:

[A1] *I saw something like the eye of ḥashmal* [Ezekiel 1:27] [6]. It was ...[7] and standing and selecting among those who descended to the *merkabah*, distinguishing him who was worthy to descend to the *merkabah* from him who was unworthy to descend to the *merkabah*. [A2] If a person was worthy to descend to the *merkabah*, they [the angels?] would say to him, "Enter"; but he would not enter. They would again say to him, "Enter"; and he would thereupon enter. They would praise him: "Surely he is one of those who descend to the *merkabah!*" [A3] But, if he was unworthy to descend to the *merkabah*, they would say to him, "Don't enter"[8]; but he would enter. They would thereupon throw iron axes [?] upon him[9].

[B] Because the guardians of the gate of the sixth palace [*hekhal*] throw and hurl upon him thousands and thousands of waves of water. Yet there is not a single drop there. If he should say, "What is the nature of these waters?", they run after him and stone him. "Fool!" they say to him. "Perhaps you are descended from those who kissed the calf, and you are not worthy to see the king and his throne[c]?" If this is true, a heavenly voice goes forth from [c]Arabot Raqia[c10]: "Well you have spoken! He is descended from those who kissed the calf, and is not worthy to

---

6 RSV: "I saw as it were gleaming bronze." The author of the *Hekhalot* passage seems to take *ke[c]en ḥashmal*, which doubtless should be translated "like the *color* of ḥashmal," in its most literal sense (*[c]ayin* usually means "eye," occasionally "color"). Cf. Schäfer, ##246–247 (Wertheimer, 24:1–2); below, chapter IX, section B2.

7 I am not sure how to translate *nizqaq* here. Perhaps it means that the eye "was engaged in standing and examining those who descended to the *merkabah*"; but the idiom seems odd. The parallel passage in text II (below) reads, in place of *nizqaq*, *muḥzaq* or *mehuzzaq* ("strengthened"?), which somewhat resemble *nizqaq* in Hebrew script. Cf. the use of *nizqaq* in Schäfer, #235 (Wertheimer, 22:1).

8 All of Schäfer's mss have the word "don't" (*'al*). Ms Budapest quotes a variant reading, "Enter" (so Wertheimer's edition), but this is perhaps a correction in accordance with text II. While text II's point is that the unworthy traveller betrays himself by entering after the first invitation, text I tells a different story: he enters despite an express warning to stay out.

9 *Migzere barzel*: perhaps translate "iron bars." (II Samuel 12:31 supports "axes," M. Sanh. 9:6 "bars" [526].) — Ms Dropsie omits this last sentence, and reads the first sentence of section B: "They would throw and hurl upon him thousands and thousands of waves of water." See below.

10 *[c]Arabot* is the name of the highest heaven in BT Hag. 12b, and in most other lists of the heavens [232]. The phrase *[c]arabot raqia[c]* is very common in the *Hekhalot* literature, independent of the system of seven heavens. Perhaps we are to translate it, not "the firmament [named] [c]Arabot" — we would expect the words to be in the reverse order — but "the plains of the firmament" (reading construct *[c]arebot*). Cf. the Apocalypse of Abraham, chapter 10: "the seventh expanse upon the firmament" (Box's translation [90]). If this is so, someone ought to investigate the relation of the *Hekhalot* phrase *[c]arebot raqia[c]* to the use of [c]Arabot as a name for the seventh heaven.

see the king and his throne." He does not move from there before they throw upon him thousands and thousands of iron axes [?].

II. Schäfer, ##407–410; part of the so-called *Hekhalot Zuṭarti* (lines 289–316, in Elior's edition [464]). Several scholars have quoted or translated parts of this passage [557]. Schäfer prints the texts of mss New York, Oxford, Munich 22 and 40, and Dropsie. I translate sections A–C from ms Oxford, but shift to ms New York for section D.

[A1] *I saw something like the eye of hashmal*, which is strengthened [? see above] and stands and selects from among those who descend to the *merkabah*, distinguishing him who is worthy to see the king in his beauty from him who is unworthy to see the king in his beauty. [A2] If a person was worthy to see the king in his beauty, they would induce him [to respond so that], when they would say to him, "Enter," he would not enter. They would again say, "Enter"; and he would thereupon enter. They would praise him: "Surely so-and-so is worthy to see the king in his beauty!" [A3] But, if he was not worthy to see the king in his beauty, they would induce him [to respond so that], when they would say "Enter," he would enter. They would thereupon squeeze him [?][d)] and throw him into Rigyon [the river] of fiery coals[11].

[B] The sixth palace looked like someone [!] at whom a hundred thousand thousands and myriad myriads of waves of the sea were being driven. Yet there was not a single drop of water, but only the light [?] of the splendor of the stones of pure marble that were built into [?] the palace [*hekhal*], which was a splendor more terrible than water [?]. The servants [that is, the angels] stand by him. If he says, "What is the nature of these waters?", they run after him and stone him. "One empty of deeds [?]," they say to him, "do you not see with your eyes? Perhaps you are descended from those who kissed the calf, and you are not worthy to see the king in his beauty?" If so, a heavenly voice [goes forth] from the seventh palace and a herald goes forth before you [!], trumpeting and proclaiming to them: "Well have you spoken! Surely he is descended from those who kissed the calf, and he is not worthy to see the king in his beauty." He does not move from there before they split his head open with iron axes [?][e)].

[C1] This is to serve as a sign for all time, that one must not make an error at the gate of the sixth palace, and see the splendor of the air [! *ziw 'awir*] of the stones, and ask, and say that they are water. He will thus not expose himself to danger. [C2] Because, even if he is not worthy to see the king in his beauty, [but nevertheless] does not ask them about the air of the splendor [! *'awir ziw*] of the stones of pure marble that were built into [?] the palace, they do not destroy him but give him the benefit of the doubt, saying: "[If] he is not worthy to see the king in his beauty, how did he manage to get into the first six palaces[f)]?"

[D] R. Akiba said: Ben Azzai[g)] succeeded in reaching the gate of the sixth palace. He saw the splendor of the air [!] of the stones of pure marble. He opened his mouth twice and said, "Water, water." Instantly they cut off his head and threw upon him eleven thousand iron axes [?]. This is to serve as a sign for all time, that one must not make an error at the gate of the sixth palace. The Lord is king, the Lord was king, the Lord will be king for ever and ever[12].

III. Schäfer, ##338–339, 346–348; from ms Munich 22. This passage occurs near the beginning of the so-called *Hekhalot Zuṭarti*. Three other manuscripts — New York, Oxford, Dropsie — have here the opening of the

---

11 We will meet the fiery river Rigyon again in chapter VIII. Johanan Levy derives its name from Greek *ryakion*, "lava stream" [567]. Scholem, whose translation of sections A3–C1 I have quoted above, renders accordingly.

12 This last sentence occurs among the daily Jewish morning prayers as part of a series of Biblical verses; it is not, however, itself from the Bible [216b,381,415]. I have the impression that the *Hekhalot* texts invoke it rather frequently. I have no idea what it is doing in this context.

passage, abbreviated: "R. Akiba said: We were four who entered *pardes*, and so forth" (Elior, line 20). All of the mss include section D, in one form or another (cf. text VII, below).

[A] R. Akiba said: We were four who entered *pardes*. One looked and died, one looked and went mad, one looked and cut the young plants. I entered safely and went out safely. Why did I enter safely and go out safely? Not because I am greater than my companions; but they [?] caused me to fulfill that which the sages taught in their Mishnah: "It is your deeds that will bring you near and your deeds that will put you at a distance" [M. ᶜEd. 5:7].

[B] These are the men who entered *pardes*: Ben Azzai, Ben Zoma, Elisha Aher, and R. Akiba. Ben Azzai looked and died. Of him Scripture says, *Precious in the eyes of the Lord is the death of his saints,* and so forth [Psalm 116:15]. Ben Zoma looked and went mad. Of him Scripture says, *If you find honey, eat only your fill,* and so forth [Proverbs 25:16]. Elisha Aher looked and cut the young plants. Of him Scripture says, *Do not let your mouth bring your flesh into sin,* and so forth [Ecclesiastes 5:5]. R. Akiba entered safely and went out safely. Of him, Scripture says, *Draw me, we will run after you,* and so forth [Song 1:4].

[C] R. Akiba said: At that time, when I ascended to heaven, I made more marks at the entrance of heaven than at the entrances of my house. When I arrived at the celestial curtain [*pargod*], the angels of destruction [*mal'akhe habbalah*] came out to injure me. God said to them: "Leave this elder alone. He is worthy to gaze at my glory."

[D] R. Akiba said: At that time, when I ascended to the *merkabah*, a heavenly voice came forth from beneath the throne of glory, speaking as follows in the Aramaic language: ... [13]

IV. Schäfer, ##671–674; from ms Oxford 1531. This passage is nearly identical to text III; but it appears, not in *Hekhalot Zuṭarti,* but as part of the cluster of *Hekhalot* material conventionally called *Merkabah Rabbah* [496,545]. The only significant differences in content between texts III and IV are: (1) IVA reverses the order of "one looked and died" and "one looked and went mad"; (2) IVB puts Ben Zoma in place of Ben Azzai ("Ben Zoma looked and died") and vice versa; and (3) text IV gives only the first words of section D, as follows: "At that time, I ascended to the *merkabah*. A heavenly voice came forth, and so forth." On the second of these points, text IV follows the tradition of PT Hag. 2:1 (77b) and *Song R.* to 1:4 [552].

Ms Munich 40 has here the opening words of the passage: "R. Akiba said: We were four who entered *pardes*, and so forth."

V. Schäfer, ##671–674. Ms New York's parallel to text IV is different enough from it to be worth translating separately.

[A] R. Akiba said: We were four who entered *pardes*. One looked and went mad, one looked and cut the young plants. I entered safely and went out safely. [This was] not because I am greater than my companions; but my deeds caused me to fulfill that which the sages taught: "It is your deeds that will bring you near, and your deeds that will put you at a distance."

[B] These are the men who entered *pardes*: Simeon b. Azzai, Simeon b. Zoma, Elisha b. Abuyah, and R. Akiba b. Joseph.

---

13 The Aramaic speech that follows, which Scholem has translated into English [602], does not concern us here.

R. Akiba said to them: "When you draw near the stones of pure marble, beware. Do not say, 'Water, water.' For it is written, *He who speaks lies shall not be established in my sight* [Psalm 101:7]."

Ben Azzai looked and died. Of him Scripture says, *Precious in the eyes of the Lord is the death of his saints,* and so forth.

Ben Zoma looked and went mad. Of him Scripture says, *If you find honey, eat only your fill, lest you become stuffed,* and so forth.

Elisha b. Abuyah cut the young plants. Of him Scripture says, *Do not let your mouth,* and so forth. It is said that, when Elisha descended to the *merkabah,* he saw Metatron, to whom permission had been given to sit one hour each day to record the merits of Israel. He said: "The sages taught that in heaven there is no standing and no sitting, no jealousy and no rivalry, no back [?] and no affliction." It occurred to him that there might be two divine powers in heaven. Thereupon they brought Metatron out from behind the celestial curtain [*pargod*] and flogged him with sixty fiery lashes. They gave Metatron permission to burn Elisha's merits. A heavenly voice went forth and proclaimed: "*Return, backsliding children!* – except for Aher."

R. Akiba ascended safely and descended safely. Of him Scripture says, *Draw me, we will run after you; the king has brought me into his chambers,* and so forth.

[C] R. Akiba said: When I ascended to heaven, I made more marks at the entrances of heaven than at the entrances of my house. When I arrived at the celestial curtain, the angels of destruction came out to injure me. God said to them: "Leave this elder alone. He is worthy to gaze at me."

[D] At that time, I ascended to the *merkabah.* A heavenly voice came forth, and so forth.

VI. Rachel Elior has published a Genizah fragment (TS K 21/95) which appears to derive from a slightly abbreviated recension of *Hekhalot Zutarti* [465]. It is not easy to define the relationship of this recension to that represented by the other manuscripts. Elior's fragment contains material corresponding to Schäfer, ##335, 337–339, 346, 348–350, 353–356; it thus includes the following:

[A–B] R. Akiba said: We were four who entered *pardes.* These are they [!]: Ben Azzai, Ben Zoma, Aher, and myself, Akiba. Ben Azzai looked and died, Ben Zoma looked and went mad, Aher looked and cut the young plants. I ascended safely and descended safely. Why did I ascend safely and descend safely? Not because I am greater than my companions; but my deeds caused me to fulfill that which the sages taught in the Mishnah: "It is your deeds that will bring you near and your deeds that will put you at a distance."

[C] R. Akiba said: When I ascended to heaven, I made more marks at the entrances of heaven than at the entrances of my house. When I arrived behind the celestial curtain [*le'ahore happargod*], the angels of destruction came and tried to drive me away, until God said to them: "My sons, leave this elder alone. He is worthy to gaze at my glory." Of him [!] Scripture says, *Draw me, we will run after you,* and so forth.

[D] R. Akiba said: When I ascended to heaven, I heard a heavenly voice issuing from beneath the throne of glory, speaking as follows in the Aramaic language: ...

VII. Schäfer, ##344–348; from ms New York. This passage occurs in ms New York near the beginning of *Hekhalot Zuṭarti,* shortly after the abbreviated opening of text III (above; Elior, lines 42–61). Scholem [593] quotes and translates parts of the passage.

[A] R. Akiba said: We were four who entered *pardes.* One looked and died, one looked and went mad, one looked and cut the young plants. I entered safely and went out safely. [This was] not because I am greater than my companions; but my deeds caused me to fulfill that which the sages taught in their Mishnah: "It is your deeds that will bring you near and your deeds that will put you at a distance."

[B] These are the men who entered *pardes*: Ben Azzai, Ben Zoma, Aher, and R. Akiba.

Ben Azzai looked at the sixth palace and saw the splendor of the air [! *ziw 'awir*] of the stones of marble that were built into [?] the palace. His body could not endure it. He opened his mouth and asked them: "What is the nature of these waters?" He died. Of him Scripture says, *Precious in the eyes of the Lord is the death of his saints.*

Ben Zoma looked at the splendor, at the stones of marble, and thought it was water. His body could endure not to ask them, but his mind could not endure it, and he went mad. Of him Scripture says, *If you find honey, eat only your fill, lest you become stuffed with it and vomit it.*

Elisha b. Abuyah descended and cut the young plants. In what way did he cut the young plants? It is said that, when he would go into the synagogues and study houses and see children successfully studying Torah, he would say [something] about them and they would be silenced[14]. Of him Scripture says, *Do not let your mouth bring your flesh into sin.*

R. Akiba ascended safely and descended safely. Of him Scripture says, *Draw me, we will run after you; the king has brought me into his chambers.*

[C is omitted.]

[D] R. Akiba said: When I ascended to the *merkabah*, a heavenly voice came forth from beneath the throne of glory, speaking in Aramaic. ...

b) The evolution of the sources. How are we to make our way through this complex and bewildering mass of data?

Our first and easiest path takes us through the five texts from III to VII. Each of these passages contains the *pardes* story. Each of them, except for text VI, tells it twice over (sections A and B). Each of them adds two brief first-person accounts of Akiba's experiences during his ascension (sections C and D; text VII, however, omits section C). Section D, which does not seem to be directly related to the *pardes* episode, is apparently unique to the *Hekhalot*. But most of the rest of the material occurs also in Talmudic and midrashic sources, from which the *Hekhalot* writers seem to have drawn it.

Thus, IIIA combines the opening of PT's version of the *pardes* story (Hag. 2:1, 77b) with a slightly expanded reworking of *Song R.*'s explanation for Akiba's success[15], and recasts the whole in the first person. IIIB closely resembles Tosefta's account (Hag. 2:3–4) as it is preserved in ms Erfurt (above, page 31). The second part of Akiba's narrative in IIIC is based on BT Hag. 15b[16], although the sentence that precedes it is apparently the elaboration of the *Hekhalot* writer. In short, the compiler of text III has brought together material from several rabbinic sources but has not in-

---

14 This rather cryptic remark, quoted directly from *Song R.* to 1:4, becomes intelligible against the background of a story found in PT (Hag. 2:1, 77b) of how Elisha would discourage young people from studying the Torah.

15 *Song R.* to 1:4: "R. Akiba entered safely and went out safely. He said: '[This was] not because I am greater than my companions; but thus taught the sages in the Mishnah: "It is your deeds that will bring you near, and your deeds that will put you at a distance." ' " This passage appears to be *Song R.*'s addition to a version of the *pardes* story that is otherwise dependent on PT [552].

16 At the very bottom of the page: "The angels tried to drive away even R. Akiba. God said to them: 'Leave this elder alone. He is worthy to make use of my glory.' "

tegrated it well enough to avoid telling his story twice. He has rewritten most of this material in the first person.

Text IV differs from III only in that it follows PT and *Song R.* in having Ben Zoma die and Ben Azzai go mad, rather than vice versa. Text V does not substantially change sections A and C, but expands section B rather considerably, on the basis of BT Hag. 14b–15a. Text VI collapses sections A and B into one continuous narrative, and retouches section C in accord with the Babylonian Talmud[h]; the writer has left the traces of his revision in his incongruous mixing of first-person and third-person narration.

So far, the *pardes* material in the *Hekhalot* seems to be little more than anthologies of the relevant rabbinic texts. With text VII, however, we are on new ground. Like text V, it leaves section A more or less untouched. It draws the details of what happened to Elisha b. Abuyah from no more exotic a source than *Song R.* But it glosses the death of Ben Azzai and the madness of Ben Zoma on the basis of the *Hekhalot*'s descriptions of the "water" trial, and thus introduces for the first time the details of this trial into a narrative of the *pardes* episode.

We have progressed from a relatively unadorned collection of rabbinic materials on the four who entered *pardes*, to a version in which these materials are expanded and combined with the details of the "water" trial. The thread that stood by itself in text III is, in text VII, woven together with a second thread. This second thread, too, seems originally to have stood alone, and to have become increasingly tangled with the rabbinic *pardes* materials.

Text I has, as far as I can see, no reminiscence whatever of the *pardes* story. Text II, by contrast, describes the "water" test so as to bring it into connection with Akiba's warning in BT Hag. 14b. Where text IB had only "there is not a single drop there," text IIB adds: " ... but only the light of the splendor of the stones of pure marble that were built into the palace" – which is surely a gloss on BT's "stones of pure marble[17]." But, while IIB thus explains Akiba's warning, it does nothing to account for the death of Ben Azzai, for the saintly Ben Azzai can hardly have been among those "unworthy to see the king in his beauty" [593]. The author of IID, which I regard as a later addition to text II (below), is the first to make this association. (He is also the first to use the Talmudic expression "water, water" in connection with the "water" test.) The writer of text VII twists the two threads still more tightly together. He interpolates the "water" test into the *pardes* story itself, and uses it to explain Ben Zoma's madness as well as Akiba's warning and Ben Azzai's death.

---

17 The variant reading "if you [plural] say" in IIB, for "if he says" (above, endnote *e*), is a further step in this direction.

Before I go on to draw a conclusion from this, I must defend my belief that IIB and IID are to be treated as distinct sources – or, to put it more exactly, that IIC and IID are additions to IIA–B. I base this view, first of all, on tensions between the two parts of text II. I have already remarked that the use of the "water" test to explain Ben Azzai's death is not really appropriate, and gives the impression of being the work of a writer who made use of an earlier source (IIB) without thinking through its implications. Similarly, IIC suggests that the unworthy mystic can fool the angelic guardians into letting him pass, if only he has the sense to keep his mouth shut at the gates of the sixth palace. But IIA–B implies that the angels, (or, at least, the source of the "heavenly voice") already know who is worthy and who is not, and use the tests as a way of making the distinction evident. I find it hard to believe that the author of these sections can also have written IIC.

To these observations, I would add a philological argument. The strange expressions "splendor of the air" and "air of the splendor" (*ziw 'awir, 'awir ziw*), used in IIC and D (and in VIIB), are best explained as based on a mistaken reading of *me'or ziw* ("the light of the splendor"; IIB) as *me'awir ziw* ("from the air of the splendor"). It follows that the author (or authors) of IIC and D already had before him a corrupted text of IIB[i)].

Let us sum up what we have discovered so far. The evolution of the sources has appeared as a process of mutual contamination of the *pardes* story and the "water" test, a process that reaches its end point in text VII. The purest, and therefore presumably the oldest, version of the "water" test is that preserved in text I. Here, and nowhere else, do we have an account of the trial that shows no sign of the influence of BT Hag. 14b. It is our only independent witness. Our discussion of the bearing of the *Hekhalot* on the problem of "water, water" must therefore focus on it[18].

c) Texts IA–B, IIA–B. Our next step must be to clarify the relationship of IA to IB, and to examine text II's adaptations of both.

Six of the seven manuscripts that Schäfer published represent IA and IB as distinct accounts of two different trials, each with its own penalty for failure. But the seventh, ms Dropsie 436, combines the end of section A and the beginning of section B into one continuous narrative:

> ... If he was unworthy to descend to the *merkabah*, they would say to him, "Don't enter"; but he would enter. They would throw and hurl upon him thousands and thousands of waves of water, without a single drop being there. If he said, "What is the nature of these waters?" [and so forth]. ...

In other words, the second trial is itself punishment for failure in the first.

---

18 This conclusion perhaps challenges the conventional view that *Hekhalot Zuṭarti* is the oldest of

In a case of this sort, I would normally assume that some editor has combined originally discrete units into one. But, in the instance before us, we have several reasons for thinking that the version of the Dropsie manuscript is primary, and that a single sequence of events has been broken into two.

To begin with, the other manuscripts also indicate some connection between the two trials, in that they open section B with the word "because" (*mippene she-*) — although it is very unclear just what the causal link is supposed to be. Further, it is a little odd that things are being thrown upon the traveller both at the very end of section A and the very beginning of section B. The brief reference to the "iron axes" at the end of section A makes a rather lame impression, as if someone had inserted it on the basis of the end of section B.

The author of IIA—B elaborates the end of section B by adding the grisly detail that the hapless traveller gets his head split open by the iron axes. But, at the end of section A, he does not mention iron axes, but speaks of the angels' throwing their victim into a river of fiery coals. Why does he make this change? I propose that he had before him a version of text I akin to that of ms Dropsie, which described how the man who failed the first trial was thrown into an apparently liquid body. But, since he wanted to identify the "water" test as the subject of Akiba's warning in BT Hag. 14b, he turned this one liquid body into two: the fiery river (the punishment for failure in the first trial), and the mirage created by the shimmering of the stones of the sixth palace (the essence of the second trial). The detail that the individual seemed actually to be thrown into the water thus lost its meaning for him; for Akiba speaks of "drawing near" the stones of pure marble, not of being cast into their radiance. The confusion of the first sentence of IIB perhaps results from the writer's half-hearted attempt to modify his source.

We have, however, a parallel to the beginning of IIB in one of the Genizah *Hekhalot* fragments that Ithamar Gruenwald published; and the resemblance perhaps suggests that the literary prehistory of text II's "water" test is more complicated than we have so far imagined. If so, I can only point to the complexities, without being able to unravel them. In the Genizah

---

the *Hekhalot* texts [542], and that its materials have an automatic claim to priority. It is worth noting, however, that the beginning of IIA1 speaks of "those who descend to the *merkabah*" (*yorede merkabah*), a curious locution which Scholem considers typical of *Hekhalot Rabbati*, as opposed to *Hekhalot Zuṭarti* [594]. (Contrast IIID and its parallels: "When I ascended to the *merkabah* ..." VB, however, has Elisha "descend to the *merkabah*.") If it is right to talk about *Hekhalot Rabbati* and *Zuṭarti* as more or less unified compositions – which, following Schäfer, I am very much inclined to doubt – we might suppose that text II is an adaptation of *Hekhalot Rabbati*'s "water" test, interpolated into *Hekhalot Zuṭarti*.

text, the angel Ozhayah tells R. Ishmael what he is to expect when he reaches the sixth palace[19]: " ... hosts upon hosts of princes and superior princes, troops and more troops. For the gate of the sixth palace pushes and drives forth and expels all at once myriads upon myriads, camps upon camps, gatherings upon gatherings. But you will suffer neither check nor harm, for you are holding a great seal, which all the angels are terrified of" [468a]. The likeness to IIB is far from exact. Yet the gushing forth of angelic throngs does remind us of the illusory gushing of non-existent waters, and some of the language used in the two passages is very similar[j]. Now, IIB lapses at one point into second person singular narration: "a herald goes forth before you" (see the conclusion of endnote *e*, above). This strange incongruity may preserve a trace of a version of the "water" test which, like the passage from Gruenwald's fragment, was an instruction in the second person. It perhaps reinforces the notion that IIB and the Genizah text are more closely related than appears at first, and that their authors may have drawn upon similar stereotypic language to express their notions of what went on at the gate of the sixth palace.

Was this locale an original part of text I, as well as text II? I am inclined to think not. The context of text I certainly does not call for a description of the gate of the sixth palace at this point. It is true that this passage comes after a description of what the traveller must encounter in his celestial journey; but we have long since left the sixth palace for the seventh (Schäfer, #235; Wertheimer, 22:1), and it is jarring now to find ourselves again before its gate. Most likely, text I's reference to the gate of the sixth palace is an addition by a later scribe, under the influence of IIA–B.

However this may be, it seems certain that the author of text I knew nothing of the idea that it was the marble stones of the sixth palace that created the illusion of water. I imagine that the author of IIA–B originated this suggestion. I further suppose that he deduced it from a comparison of BT Hag. 14b with the description of Herod's temple in BT Sukk. 51b and B.B. 4a (above, section 1b); and that we are to understand his odd reference to the marble stones as *selulot bahekhal* (which I have guessed to mean "built into the palace") in connection with the latter passage.

d) The "water" test and the Red Sea. In its earliest surviving version, the description of the "water" test had no direct connection to the *pardes* episode. It took the form of a comment on Ezekiel 1:27. This alone is enough to mark the passage as exceptional, for explicit midrash on Ezek-

---

19 I summarize and discuss the context of this passage in chapter IX, section A2b. – In the quote that follows, I have emended *sheni* ("second") to *shishshi* ("sixth"). The emendation is an easy one, and the context overwhelmingly supports it.

iel's *merkabah* is rare in the *Hekhalot* literature. It is unusual in another respect: it is practically the only *Hekhalot* source that mentions the golden calf[k]. When a *merkabah* midrash mentions both the calf and a body of water, we are bound to take notice. We are also bound to ask how the author made the connections among the *merkabah*, the waters, and the calf.

The Genizah midrashim that we examined in chapter V provide a possible model for these connections: the Israelites see the *merkabah* at the Red Sea, and therefore worship the calf. We saw in chapter III that Revelation's "glass sea" is a heavenly counterpart of the Red Sea. Can we possibly say the same for the illusory waters described in the *Hekhalot*?

I think we can. I think that it is only on this assumption that the logic underlying the "water" test becomes intelligible.

In section A, as we have seen, the waters function as an instrument of punishment. It is hard to imagine that they are not, in this role, conceived as substantial. They act much as did the waters of the Red Sea, which spared the worthy travellers (Israelites) who entered them, but destroyed the unworthy. (Pharaoh must have known well what a person feels like when angels "throw and hurl upon him thousands and thousands of waves of water.") The worthy traveller's hesitation before entering reminds us of the way the Israelites, according to rabbinic legend, stood at the shore of the Red Sea arguing about which tribe should enter first[20]. This same haggadah describes how the Israelites who first entered the sea had stones hurled at them by others (*Mekhilta*, ed./tr. 1:232 [195]; cf. Targ. Psalm 68:28); and this detail has perhaps left its trace in section B's description of how, if one fails the water test, the angels "run after him and stone him."

Text I's claim that the angels warn the unworthy visitor not to enter does not, indeed, suit this comparison very well. Both the Bible (Exodus 14:4, 17) and the haggadah [393] emphasize that God did his best to lure the Egyptians into the sea. Text II's version (A3), by contrast, is very suggestive of God's hardening the hearts of the Egyptians; and perhaps text II here preserves a more original feature of the description. This suggestion is, I realize, rather arbitrary. Yet it does have something in its favor beside that it suits my hypothesis: it is hard to imagine that any traveller to the *merkabah*, no matter how "unworthy," could be so stupid as to disregard an explicit command not to proceed. Copyists of text I may possibly have inserted "don't" into A3, in order to avoid the unpleasant implication that the angels deliberately give wrong instructions to persons seeking God.

---

20 *Mekhilta, Be-Shallaḥ* chapter 6 (ed./tr. 1:232–237 [195]). Joseph Heinemann gives a particularly useful discussion of this haggadah [408]. – BT Ber. 34a, which prescribes that a man invited to lead public prayers should first decline and afterward accept, may well have influenced the descriptions of the first trial [557]. But it does not follow that it was the only influence.

The Red Sea was the scene of a crisis in which the worthy were distinguished from the unworthy, the saved from the lost. But, according to the haggadah, it was more than that. It was the scene of a vision; and this vision led to the fresh crisis of the golden calf. Once again, the worthy folk were distinguished from the unworthy. The unworthy acted as they did because they had seen the *merkabah* at the sea.

We now have a clue to the role played by the waters in section B. The persons who first conceived the "water" test assumed that it was the experience of the *merkabah* and the waters, together, that led the Israelites to make the calf. They went from this to the idea that this combination is necessarily fatal, necessarily leads to false worship. The Red Sea in the vicinity of the *merkabah* must therefore be branded an illusion. Those who see it and know it is not really there are faithful to God, "worthy to see the king and his throne." Those who believe it is real are the ones who kiss the calf.

This reasoning is admittedly rather strange, and seems to disregard normal ideas of causation. In order fully to understand it, we may have to suppose that our linking of the *Hekhalot*'s waters to the Red Sea is only a first step, and that the Red Sea may be a screen for some other, even more important, body of water. But that will come later.

Is all of this relevant to the Babylonian expansion of the *pardes* story, and to the meaning of its warning against saying "water, water"? I have no doubt that it is. Precisely because text I gives no hint that it is directly linked to BT Hag. 14b, we can use it with some confidence as an independent witness to the ideas underlying that source. It is surely, as Scholem says, no "*post festum* interpretation of the Talmudic passage." Its testimony guides us, in our efforts to understand Akiba's warning, toward the rabbinic traditions about the *merkabah*'s appearance at the Red Sea.

I conclude by noting that Rashi interprets the crucial passage in Hag. 14b in such a way as to suggest that he envisions a predicament like that of the Israelites at the Red Sea. He paraphrases Akiba's warning: "Do not say, 'There is water, water here; how can we go further?'" Just so, the Israelites found their way blocked by the waters of the sea, and could not proceed. If we can imagine that an early tradition survived to eleventh-century France, where Rashi heard it — and the language he uses in explaining the "pure marble" may perhaps hint that he was following a tradition akin to that of the *Hekhalot*[1] — we may find in Rashi's comment some support for the idea that we are to identify the "water" of Akiba's warning as that of the Red Sea.

3. Mekhilta to Exodus 15:2

What did the Israelites see at the Red Sea?

"The salvation of the Lord," according to the Bible (Exodus 14:13). They also saw "the Egyptians dead upon the seashore," and "the great work [literally, "hand"] which the Lord did against the Egyptians" (14: 30–31, RSV). Surely we should add the "pillar of cloud" that separated the Egyptians from the Israelites, according to 14:19–20; and the "pillar of fire and of cloud" from which the Lord looked down upon the Egyptians (14:24).

The rabbis went farther. Saul Lieberman has shown that, at least as far back as early Tannaitic times, certain rabbis believed that God had revealed himself to his people at the sea with an immediacy and directness matched only at Sinai [570]. Normally, God cloaked himself with images, operated within apparently natural phenomena. At the sea, as at Sinai, he exposed himself as he was. The people, seeing him, cried out: *This is my God, and I will praise him* (Exodus 15:2). This verse is, at least ostensibly, the basis for the rabbinic belief in a theophany at the sea; the demonstrative *this* suggested to midrashic expositors that the speaker is pointing to a visible being whom he recognizes as his God.

We cannot here sift through all of the evidence that Lieberman invokes for this conception. We must single out for our attention those sources that imply some connection between God's self-revelation at the sea and Ezekiel's *merkabah*.

a) Mekhilta and Leviticus Rabbah. The earliest of these sources is preserved in both *Mekhilta*s, to Exodus 15:2 (*Mekhilta of R. Ishmael, Shirah* chapter 3, ed./tr. 2:24–25 [195]; *Mekhilta of R. Simeon,* ed. 78 [196]). It is attributed to R. Eliezer, a Tanna who was active at the beginning of the second century. There is, as we will see, circumstantial evidence that this attribution is correct.

The versions given in the two *Mekhilta*s do not significantly differ. I translate the *Mekhilta of R. Ishmael,* according to the text published by Horowitz [193] (pp. 126–127):

> R. Eliezer says: From what source [*minayin*] can you deduce that a servant-girl at the sea saw what Isaiah and Ezekiel did not[m)]? It is written, *I liken myself through the prophets* [Hosea 12: 11] [21]. It is also written, *The heavens were opened, and I saw visions of God* [Ezekiel·1:1].
>
> This may be compared to a human king who entered a province surrounded by his retinue, flanked by his mighty men, troops going before and after him. "Which is the king?" everyone

---

21 RSV: "through the prophets [I] gave parables" (Hosea 12:10, in RSV's verse numeration). "Gave parables" is RSV's translation of MT's vocalization *'adammeh*; the rabbis clearly read this word as Niph[c]al *'eddameh*, "I liken myself."

asked; for he was flesh and blood like them. But, when God revealed himself at the sea, no one
had to ask, "Which is the king?" As soon as they saw him, they recognized him. They burst out :
This is my God, and I will praise him, and so forth.

At first sight, it looks as if the two paragraphs belong together, and the
parable of the second paragraph answers the question raised in the first.
But there are several reasons for thinking this is not true. In the first place,
the contrast implied in the parable does not seem to be the same as that
stated in the question, for it is hard to believe that the author of the midrash thought that Isaiah and Ezekiel could not tell the difference between
God and his retinue. (Isaiah 6:1–3 distinguishes clearly enough between
God and the seraphim.) Second, the question "from what source can you
deduce ...?" is a technical expression, a fixed form of interrogation which
ought to be answered by a Biblical text, not by a parable. Third, if the
parable is indeed intended to be the answer to Eliezer's question, the two
Biblical quotations are left without any clear purpose.

It thus appears that the parable originally had nothing to do with Eliezer's midrash. A later editor combined the two sources, perhaps because
the image of the royal retinue suggested to him the visions of Isaiah and
Ezekiel. The answer to Eliezer's question must somehow lie in the Biblical
quotations that follow it. But how?

A passage from *Lev. R.* 1:14 (ed. 30–31 [191]) sheds some light on the
meaning of Eliezer's midrash, and helps to confirm that it is indeed Eliezer's:

> What was the difference between Moses and the rest of the prophets? R. Judah b. R. Ilai and the
> rabbis [differ on this issue].
>
> R. Judah says: All the prophets saw [the divine vision] through the medium of nine mirrors.
> So it is written: *Like the appearance of the vision that I saw, like the vision I saw when I came to
> destroy the city, and visions like the vision I saw at the river Chebar. And I fell on my face* [Ezek-
> iel 43:3]. Moses saw through the medium of a single mirror: *By vision, and not in riddles* [Num-
> bers 12:8] [22].
>
> The rabbis say: All the prophets saw [the divine vision] through the medium of a dirty mir-
> ror. So it is written: *I speak to the prophets, and I multiplied visions*, and so forth [*and I liken
> myself through the prophets*; Hosea 12:11]. Moses saw through the medium of a sparkling mir-
> ror. So it is written: *He sees the Lord's appearance* [Numbers 12:8].

As it stands, the discussion is focused on Numbers 12:8, and deduces
from two successive phrases of this verse that Moses is superior to the rest
of the prophets (God speaks to Moses [1] *by vision, and not in riddles,
and* [2] *he sees the Lord's appearance*). But, when we turn from the

---

22 The point of the midrash is that *mar'eh*, "vision," can be read as if it were *mar'ah*, "mirror."
Moses sees a single vision/mirror, while Ezekiel sees many. (Margulies, in a footnote on the passage, explains the midrashic arithmetic that yields the number nine.) Ithamar Gruenwald and
Moshe Idel have written on the conception, in ancient and medieval Judaism, that God is perceived through a mirror [231,547,564]. New Testament readers will be familiar with the idea
from I Corinthians 13:12; cf. II Corinthians 3:18, where *katoptrizomenoi* (RSV "beholding")
should perhaps be translated "seeing in a mirror."

proofs of Moses' superiority to the proofs of the prophets' inferiority, we find that these closely resemble the two verses quoted in Eliezer's midrash. One proof text, Hosea 12:11, is the same in both sources. Although not all manuscripts of *Lev. R.* actually quote the concluding words of this verse, the weight of the midrash clearly rests upon them: the expositor contrasts the cloudy and remote *I liken myself* to the direct vision that Moses saw. The other proof text is a passage from Ezekiel that refers to the prophet's "visions" (*mar'ot*). The author of the midrash in *Lev. R.*, however, used Ezekiel 43:3 rather than 1:1, since it gave him a basis for calculating the number of these "visions" (or, as he preferred to read the Hebrew word, "mirrors").

How are we to explain the relation of *Mekhilta*'s midrash to that found in *Lev. R.*? A passage in Tosefta (Zeb. 2:17) [278] gives us the clue: "Judah is the student of [his father] Ilai, and Ilai the student of R. Eliezer; therefore [Judah] repeats the teachings of R. Eliezer." If we assume that the attributions in both *Mekhilta* and *Lev. R.* are accurate, all now becomes clear. Judah b. Ilai and his contemporaries inherited from R. Eliezer a midrash which combined Hosea 12:11 and Ezekiel 1:1. They split this cluster into two, and contrasted each of the halves with a phrase from Numbers 12:8. They preserved the basic idea of Eliezer's midrash — that Moses and his contemporaries were superior to the prophets — but shifted its emphasis, contrasting the prophets only with Moses himself and not with each and every one of his followers. Judah and his colleagues differently expressed the precise nuance of the contrast. Judah further realized that his comparison of Moses' single mirror with the prophets' multiple mirrors would be more effective if he could give an exact number to these mirrors. He therefore replaced Ezekiel 1:1 with 43:3, which also mentioned *mar'ot*, and which seemed to imply that there were nine of them.

b) The meaning of Eliezer's midrash. Judah b. Ilai and "the rabbis" certainly introduced ideas into Eliezer's midrash that Eliezer himself did not intend. There is no reason to suppose that Eliezer thought of Ezekiel's *visions of God* (*mar'ot 'elohim*) as "mirrors," or that he was interested in calculating their number. But Judah's reinterpretation of the master's midrash gives us two valuable clues to its original meaning. First, we learn that Eliezer quoted Hosea 12:11 and Ezekiel 1:1, not in order to prove that the Israelites had seen a tremendous vision at the Red Sea — he evidently took this for granted — but to show that the prophets' perceptions were inferior. Second, we learn that Eliezer invoked Ezekiel 1:1 because its plural *mar'ot* proved the multiplicity of Ezekiel's perception of the divine.

We are now in a position to guess at the logic of Eliezer's midrash. Ezekiel 1:1 does not say, as one might expect, *I saw a vision of God,* but *I saw visions of God.* Eliezer interprets Ezekiel's plural in the light of Hosea 12:

11: where God *multiplies visions*[23], he is *likening himself through the prophets*; that is, he is showing the prophets images of himself, not himself as he really is. Even the *merkabah* vision, vivid and powerful as it was, was multiplex, and therefore only a series of images. It was inferior to the direct perception of God that even servant-girls had at the Red Sea.

A few other midrashim seem to support this understanding of Eliezer's exegesis. A thirteenth-century writer, Todros ha-Levi Abulafia, quotes a midrash (supposedly from the *Mekhilta of R. Simeon*, but not attested in any other source), which explains the prophets' divergent perceptions of God by quoting Ezekiel 1:1: "*I saw visions of God ...* many visions did I see before I was found worthy to receive the Shechinah" (*Mek. Simeon*, ed. 147 [196]). The implication is that Ezekiel's multiple *visions of God* were an inferior prelude to his actual experience of God's presence (not described in the Bible?). A *Tanḥuma* midrash in *Pesiqta Rabbati* 33:11 (ed. 155b [209]) explains discrepancies between Isaiah's vision and Ezekiel's by invoking Hosea 12:11, which the writer interprets: "Did I not liken myself to the prophets in many forms? ... I did not appear to you as a single vision, but rather as many visions[n])." Similarly, a very late midrash called *'Aggadat Bereshit* expounds Hosea 12:11 as follows: "Indeed *I speak to the prophets*, but *I multiplied visions*, so that one's prophecy does not resemble another's" (chapter 14, ed. 13b [183a]; *Yalquṭ Isaiah* #385). The concessive *indeed* with which the writer begins his midrash suggests that he sees this diversity as a flaw.

The second and third of these passages are presumably centuries later than R. Eliezer; and any argument for the early date of the first must depend on the not unimpeachable reliability of Abulafia's claim that it comes from the *Mekhilta of R. Simeon*. But, late as these sources may be, they confirm that the interpretation of Ezekiel 1:1 and Hosea 12:11 that I have attributed to Eliezer would have seemed plausible to midrashic expositors.

As *Mekhilta* represents it, Eliezer's midrash speaks of both Isaiah and Ezekiel. But the fact that neither *Mekhilta* nor *Lev. R.* actually quotes Isaiah leads us to suspect that Eliezer originally mentioned Ezekiel alone, specifically contrasting the theophany at the Red Sea with the *merkabah* vision; and that it was a later transmitter who added the nod to Isaiah. We find our suspicions confirmed when we turn to *Deut. R.* 7:8. Here, in the context of a discussion of the Sinai revelation, the midrash quotes the early third-century Caesarean Amora Hoshaiah: "The least in the days of Moses saw what Ezekiel, the greatest of the prophets, did not see."

---

23 It does not seem to have disturbed Eliezer that the two passages use different Hebrew words for "visions": *ḥazon* in Hosea, *mar'ot* in Ezekiel. He apparently saw the two verses as held together by their content rather than by their language. We will soon touch on this point again.

c) Hoshaiah and Origen. This last passage, with its implication that Hoshaiah knew and transmitted Eliezer's midrash, is important for another reason. With its help, we can explain an otherwise puzzling remark made by Hoshaiah's eminent Caesarean contemporary Origen.

Origen devotes his first homily on the Book of Ezekiel to a discussion of the vision of chapter 1; I will argue in chapter VIII that he got much of his material from contemporary synagogue sermons on the *merkabah* and its relation to the Sinai revelation. In the middle of his exposition, he makes the following apparently pointless comment on Ezekiel 1:1:

> It is now opportune for us to touch on certain aspects of the passage at hand. The prophet saw, not *a vision*, but *visions of God*. Why did he see not one but several *visions*? Listen to God making his promise: *I have multiplied visions* [Hosea 12:11]. [*In Ezech. Hom.* I, 7; ed. 332 [641]]

In chapter VIII, I will translate the full context in which this passage appears. It will then become clear that the passage is entirely isolated in its context, and contributes nothing to Origen's line of reasoning. We can only make sense of it if we assume that Origen took over, with the rest of the rabbinic haggadah he used, a midrash that invoked Hosea 12:11 to explain the plural *visions* of Ezekiel 1:1. I assume that this was Eliezer's midrash, which Origen quotes in a truncated form, robbed of its original point. Hoshaiah was Origen's neighbor; and, if we may rely on the parallels between the utterances attributed to the two men, his acquaintance as well [656, 664]. It is a fair guess that Origen heard Eliezer's midrash — translated into Greek, presumably — from Hoshaiah[24].

We notice that both *Deut. R.* 7:8 and Origen put offshoots of Eliezer's midrash in contexts dealing with the Sinai revelation. So does the editor of the *Mekhilta of R. Ishmael.* He applies to Exodus 19:11 an abbreviated version of Eliezer's midrash, which he here quotes without attribution:

> [*The Lord will descend on Mount Sinai*] *in the sight of all the people.* This teaches that they saw at that time what Isaiah and Ezekiel did not. So it is written, *I liken myself through the prophets.* [*Mekhilta, Ba-Hodesh* chapter 3; ed./tr. 2:212 [195]]

By the third century, it would appear, midrashic expositors had transferred Eliezer's midrash from the sea to Sinai[25]. It is probably significant, in

---

24 In chapter VIII, I will argue that some midrashim preserved in Hebrew sources were originally formulated in Greek, the language in which Origen must have learned them. Can we suppose that Eliezer originally composed his midrash in Greek, and that the Hebrew text in the *Mekhilta* is itself a translation? If so, this would neatly explain the difficulty we noted earlier, that Ezekiel 1:1 and Hosea 12:11 use different words for "visions" (*mar'ot, hazon*); for LXX has *horaseis* in both passages. But I do not consider the difficulty serious enough to demand this radical hypothesis, and prefer to hold my notion of Greek midrash in reserve until we meet situations that seem to require it.

25 *Mekhilta* twice quotes a midrash contrasting God's appearance at the sea with his appearance at Sinai (*Shirah* chapter 4, *Ba-Hodesh* chapter 5; ed./tr. 2:31–32, 219–220 [195]). This midrash

this connection, that Hoshaiah does not speak of "the least who was at the sea," but of "the least in the days of Moses." In chapter V (section 5f), I tentatively suggested that certain traditions that related the *merkabah* to the calf were shifted in the same direction. We are perhaps dealing with two aspects of the same development: the *merkabah*-Sinai association has become so important that it absorbs *merkabah* traditions that belonged originally to other contexts.

d) Conclusion. It may seem inappropriate to speak of Eliezer's midrash as a *merkabah* tradition, given that its thrust is that Ezekiel did *not* see what the Israelites saw at the sea. But psychologists teach us that denial can be itself a form of affirmation. The very fact that Eliezer singled the two visions out for contrast implies that he perceived some connection between them.

Eliezer may possibly have known traditions that claimed that God descended to the sea in a *merkabah* like the one that Ezekiel saw, and deliberately set himself against them. This would fit in with my idea that there was something about the *merkabah*'s link with the sea that made the rabbis uneasy.

I am inclined, however, to favor another explanation of Eliezer's intent. Like the authors of the midrashim on God's descent to Sinai that we examined in chapter IV (section 5), he wanted to convey that Moses' generation saw a divine vision along the lines of Ezekiel's, but vastly superior to it. But, while those authors used arithmetical multiplication to convey the idea of superiority — "twenty-two thousand chariots descended with God, each one like the *merkabah* that Ezekiel saw" — Eliezer proceeded in the opposite direction. At the sea, he declared, God showed himself in the unity that underlay all the manifestations of the *merkabah*.

In the meantime, we find our steps dogged by a problem that we have so far not even begun to confront. What led the rabbis to assume in the first place that God revealed himself at the sea? The verses from Exodus 14 that I gathered at the beginning of this section do not add up to a theophany comparable to that at Sinai; while this notion is more likely to have been read into Exodus 15:2's *this is my God* than read out of it. As this chapter progresses, we will move toward a solution of this problem.

For now, we must temporarily break off our pursuit of the theme of the *merkabah*'s appearance at the Red Sea, while we look at another Tannaitic source that seems to combine the *merkabah* and a sea.

---

is hardly compatible with Eliezer's. But the editor's repeated use of it suggests that he saw the two great theophanies as being parallel, so that a midrash originally formulated for the one could be re-used in connection with the other.

4. BT Sotah 17a, and parallels

The source in question is a brief haggadah in praise of the color blue, which both Palestinian and Babylonian rabbinic traditions attribute to the second-century Tanna R. Meir.

As usual, our first step must be to survey its variants.

a) The texts. As represented by BT (Sot. 17a; with minor variations, in Men. 43b and Hull. 89a), the haggadah runs as follows:

> R. Meir said: How is blue [*tekhelet*] different from all the other colors? The color blue resembles the sea, the sea resembles the sky, and the sky resembles the throne of glory. So it is written: *They saw the God of Israel, and beneath his feet was something resembling a construction of sapphire stone, like the heaven itself for purity* [Exodus 24:10]. It is also written: *Like the appearance of sapphire stone, the likeness of a throne* [Ezekiel 1:26].

What called forth this encomium of the color blue? It is clear from the contexts in which BT quotes this passage that the editors understood it as referring to the blue thread woven into the fringes which, according to Numbers 15:37–41, the Israelites were to attach to their clothing. "They shall place a thread of blue [*tekhelet*] in the corner fringe ... and you shall look upon it, and remember all the Lord's commandments, and do them ... and be holy to your God."

The haggadah itself does not actually mention the fringes or the blue thread, and it is not absolutely certain that the author meant to refer to them. Indeed, one late source that draws upon this midrash applies it to the blue cloth that covered the ark in the wilderness (*Numb. R.* 4:13, referring to Numbers 4:6). But the odds are that the Babylonian editors understood their source correctly. Already in the rabbinic period, the blue thread had for the most part vanished from the fringes that observant Jews wore on their clothing. (We are not entirely sure why it disappeared [376].) But the prescription from the Book of Numbers, recited every day as part of the Shema[c], kept the memory of the blue thread alive. It is reasonable to suppose that many Jews wondered why God had demanded a thread of blue, and no other color; and that some rabbis tried to find an answer.

The Palestinian tradition, represented by PT Ber. 1:2 (3c) and by *Sifre Numb.* #115 (ed. 126 [221]), combines the haggadah attributed to Meir with a distinct and originally independent midrash of Numbers 15:39. We can detect a faint trace of a seam, where the two were joined.

> It was taught in the name of R. Meir:
> [A] Scripture does not say, *You shall look upon it* [the fringe], but, *You shall look upon him* [Numbers 15:39]. This teaches that, if anyone performs the commandment of putting fringes on his clothing, it is as if he had received the Shechinah[26].

---

26 The point of the midrash is that the Hebrew word for "fringe" is feminine, while the pronoun

[B] This teaches that the color blue resembles the sea, the sea resembles grass, grass resembles the sky, the sky resembles the throne, and the throne resembles sapphire. So it is written: *I saw, above the firmament that was over the heads of the cherubim, something that looked like sapphire. Something that looked like the appearance of the likeness of a throne was visible above them* [Ezekiel 10:1]. [PT] [o)]

As Louis Ginzberg points out [285], the awkward repetition of "this teaches" at the beginning of section B marks the point at which an editor joined two distinct midrashim. BT Men. 43b quotes a somewhat different version of the first of these (section A), attributing it to Simeon b. Yohai. We may assume that Meir's name was originally attached only to section B.

The parallel in *Sifre* closely resembles PT's version, but smooths out the text by deleting "this teaches" from section B. Like BT, it quotes Ezekiel 1:26 instead of Ezekiel 10:1. Again like BT, its chain of associations has only four links (blue - sea - sky - throne), not PT's six (blue - sea - grass - sky - throne - sapphire).

Several late midrashic texts make use of both the Palestinian and the Babylonian versions of Meir's haggadah, sometimes attributing it to R. Hezekiah rather than to Meir (*Numb. R.* 14:3; *Midr. Psalms* 24:12, 90:18; ed. 105a, 197b [199]). These later sources usually abbreviate or expand the chain of associations. A *Tanhuma* version reduces the chain to three links: blue - sky - throne (*Numb. R.* 17:5; Tanh. *Shelah* #15; Tanh. Buber *Shelah* #29–30, ed. 37b [222])[p)]. But *Midr. Psalms* 24:12 (= *Numb. R.* 14:3) adds new links: blue - sea - grass - sky - rainbow - cloud - throne of glory - God's glory itself. So does *Midr. Psalms* 90:18: blue - sea - grass - trees - sky - splendor - rainbow - likeness of God.

These late versions often do not agree with the earlier sources on the proof text or texts to be used. The *Tanhuma* midrash quotes only Exodus 24:10; while both passages from *Midr. Psalms* use Ezekiel 1:28. Only one later source, *Numb. R.* 4:13, keeps both Ezekiel 1:26 and BT's four-link chain.

b) Sea, sky, throne. Thus far the evidence for Meir's haggadah. What are we to make of it? What implications does this haggadah's use of Ezekiel have for our study?

I cannot verify, but see no reason to deny, that the haggadah's nucleus indeed goes back to Meir, and that he expressed it even if he did not originate it. (The attribution of the haggadah to R. Hezekiah in a few late midrashim does not weigh very heavily against the unanimous testimony of the earlier sources.) I understand this nucleus to consist of the explanation that

---

following *upon* is masculine and must therefore refer to a masculine entity. The expositor supposes this entity to be God himself.

the color blue is special because it is a token of God's sky-blue throne, and the use of a chain of resemblances to argue for this notion. The essential point, that God's throne is blue, must have been drawn from Ezekiel's *merkabah* visions. The different versions of the haggadah, however, do not agree on exactly which Biblical text will prove this point. We must assume either that later transmitters supplied the proof texts which had been implicit in Meir's argument, or else that Meir himself quoted different Scriptural passages on different occasions.

The sources also disagree on just what links belong in the chain. All agree that blue is the color of the sky, which has the color of the throne[27]. All but the *Tanḥuma* version introduce the sea between the color blue and the sky. Some versions, apparently regarding green and blue as the same color, add "grass" or "trees." The texts that quote Ezekiel 1:28 add, on the basis of that verse, "rainbow," "cloud," "splendor," "glory," and "likeness." Not all of these variations are necessarily due to the transmitters. Meir himself may not always have used exactly the same chain of resemblances. But it does seem that the sea and the sky are essential to the haggadah in a way that the other intermediate links are not.

Why the sea? Surely it is obvious enough that the sky is blue; we do not need the sea to establish the connection. Rashi, indeed, claims (on Sot. 17a) that "blue does not particularly resemble the sky, but ... resembles the appearance of the sea, and we can see that the sea looks like the sky." But this resolution is obviously desperate; and, as we will shortly see, Rashi tries a different tack in interpreting the parallel in Men. 43b[28]. The sea must be in the chain because it has some significance of its own in connection with God's throne.

But what? Ben Zion Bokser finds here a mystical conception of cosmic unity: "The resemblance between sea and sky was a demonstration of the link between the earthly and the heavenly and the blue fringe was a precious carrier of this mystery" [377]. There is perhaps a hint of some special theosophical significance of the blue sea and the blue sky in a Greek incantation text, saturated with Jewish references, which is preserved in the Paris Magical Papyrus. "I adjure thee by him ... the heaven-like, sea-like, cloud-like ... by him that is in Jerosolymum [= Jerusalem] the pure ..." [707][9]. Or are we perhaps to explain the sea's presence in the chain by

---

27 Except for *Midr. Psalms* 90:18, which, influenced by Ezekiel 1:28, replaces the throne at the end of the chain with God's "likeness."

28 In fairness to Rashi, we must admit that one midrash, which we will discuss in detail in chapter VIII, makes a special connection between the sea and the color blue (*tekhelet*). God shows Moses what *tekhelet* is by parading before him "a troop of angels wearing clothing resembling the sea" (*Pesiqta Rabbati* 20:4, ed. 98b [209]).

the fact that the ancients extracted blue dye from a sea creature [376], a shellfish which the Talmud at one point tells us "resembles the sea" (BT Men. 44a)?

Rashi, commenting on Men. 43b, offers yet another suggestion, which is particularly interesting in the light of what we have said so far in this chapter. The sea, he says, is mentioned because "miracles were there done for Israel"; that is, at the Red Sea. And a passage that *Sifre Numbers* quotes almost immediately before Meir's haggadah perhaps supports the view that Meir's "sea" hints at the Red Sea. Of a series of etymologies proposed for the Hebrew words for "blue" and "fringe" (*tekhelet, ṣiṣit*), all are linked with the Exodus, and one with the miracle at the sea.

We cannot say that any of these suggestions is impossible, and all of them may be right. Each of the proposed associations may have had its influence on the inclusion of the sea in Meir's chain. But we can perhaps get a fresh perspective on the question if we ask not only why the sea is included, but also why the sky is included.

After all, Meir did not need the sky for his argument any more than he needed the sea. Ezekiel compares the *merkabah* throne to sapphire; to link blue to the throne, all Meir would have had to do would be to point out that blue is the color of sapphire. If Meir mentioned the sky, it must have been because a reference to the sky would add plausibility to the idea, grounded in Ezekiel, that the throne is blue. People imagined God enthroned in the sky; what could be more natural than that the throne would have a skyey color?

This same reasoning would suggest that, when Meir's haggadah mentions the sea as well as the sky, it is making an allusion to God's throne being in the sea as well as in the sky. The throne is therefore sea-blue as well as sky-blue.

At first, this seems a very daring surmise based on a very slender foundation. We certainly do not normally think of the Jewish God as enthroned in the sea. We could hardly suppose, simply on the basis of the "sea" in Meir's chain, that ancient Jews had such a conception. But we recall Revelation's "glass sea"; we recall the rabbinic evidence (which we have not yet exhausted) of the theophany at the Red Sea; we may suspect that both of these ideas reflect a more fundamental image of a God enthroned amid the waters[29]. The color of the throne that Ezekiel describes will have reinforced this image.

The source we are about to examine will take us to the heart of this issue.

---

29 So we might gather from Psalm 29:10: "The Lord sat enthroned at the flood."

5. Song Rabbah to 1:9, Exodus Rabbah 23:14

a) Armory at the sea. In chapter V, we examined a series of four dialogues, on four Biblical verses, which *Mekhilta* puts into the mouths of Pappus and R. Akiba. We noted that *Song R.*'s midrash to Song 1:9 includes these dialogues in more or less reworked and expanded form, and that the reworking and expansion of the dialogue on Song 1:9 itself is particularly drastic (section 3d). We must now look closely at *Song R.*'s additions to this dialogue, and at the parallel material in *Ex. R.* 23:14, for the light they shed on the Red Sea theophany and its relation to the *merkabah*.

I have likened you, my love, says Song 1:9, *to a mare in Pharaoh's chariotry.* In direct opposition to the intent of the original author of the Pappus-Akiba dialogues, the writer in *Song R.* attributes to Akiba a midrash which infers from this verse that God, imitating Pharaoh's actions at the Red Sea, rode first on a stallion and then on a mare. But stallions and mares do not satisfy this writer's yen for a dramatic battle scene. He spins the midrash out at great length, describing each of the weapons that Pharaoh tried to use against God at the sea (naphtha, catapult stones, arrows, and so forth), and how God matched them one by one. At last, Pharaoh's arsenal is exhausted:

R. Berechiah quoted [R. Helbo, quoting] [r] R. Samuel b. Nahman: When Pharaoh had gone through all his weapons, God began to exalt himself over him. "Wicked one," he said, "have you got a wind? Have you got a cherub? Have you got wings [30]?"

Where did God hurl them from? R. Judan said: God detached them [*shemaṭan*] from between the wheels of the *merkabah* and hurled them upon the sea.

Thus the climax of the midrash, according to *Song R.* The parallel in *Ex. R.* 23:14 presumably once included the entire passage. But, at some point, a copyist left out all but the beginning and the end, referring the reader to *Song R.* for the omitted material [s]. He resumed his copying in the middle of the climactic passage:

" ... have you got a wind? Have you got wings?" Thereupon God tore them loose, brought them from between the wheels of the *merkabah*, and hurled them upon the sea [t].

We would be unwise to rely on the scribe's assurance that the material he omits is the same as the parallel in *Song R.* The conclusion, which he copies, suggests that *Ex. R.* gives an edited version of the midrash, which smooths out the rough edges that survive in *Song R.* The reviser, it seems, omitted the attribution to R. Judan, and was thus able to work Samuel b. Nahman's statement and Judan's into a single continuous narrative. We will soon see other traces of this reviser's work in *Ex. R.* 23:14.

---

30 The reference is to Psalm 18:11: *He rode on a cherub, and flew; he soared on wings of wind.*

We have no reason to suppose that the writer in *Song R.* arbitrarily inserted the names of Samuel b. Nahman and Judan. But we can do nothing to verify the accuracy of the attributions. If they are right, we can date the two statements to the late third and early fourth centuries, respectively. Judan will then have believed that the *merkabah* was present at the Red Sea, acting as a mobile armory for God's invincible weapons — the *wind, cherub,* and *wings* of Psalm 18:11, all of which are in fact part of Ezekiel's *merkabah* (Ezekiel 1:4, 6; chapter 10)[31].

The utterance attributed to Judan speaks of God's "detaching" these items from the *merkabah.* It thus makes use of a verb (*shamaṭ*) which we have seen applied to the Israelites' separating the ox-element from the rest of the *merkabah* (*Ex. R.* 43:8 and parallels; above, chapter V, section 4e).

b) "Look what is in the sea!" Both *Song R.* and *Ex. R.* go on to provide another midrash of Song 1:9. In *Ex. R.*, this new midrash comes immediately after the passage we have just discussed; while, in *Song R.*, additional midrashim on Psalm 18:11 and Song 1:9 intervene. We have no way of knowing how much of this intervening material lay before the editor of *Ex. R.*

I translate both versions of the midrash:

[*Song R.*:]
[A] Another explanation of the words, *I have likened you, my love:* [A1] The rabbis said: The Israelites took on the likeness of mares, and the wicked Egyptians took on the likeness of lustful stallions. They chased them until they sank in the sea.

[A2] R. Simon said: The Israelites did not, God forbid, take on the likeness of mares! Rather, the waves of the sea took on the likeness of mares, and the Egyptians took on the likeness of lustful stallions. They chased them until they sank in the sea.

[B1] Each Egyptian would say to his horse: "Yesterday you wouldn't let me drag you to the Nile, and now you are drowning me in the sea!" [B2] The horse would reply: "*He has hurled* [*ramah*] *in the sea* [Exodus 15:1]. He has tricked you [*rimmah*] in the sea. Look what [*re'u mah*] is in the sea! An ambush [Greek *epithesis*] is laid for you in the sea[u)].*"

[*Ex. R.*:]
[A] What is meant by, *I have likened you, my love?* [A1 omitted.] [A2] The waves of the sea took on the likeness of mares, and the wicked Egyptians took on the likeness of lustful stallions. They chased them until they sank in the sea. [A3] So it is written: *The horse and its rider he has hurled in the sea* [Exodus 15:1].

[B1] Each Egyptian would say to his horse: "Yesterday you wouldn't let me drag you to be watered, and now you are drowning me in the sea!" [B2] The horse would reply: "*He has*

---

31 *Midr. Psalms* 18:14 (ed. 72a–b [199]) adapts this midrash as follows: "R. Berechiah quoted R. Eleazar: God began to ride on a cherub, as it is written, *He rode on a cherub* [Psalm 18:11]. 'Wicked one,' he said, 'perhaps you have a cherub?' God began to fly, as it is written, *And flew.* 'Wicked one,' God said, 'perhaps you can fly?' God began to soar from one wing to the other, as it is written, *He soared on wings of wind.* 'Wicked one,' God said, 'perhaps you can match this?' Another explanation of the words, *He soared on wings of wind*: R. Judah said: The wind comes from between the wings of the *ḥayyot*; as it is written, *He soared on wings of wind.*"

hurled [ramah] in the sea. Look what [*re'eh mah*] is in the sea! The celestial realms [*rumo shel*] ^c*olam*] ^3^2 do I see [*ro'eh*] in the sea."

Our interest in this midrash is focused on the last sentence of *Ex. R.*'s version. But we will not be able to approach this passage with any confidence unless we first clarify its relation to its context, and to the parallel passage in *Song R.*

To begin with, we are dealing here not with one midrash but with two. Section A is a midrash on Song 1:9 which, in its original form, took no notice whatever of Exodus 15:1. Conversely, section B expounds Exodus 15:1, with no concern for Song 1:9. If the author of section A had kept in mind that both *the horse and its rider* perished in the sea, he would have had no reason to turn the Egyptians themselves into stallions; he could have had the riders drawn to their deaths by their lust-maddened beasts[33]. But, thinking only of Song 1:9, he sketched a symmetrical picture: as the Israelites take the form of mares, so the Egyptians take the form of stallions. In section B, by contrast, the Egyptians remain human, and the horses are credited with carrying their unwilling masters to their doom. There is no trace of the sexual motif which the author of section A drew from Song 1:9. The expositor instead emphasizes the word *ramah*, "he has hurled," in Exodus 15:1.

As in the last passage we examined, *Ex. R.*'s version is the more smoothly polished of the two. By adding section A3, its author welds together the two distinct midrashim. By eliminating the debate from A1–2 and quoting R. Simon's opinion anonymously, he represents the more acceptable of the two views as if it were unchallenged. We cannot suppose that Simon's midrash originally stood alone and that the writer in *Song R.* added the exposition of "the rabbis." For "the rabbis'" interpretation, offensive as it is, better suits the Biblical text, where it is *you, my love* (that is, Israel) who is *likened to a mare in Pharaoh's chariotry*. The development must have gone in the opposite direction. The author of the *Song R.* passage added Simon's midrash as a corrective to that of "the rabbis"; and the author of the *Ex. R.* passage chose to retain only the corrective.

Given all this, we would be disposed to imagine that *Ex. R.* B2 is a revised version of *Song R.* B2. We are in for a surprise. Not only do the two

---

32 Literally, "the height of the world." BT twice uses this phrase for God's headquarters (Pes. 118a, Men. 29b; so the corresponding Aramaic *rum* ^c*alma*, in Targ. Jeremiah 31:14), twice as an idiom for "the highest importance" (Ber. 6b, Meg. 14a). A late midrash on the death of Moses seems to use *rum* ^c*olam* for the zenith of the sky (Jellinek [477], page 128; addition to *Deut. R.* 11:10). At Qumran, *rum* ^c*olam* means literally "the celestial heights" (*Hodayot* iii, 20; cf. tr. 158 [77], and II Baruch 51:10), and, figuratively, the peak of worldly power (1QSb v, 23; tr. 209).

33 This is, in fact, what happens in Tanh. *Shofeṭim* #14; *'Abot de-Rabbi Nathan*, version A, chapter 27 (ed. 42a [183]); *Pirqe de-Rabbi Eliezer*, chapter 42.

passages present completely different interpretations of the word *ramah*, but it is *Ex. R.*'s that seems the more primary.

Song R. interprets Exodus 15:1 by vocalizing *ramah* as if it were *rimmah*, a different verb form from an identical root, meaning "he has tricked." The expositor then explains, through the mouths of the horses, that God has tricked the Egyptians into his ambush in the sea. But *Ex. R.* treats *ramah* as if it were not a verb at all but a noun, meaning "a height, a lofty place." The phrase *ramah bayyam* thus becomes a short nominal sentence: "There is a height in the sea." Which height? The celestial heights! This interpretation of *ramah* is exactly parallel to that of the Targum to Jeremiah 31:14, which translates the place-name "Ramah" as *rum ᶜalma*, the heavenly realms.

The author of *Ex. R.*'s midrash gives an additional twist to his interpretation by playing on the similar sounds of *ramah bayyam* (*he has hurled in the sea*) and *re'eh mah bayyam* ("look what is in the sea"). He follows this with his exegesis proper. "The celestial realms," says the horse to his astonished and terrified rider, "do I see in the sea."

Ex. R.'s midrash is more plausible than that of *Song R.* The logic of the passage demands that the horses explain why they are plunging into the sea. "An ambush is laid for you in the sea" not only does not answer this question, but is an excellent reason why the horses should be going the other way. In *Song R.*'s context, the horses' call to "look what is in the sea" does not really make sense. What are the Egyptians supposed to look at? The ambush will presumably not become visible until the waters start rushing back. We must assume that the author of *Song R.* B2 replaced the midrash of *ramah* as "height" with a different midrash which, ingenious as it is, does not belong in its present context. He did not perform the operation as cleanly as he might have; and "look what is in the sea" remains as a relic of the older text.

The original meaning of the passage must be that the horses see the celestial realms in the sea and are irresistably drawn to them. It seems to be an example of the widespread folklore motif – represented in the Bible by the story of Balaam's ass (Numbers 22:21–35), in the Talmud by the notion that dogs can sense the presence of Elijah or of the angel of death (BT B.Q. 60b) – that animals can perceive supernatural realities hidden from their masters [399,822,825,843]. While the midrash on Song 1:9 speaks of a sexual seduction of the Egyptians, the midrash on Exodus 15:1 describes a metaphysical seduction of their horses.

How can we square these observations with our conclusion that the *Ex. R.* passage is dependent on *Song R.*? I think we must modify our earlier view. The author of the *Ex. R.* passage did not draw on *Song R.* as we have it, but on a now lost text which the editor of *Song R.* seems to have incorporated with few changes. The most important of these changes was in B2.

Song R.'s editor so disliked the idea that the Egyptians' horses saw the heavenly realms in the Red Sea that he slashed it out of the text, putting in its place a distinct and inappropriate midrash of Exodus 15:1.

Why did he do this? We can only guess. But our investigation so far gives a plausible direction to our guesswork. *Ex. R.* does not tell us what was in those celestial realms that the horses saw in the sea, but they presumably included God's throne[34]. (Recall that the throne is sea-blue in Meir's haggadah, and that it is set beside the glass sea in Revelation 4:6.) If we can interpret this passage in the light of the haggadah that precedes it, we may suppose that they contained the *merkabah* as well. The editor's aversion to this midrash is doubtless connected to the hints we have come across, again and again, that Jewish expositors saw something ominous in the combination of the *merkabah* and the waters.

Neither *Song R.* nor *Ex. R.* gives any clue to the author of the midrash. We cannot begin to guess when it was composed, or — since we are very unsure of the date when *Song R.* was edited — when it was cut out of its context.

c) God in the sea? Two neighboring passages in *Ex. R.* refer to God's appearance at the Red Sea. Both haggadot are of considerable general interest for what they have to tell us about how the rabbis viewed this event. Each, in addition, has a point of special relevance for our study.

The first passage occurs in *Ex. R.* 23:8. Its author is supposedly the third-century Palestinian Amora Johanan b. Nappaha[v]. It describes how the Israelite mothers in Egypt, under Pharaoh's pressure to kill their male children, abandoned their babies in the open field. These babies grew wild, cared for by God himself.

> When they were grown, they returned to their families. "Who took care of you?" they were asked. They replied: "A certain splendidly handsome young man used to come down and take care of all our needs." So it is written: *My beloved is white and ruddy, distinguished from among a myriad* [Song 5:10][35]. When the Israelites came to the sea, those children were there and they saw God at the sea [literally, "in the sea," *bayyam*]. They said to their parents: "That's the one

---

34 "God sits in the celestial realms [*rumo shel ʿolam*] and distributes sustenance to all his creatures" — BT Pes. 118a, attributed to Johanan b. Nappaha.

35 The author of the midrash seems to understand the Song of Songs' account of the lover's marvellous beauty (Song 5:10–16) as a literal description of God. Many rabbis interpreted the male figure in the Song of Songs as God — so an eerily beautiful midrash of Song 5:9–6:3 which *Mekhilta* attributes to Akiba (*Shirah* chapter 3; ed./tr. 2:26–27 [195]) — but did not always take the identification quite as literally as does our text [572,701]. On the other hand, if Scholem and Lieberman are right, it was a super-literal application of Song 5:10–16 to God's physical body that gave rise to a bizarre sub-genre of the *Hekhalot* known as *Shiʿur Qomah*, which provides meticulous yet fantastic descriptions of the measurements of God's limbs [516, 519,570,597].

who took care of us when we were in Egypt!" So it is written: *This is my God, and I will praise him* [Exodus 15:2].

The most striking feature of this haggadah is its unabashed anthropomorphism, which should permanently put to rest any notion that the rabbis need have been shocked by the far milder anthropomorphisms of the Hebrew Bible. (We will take up this issue in chapter VII.) But there is another point that catches our eye. To express that the children saw God "at the sea," the midrash does not use the phrase *ʿal hayyam*, as does the passage from *Mekhilta* that we examined in section 3. It uses *bayyam*, which can be translated "*in* the sea," as in the horses' speech (above). Is this only a variation of idiom? Or is the author trying to convey that, like the celestial realms in *Ex. R.* 23:14, the beautiful young god was actually visible in the sea?

I must admit that a parallel haggadah, in Lieberman's *Deut. R.* (ed. 14–15 [186]), says only: "When they came to the sea and saw him ... " Even if, therefore, *bayyam* in *Ex. R.* 23:8 has the significance I am proposing for it, the word may have been chosen at a late stage, perhaps under the influence of the midrash in 23:14 (which occurs three columns afterward in the printed text).

d) Descending to the sea. The second passage that concerns us appears in *Ex. R.* 23:15, almost immediately after the haggadah about the Egyptians' horses:

> R. Berechiah said: Observe the greatness of those who went down to the sea [*yorede hayyam*]! Moses had to beg and prostrate himself before God at length before he saw the divine image [*demut*] ... and was finally shown only a token of it ... [Exodus 33:18–23]. The *ḥayyot* who carry the throne do not recognize the divine image. When the time comes for them to sing their praises, they say: "Where is he? We do not know if he is here or somewhere else. But, wherever he may be, *blessed be the glory of the Lord from his place* [Ezekiel 3:12][36]." Every single one of those who came up from the sea [*ʿole hayyam*], however, could point with his finger and say: *This is my God, and I will praise him* [Exodus 15:2].

This midrash calls the Israelites first "those who went down to the sea," and then "those who came up" from it. Heinemann has shown how intimately the verb *yarad*, "to go down," came to be connected in the minds of the midrashic expositors with the Israelites' entering the Red Sea [408]. Thus, one Tannaitic midrash read the word *rodem* in Psalm 68:28 as if it were to be pronounced *(ya)rad yam* ("he went down to the sea"), and referred to the tribe of Benjamin's plunging into the Red Sea. Another found

---

36 We recall a very similar exegesis of this verse from BT Hag. 13b (above, chapter IV, sections 3b, c).

an allusion to Judah's entering the sea in the single word *rad* (understood as *yarad*, "went down") in Hosea 12:1. (Both are in *Mekhilta, Be-Shallah* chapter 6; ed./tr. 1:232–237 [195].) By shifting his terminology from *yorede hayyam* at the beginning of the midrash to *ᶜole hayyam* at its end, our author is evidently trying to convey that the Israelites have seen their God while actually crossing the sea, and that they now emerge from the waters and begin their hymn of praise (Exodus 14:29–15:1).

All of this is natural enough. After all, one usually moves downward when entering a body of water, upward when leaving it. But we know of another context that applies "descent" and "ascent," far less naturally, to the approach to the divine and departure from it. I refer to *Hekhalot Rabbati*, which speaks of descent *to* the *merkabah*, and ascent *from* it [594, 608].

Writing more than twenty years ago, Scholem called this usage "a very curious and so far unexplained change of phraseology" [594]. I am not aware that anyone has since proposed a convincing account of its logic. I here offer a fresh hypothesis: that the *Hekhalot* authors modelled the experience of the traveller to the *merkabah*, at least in part, on that of the Israelites at the Red Sea; and they therefore used language appropriate to the one situation in reference to the other. If this is so, the Red Sea and its waters — whether conceived as real or as illusory — loom even larger in the *Hekhalot* texts' image of the heavenly journey than we imagined in section 2.

6. "In the river Chebar"

With this observation, the problem that we raised at the end of section 3 becomes yet more troubling. Why is the Red Sea so important? Is it solely on account of the dramatic miracle described in Exodus that the rabbis and the *Hekhalot* writers invest these waters with enormous significance, in connection with God's revelation of himself? Or is the Red Sea a stalking-horse for some more primal, august, and ominous body of water; a mirror, fixed within Israel's history, in which those other waters are reflected?

I am thinking of the chaos-waters that existed at the beginning of creation; which, according to the first chapter of Genesis, God had to divide and limit before he was able to create the earth. I am led to this thought by two midrashim which suggest that, as the Egyptian horses saw the celestial realms in the Red Sea, so Ezekiel saw the *merkabah* and its attendants in the primordial waters.

The first of these midrashim appears in *Gen. R.* 21:9 (ed. 203–204 [188]). The second is part of the mysterious Genizah midrash called the *Visions of Ezekiel*, to which I devote much of chapter VIII.

a) *Genesis Rabbah 21:9.* The focus of this passage is the word *miqqedem* in Genesis 3:24: "He [God] drove the man out [of Eden], and he settled *miqqedem* the garden of Eden the cherubim, and the fiery sword that turned every which way, to guard the way to the tree of life."

Miqqedem can mean "to the east." It can also mean "from ancient times." This ambiguity usually poses little difficulty to modern translators and commentators, who rely on the context in which the word appears to decide between its geographic and its temporal meanings. In Genesis 3:24, there is no real question that *miqqedem legan ʿeden* means, "to the east of the garden of Eden." But midrashic expositors have no qualms about reducing a Biblical context to atoms when it suits their purposes. *Gen. R.* thus quotes two anonymous midrashim which ignore the entire first part of the verse (through "and he settled"), and read the rest as if it were: "More ancient than the garden of Eden [were] the cherubim, and the fiery sword that turned every which way ..."

One of these midrashim applies the Biblical passage to the angels; the other, to hell.

[A1] *More ancient*: angels were created earlier *than the garden of Eden*. So it is written: *This was the ḥayyah that I saw beneath the God of Israel at the river Chebar* [*binehar kebar*; literally, "in the river Chebar"], *and I knew that they were cherubim* [Ezekiel 10:20].

[A2] *And the fiery sword*: [so called] in reference to [the words,] *His* [God's] *servants are blazing fire* [Psalm 104:4].

[A3] *That turned every which way*: [meaning] that they turn themselves [into different shapes] — now men, now women, now spirits, now angels.

[B] Another explanation:

[B1] *More ancient*: hell was created earlier *than the garden of Eden*. Hell was created on the second day, the garden of Eden on the third.

[B2] *And the fiery sword*: [so called] in reference to [the words,] *The coming day shall burn them up* [Malachi 3:19].

[B3] *That turned every which way*: [meaning] that it turns itself upon a person, and burns him up from head to foot[37].

There are two serious obscurities in the way these two midrashim deal with the Bible. The first is that we do not see clearly what midrash B does with Genesis 3:24's reference to the cherubim. The two midrashim are closely parallel structurally, and neither actually quotes the words *the cherubim* from the Biblical text. Yet midrash A bases its interpretation on these words, while midrash B passes over them in silence.

---

37 The exegesis in A2 and B2 rests on the fact that the root *lhṭ* ("to blaze, burn up, be fiery") occurs in the three verses Genesis 3:24, Psalm 104:4, and Malachi 3:19. The midrash's expression "burns him up" (B3) is also from *lhṭ* – Like A2, A3 interprets Genesis 3:24 in connection with Psalm 104:4: the phrase "now spirits, now angels," is based on the beginning of Psalm 104:4, "[God] makes his angels spirits" (ʿoseh mal'akhaw ruḥot; RSV, "who makest the winds thy messengers"). – *Gen. R.* 4:6 (ed. 30 [188]) speaks of hell's being created on the second day. 11:9 (ed. 96 [188]) has hell created on the second day, the garden of Eden (perhaps understood as paradise) on the third.

We can solve this problem by assuming that both midrashim derive from a primitive exposition of Genesis 3:24, which did not even try to interpret the entire verse in a consistent way, but strung together a series of explanations of isolated phrases − *the cherubim* are the angels, *the fiery sword* is hell, and so forth[w]. Both midrashim tried to extend the interpretation of a single phrase to cover its context as well. Midrash A accomplished this more successfully than did midrash B.

The second obscurity is harder to clear up. Why does the author of midrash A quote Ezekiel 10:20? He plainly intends this verse to buttress his understanding of Genesis 3:24, that the cherubim are older than the garden of Eden. But how does the verse do this? It identifies the cherubim with the *hayyah* (singular of *hayyot*, clearly to be understood as a collective plural), but says nothing about their antiquity.

The commentators on the midrash do not help us much. Theodor, inspired by an interpretation of Genesis 3:24 in the eleventh-century commentary *Leqah Tob*, proposes that the expositor used Ezekiel 10:20 to prove that cherubim are angels. Z. W. Einhorn (d. 1862) seems to have shared this view. But, even if the midrash's author found it necessary to prove this point − which I think unlikely − Ezekiel 10:20 would not prove it, since it equates cherubim with *hayyah* but not with angels. David Luria (d. 1855) rejects this explanation, as well as the alternative proposal that Ezekiel 10:20 is supposed to show that the cherubim carry God's throne and therefore share its pre-existence. But he does not suggest anything better [188, 200].

Only one solution seems to me to offer itself. The name "Chebar" is identical in its form to an adverb *kebar*, used in rabbinic Hebrew (and in the Book of Ecclesiastes) to mean "already, long ago." Certain rabbis may have equated the two words, and assumed that Ezekiel saw his visions by "the river of Long-ago[38]." They may have gone on to equate this river with the "river flowing from Eden" of Genesis 2:10; or, perhaps, with the primordial waters in general.

---

38 Unfortunately, I can offer little evidence, besides this passage, that the rabbis so understood "Chebar." *Gen. R.* 16:3 (ed. 145−146 [188]) attributes to R. Judan the claim that the river Euphrates is also called Chebar, "because its waters disappear." The point of this etymology is not clear. Theodor quotes an anonymous commentary as explaining that "its waters disappear entirely, and people say, 'There once [*kebar*] was a river.'" (On the equation of Chebar with Euphrates, and the disappearance of its waters, see Appendix IV, section 2.) BT M.Q. 25a explains the repetition of the root *hyh* in Ezekiel 1:3 ("the word of the Lord came to Ezekiel"; see above, chapter IV, section 2g) with an obscure remark that seems to mean "it had come already [*kebar*]." This is perhaps an allusion to Ezekiel's river. I have found no other trace of any such interpretation of "Chebar" in the rabbinic literature. As far as I know, it does not occur among the Greek and Latin lists of etymologies of Biblical names, used by the early Christian writers [622a,642,650,651].

This still does not quite make the connection we need. Let us grant that certain expositors identified the river Chebar, on the strength of its name, with waters that existed at the beginning of creation, before God fashioned Eden. Let us also grant that Ezekiel saw his *hayyot*-cherubim beside these waters. It does not follow that these creatures themselves go back to primordial antiquity.

But now let us suppose that the expositor in *Gen. R.* 21:9 took the preposition *bi-* in *binehar kebar* fully literally, to mean that Ezekiel saw his *hayyot* "*in* the river Chebar." In this case, the *hayyot* became a part of these ancient waters; and the "river of Long-ago" becomes a sort of lens through which Ezekiel can see the entities that existed at the beginning of creation. Among these entities are the cherubim.

b) The "Visions of Ezekiel." This interpretation of *Gen. R.* 21:9 seems at first sight a very farfetched one, and I must admit that it would not have occurred to me if I had not been familiar with a passage in the *Visions of Ezekiel* which appears to fill in the lacunae of the *Gen. R.* text. Further, the passage in the *Visions* has a lacuna of its own; which, as we will see, we can fill from *Gen. R.* This suggests that the two midrashim are complementary, and that each is to be interpreted in accord with the other.

I will translate the *Visions of Ezekiel* in full in chapter VIII. In the meantime, I quote the material that now concerns us:

> ... God opened to Ezekiel the seven subterranean chambers, and Ezekiel looked into them and saw all the celestial entities. ...
>
> R. Isaac said: God showed Ezekiel the primordial waters that are bound up in the great sea and in layers; as it is written, *Have you come to the layers of the sea* [Job 38:16]. He showed him a mountain underneath the river, by means of which the temple vessels are to return[39].
>
> While Ezekiel was watching, God opened to him seven firmaments and he saw the *Geburah*[40]. They coined a parable; to what may the matter be likened? A man went to a barber shop, got a haircut, and was given a mirror to look into. While he was looking into the mirror, the king passed by. He saw the king and his forces through the doorway. The barber turned and said to him, "Turn around and see the king." He said, "I have already seen the mirror[41]." So Ezekiel stood by the river Chebar and looked into the water, and the seven firmaments were opened to him and he saw God's glory, and the *hayyot*, angels, troops, seraphim, and sparkling-winged ones joined to the *merkabah*. They passed by in the heavens and Ezekiel saw them in the water. So it is written: *At the river Chebar* [Ezekiel 1:1]. [229]

This midrash sets forth explicitly and clearly the conception that I have supposed to underlie *Gen. R.* 21:9. Looking into the river Chebar, Ezekiel sees the primordial waters, and the *hayyot* and other *merkabah* beings in them (understood to mean, *reflected* in them). But the passage does not

---

39 I discuss the "binding" of the waters, the "layers," and the "mountain underneath the river," in Appendix IV, sections 1–2.

40 An epithet for God, literally meaning "power" [453].

41 *Mar'ah*; obviously a play on *mar'eh*, "vision," as in *Lev. R.* 1:14 (above, section 3).

clearly explain the exegetical ground for this conception. We can hardly imagine that it sprang from the words of Ezekiel 1:1, *while I was among the captives at the river Chebar*. No one could have understood *at* in this verse to mean *in* (the Hebrew here is *ᶜal nehar*, not *binehar*, as in 10:20). Besides, 1:1 does not directly connect the words *at the river Chebar* with anything that Ezekiel saw.

Our discussion of *Gen. R.* 21:9 points us toward the solution of this problem. Like the midrash in *Gen. R.*, the haggadah in the *Visions of Ezekiel* was originally connected, not to Ezekiel 1:1, but to 10:20 (or the very similar verse 10:15). The author of the *Visions*, as we will see in chapter VIII, focused almost all of his attention on the first verse of Ezekiel; he therefore transferred to it a midrash that originally belonged somewhere else. It is only Ezekiel 10.20, with its *ḥayyah that I saw beneath the God of Israel in the river of Long-ago*, that lets us see the origin of the belief that the *merkabah* appeared in the primordial waters.

7. Reflections

Yet this explanation is no explanation at all. It clarifies the mechanics of how certain Jewish expositors rooted their strange conception of the *merkabah* and the waters in the text of Ezekiel. It does nothing to explain why they should have evolved the conception in the first place. After all, there are simpler explanations of the language of Ezekiel 10:20. Why were the expositors not satisfied with them? What did the *merkabah*'s appearance in the waters mean to these haggadists?

If we can fully clear up this question, we may hope to have the key to the parallel haggadah in *Ex. R.* 23:14, in which the celestial heights appear to the Egyptian horses in the Red Sea. We may perhaps also be a step nearer to explaining why, in some of the sources we have examined, the combination of the *merkabah* and the waters has a particularly ominous implication.

Ithamar Gruenwald, followed by Moshe Idel, explains the passage we have examined from the *Visions of Ezekiel* as a reflection of the actual practice of early Jewish visionaries, who used natural bodies of water as mirrors in which they could see supernatural beings appear in the sky [231, 547,564]. Water-divination of this sort, using a vessel filled with water (often with oil added) as a mirror in which the medium can see divine images, seems to have been common enough in the ancient world. Greek magical papyri from Egypt give several prescriptions for it, and there is evidence that some Romans practiced it around the beginning of the Christian era [716,723].

It is true that flowing rivers, which Gruenwald evidently supposes Jewish mystics to have used as aids to their visions, are bound to be less effective mirrors than the bowls of still water that we find in the pagan magical recipes. It is also true that, as far as I know, we have no direct evidence that Jews engaged in water-divination either with rivers or with bowls of water. But, for all this, Gruenwald's suggestion remains attractive, in that it allows him to make sense, not only of the *Visions of Ezekiel*, but of several other references in apocalyptic and rabbinic sources that would otherwise be puzzling. *Lev. R.* 1:14's comparison of prophetic vision to the image in a mirror is one of them. *Mekhilta*'s claim, that prophets outside Palestine only receive their visions beside bodies of water, is another (*Pisḥa*, chapter 1; ed./tr. 1:6 [195]).

I am, nevertheless, hesitant about following Gruenwald. My reservations are based only in small part on the lack of explicit evidence for Jewish water-divination, which I do not regard as a decisive objection. It troubles me more that Gruenwald's hypothesis will not account for the story of the horses' vision in the Red Sea, which seems to me clearly pertinent (and which Gruenwald does not mention). The sea is a poor mirror, and it is hard to imagine that Jewish mystics actually looked for reflections of heavenly realities in its waves.

But my main difficulty is that, even if Gruenwald is right that certain Jewish visionaries looked into rivers in order to see visions of God, this fact itself requires some explanation. After all, you do not see anything when you look at the sky's reflection in a river that you would not see (more clearly!) if you looked at the sky itself. If you convince yourself that you are going to see the *merkabah* reflected in the water, this must be because you already hold certain beliefs about water and its ability to reflect images. If we suppose that Jews at the beginning of the Christian Era held some such beliefs, and if we can guess at what these beliefs were, we may be able to explain the midrashic accounts both of the horses' vision and of Ezekiel's directly from these beliefs, without supposing any visionary practice as an intermediate link.

It is common observation that water has an uncanny power to capture whatever appears above it, and to twist the captive image into an endlessly changing series of distortions. To be sure, it is also common observation that this power is an illusion. Tellers of folk-tales all over the world know that it is only uncommon fools, like the "wise men" of Gotham or those of Chelm, who think that they can lay hold of the moon by trapping its reflection in a pool of water [823,852,857]. Yet this very fact, that stories mocking the belief in the reality of the reflection are so widespread and popular, is itself an indication that people do not find it easy altogether to shake this belief.

Thus it is that the early Gnostics, the authors of what are by all odds the most sophisticated and imaginative theosophical speculations of the first three Christian centuries, were willing to use the motif of reflection in the waters as a way of explaining how the supernal divine forces became entrapped in the nether darkness of matter. A number of Gnostic sources make use of this conception. Sometimes, indeed, they modify it with the common-sense qualification that the waters cannot *really* capture the divinity whose reflection appears in them; the evil rulers of the darkness must make a model of what they have seen in the waters, since they cannot lay hold of the image[42]. But, as Hans Jonas points out, the effect — divinity falls into the realm of matter, conveyed there by its reflection in the waters — remains the same. Jonas's remarks on the Gnostic use of the reflection motif are worth quoting:

> [This conception] implies the mythic idea of the substantiality of an image, reflection, or shadow as representing a real part of the original entity from which it has become detached. We have to accept this symbolism as convincing to those who used it for a crucial phase in the divine drama. ... The general idea common to these doctrines is as follows. By its nature the Light shines into the Darkness below. This partial illumination of the Darkness either is comparable to the action of a simple ray, i.e., spreading brightness as such, or, if it issued from an individual divine figure such as the Sophia or Man, is in the nature of a *form* projected into the dark medium and appearing there as an image or reflection of the divine. In both cases, though no real descent or fall of the divine original has taken place, something of itself has become immersed in the lower world, and just as the Darkness treats it as a precious spoil, so the unfallen deity has become involved in the further destiny of this effluence. The Darkness is seized with greed for the brightness that has appeared in its midst or on the surface of the primordial waters and, trying to mingle with it thoroughly and permanently to retain it, drags it downward, engulfs it, and breaks it up into innumerable parts [719].

I do not mean to suggest that the rabbis who composed the midrashim we have been considering were familiar with the *Hypostasis of the Archons* or other Gnostic writings, or that the Gnostics' treatment of the theme of reflection in the waters is itself rooted in some lost Jewish source — a midrash on *the spirit of God hovering over the face of the waters* (Genesis 1:2), say[43]. The Gnostic material interests me because it seems to illustrate an attitude toward reflections in water which underlies both our midrashim and the Greco-Egyptian water divination, and which can help us understand both.

Thus, the pagan magician looks for reflections of gods in a bowl of water, because he believes that water has the ability to trap at least a por-

---

42 So the Coptic Gnostic text known as the *Hypostasis of the Archons*: "As Incorruptibility looked down into the region of the Waters, her Image appeared in the Waters; and the Authorities of the Darkness became enamored of her. But they could not lay hold of that Image, which had appeared to them in the Waters ... for they were from Below, while it was from Above" (Layton's translation) [705,720].

43 I would not, however, like to rule out either possibility, especially given that the *Hypostasis of the Archons* is filled with Jewish haggadic material [548,709]. See Appendix VI.

tion of the gods' essence and hold it bound in his presence. He can then manipulate it to serve his will. For the same reason, the Jewish haggadist thinks of a body of water as a place where God is particularly likely to become immanent, where humans or specially gifted animals can see him. We begin to understand why some at least of the rabbis assumed a theophany at the Red Sea, and then tried to support this notion from the text of Exodus 14–15.

The rabbinic sources normally do not reason from this to the idea, typical of magic, that the water puts God in the power of humans, who can now make use of him as they please. But we recall that, according to certain Genizah midrashim, it is when God appears to his people at the Red Sea that they gain power over the ox-element of his *merkabah*, which they will later use for their own purposes (above, chapter V, section 5). This tradition, too, now begins to make sense.

So far, our speculations seem to have gotten us near the root of the rabbinic traditions about God's appearance at the Red Sea, and, particularly, to the explanation of the horse's cry that "I see the celestial heights in the sea." But the midrashim we examined in the last section add a new element, in that they put the primordial waters in place of the Red Sea. This substitution brings us closer to the Gnostic stories, in which it is the primordial waters that catch the reflection of divinity. It leads us to ask what the primordial waters meant to the rabbis.

I have already mentioned that ancient Near Eastern myths, known in Babylon and Ugarit, represent the chaos-waters as the primeval enemies of the gods. The gods' rulership and the well-being of creation depend on these waters' being kept in check. The Hebrews, too, were familiar with stories of this sort. Although the author of Genesis 1 practically excises them from his account of creation, scattered poetic passages in the Hebrew Bible preserve echoes of them. So do stories in the Talmud and midrash. The rabbis, it seems clear, kept alive the memory of the ancient myth of God's struggle against the waters [27,49a,107,122,417].

Further, the Bible itself gives hints (Isaiah 51:9–10, Psalm 106:9) that certain Israelite poets envisioned the miracle at the Red Sea as a replication, taking place within Israelite history, of God's prehistoric conflict with the waters [24,28,29,38,46,50,124]. We saw in chapter III that the author of the Book of Revelation seems to superimpose the image of the Red Sea upon that of the primordial waters. Can we suppose that some rabbis also took up this conception, believing that God appeared at the Red Sea as *a man of war* (Exodus 15:3), not only to fight the Egyptians, but also to fight the sea itself?

I know of no explicit evidence that they did. But, if we are willing to make this assumption, much of the data we have examined falls into place.

We can understand why the Red Sea plays a role in *Ex. R.* 23:14 parallel to that of the primordial waters in the *Visions of Ezekiel*. More than this, we can answer the question that I raised at the beginning of this section, of why the Red Sea is so important. The importance that properly attaches to the chaos-waters has been transferred to the historical incarnation of these waters.

We now have a second explanation, complementing the one that I proposed a little earlier, of why the rabbis supposed that a great theophany had taken place at the Red Sea. If the Red Sea has taken over the role, originally belonging to the primordial waters, of God's great adversary, it is natural that God would appear in his full power and glory to fight against it. This, perhaps, is the true source of the midrashic image of God's appearing to fight at the Red Sea, with the *merkabah* as his armory (*Song R.* to 1:9; above, section 4).

But why, if God comes with the *merkabah* to the sea to fight against the forces of chaos, does the image of the *merkabah* with the waters so often seem surrounded by a sinister aura? We may be able at last to solve this mystery if we assume that what seemed ominous was not the *merkabah*'s being *at* the waters, but the *merkabah*'s being *in* the waters.

When a solid object is reflected in water, it is swallowed by the water, becomes part of the water, takes on the water's chaotic fluidity. Not really, of course; as we know, and as people two thousand years ago must also have known. But the Gnostics have taught us that, when the ancients thought about reflection, their rational knowledge that the image is not the thing itself did not always outweigh a more primitive and stubborn sense that the image *is* the thing itself.

If we assume that some rabbis looked at reflections in the water the way their Gnostic contemporaries did, the implications are clear. The *merkabah* that appears in the waters has become part of the waters. Far from protecting us against chaos, it becomes one with chaos. Like the Gnostic divinity, it has become degraded in some unspeakable and possibly irreversible way. It has taken on the character of the dark and demonic forces from below[44].

---

44 One midrash, describing God's conflict with the primordial waters, hints strongly that the waters menaced God's throne. "The waters rose until they reached the throne of glory. So it is written, *The spirit of God hovered over the waters* [Genesis 1:2]; and, again, *As an eagle stirs up its nest, hovering over its young* [Deuteronomy 32:11; quoted to show that *hovering* implies contact or near-contact]" (*Midr. Psalms* 93:5; ed. 207b [199]). Had the waters swamped the throne, as they here evidently threaten to do, the effect of their victory would not have been much different from what they achieve by capturing the *merkabah*'s reflection. – We cannot be sure how old this midrash is. The *Midrash on Psalms*, the only source to quote it, is a late compilation. The editor attributes the passage to "R. Berechiah quoting Ben Azzai Ben Zoma"; the last four words are presumably corrupt, and perhaps we should side with those manuscripts that read only "Ben

I think it may be important in this connection that, when the sky's reflection appears in water, what we normally see *above* us appears *below* us. This phenomenon can only be considered a harmless curiosity as long as *above* and *below* are neutral categories, without moral or religious significance. I find it hard to believe that the average Jew in the early centuries of the Christian era would have thought of the realms above us without imagining them as the home of God and his angels, or would have conceived the nether regions without some tincture of gloom, evil, and danger.

I am not aware of any systematic study of the images of *above* and *below* in the rabbinic literature, and my evidence for this claim must necessarily be somewhat random and helter-skelter. To begin with, there is hell. It is not quite true that, as Carl Sagan once remarked, "in all the legends one gets to Hell by going down, not up" [851] — some Jewish cosmographies conceive a place of punishment in the heavens [374], and Ginzberg notes that "there is a widespread view that hell and paradise are situated side by side" [396]. Yet I have the impression that ancient Jews more commonly imagined hell as below them. There are entrances to it in Jerusalem, the desert, and the sea (BT ᶜEr. 19a). The imaginative Babylonian tourist Rabbah b. Bar Hana can hear the cries of Korah and his followers from hell by putting his ear to a crack in the ground (BT B.B. 74a). The forces of evil draw their strength from the regions below the ground: according to the Palestinian Talmud, witches become helpless when they lose contact with the earth (Hag. 2:2, 78a; Sanh. 6:6, 23c). Chaos lurks beneath the surface of the earth, its waters threatening to break upward and flood the world (BT Sukk. 53a—b and parallels [406]). It seems fair to assume that, when the rabbis quoted Isaiah's threat that the king of Babylon would be *brought down to the depths of the pit* (14:15; quoted, for example, in BT Hag. 13a), they did not imagine this to be any very friendly place; and that, if they had known Revelation's images of monsters emerging from the bottomless pit (9:1—11, 11:7), they would have agreed with the author's premise that the nether world is a source of evil and menace. The world above, by contrast, is where "our father in heaven" sits enthroned (BT Pes. 118a, for example)[45].

Azzai." The passage must be somehow linked to T. Hagigah 2:6 and its parallels [552], which have Ben Zoma argue from Genesis 1:2 and Deuteronomy 32:11 that the "upper waters" and the "lower waters" (Genesis 1:6—8) are cheek by jowl. It may perhaps also be connected to *Gen. R.* 4:6 (ed. 30 [188]), which tells us that Genesis 1:7 was "one of those Scriptures with which Ben Zoma shocked the world," without making clear just what Ben Zoma did with the verse that people found so shocking. Cf. also *Gen. R.* 5:4 (ed. 34 [188]).

45 Compare Bernard F. Batto's generalization (based on Mircea Eliade's writings) about ancient cosmology: "The farther away from the center of the cosmos one goes, the more one moves into the realm of chaos or non-creation. ... Vertically, the heavens are the source of existence and creation; the underworld and the abyss are the place of death and non-existence" [25].

When the *merkabah* appears in the waters, the upper realms are merged into the lower. Ezekiel, according to the *Visions of Ezekiel*, looks into "the seven subterranean chambers" and sees in them what ought to be in heaven. The peculiar linguistic usage of *Hekhalot Rabbati*, which speaks of descending to the *merkabah* and ascending from it, may well be connected to this reversal. I suggested, at the end of section 5, that the *Hekhalot* writers may have modelled their language after the phrases that the midrash used to refer to the Israelites' experience at the Red Sea. We are now in a position to detect the reason behind this transference. These writers had learned from midrashic traditions like the one preserved in *Ex. R.* 23: 14 that the *merkabah* had been perceptible *in* the waters of the Red Sea when the Israelites crossed it. They deduced that access to what is above lies through what is below. To get up to the *merkabah*, one must descend.

We saw in chapter V, in connection with the *merkabah*'s links to the golden calf, that some rabbis perceived in Ezekiel's vision hints of a fearful ambiguity of good and evil within God himself, and preferred not to entertain the thoughts toward which these hints pointed. The paradox of the *merkabah* in the waters points in the same direction. It brings the upper world into the nether world; it makes the distinction between *above* and *below* insignificant; it turns the *merkabah*, like any reflection in water, into part of the fluid and shapeless chaos that God once had to defeat.

We now understand more clearly why the authors of the Genizah midrashim on the *merkabah* and the calf (above, chapter V) found it appropriate to locate the Israelites' crucial encounter with the *merkabah* at the Red Sea. The water motif and the calf motif expressed, each in its own way, the divine ambiguity. Together, they reinforced each other. For precisely this reason, their combined effect was long felt to be intolerable. This is why the Genizah version of the *merkabah*-calf haggadah remained suppressed until well into the Middle Ages, while the parallel tradition that set the action at Mount Sinai was allowed to surface in the *Tanhuma* midrashim.

The peculiar diction of Ezekiel 10:20 did not by itself generate this complex cycle of meditations on God and the waters, parts of which go back to Near Eastern myths centuries older than Ezekiel himself. But it did suggest to certain *merkabah* expositors that the ancient tales of God's struggle with the waters had an important bearing on the question of what Ezekiel's vision meant. It encouraged them to suppose that they could work out the implications of these tales in the framework of the *merkabah* vision.

The conclusions they evolved were not especially comforting to those who cared about the character of their God. God had indeed, as the old traditions claimed, suppressed the chaos-waters. But chaos had its revenge. The water, by virtue of its power of reflection, ensnared its enemy's image, assimilated the *merkabah* to itself, and thus infected God with its own formlessness. That was why Ezekiel saw the *merkabah*-creatures *beneath the God of Israel in the river of Long-ago* (10:20).

But Ezekiel saw something else beneath God's throne: *a firmament the color of the terrible ice* (Ezekiel 1:22). To the early Jewish expositors, I suggest, this meant that God had frozen solid the terrible waters against which he fought, and thus defeated them[46]. By its fluidity and formlessness, chaos is the enemy of order and structure. If it can be made solid, its threat is gone. The *merkabah* expositors learned from Exodus 15:8 that God had done precisely this at the Red Sea: *the deeps congealed in the heart of the sea*.

I proposed in chapter III that the author of Revelation used these two verses — Ezekiel 1:22, Exodus 15:8 — to shape his image of a solid sea in heaven; and I drew upon the "Vita Adae" to confirm this speculation. Only now can we fully understand the author's motive: the hardening of water into glass symbolizes God's triumph over chaos.

This also is the symbolism of the "stones of pure marble" of BT Hag. 14b. We saw earlier that BT Sukk. 51b compares the marble stones of Herod's temple to "the waves of the sea" (above, section 1b). We can no longer resist the assumption that the marble stones in Akiba's warning are those that pave the heavenly Temple (thus far Maier); and that the Babylonian transmitters of the *pardes* story believed them to be the primordial waters, solidified and thus mastered. To claim that they are water is to claim that chaos is still potent. This admission is too dreadful to be tolerated. That is why he who says "water, water" *speaks lies,* and *shall not be established in* God's *sight.*

The implications of the *merkabah*-sea link, we now realize, run parallel to those of the *merkabah*-calf link. We thus understand at last why one Jewish expositor of Ezekiel 1:27, whose speculations are preserved in the *Hekhalot* literature, has the "eye of *ḥashmal*" repudiate as a worshipper of the calf anyone who thinks that the *merkabah* is to be found among the waters.

8. The anti-*merkabah*

The hypothesis I have unfolded in the last section may perhaps strike some readers as a bit top-heavy with speculation. Additional data that can confirm my inferences will be welcome.

---

46 Tryggve N. D. Mettinger has recently proposed this as the true interpretation of the verse [12a].

To this end, I now invoke a group of sources that seem to assume the existence of an "anti-*merkabah*," a mirror image of the celestial *merkabah*. In one version, this *merkabah* is located at the opposite end of the cosmos from its antitype; in another version, it is in the sea. This second version represents the watery anti-*merkabah* as evil. I did not mention these sources until now, because they occur in medieval texts and I cannot prove that their conceptions go back to rabbinic times. But I believe that these conceptions are so unusual that we cannot explain them unless we suppose that they are rooted in a cycle of ideas like the ones I posited in the preceding section. We cannot leave the subject of the *merkabah* and the waters without discussing them.

a) The merkabah in the depths. The first source that concerns us occurs in a cosmographic text called *Seder Rabbah di-Bereshit* ("The Great [Treatise on the] Order of Creation"), or *Baraita de- Ma^caseh Bereshit* ("The Baraita of Creation"). We do not know when this text was written. Nicolas Séd, who published in 1964–1965 a critical edition with a French translation, inclined to suppose that it dates in its present form from the eleventh century, but that it incorporates traditions going back to Tannaitic and Amoraic times [214].

Despite Séd's efforts, we do not have any very clear grasp of the structure of the text, or how the several recensions attested in the manuscripts relate to one another[47]. We therefore cannot be confident about the context of the passage that concerns us. Nor can we place it in the framework of the author's thought, except in the most general way.

The writer imagines a universe in which seven heavens arch over our heads and a corresponding series of seven earths stretch beneath our feet. In the pertinent passage, he is talking about the lowest of these earths:

> On the lowest earth [*ba'areṣ hattaḥtonah*] there are holy *ḥayyot, 'ofannim,* and the throne of glory. The throne of glory is the footstool of the Lord of all the earth. So it is written: *The heaven is my throne and the earth is my footstool* [Isaiah 66:1]. It is also written: *As I looked at the ḥayyot, I saw one wheel [*'ofan*] on the earth [beside the ḥayyot*; Ezekiel 1:15]. Just as his Shechinah is above, so his Shechinah is below; as it is written, *The name of the city [shall be]*, *from that day on, "The Lord is there"* [Ezekiel 48:35].

---

47 Séd distinguished two main recensions, one represented by the printed text of the *Sefer Razi'el* (Amsterdam, 1701) and by two manuscripts preserved in Jerusalem and London, the other represented by a Paris and a London manuscript. He printed these two versions in parallel columns; a third text, ms Munich 22, he printed in an appendix. Schäfer's *Synopse zur Hekhalot-Literatur* [495] includes two versions of parts of *Seder Rabbah di-Bereshit* from ms Munich 22 (##429–467, 518–540), of which Séd printed only the first. Schäfer also published parts of this text from mss Munich 40 (##714–727) and Oxford 1531 (##714–727, 743–820, 832–853), which Séd did not use at all.

So, with minor variations, run both of Séd's recensions (pp. 70−71 [213]). The text of ms Munich 22 is abbreviated; it omits the quotation of Ezekiel 1:15, and quotes the first part of Ezekiel 48:35 (*eighteen thou-sand are round about*) instead of the second (Séd, p. 98; Schäfer, #440). Ms Oxford 1531, however, gives a slightly fuller version:

> On the lowest earth there are holy *hayyot*, *'ofannim*, and the throne of glory, with the feet of the Shechinah upon their heads. So it is written: *As I looked at the hayyot, I saw one wheel on the earth,* and so forth. Just as his Shechinah is above, so his Shechinah is below. So it is written, *His glory covered the heavens and his praise filled the earth* [Habakkuk 3:3]; and, again, *The heaven is my throne and the earth is my footstool.* Thousands upon thousands and myriads upon myriads of angels surround ... the feet of the Shechinah, as it is written, *His praise filled the earth.* [Schäfer, #745]

The version of ms Oxford seems to stand midway between the text published by Séd and a parallel passage in another medieval cosmographic writing, *Midrash Konen*:

> The lowest earth is attached to the hooks of ^CArabot [the highest heaven], and the expanse of ^CArabot is in the lowest earth[48]. In them [!] are the feet of the *hayyot*, *'ofannim*, and seraphim. A firmament rests on the horns of the *hayyot*, and the throne of glory rests upon that firmament. The feet of the Shechinah are upon their heads [of the *hayyot*, that is] in ^CArabot, and their feet are in the lowest earth. How do we know that the throne of glory is in ^CArabot? *Prepare a way for the ruler in ^CArabot, by his name Yah; rejoice before him* [Psalm 68:5]. And how do we know that the feet of the *hayyot* are in the lowest earth? *As I looked at the hayyot, I saw one wheel on the earth beside the hayyot.*
>
> Just as his Shechinah is in the upper regions, so his Shechinah is on earth. So it is written, *His glory covered the heavens and his praise filled the earth*; and, again, *The heaven is my throne and the earth is my footstool.* A thousand thousand and a myriad myriads of angels stand and praise him ... all around the feet of the Shechinah in the lowest earth, as it is written, *His glory covered the heavens,* and so forth. [Ed. 33−34 [478]]

The author of *Midrash Konen* seems to develop the Talmudic image of Sandalphon (BT Hag. 13b), representing the *hayyot* as a cosmic axis that links the highest heaven and the lowest earth, cutting across all the realms in between. I have already noted that this conception left its mark on two manuscripts of the Babylonian Talmud; it influenced Muslim traditionists as well (above, chapter IV, endnote *i*; Appendix II). But the inconsistency in *Midrash Konen*'s description — are the feet of the Shechinah in the highest heaven or in the lowest earth? — suggests to me that the author has reworked and distorted an older and stranger conception, which the several versions of *Seder Rabbah di-Bereshit* preserve for us. According to this conception, the lowest of the cosmic realms contains an exact replica of the *merkabah* in the highest heaven, with the same beings attending it and the same Shechinah dwelling upon it.

---

48 The first part of the sentence implies that the two corresponding hemispheres — the highest heavens and the lowest earth — are connected by hooks or clasps at their edges. I do not know what the second part of the sentence means.

Where does the writer get this notion? Perhaps it is a dim and many times distorted echo of the "antipodes" of the ancient Greek geographers – people who walk upside-down on the opposite side of the earth from us, living in a world that reflects and reverses our own like a mirror [842][49]. The author no doubt intends it to convey the idea that God's presence is everywhere. In any case, the underlying idea seems to be mirror reflection. While the *merkabah* is located in the highest point of the cosmos, there is a mirror image of it in the lowest. We are reminded of the Gnostic motif of the divinity's reflection appearing in the nether waters.

Can we identify the "lowest earth" with these nether waters? *Seder Rabbah di-Bereshit* does not actually make this equation. But it does bring the two into close relation. In a passage that comes shortly before the one we have examined (in most texts), the author locates the "lowest earth" just beneath the rebellious waters that were barred from heaven at the time of creation (Séd, pp. 60–65, 97–98; Schäfer, ##438–439). In a passage that comes shortly afterward (in mss Munich 22 and Oxford; Séd, pp. 98–100; Schäfer, ##443–453, 750–766), he depicts a series of watery abysses sandwiched between the seven earths. Ms Oxford adds that darkness and chaos make up the outer circle surrounding "the feet of the Shechinah" on the lowest earth (Schäfer, #748). Elsewhere, the text seems to equate the seven heavens with "seven supernal fountains" and the seven earths with "seven infernal abysses"; God "established his throne in the supernal realms and placed some of his glory in the infernal ones" (Séd, p. 96, cf. pp. 48–49; Schäfer, ##431, 842).

In *Seder Rabbah di-Bereshit*, then, we find the anti-*merkabah* in the cosmic depths, probably among the waters. The writer gives no hint of tension between this lower *merkabah* and its heavenly antitype. Both, as far as we can see, are wholly divine.

b) The king of Tyre. But medieval sources also preserve a strange legend in which the *merkabah* in the waters is God's opponent. The thirteenth-

---

49 The Epicurean poet Lucretius (first century B.C.), who regarded the notion of the antipodes as absurd, described it as resting on the assumption that all things are attracted to the center of the earth. "Whatever heavy bodies there may be under the earth must then tend upwards and rest against the surface upside down, like the images of things which we now see reflected in water. In the same way they would have it that animals walk about topsy-turvy and cannot fall off the earth into the nether quarters of the sky any more than our bodies can soar up spontaneously into the heavenly regions. When they are looking at the sun, we see the stars of night; so they share the hours with us alternately and experience nights corresponding to our days" (*De Rerum Natura*, I, 1058–1067 [721]). Another distinguished skeptic spoke of "the fabled 'antipodes'" as people "who live on the other side of the earth, where the sun rises when it sets for us, men who plant their footsteps opposite ours" (Augustine, *De Civitate Dei*, XVI, 9 [618]). Science, needless to say, has since vindicated the believers.

century midrashic compilation *Yalquṭ Shim^coni* quotes one version of this legend from an unknown source (*Ezekiel*, #367). A fourteenth-century text, the Yemenite *Midrash ha-Gadol*, incorporates a slightly different version (to Exodus 7:1; ed. 108–109 [198a]). Other variants appear in modern collections of late midrashim, such as Jellinek's *Bet ha-Midrasch* [483] [50].

The legend's focus is the prophecy against the king of Tyre in the twenty-eighth chapter of Ezekiel. More especially, it is verse 2 of that chapter, where the king is told: *You became proud. You said: "I am a god; I sit in the seat of God, in the heart of the seas." Though you are a human and no god, you made yourself out to be God.* The storyteller draws upon a tradition, going back at least to Amoraic times, according to which Ezekiel's "king of Tyre" was none other than Solomon's ally Hiram. He was thus centuries old when Ezekiel spoke against him [51].

> Hiram king of Tyre [*Yalquṭ*'s version runs] was exceedingly proud and arrogant. What did he do? He went to the sea and made himself four long iron pillars^{x)} of equal measure and set them up opposite each other. He built [on top of them] seven firmaments, a throne, *ḥayyot*, thunders, meteors, and lightnings.
>
> He made the first firmament of glass, five hundred cubits by five hundred cubits. He made for it a sun, moon, and stars.
>
> He made the second firmament of iron, one thousand cubits by one thousand cubits. A pipe with water running through it separated the first firmament from the second.
>
> The third firmament was of tin^{y)}, fifteen hundred cubits by fifteen hundred cubits. A pipe with water running through it separated the second firmament from the third. He placed in the tin firmament round stones, which knocked against [?] one another and sounded like thunder.
>
> He made the fourth firmament of lead, two thousand cubits by two thousand cubits. A pipe with water running through it separated the third firmament from the fourth.
>
> The fifth firmament was of bronze; he made it twenty-five hundred cubits by twenty-five hundred cubits. A pipe with water running through it separated the fourth firmament from the fifth.
>
> The sixth firmament was of silver, three thousand cubits by three thousand cubits. A pipe with water running through it separated the fifth firmament from the sixth.
>
> The seventh firmament was of gold, thirty-five hundred cubits by thirty-five hundred cubits. In it he put precious stones and pearls, each a cubit in diameter, which he would use to create

---

50 Ginzberg gives full references to the legend and its parallels [400].

51 *Gen. R.* 85:4 (ed. 1035–1036 [188]) assumes this equation, and proposes extending it to the patriarch Judah's friend "Hirah" (Genesis 38:1). In that case, the author of the midrash points out, Hiram "will have lived nearly eleven hundred years"; otherwise, a mere five hundred or so. *Lev. R.* 18:2 (ed. 402–403 [191]), BT B.B. 85a–b, Hull. 89a, also give "Hiram" as the name of Ezekiel's king of Tyre. Christian writers of the fourth century (Jerome, Ephraem Syrus, Aphraates) refer to this identification and to Hiram's extraordinary lifespan; Jerome explicitly claims that the idea is Jewish (*Commentary* on Ezekiel 28:13; ed. 392 [622]) [373,671,672]. Already in the early third century, Origen seems to assume that Ezekiel's king of Tyre is the "Hiram" of I Kings, even while he argues for a more profound understanding of this figure as a representation of the devil (*In Ezech. Hom.*, XIII, 1, ed. 8:442–443 [641]; see below). But it may be significant that both *Mekhiltas* speak of the "prince of Tyre's" claim to divinity, yet hold back from naming him (*Mekhilta, Shirah* chapter 8, ed./tr. 2:61 [195]; *Mek. Simeon*, ed. 91–92 [196]). The expositors were perhaps not entirely sure that he was Hiram.

the illusion of lightning and meteors. When he shook himself, those stones would knock against [?] each other, and thunder was heard.

God sends Ezekiel to Hiram to remind him that he is only a human being, and carries him to Hiram's throne room by the hair of his head (as in Ezekiel 8:3). Hiram is terrified at Ezekiel's sudden appearance, but evidently not too terrified to argue:

> "I may be a human being," he said, "but I live forever. Just as God has his seat in the heart of the seas, so I have my seat in the heart of the seas. God [dwells] in seven firmaments; so do I. Furthermore, many kings died, while I endure. Twenty-one kings of the house of David, twenty-one kings of Israel, fifty prophets, and ten high priests have I buried; I am still alive. *I am a god; I sit in the seat of God, in the heart of the seas.*"

The storyteller compares Hiram, who prided himself on having sent cedars to the temple, to a slave who boasts of having made his lord's robe. To put an end to his arrogance, God destroyed the temple. According to the ending of *Yalquṭ*'s version (which *Midrash ha-Gadol* and Jellinek's text sacrifice to the new contexts in which they encase the story) God then sent Nebuchadnezzar to Hiram. He made love to Hiram's mother in front of him[52], then dethroned him and tortured him to death. As for the palace, "God split open the earth and hid it away for the righteous in the future age."

How far back can we trace this tale of seven metallic anti-heavens in the sea? We must admit that no source earlier than the Middle Ages mentions it. Rabbinic midrashim indeed develop the theme of the king of Tyre's claim to divinity, identify him with Solomon's associate Hiram, and grant him an amazing lifespan[z]. (We may well wonder why the rabbis made this farfetched and gratuitous identification in the first place; we will presently return to this question.) But only Tanh. *Bereshit* #7, itself perhaps quite late, makes any mention of his palace. This midrash tells us that "whoever wants to deify himself builds himself a palace in the midst of the waters," and cites Hiram's palace as a case in point. The author may presuppose the full account of Hiram's seven-layered construction; but, since he gives no details, we have no way of knowing. As far as I know, the earliest passably clear reference to our haggadah is a comment of Rashi's to BT Hull. 89a: Hiram "built himself seven firmaments of bronze [sic!] and climbed up and seated himself upon them."

But there is one feature of our story that suggests it may go back to antiquity: the association of Hiram's seven firmaments with seven metals.

The second-century pagan critic of Christianity, Celsus (whose polemic Origen quoted extensively in the course of refuting it), relates that the fol-

---

52 This detail evidently reverses an old legend according to which Hiram was the lover of Nebuchadnezzar's mother (*Lev. R.* 18:2, ed. 402–403 [191]). The storyteller seems not to have noticed the incongruity of Hiram's mother still being alive.

lowers of the Persian cult of Mithras used "a ladder with seven gates" as a symbol of the seven planetary spheres. "The first of the gates is of lead, the second of tin, the third of bronze, the fourth of iron, the fifth of an alloy, the sixth of silver, and the seventh of gold" (Origen, *Contra Celsum,* VI, 22 [627]). Six of the seven items on Celsus's list agree with the metals mentioned in the Hiram story, although their order is somewhat different[53].

Erwin R. Goodenough has found a comparable sequence of seven metals, perhaps representing the seven heavens rather than the planets, depicted in the painting of the "closed temple" on the wall of the third-century synagogue at Dura-Europos [715]. If Goodenough is right, Jews had assimilated the Persian idea of seven heavenly spheres made of different metals, and equated these spheres with the seven firmaments of their own tradition, no later than the third century A.D. The Hiram story draws directly on this conception. The peculiar top-heavy construction of Hiram's palace is presumably a dim reflection of the image of seven concentric spheres.

This argument for the antiquity of the tradition behind the Hiram legend would be considerably weakened if we could show that the conception of seven heavens made of seven metals survived into the Middle Ages. There are in fact medieval Muslim sources that have the several heavens made of precious metals and stones. Kisa'i's *Tales of the Prophets* (eleventh century) lists seven heavens of green emerald, ruby, topaz, silver, red gold, white pearl, and glistening light [777]. Chadwick, in his note on *Contra Celsum,* refers to a thirteenth-century Muslim work, "liber Scalae Machometi," which enumerates eight heavens of iron, bronze, silver, gold, pearl, emerald, ruby, and topaz. But the enumeration of metals in the Hiram story resembles Celsus's list far more closely than it does these medieval lists. Further, I know of no other evidence that Jews in the Middle Ages were familiar with the notion that the heavens are made of jewels or precious metals[54]. It seems simplest to assume that this idea found its way into Judaism during the rabbinic period; and that, when the author of our haggadah uses it to describe Hiram's blasphemous mimicry of the divine realms in the sea, he is drawing on early tradition.

There is even an early parallel to the transfer of the seven metallic spheres to the sea. One of the fantastic tales about the ancient Egyptian prince and magician Setne Khamwas, apparently written in Hellenistic Egypt [39], includes an episode describing the adventures of an even more ancient magician named Naneferkaptah. A priest informs Naneferkaptah of

---

53 On the "alloy," cf. endnote *y*, above.
54 Ginzberg could find no Jewish parallel to Hiram's metallic firmaments, apart from the six mountains of metal in the Book of Enoch, 52:2 [400].

the existence of a magic book, written by the god Thoth himself, to be found "in the middle of the water of Coptos in a box of iron. In the box of iron is a box of [copper. In the box of copper is] a box of juniper wood. In the box of juniper wood is a box of ivory and ebony. In the box of ivory and ebony there is a [box of silver. In the box of silver] is a box of gold, and in it is the book. [There are six miles of] serpents, scorpions, and all kinds of reptiles around the box in which the book is, and there is [an eternal serpent around] this same box" [40][55]. We need not follow Naneferkaptah's progress in finding the book and enchanting or killing its hideous guardians. What is important for us is the observation, first made at the beginning of this century by R. Reitzenstein, that the series of six boxes — seven, if "ivory" and "ebony" are counted separately — seems to represent the seven concentric spheres, transferred into the ocean [728].

What connection can there be between the Setne Khamwas stories and the haggadah of rabbinic Judaism? These Egyptian tales indeed seem remote from the materials we have been examining. Yet, as Hugo Gressmann has argued, other features of the Setne Khamwas stories (details of the punishment of the wicked in the netherworld) found their way into Judaism at the beginning of the Christian era, and left their mark on the New Testament and the rabbinic literature [69]. Similarly, when the author of the Hiram story shifts the seven heavens, in miniature, into the water, he may be taking his cue from a motif that goes back to Hellenistic Egypt.

But what did it mean to the Jewish storyteller to place Hiram's firmaments, complete with throne, *ḥayyot*, and mock luminaries, in the sea? The story itself seems to reflect a certain tension over the significance of enthronement in the waters. God himself, the author has Hiram tell Ezekiel, "has his seat in the heart of the seas." Yet the story's focus is on the sea as headquarters for the rebel — I am tempted to say rebel deity — Hiram. I suspect that this tension goes back to the ambiguity of the image of the *merkabah* in the waters. It is God's own chariot; yet its watery setting marks an element of the chaotic (and therefore anti-divine) within God. Our legend separates out this element, in the form of the anti-god Hiram and his anti-*merkabah* in the sea. God can then come and crush it.

c) The throne of the devil. We now have the clue to the meaning of a dialogue that supposedly took place early in the seventh century between the Arabian prophet Muhammad and a rival of his, a young Jewish visionary named Ibn Sayyad (or, as the Muslim traditions sometimes call him, Ibn Sa'id).

---

55 Words in brackets are the translator's reconstructions, based on the material in the sequel. – I am grateful to my friend and colleague Edmund S. Meltzer, who helped me locate this story and discussed it with me.

The Apostle of God [Muhammad] said to Ibn Sa'id, "What do you see?"
"I see a throne upon the sea," he replied, "around it the *hayyat.*"
The Apostle of God said, "He sees the throne of the devil." [772]

In an article that appeared in 1976, I gave my reasons for supposing that this discussion, and others like it recorded in the Muslim traditional literature, go back to actual encounters between Muhammad and a Jewish rival in seventh-century Medina [770]. I then proposed that the word *hayyat*, used by Ibn Sayyad, is not the Arabic word for "snakes" (its usual meaning), but an Arabicized form of Ezekiel's *hayyot*; and that Ibn Sayyad's vision, and Muhammad's verdict on it, both have something to do with Revelation's "glass sea" and Akiba's warning against saying "water, water."

Yet the dialogue remains baffling. Why does Ibn Sayyad see the throne and the *hayyot* upon the water? What prompts Muhammad to declare that what he is seeing is the throne of the devil (Arabic *Iblis*)? The material we have examined in this chapter enables us to answer both these questions. Ibn Sayyad's vision is rooted in the Jewish *merkabah* tradition. Like the midrashic Ezekiel (above, section 6), he sees the throne and the *hayyot* amid the waters. But Muhammad's response, like so much else of his teaching, is also rooted in Judaism — in the rabbis' perception that the presence of the *merkabah* in the waters is an ominous clue to the nature of its occupant. Ibn Sayyad, therefore, must be having a vision of Iblis; who, like the Hiram of the haggadah, is enthroned in the sea with his *hayyot*.

The image of the throne on the waters, and an ambivalence about its meaning, thus passed over from Judaism to Islam during the infancy of the new religion. Muslim haggadah perpetuated both the image and the ambivalence. God's throne was upon the water at the time of creation, according to the Koran (11:7). Muslim traditions about the creation, many of them claiming Muhammad's authority, make use of and develop this detail[56]. One such tradition seems to imply that God has sat on this water-bound throne since creation, distributing largesse to his creatures with one hand and judging them with the other (Tirmidhi, *Sunan*, ed. 8:213–214; Ibn Hanbal, *Musnad*, ed. 2:313, 500–501; Bukhari, *Sahih*, ed. 3:259–260, tr. 3:344 [754,741,739,740]). But Iblis also has his throne amid the waters. "Iblis's throne is upon the sea," one tradition represents Muham-

---

56 The early tenth-century Koran commentator Tabari brings together a number of these traditions in his *tafsir* (commentary) to Surah 11:7 (ed. 12:4–5 [752]). Another tenth-century writer, Maqdisi, records similar material, some of it evidently of Jewish origin (*Book of Creation and History*, ed. 1:148–150, tr. 1:137–140 [747]). Tabari, Maqdisi, and several of the standard collections of *hadiths* (traditions supposedly going back to Muhammad) all quote a brief and rather obscure series of rhymes, which have God fashion his throne on the water at the beginning of creation (Ibn Hanbal, *Musnad*, ed. 4:11, 12; Ibn Majah, *Sunan*, ed. 1:64–65; Tirmidhi, *Sunan*, ed. 8:270–271 [741,743,754]).

mad as having said, "and he sends forth his legions to tempt people" (Muslim, *Sahih*, ed. 4:2167, tr. 4:1472; Ibn Hanbal, ed. 3:314–315, 332, 354, 366, 384 [749,750,741]). The throne in the waters is plainly a headquarters for more than one sort of activity.

The Muslim texts thus replace Hiram by Iblis. By so doing, they perhaps give us a clue to Hiram's real significance in the legend we have been examining. We must consider the possibility that the author of this legend, whether consciously or not, used the relatively harmless folklore figure of Hiram as a cover for a darker and more powerful creature of evil.

This suggestion would have come as no shock to Origen, who argued powerfully that the "prince of Tyre" of Ezekiel's prophecy, whether Hiram or some other Tyrian king, was in fact a mask for the fallen Lucifer (*De Principiis*, I.v.4, tr. 47–49 [636]; *In Ezech. Hom.*, XIII, 1, ed. 8:442–443 [641]). But, however close Origen's ties to his Jewish contemporaries may have been (and we will get some sense in chapter VIII of how close they were), we cannot reason from Origen's Bible exegesis to that of the rabbis without some strong warrant for doing so.

It is more to the point that this suggestion would neatly explain the oddest detail of the rabbis' treatment of the king of Tyre: their equating him with Hiram, and the near-immortality that they give him as a result. It is true that, as Isaac Heinemann has shown, this is far from being the only case where the haggadah finds a name for an anonymous Biblical character in defiance of all historical plausibility, or where it identifies individuals whom the Bible separates from each other by centuries [405]. But this case is unusual, not only because the anachronism is so extreme, but particularly because it seems nearly impossible to point to any religious aim that might have justified it.

We can best understand what the rabbis did if we assume that, for them as for Origen, "Hiram king of Tyre" was a mask for an immortal being who set his *merkabah* upon the waters. By so doing, he drew into himself the evil that more properly belonged to the original master of the *merkabah*.

9. Conclusions

The evidence marshalled in the last section buttresses the speculations that I advanced in section 7. The primordial waters, whether they appear in their original shape or disguised as the Red Sea or the river Chebar, have powerful overtones of the chaotic and the demonic. Merged with the *merkabah*, they contaminate the divinity. Anyone who says "water, water" in the presence of the *merkabah* bears witness to God's taint. His testimony must be denounced as a lie.

This conclusion, in turn, reinforces what we gathered from our discussion of the golden calf.

Admittedly, the case of the calf differs in important ways from that of the waters. The waters and their significance are prehistoric and universal, although they may be mirrored here and there within Israel's history (notably, at the Red Sea). The calf and its implications, by contrast, are specific to Israel — unless, as our observations on Jung have perhaps suggested, they are themselves representations of something broader and dimmer, at whose shape we can only guess.

Further, the body of evidence we have examined in this chapter is somewhat different from that which we considered in chapter V. We have travelled more widely in order to find it; in particular, we have entered for the first time the territory of the *Hekhalot*. The exegetical traditions we have treated here are more diffuse, their outlines more blurred, their lines of transmission more difficult to trace. We have not, for example, been able to pose (as we did in chapter V) the question of how the "water" materials relate to the synagogue *merkabah* tradition; we had no way to find a useful answer.

But, for all this, the investigations in these two chapters have led us to essentially the same result. In both, we found that the ultimate object of the rabbis' fears was the implication that the pure and holy God is tangled, not to say alloyed, with some great evil. They directed their fears, and hence their disapproval, toward texts or statements that might serve as starting points for lines of thought leading toward this fearful conclusion: the "second story of the calf" (chapter V), or the utterance "water, water." Ezekiel's *merkabah* vision was, if not the ultimate starting point for several different lines of this sort, at least a crucial point of intersection. That is why the rabbis feared it, and sometimes tried to suppress it.

With this observation, we have completed the essential part of the work of mapping the dark side of the *merkabah*. This is not to say that we do not have discoveries of this sort yet to make. But we will come upon them in the course of exploring other aspects of the *merkabah*; and, when we find them, we will use what we have learned in the past two chapters to help us judge their significance.

We must now circle back to an earlier stage of our inquiry, and take up the synagogue tradition where we left it at the end of chapter IV. Our main task, as I then suggested, is to illuminate the Sinai-*merkabah* link and its role in the Shabu‘ot expositions, and thereby to penetrate the realities that underlie the Johanan b. Zakkai *merkabah* stories. But, before we attack this enormous problem, we must briefly turn to a more modest issue which will serve as an overture to it. This is the rainbow that Ezekiel mentions; which, we recall, plays its part in the Johanan b. Zakkai stories.

We will find that the rainbow, like the calf and the waters, managed to stir up a certain amount of rabbinic revulsion. I am not sure how important this revulsion is for the broader question of why the rabbis were afraid of the *merkabah*. It reminds us, however, that we are far from having put this question permanently behind us. Even when we walk in the chariot's light, we are apt to be startled by a shadow.

Chapter VII

The Merkabah and the Rainbow

Ezekiel 1:26–28 compares God both, to a human being and to a rainbow. The first comparison, as far as we can tell, did not seriously faze the rabbis. The second did.

This is not quite what we would expect. We tend to assume that the anthropomorphisms of the Hebrew Bible must have offended the more delicate religious sensibilities of later times. The ancient Bible translations support this assumption. LXX occasionally (less often, perhaps, than scholars tend to suppose) tones down anthropomorphic expressions [41a]. Targum scrubs them away or envelops them in clouds of euphemism. We have already seen the Aramaic translators use considerable ingenuity to this end in dealing with Ezekiel 1:26–27 (above, chapter IV). Christopher Rowland has detected in the apocalyptic visions of the *merkabah* a gradual purging of Ezekiel's anthropomorphisms [159]. Revelation 4:3, which goes rather far in this direction, is able to play down God's resemblance to a human precisely by playing up his resemblance to a rainbow.

When we find, therefore, that Ezekiel's human-like God left the rabbis unruffled, while his rainbow-like glory excited some of them and disturbed others, we are obliged to take notice.

The negative response to the rainbow is worth our attention partly because it contributes to our understanding of what there was about Ezekiel's vision that the rabbis thought worth suppressing. But the whole issue bears on our study in another, more important way. It anticipates the work with the Sinai-*merkabah* materials that we will do in the next chapter.

Like the Sinai-*merkabah* traditions, the conceptions surrounding the rainbow help us understand the supernatural phenomena in the stories of the *merkabah* expositions of Joḥanan b. Zakkai's disciples. Again like these traditions, they function as a bridge connecting the synagogue *merkabah* exegesis to the *Hekhalot*. Finally, when we examine the commotion that developed around the rainbow in Amoraic Palestine, we find at its center the man who will come to dominate our discussion of the Sinai-*merkabah* traditions. His name is Joshua b. Levi.

1. The human-like God

Before we turn to the rainbow, we must briefly consider the notion that the anthropomorphism of Ezekiel 1:26–28 was the core of what was objectionable about the *merkabah*, the supremely forbidden aspect of the vision which brought down the wrath of the rabbis on the rest.

We have several reasons for supposing this is not so. The bulk of the rabbinic literature, to begin with, does not share the Targum's horror of anthropomorphism. Rabbinic anthropomorphism is often far more daring than anything in the Bible — as we saw, in the last chapter (section 5c), from the haggadah about God's appearance at the Red Sea. (Examples of this sort could easily be multiplied.) Further, the conclusion of Ezekiel 1 is far from being the only anthropomorphic passage in the Bible, or even the most extreme one. God's feet appear in Exodus 24:10; his hand, face, and backside in 33:22–23; Daniel 7:9 describes him as an old man with white hair, sitting on a throne. But I know of no trace in the rabbinic literature that these passages stirred up anxieties comparable to those provoked by the *merkabah*.

One midrash, preserved in *Gen. R.* 27:1 (ed. 255–256 [188]) and its parallels[a], allows us to gauge how the rabbis reacted to the anthropomorphism of Ezekiel 1:26.

"Great is the power of the prophets," the expositor declares, "who liken the image [that is, the human being] to its creator!" He learns from Daniel 8:16 that God can be called "a human being" (*'adam*). But Ezekiel 1:26, with its *form like the appearance of a human being*, "puts the matter yet more clearly."

The composer of this midrash, who invokes the authority of the fourth-century Palestinians Judan and Judah b. Simon, seems to revel in the prophets' anthropomorphism. He highlights it for no more essential purpose than to prop up a highly arbitrary and fanciful interpretation of *'adam* in Ecclesiastes 2:12 (or 8:1) as referring to God. It is significant that *Gen. R.* 24:1 (ed. 230 [188]) also uses the expression "liken the image to its creator," but applies it, not to the prophets, but to sinners who foolishly imagine that God is not very different from themselves. The composer of *Gen. R.* 27:1 plainly believes that God's chosen spokesmen may take liberties forbidden to ordinary mortals.

There is no reason at all to believe that this midrash was intended to reveal to an elite circle some shocking esoteric doctrine of God's human form. The earliest sources that quote it, *Gen. R.* and *Pesiqta de-Rab Kahana*, put it into the context of a *petihah*. This points to the synagogue as its home. It suggests that the midrash was indeed intended to shock, but only in the mildest way — to startle a sleepy congregation into paying attention to the preacher. The calculated audacity of its opening certainly indicates a rhetorical purpose.

The implications of this midrash accord with those of a baraita in BT Hag. 13a, which specifically excludes Ezekiel 1:27–28 from *ma'aseh merkabah*, and therefore presumably exempts it from the restrictions imposed on *ma'aseh merkabah* [560]. Both texts suggest that Ezekiel's anthropomorphism had little or nothing to do with the rabbis' aversion to his *merkabah* vision. Whatever shock it gave them was more in the category of titillation than of appalment.

Yet some rabbis – not, to be sure, those responsible for the baraita in Hag. 13a – seem to have taken a dimmer view of the image of the rainbow. We must find out why.

2. The rainbow-like glory

a) The texts.

Like the appearance of the bow that is in the cloud on a rainy day, reads Ezekiel 1:28, *so was the appearance of the surrounding splendor. This was the appearance of the likeness of the glory of the Lord. When I saw it, I fell on my face.*

BT Hag. 16a twice quotes this verse in support of the idea that the rainbow has certain numinous properties that demand the viewer's respect and reserve. The first time is in connection with the Mishnah's assertion that "he who has no concern for the honor of his creator would be better off if he had never been born" (Hag. 2:1). The Gemara, commenting on this passage, quotes Rabbah b. Nahmani (a Babylonian Amora of the fourth century) as applying it to him "who gazes at a rainbow" (*mistakkel baqqeshet*) [554]. The anonymous compiler of the Gemara then provides the text of Ezekiel 1:28, thus explaining Rabbah's reference.

Several lines on, the Gemara attributes to the third-century Palestinian Judah b. Nahmani the remark that "everyone who gazes at three things will lose his eyesight: a rainbow, the prince, and the priests." Once again, the compiler quotes Ezekiel 1:28 to explain the first of these items.

The text itself of Hag. 16a says no more about the rainbow. Several manuscripts of the Talmud, however, contain an extremely interesting addition to this material, which the medieval scribes inserted either immediately before the utterance attributed to Judah b. Nahmani, or else in the discussion of the phrase "he who has no concern for the honor of his creator." We must hold our judgment on the source of the addition until after we have examined its text.

One manuscript, Oxford 366, gives the addition as follows:

> [A] Rava said: [A1] Whoever gazes at a rainbow must fall on his face. So it is written, *Like the appearance of the bow that is in the cloud*, and so forth.

[A2] They curse [him] in the west [that is, Palestine], because he seems to be worshipping it. [B1] He who sees a rainbow must say a blessing: "Blessed be he who remembers the covenant[1]." [B2] R. Ishmael, son of R. Johanan b. Beroqa, concludes [the blessing] as follows: "Who is faithful to his covenant and upholds his word."

En Ya[c]aqob, a sixteenth-century compilation of Talmudic *haggadot,* quotes a text of this addition which differs slightly from that of the Oxford manuscript [240a]. Its source is apparently a lost manuscript of Hag. 16a. This version says in A2 that "they curse him in the west *because it looks like heresy*"; and it adds immediately afterward: "But let him say: 'Blessed be he who remembers the covenant'" (thus anticipating B1). Abbreviated versions of *[c]En Ya[c]aqob*'s text found their way into three manuscripts: Munich 95, Vatican 134, and a Cambridge Genizah fragment (T.-S. F2[1] 204) which seems to follow a text akin to that of Vatican 134 [553][b)].

It is clear that this passage is not an original part of BT Hag. 16a. The printed edition omits it; not all manuscripts contain it[2]; those that do cannot agree on its wording or where it is to be placed. We can easily imagine why scribes might have added it — to supplement the material on the rainbow that Hag. 16a already contains — but must strain to find a reason why they would have deleted it.

What, then, is the source of Hag. 16a+ (as I will designate it from now on)? A passage in BT Ber. 59a seems at first sight a likely candidate:

[A] R. Alexander quoted R. Joshua b. Levi: [A1] He who sees a rainbow in a cloud must fall on his face. So it is written: *Like the appearance of the bow that is in the cloud,* and so forth. *When I saw it, I fell on my face.*

[A2] They curse him in the west, because he seems to be bowing to the rainbow.

[B1] But he certainly must say a blessing. What blessing should he say? "Blessed be he who remembers the covenant."

[B2] It is taught in a baraita [*matnita*]: R. Ishmael, son of R. Johanan b. Beroqa, says: "Who is faithful to his covenant and upholds his word."

[B3] Rab Papa said: He therefore ought to use both formulae: "Blessed be he who remembers the covenant, is faithful to his covenant, and upholds his word[c)]."

If we choose to argue that Hag. 16a+ was copied from this passage, we are obliged to explain several differences between the two texts. We can blame the most obvious of these differences on the scribes who presumably did the copying. How did "R. Alexander quoting R. Joshua b. Levi" turn into "Rava"? Perhaps a simple scribal blunder was responsible: someone abbreviated "Rabbi Alexander" as "Rab. A.," which a later copyist could

---

1 The reference is to the covenant that God made with Noah after the flood, according to Genesis 9:8–17: "I set my bow in the cloud, and it shall be a sign of the covenant between me and the earth. When I bring clouds over the earth and the bow is seen in the clouds, I will remember my covenant which is between me and you and every living creature of all flesh; and the waters shall never again become a flood to destroy all flesh" (RSV).

2 I have seen no trace of it in ms Munich 6, Vatican 171, Göttingen 3, or London 400.

easily have read as "Rava." Or perhaps the scribes were influenced by the context into which they inserted the material. As we saw, Hag. 16a quotes Rabbah b. Nahmani as referring to someone "who gazes at a rainbow"; and, in Hebrew script, "Rabbah" and "Rava" look almost the same[3]. Another difference between Ber. 59a and Hag. 16a+ supports the second alternative. While the former text speaks of someone "who sees a rainbow" (*ro'eh 'et haqqeshet*), the latter uses the verb "gazes" (*mistakkel*), in what seems a strained and inappropriate way. It is reasonable to assume that the scribes were influenced by the utterances that Hag. 16a attributes to Rabbah and to Judah b. Nahmani, both of which speak of "gazing" at a rainbow (above).

So far, we have seen no reason to suppose that Hag. 16a+ is anything but Ber. 59a, slightly retouched in accord with its new context. This assumption, however, will not explain a more subtle and important difference between the two passages. In Hag. 16a+, sections A and B are independent units, each of which could easily stand by itself. The editor sets them side by side on account of their common topic, but does nothing to link them. The editor of Ber. 59a, by contrast, uses section B1 to weld together the two parts of the passage. The editing of Hag. 16a+ is less polished, therefore presumably more primitive[4].

Indeed, we find a close parallel to section B standing alone in the Palestinian Talmud:

> He who sees a rainbow in a cloud should say: "Blessed are you, Lord, who remembers the covenant." R. Hiyya quoted R. Johanan[5]: "Who is faithful to his covenant and remembers the covenant." [PT Ber. 9:2, 13d]

This passage from PT helps us to explain another difference between Hag. 16a+ and Ber. 59a, concerning the blessing formulae in section B. At least as early as the second century B.C., Palestinian Jews were in the habit of saying a blessing at the sight of the rainbow (Sira 43:11). Over the centuries, shorter and longer forms of this blessing evolved. The tradition preserved in PT reported both a shorter formula ("who remembers the covenant") and a longer one ("who is faithful to his covenant and remembers

---

3 Joel Sirkes (1561–1640), who quotes Hag. 16a+ in his textual notes to Hag. 16a (printed in the standard editions of the Talmud), in fact reads "Rabbah" in place of "Rava."

4 *ᶜEn Yaᶜaqob*'s version of Hag. 16a+ bridges the two units less skillfully, by adding at the end of section A: "But let him say: 'Blessed be he who remembers the covenant'" (above).

5 Doubtless originally "R. Ishmael, son of R. Johanan b. Beroqa," as in BT. Transmitters of the tradition changed the obscure Tanna Johanan b. Beroqa into the well-known Amora Johanan (b. Nappaha), simply by omitting his father's name. A copyist misread the abbreviation for "son of" (*BEno SHel*) as if it were the abbreviation for "quoting" (*BESHem*). These two alterations yielded "R. Ishmael quoting R. Johanan." But no one had ever heard of a disciple of Johanan b. Nappaha named Ishmael. A well-meaning scribe therefore "corrected" this name to "R. Hiyya," whom rabbinic sources often represent as transmitting Johanan's utterances.

the covenant")[6]. But the Babylonians, who inherited a cognate tradition, were not sure whether their longer text was supposed to supplement the shorter or replace it. The editor of Hag. 16a+ assumed that it was a supplement: "R. Ishmael, son of R. Johanan b. Beroqa, *concludes as follows.*" But the editor of Ber. 59a supposed, probably correctly, that the two formulae were alternatives, and credited the fourth-century Babylonian Amora Rab Papa with combining them.

Let us pause and consider what we have established so far. Hag. 16a+ and Ber. 59a are independent sources which drew upon the same materials. We have not been able to discover where the scribes found the passage that they copied into Hag. 16a, and must leave this an unsolved riddle. It was these scribes who changed "R. Alexander quoting R. Joshua b. Levi" to "Rava," and "he who sees a rainbow" (in A1) to "whoever gazes at a rainbow." Apart from these two alterations, which we must correct in accord with the parallel text, Hag. 16a+ preserves its sources in a more original form than does Ber. 59a.

b) Joshua b. Levi and the rainbow. We can now move to the crux of our argument. Hag. 16a+ reports two Palestinian traditions on how one should respond to the sight of the rainbow. One of these prescribes a blessing; the other, prostration. Although the latter tradition can invoke the powerful authority of the early third-century Amora Joshua b. Levi, only the former found its way into the Palestinian Talmud. The note that the Babylonian sources add to the tradition requiring prostration — "they curse [him] in the west, because he seems to be worshipping it[7]" — suggests that PT's omission of it was deliberate.

In other words, Joshua b. Levi is reported to have deduced from Ezekiel 1:28 that the rainbow is the visible manifestation of God's glory. He who sees it must therefore respond as Ezekiel did, by falling on his face. Later Palestinians thought that this practice smacked of nature worship; they denounced it, and tried to suppress the report that Joshua b. Levi had advocated it. The Babylonians, who seem to have found it less threatening, preserved Joshua b. Levi's tradition, in Ber. 59a and in the unknown source of Hag. 16a+.

This conclusion helps us make sense of an otherwise obscure feature of an anonymous Palestinian legend about Joshua b. Levi, preserved in *Gen. R.* 35:2 (ed. 328–329 [188]):

---

6 We find PT's longer formula also in T. Ber. 6(7):5, the shorter in Genizah fragments of a lost *Tanḥuma* midrash to Genesis 8:1 [238,325].

7 These words (A2) are in Babylonian Aramaic. They are certainly a comment on the Hebrew utterance recorded in A1, and not a continuation of it.

Elijah [the prophet] and R. Joshua b. Levi were sitting together reciting traditions. When they came to one of the traditions of R. Simeon b. Yohai, they said: "Here is the master of the tradition. Why don't we enter and ask him about it?"

Elijah went in to see him [Simeon b. Yohai]. He [Simeon] asked him: "Who is with you?"

"The greatest man of this generation," he replied, "R. Joshua b. Levi."

[Simeon] said to him: "Was the rainbow seen in his time? If so, he is not worthy to see my face[d]."

The details of this story are not quite as odd as they appear at first sight. Rabbinic legend has the prophet Elijah appear to many different Tannaim and Amoraim, and Joshua b. Levi is his special favorite [370,378,388]. Once we accept that Elijah can study with the living Joshua b. Levi, we need not balk at his visiting the deceased Simeon b. Yohai, although the story does not make quite clear where the visit takes place. (One commentary on *Gen. R.*, the *Mattenot Kehunnah*, suggests that Elijah went into R. Simeon's burial cave.)

Further, we can understand why Simeon b. Yohai finds the rainbow a source of pride. "R. Hezekiah quoted R. Jeremiah: All during the life of R. Simeon b. Yohai no rainbow was seen in a cloud" (PT Ber. 9:2, 13d). Why not? Because, as an anonymous story quoted in *Pesiqta de-Rab Kahana* (ed. 190 [206]) shows, Simeon b. Yohai himself took the place of the rainbow promised in Genesis 9:8–17: he is the "sign of the world," whose merits are enough to protect the world from destruction[e]. No wonder he looks down on those lesser saints whose merits must be reinforced by an actual rainbow.

But why does he single out Joshua b. Levi for his contempt on this score? After all, it cannot be very common that not a single rainbow is seen during a person's lifetime. *Gen. R.* 35:2 (ed. 328 [188]) quotes the fourth-century Palestinian Judan as saying that there were only two periods in all post-Noachian history when the rainbow was not seen: the generation of King Hezekiah and the generation of the "men of the great synagogue." The most plausible explanation is that the author of this legend was dimly aware of some discreditable association of Joshua b. Levi with the rainbow. If the Palestinians once believed that Joshua b. Levi had proposed the rainbow as an object of worship, the snub they put in Simeon b. Yohai's mouth begins to make sense.

The Palestinians may have cursed those who prostrated themselves at the sight of the rainbow. But the notion that the rainbow is the visible glory of God had the authority of the *merkabah* vision behind it, and could not be so easily suppressed. As we saw, BT Hag. 16a attributes to Judah b. Nahmani, a Palestinian who lived a generation or so after Joshua b. Levi, the warning that anyone who stares at the rainbow will go blind. *Gen. R.* 35:3 (ed. 330 [188]) quotes an anonymous midrash which explains that the rainbow got its name (*qeshet*, in Hebrew) because it is "compared" (*muqqash*) to God — and then hurries to water down the implications of this remark.

The stories of the miracles that accompanied the *merkabah* expositions of Johanan b. Zakkai's disciples (above, chapter I) take on a special importance in this connection. Most of these miracles, as we saw, are drawn from either the Biblical or the rabbinic stories of the Sinai revelation. But one comes directly from Ezekiel's *merkabah* vision: the rainbow that appears in summertime. "Although it was a summer day, the earth shook, and a rainbow was seen in the cloud. A heavenly voice proclaimed: 'The place is cleared for you and the couch is spread for you! You and your disciples are designated for the third set!'" (PT Hag. 2:1, 77a). In view of what we have seen in this chapter, it is hard to avoid the impression that the storyteller conceives the rainbow as the visible token of God's presence.

When we first examined the Johanan b. Zakkai *merkabah* stories, I suggested that these tales derive from the synagogue, and reflect a tradition of synagogue exegesis which expounded the *merkabah* vision and the Sinai revelation together. We will pursue this tradition in the coming chapter, and will then discover that the figure most prominently associated with it is Joshua b. Levi. The veneration of the rainbow thus shares two features — its presence in the Johanan b. Zakkai stories, its association with Joshua b. Levi — with the Sinai-*merkabah* tradition. It is a tolerably short step from here to the conjecture that these two pieces of *merkabah* exegesis share a third feature as well: a home in the synagogue.

If this conjecture is right, it follows that Joshua b. Levi's injunction to throw oneself on one's face at the sight of the rainbow belongs to the *merkabah* exegesis of the Palestinian synagogues[8]. Later Palestinian rabbis saw idolatry in the practice, and recoiled from it. We may suppose, however, that Joshua b. Levi and his audiences intended nothing of the kind, and that their belief in the rainbow as divinity made visible had for them a special and entirely positive meaning. A passage from the *Hekhalot*, which we are about to examine, gives us a hint of what that meaning might have been.

---

8 Dr. Baruch Bokser has pointed out to me a passage from the so-called "Biblical Antiquities of Philo" that looks as if it ought to be relevant; only, I cannot quite define its relevance. Noah's descendants, the "Biblical Antiquities" tells us, were farmers. They would pray for rain, and God would answer their prayers. With the rain, "the bow appeared in the cloud, and the dwellers upon earth saw the memorial of the covenant and fell upon their faces and sacrificed, offering burnt offerings unto the Lord" (4:5, tr. 84 [726]). The "Biblical Antiquities," a midrashic paraphrase of Bible stories from Genesis through I Samuel which was apparently written in Hebrew but survives only in Latin translation, is certainly *not* the work of Philo. Although scholars have usually been inclined to date it to the first or early second century A.D. [711], Abraham Zeron has recently argued for a date in the third or even the fourth century [736]. If Zeron is right, it is possible that the "Biblical Antiquities" reflects popular veneration of the rainbow in third-century Palestine, which Joshua b. Levi encouraged.

c) The rainbow-being in the Hekhalot. In the remainder of this book, I will develop the argument that it is precisely the synagogue *merkabah* tradition carried to its extremes that is reflected in the *Hekhalot* literature. I here anticipate this argument with the observation that one *Hekhalot* passage, which appears in different contexts in several manuscripts but does not seem to belong to any of the conventionally defined "*Hekhalot* texts[9]," compares the body of a certain quasi-divine being to the rainbow. The writer uses Ezekiel 1:27–28 as the basis of this comparison.

The passage is, like most of the *Hekhalot,* maddeningly obscure. It speaks of a "youth" (*na^car*), also called "prince" (*śar*), who was first "given" to Moses. It seems to identify this being with the "face" of God mentioned in Exodus 33:15, and with the angel of whom God says (in Exodus 23:21) that *my name is in him*; that is, it represents him as a manifestation of God. It calls him by such names as Yophiel, Metatron, Sasangiel; and by a whole string of unintelligible epithets, some of which seem to conceal Greek and Latin words (*katharos,* "pure"; *iustus,* "just"; *kyrios,* "lord"; *krateros,* "mighty")[10]. It describes how this "prince," accompanied by fire, hail, and storm, enters the space beneath God's throne:

> When he enters, the great, mighty, and terrible God is praised three times each day[11]. He gives some of his glory to the princes [human? or angelic?] of the Gentiles; [but] the crown on his head is named "Israel." His body resembles the rainbow, and the rainbow resembles *the appearance of fire all around it* [Ezekiel 1:27][f).

Given the quotation of Ezekiel 1:27 that immediately follows, it seems clear that the reference to the rainbow is based on 1:28. The author of the *Hekhalot* passage interprets the latter verse to mean that the "prince" looks like the rainbow. If so, any rainbow that we see may turn out to be a divinity. No wonder we are expected to fall on our face before it, and go blind when we stare at it.

Another passage from ms New York (Schäfer, #385) gives a parallel description of this "prince[12]." It omits the comparison of his body with the rainbow; in place of this, it tells us that "his stature fills the world." We think of Sandalphon, the gigantic angel whose height spans heaven and earth (BT Hag. 13b; above, chapter IV, section 3c). We recall that, like Sandalphon, the rainbow seems to have its foot on earth and the top of its arch in heaven.

---

9 Schäfer, ##396–398, from ms New York (Jewish Theological Seminary) 8128; Schäfer indicates parallels. For the context in ms New York, see Appendix III; and below, chapter IX, section C4c.

10 Alan Segal's important discussion of the concept of Metatron as a junior deity [445] illuminates some of the stranger ideas summarized in this paragraph. We will return to them in chapter IX.

11 This reference to the three daily prayers of the Jewish liturgy suggests that the description of the "prince," fantastic as it is, is oriented to the synagogue.

12 See Appendix III; chapter IX, section B4.

We may suspect this is the real importance of the rainbow. The comparison of the "prince" to a rainbow, like the conception of Sandalphon, derives from that aspect of the synagogue tradition that searched for angelic mediators between God and humanity.

Who made this comparison, and when did he live? Normally, we would despair of these questions: it is usually impossible to fix the date or origin of a passage from the *Hekhalot*. But, by a bit of good luck, the writer's description of the "prince" gives us what may be a clue. God, he tells us, revealed the "prince's" name (or his own? the context is very obscure) to Moses on Sinai. Then:

> From Moses it was transmitted to Joshua, from Joshua to the elders, from the elders to the prophets, from the prophets to the men of the great synagogue. From them [it passed] to Ezra, and from Ezra to Hillel. After Hillel it remained a secret, until R. Abbahu came and said: *This is my name for ever* [Exodus 3:15]. [Schäfer, #397]

The writer has obviously taken his first sentence from the Mishnah's well-known description of the chain of transmission of the Oral Torah; the second sentence is a logical extension of it[13]. But why does he neither break off the chain with Hillel, nor simply continue it? Why does he tell us that the secret of the name was lost after Hillel's time, but rediscovered by Abbahu of Caesarea (ca. 300 A.D.)? Clearly, he regards Abbahu as being in some sense the author of the doctrine that he records.

If Abbahu had become (like, for example, Akiba) a legendary hero as well as a fairly prominent rabbinic authority, we might imagine that a person living centuries later might have arbitrarily selected him for this role. But Abbahu did not become a legendary hero. We must therefore look for the writer fairly close to Abbahu's own place and time, in circles where Abbahu would have been the outstanding candidate for the role of master of the mysteries of the ancients. (I leave open the question of what, if anything, this image of Abbahu had to do with the historical Abbahu.) We may tentatively locate these circles in fourth-century Caesarea[14].

---

13 M. Abot 1:1: "Moses received Torah from Sinai and transmitted it to Joshua, Joshua to the elders, the elders to the prophets; the prophets transmitted it to the men of the great synagogue." Jewish magicians reworked this passage and applied it to their own supposedly esoteric traditions, as we learn from the opening of the magical text that Margolioth published under the title *Sefer ha-Razim* ("Book of Secrets") [216,249a]. In chapter IX, we will see it adapted in yet another way by the *Hekhalot* writers.

14 A parallel passage, which Odeberg published at the end of his edition of *3 Enoch* (ch. 48D), tells us more about them. Metatron, we learn, revealed to Moses the secret names that he shares with God. From Moses, the secret passed to Joshua, the elders, the prophets, the men of the great synagogue, Ezra, Hillel, Abbahu, R. Zera (Abbahu's contemporary and associate), and finally to "the men of faith" and "the masters of faith." What follows suggest that these "masters of faith" used the secret names to cure illnesses (Schäfer, #80; from mss Munich 22 and Vatican 228). – The entire passage that Schäfer publishes as ##76–80 is related to ##396–398 in several ways, including the use of the names Sagnasgiel and Yephephiah (#77), which are obviously variants of

3. Conclusions

Our study of rabbinic reactions to Ezekiel 1:28 has allowed us, once again, to point to a specific feature of Ezekiel's *merkabah* that aroused the rabbis' opposition. Our sources tell us in so many words that this opposition existed, and they plausibly explain its motives. "They curse him in the west, because he seems to be bowing to the rainbow." As in our earlier studies, we find the rabbis trying to repress one of the implications of Ezekiel's vision; and we see with uncommon clarity what they thought they were doing when they repressed it.

The information we have gleaned on this hostile reaction is perhaps a little disappointing. It contributes nothing to our understanding of the divine ambiguities which (I have argued) the rabbis found hinted at in the *merkabah* vision, and which were at the bottom of their anxieties about the passage. It seems to be an objection of a more incidental sort, which by itself would hardly explain the intensity of these anxieties.

It does, however, have one important lesson to teach us; namely, that we must not try to make any too clean division between those aspects of the *merkabah* that excited and pleased the rabbis and those that frightened or appalled them. It was well that God showed himself to Ezekiel in the form of the rainbow; for this tangible appearance of the deity would naturally encourage the people's pious enthusiasm. But this enthusiasm could easily run to extremes, and itself threaten what the rabbis conceived as the purity of the people's faith. We will find this lesson of some value when we come to examine the development of the ascension theme, from the Shabuᶜot homilies into the *Hekhalot*.

The primary response to Ezekiel 1:28 – veneration of the rainbow – has proved rather more instructive than has the reaction against it. We have been able to connect this response with a specific individual (Joshua b. Levi), as well as with the stories of the *merkabah* expositions of Johanan b. Zakkai's disciples. These two links have pointed to a third, with the synagogue tradition of *merkabah* exegesis. Further, we have managed to trace a continuity between the views attributed to Joshua b. Levi and those of an anonymous *Hekhalot* author who lived a century or so later, on the rainbow as visible image of God. This continuity is important for two reasons.

First, it gives us a clue to the motives that led Joshua b. Levi to expound Ezekiel 1:28 as he did, laying what seems to us disproportionate stress on the importance of the rainbow. The crucial property of the rainbow, we gather from the *Hekhalot* source, is its ability to span heaven and earth. It

---

Sasangiel and Yophiel (#397; see above). In chapter IX, we will examine some of its other associations.

functions as does Sandalphon; and, compared with Sandalphon, it has the advantage of not being imaginary. The veneration of the rainbow thus fits securely into the agenda of the synagogue tradition of *merkabah* exegesis, with its craving for a tangible bridge between God and his worshippers.

Second, this continuity marks a line of historical development running from the synagogue *merkabah* tradition to the *Hekhalot*, with Joshua b. Levi occupying a particularly important place along that line. We must further explore this development in the next two chapters. When we do, we will again find Joshua b. Levi in a central role. We will discover, too, that the threads connecting Joshua b. Levi to the *Hekhalot* again run through the city of Caesarea. Not by way of Abbahu this time, but via another prominent Caesarean: Origen.

Chapter VIII
The Shabu^cot Cycle

One facet of the synagogue *merkabah* tradition has so far resisted our probing. This is the question of what the preachers said in the synagogue on Shabu^cot, when the Scriptures describing Sinai and the *merkabah* were read together and presumably expounded together.

We have seen several indications that these Shabu^cot sermons played an important role in the history of *merkabah* interpretation. The tenacity with which the *merkabah* held on to its position as Prophetic lection for Shabu^cot points in this direction; so do the "Sinaitic" features of the *merkabah* stories of Johanan b. Zakkai and his disciples. But, from the sources we have examined so far, we have been able to get practically no idea of what the sermons contained.

The Targum, as we saw in chapter IV, gives us little or no help in this matter. Several *Tanhuma* sources (discussed in chapter IV, section 5) perhaps allow us to conclude that a typical sermon of the third century would begin with a quotation of Psalm 68:18, followed by the explanation that "twenty-two thousand chariots descended with God to Sinai, each one like the *merkabah* that Ezekiel saw." If we are to trust these sources, the fourth-century Palestinian Berechiah added a comparison of the number of chariots to that of the Levites. But the *Tanhuma* materials leave us in the lurch at this point, and no other midrashim have so far come to our rescue.

Three rather unlikely-seeming sources, however, now carry us unexpectedly and dramatically toward our goal. The first of these is a Genizah midrash called the *Visions of Ezekiel*, usually classified among the *Hekhalot* [510, 540, 590]. The second is an account of Moses' ascent to heaven and struggle with the angels over the Torah, preserved in the twentieth section of the late midrash *Pesiqta Rabbati* and in its parallels. The third is the *First Homily* on the Book of Ezekiel, composed in Caesarea early in the third century by the great Christian expositor Origen. No one of these three texts, taken by itself, would be particularly helpful. But, when we examine them together, we will find that each helps clear up the riddles and obscurities of the others; and that the three of them point, each from a different angle, toward the *merkabah* expositions delivered on Shabu^cot in the synagogues of third-century Palestine.

I have briefly set forth the basic argument of this chapter in an article, "Origen, Ezekiel's Merkabah, and the Ascension of Moses," which appeared in *Church History* in 1981 [673]. The material deserves a more detailed and leisurely presentation, with emphasis on the Jewish sources – particularly the *Visions of Ezekiel*, an important and difficult text whose meaning and purpose have so far not been elucidated. This I now undertake.

A. The "Visions of Ezekiel"

1. Introduction

The *Visions of Ezekiel* first came to light in 1918, when Arthur Marmorstein published a one-leaf Genizah fragment from the British Museum (Or. No. 5559D, fol. 18a–b) [234]. The fragment was the end of a text, which, according to the colophon with which it concluded, was entitled "The Visions of Ezekiel the Son of Buzi the Priest" (*re'uyot yehezqel ben buzi hakkohen*)[a].

A few years later, Jacob Mann discovered in the Cambridge Genizah collection a second manuscript, nearly complete, of the entire text (Cambridge, T.-S. 8C1, fols. 3a–8a) [233]. One leaf, which should have come between 7b and 8a, was missing. Fortunately, the British Museum fragment seems to begin about where fol. 7b ends, and we do not appear to have lost more than a few words of the text. The last few lines of the *Visions* (Cambridge, fol. 8a) appear in both manuscripts[1].

Mann published a complete text of the *Visions*, based on both manuscripts. Shlomo Wertheimer followed him [502]. In 1972, Ithamar Gruenwald superseded both publications with a new edition, based on a fresh examination of the manuscripts, and accompanied by a very full commentary (in Hebrew) [229]. He later published an English introduction to the *Visions* as a chapter of his book *Apocalyptic and Merkavah Mysticism* [540]. The only English translation to have appeared so far, that of Louis Jacobs [250], is not entirely reliable.

What is the *Visions of Ezekiel*, and what does it contain? Gruenwald's description of it as "a mystical midrash on the first chapter of the Book of Ezekiel" [541] is not entirely accurate. It indeed starts out as a midrash

---

1 Ithamar Gruenwald wrote to me in 1980 that the missing leaf of the Cambridge manuscript had recently turned up. I have not been able to see a copy of it. According to Gruenwald, it does not add much to what we already know.

on the *merkabah* chapter, but it never gets beyond the first fourteen words of verse 1. It then shifts, rather abruptly, from midrash into detailed and methodical description of the seven (or eight) heavens and their contents.

Sooner or later, we will have to explain the *Visions'* peculiar structure. But this question, like the related problems of its date and its function, is best postponed until after we have laid out the text.

2. Translation

I translate Gruenwald's text, dividing it into two main sections: the midrash and the enumeration of heavens.

I have added whatever notes I think necessary to make the text intelligible. Occasionally, I have something I believe original and valuable to say about this or that problem in the text; I discuss such points at length in Appendix IV. But I have no intention of providing an English equivalent of Gruenwald's commentary. Readers who want a full discussion of every point of interest or difficulty in the *Visions*, or an extended presentation of rabbinic parallels to its ideas and expressions, must have recourse to Gruenwald's important work.

[I. The midrash.]

[A] *And it came to pass in the thirtieth* [*year*], and so forth [Ezekiel 1:1]. What was the nature of these [thirty years]? *Thirty* corresponds to thirty kings who reigned over Israel. For thus they said to Ezekiel: "Our fathers were punished in the desert forty years, *a year for each day* [that they spied out the land of Canaan; Numbers 14:34]. Similarly, we are punished for every king who arose over us."

[B] *In the fourth month, on the fifth day of the month* [Ezekiel 1:1]. What was special about Tammuz [the fourth month], that in it Ezekiel saw the [divine] Power[2]? Was it not a bad omen for Israel? So taught the sages in the Mishnah: "On the seventeenth of Tammuz the tablets were broken" [M. Taᶜan. 4:6]. But R. Levi said: [This was in order] to show the glory and power of God, that they were punished in Tammuz, and in Tammuz God's mercies were moved toward them.

[C] What does *while I was among the captivity* [Ezekiel 1:1] mean? Rabbi [Judah the Patriarch] said: Ezekiel began to complain to God. "Lord of the Universe!" he said. "Am I not a priest? Am I not a prophet? Why did Isaiah prophesy in Jerusalem, *while I* am in captivity, and Hosea in Jerusalem, *while I* am in captivity? Concerning Isaiah it is written, *The vision of Isaiah* [Isaiah 1:1]; and, concerning Hosea, *The word of the Lord that came to Hosea*, and so forth [Hosea 1:1]. Should you say that they prophesied good and I ill, the truth is that I prophesy good and they ill."

They coined a parable. To what may the matter be likened? To a human king who had many servants and appointed them to their work. He made the most intelligent of them shepherd. The intelligent servant began to cry out: "My companions are in the settlement, while I am in the desert!" [So] Ezekiel would say: "All my companions are in Jerusalem, *while I* am in captivity."

[D] Thereupon God opened to Ezekiel the seven subterranean chambers, and Ezekiel looked into them and saw all the celestial entities.

---

2 *Geburah*, a common rabbinic epithet for God [453].

These are the seven subterranean chambers: *'Adamah, 'Ereṣ, Ḥeled, Neshiyyah, Dumah, She'ol,* and *Ṭiṭ ha-Yawen.* What is the Biblical source for [believing that there exists a subterranean chamber called] *'Adamah? The ground* [*'adamah*] *was split open* [Numbers 16:31]. For *'Ereṣ? The earth* [*ha'areṣ*] *opened* [*its mouth*; Numbers 16:31]. For *Ḥeled? Give ear, all who dwell in the world* [*ḥaled*; Psalm 49:2]. For *Neshiyyah? And your righteousness in the land of forgetfulness* [*neshiyyah*; Psalm 88:13]. For *Dumah? Nor all those who descend into silence* [*dumah*; Psalm 115:17]. For *She'ol? They and all that belonged to them went down* [*alive to the netherworld* (*she'olah*); Numbers 16:33]. For *Ṭiṭ ha-Yawen? He raised me from the pit of roaring* [*from the filthy mud* (*ṭiṭ hayyawen*); Psalm 40:3][3].

[E] R. Isaac said: God showed Ezekiel the primordial waters that are bound up in the great sea and in layers; as it is written, *Have you come to the layers of the sea* [Job 38:16]. He showed him a mountain underneath the river, by means of which the temple vessels are to return[4].

[F] While Ezekiel was watching, God opened to him seven firmaments, and he saw the Power. They coined a parable. To what may the matter be likened? To a man who went to a barber shop, got a haircut, and was given a mirror to look into. While he was looking into the mirror, the king passed by. He saw the king and his forces through the doorway. The barber turned and said to him, "Turn around and see the king." He said, "I have already seen the mirror[5]." So Ezekiel stood by the river Chebar and looked into the water, and the seven firmaments were opened to him and he saw God's glory, and the *ḥayyot*, angels, troops, seraphim, and sparkling-winged ones joined to the *merkabah*. They passed by in the heavens and Ezekiel saw them in the water. So it is written: *At the river Chebar* [Ezekiel 1:1].

[G] It would have been proper for the text to say, *The heaven was opened* [*niftaḥ hashshamayim*]. What does it mean by saying, *The heavens were opened* [*niftehu hashshamayim*; Ezekiel 1:1][6]? This teaches us that seven firmaments were opened to Ezekiel: *Shamayim, Sheme Shamayim, Zebul, ᶜArafel, Sheḥaqim, ᶜArabot,* and *Kisse' Kabod*[7].

[H] R. Levi quoted R. Jose of Maᶜon, quoting R. Meir: God created seven firmaments, with seven *merkabahs* in them[8]. ... [The text is broken here, and a word or two missing.]

---

3 The expositor collects seven words or phrases which he understands the Bible to apply to the nether regions — "ground," "earth," "world," "forgetfulness," "silence," "netherworld," and "filthy mud" — and treats them as the names of seven subterranean chambers. (For reasons having to do with the rules of Hebrew vocalization, some of these names are pronounced slightly differently in their midrashic context from the way they appear in the Bible. These changes have no significance.) We will see that he uses the same method to discover the names of the seven *merkabahs* in the seven heavens. — This enumeration of the subterranean chambers has some bearing, as we will presently see, on the problem of dating the *Visions.* Later in this chapter (section B4a), we will take up the question of what led the expositor in the first place to entertain the notion (which has no evident ground in the Biblical text) that God has opened the lower realms to Ezekiel.

4 This paragraph has an important bearing on the work we did in chapter VI. I discuss its difficulties, and its implications, in Appendix IV.

5 *Mar'ah*; obviously a play on *mar'eh*, "vision."

6 That is, the expositor thinks that we would normally expect the verb "to be opened" to be in the singular, and that the Biblical text uses the plural form *niftehu* in order to convey some special point. This argument is, to say the least, eccentric. Heaven is always treated as a plural in Hebrew, and the singular *niftaḥ hashshamayim* is about the last thing we would expect [229]. Later in this chapter (section C5a), we will see what underlies this strange midrash.

7 This list contradicts the enumeration of heavens in the second part of the *Visions.* In Appendix IV, I discuss the contradictions, and show that they cannot be used as evidence that the two sections of the *Visions* were originally independent sources. Rather, the divergences of section II from the present list result from the tampering of a later editor, who wanted to conform the *Visions* to the more conventional rabbinic lists of heavens.

8 The notion that there is a distinct *merkabah* in each of the seven heavens is unique to the *Visions.* We must wait to the very end of this chapter in order fully to grasp its logic. In Appendix IV,

[J] Is it possible that God said to Ezekiel, "I am showing you my *merkabah* on condition that you describe it in full to the Israelites"? So it is written: *Tell all that you see to the house of Israel* [Ezekiel 40:4]. And it is written: *He said to me: "Son of man, keep all my words that I speak to you in your heart, and hear them with your ears. Then go to the captivity, to your people,* and so forth [*and speak to them, and say to them, 'Thus says the Lord God'"*; Ezekiel 3:10–11]. But [he was? one is?] to expound them [*ledorshan*] to an individual in such a way that his eye is able to see and his ear able to hear[9].

[II. The enumeration of heavens.]

[A1] R. Isaac said: From earth to the firmament [*raqia^c*] is a journey of five hundred years, as it is written: *In order that your days and your children's days may be multiplied on the land* [*which the Lord swore to your fathers to give them, like the days of the heavens above the earth*; Deuteronomy 11:21][10]. The thickness of the firmament is a journey of five hundred years. There is nothing in the firmament [or, perhaps, we are to take this as a proper name, *Raqia^c*], except the sun, moon, stars, and constellations.

[A2] There is one *merkabah* in it. What is the name of the *merkabah*? [The *merkabah*] of *Rekhesh*; as it is written, *Fasten the chariot* [*merkabah*] *to the horses* [*rekhesh*; Micah 1:13]:

[B] The [thickness of the] water that is upon the firmament is a journey of five hundred years. So it is written, *God called the firmament heavens* [Genesis 1:8]. Do not read *heavens* [*shamayim*]; but, *water is there* [*sham mayim*]. How is it constructed? Like a tent. So it is written: *He sits on the circle of the earth;* [*its inhabitants are like grasshoppers. He bends the heavens (shamayim) like a curtain,*] *stretches them out like a tent that is to be occupied* [Isaiah 40:22]. It is constructed like a dome, which is broader than the [disk of] earth and whose edges hang down to the sea. A wind blows between [its edges and the sea], in order to separate the upper waters from the lower.

[C1] It is a journey of five hundred years from the sea [!] to *Sheme ha-Shamayim* ["the heaven of heavens"][11]. The angels who recite the *Qedushshah* hymn[12] dwell there. You must

---

I discuss some of the names assigned to these *merkabah*s in the second section of the *Visions*, and the Biblical proof texts invoked for them.

9 I follow Gruenwald's emendation of *'i 'efshar* to *'efshar* at the beginning of the paragraph, and his understanding of the paragraph as a whole [229]. – In the last sentence, *mah sheha^cayin yekholah lir'oto* can also be translated: "to the extent that his eye is able to see." But the translation "in such a way" seems better to accord with the use of parallel expressions in the midrashic literature (below, section 3c). The sentence remains hard to understand; we will try to clear up its obscurities in what follows.

10 The expositor seems to understand *which* as referring back to *days* rather than to *land*. He then takes the second part of the verse to mean that God gave the patriarchs a life span corresponding to *the days of the heavens above the earth*; that is, the length of time it would take to travel the distance from earth to heaven. Since Abraham lived 175 years, Isaac 180, and Jacob 147, we arrive at a total of 502 years for the length of the journey; the number is then rounded to five hundred. PT Ber. 1:1 (2c) also presupposes this ingenious bit of midrash. I doubt, however, if it is really the source of the idea that a five hundred year journey separates heaven from earth. More likely, it is a clever effort to find Scriptural support for a traditional belief whose origin no one knew.

11 *Ha-* is the Hebrew definite article. Its use in this phrase is optional, and the author more commonly omits it.

12 The *Qedushshah* is an early hymn which either describes or imitates (depending on which of the two main versions one cares to follow) the praise of God by the celestial beings. It is constructed around the two Biblical verses that we dealt with in chapter II, in connection with the beginnings of the hymnic tradition: Isaiah 6:3 (*holy, holy, holy is the Lord of hosts*) and Ezekiel 3:12 (*blessed be the glory of the Lord from his place*). We cannot be sure how or when the *Qedushshah* evolved, or how the several versions preserved in the Jewish liturgy relate to one another. Some form of the hymn, at any rate, seems to have been known to the Tannaim [216d,412,416]. The authors of the *Hekhalot* thought it immensely important [401a], as we will see.

not imagine that they stay there permanently. Rather, said R. Levi, [God creates] *new ones every morning; great is your faithfulness* [Lamentations 3:23]. What are they fashioned from? The river of fire [Daniel 7:10]. As soon as they are fashioned, they stretch out their hands, take fire from the river of fire, and wash their lips and tongue. Thereupon they begin the *Qedushshah.* They do not stop singing from sunrise to sunset; as it is written, *From the rising of the sun,* and so forth [*to its setting, the Lord's name is glorified*; Psalm 113:3]. They are thereupon hidden away [?], and others fashioned in their place.

[C2] There is one *merkabah* in it [that is, in *Sheme Shamayim*]. What is the name of the *merkabah*? [The *merkabah*] of *Susim*; as it is written, *I saw in the nighttime a man riding a red horse,* and so forth [*... and following him were red, sorrel* (?) *and white horses* (*susim*); Zechariah 1:8].

[D1] It is a journey of five hundred years from *Sheme Shamayim* to *Zebul.*

What is in *Zebul*? R. Levi quoted R. Hama b. ᶜUqba, quoting R. Johanan: The prince dwells only in *Zebul,* and it is he who constitutes the fullness of *Zebul.* Thousands of thousands and myriads of myriads are in his presence, serving him. Daniel says of them: *While I was watching, thrones,* and so forth [*were set up, and the ancient of days took his seat. His clothing was white as snow, the hair of his head like pure wool. His throne was flames of fire, its wheels blazing fire.*] *A river of fire flowed* [*forth from before him. Thousands of thousands served him, and myriads of myriads stood before him*; Daniel 7:9–10].

[D2] What is his name? *Qimos* is his name. R. Isaac says: *Meᶜattah* is his name. R. ᶜAnayni b. Sasson says: *Bizebul* is his name. R. Tanhum the elder says: *'ttyh* is his name. Eleazar of Nadwad says: Metatron, like the name of the Power. Those who make use of the name say: *slns* is his name, *qs bs bs qbs* is his name, by [?] the name of the creator of the world[13].

[D3] What is the name of the *merkabah* of *Zebul*? *Ha-Lewiyyah* ["the Levites"] is its name[14]. David says of it: [*Sing praises*] *to him who rides the heavens, the ancient heavens* [Psalm 68:34].

[E1] It is a journey of five hundred years from *Zebul* to *ᶜArafel.* Its [*ᶜArafel's*] thickness is similarly a journey of five hundred years. In it is the canopy of Torah; as it is written, *Moses drew near the thick cloud* [*ᶜarafel*] *where God was* [Exodus 20:18].

[E2] In it is the *merkabah* in which God descended to Mount Sinai. What is its name? *Merkabah* of *Melakhim* ["kings"][15]. David says of it: *God's chariotry is two myriads,* and so forth [*thousands of shin'an; the Lord is among them, Sinai in holiness*]. *God's chariotry is two myriads* [Psalm 68:18][16].

[F1] It is a journey of five hundred years from *ᶜArafel* to *Shehaqim.* Its [*Shehaqim's*] thickness is similarly a journey of five hundred years. What is in it? Jerusalem rebuilt and restored; the sanctuary, temple, [tablets of] testimony [Exodus 25:16], ark, candelabrum, table [Exodus 25:23–30], and vessels; all the adornments of the temple; and the manna that the Israelites ate.

---

13 Scholem and Jacobs [598,250] translate *beshum,* "by the name," as if it were *keshum,* "like the name." The emendation seems a very plausible one. – I do not know how to vocalize *'ttyh, slns,* and *qs bs bs qbs.* We will return to these weird names, and to the entire passage containing them, in chapter IX.

14 The reference is to a midrash on Psalm 68:18, attributed in several *Tanhuma* sources to R. Berechiah (and discussed above, in chapter IV, section 5), which claims that twenty-two thousand *merkabah*s descended with God to Sinai, "corresponding to the Levitic camp" (*mahaneh lewiyyah*). In Appendix IV, I argue that the text of the *Visions* has become disarranged, and that the author originally invoked Psalm 68:18 (and not 68:34) to prove the existence of a *merkabah* named *ha-Lewiyyah.* (I also indicate a possible alternative vocalization of the name; which, however, does not essentially affect my argument.) This point is crucially important for us, in that it shows that the author of the *Visions* drew upon a synagogue midrashic tradition which used Psalm 68:18 as the link combining the Sinai revelation with Ezekiel's *merkabah.* We will later pursue its implications.

15 I discuss the meaning of this name in Appendix IV.

16 I do not know why the author repeats the opening words of the Biblical text.

How do we know that all the temple vessels are there? From what is written: *Ascribe strength to God. [His pride is over Israel, and his strength is in the clouds (shehaqim). Terrible is God from your sanctuaries. He is the God of Israel, giving strength and power to his people;* Psalm 68:35– 36.]

[F2] There is a *merkabah* in it. What is the name of the *merkabah*? [The *merkabah*] of *Kerub*, which God rode when he descended to the Red Sea [or, "to the lower regions"]. *He rode on a cherub [kerub], and flew,* and so forth [*he soared on wings of wind*; Psalm 18:11][17].

[G] It is a journey of five hundred years from *Shehaqim* to *Makhon*. *Makhon*'s thickness is similarly a journey of five hundred years. What is in it? Treasuries of snow and hail, the punishment to be inflicted on the wicked, and the reward of the righteous[18].

[H1] It is a journey of five hundred years from *Makhon* to *ᶜArabot*. Its thickness is similarly a journey of five hundred years. What is in it? Storehouses of blessing, treasuries of snow, and treasuries of peace; the souls of the righteous and the life-spirit for souls yet to be created; the punishment to be inflicted on the wicked, and the reward of the righteous.

[H2] There is a *merkabah* in it. What is its name? *ᶜAb* is its name. So it is written: *The burden of Egypt. The Lord rides on a fast cloud [ᶜab] [and comes to Egypt; all the idols of Egypt will tremble before him, and the Egyptians' hearts will melt*; Isaiah 19:1].

[J1] It is a journey of five hundred years from *ᶜArabot* to *Kisse' Kabod* ["throne of glory"]. Its thickness is similarly a journey of five hundred years. What is in *ᶜArabot* [!]? The hooves of the *hayyot* and part of the wings of the *hayyot*, as it is written, *Beneath the firmament their wings were straight* [Ezekiel 1:23].

[J2] In it is a great *merkabah* in which God will descend to judge all the nations. Isaiah says of it: *The Lord will come in fire*[19], *his chariots like a whirlwind* [Isaiah 66:15]. What is its name? "Chariots of fire and storm" [*markebot 'esh useᶜarah*].

[K] Above it are the wings of the *hayyot*, which are equal to all seven firmaments and to the thickness of all seven.

Above them is God. Blessed, praised, glorified ...[20] be the name of the king of kings of kings, blessed be he, who endures for ever. Amen, amen, eternity! *Selah*, for ever!

The visions of Ezekiel the son of Buzi the priest are completed.

3. The date of the text

When Marmorstein and Mann published their manuscripts of the *Visions,* they supposed that the text they were editing was relatively late, dating from after the end of the Talmudic period. More recently, under Scholem's influence, scholars have tended to push its date back to the fifth or even the fourth century.

---

17 The text of this paragraph is uncertain. Its opening words (that is, everything before the second "*merkabah*") fall into the gap between the end of fol. 7b of the Cambridge manuscript, and the beginning of the British Museum fragment. Mann, Wertheimer, and Gruenwald restore the missing words in essentially the same way. More important, the British Museum text is blurred at the end of the third sentence, and we cannot be sure of the destination of God's descent. For reasons which I summarize in Appendix IV, I prefer the reading *leyam suf* ("to the Red Sea"); but *lattahtonim* ("to the lower [that is, earthly] regions") is also possible, and may have been intended as a second allusion to the Sinai revelation. We will not be sure on this point, which is of some importance to us, until the newly discovered leaf of the Cambridge manuscript is published.

18 In Appendix IV, I argue that this entire paragraph is an insertion.

19 The Cambridge manuscript resumes at this point.

20 I omit six more adjectives of this sort.

"I see no reason," Scholem wrote of the *Visions,* "to consider this important text as a later pseudepigraphon. Whereas great and well-known talmudic heroes appear as the principal speakers in all the other texts about the Merkabah, no such show is made here. Only cursorily, and, as it were, in passing, are their ideas on some questions mentioned. The authorities quoted here are Palestinian rabbis of the fourth century, some of whose names are not at all familiar" [599]. Surely no one would bother to fabricate attributions to practically unknown figures like "ᶜAnayni b. Sasson" and "Eleazar of Nadwad," both of whom are quoted in connection with the name of the "prince" in the third heaven (IID2). Once we assume that the attributions in the *Visions of Ezekiel* are by and large authentic, we may feel ourselves entitled to apply to the *Visions* a criterion often used to date midrashic texts: the text is not likely to be more than a generation or two later than the last of the authorities quoted in it. Since we cannot identify any rabbi quoted in the *Visions* who was active after about 300, this line of reasoning leads us to Gruenwald's conclusion that the *Visions* must have been written in the fourth century; or, at the very latest, in the early part of the fifth [230,540].

Is this reasoning valid? Do other lines of argument support it? And, if the answer to these questions turns out to be no, where are we to look for a date for the *Visions of Ezekiel*?

a) The argument from authorities. Let us look a little more closely at the supposed authorities for the *Visions*. We find them in eleven places:

1. R. Levi (IB).
2. Rabbi (Judah the Patriarch) (IC).
3. R. Isaac (IE).
4. R. Levi, quoting R. Jose of Maᶜon, quoting R. Meir (IH).
5. R. Isaac (IIA1).
6. R. Levi (IIC1).
7. R. Levi, quoting R. Hama b. ᶜUqba, quoting R. Johanan (IID1).
8. R. Isaac (IID2).
9. R. ᶜAnayni b. Sasson (IID2).
10. R. Tanhum the elder (IID2).
11. Eleazar of Nadwad (IID2).

R. Levi and R. Isaac, who dominate this list, belong to what is conventionally defined as the third generation of Palestinian Amoraim, active around the end of the third century. So does ᶜAnayni b. Sasson, assuming that we are to identify him with the "ᶜAnani b. Sasson" who appears in BT M.Q. 24b as a contemporary of R. Ammi. R. Tanhum's title suggests that he is one of the earlier scholars of this name – perhaps Tanhum b. Hiyya, who also belongs to the third generation; perhaps Tanhum b. Hanilai, a generation earlier. As far as I know, we have no idea who Eleazar of Nadwad may have been[21].

While the author of the *Visions* leans heavily on authorities of the late third century, he never once quotes any of the fourth-century haggadists (such as Berechiah) who figure prominently in both the "classical Palestinian" and the *Tanhuma* midrashim. We might reasonably deduce that he had never heard of these rabbis, simply because he wrote before they became prominent. We would then have to date the *Visions* even earlier than Gruenwald did, to the very beginning of the fourth century.

But I am not as sure as Scholem and Gruenwald seem to be that the author of the *Visions* did not invent his attributions. The evidence bearing on this question is equivocal. The suspicions it raises, however, are enough to make me hesitate to fix a date for the *Visions* on the basis of the names that it invokes.

To begin with, the material that the writer attributes to his authorities hardly ever appears in connection with these same names in any rabbinic source. Section IH indeed traces back to R. Meir a statement concerning the seven heavens and the seven *merkabah*s that are in them; while *'Abot de-Rabbi Natan* (Version A, chapter 37; ed. 55b [183]) attributes to Meir a list of the names of the seven firmaments. But the force of this resemblance is not entirely overwhelming, since *'Abot de-Rabbi Natan* is the only rabbinic text that associates Meir with the seven heavens, and neither it nor any other source mentions the seven *merkabah*s. Moreover, this parallel stands alone. Aside from it, there is no contact between what the *Visions of Ezekiel* says certain rabbis said and what any Talmudic or midrashic source says they said.

This point does not weigh very heavily in connection with those passages (IB, C, IID1−2) that have, as far as I know, no parallel whatever outside the *Visions*. It has far more force when applied to the interpretation of Lamentations 3:23 to mean that God creates new angels each morning from the river of fire, which IIC1 attributes to "R. Levi." Palestinian and Babylonian sources record this exegesis (*Gen. R.* 78:1, ed. 915−917 [188]; *Lam. R.* 3:23, ed. 66b−67a [190]; *Ex. R.* 15:6; BT Hag. 14a). These sources indicate that both Palestinian and Babylonian traditions associated this interpretation with "R. Samuel b. Nahman quoting R. Jonathan[22]." None of them mentions R. Levi in connection with it.

---

21 Strack has brief notes on all of these rabbis, except ^cAnayni, in his *Introduction to the Talmud and Midrash*. Bacher touches lightly on ^cAnayni in his massive *Agada der palästinensischen Amoräer* [342,371].

22 They do not, however, agree on exactly what Samuel b. Nahman quoted Jonathan as having said; and BT Hag. 14a seems to reflect a confusion of Samuel b. Nahman with the Babylonian Amora Samuel.

Similarly, Palestinian and Babylonian rabbinic sources give the distance from earth to heaven as a five hundred year journey, as does section IIA1[23]. PT Ber. 1:1 (2c), like our text, invokes Deuteronomy 11:21 in support of this view. These sources usually quote the celestial measurement without any attribution, but sometimes attach a name to it — Johanan b. Zakkai (BT Hag. 13a), or Levi b. Sisi (PT Ber. 9:1, 13a). They never refer to R. Isaac. Nor do we find any of the more or less remote parallels to IE, which I discussed in chapter VI (section 6) and in Appendix IV, attributed to R. Isaac.

Can we conclude from this that the author of the *Visions* has invoked the names of Levi and Isaac without any historical basis? Not quite; for there is another explanation for the discrepancies between the *Visions* and the other sources. The *Visions,* as I will argue presently, drew on material transmitted outside the channels of tradition that fed into those rabbinic texts that we now think of as standard. Its sources thus reflect a somewhat different aspect of the rabbis' activity from those normally seen in the rabbinic literature. If this is so, we might well expect the *Visions'* combinations of names with materials to be different from the ones we find in the familiar Talmudic and midrashic sources, without being any less authentic.

This explanation will also work for another slightly peculiar feature of the *Visions'* attributions. The author twice quotes chains of authorities: R. Levi, quoting R. Jose of Ma^{c}on, quoting R. Meir (IH); R. Levi, quoting R. Hama b. ^{c}Uqba, quoting R. Johanan (IID1). Wilhelm Bacher, who has compiled the closest thing we have to an exhaustive list of the chains of transmission invoked in the rabbinic literature [797], does not list either of the *Visions'* chains. The second chain, moreover, is slightly implausible, since Levi was a student of Johanan's, and would presumably not have needed to receive his teachings through the mediation of Hama b. ^{c}Uqba[24]. But this last point is not compelling; and, in general, we can resolve the objection I raised in this paragraph in the same way that we disposed of its predecessor.

But we now come to a more serious difficulty, which I must explain at some length.

The Talmuds and the older midrashim copiously invoke the names of Tannaim and Amoraim whom they claim as their authorities. Most of the time, we have very little way of knowing if these claims are accurate. But they normally appear to be truthful at least to the extent that a saying at-

---

23 References in Appendix IV, section 4.

24 Rabbinic literature seldom or never represents Hama as transmitting Johanan's utterances. The only case Bacher lists (PT Ket. 1:10, 25d) depends on his own emendation of "Hanina" to "Johanan."

tributed to a given rabbi is an actual source that the compiler has taken up, perhaps adapted, and then combined with other materials. If the utterance in question is removed from its context, it will often (not always) be fully intelligible by itself. If, on the other hand, we were to delete from the text the names of the rabbis whom it quotes, what remained would still be uneven, an obvious composite of materials which an editor has brought together but not smoothly joined. Seams and breaks would be visible everywhere.

We find a very different situation when we turn to *Pirqe de-Rabbi Eliezer*, a late midrash which critical scholars agree was composed — not edited — during the time of Muslim rule over Palestine. Its pages, too, are peppered with the names of rabbis. But these names give the impression of being an ornamental facade. We could shift them around, or remove them altogether, without seriously disturbing the flow of the material to which they are attached. There is no doubt that the author of *Pirqe de-Rabbi Eliezer* did not invent the whole work by himself, and that he drew on earlier sources; but we cannot use the names he cites as a guide to these sources.

In this respect, the *Visions of Ezekiel* resembles *Pirqe de-Rabbi Eliezer* far more than it does the older midrashic sources. The statement attributed to R. Levi in IB could not possibly stand by itself; and, if the words "R. Levi said" were deleted, the discourse would actually flow more smoothly than before. The same is true of IIC1. Elsewhere in the *Visions*, the utterances attributed to this or that rabbi might perhaps be understandable outside their present context. But, if the names now attached to them were suddenly to vanish from the text, we usually could not tell the difference.

There are exceptions. One of them is the reference to the seven firmaments in section IH, which would seem repetitious after IG if some authority's name were not prefaced to it. Another, far more striking, is the discussion of the name of the "prince" in *Zebul* (IID2). This passage is plainly a string of divergent opinions; and, if the names of their authors were gone, we would miss them. But this passage stands out from the rest of the *Visions* in both its concerns and its style, and I am inclined to think that it is an earlier source which the author of the *Visions* has incorporated. (I will develop this suggestion in chapter IX.)

It is no accident that the unusual names that give Scholem's argument its force are all found in this one passage. For the rest, the author alternates monotonously between Levi and Isaac, breaking this pattern only with one citation of R. Judah the Patriarch (IC) and two citations of scholars whom Levi is supposed to have invoked (IH, IID1). We get the impression of a half-hearted effort to trick out a unitary composition with the names of traditional authorities, along the lines of *Pirqe de-Rabbi Eliezer*.

As I have said, these arguments are equivocal. I do not pretend to have proven by them that the names invoked in the *Visions of Ezekiel* are fictions of its author. But I have raised some doubts about the wisdom of trying to date this text on the basis of the dates of the scholars whom it purports to quote. Further, when we come to trace the sources of the *Visions'* ideas, we must be very hesitant about using these names as our leads.

The argument from authorities is, if not a broken reed, at least a fragile one. Where else can we turn for a clue to the date of the *Visions*?

b) The argument from citation formulae. Marmorstein, arguing for the late date of the *Visions*, pointed to the formula that the author uses when he wants to quote Isaiah: "Isaiah says of it" (*ʿaleha 'amar yeshaʿyah*; IIJ2). Identical expressions, quoting Daniel and David, came to light in the Cambridge manuscript (IID1, D3, E2). Marmorstein found parallel formulae used in late midrashim and in Karaite writings from the early Middle Ages.

The formula that the author uses in IB to quote the Mishnah is just as striking: "So taught the sages in the Mishnah" (*kakh shanu ḥakhamim bammishnah*). Where else do we find such a formula? Certainly not in the "classical Palestinian midrashim" of the fifth century, which introduce Mishnaic quotations with *tenenan* or *tamman tenenan* (Aramaic for "we have learned" or "we have learned there") [189a,192]. The Babylonian Talmud comes closer: it occasionally uses *shanu ḥakhamim* ("the sages taught"; Pes. 48b, Gitt. 24b, Sanh. 49b), and even *shanu ḥakhamim bemishnatenu* ("the sages taught in our Mishnah"; Yeb. 10b, B.B. 95b) [798]. The midrashim of the *Tanḥuma* genre regularly introduce quotations from the Mishnah with *kakh shanu rabbotenu* ("so our masters taught"), or, less frequently, *kakh shanu ḥakhamim* ("so the sages taught") [276].

Song R.'s version of the *pardes* story (*Song R.* to 1:4) introduces a quotation of M. ʿEd. 5:7 with the *Visions'* full formula, *kakh shanu ḥakhamim bammishnah*. *Hekhalot* sources that depend on this passage quote the same text as "the mishnah [that is, traditional teaching] that the sages taught in their Mishnah" (*hammishnah sheshshanu ḥakhamim bemishnatam*). But these passages are isolated, and the text of both is uncertain[b]. Only one midrashic text uses *shanu ḥakhamim bammishnah* as its normal way of quoting the Mishnah. This, unfortunately for us, is precisely the most mysterious and elusive of all the midrashim: the *Seder 'Eliyahu* [212, 277][25].

---

25 We find a similar formula, *shanu ḥakhamim bileshon hammishnah* ("the sages taught in the language of the Mishnah"), at the beginning of the little treatise on the merits of Torah study that has been tacked on, as a sixth chapter, to the end of the Mishnah tractate *Pirqe 'Abot*. Both the style and the contents of this treatise show that it is closely linked to the *Seder 'Eliyahu* [359]. The same formula also occurs in *Pesiqta Rabbati* 38 (ed. 165a [209]).

We know very little about this strange composition, or about the connection with the prophet Elijah that its title appears to claim. Least of all do we know its date. Proposals have ranged all the way from the third to the tenth century, with most scholars inclining toward the later end of this spectrum [248,348,357,360]. The common use of the citation formula indeed points to some link between the *Visions of Ezekiel* and the obscure circles that produced the "Elijah" literature, and we will see at the end of this chapter that this association helps us explain a difficult passage in the *Seder Eliyahu*. But it does not help us date the *Visions*, beyond reinforcing a vague suspicion that our text is late.

The sharp difference between the *Visions'* formula, and those used in *Genesis Rabbah* and the rest of the "classical Palestinian midrashim," suggests some distance between the *Visions* on the one hand and these fifth-century texts on the other. But what kind of distance? We do not have to assume that it was a separation in time. The *Visions of Ezekiel* may well have been the work of a fifth-century writer whose milieu, and hence his preferences in terminology, were different from those of his contemporaries who edited the more familiar midrashim.

The *Visions'* formula for citing the Mishnah thus seems to point to a late date, but in so equivocal a manner that we cannot rest any firm conclusions on it. We may say the same of the formula it uses for its Biblical quotations.

c) Other stylistic and linguistic indicators also point to some distance between the *Visions* and the fifth-century Palestinian midrashim, without resolving the question of whether the separation is one of date or only of milieu.

When the author of the *Visions* wants to quote a chain of three authorities (IH, IID1), he does so in the form *'amar rabbi X mishshem rabbi Y she'amar* [IID1 adds *mishshum*] *rabbi Z*. PT and the "classical" midrashim use a very different formula: *rabbi X werabbi Y* [or, *rabbi Y*] *beshem rabbi Z*.

The verb *histakkel*, "to look," which the *Visions* uses in ID and F, would be very unusual in an Amoraic source [340]. So would the expression *mashelu mashal lemah haddabar domeh* ("they coined a parable; to what may the matter be likened?" IC, F [796]). Both features would be common enough in Tannaitic materials, but there is no question of dating the *Visions* so early. If we were to exclude the possibility of diversity within the Hebrew usage of the Amoraic period, we would have no choice but to assign the *Visions* to a later time. But I am hardly ready to insist on this[26].

---

26 I owe the observations in this paragraph to a conversation, held in 1975, with Dr. Michael Sokoloff.

One expression used in the *Visions* may be particularly valuable in connection with the problem of dating. At the very end of the midrashic section (IJ), the author claims that the details of the *merkabah* "are to be expounded to an individual in such a way that his eye is able to see and his ear able to hear" (*mah sheha^cayin yekholah lir'oto umah shehe'ozen yekholah lishmoa^c*). We find parallel expressions in the two *Mekhilta*s, in both recensions of *'Abot de-Rabbi Natan*, and in *Midr. Psalms*. The idea conveyed is that Scripture occasionally compares God to one or another of his creations, not because these comparisons adequately describe God's greatness, but because they are the only way this greatness can be communicated to limited human intelligence.

Thus, *Mekhilta* tells us, Exodus 19:18 says that Mount Sinai smoked "like a furnace" when God descended on it — not because the simile is really adequate to describe the event, but "in order to give [literally, "to break"] the ear what it is able to hear" (*leshabber 'et ha'ozen mah shehi' yekholah lishmoa^c*). The expositor goes on to account for Amos 3:8, which compares God to a lion, and Ezekiel 43:2, which compares his voice to "the sound of many waters," in the same way[27]. The parallel passage in *Mekhilta of R. Simeon b. Yohai* (ed. 144 [196]) makes the same point, but uses a slightly different expression: *mashmi^cin 'et ha'ozen mah shehi' yekholah lishmoa^c* (also in the comment on Exodus 24:10, ed. 221).

In *'Abot de-Rabbi Natan,* however, the expression is transformed. One recension of this midrash ("Version B") uses essentially the same expression as do the *Mekhilta*s, for essentially the same purpose: the prophets compare God to his creations, "in order that the ear may easily be able to hear" (*bishebil shettanuah ha'ozen utehe' yekholah lishmoa^c*; chapter 3, ed. 7a [183]). But the parallel in "Version A" adds a reference to the eye. "They show the eye what it is able to see; they give the ear what it is able to hear" (*mar'in 'et ha^cayin mah sheyyekholah lir'ot umashmi^cin 'et ha'ozen mah sheyyekholah lishmoa^c*; chapter 2, ed. 7a). So does *Midr. Psalms* 1:4 (ed. 3a [199]), which uses exactly the same language but reverses the order of the clauses.

The addition of the "eye" seems illogical. All of the passages I have quoted refer to the Bible's descriptions of God and of his appearances; it is the ear's business to absorb such descriptions, not the eye's. We may well suppose that the authors of the later midrashic sources expanded an expression that had earlier been used in the Tannaitic midrashim, without quite thinking through the implications of their addition. We will later see that

---

27 *Mekhilta, Ba-Hodesh* chapter 4 (ed./tr. 2:221 [195]). *Mekhilta* uses the same expression in a more literal sense in two other places, to explain why the trumpet that the Israelites heard at Sinai (Exodus 19:16, 19) gradually swelled in volume: it started out softly, "in order to give the ear [at first] what it was able to hear" (*Ba-Hodesh*, chapters 3, 4; ed./tr. 2:218, 223).

this accusation of carelessness is not entirely just, at least as regards the author of the *Visions*. But this does not affect the point that concerns us here. By including the "eye," the *Visions* aligns itself with the later sources against the earlier ones.

d) Parallels in content. As for the contents of the *Visions*, they are so unusual that any effort to establish a date on the basis of them seems hopeless. It is not that the ideas expressed in the *Visions* are completely unparalleled; a glance at Gruenwald's commentary will show that they are not. But, with one exception to be noted below, we do not find parallels to these ideas consistently appearing in sources that are either demonstrably early or demonstrably late.

The opening explanation of Ezekiel's *thirtieth year* as "corresponding to thirty kings who reigned over Israel" (1A) illustrates the difficulties. This interpretation of Ezekiel 1:1 is, as far as I know, unique. Its underlying assumption, however, that thirty kings reigned over Israel — an assumption which it seems impossible to square with the Biblical data — has a parallel in the late midrashic material appended to *Gen. R.*, where thirty kings are said to be descended from Judah (*Gen. R.* 97:8, ed. 1207—1208 [188]) [229]. Shall we deduce from this that the *Visions'* exegesis is based on a late midrash, and must be itself even later? Perhaps. But another of the interpretation's premises, that a "year" can be understood to represent a ruler, also appears in an apocalyptic text called the *Assumption of Moses* (2:3—7) [98], which cannot be later than the first century A.D. [106, 114]. I know of no parallel to it in any later source. One of the parallels to the opening of the *Visions*, then, points to a date after the Amoraic period; another urges us to push it back as early as we can.

When we compare the *Visions'* enumerations of the seven subterranean chambers (ID) and the seven heavens (IG, II) with their counterparts in the more familiar rabbinic sources[28], we again find ourselves pulled in two opposite directions. Gruenwald [229] has shown that the names of the first four of the subterranean chambers appear in other lists among the names of the "earths" (which are arranged in layers, one above the other, our earth being the highest) or "abysses"; while the last three are properly names either of hell or regions of hell. This combination of two sets of names belonging to different contexts would naturally suggest that the list given in the *Visions* is relatively late. On the other hand, the *Visions'* list of heavens is unique, especially in that it puts ᶜ*Arabot* in the sixth rather than the seventh position; this eccentricity so disturbed one transmitter of the text that he partly rewrote it (see Appendix IV). I find it hard to imag-

---

28 Ginzberg gives full references for the English reader [391]. The best-known enumeration of the heavens is that of BT Hag. 12b. *Lev. R.* 29:11 (ed. 680—681 [191]) and its parallel in *Pesiqta de-*

ine that the *Visions'* list can have taken shape after the more familiar reckoning of the seven heavens had become standard.

In Appendix IV, I argue that we can best understand the *Visions'* strange allusion to "a mountain underneath the river" (IE) against the background of a Muslim tradition first recorded in the ninth century. This would be clear evidence for a post-Islamic date for the *Visions* — were it not for the early Muslims' well-known penchant for borrowing and adapting Jewish materials, which may be centuries older than the Muslim sources in which they appear.

e) Conclusion. Our search for a clear and unequivocal index to the date of the *Visions* thus appears to have ended in failure and frustration. Our long and tortuous examination of the problem has yielded mainly negative conclusions: the early dating defended by Scholem and Gruenwald has no solid basis in the evidence; the names of rabbis invoked in the *Visions* are likely to be false clues which lead us nowhere. We have seen a number of indications that the *Visions* is in fact a late text, but each of these indications is so very frail that even their cumulative effect is less than overwhelming.

Yet matters are not as bad as they look. The contents of the *Visions* do offer us one real clue, which we have not yet considered, to the historical context of the traditions that are preserved in this document, although probably not to its date as it stands. This clue is an odd series of parallels between the *Visions'* conception of Ezekiel and his *merkabah* vision, and the treatment of this issue in Origen's *First Homily* on Ezekiel.

I have not so far mentioned these parallels, because we are not as yet ready to deal with them. Where we now stand, they would perplex us more than they would help us. What possible link can there have been between a third-century Greek Christian homily and a Hebrew midrash, very possibly composed hundreds of years later? Only when we are in a position to understand this connection will we be ready to turn our attention to this clue, and to pursue it as far as it will lead.

4. The structure of the text

We must now examine a fresh set of questions regarding the form and the function of the *Visions of Ezekiel*. Why does the text include the material it does? Why is it organized as it is? What possible purpose can such a composition have served?

Rab Kahana, Rosh ha-Shanah #10 (ed. 343–344 [206]), list the names of both the heavens and the "earths."

These questions must be asked of any text, but they are particularly acute in connection with the *Visions*. We are dealing with a piece of work that has been very strangely put together. Why does the author begin in the format of midrash, only to abandon this format halfway through for an enumeration of the seven heavens, never to take it up again? If he intends to compose "a mystical midrash on the first chapter of the Book of Ezekiel," as Gruenwald thinks [541], why does he not let his midrash get even to the end of the first verse? Why does he insist on expounding each one of the first fourteen words of this verse, which is not even part of Ezekiel's description of the *merkabah* vision — and then leave the vision itself untouched? If his concerns are "mystical," why does he open his midrash with a series of comments which have no apparent relevance to "mysticism" of any kind (IA—C)? And why does he allow these irrelevant expositions to take up more than one third of the midrashic section, nearly one sixth of the total composition[29]?

a) Targumic Tosefta. Odd as it is, the *Visions* is not unique. A long "Targumic Tosefta" to Ezekiel 1:1[30] shares its basic structure as well as some of its themes.

As far as I know, this Targumic Tosefta has never been translated, nor has it appeared in any critical edition. M. Weiss printed the text in 1922, evidently on the basis of ms Budapest-Kaufmann 570 [227]. Shlomo Aharon Wertheimer again published it in his *Batei Midrashot* [503], claiming three Yemenite manuscripts as his basis, but omitting any information that might help us identify these manuscripts[c)].

I translate as much of the text as is necessary for us to grasp its structure and its purport. I use Wertheimer's edition, understanding that it may not be entirely reliable; since no one detail of the text is crucial for us, I do not think any mistakes of Wertheimer's are likely seriously to mislead us.

> *It came to pass in the thirtieth year*, from the time that Hilkiah the high priest found the book of the Torah in the Temple, in the court, under the porch of the Temple, in the middle of the night of the fourth of Tammuz, in the days of Josiah son of Amon, king of the tribe of the house of Judah[31]. Hilkiah the high priest found the words of the book of the Torah and gave it to Shaphan the scribe, and Shaphan the scribe read it to king Josiah [cf. II Kings 22:8—11].

---

29 Ira Chernus has noted some of these difficulties, and resolved them by supposing that "there were several redactional stages before the text reached its present form" [511]. But I do not see stylistic evidence of redactional activity in the *Visions*. (On the contradictions in the listing of the seven heavens, see Appendix IV.) In any case, we would still have to explain the editors' motives in putting together so curious a work.

30 On the "Targumic Toseftas," see above, p. 118.

31 Most of this sentence is taken verbatim from the Targum to Ezekiel 1:1 (above, chapter IV, section 2g). The conclusion of the Tosefta follows the Targum still more exactly. For "the fourth

King Josiah listened to the words of the book of the Torah, in which was written: *The Lord will exile you and the king whom you will set over you to a people which neither you nor your fathers have known. There you will serve nations who worship idols of wood and stone* [Targ. Deuteronomy 28:36]. The king thereupon tore his clothes and went and broke the wickedness of the Jews' hearts and brought them back to the words of Torah. This happened before the city of Jerusalem was handed over to Nebuchadnezzar the Chaldean.

[Nebuchadnezzar] was filled with pride in his idolatry, and spoke thus: "Is this not Jerusalem, city of the most high God, which is said to have no equal from one end of the earth to the other? It is going to be handed over to me; I will destroy it and its Temple, and I will exile its people to the country of my idols. Then I will climb to the lofty heavens and will destroy the celestial chambers; I will make war with the exalted holy ones and will set my royal throne over the cherubim." So it is written: *I will climb upon the backs of the clouds, I will be like the Most High* [Isaiah 14:14, Hebrew].

Thereupon the holy spirit answered, calling out to him: "You sinner, who rebelled against me more than all the world! How many troops have you got? How much power is at your disposal? How long are you going to live, that you can say: 'I will climb to the highest heavens and destroy the celestial chambers; I will make war with the exalted holy ones and set my royal throne over the cherubim'? ..."

The "holy spirit" proceeds to describe, at considerable length (amounting to nearly one-third of the entire Targumic Tosefta), the vast gulfs that lie between the earth and the "highest heavens." First come the seven heavens, which the author names in accord with BT Hag. 12b; each is a five hundred years' journey thick, separated from its neighbor by a five hundred years' journey. Above them are the *ḥayyot*, each of their successive organs (feet, knees, and so forth) "equivalent to [the distance from] the heights of the earth to the heights of heaven, and corresponding to the seven firmaments and their thickness." Climbing yet higher, one must pass the equally enormous throne of God; then myriads of angels; and, finally, eight hundred more firmaments under the charge of the "great prince" Metatron. And the mortal Nebuchadnezzar thinks he can "climb to the highest heavens, destroy the celestial chambers, make war with the exalted holy ones"?

"Therefore I will throw you down into the seven subterranean chambers ...[32] It is a place where the sun and the moon never rise, where human footsteps are never heard. Your soul will burn in Gehenna until the great judgment comes." So it is written: *In fact, you will be thrown down to She'ol, to the depths of the pit* [Isaiah 14:15, Hebrew].

Thereupon cruel angels were dispatched against him. They destroyed him and threw him down to *'Abaddon ʿOlam* ["eternal perdition"], where Sennacherib king of Assyria dwells.

In conversation with Sennacherib, Nebuchadnezzar promises that he will atone, if God permits, by rebuilding Jerusalem with jewels and pearls. His hope is vain. Once again (so concludes the Targumic Tosefta),

---

of Tammuz," we should doubtless read, with one of Wertheimer's manuscripts: "Tammuz, the fifth of the month." The date is of course drawn from Ezekiel 1:1.

32 My ellipsis corresponds to a list of the names of the seven chambers, of which three (*She'ol, Dumah, Ṭiṭ ha-Yawen*) also appear in section ID of the *Visions*. *Gehinnom* (Gehenna) is the third name on the list, *'Abaddon leʿOlam* ("eternal perdition") the seventh.

cruel angels were dispatched against him. They destroyed him and sent him down to *'Abaddon*. Thus it is explicitly written:

> *It came to pass in the thirtieth year,* [from the time that Hilkiah the high priest found the book of the Torah in the Temple, in the court, under the porch,] in the middle of the night, after the rising of the moon, in the days of Josiah son of Amon, king of the tribe of the house of Judah, *in Tammuz, the fifth of the month,* that the prophet said: *"I was among the captives at the river Chebar, when the heavens were opened, and I saw* in a prophetic vision that rested upon me *a vision* of the glory of the Shechinah *of the Lord"* [Targ. Ezekiel 1:1].

b) Structure of the Tosefta. The Targumic Tosefta plainly owes its nucleus — Nebuchadnezzar's threat to invade heaven, and the response of the "holy spirit" — to an older midrash of Isaiah 14:14—15. This midrash, which appears as a baraita in BT Hag. 13a (abridged in Pes. 94a—b), represents R. Johanan b. Zakkai as imagining how "the heavenly voice answered that wicked fellow [Nebuchadnezzar] when he said, *I will climb upon the backs of the clouds, I will be like the Most High."* The divine response here is considerably briefer than in the Targumic Tosefta, but its point and many of its details are the same. The human life span, explains the "heavenly voice," is far too short to permit anyone to pass beyond the several firmaments, the stature of the *ḥayyot,* the throne of glory. "You say, *I will climb upon the backs of the clouds, I will be like the Most High? In fact, you will be thrown down to She'ol, to the depths of the Pit."*

But, adapting this midrash, the author of the Targumic Tosefta has not only enriched it with all sorts of details, cosmological and other[33]. He has shifted its perspective by bringing it into connection with Ezekiel 1:1. Isaiah 14:14—15 thus loses the central place it held in the baraita. It becomes one of a series of links which bind Ezekiel 1:1 to a description of the seven heavens, and of the entities above them.

Following the Targum's lead, the author moves from Ezekiel 1:1 to II Kings 22:8—11 (paraphrased). His next step is to Deuteronomy 28:36, which introduces both the Jewish people's exile and their conqueror's idol-worship. From there he goes to Isaiah 14:14—15, which introduces the theme of invasion of heaven and which thereby leads him to his long description of the celestial and infernal worlds. He then leaps back, rather abruptly, to his starting point: Ezekiel 1:1.

We will best understand the author's proceeding if we suppose that he intended to construct a *petiḥah* — not quite classical in its form, but still recognizable — to the first chapter of Ezekiel. In a manner reminiscent of many literary *petiḥot* [303a], this *petiḥah* begins with the same verse

---

33 In the "other" category are two features of the Targumic Tosefta which will later occupy our attention: its stress on Nebuchadnezzar's idolatry (about which the baraita is silent); and Nebuchadnezzar's proposal to "destroy the celestial chambers, make war with the exalted holy ones, and set my royal throne over the cherubim."

toward which it is ultimately directed. Its effective starting point, however, is the paraphrase of II Kings 22:8—11 that immediately follows. The author leads his audience from there, by one of those rambling and convoluted paths that the composers of *petihot* so dearly loved, into a detailed account of the cosmic realms. These were, of course, what Ezekiel had seen when *the heavens were opened*. This final, essential link between the writer's cosmology and the text of Ezekiel 1:1 is what allows him to jump straight from the cosmology to the beginning of the Scripture lection for which the *petihah* is designed, with nothing in between but a picturesque description of the two wicked potentates' conversation in hell.

Rimon Kasher has meticulously collected and analyzed the Targumic Toseftas to the Prophetic books. He has found that they tend to cluster around the passages used as *haftarah* readings, particularly the beginnings of those passages. He has proposed that the Toseftas in this last group, among which he includes the Tosefta to Ezekiel 1:1, are to be seen as *peti-hot* to the lections to which they are attached [309,311]. We saw in chapter IV that the Targum as a whole is intimately connected with the public reading and translation of the Scriptures in the synagogue; it is natural to suppose that expansions of the Targum go back to synagogue sermons on the text.

Kasher's arguments, and my analysis of the Targumic Tosefta to Ezekiel 1:1, thus support each other. It appears that the title assigned this Tosefta in the Gaster Collection typescript (endnote *c*) accurately reflects the purpose for which it was composed: to serve as homiletic introduction to "the *haftarah* reading for Shabu^cot, from Ezekiel."

We may infer from the Targumic Tosefta that, at least in certain times and certain places, a Shabu^cot *petihah* might be expected to combine exposition of Ezekiel 1:1 with systematic description of the heavenly realms. This brings us back to the *Visions of Ezekiel,* and suggests a solution to the problems that we raised at the beginning of this section.

c) The Tosefta and the "Visions." The *Visions* is certainly a far more sophisticated piece of work than the Targumic Tosefta. Yet the two texts share so much, in both their structure and their content, that we may suppose them to have similar settings and parallel functions.

Both texts attach a cosmological section, in which the enumeration of the seven heavens plays a major role, to a long haggadic introduction. Both include an account of the "seven subterranean chambers"[34]; although the

---

34 They use nearly the same phrase: *shib^cah medorin shel mattah* (*Visions*); *shib^ca medorin tatta'in* (Tosefta).

Visions places this account before the description of the seven heavens, the Targumic Tosefta afterward. Both connect their cosmology with Ezekiel 1:1. The *Visions* makes this link directly, while the Tosefta prefers a roundabout approach to the cosmology; the result is that the haggadic introductions are vastly different. But the difference is not absolute. The two introductions share the theme of the punishment and exile of the Jewish people. And both texts balance this theme, near the end, with references to salvation for the Jews and punishment for the Gentiles (the fate of Nebuchadnezzar and Sennacherib, in the Tosefta; in the *Visions,* section IIJ2).

There is evidence that the author of the *Visions* made direct use of the Targumic Tosefta. Above the seventh heaven, he tells us, "are the wings of the *ḥayyot,* which are equal to all seven firmaments and to the thickness of all seven" (IIK). The detail of the immense size of the *ḥayyot*'s wings seems out of place in the cosmology of the *Visions,* and we may suspect that the author copied it from a source in which it was at home. BT Hag. 13a, which claims that every part of the bodies of the *ḥayyot* is "equivalent to all of them" (that is, the firmaments), is an obvious candidate for this source. But it is not quite suitable. It does not mention the wings of the *ḥayyot,* and its phrase "equivalent to all of them" (*keneged kullan*) is far shorter than the expression used in the *Visions.* The Targumic Tosefta, however, does include the wings; and its way of expressing size — "corresponding to the seven firmaments and their thickness" — closely resembles that of the *Visions*[d]. I infer that the author of the *Visions* drew upon the Targumic Tosefta or a similar text, and that he drew upon it as an earlier and more primitive representative of the genre to which his own composition belonged.

Not that the *Visions of Ezekiel* can be considered a *petiḥah,* in the strict sense of the word, to the first chapter of Ezekiel. A *petiḥah,* as we have seen, should start out at some other part of the Bible than the passage about to be read, and wind its way from there to the beginning of the lection. This the *Visions* does not do. But, if we define the genre of the Targumic Tosefta more broadly — a homiletic introduction to the first chapter of Ezekiel, as read in the synagogue on Shabuᶜot — the *Visions* will fit fairly comfortably within it.

The polished literary form of the *Visions* suggests some distance from the actual language of the preachers, and I would not insist that the text, as it stands, was actually delivered in the synagogue. It reads more like a literary reworking of ideas drawn from a whole series of Shabuᶜot sermons, perhaps intended as inspiration or even as a manual for future preachers. We cannot be at all confident of its relation to the oral material on which it rests, any more than we can in the case of the "literary homilies" in such midrashim as *Leviticus Rabbah* and *Pesiqta de-Rab Kahana;* which raise, in this respect, precisely the same problems [269,270,339][35]. The essential point is that the *Visions* is related to the synagogue setting; that its concerns are those of the preacher; and that we may expect its exegetical traditions to be, by and large, those of the synagogue.

We now have the answer to our question as to why the *Visions* lavishes attention on the very first verse of Ezekiel 1, and ignores the rest. Those midrashim that we call "homiletic midrashim," whose contents are ordered around the lections of the festival cycle (like *Pesiqta de-Rab Kahana*) or around the weekly readings from the Pentateuch (like *Leviticus Rabbah*)[36], do exactly the same thing.

The midrashic literature does not preserve a homily on the beginning of Ezekiel which we might compare to the *Visions*. But *Pesiqta de-Rab Kahana* contains a homily on the opening of the Book of Jeremiah (read as *haftarah* on the first of the three Sabbaths preceding the fast of the Ninth of Ab [256]), which will give us some idea of the normal pattern. The vast bulk of this homily (*Dibre Yirmeyahu*, ed. 225–239 [206]) is devoted to the first verse of the lection. Of the fifteen sections into which Mandelbaum divides the homily, the first six are *petihot*. The next six (apart from #10, which expounds Jeremiah 9:9) deal with the opening phrase *the words of Jeremiah*. #13 expounds the words *of the priests*; #14, *in the land of Benjamin*. It is only in the very last section — eight lines in Mandelbaum's edition, out of a total of nearly two hundred — that the editor of the homily moves on to Jeremiah 1:2–3.

This lopsided attention to the beginning of a Biblical passage is entirely typical of homiletic midrash. The *Visions of Ezekiel* shares this feature with *Pesiqta*'s homily on the beginning of Jeremiah and with its congeners, because it shares their origin and their function. It is a literary deposit of materials used to introduce the synagogue reading of the *merkabah* chapter.

That is why the climactic *merkabah* in the *Visions*' seventh heaven contains in its name ("chariots of fire and storm") an allusion to Ezekiel 1:4[37]. The reading of the Biblical chapter, we may assume, directly followed the introductory sermon. The *Visions* therefore concludes, appropriately, by pointing forward to the beginning of this lection. The congregation is now ready to hear Ezekiel's actual description of the *merkabah*; and it comes equipped with the hint that what the prophet saw was "the great *merkabah* in which God will descend to judge all the nations."

---

35 Indeed, the *Visions* adds a fresh wrinkle to the problem, in that we will see reason to believe that some of its oral source material was delivered in Greek. But more on this later, in section C.
36 Strack describes and catalogues the midrashim of this type [345].
37 See Appendix IV.

5. The meaning of the text

a) The function of the visionary. Our discovery in the last section, that the *Visions* emerged from a synagogue milieu, gives us the correct interpretation of a pivotal passage in the text. This passage, in turn, yields the key to the meaning and purpose of the *Visions of Ezekiel* as a whole.

The *Visions'* midrashic section concludes as follows (IJ):

> Is it possible that God said to Ezekiel, "I am showing you my *merkabah* on condition that you describe it in full to the Israelites"? ... [The author quotes two Biblical passages demonstrating that this is indeed what God said to Ezekiel.] But [he was? one is?] to expound them [*ledorshan*] to an individual in such a way that his eye is able to see and his ear able to hear.

The last sentence is puzzling. Who is the subject of the infinitive *ledorshan*, "to expound them"? From the context, we would imagine that it is Ezekiel himself. But why does the author leave this point so vague? And why does he speak of Ezekiel "expounding" his own vision? The verb *darash* is properly used for "expounding" a Scriptural passage. It is appropriate for a rabbi or a synagogue preacher with a Biblical text before him. It does not suit the prophet himself, who need only recount his vision – or "describe it in full" (*peresh*), as Ezekiel is told to do at the beginning of the paragraph.

I propose that the figure of Ezekiel in the *Visions* is, to a very great extent, a model of the contemporary preacher. The people, who address Ezekiel at the beginning of the midrashic section and receive his message at its end, represent the preacher's congregation. It is the preacher who bears the charge laid on Ezekiel, to expound the wonders of Ezekiel's vision in full detail, but in such a way that each individual can understand what he hears. Hence the author's ambiguity as to who is to do the expounding.

Equipped with this perception, let us take a fresh look at the midrashic portion of the *Visions.* We can now, I think, discover the logic that unifies it and that binds it to the cosmology.

b) The logic of the "Visions." As the *Visions* opens, we find Ezekiel's people telling him that "our fathers were punished in the desert forty years ... we are punished for every king who arose over us" (IA). What is remarkable in this passage is not the assertion itself; it is the fact that the assertion is put into the people's mouth. After all, the author could have represented Ezekiel as explaining this point to the people, or he could have left it outside quotation marks altogether. The passage becomes intelligible only if we assume that the people are complaining to Ezekiel. God treats them, they say, with grim poetic justice. They must pay with a year of exile for each of the kings who ruled them in their days of pride and independence.

We imagine at first that the people get no reply. But, as we examine the text of the *Visions* more carefully, we find their complaint both echoed and answered in several places.

Section IB, to begin with, responds to the accusation of God's cruel justice. We are shown that God does indeed operate with a sort of poetic justice; but it is a benign one, which turns the ill-omened month of Tammuz into the time when God reveals his mercy and grace. The author hints that he intends IB to answer IA, by using the verb *laqah* ("to be punished") in both paragraphs. "Our fathers were punished [*laqu*] ... we are punished [*laqinu*] ... they were punished [*laqu*] in Tammuz, and in Tammuz God's mercies were moved toward them." The people themselves, of course, do not yet know this.

Section IC takes up the theme of complaint in a different way. As the people complained to Ezekiel, so Ezekiel himself now complains to God. Why must he, alone among the prophets, prophesy in exile?

We are promptly told that God's providence has set Ezekiel at a difficult post appropriate to his talents. But the prophet himself does not seem to be given any explanation of this sort. He gets a better consolation: "Thereupon God opened to Ezekiel the seven subterranean chambers, and Ezekiel looked into them and saw all the celestial entities" (ID). We can hardly understand the connection between IC and D implied by the word "thereupon" (*miyyad*) unless we assume that the vision is God's reply to Ezekiel's complaint. This vision is not limited to the *merkabah* described in Ezekiel 1, but includes all the realms below and above, with a strong hint of future redemption for Ezekiel's people (IE). As in IB, the author implies that the vision is a token of God's grace.

If this is God's response to Ezekiel's complaint, when do the people get a response to theirs? This is what section IJ is about. The people complained to Ezekiel; Ezekiel complained to God. God showed a vision of consolation to Ezekiel. It is now Ezekiel's duty to transmit this vision of consolation back to his people. To use the *Visions'* own image, the shepherd was exiled for the sake of the flock. For their sake, too, he was shown his vision. He – or the preacher who steps into his role – must set forth its details to the people in language they can understand.

This is exactly what the preacher does in the second, cosmological portion of the *Visions*, detailing just what it was that appeared when *the heavens were opened, and I saw visions of God.*

The shift from the midrash to the cosmology no longer appears to us as abrupt as it did when we began our inquiry. We can now understand, too, why the figure of Ezekiel plays a major role up to the end of the midrashic part of the *Visions*, and is not mentioned a single time afterward. The preacher who narrates the cosmology has taken Ezekiel's place.

c) Vision and consolation. If, as appears, Ezekiel saw all the heavens and all the infernal realms opened to him, what role did the *merkabah* that he begins to describe in 1:4 play in this greater vision? The name the *Visions* gives to "the great *merkabah* in which God will descend to judge all the nations," now located in the seventh heaven, suggests that the author identified it with the entity described in Ezekiel 1 (see above). But this does not fully clear up the problem, for we may still wonder why the author also puts a *merkabah* in each of the six lower heavens.

The answer, I believe, is that the author understands each of his seven *merkabah*s as the one that Ezekiel saw, and that the multiplication of chariots is his way of resolving the tension between the vision of the opened heavens and the vision of the *merkabah*. I will not be able adequately to argue this point until the final section of this chapter, and therefore hold off discussing it.

But there is another question which I cannot postpone so easily. Exactly what is the consolation to be derived from the sights described in the *Visions of Ezekiel*? No doubt the hints of a coming redemption play some part in it. Section IE mentions the return of the Temple vessels. IIF1 has "Jerusalem rebuilt and restored" in the fifth heaven, presumably being kept in readiness for its return to its people. IIH1 speaks of future rewards and punishments. IIJ2 predicts that "God will descend to judge all the nations," as he once descended to Sinai (IIE2) and to the Red Sea (IIF2, if Mann's reading is right). Similarly, the author of the Targumic Tosefta to Ezekiel 1:1 enjoys imagining the punishment of the Jews' oppressors, and he speaks of Jerusalem being rebuilt "with jewels and pearls" (by Nebuchadnezzar, admittedly).

But, if the author of the *Visions* considered eschatological hope a major part of the "mercies" God showed when he allowed Ezekiel to see his vision, it is odd that he says so little on this subject. Rather, he seems to have believed that God's displaying the grandeur and wonder of his cosmos to his prophet was itself a consolation and act of grace. By that revelation, God showed that he was the master of that grandeur and wonder; and that, for all the punishment he had given his people, they were still his.

We must supplement the *Visions'* evidence on this point from other sources. One of these is the conclusion of *Pesiqta Rabbati's* midrash on the Sinai revelation, which will occupy us in section B of this chapter. Another, even more valuable in conveying what visionary descriptions of the heavenly realms meant to the people who heard them, is *Hekhalot Rabbati.*

Several passages in *Hekhalot Rabbati* describe the task laid upon "those who descend to the *merkabah*." Like Ezekiel in the *Visions,* they are shown what they see in order that they may describe it to their people:

Blessed [be you] by heaven and earth, you who descend to the *merkabah*[e], if you tell my children what I do during the morning, afternoon, and evening prayer, every day and every hour that the Jews say before me, *Holy*[38]. Teach them, and say to them: Lift up your eyes to the heaven above your prayer-houses when you say before me, *Holy*. For I have no such pleasure in the world that I created [as] at the time that your eyes are lifted up to mine and mine to yours, the time when you say before me, *Holy*. The breath that goes forth from your mouths[f] at that time pushes its way up before me like the sweet smell [of sacrifice].

Bear witness to them on my behalf of what you have seen. [Tell them] what I do to the image of Jacob's face that is engraved on my throne of glory. When you say before me, *Holy*, I bend over it, hug it and kiss it, embrace it so that my hands are on my shoulders[39], all three times [each day] that you say before me, *Holy*. [Schäfer, ##163–164 (I translate ms Oxford, in this and the following quotations); Wertheimer, chapter 10:5–11:2] ...

The decree of heaven will be against you, you who descend to the *merkabah*, if you do not relate what you have heard and if you do not bear witness to what you have seen. ... [There follows a reference, difficult to understand and to translate, to exaltation that takes place] in the heavens three times each day, without people being aware of it. So it is written, *Holy, holy, holy*. [Schäfer, #169; Wertheimer, 12:3–4] ...

Please, you [angels] who eagerly and whole-heartedly carry the throne of glory, sing loudly your joyful hymns before the throne of glory of ... [several cryptic names for God], the God of Israel, so that he will be in a good mood at the time of his children's prayer, and will make himself accessible[g] to those who descend to the *merkabah* at the time that they stand before his throne of glory. [Schäfer, #172; Wertheimer, 13:2]

Later on, *Hekhalot Rabbati* describes the terrifying and destructive powers that surround God in the seventh of the "palaces." However, it adds,

all those who descend to the *merkabah*[h] ascend unharmed. They see all this destruction, yet they descend safely[40]. They arise and bear witness to their terrifying vision, unlike anything that is in the palace of any human king[i]. They bless and extol ... Totrosiai[41], the Lord, God of Israel, who rejoices in those who descend to the *merkabah*, and who sits waiting for every Jew to descend into the astounding pride and strange power ... that take place before the throne of glory in the heavens three times each day from the creation to the present, for [God's] praise ...

Totrosiai, the Lord, God of Israel, looks forward [to this] as eagerly as he looks forward to the redemption and the time of salvation that is reserved for the Jews after the destruction of the last temple[42]. When will he who descends to the *merkabah* make his descent? When will he see the pride of the heavens? When will he hear the ultimate salvation? When will he see what no eye has seen? When will he ascend and tell what he has seen to the offspring of Abraham, God's lover? [Schäfer, ##216–218; Wertheimer, 18:3–5]

Scholem and Gruenwald have both classified the *Visions of Ezekiel* with the *Hekhalot* [590,540]. This judgment, despite an extremely valuable kernel of truth which it contains (to be examined in chapter IX), seems to me by and large mistaken. The *Visions* differs from the *Hekhalot* in both its

---

38 That is, when they recite the *Qedushshah* hymn (cf. *Visions*, section IIC1), with its *holy, holy, holy is the Lord of hosts*.

39 This seems to mean that God's embrace is so tight that his right hand touches his left shoulder, and vice versa. – On Jacob's face, see above, chapter IV, section 2b.

40 As usual, the terms "ascend" and "descend" are used in an extremely confusing way. Here, "ascend" seems to refer to the journey to the *merkabah*, and "descend" (in the second sentence) to the return trip.

41 A divine name fairly common in the *Hekhalot* texts.

42 I do not know what this refers to. Ms Oxford glosses *ha'aharon* ("the last") with *hashsheni* ("the second") – whether correctly or not, I cannot tell.

style and its content. As far as its structure is concerned, the carefully organized text we have been studying could hardly be more unlike the sprawling and barely coherent *Hekhalot* writings.

But, in its treatment of the role of the visionary, the *Visions* is very close to at least one current of the *Hekhalot* literature[43]. Like the Ezekiel of the *Visions*, and the preachers whom he stands for, "those who descend to the *merkabah*" are witnesses to the Jewish people of a vision of encouragement and comfort, which is bound up with their worship in the synagogue. The comfort lies in their testimony, not only to God's love for Israel, but also to the power and terror that surround the Lover.

Witnesses to the Jewish people — or only to an elite group of mystics? I have so far said nothing about the esoteric character of the ideas we have been discussing, because I do not think it exists. The evidence that the *Hekhalot* are esoteric writings seems to me far weaker than scholars normally assume; in chapter IX, we will view them in a very different light. And I do not see a particle of evidence that the author of the *Visions of Ezekiel* believed himself to be recording matters that ought to be hidden from the common view.

At one point, indeed, the author seems a little astonished at this. Is it really possible, he asks, that God can have intended Ezekiel to reveal the details of the *merkabah* to the Jewish people (IJ)? But he then answers the question with a yes — as long as the details are put in intelligible language.

In this last qualification, he has perhaps defined the essential aim of the sermons his little book represents.

6. The "Visions" and Sinai

In section IID3, the author of the *Visions* gives the name *ha-Lewiyyah*, "the Levites," to one of his seven *merkabah*s. I have suggested that this name alludes to a *Tanḥuma* midrash, discussed in chapter IV, which interprets Psalm 68:18 to mean that "twenty-two thousand *merkabah*s descended with God to Sinai, corresponding to the Levitic camp" (*maḥaneh lewiyyah*)[44]. The same midrash explains that each of these *merkabah*s was "like the *merkabah* that Ezekiel saw."

We saw in chapter IV that this *Tanḥuma* midrash represents a synagogue tradition which combined Ezekiel's *merkabah* vision (the Shabu^cot *hafṭa*-

---

43 I say "at least one current" in deference to Ira Chernus's view (which I am not sure I am prepared to accept) that communal concerns are specifically characteristic of *Hekhalot Rabbati*, and not of the *Hekhalot* in general [510].

44 See my note on section IID3; and, for a detailed argument, Appendix IV.

rah) with the Sinai revelation (the Shabuᶜot Torah reading), and used Psalm 68:18 to clip the two together. By alluding to the midrash, the author points to this tradition as a source for his exegesis.

We have now come to believe, on entirely different grounds, that the *Visions* is rooted in synagogue sermons for Shabuᶜot. Two lines of argument thus converge, each supporting the other.

But we now face a difficulty. Why does the *Visions* say so little about Sinai? Section IIE speaks of God's descent to Sinai, and refers vaguely to Moses' ascent to heaven to get the Torah. IIF2 perhaps refers to the Red Sea, which is at least part of the Exodus-wilderness story, and there is a remote chance that it may hint at the Sinai event (Appendix IV, section 3). The quotation of Isaiah 19:1 in IIH2 may also point to the Exodus. In section B4c, we will see evidence that the *merkabah*-name *Melakhim* (IIE2) may be a hidden allusion to Sinai. All told, this is not much.

The *Visions*, it seems, preserves for us traces only of those portions of the Shabuᶜot sermons that deal with the *haftarah*. The corresponding midrashim on the Torah reading, the story of the Sinai revelation, are lost.

Lost — or only unrecognized? I believe that the missing half of the Shabuᶜot cycle, whose existence we have begun to suspect, survives incognito in *Midrash Pesiqta Rabbati* and its parallels, which describe Moses' heavenly ascent. It is to these sources that we now turn.

B. The Ascension of Moses

1. Introduction

The twentieth homily of the midrash called *Pesiqta Rabbati* is focused on the opening words of the Ten Commandments, *I am the Lord your God* (Exodus 20:2). The homily begins with what appears to be a loosely organized series of expositions to Song 5:13, functioning as a *petiḥah* to Exodus 20:2. It then expounds the central text itself, with a long and amazing story about Moses' adventures in heaven.

Moses, the story goes, rides a cloud up to heaven in order to get the Torah. Hordes of angels, whose attitudes range from suspicion to savage hostility, try to block his way. He defeats them with a combination of divine patronage, forensic skill, and brute force. At the end, God opens the seven heavens to Moses and to all Israel, and angels swarm down to help the Israelites bear the mighty revelation of God's glory.

Pesiqta Rabbati is conventionally classified as a "late midrash." More to the point, it is a highly composite midrash, a compilation of homilies taken from several different sources and arranged according to the lections of the Jewish festival cycle. Homily 20 is the first of a series of five homilies which deal with the Ten Commandments, and which *Pesiqta*'s editor apparently intended to accompany the Torah reading for Shabuᶜot. Stylistically, however, it is different from the four homilies that follow it, and it seems to come from a distinct source.

What was this source? There may be a clue in the homily's opening, which introduces Song 5:13 with the formula: "This is what Solomon spoke by means of the holy spirit." Six of *Pesiqta*'s other homilies (28, 30, 34–37) begin in the same way [289,361]. There is as yet no consensus over whether this formula, which occurs in a few other midrashic sources as well, points to an early or to a late date [260]. It is perhaps significant that homilies 34–37 seem to constitute a more or less unified source, representing a Messianic doctrine which is, to say the least, very unusual. Bernard J. Bamberger has argued, on the basis of an apparent political allusion in 36:2, that the entire source can be dated precisely to between 632 and 637 A.D. [255]. If Bamberger is right (which Braude has disputed [246]), and if the common opening formula gives us warrant to reason from homilies 34–37 to homily 20, we might conclude that homily 20 was composed in its present form during the seventh century. But the possibility would remain that the portion of this homily that specifically concerns us is an older source which the seventh-century writer utilized. To fix its date, we must use evidence from within the relevant passage itself.

It is obvious, for one thing, that *Pesiqta*'s story of Moses' ascent has much in common with the *Hekhalot*. This led Leopold Zunz to conclude, a century and a half ago, that the passage had been reworked in accord with the *Hekhalot*, and could therefore be presumed late [363]. But the literary connections between homily 20 and the *Hekhalot* are not at all clear, and we do not have to suppose that the author of our passage had *Hekhalot* texts before him. (The influence could, after all, have gone in the opposite direction.) Besides, it no longer seems as obvious as it did to Zunz that the *Hekhalot* are late.

It is a more useful indication that, at least twice in his account of Moses' adventure, the author appears to betray his dependence on the Babylonian Talmud. Even if we argue, as we reasonably can, that he is using one of the Talmud's sources rather than the Talmud itself, we will presently see reason to believe that in both places he is drawing on a fairly late stratum of material. It seems a fair inference that he wrote no earlier than about the end of the Talmudic period. If he antedated the seventh century, in other words, he did not antedate it by much.

The question of dating, however, is complicated by the fact that we have two close parallels to *Pesiqta*'s narrative, which do not make the same use of the Talmud as does *Pesiqta*, and which do not seem to depend on *Pesiqta* itself. Jellinek published one of these in his *Bet ha-Midrasch*, under the title *Ma^{c}ayan Ḥokhmah*, "the fountain of wisdom" [476]⁴⁵. The other occurs in a manuscript in the Bodleian Library at Oxford. Karl-Erich Grözinger has printed it, for the first time, in the textual appendix of his exhaustive monograph on homily 20 [288].

Grözinger supposes that *Pesiqta*'s version is the latest and most developed of the group, and that the Oxford text is its forerunner; while *Ma^{c}ayan Ḥokhmah* has evolved in a separate direction [290]. I myself am not so convinced of *Pesiqta*'s relative lateness. *Pesiqta, Ma^{c}ayan Ḥokhmah,* and the Oxford text seem to me independent recensions of what is basically the same tradition; I do not think any of them draws on any of the others, and I would not try to establish their sequence. But it is clear that *Pesiqta* and the Oxford text stand closer to each other than either does to *Ma^{c}ayan Ḥokhmah*. There is one peculiar passage in *Pesiqta* which can only be explained, as Grözinger says, by assuming that the author was misled by a corruption in a text akin to that of the Oxford manuscript$^{j)}$.

The other parallel texts that Grözinger cites, such as the unnamed "haggadah" quoted several times in the twelfth-century *Maḥzor Vitry,* give the impression of being derivative. Often, they try to equate the succession of angels whom Moses meets with the series of seven heavens in BT Hag. 12b; the latter concept, as we will presently see, originally played no role at all in the ascension story. Only one of these texts will demand our attention. This is the very brief *Haggadat Shema^c Yiśra'el,* published by Jellinek [484], which is apparently drawn entirely from *Ma^{c}ayan Ḥokhmah,* but which turns the story into a first-person narrative spoken by Moses. The details of this version contribute nothing to our inquiry, but the question of why its author chose to put it in the first person will help us uncover a valuable clue to the function of the ascension tradition. We will examine this issue in section 5.

At one point in its narrative, *Pesiqta* attributes a remark to one "R. Nahum." We will see that this is a direct borrowing from the Babylonian Talmud, which neither the Oxford text nor *Ma^{c}ayan Ḥokhmah* shares. With this exception, none of the three versions interrupts its narrative at any point to introduce the name of an authority. *Ma^{c}ayan Ḥokhmah*'s story begins without a word of introduction. The author of *Pesiqta* opens his account with phrase *teno rabbanan,* "our masters taught," which the Babylonian Talmud regularly uses to signal that what follows is a baraita.

---

45 The seventeenth-century compilation *Yalquṭ Re'ubeni* contains this text, with a few omissions and insignificant variations (ed. 133–134 [236]). The compiler claims he is quoting it from something called *Pirqe Hekhalot*, "the chapters of the *Hekhalot*." Grözinger mistakenly treats *Yalquṭ*'s text and *Ma^{c}ayan Ḥokhmah* as distinct sources [290].

Only the Oxford text attributes the story to a specific rabbi: Joshua b.
Levi. We will later see that there are at least two possible explanations for
this attribution, and that I incline to suppose that it preserves an early and
authentic tradition concerning the origin of the ascension story. But this
must wait until we have examined the story itself.

2. The story

a) The ascension. Moses' adventure begins[46] when he meets a cloud
which crouches beside him on the earth, ready for him to ride. "The cloud
opened its mouth and he went inside it; as it is written, *Moses went into
the cloud* [Exodus 24:18], *and the cloud covered him* [24:16]. The cloud
carried him upward."

The Oxford manuscript and *Ma^cayan Hokhmah* leave out *Pesiqta*'s
quotation of Exodus 24:16 (whose function is not very clear in any case)
and quote verse 18 in a slightly later position. But all three versions agree
that the cloud, like an express elevator, lifts Moses straight from the ground
floor to the very top. From then on, his progress is horizontal rather than
vertical: "Moses was walking in heaven like a person walking on earth,"
we are told a little later on. There is no hint of a stage-by-stage ascent
through seven heavens[47]. Only at the very end of *Pesiqta*'s story do we find
seven heavens opened to Moses and to all Israel. We must deal with this
surprising twist when we come to it.

The three sources also agree in deriving the image of the elevator-cloud
from Exodus 24:18: *Moses went into the cloud and ascended to the mountain, and Moses was on the mountain forty days and forty nights.* We can
see how an expositor who came to this text with a prior belief in Moses'
heavenly ascent could have understood *the mountain* as heaven and *the
cloud* as Moses' way of getting there. Still, this seems to read a lot into the
text. We will presently see that another Biblical passage, from a disconcert-
ingly different context, may well have reinforced this interpretation of
Exodus 24:18.

---

46 Braude's translation of *Pesiqta Rabbati* contains the story in full [245]. Braude translated the
text published by Meir Friedmann (ed. 96b–98b), which goes back to the seventeenth-century
Prague edition; while I am working from the critical edition that Grözinger published in his
textual appendix [299], based on the fourteenth-century ms Casanata 3324. Some of the translations that I give in the following discussion will therefore differ from Braude's. In the passage
that I quote in this paragraph, for example, Friedmann's edition quotes Exodus 24:15 (*and the
cloud covered* [*the mountain*]) instead of verse 16, and Braude translates accordingly.

47 Grözinger thinks that each of the angels Moses encounters is conceived as the ruler of one of
the heavens [290]. If so, the texts have concealed this very well.

b) Moses the warrior. Moses' first encounter is with the angel Kemuel. This being, who seems to be a guard to the entrance of heaven — "he is in command of twelve thousand angels of destruction who sit at the gates of heaven" — gives Moses a savage tongue-lashing. Moses is a creature of filth; what is he doing in a place of purity? Moses stands his ground: "I am the son of Amram, and I came to get Torah for Israel." When Kemuel does not let him pass, Moses destroys him with a single blow.

The Oxford text and *Ma^cayan Hokhmah* give rather different accounts of this meeting. *Ma^cayan Hokhmah* represents Kemuel as considerably less abusive than he is in the other versions. The Oxford manuscript generally agrees with *Pesiqta*, but leaves out the conclusion that Moses annihilates Kemuel. It is not hard to see why: humans, unaided, ought not to be more powerful than "angels of destruction." The detail is indeed an odd one, and deserves our attention.

Grözinger [292] aptly compares the late midrashim on the death of Moses, in which Moses resists the efforts of the demon Sammael (who seems here to be conceived as the angel of death) to take his soul [401, 455]. In one of these midrashim, which has been added on to *Deut. R.* 11: 10 (it also appears, with variations, in one of Jellinek's texts, ed. 127–129 [477]), Moses speaks to the terrified Sammael in a way similar to that in which he here addresses Kemuel[48]. "I am the son of Amram," he says, "who came forth circumcized from my mother's womb," and so forth. Significantly, he goes on to tell Sammael, in the most martial terms, of his experience in heaven:

I ascended and trod a path in the heavens. I took part in the war of the angels and received a fiery Torah. I dwelt under a fiery throne and sheltered under a fiery pillar, and I spoke with [God] face to face. I vanquished the celestial retinue and revealed their secrets to humankind. I received Torah from God's right hand and taught it to Israel.

Grözinger prints a passage that occurs in the Oxford manuscript, apparently independent of the haggadah we have been considering (it appears about twenty lines after the material parallel to *Pesiqta* comes to an end), which reinforces this image of Moses as a warrior who invaded heaven and singlehandedly vanquished the angels. "Thereupon Moses began to fight with them [the angels] like an ox fighting with its horns [*keshor nogeah*]. When the angels saw that Moses was winning, they fled; and he returned to the people from the heavenly wars" [298].

An Aramaic hymn, preserved in the Ashkenazic liturgy for Shabu^cot, has God tell Moses to use his "horns of splendor" (*qarne hoda*) to defend himself against the angels [305]. A similar composition, also apparently in-

---

48 It is perhaps no coincidence that the two names are graphically similar. The rare name "Kemuel" [426] may be, at bottom, a variant of "Sammael."

tended for Shabu^cot, represents Moses as taunting the angels: "I will not descend, I will not descend, until I prove myself a hero, until I gore your bodies with my horns" (*beqarnay 'anaggah*) [283][49]. This notion, that Moses climbed to heaven equipped with horns which he could use as weapons against the angels, evidently underlies the Oxford manuscript's comparison of Moses to "an ox fighting with its horns." The verb the Oxford text uses, *nogeah*, is cognate to the Aramaic hymn's *'anaggah*. The same root recurs in *Ex. R.* 41:7, which describes Moses as fighting the angels with his horns (*menaggeah 'otam*).

All of these passages evidently reflect a midrashic tradition which understood *qaran ^cor panaw* in Exodus 34:29–30 (RSV: "the skin of his [Moses'] face shone") to mean, "the skin of his face had horns." This, as Joseph Heinemann has pointed out [305a], is the way Jerome understood the passage. His Vulgate translation inspired generations of artists, Michelangelo among them, to depict Moses as horned [845]. Modern scholars often smile at Jerome's supposed howler. Yet Jerome cannot have originated it. The Septuagint understood the text in Exodus, probably correctly, to mean that Moses' face was "glorified"; and Paul himself endorsed this interpretation (II Corinthians 3:7–18). We can hardly suppose that Jerome departed from it without some strong warrant, such as a Jewish tradition might have provided. He himself tells us as much, when he cites the Greek translation of the impeccably Jewish Aquila as the source for his rendering (*Commentary* on Amos 6:13; ed. 311–312 [622c]).

We must return later to the significance of the conception of Moses as warrior, and the role that his horns played in it. For now, we need note only that the author of our haggadah seems to have been a bit wary of the whole idea. He makes use of it, as we have seen, in describing Moses' exchange with Kemuel, but thereafter leaves it alone. Moses' reaction to the angels he afterwards meets is terror.

c) Hadarniel and Sandalphon. The next challenger is Hadarniel, "who is six hundred thousand parasangs[50] taller than his companions, and whose every utterance is accompanied by two flashes of lightning" (twelve thousand flashes, according to the Oxford text and *Ma^cayan Hokhmah*). Moses is so frightened of him that he wants to fall from his cloud.

But here God takes pity and intervenes, scolding Hadarniel and his fellow-angels for their quarrelsomeness. Long ago, he tells them, they tried

---

49 The poem, conventionally titled *'Angele Meroma* (after its opening words, "angels of heaven"), will presently interest us in a different connection. See section C5d, below.
50 "A parasang is 3 2/5 of a mile" (Braude [245]).

to keep him from creating Adam[51]. Now they do not want him to give Torah to Israel, even though their welfare and his own depend on Israel's accepting the Torah! Hadarniel, chastened, attaches himself to Moses, walking before him "like a student before his master."

Even Hadarniel's area of authority, however, has limits; and he cannot go beyond these limits for fear of the fire of the greater angel Sandalphon. Moses must continue alone.

At the sight of Sandalphon, Moses is again terrified, again wants to fall from his cloud. God descends from his throne and stations himself before Sandalphon (before Moses, according to the Oxford text and *Ma^cayan Hokhmah*), until Moses gets by safely. All three sources apply the words of Exodus 34:6, *the Lord passed before him*, to this incident. They then proceed to describe Sandalphon.

We have, of course, met Sandalphon before. BT Hag. 13b, as we saw in chapter IV (section 3c), identifies the *one wheel on the earth* of Ezekiel 1: 15 with a gigantic angel of that name, who "is taller than his companions by the distance of a five-hundred-year journey. He stands behind the *merkabah* and weaves wreaths for his creator." The Gemara objects that the language of Ezekiel 3:12, *blessed be the glory of the Lord from his place*, seems to imply that not even a heavenly being would know where to deposit the wreaths. It then answers its own objection with the claim that Sandalphon "speaks [God's] name over the wreath, and it goes and sits in its place."

Pesiqta, the Oxford text, and *Ma^cayan Hokhmah* do not use exactly the same language to describe Sandalphon. But all follow the contours of the Talmudic account so closely that it is hard to believe that they — or the tradition that they all share — are not dependent on it. "They said concerning Sandalphon," says *Pesiqta*, "that he is the distance of a five-hundred-year journey taller than his companions, and he serves behind the *merkabah* and weaves wreaths for his creator." (*Ma^cayan Hokhmah* follows BT yet more closely, introducing a quotation of Ezekiel 1:15 into this passage.) Lest we imagine that the angels know where they are to deposit the wreaths, Ezekiel 3:12 teaches us that they have never seen *his place*. Rather, Sandalphon "adjures the wreath, and it rises and settles on the head of its Lord."

Given this apparent dependence on BT, we may well suppose that the preceding description of Hadarniel as "six hundred thousand parasangs taller than his companions" is also modelled after BT's description of Sandalphon, but reduced to more modest proportions.

---

51 Peter Schäfer discusses the theme of the angels' opposition to the creation of Adam in his important book, *Rivalität zwischen Engeln und Menschen* [435], to which we will again have occasion to refer. So does Grözinger, in his comments on the Hadarniel episode.

The Sandalphon passage thus seems to show that our haggadah draws on ·a passage of the Babylonian Talmud in something like its present form, including a late editorial stratum of the Gemara. We might well infer that the haggadah, as our three sources transmit it to us, is a late reworking of Talmudic material. We will see that this inference is probably true, and yet, at the same time, basically misleading.

In the meantime, we have something just as important to learn from this passage: how the synagogue tradition developed the image of Sandalphon and his wreaths. *Ma^cayan Hokhmah* tells us that Sandalphon "adjures the wreath *by which they crown God's place with Qedushshah hymns.*" The writer does not make clear whether the beings who do the "crowning" are humans (as in the text from *Midrash Konen* which we examined in chapter IV) or angels. But all three sources go on to describe how a mighty *Qedushshah* of the heavenly beings accompanies the wreath's progress to the head of its master. This description, at once solemn and fantastic, is redolent of the *Hekhalot.*

I quote *Pesiqta*'s version, with a few emendations based on the parallels:

[Sandalphon] adjures the wreath, and it rises and settles on the head of its Lord. Thereupon all the celestial soldiers are seized with trembling, and the exalted *hayyot* roar like a lion. At that instant they all respond: *Holy, holy, holy is the Lord of hosts. The whole earth is full of his glory*^{k)}.

When [the wreath] reaches [God's] throne, the wheels of his throne rotate, the bases of the footstool are shaken, and trembling seizes all the heavens⁵².

When it passes by the throne, all the celestial soldiers and the wreath itself proclaim: *Blessed be the glory of the Lord from his place.*

Come and see God's praise and his greatness! When the wreath reaches his head, he gets himself ready to receive the wreath from his servants ["the prayers of the Jews," in the Oxford text]. All the *hayyot* and *'ofannim* and the wheels of the *merkabah* and the throne of glory cry out together: *The Lord will reign for ever and ever* [Exodus 15:18]. *The Lord will reign for ever, your God, O Zion, to all eternity. Hallelujah* [Psalm 146:10]⁵³.

d) Moses at the throne. After this long digression on Sandalphon, the texts return to their description of Moses' adventures. He is met by the fiery river Rigyon, whose coals are hot enough to burn up angels, let alone humans⁵⁴. He is met by the angel Gallisur, whose wings protect the angels

---

52 This last remark seems to presuppose a belief in a series of heavens, which otherwise plays no role in Moses' ascension.

53 *Ma^cayan Hokhmah*'s conclusion is yet more baroque: "... All the *hayyot* and seraphim, and the wheels of the *merkabah* and the throne of glory, and the celestial soldiers and the *hashmallim* and the cherubim, all of them magnify themselves and join together and exalt themselves, give [God] glory and splendor and declare him to be their king. All together they say: The Lord is king, the Lord was king, the Lord will be king for ever and ever. ... God himself confirms them, saying: *The Lord will reign for ever, your God, O Zion, to all eternity. Hallelujah.*"

54 We have already met Rigyon in our discussion of the "water test" in the *Hekhalot* (above, chapter VI, section 2a, text II). It is a little odd that this river, like the angels, seems to function as an active entity which "meets" Moses (*paga^c bo rigyon*) rather than as a geographical feature which

themselves from the fiery breath of the *ḥayyot*; who announces God's decrees to the world; and who, in a particularly strange passage which seems to have political overtones, uses coals from Rigyon to support the authority of earthly rulers[1]. He is met by "a troop of strong and mighty angels of destruction who surround the throne of glory," and who want to burn him with their breath.

God rescues Moses from all of these encounters. After the last of them, he extends to him the protection of his glory and his throne. From this place of safety, Moses can address the angels and convince them that the Torah is intended for humans, not for them.

Our three sources differ considerably among themselves in reporting both this climactic speech, and the action that comes right before it. *Pesiqta*'s version is the fullest.

> What did God do [to protect Moses from the angels of destruction]? He spread over him some of his splendor, set him before his throne, and said to him: "Give an answer to the angels."
>
> *When he seized the front of the throne,* [God] *spread over him the splendor of his cloud* [Job 26:9]. R. Nahum said: This teaches that the Almighty spread over him some of the splendor of the Shechinah and his cloud[55].
>
> "Master of the world," he said to him, "I am afraid they will burn me up with their breath."
>
> "Take hold of my throne of glory," [God] replied, "and give them an answer."
>
> Moses then took heart and gave the angels an answer. "The Torah says, *I am the Lord your God.* Have you another god? The Torah says, *You shall have no other gods before me.* Are you divided among yourselves? Or do you believe in two divine powers? The Torah says, *Honor your father and your mother.* Have you a father or a mother? The Torah says, *You shall not covet.* Are you prone to covetousness?"

The angels, apparently conceding Moses' point, burst into a recital of the eighth psalm: *Lord our master, your name is very great in all the earth* (8:2, or, perhaps, 8:10). We must for the time being hold off discussing the sequel to their concession.

The narrative in the Oxford manuscript is substantially shorter than *Pesiqta*'s. When the angels of destruction attacked Moses, we read there, "God spread over him some of his splendor and sheltered him with his throne of glory. So it is written: *When he seized the front of the throne,* [God] *spread over him the splendor of his cloud.*" The writer offers no explanation of this verse, nor does he mention "R. Nahum." He reports Moses' argument, too, more concisely than does *Pesiqta*. "What use is

---

Moses must pass. We will see evidence in section C that the Rigyon episode is more important than appears at first sight. — *Maᶜayan Ḥokhmah* inserts here a long description of the fiery river, which stresses its function of purifying the angels. Cf. the *Visions of Ezekiel,* section IIC1; and below, section C.

55 The midrash applies Job 26:9 to Moses. It assumes that Moses is the subject of the first verb; it understands the second verb (the cryptic *parshez*) as a sort of acronym for *PeReś SHadday Ziw,* "the Almighty spread splendor." (RSV translates the verse: "He [God] covers the face of the moon, and spreads [*parshez*] over it his cloud.")

Torah to you? Did you go out of Egypt? Is there idolatry among you?
False oaths?" The first three of the Ten Commandments are obviously irrelevant to angels; the same, the reader must suppose, is true of the rest. As
in *Pesiqta*, the angels announce their surrender by reciting Psalm 8:2.

Maᶜayan Ḥokhmah provides only the briefest introduction to Moses'
speech. "Thereupon God spread over him the splendor of his glory and said
to Moses: 'Give them an answer.'" The opening of this sentence plainly
alludes to Job 26:9, but the author does not actually quote the verse. But
then, as if to compensate for his terse introduction, he goes on to report
the speech itself in greater detail than either of the parallel texts. Moses
goes through the Ten Commandments one by one, showing why angels
have no use for them. Once again, the passage ends with the angels quoting
Psalm 8:2.

We must pause to ask who "R. Nahum" is, and why he appears in *Pesiqta* but not in its parallels. For our answers, we must turn to yet another
parallel source, which we have until now not had to reckon with.

As part of a long series of midrashim on the Sinai revelation (of which
more below), BT Shabb. 88b–89a attributes to Joshua b. Levi a haggadah
on Moses' ascension. The haggadah's framework is a midrash on Psalm 8.
The psalm begins: *Lord our master, your name is very great in all the earth
— so give your glory to heaven* (verse 2)[56]. It ends by repeating the first part
of this verse, but this time without the words *so give your glory to heaven*
(verse 10). Something, the expositor reasons, must have changed between
verse 2 and verse 10. Supposing *your glory* to be the Torah, he explains
what the change was:

> R. Joshua b. Levi said: When Moses ascended on high, the angels said to God: "Master of the
> world, what is this offspring of a woman doing among us?"
> "He has come to get the Torah," he answered.
> They said to him: "Do you really intend to give this precious treasure, which was your
> treasure for nine hundred and seventy four generations before the world was created, to flesh
> and blood? *Why should you keep humans in mind, or pay attention to men?* [Psalm 8:5]. *Lord
> our master, your name is very great in all the earth — so give your glory to heaven* [Psalm 8:2]."
> God said to Moses: "Give them an answer."
> "Master of the world," he said to him, "I am afraid they will burn me up with their breath."
> "Take hold of my throne of glory," [God] replied, "and give them an answer."
> So it is written: *When he seized the front of the throne,* [God] *spread over him the splendor
> of his cloud* [Job 26:9]. R. Nahum said: This teaches that the Almighty spread over him some
> of the splendor of his Shechinah and his cloud.
> Moses said to him: "Master of the world, what is in the Torah that you are about to give me?
> *I am the Lord your God who brought you out of the land of Egypt.*" He said to [the angels]:

---

56 So, at least, the expositor understands this verse, taking the verb *tenah* as an imperative of *natan*,
   "to give." Modern translators tend to connect it instead with the root *tny*, "to praise." Hence
   RSV: "Thou whose glory above the heavens is chanted ..."

"Were you in Egypt? Were you Pharaoh's slaves? What use is the Torah to you? ... [And so on, through the first eight commandments.]"

Thereupon they conceded to God. So it is written: *Lord our master, your name is very great in all the earth* [Psalm 8:10] — this time, however, without adding *so give your glory to heaven.*

In other words, the angels, who are assumed to be the speakers in this psalm, end by dropping their demand that God reserve his Torah for heaven.

As in *Pesiqta*, we have here a midrash of Job 26:9 attributed to "R. Nahum," invoked in such a way that it gives the impression of being an interpolation into the haggadah attributed to Joshua b. Levi. BT Sukk. 5a confirms this impression, by quoting Job 26:9 and "R. Nahum's" midrash of it in an entirely different context. Significantly, the printed text of Sukk. 5a gives the authority's name as "Tanhum," not "Nahum" (there is a difference of only one Hebrew letter between the two). Some witnesses to the text of Shabb. 88b [819], and quotations from it in *Yalquṭ Shim^coni* (*Numbers* #752, *Psalms* #641), support the reading "Tanhum[57]."

But who then is "R. Tanhum"? Schäfer supposes he is Joshua b. Levi's disciple Tanhum b. Hanilai [438]. But I think there is a better solution. Late midrashic writers often use an expression like "so expounded R. Tanhuma" as a way of indicating that they are drawing on a midrashic collection of the *Tanhuma* genre, presumably one of the prototypes of the *Tanhuma* midrashim that have come down to us [361]. The surviving *Tanhuma* sources do in fact contain expositions of Job 26:9 very similar to the one that BT attributes to "R. Tanhum": twice quoted anonymously (Tanh. Buber *Ki Tiśśa'* #13, ed. 57a [222]; *Ex. R.* 41:7), once in the name of "R. Azariah quoting R. Judah b. R. Simon, quoting R. Judah b. R. Ilai" (*Ex. R.* 42:4). It seems a fair deduction that the editors of BT found their midrash in a written source which was associated with the name "Tanhum" or "Tanhuma."

This source need not have been as late as the surviving *Tanhuma* midrashim are usually supposed to be (above, chapter IV, section 5a). But it is hard to imagine that it can have come into existence much before the end of the Amoraic period. The stratum of BT that quotes it must be late; and *Pesiqta*'s account of Moses' ascension, which seems to depend on the Talmudic passage, later still.

This argument seems to confirm the conclusion that we drew from the Sandalphon passage, that our haggadah draws on late elements of the Babylonian Talmud. But there is a new wrinkle here. BT's direct influence is evident only in *Pesiqta*, not in the parallel versions of ms Oxford and *Ma^cayan Ḥokhmah*. All three sources, and BT Shabb. 88b—89a, clearly

---

57 It is only fair, however, to add that some of the textual witnesses to Sukk. 5a have "Nahum" for "Tanhum" [819].

draw on the same fund of materials; which included, besides the speech on the Ten Commandments that Moses gives to the angels, expositions of Psalm 8 and of Job 26:9. *Pesiqta*'s parallels set forth this material in a way that more or less resembles BT's. But, unlike *Pesiqta,* they do not follow it so closely that we can argue for dependence rather than a common source.

Can we regard *Pesiqta* as a link in a chain of development between BT Shabb. 88b–89a, on the one hand, and the Oxford text and *Ma^c ayan Hokhmah,* on the other? If we do, we will suppose that the last two sources omit to quote R. Nahum/Tanhum because they have "digested" him and his midrash, assimilating what was once an intrusive element into the body of their narrative. (*Ma^c ayan Hokhmah* goes farther in this direction than ms Oxford; it does not even explicitly quote Job 26:9.) We will suppose, too, that *Pesiqta*'s author may have forgotten, and the authors of the parallels certainly have forgotten, the original point of having the angels recite Psalm 8. *Pesiqta* has them say, at the end of Moses' speech, the words *Lord our master, your name is very great in all the earth.* This could come from verse 2, or (as in BT) from verse 10. Both of the parallels, however, have the angels recite Psalm 8:2 in its entirety after their defeat – when, following BT's midrash, the words *so give your glory to heaven* would make no sense whatever. The upshot of this reasoning will be that, if BT's haggadah is late and *Pesiqta*'s is later, the Oxford text and *Ma^c ayan Hokhmah* are latest of all.

This hypothesis has its attractions. But its assumption, that the Oxford text and *Ma^c ayan Hokhmah* derive from *Pesiqta*'s version, does not do justice to the complicated relationships among the three sources (above, endnote *j*). Further, we do not have to resolve the differences between BT's use of Psalm 8 and that found in *Pesiqta* and its parallels by granting priority to the Talmud. Perhaps the earliest storytellers represented the angels as singing the whole psalm after they have lost the Torah to Moses, to express their stunned awe that God has so effectively *kept humans in mind, paid attention to men, crowned them with the glory and honor* of the Torah (verses 5–6, liberally rendered). They left it for later, more sophisticated expositors to play ingeniously with the difference in wording between the beginning of the psalm and its end.

I therefore lean to an alternative explanation, which we will see gather weight as we go on. *Pesiqta* and its parallels are not, by and large, late reworkings of Talmudic material. Rather, they represent an early ascension tradition from which the story in BT Shabb. 88b–89a itself branched off. They were written, as we now have them, after the BT materials had been edited in something like their present form. The authors therefore could embellish their traditions with some of BT's innovations – if they chose. Or, if they preferred, they could stay with an older, more traditional, form of the story. We need not assume that this older form must have been shorter and simpler than what we find in BT, or that it did not include the more striking details of our haggadah, such as Moses' encounter with Kemuel.

In the past few pages, we have found ourselves forced to consider a Talmudic version of the ascension story, side by side with *Pesiqta* and its immediate parallels. We must now widen our field of vision still more, to include two other accounts of Moses' debate with the angels. The first is an anonymous story preserved in the thirteenth-century Yemenite *Midrash ha-Gadol* (to Exodus 19:20; ed. 395–396 [198a]), which is closely parallel to BT's but diverges from it in so many minor details that I am loath to write it off as derivative. The second appears in chapter 46 of *Pirke de-Rabbi Eliezer.*

This last version differs from all the others, in that it puts the debate into the context of Moses' receiving the second set of tablets (Exodus 34) rather than the first. "Moses," the angels say, "it was for us that the Torah was intended." Moses refutes them by pointing to the fifth commandment (angels have no father or mother to honor), and to the Pentateuch's regulations concerning the impurity of corpses (angels do not die). We see here another distinction between *Pirqe de-Rabbi Eliezer* and the other versions: Moses does not restrict his arguments to the Ten Commandments. The writer has apparently been influenced by another cycle of *haggadot*, in which God himself — not Moses — persuades the angels that the Torah's prescriptions are for beings who are impure and mortal[58].

Pirqe de-Rabbi Eliezer, we recall, is a late midrash, certainly written after the rise of Islam. We do not know precisely what sources the author used, nor can we be sure how freely he may have reworked his source for any given passage. But we cannot rule out the possibility that he may preserve a trace of an independent variant.

In any case, we now have six parallel sources on the table before us, in place of our original three. We must take all of them into account when we consider the next episode of the story, the aftermath of Moses' victory.

e) "You took gifts for humanity." So far, we have reached the point in the narrative where the angels concede to Moses' arguments and abandon

---

58 Schäfer cites the following sources for this variant of the debate motif: *Pesiqta Rabbati* 25:3 (ed. 128a–b [209]); *Midr. Psalms* 8:2 (ed. 37b–38a [199]); *Song R.* to 8:11; Tanh. Buber *Be-Ḥuqqotay* #6 (ed. 56b [222]; = Tanh. *Be-Ḥuqqotay* #4). He also quotes and discusses many of the sources that directly concern us, in which Moses is the angels' opponent. So, less thoroughly, does Joseph P. Schultz [436,440].

their resistance to his taking the Torah. The Torah, however, is not all that he brings with him from heaven.

Not only, says *Pesiqta*, did the angels concede to Moses, "but the angel of death transmitted something to him. So it is written: *You ascended on high, you took a captivity captive, you took gifts for humanity* [Psalm 68: 19]." Numbers 17:11–13 represents Moses as telling Aaron how to use incense to stop a plague, so that Aaron *stood between the dead and the living.* If the angel of death had not taught him this trick, *Pesiqta* asks — shifting, for the first time, from Hebrew into Aramaic — "how would Moses have known what he had to do?"

As above, *Pesiqta's* version shows the influence of BT. According to Shabb. 89a, each of the angels "became his friend and transmitted something to him. So it is written: *You ascended on high, you took a captivity captive, you took gifts for humanity*; that is to say, *you took gifts* as a reward for their having called you *a human being.* Even the angel of death transmitted something to him." The Talmud alludes to Numbers 17:11– 13; then asks, in Aramaic: "If [the angel of death] had not told [Moses how to do this], how would he have known?" This last sentence is plainly the source of *Pesiqta's* Aramaic finale.

But, if *Pesiqta's* author follows BT, he does not go with it all the way. He seems to take Psalm 68:19's *laqahta mattanot ba'adam* in its simplest sense: Moses *took gifts,* namely secrets of healing, *for humanity.* BT had taken advantage of the ambiguity of *ba'adam* to construct an ingenious if rather forced midrash, the point of which was that the angels had contemptuously called Moses a mere *human being* (cf. Psalm 8:5), and now give him presents to make up for it[59]. But *Pesiqta's* author will have none of this refinement. He remains with the more straightforward exegesis shared by the parallel sources.

Take *Midrash ha-Gadol,* for example:

> When the angels saw that God had given [Moses] the Torah, they too revealed to him a multitude of secrets. So it is written: *You ascended on high, you took a captivity captive, you took gifts for humanity.* When the angel of death saw that all the angels were revealing secrets to him, he, too, revealed secrets. "When a plague breaks out," he said, "burn incense and it will stop." ... [Reference to Numbers 17:11–13.]

Or, *Pirqe de-Rabbi Eliezer:*

> When the angels saw that God had given Moses the Torah, they also gave him gifts: healing amulets for humans. So it is written: *You ascended on high, you took a captivity captive.*

---

59 I follow Rashi. – At the root of this interpretation is an understanding of *ba'adam* as "on account of a human being," which BT expands into "on account of *their calling you* a human being." Several midrashic sources preserve a variant interpretation, which takes *ba'adam* to mean "for the sake of a human being"; this human being may be identified with Abraham (PT Shabb.

The Oxford manuscript relates that each of the angels "became his friend. Each transmitted a secret of healing to him. Even the angel of death transmitted his secret to him." The writer alludes to Numbers 17:11—13, but does not quote Psalm 68:19.

In this last respect, the Oxford text stands alone. Even *Ma^cayan Hokhmah* — which, as we will see presently, goes off at this point in a highly individual direction of its own — quotes Psalm 68:19, and applies it to the secrets of healing that Moses received from the angels. The near-ubiquity of this verse, at a particularly crucial juncture of the ascension story, suggests that it may have played a particularly crucial role in the genesis of the tradition. To test our suggestion, we must look more closely at how the rabbis understood this obscure and tantalizing bit of Scripture.

More than a dozen other passages in the rabbinic literature quote Psalm 68:19 [294,804]. All assume that it refers to the Torah. Almost all either state or imply that the person addressed is Moses, while the "captivity" he takes is the Torah itself.

The use of the word "captivity" implies that Moses captured the Torah in battle; and several rabbinic passages make this point explicitly. *Ex. R.* 28:1 explains that *you ascended* means "you wrestled with the angels of heaven," and that "no creature ever exercised power in the celestial realms the way Moses did." *Ruth R.* 2:3 quotes an otherwise unknown "R. Menahem b. Abin" as identifying the name *Yashubi-lahem* (I Chronicles 4:22, Hebrew text) with Moses, "who ascended to heaven and took the Torah captive. So it is written, *You ascended on high, you took a captivity captive.*" The expositor plainly derives *Yashubi* from *shabah*, "to take captive," and connects *lahem* with the root meaning "to make war" (Einhorn [200]).

Sifre Deut. #49 (ed. 114—115 [220]), the only passage that applies Psalm 68:19 to the individual Jew rather than to Moses, nevertheless has as its background tales of Moses' martial feats. "If you adhere to the sages and their disciples, I will consider this as if you had ascended to heaven ... made war, and taken away [the Torah]. So it is written: *You ascended on high, you took a captivity captive.*"

Behind the modest hints of these midrashim we can detect tales, akin to those of *Pesiqta* and its parallels, of how Moses climbed to heaven and struggled with hostile angels over the Torah. We cannot assume that all of these stories were entirely consistent with each other. In one, for example, Moses seems to take away his "captivity" by stealth rather than by force:

16:1, 15c; *Ex. R.* 28:1), with the Israelites (*Pesiqta Rabbati* 47:4, ed. 191b [209]), or with those for whom the Torah's purity laws are intended (Tanh. *Ki Tissa'* #17).

R. Joshua b. Levi said: When Moses ascended on high, the angels tried to kill him. He said to them: "Do you really plan to kill me for the sake of two [paltry] objects that I was given in heaven?" They let him alone. ... [But in fact] he had a great gift with him. So it is written: *You ascended on high, you took a captivity captive, you took gifts for humanity.* [Tanh. Buber *Ha'azinu* #3, ed. 26a–b [222]; cf. Tanh. *Ha'azinu* #3] [439]

The story seems to contradict the haggadah which BT Shabb. 88b–89a attributes to Joshua b. Levi, as well as *Pesiqta* and its parallels. It assumes that the angels' hostility persists after Moses has received the Torah — or, more exactly, the two tablets of the Ten Commandments — and is returning to earth with them. Further, it understands the *gifts* of Psalm 68:19 as the Torah itself; not, as in the passages I quoted earlier, additional presents which the now friendly angels shower on Moses. The equation of *gifts* with Torah (which we also find in *Ex. R.* 28:1, 33:2, and *Midr. Psalms* 68:11, ed. 160a [199]) seems the more natural interpretation. I will later suggest that certain groups which took a particular interest in magical healing adapted the exegesis of the verse to suit their own concerns.

None of these variations, however, is crucial. *Pesiqta* and its parallels share with the other midrashim on Psalm 68:19 the essential themes of Moses' ascent, conflict with the angels, and final victory. This basic agreement suggests that this verse is not merely one more of the twenty or so Biblical texts that *Pesiqta* quotes, but is centrally important; is, in fact, one of the roots of the whole ascension tradition.

How did the expositors know in the first place that Moses had ascended to heaven; and not, as the ordinary reader of the Book of Exodus would imagine, to the top of Mount Sinai? BT Sukk. 5a invokes Exodus 19:3, *Moses ascended to God,* as evidence that Moses reached heaven [291]. But an interpreter can understand the verse in this way only if, dominated by a preconceived notion of what it must mean, he ignores its very next words: *the Lord called to him from the mountain.* The same is true of Exodus 24:18, with which *Pesiqta* and its parallels begin their story of the heavenly journey. The rabbis are clearly forcing a heavenly ascent into these verses rather than reading it out of them. We must ask if there is any Biblical text which will yield on its own, naturally and without compulsion, the belief that Moses went up to heaven.

There is. It is Psalm 68:19. This verse, to be sure, does not specify who the *you* is who *ascended on high.* But any ancient expositor would find this clear from its context:

[18]God's chariotry is two myriads, thousands of *shin'an*;
The Lord is among them [at?] Sinai in holiness.
[19]You ascended on high, you took a captivity captive,
You took gifts for humanity ...

Once verse 18 has set the scene at Sinai, the interpreter will have no difficulty identifying *you* as Moses, his *ascent on high* as the ascent described in Exodus 19:3. The *captivity* could be nothing other than what Moses brought back from his meeting with God; that is, the Torah, seized as spoils of war. The only ambiguous point is, as we have seen, the *gifts for humanity*.

But, as we have seen again and again, Psalm 68:18 is a highly important passage in its own right. A synagogue tradition, which perhaps goes back to pre-Christian Alexandria — and which, more to our purpose, was used by the author of the *Visions of Ezekiel* — used this verse to link the Torah reading and the *haftarah* for Shabu*c*ot, the Sinai revelation and the *merkabah* vision.

When we take verses 18 and 19 together, we find that this unit is doubly pivotal. It serves, on what we may conceive as the horizontal plane, as a clasp holding Exodus 19–20 and Ezekiel 1 together. Vertically, it is the seed from which the ascension narrative shoots upward. This is why *Pesiqta* and its parallels, BT Shabb. 88b–89a, and Tanh. and Tanh. Buber *Ha'azinu* #3, all begin with the words "when Moses ascended on high" (*besha*c*ah she*c*alah mosheh lammarom*). They are imitating the language of their common source, Psalm 68:19's *you ascended on high* (*c*alita lammarom*).

This is not to say that we can fully understand the ascension stories on the basis of Psalm 68:18–19 alone. The detail of Moses' riding the cloud, to give only one example, remains somewhat obscure; and we will need light from another direction to make it entirely clear. But I think that these two verses give us our most important clue to the problem of how the concept of Moses' ascent, and of heavenly ascension in general, developed in connection with Ezekiel's *merkabah* and in the framework of the Shabu*c*ot cycle. In what follows, we must return to them again and again.

f) The story concluded. In the meantime, let us see Moses' adventure to its end.

As I have said, *Ma*c*ayan Hokhmah* goes its own way after it has reported the angels' concession. Here is how it finishes the story:

> God taught [Moses] the whole Torah in forty days. He was about to descend, when he saw the full terror of the angels, the troops of terrifying, dreadful, horrifying angels. Trembling seized him, and he forgot [the Torah] all at once.
> So God summoned Yephephiah the prince of Torah, and he transmitted the Torah to him in perfect order, so that he could keep it in his memory[60]. The angels all became his friends, and each of them transmitted to him a method of healing and a secret of the [magical] names that can be constructed from each section of Scripture, [with] all their uses. So Scripture says: *You ascended on high, you took a captivity captive, you took gifts for humanity.*

---

60 So I understand *c*arukhah bakkol ushemurah*; literally, "ordered in all respects and preserved." In chapter IX, we will look more closely at the concern that underlies this passage: how the individual is to remember the Torah that he has learned.

Even the angel of death transmitted something to him. So it is written ... [allusion to Numbers 17: 11–13].

This is the august [magical] usage which the angels transmitted to him through Yephephiah prince of the Torah, and through Metatron prince of the presence. Moses transmitted it to Eleazar [the son of Aaron], and Eleazar to his son Phinehas, who is Elijah the great high priest of blessed memory. Amen.

We must postpone to chapter IX all discussion of the significance of this strange story, and the importance of the new characters, Yephephiah and Metatron, whom it introduces.

Pesiqta and the Oxford text have no trace of this ending. Indeed, they do not properly end the story of Moses' ascent at all. They break off right after describing the angels' gifts, and jump straight into a new episode which does not seem to follow from what precedes. The seven heavens, of which we have so far heard no hint, are suddenly introduced; and God opens them to Moses, as if Moses were not himself in heaven.

[A] Thereupon God opened seven firmaments and showed him the heavenly temple. He also showed him the four colors from which he [God? Moses?] made the tabernacle. So it is written: *You must set up the tabernacle [according to its plan, which you were shown on the mountain;* Exodus 26:30].

[B] "Master of the world," he said to him, "I do not know what the four colors look like[61]." ... [God solves this problem by showing Moses four bands of angels wearing clothing of different colors, which God then identifies with the four colors of Exodus 26:31].

[C] Thereupon God opened the doors of the seven firmaments and revealed himself to the Israelites' sight, in his beauty and glory and splendor, his crown and the appearance of his glory[62].

[D] When they heard, *I am the Lord your God* [Exodus 20:2], their souls left them. God sent down the dew with which he is going to bring the souls of the saints to life, and brought them back to life. So it is written: *You shed gracious rain, O God. When your heritage was exhausted, you restored it* [Psalm 68:10][63].

[E] What did God do? He sent twelve hundred thousand ministering angels down to earth to them. Two angels laid hold of each Israelite: one put his hand over his heart so that his soul would not leave him, while the other lifted up his neck so that he could see God face to face.

[F] Why did he reveal himself to them face to face? He said to them: "See that I have revealed myself to you in my glory and my splendor. Should there be a generation that leads you astray and says, 'Let us go worship other gods,' then say to them: 'We have a Lord whom we

---

61 Braude translates, "I do not know the earthly counterparts of these four colors," obviously in order to avoid contradicting section A. This translation, and Grözinger's defense of it [295], seem to me strained. I prefer to leave the contradiction, as one of several indications that the author is pasting scraps of material to the end of his narrative without integrating them.

62 The printed edition and ms Oxford omit "the doors of," so that section C begins exactly as does A. This is perhaps the older tradition. – The printed text (which Braude translates) has "stature" for "splendor," "throne" for "appearance." Ms Oxford speaks only of God's "beauty and his glory and his crown."

63 The Oxford manuscript apparently ends its quotation of this narrative with the first sentence of section D, to which it adds, "and so forth." Grözinger's transcription, at any rate, stops at this point. The copyist perhaps felt that the following material so closely resembled BT's Sinai *haggadot* (see below) that there was no need to transcribe it. – The printed edition omits the reference to the dew of resurrection, obviously as a result of scribal error (the copyist's eye jumped from *nishmatan* to *nishmatan*). So, therefore, does Braude.

serve. When we abandon him, he sends us down to hell. And God will establish his kingdom over all Israel.' "

With this loosely connected string of *haggadot*, homily 20 of *Pesiqta Rabbati* comes to an end.

3. The sources of the ascension story

a) Introduction. It is obvious that the ascension stories in *Pesiqta* and its parallels are both late and composite. We have seen convincing evidence for their lateness in the fact that all seem to draw, in a greater or lesser measure, from the Babylonian Talmud. As for their being composite, the series of items that *Pesiqta* and the Oxford text try to make into a conclusion for the narrative do not hang together with what precedes them, or with each other.

In section A, the author seems to have forgotten that Moses is already in heaven. In section B, Moses complains that he does not know what the four colors of the tabernacle look like, even though he has been shown them in section A [366]. Section D, in which it is God's word rather than his appearance that takes the Israelites' souls away, fits badly with the surrounding material [296]. Most awkward of all, the author suddenly abandons Moses after section B; and it is the whole Israelite people who see the seven heavens opened.

But, as we have seen, we do not have to suppose that *Pesiqta* and its parallels offer nothing more than late combinations and expansions of material that was at hand in the Talmud and perhaps other rabbinic sources. We must also reckon with the possibility that, for all their late "improvements" of the story (that is, details drawn from BT), they basically represent an early ascension tradition which itself underlies BT's materials. If so, we may be prepared to imagine a primitive unity of some kind underlying the multiplicity of *Pesiqta*'s narrative. This unity will perhaps explain why the author has tried to put together a conclusion from a set of *haggadot* that harmonize so badly with each other.

The job that lies before us is to raise this possibility to something more than conjecture, and to trace the shape of the underlying unity.

Let us take Karl-Erich Grözinger's analysis as our starting point.

b) Grözinger sees the main account of Moses' ascent and struggle with the angels — that is, the story that precedes *Pesiqta*'s concluding *haggadot* (which I have designated sections A–F) and the alternative ending of *Ma^cayan Ḥokhmah* — as a combination of two originally independent sources. The first of these is a "midrash of R. Joshua b. Levi," preserved for us in BT Shabb. 88b–89a (above, section 2d–e). The second is an "apocalypse of Moses," which described Moses' ascent through seven (or, in a different version, three) heavens. The original climax of the "apocalypse" was not a debate with angels or the capture of the Torah, but a vision of God enthroned. Almost all surviving versions of the story, however, have replaced the original ending of the "apocalypse" with material drawn from the "midrash" [290].

Grözinger defines fairly precisely which parts of our haggadah are from each of the two sources. The opening words, "when Moses ascended on high ...," are from the "midrash." So is the Oxford text's opening attribution to Joshua b. Levi, which is exactly the same as the beginning of the story of BT Shabb. 88b–89a. The haggadah then turns to the "apocalypse" for the details of Moses' ascent, returning to the "midrash" only when God gives Moses the protection of his throne and tells him to answer the angels. The rest of the story, through the episode of the angels' gifts, is from the "midrash."

How shall we judge Grözinger's proposal? One feature of it, his reconstruction of the "apocalypse of Moses," seems to me very doubtful. *Pesiqta* and its parallels know nothing, as far as I can see, of any ascent through a series of heavens, three or seven. The sources that assign each of *Pesiqta*'s angels to a different heaven, like the haggadic fragments quoted in *Maḥzor Vitry* [297], are probably trying to harmonize *Pesiqta* or some similar text with the familiar Talmudic sequence of seven heavens (BT Ḥag. 12b). I am therefore suspicious when Grözinger claims that one of the *Vitry* fragments, and it alone, preserves some trace of the original end of the "apocalypse": "Moses went from heaven to heaven until he came to the seventh heaven and saw the Lord sitting on a high and exalted throne."

None of this proves that an "apocalypse of Moses," without the seven heavens, cannot have existed. It would be dogmatic to deny that the original ending of the "apocalypse" might have been lost, and that the passage quoted in *Maḥzor Vitry* might have either preserved or re-created it. But there is another problem, namely that I do not understand the motivation of any of the characters in Grözinger's "apocalypse." Why should Moses, who after all had enough contact with God on earth, be willing to undergo harrowing dangers in order to see him enthroned in heaven? Why should the angels want to stop him? It is true that we find a similar theme, of angels resisting the efforts of humans to travel to heaven and see "the king and his throne," in the *Hekhalot* literature. The "water test" (above, chapter VI) is a classic example. But this does not help us very much, since the motives of the opposing parties are no clearer in the *Hekhalot* than they are in the "apocalypse." Only when we take *Pesiqta*'s narrative as a whole do we understand why Moses and the angels are fighting. They have something that he wants very much, and they do not want him to get it away from them[64].

Even if I have shown, however, that the "apocalypse of Moses" never existed as an independent source, this does not rule out a second possibility. The author of *Pesiqta*'s haggadah may have taken BT Shabb. 88b—89a as his starting point; but, not finding it exciting enough, "improved" it with lurid details whose mental atmosphere is that of the *Hekhalot*. This hypothesis will prove a good deal harder to refute. It is a point against it that, as we have seen, ms Oxford and *Ma*ayan Hokhmah* do not share *Pesiqta*'s clear dependence on BT, in the passages that describe the action before and after Moses' speech. But this does not prove that they did not use either BT or *Pesiqta* itself, although it is rather hard to see why they would have changed their source's language as they did.

c) *The midrash of Joshua b. Levi.* We can get some perspective on this issue, if we recall that there is more than one "midrash of R. Joshua b. Levi" that bears on our problem. In BT Shabb. 88a—89b, we find a long string of *haggadot* on the Sinai event, of which no fewer than eight in a row (accounting for about half of the contents of the Sinai section) are attributed to Joshua b. Levi. Of these eight, the first two are of no concern to us. But, with the third, we find ourselves on familiar ground.

[3] R. Joshua b. Levi said: At each of God's utterances, the Israelites' souls left them; as it is written, *My soul left me when he spoke* [Song 5:6]. But, if their souls left them at the first word, how were they able to receive the second? [God] sent down the dew with which he is going to resurrect the dead, and he brought them back to life. So it is written: *You shed gracious rain, O God. When your heritage was exhausted, you restored it* [Psalm 68:10].

[4] R. Joshua b. Levi said: At each of God's utterances, the Israelites retreated twelve miles. The angels helped them walk back. So it is written: *The angels of the hosts*[65] *wander, they wander* [Psalm 68:13]. Do not read *yiddodun*, "they wander," but *yedaddun*, "they help them to walk." [Shabb. 88b]

The fifth of these "Joshua b. Levi" *haggadot* is the account of how Moses debated the angels and received their gifts, which we have earlier discussed. Of the last three, only the opening sentences concern us: "when Moses ascended on high ..." (nos. 6, 8); "when Moses descended from God's presence ..." (no. 7).

It is clear enough that the author of *Pesiqta*'s ascension narrative is using "Joshua b. Levi" material both in the main account of the ascent and in his concluding *haggadot*. It is not so clear that he is drawing this material from the Talmud. Section D of *Pesiqta*'s conclusion is indeed very similar to the

---

64 As we will see in chapter IX, this observation sets us on our way to solving the problem of the conflict in the *Hekhalot*.

65 The Masoretic Text has here *malkhe ṣeba'ot*, "the kings of the armies" (so RSV). But the expositor reads the first word as if it were *mal'akhe*, the "angels" who attend the "hosts" of Israel (below). I will presently suggest that the author of the *Visions of Ezekiel* alludes to this verse when he gives one of his *merkabah*s the name *Melakhim*, "kings."

third of the *haggadot* in Shabb. 88b. But the relation of section E to the
fourth Talmudic haggadah is more complex. The two share the basic theme
that angels encouraged the Israelites and helped them to bear the force of
the revelation. But *Pesiqta* expresses this idea with details — the twelve
hundred thousand angels, their way of physically supporting each Israelite
— which the "Joshua b. Levi" passage may well presuppose, but does not
explicitly state.

To find these details set forth in black and white, we must turn to other
rabbinic sources:

> R. Simai expounded: When the Israelites said *we will do* before they said *we will hear* [Exodus
> 24:7], there came to them six hundred thousand angels, one for each Israelite. They made for
> them two wreaths [apiece], one for *we will do* and one for *we will hear*. But when the Israelites
> sinned [with the calf], twelve hundred thousand angels of destruction came down and took them
> away. So it is written, *The children of Israel were stripped of their ornaments from Mount Horeb*
> [Exodus 33:6]. [BT Shabb. 88a]

> *They stood at a distance* [Exodus 20:15], of more than twelve miles. This teaches that the
> Israelites recoiled twelve miles [at hearing each of the Ten Commandments] and then had to
> walk back twelve miles ... with the result that they walked two hundred and forty miles on that
> one day. God said to the angels: "Go down and help your brothers." So it is written: *The angels
> of the hosts help them to walk, they help them to walk* [Psalm 68:13] — *they helped them*
> going, *they helped them* coming back. Not only did the angels [help them], God did too. So it is
> written: *His left hand is under my head, his right hand embraces me* [Song 2:6]. [*Mekhilta, Ba-
> Hodesh* chapter 9, ed./tr. 2:269–270 [195]]

It requires some strain to imagine that *Pesiqta*'s author has pieced his
section E together from these several passages. The strain is relieved if we
suppose that he has drawn it from a tradition cognate to all of them. The
sources related to this tradition are, as we have seen, an anonymous passage
in the third-century *Mekhilta*; an utterance attributed to the early third-
century R. Simai; and another utterance attributed to Simai's younger contemporary Joshua b. Levi. It seems likely that *Pesiqta*'s source, too, goes
back to early third-century Palestine.

Joshua b. Levi's name has begun to crop up rather frequently. Apart from
the *haggadot* quoted in BT Shabb. 88b–89a (and, of course, the beginning
of the Oxford text), we have seen that *Tanḥuma* attributes to Joshua b.
Levi a midrash which applies Psalm 68:19 to Moses' hazardous adventures
in heaven (above, section 2e). PT Shabb. 16:1 (15c) again connects this
scholar to this verse. Joshua b. Levi claims to have learned from a "hag-
gadah-book" that one hundred and seventy-five sections of the Torah begin
with God "saying" or "commanding" something, and that this number corresponds to the years of Abraham's life. "So it is written, *You took gifts
corresponding to a human being* [Psalm 68:19][66]; and [this *human being*

---

66 This is a thinkable, but excessively strained, way of understanding the word *ba'adam* (cf. above,
    section 2e). – *Midr. Psalms* 22:19 (ed. 95a–b [199]) and *Soferim* 16:10 draw on the PT passage.

must be Abraham, for] it is written, *The human being* [understood as Abraham] *who was great among the Anakim* [Joshua 14:15]."

Obviously, if the attributions in the two Talmuds and *Tanḥuma* are all accurate, Joshua b. Levi must have changed his mind more than once about the meaning of the words *you took gifts for humanity*. But all of these passages agree that Joshua b. Levi was concerned with the exegesis of Psalm 68:19, which we have seen to be the single most important Scriptural basis for the story of Moses' ascension.

Abraham Weiss, discussing the pre-existent collections incorporated into the Babylonian Talmud, has suggested that the "Joshua b. Levi" *haggadot* in BT Shabb. 88b–89a once constituted an independent source [353]. This seems plausible enough. Yet it is worth trying to imagine what this source might have looked like or what situations it could have been employed in. As a literary text, as a sermon, or even as a lecture to students, it seems too truncated and disconnected within itself to be of much value.

But now let us suppose that it is itself part of a larger whole, which included also the expositions of Psalm 68:19 that PT and *Tanḥuma* attribute to Joshua b. Levi. Let us also suppose that this greater entity corresponds to the ascension tradition that we have tentatively imagined to underlie *Pesiqta* and its parallels; and that Joshua b. Levi was in fact its author. Let us suppose, in other words, that the author of the Oxford text does not merely quote verbatim from BT Shabb. 88b when he attributes the ascension story of Joshua b. Levi (as Grözinger thinks [200]), but is transmitting accurate information about its origin.

What kind of entity can this have been? The several different interpretations of *you took gifts for humanity*, to say nothing of the contradiction between *Tanḥuma* and BT Shabb. 89a over whether the angels stay hostile to Moses after he has received the Torah, rule out a single speech or a single treatise[67]. But we can explain those inconsistencies if we suppose that Joshua b. Levi delivered, over a more or less extended period of time, a number of sermons on the theme of Moses' heavenly ascension, within the context of the Sinai revelation. The details changed from time to time, but the essential point stayed the same. Moses braved the terror of the angels in order to take Torah from heaven with his own hands. The angels, violently hostile at first, became supporters and benefactors of Moses and the whole Israelite people.

The most likely occasion for these sermons, we may well suppose, was Shabuᶜot. When we come to examine the detail of the opening of the seven heavens, we will see this supposition confirmed.

---

67 The context of the passage in PT Shabb. 16:1 seems to argue against the possibility of a treatise, in that it suggests rather strongly that Joshua b. Levi did not care much for the practice of writing down haggadah.

d) Conclusion. How are we to conceive the relation between the cycle of Shabu^c^ot sermons that I have hypothesized, on the one hand; and the versions of the ascension story in *Pesiqta* and its parallels, on the other?

I find myself imagining a series of twentieth-century reconstructions of an antique building of some very stylized type — a Roman amphitheatre, perhaps, or a Gothic cathedral. The original buildings have been destroyed, let us say, with only some fragments remaining (corresponding to the utterances attributed to Joshua b. Levi in BT Shabb. 88b–89a). Some of these surviving fragments have since been decorated in a relatively modern style (as BT decorates its account of Moses' seizing the throne with a citation of "R. Tanhum").

The twentieth-century architects who design the reconstructions have a generally good idea of what the structure is to look like and how its parts are to fit together. They sometimes commit anachronisms, such as copying the modern features that have been added to some of the fragments. (The analogue to this is *Pesiqta*'s use of the "Tanhum"/"Nahum" quotation.) They sometimes are not sure exactly how to arrange the truly antique features that they know ought to be part of the structure, and incoherence results. (This time, the analogue is the confusion that we have seen in *Pesiqta*'s concluding materials.) But, by and large, they produce reasonably authentic replications of the ancient structure. Their constructions are modern, as examination of the building materials will show. Yet in another sense they are ancient; and this sense will be the more important one to future historians who otherwise have no way of knowing what an amphitheatre or a cathedral looked like. This is why I said that it is true and yet misleading to speak of *Pesiqta* and its parallels as late reworkings of Talmudic sources.

The fact that I can find an analogy to make my hypothesis more graphic is, of course, no proof that it is true. The reader may reasonably judge that it is still trapped at the level of conjecture. I have argued so far that we cannot sustain Grözinger's division of the ascension story into two originally independent sources; that the assumption that the story depends essentially on BT's "Joshua b. Levi" materials is also flawed; and that the story's relation to these materials best makes sense if we suppose it replicates more or less faithfully what Joshua b. Levi preached on various Shabu^c^ot festivals early in the third century. But the advantages of this model are not so dramatic that we can dispense with what would be the most important evidence in its favor: attestation of sermons of this sort from the third century itself.

I will provide this evidence in section C. In the meantime, I must continue to ask the reader for patience while I develop the argument in a fresh direction, which will lead us back to where we stood at the end of section A. The Sinai-ascension *haggadot* represented in *Pesiqta* and its parallels, I now suggest, are one wing of a duplex structure. The other wing is represented by the *Visions of Ezekiel.*

4. The ascension story and the "Visions of Ezekiel"

a) The heavens opened. The most evident link between the two parts of the structure is *Pesiqta*'s detail that God opened the seven heavens – to Moses at one point, to all the Israelites at another.

BT's "Joshua b. Levi" *haggadot* have no parallel to this detail. We do, however, find something very similar in one *Tanḥuma* text, a recension of *Deuteronomy Rabbah* published by Saul Lieberman:

> On the day the Torah was given, God tore open (*qara^c*) the heavens and showed the Israelites everything that was above.
>
> R. Phinehas quoted R. Levi, quoting R. Simeon b. Laqish[68]: God tore open seven firmaments for them. Just as he tore open the upper realms, so he tore open the lower ones. So it is written: [*You shall not make ... a likeness of anything*] *that is in the heaven above or the earth beneath* [Exodus 20:4].
>
> He said to them: "See that there is none beside me!" So it is written: *You were shown that you might know* [*that the Lord is God, there is none beside him*; Deuteronomy 4:35]. *You must know today,* and so forth [*and keep in your mind that the Lord is God in heaven above and on earth beneath, there is no other*; 4:39].
>
> "If you want to choose a god for yourselves, [God continued,] just as all the nations have chosen from the angels who serve me by the thousands, go ahead and choose from them!" They said to him: "*It is you, out of all the myriads, who are holy* [Deuteronomy 33:2][69]. You are our God, you are our portion, you are holy." [*Deut. R.* Lieberman, ed. 65–66 [186]]

This passage explains the purpose of the opening of the seven heavens much as does *Pesiqta*. The Israelites choose God in full knowledge of his unique greatness, and therefore will not be seduced away from him. But the author here allows them to see a great deal more than they do in *Pesiqta*. God's challenge implies that they have seen not only himself, but all the angels as well. We are told explicitly that they have seen what is in the lower realms as well as what is in the upper.

What Scriptural evidence is there that the seven heavens were opened at Sinai? *Pesiqta* offers none. *Deuteronomy Rabbah* quotes only Exodus 20:4 and two verses from Deuteronomy 4, which indeed fit in well with this notion but which, by themselves, are hardly enough to support it.

---

68 This Palestinian scholar lived a generation after Joshua b. Levi. It is possible to emend the manuscript's abbreviation *bšršbl* ("in the name of R. Simeon b. Laqish") to *bšrybl* ("in the name of R. Joshua b. Levi"). But this alteration has no support other than that it fits my hypothesis, and it is open to a serious objection: there is apparently no other case of Levi's transmitting an utterance of Joshua b. Levi, who lived two generations earlier [797].

69 RSV: "he came from the ten thousands of holy ones." The midrash reads *we'atah*, "he came," as if it were *we'attah*, "you"; and treats "holy" as a clause separate from "myriads."

The source for the idea must have been Ezekiel 1:1 (*the heavens were opened*), which was understood as it is in the *Visions of Ezekiel*, but transferred from the *merkabah* vision to Sinai. The Sinai texts then repaid their debt to the *merkabah* by suggesting (Exodus 20:4, Deuteronomy 4:39) that *the earth beneath* is parallel to *the heaven above*. It follows that, just as the seven *heavens above* were opened to Ezekiel, so were the seven *earths beneath*. That is why the *Visions* has Ezekiel see the subterranean realms as well as the heavens, and why *Deuteronomy Rabbah* has the Israelites see both.

The parallel between the two revelations extends to their details. The Israelites see throngs of angels (*Deut. R.*); Moses sees the heavenly temple (*Pesiqta*). All are part of the seven heavens of the *Visions* (IIC1, D1, F1). *Pesiqta*'s language, "God opened seven firmaments" (section A), is very close to that of the *Visions*.

But it is a long way from Sinai to Chebar, and we must explain what led the expositors to shift details back and forth between the two revelations. These transfers must have taken place inside a framework which brought the two episodes together, so that is was an easy step from one to the other rather than a drastic leap. The obvious candidate for such a framework is Shabu^c ot. The synagogue interpretation of the *haftarah*, which the *Visions* preserves for us, naturally had its impact on the synagogue interpretation of the Torah reading; and the other way round.

This link encourages us to look for other connections between the "Sinai" and the "*merkabah*" parts of the homiletic structure. Lieberman's *Deuteronomy Rabbah* contains a second passage which may help us.

Expounding Deuteronomy 34:1−4, the midrash elaborates the vision of the promised land which God showed Moses before his death. It is true that Moses sees this vision, not at Mount Sinai, but at Mount Nebo forty years afterward. But some of its details resemble those of the *Visions of Ezekiel*; they may possibly have first become attached to Moses through the Sinai-*merkabah* link, and then transferred from one of Moses' revelations to another.

> God sharpened Moses' eye so that he could see all the boundaries of the land of Israel, the Temple Mount first of all. ... He saw the First and the Second Temples. ... [God] showed him the twelve territories [of the tribes], just as Ezekiel saw twelve jewels in paradise; as it is written, *You were in Eden the garden of God*, and so forth [Ezekiel 28:13]. He showed him *Neshiyyah* and *Tahtit*, ^c *Efatah* and *Tit ha-Yawen*, *She'ol* and *'Abaddon* and *Be'er Shahat*[70]. He showed him Behemoth and Leviathan and the dragon [Isaiah 27:1], and the couches of the righteous in paradise. He showed him *heaven and the heaven of heavens* [*shamayim usheme hashshamayim*,

---

70 Of these seven names for the infernal regions, all but two appear in the *Visions* or the Targumic Tosefta to Ezekiel 1:1, or both.

Deuteronomy 10:14]. He showed him the paths taken by the rivers of fire and by the *hayyot*. He showed him pits and ditches and caves, seas and rivers and springs. ... He showed him the great sea and the ultimate sea[71]. He showed him the righteous who will rise even before the resurrection. He showed him the torments of the wicked in hell.

So it is written: *The Lord said to him: "This is the land* [*that I swore to Abraham, Isaac and Jacob: 'To your offspring will I give it'"* Deuteronomy 34:4]. "When you go to your ancestors," he said to him, "tell them that I did not lie to them. ... In this world, I have given you one land. But, in the future [world], I will give each tribe a land of its own." So Ezekiel sees, and specifies[72] for each tribe: *One for Dan* [...] *one for Asher* [...] *one for Naphtali*, and so forth [Ezekiel 48:1–3]. [*Deut. R.* Lieberman, ed. 51–52 [186]]

Here and in the *Visions,* the prophet sees the temple, the seven infernal realms, and a series of heavens. (*Deut. R.* mentions only two heavens; but these correspond to the first two of the *Visions.* See Appendix IV, section 4.) Like Ezekiel (*Visions*, IE−F), Moses sees "seas and rivers." He also sees "the paths taken by the rivers of fire and by the *hayyot*," a detail which suggests the description of the heavenly realms in the *Hekhalot*.

It is perhaps significant that the *Deut. R.* passage twice compares what Moses sees to Ezekiel's visions − although, admittedly, these are not visions of the *merkabah*.

b) Prophet and people. In one passage from Lieberman's *Deuteronomy Rabbah*, then, the visionary who corresponds to Ezekiel is Moses himself. In the other, it is the entire Israelite people at Sinai. We saw the same variation, in a much shorter space, in *Pesiqta*'s concluding *haggadot*: the seven heavens are at one point opened to Moses, at another to all Israel.

This idea of dual revelation, to the prophet and to his people, follows naturally enough from the Bible's account of the Sinai revelation, where God reveals himself both to Moses and to the Israelites. What is important for us here is that the same idea may underlie the charge God gives Ezekiel in a crucial passage of the *Visions*: "I am showing you my *merkabah* on condition that you describe it in full to the Israelites ... expound[ing] them to an individual in such a way that his eye is able to see and his ear able to hear." The reference to the eye seeing, which seemed at first so incongruous (above, section A3c), now begins to make sense. Through Ezekiel's expositions, the people are to "see," vicariously, the wonders of the opened heavens. "Ezekiel," as we have seen, stands here for the contemporary preacher. We may assume that the preacher's audience is to have the vicarious experience implied in the *Visions*.

---

71 In the Bible, *hayyam haggadol* and *hayyam ha'aharon* (Deuteronomy 34:2) are two names for the Mediterranean. Lieberman, basing himself on the context and on the exegesis of Deuteronomy 34:2 in *Sifre Deut.* #357 (ed. 426 [220]), emends *yam* ("sea") to *yom* ("day"). The emendation is plausible enough. Yet the fact that Ezekiel also sees "the primordial waters that are bound up in the great sea" (*Visions*, section IE) makes me hesitate to adopt it.

72 *Mefaresh*; the same verb that I translated "describe in full" in *Visions*, section IJ.

What were the people to gain from this experience? We have already broached this question in section A (5c), and tried to answer it on the basis of the *Visions* and of passages from *Hekhalot Rabbati*. We concluded, briefly, that they were to be assured of God's immense power and grandeur, and at the same time of his abiding love for them. We now can confirm and supplement this deduction, from the accounts of the opened heavens in *Pesiqta* and *Deut. R*. God here shows himself and his heavens to the Israelites, so that they may choose him above all possible competitors, and know ever after that they have made the right choice. "Should there be a generation that leads you astray and says, 'Let us go and worship other gods,' then say to them: 'We have a Lord whom we serve. When we abandon him, he sends us down to hell. And God will establish his kingdom over all Israel'" (*Pesiqta*).

The last sentence is reminiscent of the eschatological reference near the end of the *Visions,* to the "great *merkabah* in which God will descend to judge all the nations" (IIJ2), as he descended in his *merkabah* to Sinai (IIE2). But *Pesiqta* adds an element of religious polemic that we do not find in the *Visions*: someone is trying to discredit Judaism and tempt Jews away. The Targumic Tosefta to Ezekiel 1:1 also introduces religious conflict. Only here it is sharper, the enemy more powerful and more arrogant. In contrast to the Talmudic haggadah on which it is based (Hag. 13a), which gives no motivation for Nebuchadnezzar's plan to invade heaven, the Targumic Tosefta explains that he is "filled with pride in his idolatry." Having destroyed the earthly Jerusalem and its temple, he will go on to "climb to the lofty heavens and destroy the celestial chambers." We must explore the significance of this polemic, and of its sharpening in the Targumic Tosefta, when we discuss the historical context of the Shabu^cot sermons in the next section.

c) Psalm 68. I have already stressed that Psalm 68:18–19 is central to the Sinai-ascension *haggadot*, both as the germ of the ascension story and as its link with the *merkabah*. Some of this passage's importance seems to have spilled over to other parts of the psalm.

Thus, BT Shabb. 88b–89a represents Joshua b. Levi as quoting 68:10 and 13 as well as 19 (above, section 3c); and Shabb. 88b quotes 68:12 in a haggadah on God's speech at Sinai, which is attributed to the third-century R. Johanan. The notion that the number of angels is either equal to or double that of the Israelites (*Pesiqta*; R. Simai in BT Shabb. 88a) may contain a hidden allusion to exegetical traditions surrounding Psalm 68:18, which compare the heavenly *myriads* and *thousands* to the *myriads and thousands of Israel* (Numbers 10:36)[73].

---

73 *Sifre Numbers* #84 (ed. 83–84 [221]): "The Shechinah dwells in the upper realms only among

Psalm 68 also seems to have been a favorite of the author of the *Visions*. He quotes verses 18 (IIE2), 34 (IID3), and 35 (IIF1). I suggest, in Appendix IV, that the entire passage 68:33–36 was once the proof text for the *merkabah* of *Melakhim* ("kings"). I now propose that the name *Melakhim* has a double reference. It indeed points to the "kingdoms" (*mamlekhot*) of Psalm 68:33, as I argue in the appendix. But it also refers to the *malkhe ṣeba'ot*, "kings of the armies" (RSV), of 68:13. We have seen that BT Shabb. 88b and *Mekhilta* understand this phrase as if it were *mal'akhe ṣeba'ot*, "the angels of the hosts," who stand by the Israelites during the Sinai revelation. The *Visions* presupposes this exegesis.

The Sinai midrashim and the *Visions* thus share a concern with the psalm used by synagogue expositors to connect Sinai with the *merkabah*. Once again, echoes from one part of the homiletic structure are audible in the other.

5. Haggadat Shema^c Yiśra'el: "you saw with the understanding of your heart"

I spoke, a few pages back, of the synagogue audience's vicarious experience of God's revelation. A brief text published by Jellinek [484], under the title *Haggadat Shema^c Yiśra'el*, helps us understand what this experience involved.

> *Hear, O Israel* [*shema^c yiśra'el*], *the Lord is our God, the Lord is one* [Deuteronomy 6:4]. Moses said to the Israelites: "Hear, O Israel, all the nation! I ascended on high and saw all the celestial princes. I saw Kemuel the gate-keeper, the angel in command of twelve thousand angels of destruction who stand at the gate of heaven. ..."

Moses proceeds to describe his meetings with Hadarniel, Sandalphon, and the rest, in a narrative that seems to be based entirely on *Ma^cayan Ḥokhmah*[74]. But the story breaks off before Moses' address to the angels, with the remark that it was the fear of God that kept "the angels of terror who surround the throne of glory" from hurting Moses. The narrator then draws his conclusion:

---

thousands and myriads; as it is written, *God's chariotry is two myriads, thousands of shin'an* [Psalm 68:18]. Similarly ... the Shechinah dwells in the lower realms only among thousands and myriads ... *Return, Lord, to the myriads and thousands of Israel* [Numbers 10:36]." *Genesis Rabbah* at one point identifies Jacob's *camp of God* (Genesis 32:1–2) with the *chariotry* of Psalm 68:18, and at another calculates the number of angels in the *camp* by analogy with the Israelites at Sinai (74:17, 75:10; ed. 876–877, 888–889 [188]). It does not, however, take the final step of comparing the *chariotry* to the Israelites. Cf. chapter IV, section 5d.

74 Grözinger calls attention to some of the evidence for this dependency, but he does not seem to be willing to follow its implications. He translates the entire text, except for its conclusion (which I translate below), into German [290].

You too saw, with the understanding of your heart and your mind and your soul [*bebinat lebabekhem weśikhlekhem wenishmatekhem*] how [God] revealed himself at the sea, how he bent the upper heavens and descended in his glory on Mount Sinai, with a *chariotry of myriads, thousands of shin'an* [Psalm 68:18]. You saw how the whole host of heaven was frightened of his holy word, how *the earth trembled* before him, *the heavens dripped* [water] [Psalm 68:9], and *the mountains danced* [Psalm 114:6]. All human beings were astonished and terrified of him, all animals and birds silently trembled for fear of him. The sea was split, the earth trembled, the sun and the moon stood still.

Therefore, Israel, holy nation all, you must hear and understand and know that *the Lord is our God*, by whose name we are called, in unity; *the Lord is one*. He has no second; there is nothing like him or any partner for him — not in heaven and not on earth and not in the abyss, not in this world or in the next.

The first sentence seems incongruous. After all, the Israelites saw the great theophanies with their own eyes, not "the understanding of your heart and your mind and your soul." We can only explain this reference if we suppose that the speaker here steps out of his assumed role and betrays his own identity.

He is a preacher. He relates the wonders and terrors of the heavens as if he, in the role of Moses, had seen them with his own eyes. His intent is that his hearers also see them as if with their own eyes, and know what it means to be the chosen people of the one God. He is thus a partner to the preachers who stand behind the figure of Ezekiel in the *Visions*, and to "those who descend to the *merkabah*" who speak in *Hekhalot Rabbati*.

With *Haggadat Shema^c Yiśra'el*, the phenomenon of the speaker who takes on the role of witness, and makes his audience witnesses with him, becomes a thread tying together the Sinai-ascension tradition, the *Visions of Ezekiel*, and the *Hekhalot*.

A passage in the Gemara to BT Meg. 24b tightens the knot. The Gemara is commenting on M. Meg. 4:6: "R. Judah says: Anyone who has never seen the luminaries should not *pores 'et shema^c*." To this end, the Gemara quotes the Babylonian version of the baraita that gives the response of R. Judah's anonymous opponents: "Did not many hope to expound the *merkabah*, and yet they never saw it[75]?" The author of the Gemara then tries to imagine how Judah would have argued back. In the case of the *merkabah*, he claims Judah would have reasoned, "the matter depends on the understanding of the heart" (Aramaic *'obanta delibba*); while the blind man who wants to *pores 'et shema^c* is in an altogether different situation.

We need not discuss the question of whether or not this anonymous fifth- or sixth-century Babylonian writer has correctly reconstructed the thoughts of Judah b. Ilai. The important point is that he regards "expound-

---

75 On the baraita, see above, chapter I, sections 1 and 7. I discuss the text and interpretation of the Gemara in *The Merkabah in Rabbinic Literature* [552].

ing the *merkabah*" as a form of contemplation with "the understanding of the heart" [552], and expresses this idea with an Aramaic phrase that corresponds exactly to the Hebrew *binat lebab* used in *Haggadat Shema‘ Yiśra'el.*

The concept of seeing with "the understanding of the heart," then, makes yet another connection between the Sinai revelation and the vision of the *merkabah*. In section C, we will see that Origen attests and reinforces this link, thereby assuring us that it cannot have been forged any later than the early third century.

6. Ascension or invasion?

We cannot pass on to Origen without first treating one more question. Does the theme of the heavenly ascension, which plays such a huge role in the "Sinai" part of the Shabu‘ot homiletic structure, have any echo in the "*merkabah*" part?

If we base ourselves only on the *Visions of Ezekiel,* the answer must be no. Ezekiel, and through him his audience, sees the seven heavens opened. But neither he nor anyone else is described as climbing up there[76].

When we turn to the Targumic Tosefta on Ezekiel 1:1, however, we find a heavenly ascension projected, although not actually carried out.

"... I will climb to the lofty heavens and will destroy the celestial chambers; I will make war with the exalted holy ones and will set my royal throne over the cherubim. ... *I will climb upon the backs of the clouds, I will be like the Most High* [Isaiah 14:14]."

The speaker, of course, is Nebuchadnezzar. And the invasion of heaven that he plans turns out to be astonishingly like the one that Moses executes.

I will climb upon the backs of the clouds. We have seen that Moses rides to heaven inside a cloud. This detail indeed rests partly on Exodus 24:18 (*Moses went into the cloud and ascended to the mountain*), but it cannot be explained entirely on the basis of that verse. When Exodus 24:18 and Isaiah 14:14 are read together, however, they yield a picture of a heavenly ascent very like that of *Pesiqta* and its parallels[77].

---

76 Section IIE1, however, seems vaguely to hint at Moses' ascent.

77 A full quotation of Isaiah 14:12–15 will be helpful at this point: [12]*How have you fallen from heaven, Morning-star, son of the Dawn! You have been cut down to earth, you who cast lots* [?] *over the nations.* [13]*You said to yourself, "I will climb to heaven, I will lift up my throne above the stars of God, I will sit on the mountain of meeting in the far reaches of the north.* [14]*I will climb upon the backs of the clouds, I will be like the Most High.*" [15]*In fact, you will be thrown down to She'ol, to the depths of the pit.* — Notice that verse 13 has *the mountain of meeting* (har mo‘ed) as the speaker's destination; while, in Exodus 24:18, Moses goes up to the *mountain* (har) to meet God.

A midrash quoted in *Mekhilta* and in the Tosefta[78] suggests that some at least of the rabbis imagined Nebuchadnezzar's cloud as looking very much like Moses':

> Nebuchadnezzar said: "I am going to make myself a little cloud and live inside it." So it is written: *I will climb upon the backs of the clouds,* and so forth. [*Mekhilta, Shirah* chapter 6; ed./tr. 2:46 [195]]

As the parallel in T. Sotah 3:19 makes clear, the point of the midrash is that Nebuchadnezzar thinks he is too good for human society and therefore wants to live by himself in the sky. God punishes him, suitably, by driving him off to live with the beasts (Daniel 4). The midrash does not speak, as does the Targumic Tosefta, of an invasion of heaven. But we learn from it that some expositors envisioned a passenger-carrying cloud, rather like a flying saucer, when they read Isaiah 14:14. This image left its mark on the traditions of Moses' ascension.

I will climb to the lofty heavens and ... make war with the exalted holy ones. The language recalls Moses' boast that "I ascended and trod a path in the heavens. I took part in the war of the angels ... I vanquished the celestial retinue ..." (*Deut. R.* 11:10, quoted more fully above). One detail of this "war" survives, as we have seen, in *Pesiqta*'s description of how Moses smashed the angel Kemuel.

We have also examined a passage from the Oxford manuscript, in which Moses fights the angels "like an ox fighting with his horns" (*keshor nogeaḥ*). The verb, from the root *ngḥ*, seems to reflect a midrashic image, based on Exodus 34:29—30, of Moses with horns (above, section 2b). It crops up again, in a slightly different grammatical form, in *Ex. R.* 41:7. The sin of the golden calf, the expositor tells us, greatly weakened Moses' ability to fight the angels. "Just recently, he was fighting them with his horns [*menaggeaḥ 'otam*][79]; now he is frightened of them." The author of the *'Angele Meroma* poem uses the cognate Aramaic verb, when he has Moses promise the angels he will "gore your bodies with my horns" (*beqarnay 'anaggaḥ*) [283]. Significantly, the Targumic Tosefta has Nebuchadnezzar use an Aramaic idiom based on the same root: *'aggiaḥ qeraba,* "I will make war."

I will set my royal throne over the cherubim. That is, Nebuchadnezzar will replace God as the one enthroned over the cherubim (I Samuel 4:4, and elsewhere). This threat is plainly based on Isaiah 14:13: *I will lift up my throne above the stars of God.*

---

78 By "Tosefta," of course, I here mean the collection of Tannaitic materials that goes by that name, and not the "Targumic Tosefta."

79 Or, "fighting them as if with horns," depending on how literally we suppose the expositor to have taken Exodus 34:29—30.

Now, Moses never does anything quite this drastic. But we have seen that several versions of the ascension story, including BT Shabb. 88b–89a, apply to Moses the words of Job 26:9: *he seized the front of the throne.* I agree with Joseph P. Schultz that this detail is likely to be a watered-down version of a tradition that Moses was seated on God's throne at the time of his ascension [444]. A Hellenistic Jewish dramatist of the second century B.C., named Ezekiel (by coincidence, I assume!), makes use of this tradition in his Greek play *The Exodus.* Significantly, he has the stars fall at Moses' feet, a detail which suggests Isaiah 14:13 [710,716a,735][80]. Samaritan literature from the early centuries of the Christian Era also reflects belief in an enthronement of Moses.

All of these sources, of course, have Moses seize God's throne with the permission of its occupant. But the image they project is disturbingly close to that of the rebel of Isaiah 14; who is, this time, successful.

The ascension of Moses and the ascension of Nebuchadnezzar thus seem to be the negative and the print of the same photograph, and it is not easy to decide which is the primary image and which its reversal. Our old bugaboo of moral ambiguity, which we thought we had left behind with the calf and the waters, has suddenly met us again where we least expected to see it. Only this time the ambiguity is not that of God, but of the quest for heaven.

This ambiguity may be even deeper than it first appears. Modern scholars agree that behind the historical figure of the "king of Babylon," against whom Isaiah 14:3–23 is supposedly directed (and who the rabbis assumed was Nebuchadnezzar)[81], lurks the mightier mythological figure of a rebellious star god [28a,33a,40a,51a,125]. *How have you fallen from heaven, Morning-star, son of the Dawn!* Isaiah 14:12 addresses him; and Christian tradition, taking its cue from Luke 10:18 ("I saw Satan fall like lightning from heaven"), gives him back his ancient demonic character. *Lucifer,* "light-bearer," as Jerome translates *Morning-star* in his Vulgate, thus becomes another name for Satan. The parallels we have considered in the past few pages tempt us to look for an intersection of the horned devil of Christian iconography and the horned Moses of midrash.

---

80 *The Exodus* no longer survives. We know it only from quotations by the Christian writers Clement of Alexandria and Eusebius, the latter of whom preserves the enthronement episode.

81 The only case I know of where the rabbis apply any part of 14:12–15 to something other than Nebuchadnezzar is a midrash on the opening words of verse 12, found in *Mekhilta* (*Shirah* chapter 2; ed./tr. 2:20 [195]), *Song R.* 8:12, and Tanh. *Be-Shallaḥ* #13. This midrash identifies the *Morning-star* with the heavenly patron of Babylon, whose fall must precede that of Nebuchadnezzar himself (to whom the rest of verse 12 refers). – The author of chapters 12–17 of the "Vita Adae," however, whom I assume to have been Jewish, agrees with the Christian tradition in applying Isaiah 14:12–15 to the devil (above, chapter III, section 5e).

Even if we resist this temptation — which is perhaps the wiser course — we cannot avoid speculation of a more modest sort. We have seen the heavenly ascension, central to the Sinai materials of the Shabuᶜot cycle, cast a dark shadow into that portion of the cycle that deals with the *merkabah*. We may guess that the people who preached and who heard the Shabuᶜot sermons were, on some level, dimly aware of this shadow clinging to Moses' triumph. We may further guess that this applies also to those who dreamed of the "descent to the *merkabah*." But we need not consequently suppose that awareness of the rebellious overtones of the heavenly ascent would have had to repel them. It may have been precisely these overtones that attracted them to it.

In chapter IX, we will see why.

C. Origen

1. Introduction

a) Origen and the church. We first made Origen's acquaintance in the introduction to this book, and we have run into him from time to time in the chapters that followed. Let us review what we said about him when we first met. He was born about 185. He lived and worked in Alexandria until about 232, when a bitter conflict with his bishop forced him to leave. He then settled in Palestinian Caesarea, where he spent the rest of his life — despite, if we are to trust his latest biographer (Pierre Nautin), periodic efforts to make a place for himself in more prestigious intellectual centers [686]. He died between 251 and 255, probably as a result of tortures he suffered during the emperor Decius's persecution of Christianity.

Origen was an excitingly original theologian and a profound Bible scholar[82]. In the masterwork of his youth, which we know as *De Principiis* ("On First Principles"), he set forth a brilliant synthesis of Christianity with Platonic philosophy [636,708]. In one of the great achievements of his later years, the Hexapla, he gave the Greek-speaking Christian a tool which he could use to work his way back to the original text of the Old Testament [644,690]. He wrote commentaries on Biblical books, and delivered at Caesarea countless homilies on the portions of the Old and New Testa-

---

82 I did not have the opportunity to consult Joseph Wilson Trigg's lucid and comprehensive *Origen: The Bible and Philosophy in the Third-century Church* [700] until after I had finished the manuscript.

ments read aloud in church. More than any other early Christian thinker, he showed Christianity how to find a place in the Greco-Roman intellectual world, and how at the same time to understand and keep its allegiance to its Biblical past.

The church was not altogether grateful. Its bishops, in Alexandria and later in Palestine, did not exactly shower Origen with appreciation[83]. To judge from his complaints, his congregants did not appreciate his sermons a fraction as much as we do. They come to church rarely, he says, pay no attention to the preacher when they are there, instead spend their time gossiping, and so forth [676]. In the centuries that followed, Origen had his enthusiasts. But he was also harshly criticized, and periodically denounced for heresy.

One of the results of these condemnations has been that only a fraction of his massive output survives in the original Greek. The rest is either lost altogether, or survives only in Latin translations made by Jerome and his sometime friend Rufinus around the end of the fourth century.

The reliability of Rufinus's translations is not unimpeachable. In his prefaces to his translation of *De Principiis,* he announces proudly that he has excised those unorthodox passages that he is sure heretics have interpolated [637]. Comparison with the surviving Greek fragments suggests that we in fact have in the Latin *De Principiis* a drastically bowdlerized Origen. We cannot be sure to what extent he has also rewritten those of the homilies that he has translated; these texts deal with subjects that are theologically far less ticklish than those of *De Principiis*, and presumably offered less temptation to the censor in Rufinus[84].

Jerome, by contrast, translated less of Origen's work, but his translations are more likely to be faithful. After copiously using Origen's exegetical work in his own commentaries, and occasionally taking credit for Origen's fieldwork among Jewish scholars [654], Jerome turned around and denounced Origen as a heretic. We may therefore expect that Jerome would be less tempted than the more loyal Rufinus to clean and dress up Origen in accord with the expectations of the late fourth-century church. Luckily for us, it is Jerome who translated the most important passage we have to consider in this section, Origen's first homily on Ezekiel.

---

83 To be fair, Origen's theories about ideal church leadership must have made him a hard person for the actual leadership to deal with [699].

84 Annie Jaubert's comparison of several passages of the Latin translation of the *Homilies on Joshua* with Greek fragments suggests that Rufinus has faithfully preserved Origen's thought, although not his exact language [631]. On the other hand, Rufinus admits at one point that he has given rather free and expansive translations of the homilies on Genesis, Exodus, and especially Leviticus [688].

b) Origen and the Jews. This man, who cast so gigantic a shadow over the intellectual history of Christianity, also plays a part in the history of Judaism. As far as we can judge, Origen was in touch with Jewish thinkers all of his adult life; and, as we will see, there is evidence that both he and they learned from these contacts. Even in Alexandria, where the Jewish community seems to have been decimated after an abortive uprising early in the second century, Origen knew a "Hebrew," perhaps converted to Christianity, whom Nautin regards as one of his "two teachers of Christian life" [694]. (The other was his martyred father.) He certainly seems to have had some knowledge of rabbinic tradition during his Alexandrian period, for the Alexandrian *De Principiis* mentions the rabbinic institution of the Sabbath limit (IV.iii.2; tr. 291 [636]). Expelled from Alexandria, he found himself in a city which, if an intellectual backwater in other respects, was at the time becoming a major center of rabbinic Judaism [421]. He took advantage of his new surroundings to learn what Jews were saying about their Bible, its language, and its religious conceptions.

We thus find Origen turning to Jewish scholars (with disappointing results) to find out what the Hebrew names would be for the two trees mentioned at the end of the Apocryphal *Story of Susanna* (*Epistle to Africanus*, tr. 375—376 [635]). He discusses Isaiah's prophecies of the "suffering servant" with Jewish interpreters (*Contra Celsum*, I, 55; tr. 50—51 [627]). He learns about the authorship of certain Psalms from a patriarch "Iullus" (Hillel? [402]), and from another "who bore the title of 'sage' among the Jews," whose identity we will presently guess at [635a, 689]. Thus equipped with a lifetime of first-hand knowledge of Jews, Origen can represent himself in his polemic *Contra Celsum* as something of an expert on Judaism; he can weigh the pagan Celsus's knowledge of the Jews and their faith against his own, and find it absurdly wanting [667][85].

"Origen does not care for the Jews," Gustave Bardy commented in 1925 [653]. More recently, Robert M. Grant has warned, in a review of N. R. M. de Lange's *Origen and the Jews,* against imagining too cozy an ecumenicity between Origen and his Jewish acquaintances in third-century Caesarea [672a]. There is no question that, when Origen talks about Jews, he normally does so disparagingly. But, even while abusing Judaism, Origen often shows how important Jewish ideas were for his own thinking.

There is an amusing example of this in the fifth homily on Exodus, which deals with how the Israelites left Egypt and crossed the Red Sea. Origen begins the homily by warning against trying to interpret the text literally, as do the Jews and certain unnamed Christians who want to follow

---

85 The joke is perhaps on Origen. Celsus may accurately represent the attitudes of Jews who were far more thoroughly Hellenized than the rabbis whom Origen knew at Caesarea [666].

them. To turn to "Jewish tales" to interpret the Scripture, he declares, "is to surrender to the enemies of Christ" (V, 1; ed. 6:184 [639]). Yet, at the end of the homily, he does exactly what he denounces. "I have heard transmitted from the elders [*audivi a maioribus traditum*]," he says, that twelve divisions were made in the Red Sea, one for each of the tribes of Israel; and he proceeds to reproduce, with some precision, a midrash on this subject which happens to be preserved in rabbinic sources (V, 5; ed. 6:190) [682]. Origen evidently had few qualms about passing off "Jewish tales" which caught his fancy as traditions of "elders," whom the hearer was bound to suppose to be Christian. He thus had the benefit of an exciting story which he could add to Christianity's arsenal against Judaism. We will presently see him performing a similar, if more complex, operation with the Shabu^cot cycle.

It follows from the example I have just given that Origen does not always footnote his Jewish sources. His debt to Judaism, we must suppose, is greater than he is willing explicitly to admit.

No wonder, then, that the question of Origen and Judaism has attracted much scholarly attention, particularly in the past fifteen years. Henri Crouzel's *Bibliographie Critique d'Origène* [661] lists the literature published before 1970. De Lange's fine study *Origen and the Jews* (1976) [664] systematically brings together the discoveries of earlier investigators, and adds much that is new[86]. Three recent articles are particularly important. In a piece that first appeared in English in 1971, Ephraim E. Urbach argues that rabbinic exegesis of the Song of Songs deeply influenced Origen's approach to that book [701,702]. Reuven Kimelman (1980) develops Urbach's arguments, suggesting that the influence may have gone in two directions, and that some rabbinic cómments on the Song of Songs may be reactions to Origen's interpretations [679]. And Abraham Wasserstein (1977) shows neatly that an exposition of Ezekiel 14:14, which Origen claims in his fourth homily on Ezekiel to have "once heard from a certain Hebrew" (*audivi quondam a quodam Hebraeo hunc locum exponente*), in fact turns up in the *Tanḥuma* midrashim [703][m].

But the single most brilliant and most unjustly neglected study of Origen's relations with his Jewish contemporaries is Dominique Barthélemy's "Est-ce Hoshaya Rabba qui censura le commentaire allegorique?", first published in 1967 [656]. Barthélemy takes as his starting point a series of peculiar textual variations found in certain manuscripts of Philo. These variants seem to be deliberate "corrections" of the writings of the Alexandrian Jewish philosopher, designed to bring them into harmony with the ideas of

---

86 An earlier monograph, Hans Bietenhard's *Caesarea, Origenes, und die Juden* (1974) [658], is far less satisfactory.

rabbinic Judaism and to eliminate bits of aid and comfort that they might provide to Christianity. But when, after the rise of Christianity, might the rabbis and their followers have been studying and editing Philo's Greek compositions? Barthélemy argues dazzlingly that our textual tradition of Philo goes back to Origen's Caesarea, and that we have of Philo's writings essentially those books that Origen was able to carry with him from Alexandria to Caesarea. It was Origen who introduced the rabbis of Caesarea to their forgotten sage, and it was these rabbis who "corrected" some of Origen's manuscripts in accord with their ideas of what a Jewish philosopher should have written. Foremost among them was the Caesarean Hoshaiah Rabba, "Hoshaiah the Great," whose exposition of the first verse of Genesis (*Gen. R.* 1:1, ed. 1—2 [188]) closely resembles one "corrected" Philonic text[87].

It is easy to dismiss Barthélemy's reconstruction as conjecture. Of course it is conjecture. But it is a conjecture that does rare justice not only to the gritty little data that Barthélemy sets out to explain — the Philonic variants — but also to the monumental fact that the outstanding thinkers of two religions, who had every reason to be interested in each other, were in the same town during the first half of the third century. Their contacts need not have been affectionate, but Origen's explicit evidence must convince us that they were real. Yet, when we try to envision these contacts, we normally come away as hungry and frustrated as voyeurs at a cloudy window. At the cost of a number of imaginative leaps, Barthélemy has given us a remarkable stretch of clear window-pane.

Our own task in what follows will be similar to Barthélemy's. Unlike Barthélemy, we will be dealing with the Jews' influence on Origen rather than his on them. But we will make use of one of Barthélemy's most important insights: that the exchanges between Origen and the Jews must have been conducted in Greek, and are likely to have involved the use of Greek materials.

This has an exciting implication for the history of rabbinic thought. From the surviving rabbinic sources, we would never dream that any rabbi had heard of Philo; while, if Barthélemy is right, some at least of the Caesarean rabbis were interested enough in him to prepare an "orthodox" edition of his Greek writings. We may suspect that the Talmud and midrash allow us to see only one aspect of the rabbis, the one that by and large faced away from the Greek-speaking world. Any reflection of their other faces, normally hidden, will be welcome. This is yet another reason why Origen, and the Shabu^c ot cycle on which he draws, are so important to us.

---

87 Several scholars since the late nineteenth century have suggested that Origen and Hoshaiah were acquainted [421,652,664]. I have earlier proposed that Hoshaiah was the channel by which Eliezer's midrash of Ezekiel 1:1 and Hosea 12:11 reached Origen (above, chapter VI, section 3c).

2. The First Homily on Ezekiel

The more dependable of Origen's two Latin translators, Jerome, has preserved for us the text of the fourteen *Homilies on Ezekiel*. Of the original Greek we have only a few isolated fragments[88].

The first of these homilies, by far the longest of them, is about the *merkabah*. The opening two-thirds of the homily expounds Ezekiel's preface to the *merkabah* vision, and examines what it has to tell us about God's justice and his mercy (I, 1—10). The remainder is a cursory and not very systematic exposition of the vision itself (I, 11—16).

Origen's central point in this homily is that the God of the Old Testament, far from being the vindictive horror imagined by the Marcionite "heretics[89]," is in fact the same stern but loving father who is described in the New. Indeed, if any distinction at all is to be made between the values preached in the two Testaments, it is the Old Testament that is the more humane (I, 9). Its God indeed punishes; but he punishes like a doctor giving bitter medicine, like a father, like a kind lord (I, 2). The purpose of punishment is to reform and ultimately to heal the sinner.

This theme is a familiar one with Origen [675]. But how does he find it in the first chapter of Ezekiel? First, in the fact that God exiled a small number of just men — Daniel, Hananiah, Mishael, Azariah, and of course Ezekiel himself — to Babylonia together with the sinners. They were exiled, not because they had themselves sinned, but in order that they might sustain and bring to repentance those who had (I, 1—2). Second, in some of the details of the vision itself. Thus, Ezekiel sees God as a being of fire; but only from the waist down (Ezekiel 1:27), which signifies the region of the body whose lusts the fires of hell must punish. From the waist up, he appears as electrum (so the Septuagint translates *hashmal*), the shining metal that is more precious than gold or silver. "God has not only torments to offer, but comforts as well. ... God is fiery, but not all of him is fiery" (I, 3).

This approach explains why Origen consistently interprets the details of the *merkabah* as tokens of grace. Following the Septuagint, he understands

---

88 As far as I know, the *Homilies on Ezekiel* have never been translated into any modern language. All the quotations that follow are my own translations.

89 Marcion was a Christian teacher of the mid-second century, whose version of Christianity competed for centuries with the one we have come to know as "orthodox" [657]. He taught that the "just God" who created the world and revealed the Old Testament was an entirely different being from the far superior "good God," who sent Jesus Christ to redeem humankind from the "just God" and all his works [718]. — Harnack has observed that, while we find polemic against the Marcionite "heresy" throughout Origen's exegetical writings, it is particularly strong in the *Homilies on Ezekiel* [677]; the first homily is largely given over to it. This point may, in expert hands, turn out to be a clue to the difficult problem of dating these homilies.

the "storm wind" of 1:4 as a "spirit lifting up[90]." It comes to lift away evils from your soul, paving the way for your happiness. That done, you are ready for the "great cloud" which comes to rain spiritual benefits upon you (I, 12). If the "spirit" cannot purify you, the "fire" (still, of 1:4) must do the job. But, characteristically, the "fire" is coupled with "splendor." "Even those details that appear to be sad," says Origen, "are balanced by the nearness of more joyful ones" (I, 13). Jerome, writing his own commentary on Ezekiel nearly two hundred years later, explains that some people interpret Ezekiel 1:4 "in a positive sense, others the reverse" (*ab aliis in bonam, ab aliis in contrariam partem*); his explanations *in bonam partem* (*Commentary* on 1:4; ed. 7–9 [622]) turn out to be, for the most part, Origen's.

a) Jewish sources? Where did Origen get this approach to the *merkabah*? Several features of the first homily, not themselves directly connected to the *merkabah*, point to some contact with Jews. They perhaps encourage us to look to a Jewish source for the *merkabah* exegesis itself.

Thus, Origen remarks at one point that "the Jewish new year is now drawing near" (*novus annus imminet iam Iudaeis*). The context – an effort to prove that Ezekiel's *fourth month* is January, the month of Christ's baptism – shows that he is talking about the autumn Rosh Hashanah (I, 4). In another place, he casually equates the Babylonian exile with Adam's being expelled from paradise: "Adam was indeed in paradise. But the serpent became the cause of his captivity, and brought it about that he should be expelled, be it from Jerusalem or from paradise, and come into this place of tears" (I, 3). A similar comparison, bordering on equation, occurs in a *petihah* for the fast of the Ninth of Ab, attributed to "R. Abbahu quoting R. Jose b. Hanina" (*Gen. R.* 19:9, ed. 178–179 [188]; *Lam. R.*, Proem 4, ed. 3a [190]; *Pesiqta de-Rab Kahana, 'Ekhah* #1, ed. 249–250 [206]). Both of these rabbis were Caesareans, and Jose b. Hanina was a younger contemporary of Origen[91].

Finally, Origen indicates that the people who died in Noah's flood, Sodom and Gomorrah, the Egyptians, and the six hundred thousand Israelites who died in the desert, all received punishment in this world so that they should not be continuously punished in the next (I, 2). M. Sanh. 10:3 expresses a similar idea[92]. We must admit, however, that, if Origen

---

90 Greek *pneuma exairon*, for Hebrew *ruah se^c arah*.

91 The fast of the Ninth of Ab falls about seven weeks before Rosh Hashanah. If we wanted to let our imaginations run free, we might speculate that Origen heard Jose b. Hanina's exposition in a Caesarean synagogue on the Ninth of Ab, and made use of it in a sermon that he preached a few weeks later, shortly before Rosh Hashanah.

92 "The generation of the flood has no share in the world to come, but will not suffer judgment. ...

indeed borrowed this idea from the Jews, he must have done so well before he came to Caesarea; for we find it already in the Alexandrian *De Principiis* (II.v.3; tr. 104 [636]).

At first sight, it seems unlikely that Origen took his treatment of the *merkabah* from Judaism. For one thing, his interpretation of Ezekiel 1:4 rests on the Greek rather than the Hebrew text of that verse. For another, the rabbinic sources, insofar as they give us any clue to the overall implications of the *merkabah* vision, seem more in accord with Jerome's interpretations *in contrariam partem* (which, incidentally, Jerome bases on the *Hebrew* text of 1:4) than with Origen's. Thus, we saw in chapter IV that BT Hag. 13b interprets Ezekiel 1:4 to mean that the *merkabah* "went to subdue the entire world beneath the power of wicked Nebuchadnezzar." We saw also that the *hayyot* appear in the Targum as agents of God's wrath; and that, in the parallels to *Gen. R.* 65:21, they shift from "angels" into "angels of destruction."

b) Homily I and the "Visions." But Origen's *merkabah* exegesis has one close companion on the Jewish side. This is the *Visions of Ezekiel.*

Like Origen, the author of the *Visions* understands the *merkabah* as a sign of mercy and grace. "They were punished in Tammuz, and in Tammuz God's mercies were moved toward them" (IB). The thrust of the *Visions*, as I have understood it, is strikingly similar to the point of Origen's first homily. Both preachers aim to clear God of the charge that he operates with a cruel and unyielding justice. For Origen, it is the Marcionites who make this charge; while the *Visions* represents it as the not very well articulated grumbling of the Jewish people. But the basic idea is the same.

The resemblance between the two sources extends to the details of their exegesis.

Thus, we saw that the author of the *Visions* takes *wa'ani betokh hag-golah* (*while I was among the captivity,* Ezekiel 1:1) to express Ezekiel's complaint that Isaiah and Hosea were allowed to "prophesy in Jerusalem, while I am in captivity." The Septuagint translates *wa'ani* with *kai egō,* which Origen understands as *even I* (Latin, *et ego*). Travelling by a some-

---

The people of Sodom have no share in the world to come ... but they will suffer judgment. R. Nehemiah says: Neither will suffer judgment. ... The generation of the desert has no share in the world to come, but will not suffer judgment ... in the opinion of R. Akiba." – Marc Bregman has pointed out that the best witnesses to the text of the Mishnah, reinforced by a very early Genizah fragment of *'Abot de-Rabbi Natan,* make these judgments about these three groups alone [260a]. (Most Mishnah editions add the generation of the tower of Babel, and the spies of Numbers 13–14.) This shorter, more authentic list is very close to Origen's. – The Aramaic story of Aher quoted in BT Hag. 15b, although certainly later than this Mishnaic passage, gives us an idea of how its ᶜomedin baddin (which I have translated "suffer judgment") is to be understood.

what different route, Origen thus arrives at an understanding of the phrase which is essentially the same as that of the *Visions*:

> It appears to me to have been spoken ironically. *Even I was in the midst of captivity. Even I*; as if the prophet were saying: "*Even I*, who was not caught in the sins of the people, *was in the midst of captivity*." Such is the literal meaning of the passage. Understood allegorically, however, it is Christ who speaks: *Even I* came to a place of *captivity*; I came to regions of enslavement, where captives are held. [I, 5]

We need not follow Origen as he develops his allegory, and finds in the Psalms and the prophets the voice of Christ protesting the unworthiness of those whose captivity he came to share. His notion that Ezekiel is a "type" of Christ, who also saw the heavens opened while he was at a river, will occupy us more fully below[93]. For now, the point that concerns us is that Origen and the *Visions* agree that a complaint is expressed in Ezekiel 1:1.

How little this interpretation is self-evident may be seen from the fact that it has practically no parallel in Christian sources, and none at all in rabbinic literature. An anonymous midrash quoted in *Lam. R.*, Proem 34 (ed. 19b [190]), understands *wa'ani betokh haggolah* very differently. The *wa-* (literally, "and") of *wa'ani* is said to imply that God was with Ezekiel in captivity; as if the text had said, [*he*] *and I among the captivity*[n]. On the Christian side, the fifth-century Theodoret of Cyrus does give a similar explanation of Ezekiel 1:1 in his *Commentary* (ed. 820–821 [646]). But we can hardly understand Theodoret's point without supposing Origen's first homily as its background, and we may assume that the first homily was in fact its source. Jerome ignores the idea altogether.

We have already seen why, according to Origen, God exiled a few of the pious together with the impious. A Greek fragment of Origen, evidently related to Homily I, 5, but not identical to it (ed. 329 [641]), expresses the reason for Ezekiel's exile in two words: *di' oikonomian*, "for the sake of *oikonomia*." It is not easy to translate this last word. Christian writers use it to mean "plan of salvation," "administration of salvation ," or "order of salvation." But, more basically, the word refers to the administration of a household or estate [818a]. Origen's use of it is thus reminiscent of the *Visions'* parable of a "king who had many servants and appointed them to their work," and made the most intelligent of them shepherd in the desert (IC). Ezekiel's people — the shepherd's flock — are as important to Origen

---

93 This, of course, is why Origen is concerned to show that Ezekiel's *fourth month* is the month of Christ's baptism (above). – Origen uses this typology, combined with an etymological interpretation of Ezekiel's name and that of his father, as fuel for his polemic against the Marcionites. *Ezekiel*, he tells us (not quite accurately), means "power of God," which can refer to nothing but the Lord Christ. He is *son of Buzi*, which means "held in contempt" – exactly what the "heretics" do to Christ's father the Creator (I, 4).

as they are to the author of the *Visions*, and they are important in much the same way. We will return to this point below.

"Thereupon," continues the *Visions*, "God opened to Ezekiel the seven subterranean chambers, and Ezekiel looked into them and saw all the celestial entities" (ID). I have suggested (section A5b) that we cannot understand the use of "thereupon" unless we suppose that the vision was intended to console Ezekiel for his exile. So Origen. After describing at length God's goodness in sending the righteous to care for the exiled sinners, he continues:

> That is why the prophet was in captivity. Consider now the things that he saw, in order that he might not feel the sorrows of captivity. Below [that is, on earth] he sees hardships. But when he lifts up his eyes he sees *the heavens opened*, gazes at heavenly things, sees the likeness of the glory of God, the four living creatures ... the driver of the four living creatures, the wheels containing each other. [I, 3]

The purpose clause, "in order that he might not feel the sorrows of captivity" (*ne dolores sentiat captivitatis*), conveys the same idea as does the *Visions'* "thereupon."

But it is with Origen's interpretation of the words *the heavens were opened* that his link to the *Visions of Ezekiel* appears most clearly:

> *The heavens were opened.* It was not enough that one heaven be opened; several were opened, so that the angels might descend to those who are to be saved, not from one, but from all of the heavens ... [I, 7]

It is hard to see how the point that Ezekiel saw several heavens opened, rather than just one, can have had much significance for Origen. He elsewhere shows that he is familiar with the idea that there are several heavens, but is not very interested in it (*De Principiis*, II.iii.6, tr. 90–92 [636]; *Contra Celsum*, VI, 19–21, tr. 331–334 [627]). We must assume that he stresses this notion here because he is following a source in which it does play an important role. This source is presumably a Jewish tradition, which also underlies section IG of the *Visions*. We will presently see that this connection not only explains Origen's emphasis on the plurality of heavens, but also gives us our clue to the peculiar exegesis that the *Visions* uses to prove this plurality.

With the opening of the "several" heavens, we come to the end of our series of parallels between the first homily and the *Visions*. We reach, simultaneously, the beginning of the first homily's parallels with the Sinai *haggadot*.

c) Homily I and the Sinai haggadot. To make my point, I must quote Origen at some length:

> *The heavens were opened.* The heavens had been closed. When Christ came, they were opened; so that, once they had been unlocked, the holy spirit might come upon him in the form of a dove [Matthew 3:16 and parallels]. For it would not have been able to frequent us, had it not first

descended to its natural consort. Jesus *ascended on high, took a captivity captive, received gifts for humanity* [Psalm 68:19]. *He who descended is he who ascended above all the heavens, that he might fulfill all things. He made some apostles, others prophets, others evangelists, others pastors and teachers, for the perfection of the saints* [Ephesians 4:10–12][94].

The heavens were opened. It was not enough that one heaven be opened; several were opened, so that the angels might descend to those who are to be saved, not from one, but from all of the heavens. [These were the] *angels who ascended and descended over the son of man* [John 1:51], *and came to him and ministered to him* [Matthew 4:11]. The angels descended, however, because Christ had descended first. They had earlier been afraid to descend, before the lord of the powers and of all things went before them. When they saw, however, the leader of the celestial army [cf. Luke 2:13] lingering in earthly places, they went forth through the opened way, following their lord and obedient to the will of him who distributed them as the guardians of those who believe in his name.

You who were yesterday under a demon are today under an angel. *Do not,* says the Lord, *scorn any of these little ones* who are in the church, *for indeed I say to you that their angels always see the face of my father who is in heaven* [Matthew 18:10].

Angels serve your welfare. They are committed to the service of the son of God. They say among themselves: "If *he* descended, and descended in a body, if *he* put on mortal flesh and suffered the cross and died for humanity, why then do we sit quietly, and why do we spare ourselves? Come, all angels! Let us descend from heaven." Just so, there was *a multitude of the celestial army praising and glorifying God* [Luke 2:13] when Christ was born.

All things are filled with angels. Come, angels, support an old man converted from his early error, from the doctrine of the demons, from *iniquity speaking on high* [Psalm 73:8]. Take him into your care like a good doctor; care for him and build him up. He is a little one, an old man born today, a new little old man made a child again[95]. When you take him into your care, give him the baptism of the second birth [*baptisma secundae generationis*; cf. Titus 3:5], and call to your other fellow-servants, so that all of you may equally instruct toward faith those who were once deceived. *For there is more joy in heaven over one sinner who repents than over ninety-nine just people who have no need of repentance* [Luke 15:7].

All creation exults, applauds, and shares in the happiness of those who are to be saved; *for the creation waits with eager longing for the revelation of the sons of God* [Romans 8:19]. Admittedly, those who falsify apostolic writings do not like their books to contain passages of this sort, by which Jesus Christ may be shown to be the creator[96]. Yet all creation is there said to await the time when the sons of God are to be freed from sin, taken from the devil's hand, reborn by Christ.

But it is now opportune for us to touch on certain aspects of the passage at hand. The prophet saw, not *a vision,* but *visions of God* [Ezekiel 1:1]. Why did he see not one but several *visions*? Listen to God making his promise: *I have multiplied visions* [Hosea 12:11].

In the fifth day of the month, which was the fifth year of king Jehoiachin's captivity [Ezekiel 1:2]. In *the thirtieth year* [1:1] of Ezekiel's age, and the fifth of Jehoiachin's captivity, the prophet was sent to the Jews. The most merciful father did not despise, nor did he leave the people for long without someone to remind them. It was *the fifth year.* How much time intervened?

---

94 The-author of the Epistle to the Ephesians (traditionally identified as Paul) gives a free quotation of Psalm 68:19 in 4:8, then expounds it in the following verses [73]. Significantly, Origen quotes Psalm 68:19 itself, with its *received gifts* (MT *laqaḥta mattanot;* LXX *elabes domata;* Origen, *accepit dona*), and *not* Ephesians 4:8, with its *gave gifts* (*edōken domata;* Vulgate, *dedit dona*); although, like the author of Ephesians, he naturally changes the verbs from second to third person. We will soon see the importance of this.

95 This awkward phrase is the best way I can think of to render the charming *novellus senex repuerascens.* The idea is roughly similar to that expressed in I Corinthians 3:1–2.

96 Harnack understands this to mean that the Marcionite text of the Epistle to the Romans did not include 8:19 [678].

Five years, of [that time during] which the captives labored. Thereupon the holy spirit descended, *the heavens were opened,* and those who were oppressed by the yoke of captivity saw those
things that were seen by the prophet. For when he says, *the heavens were opened,* in a certain
way they too contemplated with the eyes of the heart that which he observed even with the eyes of
the flesh [*quodam modo et ipsi intuebantur cordis oculis, quae ille etiam oculis carnis adspexerat*].
[I, 6–8]

This luxuriant account of how the angels descend to aid and support the
believers is certainly not taken from Ezekiel. Nor will any of the New
Testament passages that Origen quotes yield it naturally, although we can
perhaps extract it from John 1:51 ("you will see heaven opened, and the
angels of God ascending and descending upon the Son of man") if we are
prepared to use some force. It reads far more like a Christianized version
of the Sinai *haggadot* that we considered in section B of this chapter. "God
opened the doors of the seven firmaments and revealed himself to the Israelites' sight. ... He sent twelve hundred thousand ministering angels down
to earth to them. Two angels laid hold of each Israelite: one put his hand
over his heart so that his soul would not leave him, while the other lifted
up his neck so that he could see God face to face" (*Pesiqta*). "God said to
the angels: 'Go down and help your brothers.' So it is written: *The angels
of the hosts help them to walk, they help them to walk* [Psalm 68:13]"
(*Mekhilta*).

We notice that both Origen and the Sinai stories have the angels help
not only the community as a group, but also each individual within it. We
notice that Origen seems to imagine his community as having been, like the
Israelites at Sinai, freshly initiated into a faith and a covenant to which they
had been strange. (I do not know to what extent this would correspond to
the actual experience of the Christian community at Caesarea.) The initiate,
Origen tells us, has turned away "from his early error, from the doctrine of
the demons, from *iniquity speaking on high.*" The Israelites at Sinai, too,
have learned how to respond to "a generation that leads you astray and
says, 'Let us go worship other gods'" (*Pesiqta*). They have seen that there is
none beside God, and know that "you are our God, you are our portion,
you are holy" (*Deut. R.*).

Origen calls on the angels to support the believer, who is like a frail
child, and to give him "the baptism of the second birth." Both of these
images have their parallels in the Sinai *haggadot*. The picture of the angels'
helping the Israelites to walk, which *Mekhilta* and BT Shabb. 88b read into
Psalm 68:13, is modelled after that of a mother helping her young child
(Rashi to Shabb. 88b; cf. M. Shabb. 18:2). Origen's "baptism of the second
birth" is presumably influenced by Titus 3:5, which speaks of baptism as
the "washing of regeneration" (*palingenesias,* literally "rebirth"). But the
image strongly suggests the dew of resurrection with which God revives the
Israelites when they die after hearing the beginning of his speech (*Pesiqta,*
BT Shabb. 88b).

Ira Chernus has recently made a strong case for supposing that the haggadic theme of the Israelites' death and resurrection at Sinai is an example of the widespread cross-cultural motif of "initiatory death," followed by rebirth into new and perhaps eternal life [512]. If Chernus is right, Origen's assimilation of the rabbinic dew of resurrection to the waters of Christian baptism comes to seem particularly apt. We must return to this point in a little while, when we examine another of Origen's homilies which represents baptism as a lawgiving taking place in the presence of angels.

I note parenthetically two more, rather doubtful, points of contact between Origen's first homily and *Pesiqta Rabbati*'s twentieth. First, Origen's reference to Christ as "leader of the celestial army" (*principem militiae caelestis*), although certainly based on Luke 2:13 — which Origen goes on to quote — is reminiscent of the "celestial soldiers" (*ḥayyele marom*) of *Pesiqta* and its parallels (above, section B2c). Second, the *petiḥah* expositions of the twentieth homily include a haggadah describing how the earth rejoiced and praised God when Israel received the Torah, while the heavens mourned (20:1; ed. Friedmann, 95a [209]; ed. Grözinger, 305 [288]). The first part of this description, if not the second, perhaps suggests Origen's exposition of Romans 8:19: "All creation exults, applauds, and shares in the happiness of those who are to be saved ..."

d) Sinai and merkabah. There is one passage of the first homily, in particular, which seems to make no sense unless we assume that Origen is drawing on Sinai traditions to explain Ezekiel's vision. This is his strange claim, at the end of the long passage quoted above, that "the holy spirit descended, *the heavens were opened,* and those who were oppressed by the yoke of captivity saw those things that were seen by the prophet" — if only, as he goes on to say, "with the eyes of the heart." The text of Ezekiel does not give the slightest justification for believing that anyone besides Ezekiel himself saw what he saw when *the heavens were opened.*

At Sinai, by contrast, God opened the seven firmaments to all Israel (*Pesiqta, Deut. R.*). We have seen (above, section B4a) that the Shabu^cot preachers did not force the Sinai revelation and the *merkabah* vision into separate airtight compartments, but freely transferred details from one episode into the other. Thus, *Pesiqta* and *Deut. R.* transfer Ezekiel's opened heavens to Sinai. From such texts as Exodus 20:4 and Deuteronomy 4:39, *Deut. R.* evolves the notion that the seven subterranean chambers were opened, mirroring the opening of the heavens. The *Visions of Ezekiel* then carries this conception back from Sinai to the *merkabah.*

Origen, or his source, must have made a transfer of precisely this sort, from the Sinai revelation to the *merkabah.* We are to explain it in precisely the same way. Origen knew a cycle of Shabu^cot sermons like the ones I have supposed to lie behind the *Visions of Ezekiel* and the Sinai-ascension *haggadot*. He used them extensively for his own homily on the *merkabah*, together with other Jewish material[97]. Following his sources, he transferred the detail of God's revealing himself to the entire people, as he transferred the angels' descent, from the setting of the Torah reading into that of the *haftarah*.

But Origen now provides us with a fresh puzzle. Elsewhere, he denies that Ezekiel can have seen the heavens opened except in his mind. "For I do not imagine that the visible heaven was opened, or its physical form divided, for Ezekiel to record such an experience" (*Contra Celsum*, I, 48; tr. 44 [627]). Other remarks that he makes here and there in his writings seem to confirm that this was indeed how he normally understood Ezekiel's vision (*Contra Celsum*, VI, 4, tr. 319 [627]; *De Principiis*, I.i.9, II.iv.3, tr. 14, 99 [636]; fragments of the *Commentary* on John 1:31 and 1:51, ed. 4:499–501, 567 [638]). Why, then, does he appear to reverse himself in the first homily, and declare that the people "contemplated with the eyes of the heart that which [Ezekiel] observed even with the eyes of the flesh"?

The solution, once again, lies in Origen's Jewish source. In *'Aggadat Shema[c] Yiśra'el*, the preacher (purportedly Moses) tells his audience that "you too saw" God's descent on Sinai "with the understanding of your heart and your mind and your soul" (*bebinat lebabekhem weśikhlekhem wenishmatekhem*). The writer of the Gemara in BT Meg. 24b thinks that "expounding the *merkabah*" is a sort of contemplation that "depends on the understanding of the heart" (*'obanta delibba*; above, section B5). The preacher's aim, on Shabu[c]ot, is to create precisely the effect that Origen describes. His people are to see with the "eyes of the heart" the wonders that Moses and Ezekiel saw with the "eyes of the flesh."

This is all that the ordinary preacher can hope to achieve. But the stories of Johanan b. Zakkai's disciples, which we examined in chapter I, spin extravagant fantasies of the far more dramatic successes that certain extraordinary preachers had when they expounded the *merkabah*. In these fantasies, the wonders of Sinai actually become visible. It is no coincidence that attending angels play a large role in these stories, as they do in Origen's first homily. We will presently come across another key feature of the Johanan b. Zakkai stories, the enveloping fire, in Origen's *Commentary on John*.

e) The ascension of Moses. In the meantime, let us look at what we have achieved so far. We have seen evidence that Origen drew upon the *mer-*

---

97 Above, section 2a. I have suggested (chapter VI, section 3c) that the apparently gratuitous passage near the end of our long quotation, in which Origen interprets the plural *visions* in the light of Hosea 12:11, is a distorted form of an independent midrash authored by R. Eliezer.

kabah exegesis of the *Visions of Ezekiel*, and upon the Sinai *haggadot* of *Pesiqta Rabbati*. More important, we have seen evidence that he knew these two clusters of material as parts of a single package; details move easily from one to the other. This package must have existed in the third century, most likely in the Caesarean Jewish community.

What did the package look like? I cannot imagine that it consisted of a single sermon. Such a sermon would have had to be enormously long, and would have exhausted rather than edified its hearers. Rather, I imagine a cycle of potential sermons, standing to the use of the synagogue preachers. The individual expositor could make his selection as he pleased. Now he might preach on the wonders that Ezekiel saw, as in the *Visions of Ezekiel*; now he might hold his audience spellbound with Moses' terrifying journey to the heights, as in *Pesiqta Rabbati*.

But here the reader may draw back. I have shown, he may grant, that Origen drew on some of *Pesiqta*'s Sinai *haggadot*; it does not automatically follow that these *haggadot* must have included *Pesiqta*'s description of the ascension of Moses. This is true. But I think Origen has indeed left a trace of the ascension stories in his first homily, in the form of a seemingly irrelevant and unnecessary quotation of Psalm 68:19, at the beginning of his exposition of *the heavens were opened* (above, page 332).

It is natural, given his Ezekiel-Christ typology, that Origen should apply Ezekiel 1:1 to the opening of the heavens at Jesus' baptism, when the holy spirit descended on Jesus in the form of a dove (Matthew 3:16 and parallels). But why does he go on to quote Psalm 68:19; which, interpreted through the following quotation from Ephesians, must refer to Christ's ascension after his death and resurrection? Origen's argument would be smoother and make better sense if both Psalm 68:19 and Ephesians 4:10–12 were deleted. And, if he has to include some reference to Jesus' ascension, why not simply quote Ephesians 4:8–12 as a block? Why quote, first the Old Testament passage, then its New Testament expansion?

The answer, I think, is that Origen knows the Jewish stories of Moses' ascension; he knows that their germ and nucleus is Psalm 68:19; and he knows that they are connected, through this verse, to Ezekiel's *merkabah*. By replacing the ascension *haggadot* with Ephesians 4:10–12, he lets Jesus take the place of Moses as the hero who invades heaven and brings back *gifts for humanity*, including the institutions of a new covenant and the help of the angels. This supposition, that Jesus has ousted Moses, explains why Origen does not leave any explicit reference to Sinai in his first homily. It indeed demands some explanation of its own, which we will presently look for in the third-century polemic between Judaism and Christianity.

But there is another question that must occupy us first. Is the first homily on Ezekiel the only composition of Origen's that draws upon the Shabu^cot homilies, or do we see the cycle reflected in other passages as well? I believe that we do; and that these other passages not only confirm our deductions from the first homily, but add to our knowledge of the Shabuᶜot homilies and their role in third-century Judaism.

3. Origen on Joshua, Luke, John

a) The dating of Origen's homilies. There is, as far as I know, no serious question that the homilies preserved in Origen's name reflect sermons that he gave during the two decades or so that he spent at Caesarea. But can we date them more precisely? In this section, we are about to compare three different homilies with one another, and with Book VI of the *Commentary on John.* It would be desirable to know which of these sources is earlier and which later; whether they are more or less contemporary, or whether ten or twenty years separate them. We cannot go further until we have at least faced this issue.

A remark that Eusebius makes in his account of Origen's life suggests that the homilies come from Origen's last years: "... it was natural that Origen, now over sixty and with his abilities fully developed by years of practice, should, as we are told, have allowed his lectures to be taken down by shorthand-writers, though he had never before agreed to this" (*Ecclesiastical History*, VI.xxxvi.1; tr. 271 [620]). Scholars have normally accepted Eusebius's testimony. They have supposed it confirmed by a passage from the ninth homily on Joshua — coincidentally, one of the homilies that we are about to draw on — which has seemed to refer to Decius's persecution of Christianity (250–251).

Pierre Nautin has disposed of these arguments, and has made an extremely ingenious case for a much earlier dating. Origen, Nautin thinks, delivered all of his homilies to the Old and the New Testaments in one three-year period, in the course of which both Testaments were read concurrently in the Caesarean church. These three years are likely to have been either 238–241 or 239–242 [693]. If Nautin is right, the three homilies that concern us (on Ezekiel, Joshua, and Luke) are not likely to be more than a year or two apart. None of them needs to be more than a few years later than the sixth book of the *Commentary on John,* which can be dated fairly securely to the beginning of the Caesarean period[98].

Attractive as Nautin's hypothesis is, and convenient as it is for my own argument, it seems to me seriously flawed. His assumption that the homilies as we have them are transcripts of an orderly sequence of sermons,

---

98 Evidence in Origen's introduction to Book VI, sections 1–12 (ed./tr. 128–137 [629]) [691].

delivered in accord with the church's lectionary calendar, would lead us to expect that Origen's homilies on the Old Testament will cover approximately equal stretches of the Biblical text, at least within any given book. It does not prepare us for the fact that, of the sixteen *Homilies on Genesis* [632,688], fully twelve are devoted to the stories of Abraham and Isaac in chapters 17—26; that is, three-quarters of the homilies for one-fifth of the text. Nor would we have expected to find that at least four of the *Homilies on Isaiah* [641] (I, IV, V, VI; also IX, if we suppose it is authentic) expound the vision of chapter 6, often going over the exact same verses; or that the first of these homilies, in particular, is so jagged and obscure in its style that it reads more like notes for a sermon than a transcript of one. The relation between the literary homilies and what Origen actually preached in church appears to have been far more complex than Nautin supposes[o]. Since Nautin's argument for the date of the homilies rests on his assumption about what the homilies are, questioning the one requires us to question the other.

I cannot, however, improve on Nautin. At present, I believe, we have no way of knowing when Origen wrote or spoke the homilies that concern us. They may be later than Nautin thinks; or, conceivably, even earlier. There is no reason why any long period of time *must* have separated them from each other, or from the sixth book of the *Commentary on John*. This is worth keeping in mind as we proceed.

b) The first passage we must consider is from the *Homilies on Joshua, IX, 4* (ed./tr. 250—255 [630]). Origen is expounding the Septuagint text of Joshua 8:32: *Jesus* [that is, Joshua] *wrote Deuteronomy upon the stones in the presence of the children of Israel*[99].

Taken literally, Origen argues, the text is absurd. Let "those Jews, advocates of the literal meaning, who do not know the spirit of the law," explain to him how Joshua could possibly have found time to write out the whole Book of Deuteronomy during a public assembly, or space on the stone altar to write it in! But, if the text is understood allegorically,

> our Lord Jesus needs no long time to write Deuteronomy, to carve the second law into the hearts of the believers, to impress the law of the spirit upon the minds of those people who are worthy

---

99 RSV translates MT Joshua 8:32 as follows: "And there, in the presence of the people of Israel, he [Joshua] wrote upon the stones a copy of the law of Moses, which he had written." LXX gives, for the Hebrew *mishneh torat mosheh* (literally, "the repetition of the Torah of Moses"), the double translation "Deuteronomy, the law of Moses." (Origen perhaps used a variant text of LXX, which omitted "the law of Moses.") *To deuteronomion*, which LXX also uses to translate *mishneh hattorah* in Deuteronomy 17:18, is Greek for "the second law." Origen can understand it to mean either the Book of Deuteronomy, or the "second law" of Jesus, as it suits him [674].
– "Jesus" (*Iēsous*) is simply the Greek form of "Joshua," used throughout the LXX Joshua. Origen gets endless mileage out of this in his *Homilies on Joshua*.

to be chosen [as stones] for the building of the altar. As soon as a person believes in Jesus Christ, the law of the Gospel is written in his heart; and it is *in the presence of the children of Israel* that it is written.

For, at the time that you received the sacrament of the faith, there attended you heavenly powers, throngs of angels, *the assembly of the first-born* [Hebrews 12:23]. If we correctly understand "Israel" to mean "one who sees God with his mind[100]," this [designation] is most appropriate for the ministering angels. We know this from the fact that the Lord says about the little children – which is what you were when you were baptized – that *their angels always see the face of my father who is in heaven* [Matthew 18:10]. It was, then, *in the presence* of these *children of Israel*, who see the face of God, who were in attendance when you received the sacraments of the faith, that Jesus wrote Deuteronomy in your heart.

Shall we prove to you yet more clearly from the holy scriptures that *Jesus wrote the second law in the presence of the children of Israel*? The apostle makes this point plainly when he writes to the Hebrews: *You have not drawn near to the sound of the trumpet and the mountain blazing. Rather, you have drawn near to Mount Zion and the city of the living God, the heavenly Jerusalem; to the assembly of the first-born that is inscribed in heaven; to a throng of angels praising God*[101]. It was, you see, *in the presence* of all these, who are properly called *children of Israel* because they always see God, that Jesus wrote his law in the hearts of the believers.

We have this passage only courtesy of Rufinus, and therefore must not lay too much weight on its exact wording. But the essential point seems clear. Origen treats baptism as a lawgiving, and assumes that throngs of angels attend it. As in the first homily on Ezekiel, he speaks of those who receive this "law" as little children, and quotes Matthew 18:10 in reference to them and their attending angels[102]. But Matthew 18:10 will hardly yield the image of angels at a lawgiving, any more than will Joshua 8:32 itself. It is important that, as soon as Origen is through expounding Joshua 8:32, he drops his identification of "Israel" with the angels, and returns to his more usual (and traditional) explanation of the name as referring to the new "Israel of God," the Christian people (IX, 5, 7–10; referring to Joshua 8: 33, 35, 9:2). Clearly, this identification is a temporary expedient[103] which enables Origen to apply to Joshua 8:32 a ready-made image of angels at lawgiving. His most likely source for this image is the Sinai *haggadot.*

Indeed, he practically tells us as much with his quotation from Hebrews 12. This quotation draws our attention to Sinai, and tells us at the same

---

100 This is based on the Hellenistic Jewish derivation of "Israel" from '*ish ro'eh 'el*, "man who sees God," which goes back at least to Philo [719a,719b,733]. Origen often makes use of it.

101 This is a very free quotation of Hebrews 12:18–19, 22–23; see below.

102 This is not the first time Origen makes use of Matthew 18:10. He quotes it already in the Alexandrian *De Principiis* (I.viii.1, tr. 66 [636]), in support of his doctrine of the guardian angels of the church [662]. I do not suggest that Origen owes his belief in guardian angels to the Jews of Caesarea, but only that their stories of Sinai contributed some fresh shades to it.

103 I must admit that, while it is unusual, it does occur elsewhere. In the *Homilies on Numbers*, XI, 4–5 (ed. 7:82–87 [640]; tr. 213–223 [633]), Origen explains that the "first fruits" that the Israelites are to offer (Numbers 18:8–13) represent the souls of the believers. The "Israelites" themselves stand for the angels, "the true and heavenly Israelites."

time that Sinai has been superseded. By stressing that the lawgiving in question is *not* that of Sinai, Origen hints that it once was. He thus takes the energies of the Jewish tradition and directs them against Judaism.

The quotation itself is significantly distorted. *For you have not come,* Hebrews 12:18–19 runs (in the RSV), *to what may be touched, a blazing fire, and darkness, and gloom, and a tempest, and the sound of a trumpet, and a voice whose words made the hearers entreat that no further messages be spoken to them.* Origen's *mountain blazing* seems instead to go back to such Old Testament passages as Exodus 19:18, Deuteronomy 4:11, 5:20, 9:15. It may of course have been Rufinus who made the change, but it is hard to see why he would have made it. Considered as Origen's own error, the misquotation appears as a Freudian slip, suggesting that Sinai was more on Origen's mind than he was willing to admit.

c) We have our next passage, from the *Homilies on Luke, XXVII, 5* (ed./ tr. 348–349 [634]), through the more reliable mediation of Jerome. Origen here expounds the description of Jesus' baptism in Luke 3:21–22, which he conflates with the parallel Matthew 3:16–17:

> The Lord was baptized, *the heavens were opened, the holy spirit descended upon him,* and a voice thundered from heaven: *This is my beloved son, with whom I am pleased.* It must be said that the heaven was unlocked at the baptism of Jesus. The heavens were opened to grant remission of sins – not his, indeed, *who did no sin, in whose mouth no deceit was found* [Isaiah 53:9, I Peter 2:22] ; but the sins of all the world. The holy spirit descended, in order that, after the Lord had *ascended on high leading a captivity captive* [Psalm 68:19, Ephesians 4:8], he might grant us the spirit that had come to him. Indeed, he also gave [the spirit] at the time of his resurrection, saying: *Receive the holy spirit. If you forgive the sins of anyone, they are forgiven; if you retain the sins of anyone, they are retained* [John 20:22–23].

We need not examine the continuation of this passage, in which Origen discusses the image of the holy spirit as a dove; and, for what this may be worth, quotes in this connection another verse from Psalm 68 (14). What is important for us is that Origen here reinforces the impression he has given in his first homily on Ezekiel, that he imagines Jesus' ascension as somehow connected with his baptism – or, perhaps more to the point, with the opening of the heavens. He even distinguishes a gift of the spirit made at the time of the ascension and another made at the time of the resurrection, implying that he regards these as two separate occasions[p).

It is not easy to square the emerging picture with the New Testament, much less derive it from there. More likely, Origen is imposing on his New Testament texts an image he has drawn from elsewhere: the ascension of Moses, according to the Shabu^c ot cycle.

d) It is in his *Commentary on John, Book VI,* that Origen gives his most vivid and detailed account of the ascension, and here we luckily have the original Greek.

The passage that concerns us is part of an extremely long and involved exposition of John 1:29, which calls Jesus *the lamb of God who takes away the sin of the world.* In this act of redemption, Origen says, Jesus *disarmed the principalities and powers and made a public example of them, triumphing in the tree* (Colossians 2:15)[104]. Origen goes on to describe in some detail the sequel to Jesus' victory:

Having destroyed his enemies through his passion, *the Lord powerful and mighty in battle* [Psalm 24:8] needs for his valorous feats a purification that only the father can give him. He thus prevents Mary [Magdalene] from touching him, saying: *Do not touch me, for I have not yet gone up to the Father. But go and tell my brothers: I am going to my Father and your Father, my God and your God* [John 20:17].

When, conquering and triumphant, he goes with his body resurrected from the dead — for how else can one understand the words *I have not yet gone up to my Father* and *I am going to my Father?* — certain powers then say: *Who is this who comes from Edom, his garments crimson from Bosor, so lovely?* [Isaiah 63:1]. Those who accompany him say to the guards of the celestial gates: *Open your gates, O princes, and be opened, O eternal gates, that the king of glory may enter* [Psalm 24:7, LXX]. As if (if one may speak thus) they see his right hand bloodied and entirely filled with heroic feats, they continue to inquire: *Why are your garments crimson, and your clothing like the remains of a full winepress pressed out?* [Isaiah 63:2–3, LXX]. He then answers: *I have crushed them* [63:3].

It was surely on account of these things that he had to wash *his robe in wine, and his garment in the blood of grapes* [Genesis 49:11]. For, having taken our weaknesses and borne our illnesses [cf. Matthew 8:17, Isaiah 53:4], and having taken away the sin of the entire world, and performed so many benefits, he thereupon received a baptism greater than anything humans could guess at. I believe it was concerning this that he said: *I have a baptism to be baptized, and how I am constrained until it is accomplished!* [Luke 12:50]. In order that, examining the text, I may stand more boldly against the conjectures of the majority, let me ask those who think that his martyrdom was this greatest baptism — beyond which no other baptism could be conceived — why afterwards he said to Mary, *Do not touch me.* He should rather have make himself available to be touched, inasmuch as he had received the perfect baptism through the mystery of his passion.

But when, as we have said, he had performed his valorous feats against the hostile forces and he needed to wash *his robe in wine and his garment in the blood of grapes,* he went up to the Father, the vinedresser of the true vine [John 15:1]. This was in order that he might wash himself clean — after he *ascended on high, having taken the captivity captive* [Psalm 68:19, Ephesians 4:8] — and descend bearing the manifold gifts, the *tongues as of fire* distributed to the apostles [Acts 2:3], and the holy angels to stand by them and protect them in all their deeds.

For, before these arrangements[105], they had not yet been purified, and therefore could not support the presence of angels among them. Perhaps the angels, too, did not want to be with those whom Jesus had not yet prepared and purified. For only Jesus so loved humanity that he would eat and drink with sinners and tax-collectors [Mark 2:16], give his feet to [be washed by] the tears of the repentant sinning woman [Luke 7:38], and go down to death on behalf of the

---

104 Quoted in *Commentary*, VI, 285 (ed./tr. 2:346–347 [629]). I have followed RSV except for the last three words, where Origen either paraphrases Colossians or quotes a different text (*en tō xylō* for *autous en autō*). Blanc discusses this variation at some length in her note on the passage [629]; cf. above, chapter III, endnote g. — The *principalities and powers* are usually taken to be some sort of demonic rulers of the cosmos [60]. This is certainly how Origen understands the verse.

105 The word that I translate "arrangements" is the plural of *oikonomia* (above, section 2b). I do not know how to render it adequately into English. Blanc translates: "avant l'accomplissement de ces mystères."

impious [Romans 5:6]; not considering his being equal to God a thing to be held on to, but emptying himself and taking on the form of a slave [Philippians 2:6–7]. [VI, 287–294; ed./tr. 2: 348–353 [629]]

This long and complex passage has two points of contact with the passage from the first homily on Ezekiel that I quoted in section 2c. One is the use of Psalm 68:19. The other is the description of the angels' descent, in Jesus' train, to support and protect the believers. But the two passages differ in the space that they allot to these elements. Origen allows his account of the angels to mushroom in the first homily; he keeps it to a minimum in the *Commentary*. The quotation of Psalm 68:19, by contrast, which is left in the first homily without any explanation apart from a further quotation of Ephesians 4:10–12, here becomes part of an elaborate midrashic web on the theme of Jesus' ascension. The other main threads of the web are Psalm 24:7–10, Isaiah 63:1–6, John 20:17, Genesis 49:11, and Luke 12:50.

When we look at the last three verses more closely, we see that Origen is using them here in a very unusual way, which goes even against his own treatment of them in his other writings. He insists that Luke 12:50 cannot refer, as most people think, to Jesus' death, but must speak of some mysterious "baptism" that follows. But he himself gives elsewhere precisely the interpretation that he here argues against (*Exhortation to Martyrdom*, chapter 30, tr. 61–62 [628]; *Homilies on Judges*, VII, 2, ed. 7:507 [640]). Since Origen here interprets Genesis 49:11 in the light of his understanding of Luke 12:50, it follows that he must break with a century of Christological exegesis of this passage and deny that the *wine* is Jesus' own blood. Yet, expounding Leviticus 16:26 in his *Homilies on Leviticus* (IX, 5; ed. 6: 424 [639]), Origen himself claims that Jesus "*washed his robe in wine* — that is, in his blood — in the evening, and was made clean. That was perhaps why he said *Do not touch me* to Mary when she wanted to hold his feet after the resurrection."

It is striking that Origen gives, in this passage from the Leviticus homilies, a far more plausible explanation of John 20:17 than he does in his *Commentary on John*. Jesus has just been purified by his own blood, as Genesis 49:11 prophesies. He therefore cannot allow himself to be again contaminated by a woman's touch. Origen's contrasting claim in the *Commentary*, that Jesus did not want Mary Magdalene to touch him *before* he had been purified, makes far less sense; for what harm could Mary's touch have then done Jesus[106]?

Some external force has evidently pulled Origen's exegeses of John 20: 17, Genesis 49:11, and Luke 12:50 into a new and unfamiliar shape. We

---

106 I give fuller references in my *Church History* article [673].

may suspect that it is this same force that has induced Origen to apply to Christ's ascension the blood-glutted language of Isaiah 63. Christian interpretation since the middle of the second century had understood the dialogue of Psalm 24:7–10 to refer to the ascension. But it was Origen who first added the far more martial passage from Isaiah [663].

In Origen's version, Jesus not only is *the Lord powerful and mighty in battle*, but enters heaven with "his right hand bloodied and entirely filled with heroic feats." "Conquering and triumphant," he has "destroyed his enemies," "performed his valorous feats against the hostile forces." He is, I propose, modelled after the Moses who invades heaven and wipes out Kemuel with a single blow; who "took part in·the war of the angels and received a fiery Torah ... vanquished the celestial retinue and revealed their secrets to humankind" (*Deut. R.* 11:10).

You ascended on high, you took a captivity captive, you took gifts for humanity. The Jesus of the New Testament and Christian tradition dies, is buried, descends "into the lower parts of the earth" (Ephesians 4:9). He is then resurrected and ascends to heaven, where he remains sitting on the right hand of the Father. But the Jesus of this passage of the *Commentary on John*, like the Moses of the Sinai-ascension stories, goes first up to heaven and then back down. He returns "bearing the manifold gifts, the *tongues as of fire* distributed to the apostles, and the holy angels to stand by them and protect them in all their deeds."

The "manifold gifts" (*poikila charismata*) are presumably those enumerated in Ephesians 4:11–12. They are the institutions of the new covenant, corresponding to Moses' "great gift" of the Torah (Tanh. Buber *Ha'azinu* #3; quoted above, section B2e). Acts 2:3 speaks of *tongues as of fire* resting on the apostles. The New Testament gives no clear support for Origen's image of the attending angels. But both angels and fire are part of the Sinai *haggadot*; and both, as we saw in chapter I, reappear when Johanan b. Zakkai's disciples expound the *merkabah*.

But what of the great baptism, "beyond which no other baptism could be conceived," which Origen reads into Luke 12:50? Does Moses undergo anything of the kind? At first, we are disposed to answer no. But then we recall the odd detail, in *Pesiqta* and its parallels, that the fiery river Rigyon "meets" Moses. We also recall that the *Visions of Ezekiel* (section IIC1) has the angels performing their ablutions in the "river of fire."

The *Visions,* moreover, does not stand alone [229,492a]. "When the angels come to judgment," says *Ma'ayan Ḥokhmah* in its description of Rigyon, "they are renewed and bathe in that river of fire." A passage in the *Hekhalot* text that Odeberg published as "3 Enoch" [490] tells how, "when the angels want to sing their hymns ... they go down to the river of fire and bathe in the river of fire, washing their tongues and mouths seven times in the river of fire" (Schäfer, #54; Odeberg, ch. 36). Another passage, which occurs in different contexts in several *Hekhalot* manuscripts, gives a more elaborate account of these ablutions (Schäfer, ##180–186, 530–536, 790–796, 810–816). The angels, we are told here, need purification because they spend time on earth and pick up something of the stink of unclean humanity[107].

This last point reminds us of Kemuel's claim (in *Pesiqta* and the Oxford text) that Moses, a human being from a place of filth, must not enter the realms of purity. Kemuel is, of course, a hostile critic. But the point he makes is a valid one, and suggests that Moses will need to be purified sooner or later. We may guess that the detail of Rigyon's meeting Moses is a trace of a description of some such purifying immersion in the fiery river. We best understand Origen's dark hints at "a baptism greater than anything humans could guess at" if we suppose that he knew a version of the Jewish ascension story that explicitly related the purification of Moses, and that he transferred it from Moses to Jesus[108].

Just as we can use Origen's first homily on Ezekiel to flesh out the spare references to the attending angels in his *Commentary on John*, so we can use the *Commentary* to discover what lies behind his quotation of Psalm 68:19 in the first homily. In both texts, Origen gives a Christianized version of the Sinai-ascension legend preserved in *Pesiqta Rabbati*, in which Jesus replaces Moses as the ascending hero and the original ties with Sinai are effaced as completely as possible.

Like *Pesiqta*, Origen represents the descent of the angels as following upon the ascent of the hero, and implies that there is a causal link between the two. This seemingly minor point takes on great importance when we realize that it echoes a theme that we detected back in chapter III, particularly in connection with the ascensions of Enoch and Abraham (sections 3e, 5e, 6f). In some way we could not then explain, the exaltation of the human being seemed linked to the degradation of heavenly beings.

We also recall from chapter III that the Apocalypse of Abraham models Abraham's ascent after Moses', and that the threats that Azazel there uses to scare Abraham away from making the climb reflect the terrifying experi-

---

107 Versions, or portions thereof, have been published by Jellinek, Wertheimer, and Scholem [482, 498a,600]. – It is odd that the text speaks of the angels, after their immersion, becoming "*like* the angels of *^CArabot Raqia^C*"; as if the writer cannot get out of his head a version in which the purified beings are humans advanced to angelic status.

108 In his twenty-fourth homily on Luke (ed./tr. 326–327 [634]), Origen gives a very strange description of a baptism in a fiery river which Jesus himself administers to those souls who want to pass over to paradise [670]. Roberta Chesnut has called my attention to the motif of the "sea of fire" in the Syriac homilies of the Monophysite theologian Jacob of Sarug (d. 521), which may perhaps draw on Jewish *merkabah* traditions [660]. These data seem relevant to the current discussion, but I am not sure just how to integrate them.

ences that Moses actually has. We may now begin to suspect that Azazel's motives in the apocalypse cast light on the motives of the angels who oppose Moses. What is at stake, perhaps, is not only the possession of the Torah, but an attack from below that threatens to tear the angels down from their thrones of power.

We will pursue this suspicion in chapter IX. In the meantime, let us come back to Origen, and see if we can trace the channels by which the materials of the Shabu^cot cycle reached him.

4. Origen and Joshua b. Levi

The most important channel, I believe, was R. Joshua b. Levi.

Earlier in this chapter, we saw reason to believe that we could trace the Sinai-ascension *haggadot* back to a series of sermons delivered by Joshua b. Levi, presumably on Shabu^cot. We now have evidence that Origen, who was active in Caesarea at about the same time that Joshua b. Levi was active in Lydda, made use of a cycle of Shabu^cot sermons very much akin to those we postulated for Joshua b. Levi. We must add that Saul Lieberman has argued that the editors of the "Talmud of Caesarea" incorporated the work of the Lyddan scholars, which seems to point to particularly close ties between these two centers [321]. We must add, too, that Joshua b. Levi himself was no stranger to Caesarea; in PT Ber. 5:1 (9a) we find him and Hanina b. Hama respectfully received in the proconsul's court there [369]. Given all this, it seems very plausible that Origen had access to Joshua b. Levi's teachings, and that he may have known the man personally.

Origen perhaps tells us as much. In what appears to be a fragment of the introduction to his great commentary on Psalms, written at Caesarea [689], Origen remarks that "I was discussing certain oracles of God with Iullus the patriarch and with someone who bore the title of 'sage' among the Jews." He learned from them, he says, that a name attached to the beginning of any given psalm ("a psalm of David," "a psalm of Asaph," or the like) announces the author, not of that psalm alone, but also of whatever anonymous psalms come right after it. Moses was thus the author of Psalm 90 ("a prayer of Moses the man of God"), and also of the ten anonymous psalms that follow [635a].

In itself, this tradition does not interest us in the least; nor have we any reason to entangle ourselves in the century-old controversy over who it was that Origen meant by "Iullus the patriarch" [665]. What does concern us is that, as Grätz pointed out in 1881 (and Krauss after him), the substance of the tradition that Origen heard from Iullus and his fellow-"sage" crops up in rabbinic sources [402,683]. "Moses uttered eleven psalms, corresponding to the eleven tribes that he blessed [Deuteronomy 33]." Psalm

90 is the psalm for the tribe of Reuben; Psalm 91 is Levi's, Psalm 92 Judah's, Psalm 93 Benjamin's, Psalm 94 Gad's, Psalm 95 Issachar's. "R. Joshua b. Levi said: The tradition I received extends this far. From here on you must work it out for yourself[109]."

That is, Joshua b. Levi transmits and comments on an anonymous tradition which is very similar to the one that Origen heard from Iullus and the other "sage." It hardly seems fantastic to suppose that this "sage" was Joshua b. Levi himself.

5. The Greek midrash of Caesarea

Origen's command of Hebrew was feeble at best [665]. Whether we suppose that he learned the Shabuᶜot expositions directly from Joshua b. Levi, or indirectly, through the Caesarean community, the language he learned them in must have been Greek. This poses no problem for our reconstruction. It is hard to imagine Joshua b. Levi appearing at the proconsul's court in Caesarea (above) without some ability to communicate in Greek, and we would expect the rabbis who actually lived in Caesarea to be yet more fluent.

Moreover, to judge from the rabbinic and archaeological evidence that Lee I. Levine has collected, many Caesarean Jews knew no more Hebrew than Origen did. "R. Levi b. Hita came to Caesarea and heard voices reciting the *Shemaᶜ* in Greek. He wanted to stop them. R. Jose heard about it and became angry [with R. Levi]. He said: 'This I say: If they cannot say it in Hebrew, should they then not say it at all? Rather, they are permitted to say it in any language[110].'" We can hardly expect that people who could not even say the *Shemaᶜ* in Hebrew would have gotten much out of a sermon delivered in that language. It follows that the rabbis who preached in

---

109 That is, you must figure out for yourself which tribes the next five psalms were written for. – The passage occurs in *Midr. Psalms* 90:3 (ed. 193b–194a [199]) and among the additions to *Pesiqta de-Rab Kahana* (*We-Zot ha-Berakhah*; ed. 441–443 [206]). I have translated *Pesiqta*'s text of the first sentence, but followed *Midr. Psalms* for the rest. – The context of the midrashic passage may perhaps explain a peculiar blunder that Origen attributes to one of his Jewish informants: "He said at first that there were thirteen [psalms] of Moses." This would be strange arithmetic indeed. But the sequence of expositions that includes our midrash begins: "R. Helbo quoted R. Huna: Moses wrote out thirteen copies of the Torah on the day he died. Twelve were for the twelve tribes; one he deposited in the ark, so that no one would be able to alter its text" (*Midr. Psalms;* *Pesiqta*'s version is slightly different). Perhaps Origen or one of his informants confused Moses' *thirteen* copies of the Torah with his *eleven* psalms.

110 PT Sotah 7:1 (21b), following Levine's translation [422]. Admittedly, Levi b. Hita (or Hayta) seems to have lived more than a century after Origen [805]. But I see no reason to suppose that knowledge of Hebrew was any more widespread among the Jews of Caesarea in the third century than it was in the fourth.

some at least of the Caesarean synagogues must have preached in Greek. To judge from an inscription found in one of these synagogues, they may sometimes have used the Septuagint as well as the more "orthodox" translation of Aquila as their Bible text [422].

All of this suggests the possibility that Origen did not need to have anyone translate the Shabu^cot expositions into Greek for his benefit. Greek may have been their original language.

a) "The heaven was opened." If so, we can understand why certain passages in the *Visions of Ezekiel* seem best to make sense on the assumption that they were formulated in Greek, or based on the Septuagint text of the Bible.

The clearest case is the exposition, in section IG, of the words *the heavens were opened.* "It would have been proper for the text to say, *The heaven was opened* [*niftah hashshamayim*]. What does it mean by saying, *The heavens were opened* [*niftehu hashshamayim*]? This teaches us that seven firmaments were opened to Ezekiel. ..." This argument is, as Gruenwald observed, complete nonsense [229]. "Heaven" (*shamayim*) is always treated as a plural in Hebrew (and Aramaic); no one could possibly have expected to find the singular verb *niftah* used with it.

But, as we have seen, Origen made use of this exegesis in his first homily on Ezekiel, and therefore must have known it in Greek. If we assume that its Jewish author originally formulated it in Greek, and derived it from the Septuagint rather than the Masoretic Text, its logic makes perfect sense. Like MT, LXX Ezekiel 1:1 uses plural for both the noun and the verb (*ēnoichthēsan hoi ouranoi*). In the Greek of LXX, however, "heaven" is normally singular. A Greek-speaking Jewish expositor therefore might well base a midrash on the unusual plural of this passage[111]. The author of the *Visions of Ezekiel* (or, more likely, one of his sources) tries to perform the impossible task of carrying this midrash over into Hebrew; and the result is absurdity.

b) "The sparkling-winged ones." According to section IF of the *Visions,* Ezekiel "saw God's glory, and the *hayyot*, angels, troops, seraphim, and sparkling-winged ones joined to the *merkabah.*" The "sparkling-winged ones" (*nosese kanaf*) are plainly drawn from Ezekiel 1:7: *Their legs were straight, and the soles of their feet were like the soles of a calf's foot, and they sparkled* [*nosesim*] *like polished* [?] *brass.*

---

111 Out of approximately six hundred occurrences of *ouranos* recorded in Hatch and Redpath's *Concordance to the Septuagint* [803], I count forty-nine uses of the plural, of which seven are in the Apocrypha. In the surviving fragments of Aquila, Symmachus, and Theodotion, the plural is proportionally more common than in LXX, but still relatively rare.

Gruenwald has compared the usage of the liturgical poems (*piyyuṭim*) of
the early Middle Ages, which, obviously on the strength of this verse, refer
to angels as "sparkling ones" (*noṣeṣim*; examples in Ben Yehuda's *Thesaurus* [799]). But Ben Yehuda lists no parallels to the designation "sparkling-*winged* ones"; and it is hard to see how these "wings" can have come from
the Hebrew text of Ezekiel 1:7^{q)}.

Wings, however, figure prominently in the LXX translation of this verse:

> Their legs were straight, and their feet were winged, and [were?] sparks like flashing brass; and
> their wings were swift.

This seems the most likely understanding of the Greek text. By stretching the language, however, it is possible to take *hai pteryges autōn* as the
subject of *spinthēres hōs exastraptōn chalkos*, and to understand the verse:

> Their legs were straight, and their feet were winged; and their wings were sparks like flashing
> brass, and were swift.

I think it likely that it is the LXX text, so understood, that underlies
the epithet "sparkling-winged ones" of the *Visions*.

c) "Am I not a priest?" Ezekiel, the author of the *Visions* tells us (section IC), "began to complain to God. ... 'Am I not a priest? Am I not a
prophet? Why did Isaiah prophesy in Jerusalem, while I am in captivity,
and Hosea in Jerusalem, while I am in captivity?'"

Why should a "priest" and a "prophet" not have gone into captivity?
Gruenwald has given a fairly plausible explanation of the "prophet" part of
Ezekiel's protest; it is probably connected to the belief, expressed in some
rabbinic sources, that revelation does not occur outside Palestine [229]. It
is less clear why Ezekiel invokes his priesthood. Two Biblical passages,
Ezekiel 4:13–14 and Amos 7:17, perhaps hint that it is a special indignity
for a priest to be in an unclean land. But the logic of this part of Ezekiel's
argument is still shaky. Our hypothesis, that Greek Jewish sources lie behind the *Visions*, may help strengthen it.

Daniel R. Schwartz has recently discussed a difficult passage in Josephus's *Antiquities* which seems to contrast Jeremiah and Ezekiel. Both were
"priests by descent" (*tō genei hiereis*); but Jeremiah spent much of his
adult life in Jerusalem, while Ezekiel went into exile as a boy (X, 80; referring ahead to X, 98). Josephus's point, Schwartz argues, rests on a difference in meaning between the Hebrew term for "priest" (*kohen*) and the
Greek word used to translate it (*hiereus*). Anyone who can claim descent
from Aaron is a *kohen,* whether or not he functions as a priest; while a
hiereus is someone who actually officiates in a cult. Josephus therefore
consistently distinguishes a man who (like Jeremiah) has at least the potential to serve as priest, from a descendant of Aaron without such potential
– because, for example, he has a physical defect, or (like Ezekiel) he can-

not get to Jerusalem. The former is a *hiereus*, the latter only a *"hiereus* by descent."

Centuries later, Jerome makes a similar distinction in his Latin terminology: Josephus of Jerusalem is a "priest" (*sacerdos*), while Philo of Alexandria is only "of priestly race" (*de genere sacerdotum*). Schwartz can thus argue from Josephus's usage, and from Jerome's, that Greek and Latin writers on Jewish subjects sensed that *hiereus* and its Latin equivalent were not quite appropriate for a *kohen* who had no chance actually to function as a priest [730].

Now, LXX Ezekiel 1:3 calls Ezekiel a *hiereus*; and, unlike MT, makes clear that it is he and not his father who bears this title. Spoken in Greek, therefore, Ezekiel's protest makes good sense. God himself has attested, through the words of Scripture, that Ezekiel is a *hiereus*. Now, by sending him into exile, he makes it impossible for him to be a real *hiereus*! The author's point was lost only when his midrash was translated into Hebrew; and when *kohen*, with its different range of meanings, was substituted for *hiereus*[112].

d) "Angels of heaven, open to me!" So far, our argument for Greek originals for the Shabu[c]ot homilies has rested entirely on the *Visions of Ezekiel.* I know of no comparable evidence from *Pesiqta*'s Sinai-ascension *haggadot.*

This difference will not surprise us if we suppose that we have received the Sinai-ascension materials through the more or less regular channels of transmission of midrashic literature, where generations of Hebrew- and Aramaic-speaking redactors could rub away whatever traces these texts once bore of their Greek origins. The solitary and eccentric *Visions,* surviving only in two isolated Genizah manuscripts, presumably comes to us by less familiar paths. It reaches back more directly to the Greek midrash of third-century Caesarea, and reflects some of its peculiarities relatively undistorted. We noticed in section A that the *Visions* is a slightly odd text, whose style and contents do not quite jibe with what the more familiar midrashim would lead us to expect. We now perhaps understand why.

---

112 One problem raised by this passage, however, remains unsolved. Why does the author have Ezekiel quote Isaiah 1:1 and Hosea 1:1 in support of his claim that Isaiah and Hosea prophesied in Jerusalem? The former passage indeed mentions Jerusalem, but not as the place of Isaiah's prophecy; the latter does not mention it at all. It is probably significant that Hosea is the first book of the Twelve Minor Prophets; Ezekiel thus contrasts the beginning of his book with the beginnings of two of the three other major Prophetic works. It is therefore doubly odd that he does not mention Jeremiah, who did in fact prophesy in Jerusalem while Ezekiel was in the exile. Perhaps he omits Jeremiah because his theoretical objection, "they prophesied good and I ill," would be nonsense if applied to Jeremiah? (*Pesiqta de-Rab Kahana, Dibre Yirmeyahu* #2, ed. 226–227 [206], seems to imply that Ezekiel was considered a prophet of good, Jeremiah of ill.)

There is one possible source for early Sinai-ascension material, however, which we have so far neglected. It is the bits and pieces of Aramaic liturgical poetry that Joseph Heinemann has collected and discussed [304]. If Heinemann is right, these texts are extremely early and primitive, and are connected with the translation and exposition of the Scriptures in the synagogue. As far as oddity goes, they yield nothing to the *Visions of Ezekiel.*

Two of Heinemann's pieces, mentioned above (section B2b) in connection with the horns of Moses, deal with Moses' ascension and his conflict with the angels. One of these, the poem called *'Angele Meroma*, describes a dialogue of Moses with the angels at the gates of heaven. He wants to get in; they want to keep him out [283,305].

All of the passages Heinemann quotes use Greek words frequently and in very unusual ways. For example, they often call God *qyrys*, which is certainly Greek *kyrios*, "Lord." In this respect, *'Angele Meroma* is particularly rich:

> "Angels [*'ngly* = Greek *angeloi*] of heaven, open to me, that I may enter!"
> says Moses.
> "We won't open, for we have no power to open,"
> say the angels [Aramaic *mal'akhayya*] to Moses the prophet.
> "I am crying out to you: open the heaven [*'wrnws* = *ouranos*] to me!"
> says Moses.
> "Why are you crying out to us? You ought to cry out to the Lord [*qyrys* = *kyrios*],"
> say the angels to Moses the prophet.
> "I am a man of the race [*gynws* = *genos*] of righteous Abram,"
> says Moses.
> "You are a man, son of woman. How can you climb to a place of fire?"
> say the angels to Moses the prophet.
> "Mighty ones, open to me quickly!"
> says Moses.
> "Our creator knows that we haven't the authority,"
> say the angels to Moses the prophet.
> "If you don't open to me, you'll open sooner or later,"
> says Moses.
> "If you've come up, you'll go down sooner or later,"
> say the angels to Moses the prophet.

In the second part of the poem (omitted by Heinemann), Moses declares over and over that he will not go down until he has battled the angels and received the Torah: "until I take my bride and go, until I take my Torah and descend" [283].

The contents of *'Angele Meroma* obviously link it to the Sinai-ascension *haggadot*; while Moses' demand that the angels "open the heaven" suggests Ezekiel 1:1. Its language is Aramaic. But it perhaps betrays a Greek Jewish source, not only in its heavy and apparently needless use of Greek words — *angeloi, ouranos,* and *kyrios,* at least, have perfectly satisfactory equivalents in Aramaic or Hebrew — but also in what seems to be the influence of the LXX text of Psalm 24:7–10.

Lift up your heads, O gates, the Hebrew text of Psalm 24 demands twice. But the Greek has instead: *Open your gates, O princes, and be opened, O eternal gates, that the king of glory may enter.* Early Christian exegesis, as we saw in connection with Origen's *Commentary on John,* often applies LXX Psalm 24:7–10 to Christ's ascension: he, or his attendants, demand that the guardians of heaven open their gates to him [28a,663, 698a][113]. In *'Angele Meroma,* we find Moses standing in Jesus' place and making the same demand. Here, too, the Greek text of the twenty-fourth psalm seems to be in the background.

Admittedly, the Biblical passage's description of the *king of glory* seems better to suit Jesus than Moses. Perhaps Christian exegesis had its own influence on the Shabu{c}ot homilies of the Greek-speaking synagogues; and perhaps Jews were no less willing than was Origen to put one champion in the place of the other.

e) Implications. In a series of classic studies on Greek and Hellenism in Jewish Palestine, Saul Lieberman has collected evidence from the rabbinic literature for the rabbis' use of the Greek language and of Hellenistic patterns of thought [422a,423,424]. Barthélemy's arguments (above, section 1b), and the evidence we have examined in this section, suggest that Lieberman's data represent only a small part of the reality. We must imagine Greek as standing beside Hebrew and Aramaic, as a language which the rabbis used to formulate their religiosity and to convey it to their followers.

We need not suppose that this "rabbinic Greek" was the refined and subtle medium that we know from classical and Christian literature, or that the Caesarean rabbis' use of it implies that they had absorbed much of Greek culture[114]. "Jews are not at all well read in Greek literature," says Origen, correcting what he thinks is an error of Celsus (*Contra Celsum,* II, 34; tr. 94 [627]). He reports in his *Epistle to Africanus* that his Jewish informants were not able to suggest a translation of the Greek puns in the *Story of Susanna* back into their supposed Hebrew original (tr. 375–376 [635]). We have no reason to doubt Origen's testimony, but we must look at it in perspective. By the standards of an Alexandrian intellectual, the rabbis of Caesarea no doubt spoke a crude, clumsy, and unlettered Greek. This does not prevent them from having used it as a medium in which they could ca-

---

113 Professor Daniel Sheerin has so far, to my knowledge, not published his important studies of the development of Christian exegesis of Psalm 24:7–10.

114 I do not deny the possibility that there may have existed in third-century Caesarea some form of Hellenized Judaism, independent of and perhaps opposed to that of the rabbis. But, if there was such a Judaism, it is not what we are concerned with here. We are talking about *rabbinic* Judaism, expressing itself in Greek.

pably and forcefully develop their distinctive ideas from their Greek Scriptures.

The implications of this are considerable, and go well beyond the scope of this book. If, only in this one town of Caesarea, rabbis preached Greek sermons Sabbath after Sabbath, festival after festival, year after year, they must have created an enormous mass of oral material in Greek. What happened to it all? Do we have its essentials, reshaped into Hebrew or Aramaic, in the familiar rabbinic sources? Or do we have only those aspects of it that the editors of our Talmudic and midrashic texts thought interesting and useful, and therefore did not allow to perish? The second alternative seems the more likely. If the synagogue homilies of Caesarea could be recovered in their original Greek, we might well find different emphases in it from those of the surviving literature[115]. The historical Joshua b. Levi, the historical Hoshaiah and Jose b. Hanina and Abbahu, might turn out to be far more complex characters than our Hebrew and Aramaic sources allow us to see.

This is, of course, a dream. The Greek rabbinic literature, if it was ever written down, has vanished — probably forever. We do not know what aspects of the rabbis' intellectual life have disappeared with it. Only on rare occasions, and by dint of highly unconventional and speculative methods, can we recover fragments of what has been lost. This has been Barthélemy's contribution. If the reader is prepared to accept the arguments I have offered, it is now ours as well.

Read with Origen's help, the *Visions of Ezekiel* is a mirror to a hidden face of third-century rabbinic Judaism.

6. The Shabu^c ot cycle and Jewish-Christian polemic

We are now at last in a position to understand the element of religious polemic that we have found here and there in texts representing the Shabu^c ot cycle (above, section B4b).

"See that I have revealed myself to you in my glory and my splendor," God says to the Israelites at the conclusion of *Pesiqta*'s story. "Should there be a generation that leads you astray and says, 'Let us go and worship other gods,' then say to them: 'We have a Lord whom we serve. When we abandon him, he sends us down to hell. And God will establish his kingdom over all Israel.'"

---

115 We might, for one thing, find in this Greek material a reasonably clear picture of the rabbinic reactions to the specific claims of Christianity, of which our surviving rabbinic sources give only the most sparse and unsatisfying hints [414,425].

In the Targumic Tosefta to Ezekiel 1:1, seduction has turned to force. Nebuchadnezzar "was filled with pride in his idolatry, and spoke thus: 'Is this not Jerusalem, city of the most high God, which is said to have no equal from one end of the earth to the other? It is going to be handed over to me; I will destroy it and its Temple, and I will exile its people to the country of my idols. Then I will climb to the lofty heavens and will destroy the celestial chambers; I will make war with the exalted holy ones and will set my royal throne over the cherubim. '"

I propose that these two passages reflect two stages of the struggle between Judaism and Christianity. The first is from the propaganda war of the third century. The second is from the time after Constantine's conversion in the early fourth century, when Christianity gained access to the centers of power.

Among the projects of the Christian emperors, from the fourth century on, was to turn Palestine into the Christian Holy Land and Jerusalem into a showcase for the Christian victory. To this end, they made the Temple site into a desolation. They permitted Jews to visit it only once a year, on the fast of the Ninth of Ab, in order to mourn over the Temple. The ordinary Christian was invited to consider the contrast between the ruins of the Temple on the one hand, and the splendor of the Church of the Resurrection and the churches on the Mount of Olives on the other. He could hardly doubt that, as Ezekiel prophesied (11:23), the glory of the Lord had abandoned the Temple for the mount of the Savior's ascension; that God had forsaken the synagogue for the church, the old Israel for the new [368, 442, 622b].

For the third-century Shabu^cot preachers, it might have been answer enough to Christian enticements to point to the "glory and splendor" that descended with God to Sinai, and which remains with him in heaven. But after the Christian triumph of the fourth century, the point had to be sharpened. The preachers now declared: Let the modern Christian Nebuchadnezzars boast of having turned God's earthly Temple into a ruin! His "celestial chambers" remain inviolate. The Christians are fools if they think they can touch them.

Indeed, we can perhaps best understand the lavish descriptions of the heavenly structures in the *Hekhalot* literature as a Jewish answer to the splendid religious edifices built by Constantine and his successors, which both advertised the church's victory on earth and symbolized its greater unseen glories[116]. In this world, Jews could hardly hope to compete. But

---

116 Eusebius's oration over Constantine's great cathedral at Tyre, quoted in the tenth book of the *History of the Church* (X, iv; tr. 383–401 [620]), gives a vivid picture of what these edifices meant to fourth-century Christians.

what they could not build on earth their fantasy let them build in heaven. We may guess that, as the humiliation of God's earthly *hekhal* ("temple") dragged on, the glories of the heavenly *hekhalot* became more and more important to certain preachers and certain of their hearers. The need for such fantasies may have been one of the motives that generated the *Hekhalot* literature.

The polemic of the "Targumic Tosefta" was, we may imagine, a one-way street. Even if the Christians of fourth-century Palestine came by some chance to hear of it, they would have needed no reply to it. For them, the evident glories of Christian Jerusalem would have been answer enough.

But things were different a hundred years before. We gather from Origen's complaints that some among his Caesarean flock were more than a little attracted to Judaism, and sometimes found themselves in synagogue as well as in church [668]. There, no doubt, they heard sermons preached to them in Greek; including, if they came on the right festival, some of the homilies of the Shabu^cot cycle. These vivid and exciting sermons could easily have drawn them, with their Jewish neighbors, toward the God and the Torah of Sinai[117].

Origen struck back. We have seen how easily he could convert midrashic legends into traditions of supposedly Christian "elders," and use their energies in the service of Christianity (*Homilies on Exodus*, V, 5; above, section 1b). In the same way and for the same purpose, he detached the Shabu^cot themes from the Old Covenant and transferred them to the New. In Origen's reworking of these themes, therefore, the ascending and triumphant Moses must vanish entirely, to be replaced by the ascending and triumphant Jesus.

You have come to Sinai, the Jewish preachers told their hearers in effect, *and you have seen there the heavenly glory.* To which Origen replied, misquoting the twelfth chapter of Hebrews: *You have not drawn near to the sound of the trumpet and the mountain blazing. Rather, you have drawn near to Mount Zion and the city of the living God, the heavenly Jerusalem; to the assembly of the first-born that is inscribed in heaven; to a throng of angels praising God* (*Homilies on Joshua,* IX, 4).

---

117 Origen leaves little doubt that the Jews of Caesarea were interested in making converts. "At this the Jew said that these prophecies [of Isaiah 53] referred to the whole people as though of a single individual, since they were scattered in the dispersion and smitten, that as a result of the scattering of the Jews among the other nations many might become proselytes" (*Contra Celsum,* I, 55; tr. 50 [627]).

7. Conclusions

The Shabu^cot cycle rests upon three key Biblical passages: Exodus 19, Psalm 68:18–19, and Ezekiel 1. These three texts combine in different ways, drawing dozens of other Scriptures into their couplings. They beget swirls of vivid images.

The heavens open; the hidden wonders are seen; the *merkabah* comes down, perhaps in thousands. Moses ascends on high, takes a captivity captive, brings gifts for humanity. Fire and angels are everywhere, perhaps benign, perhaps hostile. God gives Israel his Torah, and endorses it with his glory. The prophet Ezekiel sees the glory mirrored in the *merkabah*. All Israel sees it, too, at Sinai. And all Israel sees it now, in the synagogue, when the *merkabah* is read and preached.

You see it too. This is perhaps the central message that underlies the complex and interwoven themes. *Haggadat Shema^c Yiśra'el* puts it well: "You too saw, with the understanding of your heart and your mind and your soul, how [God] ... descended in his glory on Mount Sinai. Therefore, Israel, holy nation all, you must hear and understand and know that *the Lord is our God,* by whose name we are called, in unity; *the Lord is one.*"

In this, we hear the most powerful message that the synagogue *merkabah* tradition spoke to the Jewish people. We recognize the echo of it that we heard at the very beginning of our study, when we examined the stories of the *merkabah* expositions of Johanan b. Zakkai's disciples. We now can grasp why people nurtured on the synagogue tradition were ready to believe that the fire and the angels of Sinai appeared when Johanan b. Zakkai and his disciples spoke.

Were they prepared to believe even more than this? The question becomes urgent when we turn to the *Hekhalot* literature. This literature combines the themes of Ezekiel's *merkabah* and heavenly ascension, without ever explaining — it seldom explains anything about itself — why it combines them. It is in the Shabu^cot cycle that we find, for the first time in rabbinic material, the same combination. The Shabu^cot cycle, too, helps us identify Psalm 68:18–19 as the Scriptural inspiration for this linkage. This naturally suggests that the clue to the genesis of the *Hekhalot* lies in the Shabu^cot cycle.

Here and there, the Shabu^cot materials bear what seem to be traces of this relationship. The *Visions of Ezekiel* is not part of the *Hekhalot* literature, but it has at least two important points of contact with it. One is the conception of the visionary as witness and reporter (*Visions,* section IJ; above, section A5c). The other is the strange discussion, which we have so far neglected, of the "prince" in *Zebul* (*Visions,* section IID).

The ascension story of *Pesiqta* and its parallels shares the *Hekhalot* literature's portrayal of heaven as a terrifying place, filled with monstrous angels bearing fantastic names. It also shares a concern with the details of the heavenly liturgy, as we see from *Pesiqta*'s account of the progress of Sandalphon's wreaths toward God's head. We will see in the next chapter that the ascension story, particularly in *Ma^cayan Hokhmah*'s version, is tied to the *Hekhalot* in ways that we have not yet suspected.

One question, however, remains on our agenda for this chapter. What is the meaning of the seven *merkabah*s in the *Visions of Ezekiel*? I have already (at the beginning of section A5c) hinted at a solution to this problem. But I could not give a clear and convincing statement of the solution before we had thoroughly explored the Shabu^cot cycle. We are now ready for it.

8. Postscript: the seven *merkabah*s

The inspiration for this solution is a passage in the most cryptic of all rabbinic texts: *Seder 'Eliyahu*, which we have already seen to be linked with the *Visions of Ezekiel* through its formula for quoting the Mishnah (above, section A3b). Our study of the Shabu^cot cycle gives us the key to the difficulties of this passage. *Seder 'Eliyahu* then returns the favor.

Chapter 7 of *Seder 'Eliyahu Rabbah* (ed. 34 [211]) introduces the *merkabah* in connection with the word *'adam* ("man") in Leviticus 1:2[118]:

> ['Adam] is the language of brotherhood, the language of satisfaction [? ^catirah], the language of friendship. [Similarly,] God called Ezekiel, son of Buzi the priest, *son of man* [*ben 'adam*; Ezekiel 2:1, and often in Ezekiel]: son of proper men, son of righteous men, son of men who perform kind deeds, son of men who always despise themselves[119] for the sake of my honor and Israel's honor.
>
> Another explanation of *son of man*: We may liken the situation to that of a human king whose wife and children behaved unfaithfully toward him, so that he drove them out of his house. Some time later, he sent for one of the sons she had born him. "Son of So-and-so [the woman's name]," he said to him, "let me show you my house and the house that I built for your mother. Are my glory, and the house that I built for your mother, at all diminished?"
>
> That was Ezekiel's situation. So it is written: *In the thirtieth year, in the fourth month, on the fifth of the month*, and so forth, *which was the fifth year*, and so forth, *the word of the Lord came to Ezekiel*, and so forth [Ezekiel 1:1–3]. This is the first episode [*shitah*]. What does [Scripture] say in the second? *I looked, and behold, a storm wind was coming from the north*, and so forth [1:4].

---

118 Older editions give this as chapter 6. – The passage was copied, with minor variations, from *Seder 'Eliyahu Rabbah* into some manuscripts of *Leviticus Rabbah*; it appears in the printed editions as *Lev. R.* 2:8 (ed. 46–47 [191]). Shalom Spiegel, to whose discussion of the passage we will return, did not realize that it is not an original part of *Leviticus Rabbah* [16].

119 *Mebazzin 'et ^casman*; obviously a play on "Buzi." We have seen parallel interpretations of the name of Ezekiel's father in a "Targumic Tosefta" to Ezekiel 1:3 (chapter IV, endnote *h*) and in Origen (above, section 2b).

After [God] had shown him[120], he said to him: "Son of man, this is my glory, by which I exalted you above the Gentiles. Are my glory, and the house that I built for you, at all diminished? So it is written: *If they are ashamed of what they have done, [make known to them] the design of the house and its description,* and so forth [Ezekiel 43:11]. Do you imagine that I have no one to serve me? Do I not have four hundred ninety-six thousand myriads of angels attending me, endlessly sanctifying my great name – saying *Holy holy holy* from sunrise to sunset, and *Blessed be the glory of the Lord from his place* from sunset to sunrise – not to speak of the seventy Gentile nations[r])? Why do you follow ugly ways and do unsightly things, stubbornly resenting the punishments that fall on you? But what am I to do? I must act for the sake of my great name, by which you are called." So it is written: *I acted for the sake of my name, so as not to profane it,* and so forth [Ezekiel 20:14].

The general drift of this passage seems clear enough. But what does the writer mean when he speaks, in the third paragraph, of "the first *shiṭah*" and "the second"? And why does he seem to assume that God showed Ezekiel his "house" – which must mean the heavenly temple – in the *merkabah* vision?

The word *shiṭah,* according to Jastrow [808], means literally *row, line;* hence, *line of thought, opinion, principle, system. Seder 'Eliyahu* seems to use it in a special sense that is not very easy to define. Thus, in chapter 31(29) (ed. 160 [211]) we are told that God "created his world in two *shiṭot.*" The writer explains "the first *shiṭah*" as the multitudes of angels of different kinds, the throne of glory, and the "sapphire" of Ezekiel 1:26. He does not tell us what the second *shiṭah* is, but we may assume he intends the natural order of creation described in the first chapter of Genesis. A few pages later, we read that "from the flood to the time of Manasseh [king of Judah] was one *shiṭah,*" and "from the time of Manasseh to the building of the Second Temple was one *shiṭah*" (ed. 162–163). Another page later, the author asks to what God likens "the faces of the righteous in the future, in the first *shiṭah,*" and answers this baffling question with an even more perplexing parable (ed. 164).

The use of *shiṭah* that best bears comparison with our passage occurs almost immediately before it in chapter 7(6) (ed. 33). The writer gives an abbreviated quotation of Amos 7:1–3 (Amos's vision of locusts). Then: "This is the first *shiṭah.* In the second, [Scripture] says: ..." There follows a similarly abbreviated quotation of Amos 7:4–6 (vision of "judgment by fire"), concluding with the words: "[God] gave revelation twice to the prophet Amos." The author plainly uses the words "first *shiṭah*" and "second" to set apart two consecutive but distinct visionary episodes. We may assume that he uses these words in the same way on the next page, in connection with Ezekiel. That is why I chose to translate *shiṭah* as "episode."

But this usage, clear enough where the two visions of Amos 7:1–6 are involved, is puzzling in connection with the *merkabah.* How could Ezekiel

---

120 The text copied into *Leviticus Rabbah* supplies "all the *merkabah*" as object.

1:1–3 be considered a separate vision from verse 4 and what follows? This difficulty moved Shalom Spiegel to suggest that the midrash refers to a lost oracle of Ezekiel which once came before 1:4, but which was later suppressed [16]. But it hardly seems likely that the memory of a lost oracle, which left no trace on any other text, would have survived to the time of the *Seder 'Eliyahu*. We must look for another solution.

The *Visions of Ezekiel* indicates the direction in which we are to look. It shows us that, like homiletic midrash generally, the Shabuᶜot homilies on Ezekiel 1 tended to focus on the very beginning of the lection (above, section A4c). Thus, the *Visions* developed from the words *the heavens were opened* an elaborate description of the wondrous things that Ezekiel saw in the opened heavens. The author of *Seder 'Eliyahu*, taking this synagogue tradition for granted, could not read *the heavens were opened* without thinking of the whole body of cosmological lore that the preachers piled upon these words. The result was that he conceived Ezekiel as having received revelation in two "episodes" – the vision of the opened heavens; and the distinct vision of *ḥayyot*, wheels, and so forth – which have exactly the same relation to each other as do Amos's two visions.

We may also compare Ezekiel's *shitot* to the two *shitot* of creation (above). The second *shitah* is explicitly described in the Biblical text; while the first is read into it by the haggadic tradition.

We now understand why the author assumes that Ezekiel saw the heavenly temple. This structure appears in the fifth heaven of the *Visions* (section IIF1). Moses saw it, according to one of *Pesiqta*'s concluding *haggadot*, when God opened the seven heavens to him. The author of *Seder 'Eliyahu* could thus take for granted that it was part of Ezekiel's "first episode." So, presumably, were the throngs of angels who attend God, "endlessly sanctifying [*maqdishin*] my great name"; that is, reciting the *Qedushshah*. In the second heaven of the *Visions* (IIC1), the angels who utter the *Qedushshah* "do not stop singing from sunrise to sunset."

We have learned so far that the author of *Seder 'Eliyahu* felt a tension between the vision of the opened heavens and the *merkabah* vision proper, and that he resolved it by distinguishing the two "episodes." The author of the *Visions*, we must suppose, felt the same tension. But he responded differently. Instead of separating 1:1 from 1:4–26, he tried to integrate the details of 1:4–26 into his understanding of 1:1.

This is the logic behind the *Visions'* seven *merkabah*s. If Ezekiel starts his account of the vision by telling us that he saw the seven heavens, it stands to reason that he must have seen the details that follow in each of the seven. Otherwise, thinks the author, one cannot understand the relation of verse 1 to the rest of the chapter. He thus infers that Ezekiel saw not one *merkabah* but seven. I show in Appendix IV how he learns their names, and sometimes also their histories, from other passages of Scripture.

Chapter IX

The Merkabah and the Hekhalot

A. The Problem of the Hekhalot

1. Introduction

The materials that go by the name of *Hekhalot* ("Palaces") are so utterly bewildering that one hardly knows where to begin asking about them. Let us start our discussion with a few conventional suppositions, which we will presently turn around and question.

Let us assume that we are dealing with a series of treatises, composed mainly in Hebrew but also partly in Aramaic. Let us again assume that the main subject of these treatises is the heavenly ascent and how one goes about achieving it. We then find ourselves asking who wrote these texts, and when. If they in fact go back to the rabbinic period — and we will see that there is fairly solid evidence that they cannot have been written later than about 800 — are they the work of the rabbis and their followers, or of fringe Jewish groups whom the rabbis would have rejected as heretics? Do they describe something that their writers and readers were in fact doing? By this, I of course do not mean that they actually and literally travelled to heaven, but that they actually went into trances of some sort and convinced themselves that they had spent the trance making the celestial journey.

Finally, we must pose the questions that bear most directly on our study. What, if anything, have these real or alleged trance journeys to do with the *maʿaseh merkabah* of the rabbinic sources that occupied us in chapter I? What have they to do with the traditional lines of *merkabah* exegesis that we have spent the rest of the book examining?

a) Scholem's solution. The eleventh-century scholar Hai Gaon, as we saw in our Introduction, answered all of these questions unambiguously.

The trances, if not the trips taken in them, were real. If (Hai wrote) a person wants "to look at the *merkabah* and to peer into the palaces of the celestial angels ... he must sit fasting for a specified number of days, place his head between his knees, and whisper to the earth many prescribed songs and hymns. He thus peers into the inner rooms and chambers as if he were seeing the seven palaces with his own eyes, and he observes as if he were going from palace to palace and seeing what is in them." The persons who undertook these experiences were the great Tannaim. Concerning them they taught two *mishnayot*, called the "Greater" and the "Lesser" treatises on the "Palaces" (in Hebrew, *Hekhalot Rabbati* and *Hekhalot Zuṭarti*). In reference to them, they legislated against a person's expounding the *merkabah* "unless he is a scholar and has understood on his own" (M. Hag. 2: 1). Again in reference to them, they told the strange story of the four rabbis who entered *pardes* [241].

Gershom Scholem brought his massive twentieth-century erudition to the support of Hai Gaon's views [589,605]. He did not, of course, uphold them in their eleventh-century form. Hai had seen much of *Hekhalot Rabbati* and *Zuṭarti* introduced as utterances of R. Akiba or R. Ishmael, and had uncritically assumed that these attributions were true. Scholem could hardly do this. But he found reasons of his own for believing that the *Hekhalot* were early. They were certainly not, as the nineteenth-century scholars Heinrich Grätz and Philipp Bloch believed [528,509], products of the early Islamic period. They must be dated to the Talmudic era; and, as Scholem's thinking about them developed, he pushed them further and further back within it. Their central ideas, he claimed at last, belong to the first and second centuries A.D. [613]. Further, their pious acceptance of rabbinic *halakhah* shows that "their writers lived near the center of rabbinic Judaism, not on its fringes" [592]. We might well suppose from Scholem's arguments (although I do not recall that Scholem himself actually says this) that the texts' claims to originate from the teaching of Akiba and Ishmael are not far wrong.

What was Scholem's evidence? Obviously, the *Hekhalot* cannot be older in their present form than Akiba and Ishmael themselves, and therefore must be later than about 100 A.D. At the other end, we have not only Hai Gaon's testimony to their existence, but a few earlier writings that seem to reflect them. The early tenth-century Karaite writer Salmon b. Yeruhim, mightily polemicizing in Hebrew rhymes against the rabbis and their un-Scriptural abominations, concludes his *Book of the Wars of the Lord* with extended abuse of allegedly rabbinic traditions which are closely related to material that we now have in the *Hekhalot* (chapters 14–17 [244])[1]. A century before Salmon, Bishop Agobard of Lyons seems to include the

---

1 I translate chapter 17 of the *Book of the Wars of the Lord* in Appendix VII.

Hekhalot in his attack on "Jewish superstitions" [491,528,563]. Plainly, the *Hekhalot* belong somewhere between 100 and 800 A.D.

Scholem's preference for an early date within this range rests on a long series of correlations of the language and ideas of the *Hekhalot* with language and ideas found in other, more securely dated, sources. He sets forth an impressively detailed, although rather unsystematic, argument to this effect in his book *Jewish Gnosticism, Merkabah Mysticism, and Talmudic Tradition.* I cannot possibly do justice here to the wealth of his argumentation. But I can give some impression of its technique with a few examples.

The heavenly ascensions to which the *Hekhalot* are supposedly devoted continue in the tradition of such apocalyptic texts as the Apocalypse of Abraham and I Enoch 14. The hymns they describe the angels as singing suggest those found in the Apocalypse of Abraham and the Book of Revelation; their style is particularly reminiscent of the Qumran "Angelic Liturgy." All of this points to the antiquity of both the ascension tradition and the hymns. Indeed, one hymn quoted in *Hekhalot Rabbati* (and elsewhere) seems to underlie a passage which rabbinic texts quote in the name of the third-century Amora Isaac Nappaha. It is therefore at least as early as the third century [595,607].

In the third century, too, Origen tells us (in the introduction to his *Commentary on the Song of Songs*) that the Jews are reluctant to let their children study the Song of Songs. He thus bears witness to the existence of the *Hekhalot* subgenre that we call *Shiᶜur Qomah* — fantastic descriptions of the names and dimensions of God's limbs, which are rooted in the Song of Songs' descriptions of the divine Lover [597].

The material reality presupposed is that of Roman Palestine. Thus, one passage in *Hekhalot Rabbati* compares the terrible horses of heaven and the mangers from which they eat to the gate and the mangers of Caesarea[a]. Scholem sees here a reference to the Hippodrome of Caesarea. Since rabbinic literature never mentions the Hippodrome, it follows that the allusion cannot be drawn from rabbinic texts, but must be based "on a concrete Palestinian reality known to the writer" [596].

The keystone of Scholem's argument, however, is his correlation of the *Hekhalot* materials with the Talmudic *maᶜaśeh merkabah*. The *Hekhalot* are mystifications without a context. Rabbinic allusions to *merkabah* and *maᶜaśeh merkabah* provide a frame suited for such mystifications, but leave a great gap where the frame's contents ought to be. That is, they darkly mutter about dangerous secrets connected with Ezekiel's *merkabah*, but, naturally enough, do not actually communicate these secrets. Equate the *Hekhalot* with the rabbinic *maᶜaśeh merkabah*, fit them into the contextual framework that the rabbinic sources provide, and each body of data will fill the other's lack. The rabbinic texts teach us that the *Hekhalot* are esoteric teachings based ultimately on meditations on Ezekiel's vision; the

Hekhalot teach us that these esoteric teachings centered on the practice of mystical ascent. The *Hekhalot* thus give us the key to such cryptic Talmudic passages as the story of the four who entered *pardes*; while these Talmudic passages give us our grounds for believing that the *Hekhalot* come from early in the rabbinic period.

In earlier chapters, I have indicated some of my disagreements, great and small, with Scholem's positions. Origen's testimony to Jewish restrictions on the Song of Songs will bear a simpler explanation than Scholem's (above, chapter I, section 5). The relation of the *pardes* passage to the pertinent *Hekhalot* sources is far more ambiguous and complex than Scholem thought; and the complexity increases when we recall that the point of contact between the two bodies of data lies in the specifically Babylonian version of the *pardes* episode (chapter VI, section 2). Most important, the neat fit that Scholem proposed for the rabbinic *merkabah* sources and the *Hekhalot* does not seem to me to work. In chapter I, and at more length in *The Merkabah in Rabbinic Literature* [552], I have shown why.

Like Scholem, although not for all of the same reasons, I view the *Hekhalot* as essentially products of the rabbinic rather than the Islamic era. Within that period, I am inclined, against Scholem, to look more to late Amoraic Babylonia than to Tannaitic Palestine. Among the rabbinic sources, it is only Babylonian material of the fourth century or later that appears to extend the category of *maᶜaśeh merkabah* to include heavenly ascensions reminiscent of the *Hekhalot*. This observation well fits with two passages from the *Hekhalot* themselves, to be examined below, which point to Babylonia as their home. On the other hand, I cannot argue against all of the many converging lines of evidence that Scholem sets forth for an earlier Palestinian dating. I have perhaps even added to them, by advancing an argument of my own for connecting some *Hekhalot* materials with fourth-century Caesarea (chapter VII, section 2c) — which supports Scholem's suggestion that the author of at least one passage of *Hekhalot Rabbati* was familiar with the public buildings of Roman Caesarea (above). In any case, I do not see the issue of dating as the crux of my disagreement with Scholem.

Nor would I propose, against Scholem, that we entirely segregate the *Hekhalot* from the rabbinic *merkabah* traditions. The goal of the *Hekhalot* visionary's journey is the *merkabah*, and the surrounding entities which often appear in the *Hekhalot* texts — *ḥayyot,* cherubim, *'ofannim, ḥashmal,* and the like — are obviously drawn from *merkabah* materials. In their very choice of terminology, therefore, the *Hekhalot* proclaim that they have something to say about Ezekiel's *merkabah*. It would surely be perverse for us to allow, as we have, the Book of Revelation to speak its piece on this subject, and yet to keep the *Hekhalot* sealed away in silence.

My dispute with Scholem, then, does not fundamentally concern the antiquity of the *Hekhalot*, or their relevance to the problems of the *merkabah*. It concerns the issue of where they lie among the currents of Jewish *merkabah* interpretation, and thus among the currents of ancient Judaism itself. In considering this issue, we are back with the questions of who wrote the *Hekhalot*, for whom, and for what purpose.

We have already heard Scholem's views on these questions. We cannot effectively contest them without offering some sort of plausible alternative. And we cannot do this without taking up the questions that we postponed at the beginning of this chapter. Are we sure we know what the *Hekhalot* are, and what they are talking about?

b) Texts and publications. The "canon" of the *Hekhalot* literature is, for reasons which we will presently see to be excellent, only very vaguely defined. Scholem, Jonas Greenfield, and Peter Schäfer have provided annotated lists of what are conventionally regarded as the major texts, and Ithamar Gruenwald has devoted the second part of his *Apocalyptic and Merkavah Mysticism* to detailed summaries and discussions of these texts [590, 531,496,586,535]. The lists vary somewhat, but several texts occur regularly.

There are, to begin with, the two "mishnahs" mentioned by Hai Gaon, *Hekhalot Rabbati* [463,500] and *Hekhalot Zuṭarti* [464]. There is a work which was at one time entitled, to judge by its manuscripts, *Sefer Hekhalot* ("the Book of *Hekhalot*"); but which has come to be better known by the name its twentieth-century editor and translator called it, *3 Enoch*[2]. There is a *Merkabah Rabbah* ("the Great [Treatise on the] *Merkabah*"), so named on the basis of the manuscripts [584]; a text which Scholem published under the title *Maᶜaśeh Merkabah* [603]; and yet another, unrelated, text, which Wertheimer published as *Maᶜaśeh Merkabah*, but which is more generally known as *Massekhet Hekhalot* ("Treatise on the *Hekhalot*") [479, 499]. There are some extraordinarily interesting fragments from the Cairo Genizah, which Gruenwald published in 1968, and which include portions

---

2 Hugo Odeberg's *3 Enoch, or The Hebrew Book of Enoch* [490], first published in 1928, was until very recently the only critical edition of a *Hekhalot* text to appear in print (more on this below). It is still the only publication to supplement the critical text with a translation into a European language (in this case, English), a scholarly introduction, and a full commentary. — In choosing a title for this text, Odeberg imitated the style of Charles' *Apocrypha and Pseudepigrapha of the Old Testament*, which listed an Ethiopic and a Slavonic book of Enoch (1 and 2 Enoch, respectively). Like nearly everything else in Odeberg's edition, the title has been much criticized: it has only a slender manuscript basis; and its implication, that this *Hekhalot* text ought to be enrolled among the Biblical Pseudepigrapha, is misleading. Yet it is also perversely appropriate. *3 Enoch* indeed continues the tradition of the pseudepigraphic Enoch literature, with a startling new twist which we have presently to examine. The name *3 Enoch* has therefore stuck, over all protest, and replaced the colorless *Sefer Hekhalot*. I use it throughout this book.

of texts evidently known as *Ḥotam ha-Merkabah* ("Seal of the *Merkabah*")
and *Śar Torah* (literally, "Prince of the Torah"; more on this below) [466,
474]. *Shiᶜur Qomah*, often listed among the *Hekhalot*, probably ought to
be considered a generic term for materials describing God's organs rather
than a single text [496,586]. I have already given my reasons for thinking
that the *Visions of Ezekiel*, which appears in nearly all the lists, is not a
Hekhalot text at all.

Apart from *3 Enoch* (see below), very little of this material is available
in English. Until very recently, it was also largely inaccessible even to people who read Hebrew and Aramaic. Important parts of it — *Hekhalot
Zutarti*, and much of *Merkabah Rabbah* — had never appeared in print at
all. Those publications that did exist [475,489,497,603] did not exactly
inspire the reader's confidence that he had before him the material more or
less as its author had written it, and not the garblings of later scribes and
printers. With the exception, again, of *3 Enoch,* there was nothing like a
critical edition of any *Hekhalot* text[3]. Hugo Odeberg's edition of *3 Enoch,*
flawed as it was [529], proved easier to criticize than to emulate.

The most obvious difficulty was that there was no way to get a foothold
in the material. It is very hard to begin preparing a critical edition before
you have some idea what the text you are editing ought to be saying.
Without this, you have no criterion for selecting any manuscript as your
base text, especially if all the available manuscripts seem about equally unintelligible. Still less do you have any ground for putting together an eclectic text, unless you are prepared to write your own *Hekhalot* literature.
And, precisely because the existing printed texts were so unreliable, the
would-be editor could not approach the confusing and often barely legible
manuscripts with any sense that he knew what he was looking for.

His problems went still deeper. Upon examining the manuscripts, he
would discover that it was far from clear just what the text he was supposed to be editing actually contained. Its beginning and its end might be
unmarked, or might be marked differently in different manuscripts. One
manuscript might include within the confines of the text large chunks of
material that other manuscripts omitted entirely, located within other
Hekhalot texts, or placed in a different position in the same text. Given this
situation, and given that the *Hekhalot* do not have enough coherence to
guide a decision about what a text of this type ought to contain, how could
he decide even what it was that he was going to edit? He might well conclude that the *Hekhalot* texts, as texts, do not exist; and that their titles
are arbitrary labels which medieval scribes attached to stretches of material
whose extent they themselves barely knew how to define.

---

3 I explain what a "critical edition" is in Appendix I, section 5.

In the light of these difficulties, one can appreciate the achievement of Rachel Elior, the first scholar since Odeberg to publish a critical edition of a *Hekhalot* text (*Hekhalot Zuṭarti*, 1982 [464])[b]. The drawbacks of this edition, which are considerable [562], do not reflect on Elior's care or her competence, but rather point to the nearly insuperable character of the obstacles that any editor must face. If, however, we cannot get over these obstacles, we can perhaps find a way around them. So Peter Schäfer and his colleagues in Germany have taught us in their masterful *Synopse zur Hekhalot-Literatur*; which, published near the end of 1981, has opened a new epoch in the study of the *Hekhalot* [495,562].

Schäfer and his colleagues have postponed indefinitely any hope of preparing critical editions of *Hekhalot* "texts," which are ill-defined and dubious at best, and focused instead on publishing *Hekhalot* manuscripts. To be precise, they have selected seven particularly important manuscripts, containing most of the conventionally delineated "texts," and printed them verbatim. Where appropriate, they have laid them out in parallel columns, so that the reader can make his own comparisons of them and decisions among them. The resulting synopsis much resembles — except, perhaps, for its greater complexity — one of those volumes, familiar to students of the New Testament, which print the three Synoptic Gospels in parallel columns, often repeating material so that the reader can examine side by side units of tradition that occur in different sequences in the parallel sources.

Schäfer's manuscripts include, among them, *Hekhalot Rabbati* and *Zuṭarti, 3 Enoch, Merkabah Rabbah*, and Scholem's *Maʿaśeh Merkabah*. These "texts" float in a larger mass of unassigned *Hekhalot* material, like partly coagulated globs floating in a thick and murky liquid. The manuscripts, and therefore the *Synopse*, also contain *Seder Rabbah di-Bereshit* ("the Great [Treatise on the] Order of Creation"), a medieval cosmological text which has already presented some points of interest for us [213]; and a magic book called *Ḥarba de-Mosheh* ("Sword of Moses"), whose relevance to the *Hekhalot* is unclear. Unfortunately, they do not include *Massekhet Hekhalot*, for which we must still use the editions of Jellinek and Wertheimer. Naturally enough, they do not include the Genizah fragments that Gruenwald discovered. Also naturally, as far as I am concerned, they do not include the *Visions of Ezekiel*.

If Schäfer has at last laid the world of the *Hekhalot* open before students who can read Hebrew and Aramaic, those restricted to English or to another European language remain in much the same situation as before. Schäfer proposes (in his foreword) a translation of the *Hekhalot* texts he has published. But this will doubtless be in German; and, in any case, there is no telling when it will appear.

In the meantime, translations of the *Hekhalot* barely exist. *3 Enoch* is, of course, an exception. Odeberg published an English translation of this text with his critical edition of the Hebrew; and the new Doubleday edition of the Pseudepigrapha contains a fresh translation by P. Alexander — locating it, as Odeberg would doubtless have wished, right after the Ethiopic and Slavonic Books of Enoch [459a]. Lauren Grodner has translated a substantial portion of *Hekhalot Rabbati,* for David R. Blumenthal's anthology *Understanding Jewish Mysticism* [463]. (Morton Smith has never published his complete translation of this text, although he has summarized and discussed it [614].) Scholem cites a German translation, by August Wünsche, of *Massekhet Hekhalot* [504,590]. Beyond this, as far as I know, the English reader must rely on the snippets translated by Scholem and other scholars [493,584], and on Ithamar Gruenwald's summaries of the major texts [535][4].

In exploring the *Hekhalot,* then, we are moving into a thicket which even readers of Hebrew have only recently been able to penetrate. Those who do not read Hebrew can penetrate it hardly at all. For this reason, I will be obliged to spell out my arguments here in even more detail than I have done until now, and support them with yet more extensive translations of the sources.

I base my translations on the manuscripts that Schäfer published, and cite them by the paragraph numbers that Schäfer assigned to them[5]. Where the passage occurs in one or another of the edited *Hekhalot* texts — Wertheimer's *Hekhalot Rabbati,* Elior's *Hekhalot Zuṭarti,* Odeberg's *3 Enoch,* or Scholem's *Maᶜaśeh Merkabah* — I cite the pertinent edition as well, using the editor's chapter, paragraph, or line numbers. For *Massekhet Hekhalot,* of course, I must rely on the editions of Jellinek and Wertheimer; for the Cairo Genizah fragments, Gruenwald's *Tarbiz* article. Wherever a translation exists, I will make reference to it.

2. Locating the center: the heavenly journey

a) Introduction. Describing the *Hekhalot* sources is, for all its complexity, a fairly straightforward matter. Defining what they are about is vastly harder.

---

4 Nicolas Séd has translated *Seder Rabbah di-Bereshit* into French [213]. But this text is, at most, on the borders of the *Hekhalot* literature.

5 Schäfer and his colleagues divided the material in their synopsis into 985 brief units of content, which I here call paragraphs. They have nothing to do with the chapter divisions used in some of the older publications.

The difficulty is locating the center. Open Schäfer's *Synopse* at any point − it usually does not much matter where you start a *Hekhalot* text − and you find yourself plunged into a swirl of hymns, incantations, divine names, and fantastic descriptions of heavenly beings. All of this usually seems to be assembled in no discernable pattern and to no discernable purpose. Every now and then the name of a rabbi, usually "Ishmael" or "Akiba" or "Nehuniah b. ha-Qanah," floats to the surface. Very occasionally, there is something that looks like a narrative. Thus, in *3 Enoch*, the supreme angel Metatron describes to R. Ishmael how he, Enoch son of Jared, was raised from earth and transformed into a celestial creature (Schäfer, ##5−19; Odeberg, chs. 4−15). In *Hekhalot Rabbati*, R. Ishmael describes how R. Nehuniah b. ha-Qanah sent him down to the *merkabah* to investigate why Rome was allowed to decree the execution of several Jewish sages[c]; and how, in the same situation, Nehuniah explained to Ishmael and his colleagues the technique of the journey (Schäfer, ## 107−111, 198−240; Wertheimer, 5:4−6:2, 7:3, 15:1−23:1; tr. Grodner). These narratives often seem intended as frameworks, to give some sense and coherence to the masses of details and names. They accomplish this, at best, for only a fraction of the literature. For the rest, the modern reader must discover on his own whatever unifying principle there may be.

Most scholars find this principle in the idea of the heavenly ascent (or "descent"). The *Hekhalot*, they tell us, are fundamentally manuals for the journey into the divine presence, intended to provide the would-be ecstatic with the equipment he needs for the journey and the knowledge he needs to ward off its dangers. He will need to know the right names to invoke and the right songs to sing; he must be armed with the proper "seals"; he must have some idea of what he can expect to see, and what pitfalls will be waiting for him. (We saw a detailed example of a pitfall in the "water test"; chapter VI, section 2.) Everything in the *Hekhalot* either serves this theme; or, like the *Śar Torah* (below), may be considered a lapse from it.

Those who hold this view can point to the sentence that opens *Hekhalot Rabbati*, which the writer may have intended to define its contents: "R. Ishmael said: What are those songs that a person should utter if he wants to gaze at the sight of the *merkabah*, to descend safely and to ascend safely?" (Schäfer, #81; Wertheimer, 1:1).

They can also point to passages of the *Hekhalot* that explicitly represent themselves as instructions for the journey. The best known of these is Nehuniah b. ha-Qanah's speech to his colleagues in *Hekhalot Rabbati*, which I have just mentioned, and which I briefly discussed at the beginning of chapter III [524a,568,587,588,591]. The reader may form his own impression of this passage from Grodner's full translation of it [463]. But another passage, from one of Gruenwald's Genizah fragments, is no less impressive [468]. Gruenwald gives a few quotations from it in English [546], but it has not otherwise been translated, nor is it often discussed[5a]. It therefore deserves that we linger with it a little.

b) In this passage, which I will henceforth refer to as *the Ozhayah text*, an angel called Ozhayah addresses R. Ishmael as follows:

> "Now, friend, return to the study of the descent to the *merkabah*. I have been instructing you in it: how one descends and how one ascends; what the character of the first palace is; how one gets [angels] into his service and how one adjures them. I have given you the authoritative information on this[d]. You must write down the seal of the descent to the *merkabah* and bequeath it to humanity, for your own benefit and for the benefit of whoever wants to descend and to look at the king and his beauty. If he takes this path, he will descend and see, and no harm will come to him.
>
> "I set it forth for you on the scroll and I saw it [?]. Then you descended and saw; you tested it, and no harm came to you. The reason is that I have made the paths of the *merkabah* like light for you, and the roads of heaven like the sun. You were not like those who came before you, who were greatly disgraced. They were like a person who is lost in the desert, and who takes a road which leads him into a teeming forest. There he finds everywhere lions' dens, leopards' dwellings, wolves' haunts. He stands among them and has no idea what to do. One animal mauls him; another one drags him off.
>
> "This is what happened to your colleagues who descended before you. I swear to you, friend, by [God's] exaltation, that they dragged Ben Zoma a hundred times[e] through the first palace – I was witness, I counted how many times they dragged him and his companion[s?], whether they rescued him or not, whether they were spared or injured – two hundred times through the second, four hundred times through the third ... [and so on, up to] 6400 times through the seventh. But you will not get a scratch from the princes, from the guards of the palaces, from the angels of destruction."

When Ishmael gets to the sixth palace, Ozhayah goes on, hordes of angels will burst forth upon him from the gate of the palace. But he will not be hurt, "because you are holding a great seal, which all the angels are terrified of." He must not be frightened by the fires he sees spurting from the seventh palace into the sixth, but must stand to one side. The text then refers obscurely to a "voice," and continues: "If you are standing, [sit down]. If you are sitting, lie down. If you are lying on your back, lie on your face. If you are lying on your face, stick your fingernails and toenails into the ground of heaven [!]. Stuff wool into your ears and nose and anus, so that your soul cannot escape before I can get there and revive you[6]."

5a Professor Martha Himmelfarb discusses the text, and translates some passages from it, in an unpublished manuscript: "Heavenly Ascent and the Relationship of the Apocalypses and the Hekhalot Literature." Himmelfarb's observations on the *Hekhalot*, which I did not see until after I had finished this book, are often parallel to my own.

6 This remarkable passage is reminiscent of the seventeenth chapter of the Apocalypse of Abraham (above, chapter III, section 6c): " ... fire came against us round about. ... And the angel bent his head with me and worshipped. And I desired to fall down upon the earth ... [but] there was no earth to fall upon." Less imaginative, the author of this *Hekhalot* text provides Ishmael with a "ground of heaven." – Ira Chernus has aptly compared this passage, with its apparent fear that

Ozhayah goes on to assure Ishmael, and through him the readers of the book that he is supposed to write, that they can always count on his services.

"Whenever you want to descend to the *merkabah* and to look at the king and at his beauty – you and anyone else who wants to descend to the *merkabah*, whether in your own generation or in future generations – let him mention my name and call for me in a soft voice at every palace. Then nothing will be able to hurt him or come near him, and he can see the astounding exaltation and the splendid beauty."

The text is badly broken for the next several lines. When it again becomes fully clear, we are in the seventh palace. The angelic guards have put away their weapons, and covered their faces. God welcomes the traveller: "Whoever knows that he is pure of sin and bloodshed, and has Torah, let him enter and sit before me!" He is received by yet another being, whose significance we are not yet ready to appreciate.

"Look at the youth [*naᶜar*] who comes forth from behind the throne to greet you! Do not prostrate yourself before him, even though his crown is like his king's crown, his shoes [?] like his king's shoes, his robe like his king's robe. A robe of ... [?] is tied around his waist. The sun goes forth [?] from the belt that is in front of him, the moon from the knots at his back. His eyes blaze like torches, his eyeballs like lamps. His splendor is like his king's splendor, his glory like his creator's glory. Zehubadiah is his name. He will take your hand and seat you in ... [?]. It is not only that you came with his permission; he seats others as well on a seat that is fixed in the presence of the throne of glory."

With this mysterious "youth," Ozhayah's description of the journey comes to an end. The text concludes with Ishmael's testimonial:

R. Ishmael said: I did not move from that spot until I had completed and adorned it [the book he is writing, apparently], for descent and for ascent ... [a few words are missing] so that scholars in future generations can descend and ascend. I have written it about the palace and its princes, and I have set forth in detail[f] those hundred and nineteen [magic words or formulae, evidently] that are written at the beginning of this book[7].

R. Ishmael said: I did it. But I still could not believe, until the least of the students in our college [*haburah*] also did it. He descended ... [several words missing] and said to me: "Go up and bear witness in the college." For it is written that the testimony of the seal of the *merkabah* becomes visible [or, "is found acceptable"?] four times[g], to descend by means of it to see the king in his beauty; and thereupon the world is redeemed. The friend [=R. Ishmael?] and his student are two of these. There will be two more at the end of the years, in the days of the house of the master; and thereupon salvation comes to Israel.

The last three sentences (which are the final words of the text identified by the copyist as *Hotam ha-Merkabah*) are very obscure, and I am far from certain that I have translated them correctly. The cryptic reference to the

the experience of the fire and the "voice" will cause the traveller's soul to leave him, to one of the Sinai *haggadot* we examined in the last chapter, in which the Israelites' souls actually do leave them when they hear God speaking from the fire (sections B2f, 3c) [514]. We must return to the implications of Chernus's observation.

7 The beginning of the book is now missing.

"days of the house of the master" points back to a passage earlier in the text (not translated here), where God describes in very mysterious terms how he has prepared a name and reserved it, not for any angel, "but for a certain scholar who will arise at the end of the years in the master's house, who is going to be established before me in Babylonia. Through the agency of that house, Babylonia will weave two wreaths, one from the six days of Creation and the other for the end of the years" [467].

Gruenwald may be right in supposing that we have here a piece of political propaganda on behalf of some specific Babylonian Jewish leader, whose identity we can no longer guess at [546]. If so, the author of our text seems to have regarded him as a more or less Messianic figure, whose activity "at the end of the years" brings salvation to Israel and to the world. In the best tradition of apocalyptic pseudepigraphy, the writer turns R. Ishmael into a prophet of his advent. If *Hotam ha-Merkabah* is indeed, as it appears to be, a manual for the ecstatic "descent to the *merkabah*," the allusion seems to confirm my suggestion (above) that Babylonia was the home of this activity.

But the text has other interesting things to teach us about the "descent." It is a horribly dangerous activity; but only if one does not know the right technique, which makes "the paths of the *merkabah* like light." It is the book's business to provide this technique to its readers — without, we gather, much discrimination. True, God seems to welcome only a person who "knows that he is pure of sin and bloodshed, and has Torah." But Ishmael's subsequent testimonial, that "the least of the students in our college" could use the technique as well as he could, suggests that the amount of Torah demanded is not overwhelming. The testimonial itself, like Ozhayah's earlier promise to help anyone who asks for it, seems intended to encourage anyone who wants to undertake the "descent." If there is anything esoteric or restricted about this activity, the text does not show it.

Ecstasy for the masses? Perhaps. But let us continue to suspend judgment on the question of who, if anyone, was actually undertaking these trance-journeys, and consider for a moment a related question: what was the purpose of the journey supposed to be?

At first sight, the answer seems not only obvious, but also stated explicitly: the traveller wants "to look at the king and at his beauty." But this reply is not very satisfying, because it goes on to provoke the question of why anyone should want to do *that*. The *Hekhalot* do not represent the divine vision as inherently pleasurable or sustaining. On the contrary, for all its "beauty," it is at least as terrifying and destructive as the journey that preceded it [515]. What, then, does the successful traveller get out of his trip that makes its hazards worthwhile?

Does the sight of God insure his future happiness? The happiness of his community? The end of *Hotam ha-Merkabah*, which suggests that the re-demption of the world is bound up with the descent, perhaps indicates that this is part of the answer. Or does the visionary, by virtue of his experience, gain status within the community? This suggestion has a plausible sound to it, and finds some support in the passages from *Hekhalot Rabbati* that I quoted in the last chapter (section A5c). These texts, like *Hotam ha-Merka-bah*, seem to encourage any interested person to make the descent. God, we are told, "rejoices in those who descend to the *merkabah*, and sits waiting for every Jew to descend into the astounding pride and strange power." In the meantime, those who do make the descent are God's special messengers to the rest of the people, who "see what no eye has seen" and return to tell it to Abraham's offspring.

These answers, reasonable as they are, have a makeshift quality to them. Sooner or later, we will have to propose a comprehensive answer to a ques-tion which we can fully state as follows: If a person undertakes the trance-journey, what satisfaction does he expect from making it? If he does no more than believe that others have made it in the past, or that he can make it in the future, what satisfaction does he get from that belief? When we answer this question, we will also have an answer to the related question of why the journey is so dangerous, and why the angels the traveller meets seem so anxious to block him[8].

If we are to find our way toward a solution, however, we must broaden our inquiry. The questions that pertain directly to the trance-journey, im-portant as they are, do not by any means exhaust the problems we face. For – and here we come back to where we were at the end of section 2a – the vividness of the Ozhayah text and of R. Nehuniah's instructions for the heavenly journey must not dazzle us into forgetting that these passages are not at all typical of the *Hekhalot*. Indeed, anyone who reads Scholem and then works his way through Schäfer's *Synopse* will be surprised at how few and far between prescriptions of this sort turn out to be. He will find much information about the heavenly realms, but few suggestions that he himself ought to go visit them. Other concerns, linked more to earth than to heav-en, often seem to occupy the writers. What these concerns are, we will see in more detail as we go on.

Schäfer thus has sound reason for proposing that the *Hekhalot* have, beside the theme of heavenly ascension, a distinct concern with the adjura-tion of angels. Here the human does not travel to the angels' realms, but uses his magical knowledge to force them onto his own territory and into

---

8 This question is not often asked. Many scholars, starting from the premise that the trance-journey is "real," seem to forget that the entities the traveller encounters have no existence outside his imagination, and that their motives must be explained in terms of his own.

his service. These two types of material, originally independent (Schäfer argues), appear side by side in the *Hekhalot* [581].

Schäfer is right, I believe, in making this distinction; and again right in refusing to force the adjuration material into subordination to the supposedly cardinal issue of ascension. I cannot agree, however, that the two categories are originally unconnected. We will see that the two are indeed linked; and that it is this link that will finally explain the function and motivations of the heavenly journey.

c) The concluding passages of Hekhalot Zuṭarti give particularly valuable testimony on the relation of the ascension theme to the *Hekhalot*'s more mundane interests. Before we leave (for the time being) the issue of the heavenly journey, we must therefore examine these passages in some detail.

The materials that concern us begin with the description, which I have earlier fully translated, of the two tests that the traveller must undergo at the gate of the sixth palace (Schäfer, ##407–410; Elior, lines 289–316; above, chapter VI, section 2a). The text then describes the splendid welcome the traveller receives in the seventh palace (having presumably passed the ordeals at the gate of the sixth), and his contemplation of his king (##411–412; Elior, lines 317–348)[h)]. Next, it offers the reader, on the authority of R. Akiba, the names of the seven princes who guard the gates of the seven palaces and the names of their seals; when you show each one his seal, he will let you into his palace (##413–417; Elior, lines 349–388). Not only that: the seventh of them will lift you straight into God's lap (#417).

> Make your request: May it be your will, Lord, God of Israel, our God and God of our fathers ... [there follow the divine names given to the seven seals] to give me grace and favor and mercy before your throne of glory and in the view of all your servants, and to put all your servants at my disposal, to do such and such.
> Great, mighty, terrible, powerful, exalted, strong God! *My beloved is white and ruddy,* and so forth; hosts. *His head is pure gold,* and so forth; hosts. ... [And so on, through the rest of Song 5: 10–16.] Ground well, purity. Yah, Yod, Yod, Yah, Yah. Powerful, Yah. Holy, Yah. *Holy, holy, holy is the Lord of hosts, the whole earth is full of his glory* [Isaiah 6:3]. Repeat this mishnah every day after prayer. [##418–419; Elior, lines 389–443][9]

I would not entirely vouch for my translation of the incantations in the second paragraph. But the passage is by and large clear. It is also clear that we are dealing with something considerably more (or less) than the peak of a mystical experience. The traveller's motive for wanting to sit in God's lap is far more concrete than pure yearning for the divinity. And, once we

---

9 For reasons I do not understand, Elior concludes her edition of *Hekhalot Zuṭarti* just before the end of this passage, printing "repeat this mishnah every day after prayer" and all that follows as an appendix (without critical apparatus or notes).

grant that the trance-journey functions as a means to an unspecified but presumably practical end ("to do such and such" really means "fill in the blank"), we may raise the question if it is essential actually to make the journey. Can the individual use the names of the seven seals to invoke God, as he does here, without believing that he has used them actually to pass through the seven palaces? Can he speak the powerful prayer *as if* he is sitting on God's lap?

The concluding sentence, "repeat this mishnah every day after prayer," gives some weight to these questions. We may perhaps infer from it that the trance-journey had become part of the individual's daily routine. But it seems more likely that he believed "this mishnah" to have some power when used daily, even without the trance-journey. We will see this suspicion strengthened as we go on.

R. Ishmael is the speaker in the next passage. In very difficult language, he describes an angelic "prince," at the sight of whom "my hands were burned up, and I found myself standing without hands or feet until Prince Panion of the exalted servants appeared to me." This "Panion," it seems, shares God's name and serves at his throne. He also

opens the gate of salvation, to show him grace and favor and mercy in the eyes of all who see him. Whoever sees him – be it young man or woman, youth or elder, man or woman, Gentile or servant-girl [?] or Jew – they will run to meet him and love him [and look out for] his welfare and want the best for him and be glad to support him, whether they like it or not[10].

^CAnafiel [another angel, whom we will meet again later] said: If anyone wants to pray this prayer and contemplate the work of his creator, let him mention just one of these letters and I will not turn to my right or my left before I turn [to him] and do whatever he wants. I will wipe out anyone who slanders him, apart from an angel who is emissary of the king of glory. ... [String of incomprehensible words.]

The great, mighty, terrible, awesome, strong God is hidden from all creatures and concealed from the angels. But he revealed himself to R. Akiba in the *ma^caśeh merkabah*, in order to do his will. So it is written: *Whoever is called by my name* [Isaiah 43:7][11]. So may he do my will, my desire, and everything I want! Amen, amen, selah. The Lord is king, the Lord was king, the Lord will be king for ever and ever.

R. Akiba said: When I set forth this method of ascending and descending to the *merkabah*, they fixed for me a daily blessing in the heavenly court and in the earthly court.

---

10 Who is this lucky man? Scholem, whose translation of this passage overlaps with mine, renders the beginning: " ... opens the Gates of Salvation to show favor and loving kindness and mercy to all those who ascend to the Merkabah" [601]. He plainly draws the last eight words of his translation from the reading of ms New York, *lekhol ha^colin lammerkabah*. But only this one manuscript has these words, which fit in badly with what follows, and which are best regarded as a gloss. It is evidently the person who makes use of the formulae given here, whether or not he has travelled to the *merkabah*, who gets the benefit of Panion's favor.

11 RSV translates this verse: " ... every one who is called by my name, whom I created for my glory, whom I formed and made." The author of our passage seems to have understood it somewhat as follows: "Whoever calls upon my name and invokes my glory ... I have done [his will] for him." That is, he understands the verb with which the verse ends (^caśitiw) as meaning the same as it does in his own usage: *kakh ya^caśeh*, "so may he do ..."

R. Akiba said further: A heavenly voice announced to me from beneath the throne of glory: "For my friend, who endures the suffering of descending and ascending to the *merkabah*, I have fixed a blessing [to be recited] three times a day in the heavenly court and in the earthly court. I will love and I will redeem any household where it is repeated."

R. Akiba said: Anyone who wants to repeat this mishnah and to utter this name explicitly must sit fasting for forty days. He must put his head between his knees until the fast gets control of him. He must whisper[1]) toward earth and not toward heaven, so that earth may hear and not heaven. If he is an adolescent[12], he may say it as long as he does not have an emission. If he is married, he must be prepared [that is, continent] three days in advance; as it is written, *Be prepared for the third day [do not come near a woman*; Exodus 19:15][13].

If he tells it to his friend, he must tell him one letter from among the first ones and one letter from among the last ones; he should not make the combination for him, lest he make a mistake and destroy God's world[14]. If he wants to test him, he may test him once but not twice. He must supervise him carefully, lest he make a mistake and destroy God's world. He should make regular use of it month by month and year by year, thirty days before Rosh Hashanah, [to cover the forty-day period?] from the first day of Elul to Yom Kippur, to keep Satan from accusing him and ruining his entire year. [##420--424; Elior, appendix]

The last paragraph is especially interesting, not least because it is evidently the source from which Hai Gaon drew his classic description of how the *merkabah* traveller goes into his trance. Anyone who turns back to my quotation from Hai at the beginning of this chapter (section 1a) will see how closely this passage resembles his account; and there is no other passage in the *Hekhalot* that comes anywhere near it [562]. But, when we consider our text a little more closely, we will find it hard to escape the impression that Hai misunderstood his source. Although the aim of the ritual is not entirely clear, there is no hint that it has anything to do with heavenly journeys. The conclusion speaks of it as something that one is to do regularly, particularly in the crucial time before the yearly judgment of New Year's Day, to make sure that one is slated for good luck in the coming year. This does not sound very much like a visit to the *merkabah*.

Indeed, the drift of the text has gradually carried us away from the idea that its reader is expected to undertake a journey to the *merkabah*. He will indeed benefit from the magic he has learned, but in a less strenuous way. He need only mention the sacred formulae, and ᶜAnafiel's power will be at his disposal. He need only repeat the blessing fixed for R. Akiba, and he will share vicariously in the benefits of Akiba's "suffering of descending and ascending to the *merkabah*." There is no reason to suppose that he himself needs to take on this suffering. Akiba's visiting the *merkabah* is important for him, not because he is necessarily going to imitate it, but

---

12 *Naᶜar*; the same word that I translated "youth" in the Ozhayah text (and below, sections B4, C4). The importance of this will become clear at the end of the chapter.

13 Perhaps significantly, this verse refers in its Biblical context to the Israelites' preparation for the Sinai revelation. See below.

14 Ms Munich 22 adds at this point: "If he is in jail, he may utter it in the daytime in order to save his life. But he may not utter it by night, lest he make a mistake and destroy God's world."

because it has opened channels of power from which he can now profit. The hidden God "revealed himself to R. Akiba in the *ma^ca´seh merkabah*, in order to do his will. ... So may he do my will, my desire, and everything I want!"

The concluding passages of *Hekhalot Zuṭarti* thus urge us to modify the impressions we have gotten from R. Nehuniah's speech in *Hekhalot Rabbati*, and from the Ozhayah text. The *Hekhalot* do indeed deal with the heavenly journey; and they indeed deal with it in the context of practical instruction, as opposed to telling an exciting story or revealing cosmic secrets of purely theoretical interest. But we are no longer so sure that the essential concern of this instruction is how to get to the *merkabah*. It may be the winning of other supernatural benefits, which are bound to the heavenly journey in a way that we have yet to discover, but which do not require that the individual believe himself actually to have made the journey.

Before we probe the question of just what these benefits might be, we must touch on another issue, which has already come up in connection with the Ozhayah text. Whom does the author expect to be making use of the techniques he describes? It is clear from the last paragraph that he regards these techniques as being dangerously powerful: make a mistake with them, and you destroy God's world. He adds a postscript warning his reader not to transmit the "secret" he has learned to an unworthy person[15]. From this, we seem indeed to be dealing with highly esoteric and restricted material. But then we are astonished to find, in the next-to-last paragraph of my quotation, that the author expects his audience to be largely composed of adolescent boys! We are miles away from those rabbinic restrictions, described by Origen and hinted at in the Babylonian Talmud, which reserved the study of Ezekiel's *merkabah* for the mature. Like the heavenly journey in the Ozhayah text, the "secrets" of *Hekhalot Zuṭarti* do not appear to be set aside for any very narrow elite. This feature, and the "secrets'" particular interest for adolescents, will become clearer as we go on.

---

15 Schäfer, ##425–426 (Elior, appendix): "R. Ishmael said: Severa, prince of the [divine] presence, said to me: I am revealing this secret to you. If anyone reveals it to a person who is not worthy, he will be driven out of this world and his dwelling will be at the bottom of hell. ... Whoever is careful with this book and purifies himself will be beloved of the angels, troops, seraphim, cherubim, *'ofannim*, and the throne of glory. Saints and righteous men and the patriarchs will pray for his life, and he will inherit paradise." – This is practically the only passage in the *Hekhalot* literature that imposes any restriction, however vague, on the transmission of the material. See below, section 4.

3. Locating the center: *Sar Torah*

A large proportion of what Schäfer designates as "adjuration" material in the *Hekhalot* is directed toward the specific aim of mastering the Torah. Following the hints given by the copyists of the *Hekhalot* manuscripts, scholars usually treat this material as a distinct sub-genre of the *Hekhalot*, called *Sar Torah*, "Prince of Torah" — presumably, after an angelic being whom we would expect to be prime target of the adjurations[16]. The relation of the *Sar Torah* material to the theme of the heavenly journey is not easy to define; and, as we will see, scholars have not been very sure what to do with it.

Let us begin our examination of *Sar Torah* with a brief text which appears in several slightly different versions, in different contexts. As far as I know, it has been published only once before Schäfer (in Musajoff's *Merkabah Shelemah* [489], pages 4a–b), has never been translated, and has attracted little attention[17]. Yet it is outstandingly important; for the motivations and concerns of writer and readers, usually so inscrutable in the *Hekhalot* literature, are here transparent.

  a) The Hekhalot Rabbati interpolation. The simplest and most basic version of the text appears in two manuscripts of *Hekhalot Rabbati* (Budapest, Munich 22), right before the long *Sar Torah* myth that will engage our attention later in this chapter (section C5b). It is obviously not an original part of *Hekhalot Rabbati*. Indeed, ms Budapest brackets it at its beginning and end with the word *tosefet,* "addition."

> R. Ishmael said: When I was thirteen years old, R. Nehuniah b. ha-Qanah found me in a state of self-affliction, great suffering, and great danger. The Scripture that I read today I would forget tomorrow. The Mishnah that I studied today I would forget tomorrow. What did I do? When I realized that Torah did not stay with me, I took myself in hand and abstained from eating, drinking, bathing, and oiling. I kept myself from sex. I neither rejoiced nor laughed, and no word of song came forth from my mouth.
>
> My teacher, R. Nehuniah b. ha-Qanah, then took me from my father's house and brought me into the chamber of hewn stone[18]. He adjured me by the great seal and the great oath that be-

---

16 This explanation is not entirely satisfying. The "prince of Torah" seldom actually appears in these texts (we will presently examine one exceptional passage). Manuscript variants in the *Sar Torah* section of *Hekhalot Rabbati* (Schäfer, #297–306; Wertheimer, 31:5–32:3, 40:3–5; see below) alternate *sar torah* with *sod torah* ("secret of Torah"), and the latter is sometimes perhaps the better reading. It is used in the passage I am about to quote.

17 To my knowledge, only Joseph Dan [522a] has touched upon it.

18 That is, the chamber in the Temple that supposedly served as the seat of the Great Sanhedrin (M. Sanh. 11:2, Midd. 5:4). This anachronistic reference has a parallel in *Hekhalot Rabbati*'s description of Nehuniah's lecture on the technique of "descending to the *merkabah*": "R. Ishmael said: Thereupon I arose and assembled all the Greater Sanhedrin and all the Lesser Sanhedrin to the third entrance of the house of the Lord. He [Nehuniah] sat on a stool of pure ivory ..." (Schäfer, #202; Wertheimer, 16:2). We will meet the "third entrance" again, in the *Sar Torah* myth.

long to Zekhuriel Yahweh, God of Israel, who is Metatron Yahweh, God of Israel, God of heaven and God of earth, God of all the gods, God of the sea and God of the dry land[19]. He revealed the method of the secret of Torah [*sodah shel torah*]. Thereupon my heart was enlightened like the gates of the east, and my eyes saw into the depths and the paths of the Torah. I never again forgot anything of what I heard from my master or from my studies [perhaps read, "from the students"]. Of the paths of Torah that I explored in truth, I never again forgot anything.

R. Ishmael said: Even if I had never studied any Torah, this method that I established in Israel would be enough for me, and equivalent to the entire Torah. [Its purpose is] that Torah be multiplied without effort. [Schäfer, ##278–280]

This is the entire text. It has a very modern ring to it. More specifically, it reminds me of the toothpaste advertisements that used to appear, if I recall correctly, in the comic pages of the newspapers. An apparently attractive girl cannot find a boyfriend, and is frustrated and puzzled until a particularly good friend lets her in on the secret that it is all because she isn't using the right toothpaste. She switches to the advertised brand; and the last frame shows her being happily romanced.

Guided by this parallel, which admittedly leaps over a considerable gap of history and culture, we can begin to imagine the audience for whom our text was intended. They can hardly have been latter-day equivalents of the historical R. Ishmael; that is, accomplished and recognized scholars. Rather, we must think of people for whom the Bible and the Mishnah are more or less esoteric and inaccessible, for whom the learning of an Ishmael or a Nehuniah b. ha-Qanah is a glamorous and uncanny achievement that can only have been attained through magic. This is not to say that they are indifferent to it. On the contrary: they admire Ishmael and his learning, and are so eager to have what he had that they are prepared to believe that they can get it "without effort," if only they know the right hocus-pocus.

Who are they? We note that the sad and frustrated Ishmael with whom they are supposed to identify is thirteen years old, and we recall that the ritual with which *Hekhalot Zutarti* closes (above) is at least partly intended for adolescents. This can easily lead us to the conclusion that *Şar Torah*'s appeal was for the less successful student of Torah[20]. This is reasonable, but I do not think it is the whole truth. We will soon see traces of a more clearly definable viewpoint, with a more polemical intent, behind the reference to the "multiplication" of Torah, and behind Ishmael's remark that "even if I had never studied any Torah, this method that I established in Israel would be enough for me."

---

19 The name "Zekhuriel" is particularly appropriate for an incantation that is supposed to help improve memory, for the Hebrew root *zkr* means "to remember." I therefore suppose that "Zekhuriel" is the correct reading; and that "Zebudiel," found in parallel texts, is derived from it by scribal error. About "Metatron," with whom Zekhuriel is here identified, we shall have a great deal more to say.

20 According to M. 'Abot 5:21, five is the age to begin studying Scripture, ten the age to begin Mishnah.

b) The Chapter of R. Nehuniah b. ha-Qanah. In the meantime, let us look at a somewhat more elaborate version of the text. It appears as a short and apparently independent *Hekhalot* text called "The Chapter of R. Nehuniah b. ha-Qanah," which ms Vatican 228 places right after the *Śar Torah* section of *Hekhalot Rabbati* (Schäfer, ##307–314). After an opening paragraph praising God, it begins almost exactly like the *Hekhalot Rabbati* interpolation. It starts to go its own way after Nehuniah brings Ishmael into the chamber of hewn stone:

... He adjured me by the great seal, by the great oath, in the name of Yad Naqof Yad Naquy Yad Heraṣ Yad Ṣuqaṣ; by his great seal, by Zebudiel Yah, by Akhtariel Yah, by heaven and by earth.

As soon as I heard this great secret, my eyes became enlightened. Whatever I heard – Scripture, Mishnah, anything else – I forgot no more. The world was made new for me in purity, and it was as if I had come from [!] a new world.

Now: Any student [*talmid*] who knows that what he learns does not stay with him should stand and say a blessing, rise and speak an adjuration, in the name of Margobiel Giwat'el Ziwat'el Ṭanariel Hozhayah Sin Sagan Sobir'uhu, all of whom are Metatron. Marg[obiel] is Metatron; Giw[at'el] is Metatron; Ṭanariel is Metatron; Hozhayah is Metatron; Sin is Metatron; Sagan is Metatron; Sobir'uhu is Metatron. Because they love him so much in heaven, they call him Ziwat'el servant of Zebudiel Yah, Akhtariel Yahweh God of Israel, *Yahweh, Yahweh, merciful and gracious God, slow to anger and full of faithfulness and truth* [Exodus 34:6]. Blessed be the wise one who knows secrets, the master of mysteries.

Chapter Two[21]. R. Ishmael said: How should a person make use of this? He should count on his fingers as he speaks the names, one hundred and eleven times. He must not fall short [of this number] or add to it. If he adds to it and suffers injury, his blood is on his own head. When he speaks the adjuration, he should stand and fulfill [the requirement that he recite?]: "In the name of Margobiel," and so forth, as in the first chapter, until he gets to "*slow to anger and full of faithfulness.*" Blessed be you, Lord, who brings the dead to life.

R. Ishmael said: Any student [*talmid ḥakham*] who recites this great secret will have a pleasant appearance, people will like the way he talks, everyone will be afraid of him, he will not have bad dreams, and he will be safe from all kinds of catastrophes, from witchcraft, and from hellfire.

R. Ishmael said: Any student [*talmid ḥakhamim*] who recites this great secret should recite it regularly [? *bemishnah*], and say: Blessed be you, Lord, teach me your laws. You are good and do good; teach me your laws.

R. Ishmael said: When I was thirteen years old, I pondered this matter, and went back to my teacher, R. Nehuniah b. ha-Qanah.

I said to him, "What is the name of the prince of Torah [*śarah shel torah*]?"

He said to me, "His name is Yofiel."

I then arose and afflicted myself for forty days, and spoke the great name until I brought him down. He came down in a flame, his face like the appearance of lightning [cf. Daniel 10:6]. When I saw him, I was terrified, and shook, and I sank [?] backwards.

He said to me: "What are you, son of man, that you have disturbed the great retinue?"

I said to him: "He who spoke and the world came into being knows perfectly well that I did not bring you down for your [sic] own glory, but in order to fulfill the will of your creator."

He said to me: "Son of man, stinking drop, worm and maggot ..." [It is not clear whether what follows is a continuation of this address.]

Whoever wishes that he [the "prince of Torah," presumably] be revealed to him should sit fasting for forty days, and immerse himself twenty-four times each day. He must not taste any

---

21 The copyist evidently conceived the text as divided into two chapters.

filthy thing [*dabar mezuham*]. He must not look at a woman. He must sit in a darkened house. Shalom. In the name of Gamnuni Yakhtada^c Tartara^c ...

The string of magic words, which may or may not be intended as secret names of God, goes on for several lines. It concludes, and the text with it: "Holy, holy, holy. Blessed be the name of his glorious kingdom for ever and ever."

This "Chapter of R. Nehuniah b. ha-Qanah" gives us a considerably more detailed picture than did our first text of how the rituals of *Śar Torah* are to be carried out, and what the "student" who undertakes them expects to get out of them. Several details suggest other parts of the *Hekhalot*. The forty-day fast (mentioned twice) and the avoidance of women are reminiscent of the end of *Hekhalot Zuṭarti*. As in the *Hekhalot Rabbati* interpolation, Nehuniah b. ha-Qanah initiates Ishmael into the secrets of magical technique. This situation recalls the passage from *Hekhalot Rabbati,* to which I have already referred several times, in which it is Nehuniah who instructs Ishmael and his colleagues in the "descent to the *merkabah.*"

The "Chapter of R. Nehuniah" offers a particularly striking parallel to the beginning of Nehuniah's speech in *Hekhalot Rabbati*. "Whenever a person wants to descend to the *merkabah,*" Nehuniah there tells his listeners, "he calls upon Severa, prince of the [divine] presence, and adjures him one hundred and twelve times by Totrosiai Yahweh, who is called ..., [there follows a string of bizarre-sounding names]. He must not go over one hundred and twelve times or fall short of them. If he goes over or falls short, his blood is on his own head. He should count to one hundred and twelve on his fingers as he speaks the names. Thereupon he descends, and has control over the *merkabah* [! *sholeṭ bammerkabah*]" (Schäfer, ##204 –205; Wertheimer, 16:4–5). The "Chapter of R. Nehuniah" (at the beginning of "Chapter Two") prescribes one hundred and eleven repetitions, as opposed to *Hekhalot Rabbati*'s hundred and twelve; but otherwise both the idea and the way it is expressed are practically the same[22]. This parallel strongly suggests that the "descent to the *merkabah*" and the *Śar Torah*, however diverse their purposes may seem, somehow belong together, and cannot be fully explained apart from each other.

The author of the "Chapter of R. Nehuniah" plainly thinks of his ideal reader as a student of Torah, for he calls him that in so many words (*talmid, talmid ḥakham, talmid ḥakhamim*). It is odd, however, that he has to warn him against eating "any filthy thing" during the forty days of his fast.

---

22 The demand that the magician repeat the "names" precisely one hundred and eleven times recurs in our third *Śar Torah* text (below). In *Maʿaśeh Merkabah*, the beings that attend the *merkabah* "speak God's name, using the name Totrosiai Yahweh, one hundred and eleven times" – and there follows a long string of arcane names. (Schäfer, #590; Scholem, #30 [603]. Ms New York has "twelve" in place of "eleven.")

We can hardly imagine that he means, literally, filthy or disgusting food; for why should he have to urge his reader not to eat it? He must, it seems, refer to food that is ritually forbidden. If so, his implication is that the "student" might normally allow himself to eat such food, but must be strict about abstaining from it when invoking the "prince of Torah." This seems a strange sort of Torah student indeed. We will need eventually to go beyond the category of "student" in order to explain who he is.

c) Merkabah Rabbah. The third, and last, *Śar Torah* passage that we must examine in this section belongs to the materials conventionally labeled *Merkabah Rabbah* (Schäfer, ##675–687)[j].

The passage opens with R. Ishmael exclaiming: "Happy is the man who recites this secret in full every morning! He gets this world, the next world, and eternity. He is found worthy to receive the Shechinah when it returns in the future" (#675). After more encouragement of this kind, we read:

> Be sanctified and praised forever, Yahweh, God of Israel, king of kings of kings! You dwell on an exalted throne, in chambers in the height of the palace of pride. For you have revealed mysteries and inner mysteries. You revealed secrets and inner secrets to Moses, who transmitted them to Joshua, Joshua to the elders, the elders to the prophets, the prophets to the pious men [*hasidim*], the pious men to the God-fearers, the God-fearers to the men of the great synagogue. The men of the great synagogue revealed them to all Israel. By means of them, the Israelites performed the Torah and multiplied learning. They mentioned before you each secret [name?] by itself. They performed and uttered and acted, were wise and made themselves wise. They hymned ... [##675–676]

At this point the text plunges briefly into unintelligibility. When it surfaces again, it is talking about the praise of God by his heavenly throngs, and reciting magic words. "The creatures of heaven and earth praise you. Blessed be you, Yahweh, wise one who knows mysteries, lord of all secrets" (#676).

Now comes Ishmael's testimonial to his unhappy and frustrated youth, and to the success of the method that Nehuniah b. ha-Qanah taught him, in a form so nearly identical to the *Hekhalot Rabbati* interpolation that there is no point in repeating it (##677–679). An important addition follows:

> R. Ishmael said: When I heard this great secret, the world turned pure for me. I felt [as I did] when I entered a new world. It seemed each day [as it was] when I stood before the throne of glory. [#680]

In the last two sentences, I have translated the Hebrew fairly conservatively. But I suspect it would be better to render more freely: "I felt *as if I were* entering a new world. It seemed each day *as if I were* standing before the throne of glory[23]." (Cf. #309 from the "Chapter of R. Nehuniah," which explicitly says *ke'illu ba'ti*, "as if I had come.") If my suspicion is

---

23 *Wehayah libbi keshebba'ti le^colam hadash* [two mss add *ubekhol*] *yom weyom domah ^calay nafshi keshe^camadti lifne kisse' hakkabod.* It is possible to vocalize *la^colam* (instead of *le^colam*),

right, the text has just thrown up a bridge between *Śar Torah* and the "descent to the *merkabah*." In the enthusiasm of his enlightenment, the person who uses the "secret of Torah" feels *as if* he is in God's presence. This accords with the interpretation I proposed for the concluding sections of *Hekhalot Zuṭarti*, where the adept seems able to manipulate his formulae *as if* he is sitting on God's lap. We will soon see another bridge between *Śar Torah* and the heavenly journey, which again fits in with this understanding.

R. Akiba now speaks to R. Ishmael, warning him of the danger of the method he has learned from R. Nehuniah. "You might make an error and use it improperly, and do something that is not appropriate, and they would then cause you harm" — as "they" earlier inflicted damage on certain anonymous persons (ms New York: *peloni we'almoni*) who had made mistakes. Ishmael goes back to Nehuniah, who grimly confirms Akiba's warning. "Were it not for the covenant made with Aaron, and the branch from which you spring, they would already have caused you harm and destroyed you entirely k)." We are not told who "they" are, but the advice Nehuniah adds suggests he has angels in mind: "One adjures servants by their king; one adjures a slave by his master." Nehuniah ends with the warning, with which we are by now familiar, that the "names" be repeated precisely one hundred and eleven times (#681).

Ishmael goes on to explain the rituals to be performed by "every student [*talmid ḥakham*] who knows this great secret." He must use the arcane names of Metatron (#682). He "must fast forty days in a row. He must eat bread that he has himself baked, and drink water that he has himself drawn. He may not eat meat or drink wine or taste a vegetable of any kind. If he has an emission, he must go back to the beginning" (#684).

Now, as at the end of *Hekhalot Zuṭarti*, comes a reference to Akiba's "descent to the *merkabah*":

> R. Ishmael said: On this account did R. Akiba descend to inquire of the *merkabah*[24]. He said: "Is it the will of Zebudiel Yahweh, God of Israel, king of kings of kings; king who is praised from among [?] names, for his names are sweeter than milk and honey; king whose name is called by ten names ... [list of names, which do not seem to add up to ten] to Marge'el who is Metatron, *in him*[25]. I^cadyah [?] holy. On account of the love they have for him in heaven, the princes of

---

and to translate "as if I were newly born" in place of "as if I were entering a new world." Schäfer, indeed, prefers this option, thinking that it yields a more meaningful translation. But he admits that the rendering I have chosen better suits the language [585].

24 *Lidrosh bammerkabah.* In another context, such as the rabbinic passages we examined in chapter I, this would mean "to expound the *merkabah*."

25 *Beqirbo*, "in him," is the last word of Exodus 23:21: God warns the Israelites to obey the angel whom he will send to lead them to the land of Canaan, and not to rebel against him, *for my name is in him.* BT Sanh. 38b and several *Hekhalot* passages apply this verse to Metatron, "whose name is like the name of his master" (BT), and whom the *Hekhalot* conceive as a junior deity (below) [446,598,611]. The text before us seems to be a particularly obscure formulation of the idea, which we will meet again, that God transferred some of his own names to his viceregent Metatron.

the heavenly host call him Ziwatiel, servant of Yahweh, God of Israel, blessed be he. *Yahweh, Yahweh, merciful and gracious God, slow to anger and full of faithfulness and truth* [Exodus 34:6]."

R. Akiba said: When I went and asked this question before the throne of glory, I saw Yahweh, God of Israel, become so happy that he stretched out his two hands and slapped the throne of glory. "Akiba my son," he said, "[I swear] by this throne of glory that I sit on, this precious object that my two hands established, that I will attend even to someone who has just this moment converted to Judaism, as long as his body is pure of idol-worship and bloodshed and illicit sex. I will attach my servant Metatron to his footsteps, for much learning of Torah."

As I was being dismissed from before the throne of glory, to go down and be with humanity, he said to me: "Akiba, go down and bear witness to people of this method." So R. Akiba went down and taught people this method. [##685–686]

What was the question Akiba went to the *merkabah* to ask? The text, oddly enough, seems never to get around to reporting it, and we must infer it from God's reaction in the next paragraph. Akiba, we gather, must have asked whether God really approves of people learning Torah through the magical techniques of *Śar Torah*. God's response is, as the phrase goes, overwhelming. Even a fresh convert who uses the "method" that Akiba brings back with him from the *merkabah* can count on God and Metatron helping him to learn Torah.

In these last words, we have a fresh index to the people for whom the *Śar Torah* texts were written. I do not mean that they were all recent converts. In God's speech to Akiba, the convert seems to mark the outer boundary of his concern[1]. But the speech makes little sense unless the text's audience lies not far within those bounds. It points toward people far removed from the rabbinic intelligentsia, from the circles of the "sages" and their "disciples," who nevertheless revere the ancient sages and think of themselves as students – albeit students in dire need of God's help. They are pure of idol-worship and bloodshed and illicit sex, but are perhaps not always strict about all of the Torah's regulations. We recall that the "Chapter of R. Nehuniah b. ha-Qanah" seems to assume that its "student" will not always avoid forbidden food.

With this in mind, let us look again at the chain of transmission set forth in #676. Plainly enough, it is adapted from the beginning of *Pirqe 'Abot*, which enumerates the links in the chain of transmission of the Oral Torah. (This is neither the first nor the last time we see the *Hekhalot* making use of this familiar passage; above, chapter VII, section 2c, and below, section C5b.) "Moses received Torah from Sinai and transmitted it to Joshua, Joshua to the elders, the elders to the prophets; the prophets transmitted it to the men of the great synagogue" (M. 'Abot 1:1). From there, the following mishnahs in tractate *'Abot* tell us, successive pairs of sages handed down Torah until it reached Hillel and Shammai. It then became the inheritance of Hillel's descendants, the patriarchal house ('Abot 1:16–2:5); or, according to a variant and perhaps hostile tradition reflected in 'Abot 2:8, of Hillel's alleged disciple Johanan b. Zakkai. Whichever version we accept, the essential claim of *'Abot* is the same: the Torah and its authority descended from Moses, through the "men of the great synagogue," to the rabbis and their leaders.

The *Hekhalot* text before us seems deliberately to challenge this claim. The men of the great synagogue did *not* hand the secrets that were Moses' heritage over to a rabbinic elite, but to "all Israel." Armed with these secrets, all the Jewish people, down to the fledgling convert, can perform the Torah and multiply learning.

Use of the occult procedure has its dangers. Vengeful angels lie in wait for the practitioner, ready to do him harm if he makes the slightest error — such as uttering the mighty "names" either more or less than one hundred and eleven times. In this respect, *Sar Torah* is very like the "descent to the *merkabah*." Again as in the journey to the *merkabah*, the angels who block the way are not all-powerful. "One adjures servants by their king; one adjures a slave by his master." (R. Ishmael's Aaronic descent helps protect him in both undertakings from the angels' hostility; above, endnote *k*.) The man enlightened through the magic of *Sar Torah* is as if he had achieved the goal of the "descent to the *merkabah*," and stands before God's throne. The charter of *Sar Torah* comes from the throne, mediated through Akiba's journey to the *merkabah*[26]. To put it a little differently: because Akiba travelled to the realms of the *merkabah*, the Torah can become the possession of all Israel.

4. Conclusions

Of the many questions that we raised near the beginning of this chapter, the one that has mostly occupied us so far has been the problem of defining what the *Hekhalot* are essentially about. We have searched through this chaotic bulk of material for some central concern which, once assumed, will give order and coherence to the rest.

Scholem and his followers have good reason for supposing that the heavenly ascent is one such central concern. But it does not seem likely that it is the only center, or even the principal one. Prescriptions for the heavenly ascent are too rare in the *Hekhalot*; there is too much in these texts that

---

26 Just as Akiba is here told to "go down and bear witness to people of this method," so, at the end of the Ozhayah text (above, section 2b), Ishmael is told to "go up and bear witness in the college" of the technique for descending to the *merkabah* [470]. The stress that the Ozhayah text places on "the least of the students in our college" becoming as accomplished in the descent as Ishmael himself [470] is plainly related to *Sar Torah*'s purpose of spreading Torah throughout "all Israel." We will presently see in another *Sar Torah* text an important parallel to the testimonial with which the Ozhayah text concludes (below, section C5b).

cannot reasonably be derived from a central interest in ascending, or descending, to the *merkabah*.

Schäfer thus appears to have a strong case for distinguishing a second category of *Hekhalot* materials, originally independent of those involving the heavenly ascent [581]. This second category focuses on the adjuration of angels; and, insofar as the aims of these adjurations are made explicit, the chief benefit expected is a magical ability to master the Torah without effort. But we cannot go all the way with Schäfer. The *Sar Torah* theme, while not derived from that of the heavenly ascent, is nevertheless closely bound to it. This follows from the parallel techniques used for *Sar Torah* and for heavenly ascent, the parallel claims made for these techniques, and the parallel language in which both are set forth. It also follows from *Merkabah Rabbah*'s explicit linking of Akiba's journey to the *merkabah* with the practice of *Sar Torah*. These two aspects of the *Hekhalot* are intertwined. It is up to us to discover how.

Scholem, while admitting early elements in *Sar Torah*, believed that by and large it was a late and degenerate stage of what had originally been ecstatic mysticism, "when the ecstatic ascent had already lost much of its freshness and had been superseded by a greater stress on the magical elements" [592]. Gruenwald followed Scholem on this point; and the relatively late date of *Sar Torah* has become a conventional postulate of *Hekhalot* research [512b,543] [27]. But I can see nothing in the texts to support the idea that passages speaking of heavenly ascent are older than the *Sar Torah* materials [28]. This view seems to rest mainly on the prejudice that whatever sounds more purely "mystical" must be more authentic, and therefore earlier.

On the contrary, the *Sar Torah* incantations have a claim to priority in that their purpose, unlike that of the trance-journey, is basically intelligible. Given the importance of Torah learning as a source of status in the rabbinic world (a point to which we will return later), we can see why people would be interested in a method for learning Torah without effort. It is not so easy to see why anyone would care about "descent to the *merkabah*"; unless, as *Merkabah Rabbah* suggests, he saw in this journey a source and legitimation for *Sar Torah*.

---

27 Joseph Dan partly dissents [522a].

28 It is true that the legitimating myth of *Sar Torah*, which will occupy us near the end of this chapter, gives clear indications that, at least in its present form, it comes from Babylonia (below, section D2b). But we can say the same for the Ozhayah text, which offers the most vivid and credible description of the ecstatic journey in the entire *Hekhalot* literature. Ithamar Gruenwald has pointed out (although he seems reluctant to accept the implications of his observation) that *Hekhalot Rabbati* presupposes the Babylonian practice of daily reciting the *Qedushshah* [550].

This is not, of course, the first time we have come across the theme of heavenly ascent yielding Torah for all Israel. We saw it in chapter VIII, in the legends of Moses' ascension. I now propose that these Sinai-ascension *haggadot* provide the model both for the *Hekhalot*'s trance-journey material and for *Sar Torah*. They form a framework inside which the trance-journey and *Sar Torah* fit together, and each becomes comprehensible in the light of the other.

More specifically, I suggest that certain people, nurtured on the stories of how Moses climbed to heaven and seized Torah from the angels, used these images to express and to satisfy their own yearning to have Torah made accessible to them. They imagined more recent heroes, Ishmael and Akiba and Nehuniah b. ha-Qanah, replicating Moses' feat, and then making the results available to others through magical technique. They sometimes believed that they themselves could (or perhaps must) make the daring journey, using a similar magical technique for this purpose. Hence, *Hekhalot Rabbati*'s and the Ozhayah text's instructions in the "descent to the *merkabah*." But this feature was neither invariable nor essential. What was important was the profit of the magic, in the form of easy expertise in the Torah, whether the individual won it through his own psychic adventuring or whether he enjoyed the fruits of Akiba's "suffering of descending and ascending to the *merkabah*" (*Hekhalot Zutarti*). Whichever he did, angels stood ready to block him and perhaps injure him. In the same way, and presumably for the same reasons, they had threatened the ascending Moses.

I have just set forth a preliminary sketch of my solution to the problem of the *Hekhalot*. It raises, I am aware, nearly as many questions as it answers. I have spoken of "certain people," but have not yet tried to explain who these people were. I have not yet explained why the legends of Moses' ascent had so powerful an effect on them, or why they tried to translate them into reality in so extraordinary a way. I have barely begun to clarify the role of the opposing angels.

We will deal with all of these questions before we are finished. But we must set them aside for a while, in order to explore the proposition that I would take as my starting point for investigating them. It is this: we are not to look for the originators of the *Hekhalot* in any esoteric clique, but among the Jewish masses.

What we have seen of *Sar Torah* supports this claim, and I see no reason to suppose that what is true of *Sar Torah* is not also true of the rest of the *Hekhalot*. These texts, by and large, do not give the impression of being

---

If, therefore, ties with Babylonia imply a late date, this judgment applies as much to the ascension materials in the *Hekhalot* as it does to *Sar Torah*.

hidden doctrine whispered only into trustworthy ears. They talk a great deal about "secrets," but the importance of these secrets is that they are now about to be revealed.

Gruenwald, for one, is well aware of this, but seems reluctant to draw from it what I regard as the natural conclusion. "No secrecy," he remarks at one point, "is demanded from the initiate, and although we may assume that such secrecy is elementary, one still remains puzzled by the outright manner in which the material is displayed" [539]. Discussing the passages from *Hekhalot Rabbati* that demand that the *merkabah* traveller describe what he has seen to the Jewish public (above, chapter VIII, section A5c), he goes still farther: the *Hekhalot* are not esoteric. "Of course, one may argue that the ones to whom the mystics have to report their experiences are none other than the members of the mystical group. But, one should notice that the *Hekhalot* writings almost never require secrecy" [544].

There are exceptions. *Hekhalot Zuṭarti* ends with a curse on anyone who transmits "this secret ... to a person who is not worthy," followed by a blessing on "whoever is careful with this book and purifies himself" (Schäfer, ##425−426; above, section 2c). If "careful" (*nizhar*) means "careful to keep it secret" − which is not at all clear − then there are similar hints of secrecy in ##477 and 500, neither of which belongs to any of the conventionally designated texts. A difficult magical text in Aramaic, which no one but Schäfer appears to have published, invokes a curse on anyone who sells the book (#489), and an extravagant blessing on "whoever does not reveal this great name" (#490). Ms Munich 22 refers at one point to copyists' alleged suppression of details of *Shiᶜur Qomah* (#468); and an instruction on how to get revelation in a dream considers the possibility that the recipient may not be allowed to pass on this revelation (##506−507). That is all I have found in the *Hekhalot* that even hints that anything in them is to be kept secret, and it is not much. We would expect an esoteric literature to take more pains to guard itself.

The conventional opinion that the *Hekhalot* are esoteric seems to me to rest, not on any internal evidence, but on the assumption that the *Hekhalot* belong together with the rabbinic sources speaking of *maᶜaseh merkabah*, and that each of these bodies of data can be used to interpret the other (above, section 1a). If the *Hekhalot* represent the core of that *merkabah* which, the Mishnah tells us, may not be expounded by an individual "unless he is a scholar and has understood on his own" (Hag. 2:1), it almost goes without saying that they are esoteric. Discard this assumption, as I have urged (chapter I), and matters begin to look very different.

Does this separation I have proposed, between (*maᶜaseh*) *merkabah* and the *Hekhalot*, imply that the *Hekhalot* have no bearing on the exegetical traditions about Ezekiel's *merkabah*, which I have spent this book tracing?

We must admit that exegesis, of Ezekiel or of any other Scripture, does not rank very high on the agenda of the *Hekhalot*. The authors of these texts normally use the word *merkabah* to designate the goal of the heavenly journey, not a Biblical text which they set themselves to expound. They indeed make use of Ezekiel's language in their descriptions of the *merkabah* and its surroundings, but show no very nice regard for the texts from which they draw it. Thus, we regularly find *ḥayyot* and cherubim side by side in the *Hekhalot* (for example, *3 Enoch* chs. 20—22; Schäfer, ##31—34), in spite of Ezekiel 10's clear assertion that they are different names for the same beings.

Still, the *Hekhalot* do not cut the *merkabah* world and its furnishings entirely free of the Scripture from which they emerged. Their writers are aware that the *merkabah* is, strictly speaking, Ezekiel's vision. One of Gruenwald's fragments quotes Ezekiel 1:26 as being from among "the words [or, "matters"] of *merkabah*" (*dibre merkabah*; see Appendix V) [473]. And, scattered here and there among the hymns and incantations, we find traces of exegetical traditions rooted in the text of Ezekiel.

These traditions do not, indeed, yield the mystical exegeses of Ezekiel, suitable for being handed down in whispers among an elite, that Scholem and Gruenwald might lead us to expect. But they make a contribution to our study that is nearly as important. I have suggested that the *Hekhalot* are rooted in the Sinai-ascension *haggadot,* which I have earlier connected with the popular synagogue tradition of *merkabah* interpretation. If this is true, we might well expect them to show their orientation toward this tradition in their explicit exegeses of Ezekiel's text. By examining what they say about the Biblical passage, we can get some idea of how they stand with regard to the streams of *merkabah* exegesis that we have spent so long exploring, particularly the stream that ran through the synagogue.

Equipped with the fresh knowledge this inquiry will yield, we will be ready to launch a more effective attack on the problems of *Śar Torah,* and of the *Hekhalot* in general.

B. The Merkabah Exegesis of the Hekhalot

In the pages that follow, I select and arrange the texts in accord with the patterns of exegesis that I see emerging from them. This procedure, I am aware, is apt to let my conclusions prejudice my presentation of the data. But any more dispassionate arrangement of the material — in the sequence of Schäfer's *Synopse*, for example, or of the verses from Ezekiel that the *Hekhalot* writers are interpreting — would have an even more serious drawback, in that it would force the reader to wade through a large and chaotic mass of data before getting any inkling of the coherence that I see in it.

I attach, as Appendix V, what I intend to be a complete index of the passages of the *Hekhalot* that either quote or allude to verses from the *merkabah* visions of the Book of Ezekiel. I there summarize those passages, about one-quarter of the total, that I have left out of the following discussion. This appendix, I hope, will give the reader some independent control over the pertinent material, and allow him to judge whether a different presentation of it would have yielded results different from the ones I am leading him toward.

1. Two passages of *Hekhalot Zuṭarti*

a) An Aramaic account of the ḥayyot. Early in *Hekhalot Zuṭarti*, there is a passage that seems almost to be a digest of the *merkabah* exegesis of the *Hekhalot*. The text is in Aramaic, and is devilishly difficult. I do my best to translate it:

> R. Akiba said: I heard them saying on [God's] right and his left: If anyone wants to learn this name, let him learn this wisdom. If anyone wants to learn this wisdom, let him learn this secret. If anyone wants to learn this secret, let him learn knowledge from the *ḥayyot* [*ḥayyata*] that are before him [God? or the inquirer?]: their movement, their appearance, their faces, their wings. Their movement is *like the appearance of bazaq* [Ezekiel 1:14]. Their appearance is like the appearance of the rainbow in the cloud [cf. Targ. Ezekiel 1:28]. Their faces are like the appearance of a bride [?]. Their wings are like the splendor [?] of clouds of glory.
>
> Each one has four faces, four faces to a face; four faces for each face; sixteen faces for each face; sixty-four faces for each creature [*birya*]. The total number of faces of the four creatures [*biryan*] is two hundred and fifty-six. Each one has four wings, four wings to a wing; four wings for each wing; sixteen wings for each wing; sixty-four wings for each creature. The total number of wings of the four creatures is two hundred and fifty-six.
>
> When they want to look, they look forward toward the east. When they want to gaze, they gaze behind them toward the west. When they fly, they fly with their outer wings and cover their bodies with their inner wings. When they pray, they pray with their inner wings and cover their bodies with their outer wings. When they turn sideways, they turn sideways with their outer wings and cover their bodies with their inner wings. When they fall silent, they fall silent with their inner wings and cover their bodies with their outer wings. When they speak, they shatter and shake the world with their speech [*kad memall(el)an raᶜaᶜan umeraᶜashan ᶜalma bemillulehon*]. When they begin to sing hymns before holy El Shaddai, [a verb seems to be missing here] with their mouths, their faces, and their wings[m]. [Schäfer, ##353–355; Elior, lines 100–119]

The author goes on to describe the concentric circles of hail, wind, fiery rivers, and so forth, that surround the feet of the *ḥayyot* (*parsot ragle hahayyot*; much of this part of the text is in Hebrew). The account quickly lapses into unintelligibility. It emerges again with a reference, the application of which is very unclear, to

> the feet of the *ḥayyot* [*parsot ragle hahayyot*], like the sun, like the moon, like the stars; the human face, the eagle's wings, the lion's claws, the ox's horns. His face has the likeness of the wind and the shape of the soul[n], which no creature can recognize. His body is like *tarshish* [Daniel 10:6], filling the whole world. Neither those near nor those far away can look at him. May his name be blessed for ever and ever! [#356; Elior, lines 130–134]

Where does the writer get his description of the *ḥayyot*? Much of it is so close to what we find in the Targum to the first chapter of Ezekiel (above, chapter IV, section 2) that we can hardly avoid the conclusion that he is using either the Targum itself or some very closely related text or tradition. This is clearest in the second paragraph of his description (#354). The writer follows Targ. Ezekiel 1:6 practically verbatim — notice how he shifts in this paragraph from *ḥayyata*, an Aramaized form of *ḥayyot*, to the Targumic *biryan* — but goes beyond it in giving the *ḥayyot* a total of two hundred and fifty-six faces as well as wings. The result is that his calculations make even less sense than those of the Targum.

But the Targum has left other traces as well in the *Hekhalot* passage. When the author speaks of the *ḥayyot* as singing hymns "before holy El Shaddai" (*qodam 'el shadday qaddisha*), we hear an echo of the Targum's comparison of the sound of their wings to "a voice from before Shaddai" (*keqala min qodam shadday*, 1:24). "When they fall silent" (*mishtatteqan*) reflects Targ. Ezekiel 1:24, "when they stood, they silenced [*meshatteqan*] their wings." The sentence, "when they speak, they shatter and shake the world with their speech," combines two passages from the Targum. "They shake the world as they travel" (*mezi^can ^calma bimehakhehon*), says Targ. Ezekiel 1:7 of the *ḥayyot*; while 1:24 equates "the voice of their wings ... when they went [*bimehakhehon*]" with "the sound of their speech [*millu-lehon*] as they praised and blessed their everlasting Lord, ruler of the worlds." The *Hekhalot* writer thus uses the Targum of 1:24 to interpret the Targum of 1:7, and then incorporates the result into his description of the *ḥayyot*^o).

The writer takes for granted that the *ḥayyot* use their wings as organs of song. They both "pray" and "fall silent" with their inner wings; they apparently sing hymns with "their mouths, their faces, and their wings." This belief is, of course, one which the author shares with the Targum. But it is also, as we have seen, one of the most ancient and widespread elements of the synagogue tradition of *merkabah* interpretation. It is perhaps not enough to explain its presence here as due to the writer's dependence on the Targum. We should rather consider it a mark of his more general affiliation with the synagogue tradition, which itself explains why he is so ready to use the Targum as a guide in sketching his picture of the *ḥayyot*.

When, therefore, we find that both Targ. Ezekiel 1:6 and *Hekhalot Zutarti* offer the same fantastic multiplication of the organs of the *ḥayyot*, we should not explain the resemblance by supposing that there is something "mystical" or "esoteric" about these extravagances, and that the Aramaic translator is here flirting with "*merkabah* mysticism." We are rather to deduce that the *merkabah* exegesis of the *Hekhalot* develops the popular tradition of the synagogue, dwelling with particular fondness on its more bizarre features.

b) Ḥayyot and throne, in ms New York. A second passage, equally rich in *merkabah* exegesis, occurs in ms New York of *Hekhalot Zuṭarti* (Schäfer, ##368–373; Elior, lines 239–280). The passage's relation to its context is not at all clear. Its first part, amounting to about one third of the total, also occurs in a slightly different form and an entirely different context, among the material conventionally — whether appropriately or not is another matter — labeled *"Shicur Qomah*[29]*."* We might suppose from this that it is an interpolation by the copyist of the New York manuscript from a distinct source, and had originally nothing to do with the surrounding material in *Hekhalot Zuṭarti.* Yet the parallel manuscripts of *Hekhalot Zuṭarti* (Oxford, Dropsie, Munich 22 and 40) do include a brief passage parallel to the beginning of ms New York's material, listing the names of the four legs of the throne and of the four *ḥayyot*; but, unlike ms New York, not identifying the two (Schäfer, #368).

Tracing the relationship of the several variants to each other and to their context thus turns out to be an extremely complicated problem, for which I am able to offer no solution. I content myself with translating the text of ms New York, minus its strings of occult names.

> [#368] The legs of the throne of glory are identical with the *ḥayyot* that stand beneath it. The first leg of the throne, which is a *ḥayyah*, is named ... The second ... third ... fourth ... is named ... The likeness of their faces is the stamp of a lion, the seal of an eagle, [the likeness of an ox], and a human face sealed up[P]. Each one has four faces; four faces to a corner [*pinnah*; see below]; four faces for each corner; sixty-four faces for each *ḥayyah.* Each one has four wings; four wings to a wing; four wings for each wing; sixty-four wings for each *ḥayyah.*
>
> [#369] The prince of the human face is named ... The prince of the lion's face ... ox's face ... eagle's face is named ... When the Israelites sinned[30], the ox's face was concealed [*nignaz*] and a cherub put in its place. The prince of the cherub's face is named ... [The *"Shicur Qomah"* parallel ends at this point.]
>
> [#370] When the *ḥayyot* fly, they fly with thirty-two [wings], and they cover their bodies [cf. Ezekiel 1:11] with the other thirty-two. They fly on wind, for they are made entirely of fire, and fire is lighter than wind. That is why wind helps fire [to spread]. So it is written: *Wherever the wind went,* and so forth [*they went*; Ezekiel 1:12, cf. 20][31].
>
> The sound of the wings of the *ḥayyot* was the *quaking* mentioned by Elijah. *The Lord passed by, with a great and mighty wind* [I Kings 19:11]. Here we have the *wind. After the wind was a quaking* [19:11]. The *quaking* was like the sound of mighty waters, as it is written: *I heard the sound of their wings like the sound of many waters* [Ezekiel 1:24]. *After the quaking was a fire*

---

29 Schäfer, ##954–955, from ms Munich 40. The larger context in which this text occurs (##939 –977) corresponds to pages 34a–43a of Musajoff's *Merkabah Shelemah* [489], and to the *Shicur Qomah* text that Martin Samuel Cohen has translated and annotated [516]. The version of our passage that Munich 40 represents therefore appears, as "section J," in Cohen's translation. It is also part of a far less scholarly translation of *"Shicur Qomah,"* done by somebody or something called "The Work of the Chariot," published in David Meltzer's *The Secret Garden* [488].

30 The parallel in the *"Shicur Qomah"* version (#955, from ms Munich 40) is more explicit: "When the Israelites sinned by making the calf ...."

31 Understanding *ruaḥ*, normally translated "spirit" in this verse, to mean "wind."

[I Kings 19:12]. This is the fire that Daniel mentioned: *Its wheels were blazing fire,* and so forth. *A river of fire flowed from before him. Thousands of thousands served him, and myriads of myriads* and so forth [Daniel 7:9–10].

[#371] The throne rests on the four *hayyot.* The throne resembles the sky, the sky resembles the waters of the sea, the waters of the sea resemble the color blue [*tekhelet*], while the color blue is sapphire. Pure clouds surround the throne, sending forth lightning flashes like the flashing of *tarshish* [Ezekiel 1:16]. The splendor of the flashing of the throne, which is like sapphire, combined with the flashing of *tarshish,* make up *the radiance* [*hannogah*; Ezekiel 1:28]. The *hashmal* resembles the appearance of sapphire and *tarshish* together. It looks like fire; yet not like fire, but like flames of different colors mixed together, so that the eye cannot grasp them. *Fire flashing* [Ezekiel 1:4], because it is so brightly polished and because of all the flashings that appear [?], surrounds the throne.

The *hayyot,* which are the legs of the throne, appeared to Ezekiel from the midst of all these awesome sights [cf. Ezekiel 1:5]. Each leg has four faces of different types, and four wings. The four legs thus have sixteen faces and sixty-four wings in each direction.

[#372] Above the throne is the great fire ... [three words that I do not understand] from the curtain of fire spread before him. Seven mighty servants are inside this curtain. Twelve stand around the throne, three in each direction. Their names are ...

[God] sits in the middle, his glory *like the color of hashmal* [Ezekiel 1:27]. On his forehead is the wreath of the ineffable name, woven of fire. On his head is a crown of splendor. So·it is written: *From the radiance opposite him* [*coals of fire burned*; II Samuel 22:13, cf. Ezekiel 1:13]. Life is on his right hand, death on his left. He holds rods of fire in his hand. On his right are two mighty princes, named Shebabiel and Piriel. On his left are two mighty ones who carry out [harsh] decrees, named Creator [!] and Gallisur[32].

[#373] The throne of glory is the dwelling of his glory. The *hayyot* carry the throne. The *'ofannim* are the wheels of the *merkabah* [*galgalle merkabah*]. All of them are fire mixed with fire. So it is written: *Their appearance was like coals of fire* [Ezekiel 1:13].

Like the author of the Aramaic text we examined above, this writer follows the Targum in multiplying the *hayyot*'s faces and wings. Or, perhaps, he draws upon the Targum's tradition as it is mediated through this Aramaic *Hekhalot* passage, even when this means contradicting the Targum itself. Against the Targum, but in accord with the Aramaic passage in *Hekhalot Zuṭarti,* he gives each of the *hayyot* sixty-four faces as well as sixty-four wings. (He seems, however, to revert to the Targumic computation at the end of #371.) When he claims that the *hayyot* fly with thirty-two of their wings and cover their bodies with the other thirty-two, he is evidently developing the Aramaic *Hekhalot* text: "When they fly, they fly with their outer wings and cover their bodies with their inner wings" (#355).

At one point, the writer seems to have difficulty reproducing his Aramaic source in Hebrew. The *hayyot,* he tells us in #368, have "four faces for each *pinnah*"; and I have naturally translated *pinnah* as "corner." But a variant spelling in the *"Shiʿur Qomah"* version (#954), supported by the par-

---

32 The first two names are apparently derived from Aramaic *shebiba* ("flame") and Greek *pyr* ("fire"), respectively. Gallisur, we recall, is one of the angels who meets Moses in the Sinai-ascension *haggadot*; one of his normal functions there is to announce God's decrees to the world. We will come back to him later on. "Creator" (*habbore'*) perhaps reflects Gnostic influence on this passage; see the end of Appendix VI.

allel "four wings for each wing," suggests that what he originally wrote was *paneh*, the non-existent singular of *panim*, "faces." Evidently, he has tried unsuccessfully to translate the singular noun *'appa*, "face," which is normal in Aramaic. It follows that the haggadic tradition multiplying faces and wings must have come to him from Aramaic; and we need not hesitate to find its roots in the Targum.

I know no parallel to the author's remarkable midrash of I Kings 19:11—12, comparing Elijah's vision with those of Ezekiel and Daniel. But this midrash seems silently to assume the Targum's exegesis of Ezekiel 1, with or without the mediation of the Aramaic *Hekhalot* passage. It equates Elijah's *quaking* (*ra'ash*) with Ezekiel's *sound of their wings like the sound of many waters*. This makes no sense, unless we also know that the wings of the *hayyot* sound like a "quaking." Ezekiel 3:12—13 indeed tells us as much; but then it is odd that the writer does not quote this text instead of 1:24. He must presuppose an exegetical tradition which included "quaking" among the effects of the wings of the *hayyot*, "when they went" (1:24). We find this tradition reflected in Targ. Ezekiel 1:7; and, in a different form, in *Hekhalot Zuṭarti* (#355).

We find a few other familiar elements in this passage, apart from those we recognize from the Targum. #369 draws upon the haggadah, which we have traced back to the Palestinian synagogue tradition, of the cherub's face replacing the ox's (above, chapter V, section 2). The beginning of #371 incorporates, in reverse order, R. Meir's chain of resemblances linking the color blue with the throne of glory (chapter VI, section 4).

The writer's equation of the *hayyot* with the legs of the throne is so far new to us. So is his description of God's surroundings, in #372. The second of these features, however, crops up in an account of the divine throne and its surroundings, in chapter 4 of the late midrash *Pirqe de-Rabbi Eliezer*; while the same midrashic source offers a close parallel to the first feature. This link is part of a complex chain of associations that leads us, through a passage in the *Midrash on Psalms*, to the Coptic Gnostic texts, and back again to the Targum to Ezekiel 1:6 (details in Appendix VI).

How are we to explain these connections? Scholars occasionally look upon *Pirqe de-Rabbi Eliezer* as a semi-esoteric work, which enshrines fully esoteric traditions on the *merkabah*. (The remarks of Chernus and Gruenwald to this effect are fairly typical [512a,551a].) I see no justification for any such estimation of *Pirqe de-Rabbi Eliezer*, and would explain its links to the *Hekhalot* in an entirely different way. I have mentioned (chapter V, section 5c) that this midrash is related to the Palestinian Targumic tradition [410]. We might therefore expect it to preserve some early synagogue *merkabah* exegeses which the older sources neglect; and the evidence considered in Appendix VI suggests that that is precisely what we have here. The parallels between *Pirqe de-Rabbi Eliezer* and the *merkabah* exegesis of the New York text of *Hekhalot Zuṭarti* are thus one more bit of evidence that this exegesis derives from the synagogue.

Our second *Hekhalot Zuṭarti* passage contains a few elements I do not recognize from anywhere else: its midrash of I Kings 19:11–12 (above); its discussion of the relationship among sapphire, *tarshish*, and *ḥashmal*; its oddly rationalizing explanation that the *ḥayyot* are carried as fire on the wind. But, where we can trace its affiliations, they are with the synagogue tradition. My deductions from the first *Hekhalot Zuṭarti* passage we examined have so far held up.

2. *Hekhalot Rabbati*: the terror of the eyes

Ezekiel gave the *ḥayyot* a total of sixteen faces. The Targum, as we have seen, multiplied this number to sixty-four; while two passages from *Hekhalot Zuṭarti* multiplied it yet again to two hundred and fifty-six.

A passage in *Hekhalot Rabbati* presupposes this last, most generous calculation. More important, it incorporates the number into a remarkable account of the *merkabah* traveller's terrifying encounter with the *ḥayyot*, which gives us a rare clue to the psychological reality underlying the description. This mesh of exegesis and experience deserves our closest attention[33].

The passage in question (Schäfer, ##245–250; Wertheimer, 23:5–24:5) evidently belongs to Nehuniah b. ha-Qanah's instruction on the "descent to the *merkabah*." This instruction has earlier taken us to the gate of the seventh palace and introduced us to its guards, chief among whom is the great "prince" ᶜAnafiel (#241). ᶜAnafiel, we learn, is one of the most exalted beings in heaven, comparable to the Creator. Like Metatron in other sources, he is "a servant who is named after his master" (#242, 244) [517]. He opens and shuts the doors to the seventh palace,

and he stands by the gate of the seventh palace. The holy *ḥayyot* are by the gate of the seventh palace; the cherubim and *'ofannim* are by the gate of the seventh palace; the two hundred and fifty-six faces[q] of all the holy *ḥayyot* are by the gate of the seventh palace.

[#246] Greater than all of them[34] are the five hundred and twelve eyes of the four holy *ḥayyot* by the gate of the seventh palace. They have all of the facial forms of the sixteen faces of each of the *ḥayyot*, by the gate of the seventh palace[r].

---

33 I discuss it more fully in a recent article [562a].

34 This formula, *gedolah mikkullam*, is used repeatedly at the beginning of *Hekhalot Rabbati*, in an entirely different context (Schäfer, #81–92; Wertheimer, 1:2–2:3; partially translated below, section D3). We find it again in the late *Midrash on Proverbs*, applied to the various sciences associated with "the viewing of the *merkabah*" (chapter 10; ed. 33b–34a [198b]; partially translated by Scholem and Cohen [611a,516a]). It seems out of place here.

[#247] Whenever someone wants to descend to the *merkabah*, prince ^cAnafiel opens for him the doors of the gate of the seventh palace. The man goes in and stands on the threshold of the gate of the seventh palace. The holy *hayyot* then look at him with their five hundred and twelve eyes. Each one of the eyes of the holy *hayyot* is split open [*pequ^cah*], the size of a large winnowers' [?] sieve[s]; and their eyes look as if *they race like lightnings* [Nahum 2:5; cf. Ezekiel 1:13–14]. Besides them, there are the eyes of the mighty cherubim and of the *'ofannim* of the Shechinah, which look like torches and flaming coals.

[#248] The man shudders and trembles and recoils; he faints in terror and collapses. But prince ^cAnafiel, and the sixty-three guards of the gates of the seven palaces, all support him and help him. "Don't be afraid, child of the beloved seed," they say to him. "Go in, see the king in his beauty. You won't be destroyed and you won't be burned up." ...[35] [#250] They give him strength.

A trumpet then blows *from above the firmament that is over their heads* [Ezekiel 1:26]. The holy *hayyot* cover their faces, the cherubim and the *'ofannim* turn their faces away. [The man] goes in and stands before the throne of glory.

The center of this description is the five hundred and twelve huge eyes of the *hayyot*, and the terror they evoke. The passage clearly presumes the Targumic tradition of the multiplication of the creatures' faces, in the extravagant form in which it appears in *Hekhalot Zutarti*: two hundred and fifty-six faces will contain five hundred and twelve eyes. (The second sentence of #246 seems to me an interpolation, its purpose to reduce the number of faces to the more modest Targumic figure of sixteen apiece. See also endnote *q*.)

It is equally clear, however, that we need more than the Targumic tradition to explain the passage. The text before us evokes a real sense of the uncanny, which is entirely missing from Targ. Ezekiel 1:6 and the *Hekhalot Zutarti* passages. I believe that its uncanny quality is rooted in a single point: the remark, which at first sight seems hardly intelligible, that the *hayyot*'s eyes are split open, and are the size of enormous sieves. To understand how this can be, we must look more closely at this image.

Where else do we find the image of a sieve split open? As far as I know, the precise language used here recurs nowhere else. But there is a very similar phrase in another passage from *Hekhalot Rabbati* (Schäfer, #189; Wertheimer, 13:4):

> When the time for the afternoon prayer arrives each day, the splendid king sits and raises up the *hayyot*. Before he is through speaking, the holy *hayyot* come out from beneath the throne of glory. Their mouths are full of song, their wings full of joy; their hands play music and their feet dance. They surround their king, one on his right and one on his left, one in front of him and one behind him. They hug him and kiss him, and uncover [*mefare^cot*] their faces. They uncover, while the king of glory covers his face[t]. ^cArebot Raqia^c splits open like a sieve [*mitbaqqea^c kikhebarah*] before the splendor, radiance, beauty, appearance, desire [*hemdat*], compassion, passion [*ta'awat*], shining light, magnificent appearance of their faces[u]. So it is written: *Holy, holy, holy is the Lord of hosts, the whole earth is full of his glory* [Isaiah 6:3].

---

35 I leave out #249, which contains nothing but a string of attributes of God's royalty: "He is a righteous king, he is a faithful king," and so forth.

The overtones of this passage are even more erotic than appears at first sight. Two of the words in the long string of nouns that describes the faces of the *hayyot*, *hemdah* and *ta'awah*, are regularly used of sexual lust (particularly *ta'awah*). The root *pr^c*, used here for the uncovering of the faces of the *hayyot*, is also used in connection with circumcision, for the uncovering of the corona. When, therefore, the heavenly realm "splits open like a sieve" before the splendor and passion of the *hayyot*'s denuded "faces," we do not have to look very far beneath the explicit scene to find a sexual act described only slightly less explicitly. The sieve split open is then an image for the female genitals. The nearly identical image in #247 surely has the same meaning[36].

The traveller to the *merkabah*, then, is confronted with five hundred and twelve gigantic vaginas staring at him, and it is no wonder that he loses his nerve. Freud and his followers have offered various explanations of why certain men should be terrified of female genitals: primitive dread of castration (Freud himself), traumatic early experiences with angry and seductive mothers (Philip Slater, Melford Spiro). We may or may not care to accept their speculations. Their researches seem at any rate to have established that this terror does exist, and has left its traces in the mythology of widely separated cultures [853,856][37]. The best known of these is the Greek myth of Medusa, whose face is so dreadful that he who sees it turns to stone [837a]. The terror of the *merkabah* traveller is not quite so extreme. He faints; but the comforting male figure of ^cAnafiel brings him back to consciousness, and the *hayyot* cover their terrible "faces[38]."

I find it very hard to believe that the author of this account of the trance-journey deliberately and consciously constructed this powerful image of dread. More likely, it came to him from a real hallucinatory experience of some kind, which fused his unconscious sexual fears with his

---

36 I have shown elsewhere that the rabbinic use of the "sieve" to describe Miriam's well (especially in T. Sukkah 3:11), and the sexual associations that the ancient Greeks attached to the similar winnowing-basket, confirm this interpretation [562a].

37 In one dream Freud analyzes, the dreamer saw himself chasing a boy, who *"fled for protection to a woman, who was standing by a wooden fence, as though she was his mother. She was a woman of the working classes and her back was turned to the dreamer. At last she turned round and gave him a terrible look so that he ran off in terror. The red flesh of the lower lids of her eyes could be seen standing out."* Freud argues persuasively that the terrible red eyes are the dreamer's distorted memory of a childhood view of female genitals [835]. The parallel to the terrifying eyes of the *hayyot* is obvious.

38 We recall that in #189 the *hayyot* uncover their faces, while God covers his. Another description of the hymning of the *hayyot*, from an independent source which ms New York inserts into *Hekhalot Rabbati* immediately before #189, reverses these actions: the *hayyot* cover their faces, God uncovers (*porea^c*) his (Schäfer, #184 and parallels). In the Ozhayah text, summarized earlier in this chapter, the terrifying angelic guards "cover their faces, and great silence is upon their faces" [469].

consciously acquired expectations of what the world of the *merkabah* should look like. This conscious component derived from the Targumic tradition; hence, from the synagogue.

The line of development that led from the Targum's sixty-four faces, through the two hundred and fifty-six faces of *Hekhalot Zuṭarti*, to the five hundred and twelve terrifying eyes of *Hekhalot Rabbati*, did not end there. Extended to Ezekiel 1:27, it expressed itself in the image of a fearful "eye of *ḥashmal* ... standing and selecting among those who descended to the *merkabah*, distinguishing him who was worthy to descend to the *merkabah* from him who was unworthy to descend to the *merkabah*" (*Hekhalot Rabbati*; above, chapter VI, section 2).

So, at least, I would explain the origin of this interpretation of Ezekiel 1:27, which is the most original and distinctive piece of *merkabah* exegesis in the *Hekhalot*.

3. The synagogue tradition, elsewhere in the *Hekhalot*

The passages from *Hekhalot Zuṭarti* and *Rabbati* that we have so far considered do not stand alone. Traces of the synagogue tradition's influence are scattered through the *Hekhalot*.

As we follow these traces, we can no longer make much use of the theme that has largely guided us until now, of the fantastic multiplication of the *ḥayyot*'s organs. Several passages of *3 Enoch*, it is true, share with Targ. Ezekiel 1:6 the general idea that heavenly beings can be expected to have some grotesque number of faces and wings. But the numbers they give are usually not the same as the Targum's; and, while we may suppose that the Targum has helped shape the imaginings of their writer (or writers), we cannot clearly mark its influence[v].

We must look rather to fresh elements of the synagogue *merkabah* exegesis that crop up in the *Hekhalot*. Some of them we will be able to recognize as such, as we have normally done hitherto, by comparing the *Hekhalot* passages with the Targum to Ezekiel. But often we must use as our touchstone other exegetical traditions, preserved not in the Targum but in Talmud or midrash, which I have connected in chapter IV — sometimes more, sometimes less securely — with the synagogue.

a) Targ. Ezekiel 1:14. The author of *3 Enoch* inserts a brief midrash of Ezekiel 1:14 into a long list of the different kinds of *merkabah*s that God has at his disposal (Schäfer, #37; Odeberg, ch. 24). This list will engage our attention later in this chapter, when we compare the *Hekhalot* with the *Visions of Ezekiel*. It is the midrash that concerns us now.

The hayyot went forth/ran and returned. They run with [God's] permission and return with [God's] permission, for the Shechinah is upon the height of their heads.

My literal translation of the last words, *ᶜal rum rashehem* (Odeberg renders "above their heads"), conveys the awkwardness of the Hebrew expression. True, we find a similar expression a few paragraphs earlier, where we read that the wings of the cherubim are *berum rashehem,* "at the height of their heads" (Schäfer, #34; Odeberg, ch. 22). But that does not make it any less peculiar here.

The writer seems to have been influenced by Targ. Ezekiel 1:14: "When the creatures are sent forth to do the will of their Lord, who established his Shechinah in the heights above them ... " (*de'ashre shekhinteh bimeroma ᶜela minhon*). He may possibly have chosen to speak of God's "permission" (*reshut*) because of the Hebrew word's resemblance to the Targum's *reᶜut,* "will."

A later passage of *3 Enoch* refers to angels who "run as messengers" (*raṣin bishelihut*; Schäfer, #52; Odeberg, ch. 35). This seems to be an allusion to Ezekiel 1:14, interpreted along the lines of the Targum (*be'ishteluhehon,* "when they are sent forth") and *Gen. R.* 50:1 (ed. 515–516 [188]: *roṣot laᶜaśot shelihutan,* "they desire to fulfill their mission").

We may perhaps detect another echo of this exegesis in a description of the angels in *Massekhet Hekhalot,* ch. 6 (Wertheimer, page 69): "In fear and trembling, they are ready to execute the will [*raṣon*] of their creator. Some of them stand, a thousand holy camps. Others, a myriad hosts, run as messengers [*raṣim ... bishelihut*]."

b) Targ. Ezekiel 3:12. A passage in ms Munich 22 of *Maᶜaśeh Merkabah* describes the *merkabah* beings as uttering, "with the voice of a great quaking" (Ezekiel 3:12–13), the formula: "Blessed be the name of his glorious kingdom for ever and ever, from the place of the dwelling of his Shechinah [*mimmeqom bet shekhinato*]" (Schäfer, #553)[39].

This formula is obviously supposed to take the place of Ezekiel's *blessed be the glory of the Lord from his place.* It fuses the liturgical utterance, "Blessed be the name of his glorious kingdom for ever and ever," with a Hebrew re-translation of Targ. Ezekiel 3:12: "Blessed be the glory of the Lord from the place of the dwelling of his Shechinah" (*me'atar bet shekhinteh*).

c) The synagogue exegesis of Ezekiel 1:24–25 has left its marks on the *Hekhalot,* in several different ways.

It has taught the *Hekhalot* writers that the *hayyot* use their wings as

---

39 This and similar formulae recur in #555 (Scholem, #6) [460]. The manuscripts differ considerably on their wording.

organs of song. We have already found this notion expressed, in language borrowed from Targ. Ezekiel 1:24, in *Hekhalot Zuṭarti*'s Aramaic description of the *ḥayyot*. A few other passages also state it, or take it for granted.

Without it, we can hardly make sense of the allusion to the *ḥayyot*'s wings in the remarkable description, quoted above (section 2) from *Hekhalot Rabbati*, of how the *ḥayyot* come forth daily from beneath the divine throne to dance with their king. "Their mouths are full of song, their wings full of joy; their hands play music and their feet dance" (Schäfer, #189; Wertheimer, 13:4).

Less ambiguously, *3 Enoch* describes the cherubim, which it represents as standing beside the *ḥayyot* (!): "The wings of the cherubim ... are spread out, so that they can sing with them to the dweller in the clouds, offer praise with them to the king of kings" (Schäfer, #34; Odeberg, ch. 22).

Maʿaśeh Merkabah, in the context of a description of how the heavenly beings praise God, offers the line: "Clouds of comfort [?], holy *ḥayyot*, utter [*memallelin*] song, ... [unintelligible word] their mouth, their wings water" (Schäfer, #593; Scholem, #32; cf. Altmann [461]). This sentence is of more than average obscurity. But "their wings water" (*kanfehem mayim*) is evidently linked to Ezekiel 1:24, "the sound of their wings like the sound of many waters." The writer's choice of the word *memallelin* points to the synagogue interpretation of this verse, reflected in a baraita in BT Hag. 13b, in which the *ḥayyot* utter (*memallelot*) God's praise — with their wings, presumably[40].

The baraita to which I have just referred runs as follows:

> At times they [the *ḥayyot*] are silent, at times they speak. When revelation goes forth from God's mouth, they are silent. When no revelation goes forth from God's mouth [*beshaʿah she'en haddibbur yoṣe' mippi haqqadosh barukh hu'*], they speak.

Compare the following passage from *Hekhalot Rabbati* (Schäfer, #272; Wertheimer, 27:1):

> You revealed your secret to Moses, and did not conceal your mighty deeds from him. When no revelation went forth from your mouth [*bizeman she'en haddibbur yoṣe' mippikha*], all the high mountains trembled and stood before you in great terror. When revelation did go forth from your mouth, flames burned them all up.
> You test the conscience and choose faithfulness. You dwell amid fire and flame[w]. You are the mightiest of the exalted ones [*geʾim*], exalted over everything, exalting yourself over everything, bringing down the exalted and raising up the lowly.

---

40 Interpreting the baraita in accord with Targ. Ezekiel 1:24–25; see above, chapter IV, section 3c. — Another hymn, found a little later on in *Maʿaśeh Merkabah*, contains the line: "Their wings are spread, their hands are stretched out, the sound of their wings is like the sound of many waters" (Schäfer, #596; Scholem, #33; cf. Altmann [462]). The first clause is from Ezekiel 1:11, the last from verse 24; the one in between may be linked to the exposition of 1:8 in BT Pes. 119a (above, chapter IV, section 2e).

The language of the first paragraph is so close to the baraita's that we can hardly deny the baraita is its source. We have already seen (chapter IV, section 3c) that the baraita is rooted in the Targum's exegesis of Ezekiel 1: 24–25. But it tears the interpretation out of its original context, turning it into an etymology for the word *ḥashmal* (treated as a compound of *ḥashot*, "they are silent," and *memallelot*, "they speak").

We now find that the *Hekhalot* writer re-applies the language of the baraita itself, this time to the Sinai revelation. This is clear from his talk about high mountains burned up by flames, and is supported by his references to Moses and to the burning bush (endnote *w*); which, according to Exodus 3:1, was located on Horeb = Sinai.

This transference is extremely important for us, in the light of the synagogue tradition's combination of the Sinai revelation with the *merkabah* vision (above, chapters I, IV, VIII). We will have more to say about it in section C, when we consider the relation of the *Hekhalot* to the Shabuᶜot cycle.

We saw in chapter IV (section 4) that the synagogue tradition developed the Targum's exegesis of Ezekiel 1:24–25, with its periodic silences of the *ḥayyot*, into the notion that the angels cannot sing their own praises of God until he has had a chance to hear the prayers and hymns of the Jewish people. We find the same idea in the *Hekhalot*. According to *Hekhalot Rabbati*, for example, God begins each day by praising the *ḥayyot*, blessing the hour he created them – and then ordering them to silence all creatures, "so that I can listen and pay attention to the sound of my children's prayer" (Schäfer, #173; Wertheimer, 13:3).

Grözinger and Schäfer quote several passages of this sort, which give an overall picture close to that of the midrashic material we examined in chapter IV [533b,534a,582]. As a rule, they show no direct evidence of having been inspired by Ezekiel 1:24–25; and it is only this that keeps me from classifying them as offshoots of the synagogue exegesis of these verses[41]. There is, however, an important exception to the rule. This exception, and the context in which it occurs, will occupy us in section 4.

d) The faces of the ḥayyot. *Hekhalot Rabbati* records, immediately after the passage that I quoted five paragraphs above, an impressive hymn on the four creatures represented in the faces of the *ḥayyot* (Schäfer, #273; Wertheimer, 27:2–5; Maier translates the passage into German and discusses it [576]).

---

41 Sometimes, however, they quote Job 38:7, which has also figured in our discussions in chapter IV.

The human being is the most exalted [*ge'eh*] of creatures. You fixed [*qaba^cta*] a human's likeness in your throne. They have a human face, *and human hands under their wings* [Ezekiel 1:8].
They run like a human being, they labor like a human being, they prostrate themselves when they
sing hymns like a human being. Your fear, O king, is upon them.
The ox is the most exalted of animals. You fixed an ox's likeness in your throne. They run
like an ox, they labor like an ox, they stand in their positions like an ox. Your fear, O holy one,
is upon them.
The lion is the most exalted of beasts. You fixed a lion's likeness in your throne. They roar
like a lion, they are terrifying as a lion, they are fearful as a lion, they are strong as a lion. Your
fear, O mighty one, is upon them.
The eagle is the most exalted of birds. You fixed an eagle's likeness in your throne. They run
like an eagle, they are swift as an eagle, they fly like an eagle, they soar like an eagle. Your fear,
O pure one, is upon them.
All together, they praise your holiness with a threefold sanctification. So it is written: *Holy,
holy, holy is the Lord of hosts; the whole earth is full of his glory* [Isaiah 6:3].

At first sight, this hymn seems obviously to be based on BT Hag. 13b's
midrash of the four faces, which I translated as paragraph F in chapter IV,
section 3b. When we look closer, however, it appears that the *Hekhalot*
writer is instead following one of the Palestinian versions of the haggadah[42];
for the source used by BT, unlike its Palestinian parallels, does not speak of
each animal as "exalted" in its category, nor does it use the verb "fixed."

This haggadah of the four exalted creatures has left a few other traces
in the *Hekhalot* literature, particularly *Hekhalot Rabbati*. One of these is
in the passage, quoted above, that comes right before the hymn and presumably serves as introduction to it: "You are the mightiest of the exalted
ones [*ge'im*], exalted over everything, exalting yourself over everything,
bringing down the exalted and raising up the lowly" (Schäfer, #272; Wertheimer, 27:1). Another of *Hekhalot Rabbati*'s hymns tells us that there
stand beneath God's throne "the most exalted ones [*ge'e ge'im*] ... and all
the kings, leaders of the categories that you created. They are bound, and
stand beneath your throne of glory" (Schäfer, #98; Wertheimer, 3:3)[x)].
The reference to the *hayyot* as "kings" (*malkhe*; ms Vatican corrects to
mal'akhe, "angels") perhaps reflects the Talmud's version of the haggadah,
which speaks of the lion as "king of beasts," and so forth. In yet another
hymn, God is "the exalted one who exalts himself over the exalted" (*ge'eh
hammitga'eh ^cal hagge'im*; Schäfer, #254, cf. #263 and #975; Wertheimer,
25:2).

---

42 *Song R.* to 3:9–10; *Ex. R.* 23:13; Tanh. Buber *Be-Shallah* #14, ed. 31a [222]; *Midr. Psalms*
103:16, ed. 219a–b [199]. See above, chapter IV, section 3d. I translate the version in Buber's
Tanhuma: "*I will sing to the Lord, for he is highly exalted* [Exodus 15:1]. R. Abin ha-Levi said:
There are four exalted creatures in the world. The lion is the most exalted [*ge'eh*] of beasts. The
ox is the most exalted of animals. The eagle is the most exalted of birds. The human being is
exalted over all of them. God took them and fixed them [*qeba^can*] in the throne of glory, for he
exalts himself over the exalted [*mitga'eh ^cal ge'im*]. Hence, *I will sing to the Lord, for he is highly exalted.*"

"Be exalted," a hymn in *Maᶜaśeh Merkabah* tells God, "over the *ḥayyot* and over the chariots of your power" (Schäfer, #585; Scholem, #25). *Hekhalot Zuṭarti* seems also to reflect this image when it speaks of an angel who "exalts himself with the king of the world" (*mitga'eh 'et* [!] *malko shel ᶜolam*; Schäfer, #416; cf. Elior, line 372). *Seder Rabbah di-Bereshit* explains that the *ḥayyot*, enormous as they are, are only a tiny fraction of God's size. "That is why Scripture says, *The Lord is high above all nations* [Psalm 113:4]. Do not read *goyim*, 'nations,' but *ge'im*, 'exalted ones.' This refers to the holy *ḥayyot*, who, on account of their enormous stature, exalt themselves over all categories of being in heaven and earth. But God exalts himself over all of them" (Schäfer, ##518, 778).

The *Hekhalot* have a few other references to Ezekiel's four facial forms. The conclusion of *Hekhalot Zuṭarti*'s Aramaic description of the *ḥayyot* seems, as far as we can tell (the context is very obscure), to combine the four into a grotesque being with a human face, eagle's wings, lion's claws, ox's horns (Schäfer, #356; above, section 1a). Ms New York of *Hekhalot Zuṭarti*, and its parallels, list "the stamp of a lion, the seal of an eagle, the likeness of an ox, and a human face sealed up" (Schäfer, #368; above, section 1b). I know of no parallel to the conceptions expressed in either passage. But ms New York, as we have seen, goes on to list the names of the "princes" of the four faces, and adds: "When the Israelites sinned, the ox's face was concealed and a cherub put in its place" (Schäfer, #369, cf. #955). The writer plainly draws on a haggadah, by now familiar to us, which I have claimed for the Palestinian synagogue tradition.

Unhappily, I cannot confidently make a parallel claim about the haggadah of the four exalted creatures, which seems more usually to have yielded the *Hekhalot* writers their material for reflection on the *ḥayyot*'s faces. We saw in chapter IV (section 3d) that this haggadah must have been very popular in the third and fourth centuries, for Christians as well as Jews seem to have been familiar with it; but I could not prove that the synagogue was the source of its popularity. The liturgical use to which *Hekhalot Rabbati* puts it would itself perhaps point to a synagogue origin. This reasoning, however, comes dangerously close to being circular.

e) Targum, outside Ezekiel. We are not yet quite done with the Targum to Ezekiel. A passage from a *Shiᶜur Qomah* text seems to have drawn on Targ. Ezekiel 1:27, and we will need to ponder the implications of this dependency. This discussion, however, is better postponed to section 5, below.

I have made no effort systematically to examine the Targums to other parts of the Bible, outside Ezekiel's *merkabah* visions, with the aim of tracing their influence on the *Hekhalot*. I have, however, come upon a few items worth noting.

Schäfer, #183, with its parallels, describes how the angels stand in terror and humility, "and cover their faces with their wings, that they may not recognize the likeness of God who dwells in the *merkabah*." *Massekhet Hekhalot*, ch. 6 (Wertheimer, page 60), makes a similar point. We recognize here the synagogue's exegesis of Isaiah 6:2, reflected in the Targum to that passage and in *Lev. R.* 27:3 (ed. 625—627 [191]; above, chapter V, section 2).

Schäfer, #468, tells us that "the chariots of [God's] glory" (*markebot yeqaro*) number three hundred. (The parallels in #376 and #728 miscopy *yeqaro*.) This Hebrew expression seems to be based on Aramaic *markebat yeqareh*, in Targ. Habakkuk 3:4 (cf. 3:8).

Finally, a passage near the beginning of ms New York's text of *Hekhalot Zutarti* (Schäfer, #343; Elior, lines 34—35) speaks of the miracle at the Red Sea, and purports to reveal the name by which Moses "made the water into lofty walls" (*ᶜabad mayya shurin remin*). This Aramaic phrase is surely drawn from Targum Pseudo-Jonathan to Exodus 14:22: "The waters were congealed like walls three hundred miles high" (*umayya qarshun he keshurin remin telat me'ah milin*). In Appendix IV, section 1, I show reason to believe that a peculiar passage in the *Visions of Ezekiel* (section IE) is based on a misunderstanding of a Targum to this passage.

4. The "youth," and the synagogue tradition

We recall from the Ozhayah text that the traveller to the *merkabah* can expect to be greeted by a mysterious "youth" (*naᶜar*), whose "splendor is like his king's splendor, his glory like his creator's glory." So impressive is he, that the visitor must take care not to treat him as divine.

We find this "youth" again in a number of *Hekhalot* passages, which crop up in the manuscripts in a bewildering variety of contexts and combinations. Each passage exists in several different versions, and these flow into each other in such a complex way that I cannot even attempt to classify them or trace their evolution. Most of this material is conventionally considered part of the *Shiᶜur Qomah* — a judgment which does not give us any help in understanding it, but which has the welcome result that it is available in Martin Samuel Cohen's scholarly English translation of *Shiᶜur Qomah* [516].

These passages often give this "youth" the title of "prince" (*śar*). They call him by many names, the most prominent of which is "Metatron." He is thus identified with a being whom we have already met several times (most recently in connection with *Śar Torah*), but have not yet paused to examine. *3 Enoch*, as we will later see in more detail, maintains this identification but changes its emphasis, so that "youth" appears as a somewhat eccentric nickname for Metatron.

We will come back again and again to the "youth"; only at the end of this chapter will we fully unravel his mystery. For now, we will consider the aspects of him revealed in a complex text that occurs in ms New York, in two parallel versions set one after the other (Schäfer, ##384–394, 395–400). I have touched on the second of these versions in chapter VII, section 2c, in connection with Joshua b. Levi's views on the rainbow; I will later take it up in more detail. I now concentrate on the first version [43].

The passage starts with a description of God's surroundings. After a long series of images, we read of "the seal-ring of a lion, the seal of an eagle, the likeness of an ox, and a human face kept secret [? cf. above, section 1a]. God's hand rests on the head of the youth, named Metatron" (#384). Parallels to this passage, which other manuscripts preserve in different contexts, have for the last sentence: "His hand [*weyado*] rests on the youth." It seems likely that "God" and "Metatron" are glosses by the copyist of ms New York or his source, and that the original text spoke only of the "youth," without identifying him[44].

However this may be, ms New York goes on to describe the youth's entrance beneath the throne of glory. Fire, hail, and wind accompany his progress toward it. Then:

> When the youth enters beneath the throne of glory, God embraces him with a shining face[y]. All the angels gather and address God as "the great, mighty, terrible God"; and they praise God three times a day through the agency of the youth [*ʿal yad hannaʿar*]. God gives some of his splendor and glory to the Gentile kings. The youth's stature fills the world, and God calls him "youth." [#385]

The text identifies (or, again identifies) the youth as Metatron (#386). In a long passage which we will meet again in a different context (section C3d), it lists his seventy names and describes how he revealed Torah to Moses (##387–388). It lavishly praises his importance among the heavenly beings, and lists, among his titles, "prince of the presence" (*śar happanim*) and "prince of Torah" (*śar hattorah*; #389). It concludes with a strange scene:

> [#389] The angels that are with him come and surround the throne of glory. They are on one side, the *ḥayyot* on the other, and the Shechinah on the throne of glory in the middle.

---

43 To avoid misunderstanding, I must stress that none of this material is unique to ms New York. But the manuscripts that contain parallel material (easily to be found in Schäfer's *Synopse*) organize it differently from ms New York, and I find ms New York's arrangement the most convenient to work with. – If the reader has difficulty visualizing the layout of the material, on the basis of the summaries and partial quotations I give here and in chapter VII, the overview in Appendix III may prove helpful.

44 I suspect that this text is based on the *Ketib* of Ezekiel 1:8 (*weyado ʾadam*; above, chapter IV, section 2e), and that its author conceived the "hand" as belonging to the "human face" (*pene ʾadam*).

[#390] One *hayyah* rises above the seraphim, descends upon the tabernacle of the youth named Metatron, and speaks with a loud voice of gentle stillness ...[45]. The angels fall silent. The watchers and holy ones become quiet. They are silent, and are pushed into the river of fire. The *hayyot* put their faces to the ground, and the youth named Metatron brings the fire of deafness and puts it into their ears, so that they cannot hear the sound of God's speech or the ineffable name[2].

The youth named Metatron then invokes, in seven voices, his living, pure, honored, terrible ... [etc.] name [which the text then sets forth].

I do not understand all the details of this account. But I can detect in #390 a variation on the theme, which we touched on in section 3c, of God silencing the angels so that he can hear the prayers of Israel. The reference to "one *hayyah*," at the beginning of #390, is very reminiscent of another *Hekhalot* source in which "one *hayyah*, whose name is Israel and who has 'Israel' inscribed on its forehead," stands in the middle of heaven and leads the angels in the morning prayer[46]. The youth himself, according to #398 (parallel to #385), wears a crown called "Israel." In #385, it is his approach to God's throne that allows the angels to offer their own praises. In #390, they are silenced, or even annihilated, in his favor. When we find him stuffing "the fire of deafness" into the ears of the *hayyot*, we may suspect that he is reversing an action prescribed in the Ozhayah text[47]. There, the human visitor to the sixth palace must fill his ears with wool, lest his soul escape in that fiery realm. Here, the human figure has the upper hand.

The angels become silent, not only before the youth's invocation, but also before "the sound of God's speech" — or, in #399 and its parallels, just "the sound of speech" (*qol dibbur*). We recognize here a fingerprint of the tradition found in Targ. Ezekiel 1:24—25, and in the Talmudic baraita that develops it (above, chapter IV, sections 2c, 3c). According to the Targum, the living creatures silence the praises of their wings before God's revelation (*dibbera*) to the prophets. The baraita in BT Hag. 13b makes the same point: "When revelation [*dibbur*] goes forth from God's mouth, they are silent."

The *Hekhalot* writer combines this theme with another one, also drawn from the synagogue tradition. "The youth's stature fills the world" (#385). We cannot understand why he should need this gigantic size, unless we sup-

---

45 *We'omeret beqol gadol qol demamah daqqah zakh kisse' hakkabod.* The sentence of course contradicts itself; and I do not know how to connect the last three words (omitted from my translation) with what precedes. The parallels that Schäfer prints, here and opposite #399, give several variants, but they do not help us. — All the parallels omit the words "named Metatron" throughout the paragraph. They are obviously a gloss.

46 Schäfer, ##296, 406. Wertheimer prints the passage, probably wrongly, as part of *Hekhalot Rabbati* (31:4). Grözinger and Schäfer translate it into German [533a,582]. — In Appendix VI, I discuss the parallels from chapter 4 of *Pirqe de-Rabbi Eliezer*, and from the Gnostic *On the Origin of the World*.

47 Cohen has noticed the resemblance of the two actions, but explains it differently [516b].

pose that he has stepped into the role of the Talmudic Sandalphon, "who stands on the earth and whose head reaches to beside the *ḥayyot*" (Ḥag. 13b), and who can thus lift the Jews' prayers directly to God (above, chapter IV, section 3c).

Shall we suppose, then, that the youth is Sandalphon, equipped with a new set of names? I prefer to put it differently: the youth functions here, in a way similar to Sandalphon's, as a personification of the prayers of the synagogue. I am far from claiming that this exhausts his significance. On the contrary; we have a long way to go before we begin to grasp all that the youth meant to those who believed in him. Only then will we understand how the role in which he operates here fits into his total meaning.

If the first version of ms New York's account of the youth links him to the synagogue exegesis of Ezekiel 1:24—25 and 1:15 (Sandalphon), the second version introduces Ezekiel 1:27—28. Where #385 has the youth's stature fill the world, the parallel in #398 declares: "His body resembles the rainbow, and the rainbow resembles *the appearance of fire all around it* [Ezekiel 1:27]." As I have argued in chapter VII, the rainbow of Ezekiel 1:28 takes Sandalphon's place as bridge between earth and heaven; and the youth (now called "prince") is identified with it.

Fifteen lines further in the New York manuscript, Ezekiel 1:27—28 is again applied to the youth. #400, which concludes the second version of the passage on the youth (or, perhaps, begins a fresh series of very obscure materials), seems to say that God and the youth "resemble each other from the loins downward [*mimmotnaw ulemaṭṭah*], but do not resemble each other from the loins upward [*mimmotnaw ulemaᶜlah*]." The language is very close to that of Ezekiel 1:27, and we can hardly doubt that this text inspired the writer. The *Hekhalot* author is evidently not sure whether the human-like being that Ezekiel saw on the sapphire throne was God himself, or the lesser figure of the youth. He expresses this uncertainty by hinting that 1:27 can apply more or less to both.

5. Anthropomorphism: Targ. Ezekiel 1:27 and *Shiᶜur Qomah*

The author of yet another passage from ms New York, plainly belonging to the *Shiᶜur Qomah* genre, is less timid on this point[48]. R. Akiba here quotes "Metatron, the beloved servant, the great prince of the testimony," as detailing the measurements of the different parts of God's body. "From

---

48 Schäfer, #376; with parallels from three other manuscripts. Cohen (section B) and Meltzer (chapter 1) translate texts fairly close to that of ms New York [516,488].

the dwelling-place of his glory and upward [*mibbet moshab yeqareh ule^cela*], he measures 1,080,000,000 parasangs; from the dwelling-place of his glory and downward [*mibbet moshab yeqareh ulemaṭṭah*], 118,000 parasangs[49]. He is [a total of] 2,360,000,000 parasangs tall."

"The dwelling-place of God's glory" must be somewhere around the middle of his body. It is evidently the "loins" of the figure on the sapphire throne, seen through the lens of the Targum to Ezekiel 1:27. MT describes this figure "from the appearance of his loins," upward and downward. Targum substitutes an elaborate circumlocution: "An appearance of glory which the eye could not look at and which it was impossible to contemplate, and upward ... and downward" (*hezu yeqar dela yakhela ^cena lemihze wela 'ifshar le'istakkala beh ule^cela ... ulera^c*). This Targumic passage must have influenced the *Hekhalot* writer; for we cannot otherwise explain why, in the middle of a passage that is mostly written in Hebrew, he shifts suddenly from Hebrew (*mibbet moshab*) to Aramaic (*yeqareh ule^cela*).

This leads us to a paradoxical conclusion. The Aramaic translator of Ezekiel 1:27 had recoiled from its anthropomorphic reference to God's loins, and had therefore shrouded these parts in an impenetrable fog of euphemism. Now comes a writer who is so under the spell of the Targum to this passage that he cannot resist imitating its language – and he uses the Targum's phraseology in the course of a limb-by-limb description of God's utterly human-like body! If the Targum so influenced him, why did its lesson, that one may not describe God in human terms, have so little impact on him?

This question brings us up against a more general difficulty. I have argued at some length that the *Hekhalot* writers drew their ideas about Ezekiel's *merkabah* mainly from the synagogue tradition of *merkabah* exegesis, and most particularly from those elements of the tradition that we find in the Targum. Yet one of the most striking characteristics of the Targums in general is their almost obsessive resistance to any hint of anthropomorphism of any kind, including much that modern Bible readers would find innocuous. The *Hekhalot*, by contrast, indulge in anthropomorphism to a degree that must be unsurpassed, and perhaps unequalled, in any of the literature of the Judaic religions. Even aside from *Shi^cur Qomah*, writers who have God "bend over [the image of Jacob's face], hug it and kiss it, embrace it so that my hands are on my shoulders" (above, chapter VIII, section A5c), or say that he "stretched out his two hands and slapped the

---

49 We must change both figures to 1,180,000,000 to get the arithmetic to come out right. Both emendations are easy: insert ^caśar before 'elef in the first number, rebabot after 'elef in the second.

throne of glory" (chapter IX, section A3c), plainly have no inhibitions about imagining God in human form.

There is a real tension here. But it does not invalidate the evidence I have presented, that the *Hekhalot* writers make heavy use of the Targum to Ezekiel and develop its exegetical traditions. We have, I think, another way out of the difficulty; and it lies in the obsessive character of the Targum's hostility to anthropomorphism.

When the Targum's translators relentlessly throttle back anything that might imply God has a human-like body, I suspect that they are repressing what they know to be powerful tendencies in themselves and in their hearers. Unchecked, these tendencies might burst forth into what most monotheists would regard as lunacy. And burst forth they do, in *Shi'ur Qomah* and the rest of the *Hekhalot*.

Put another way, the anthropomorphism of the *Hekhalot* represents the synagogue tradition's urge to make God as concrete and tangible to his worshippers as possible. The anti-anthropomorphism of the Targums represents the tradition's effort to police its own impulses.

Perhaps we can also detect a few attempts to satisfy both of these tendencies, to bring a human element into the realm of the divine while at the same time keeping God himself pure and safe from this element. The belief that Jacob's image is on God's throne, which I have derived from Targumic exegesis of Ezekiel 1:26 (above, chapter IV, section 2b), may be the fruit of one such compromise. The belief in a godlike "youth" or "prince," who can take God's place on the sapphire throne, may be another.

If so, both attempts backfired. The God of the *Hekhalot*, shamelessly anthropomorphic, hugs and kisses the image of Jacob's face, embraces with radiant face the youth who enters beneath his throne. Not only is he not transcendent; with the youth's appearance, he is not even unique. Human nature has infiltrated heaven. Human invasion is now thinkable.

This, I will suggest, is the underlying theme of the *Hekhalot*.

C. The Hekhalot and the Shabu'ot Cycle

1. Introduction

Through all this discussion of the *merkabah* exegesis of the *Hekhalot*, we have so far seen nothing of Ezekiel 1:1. Given the central importance of this verse for the author of the *Visions of Ezekiel*, we may well wonder what, if anything, the *Hekhalot* writers do with it.

As it happens, there is one passage in the *Hekhalot* that quotes 1:1

(Schäfer, ##514–515). At first glance, it does not look very promising. It is part of a rather incoherent chain of materials devoted mostly to sacred names and how to use them. It does not belong to any of the conventionally defined texts; and, with most of its context, it is found only in ms New York.

#514 begins: "This is the great name that the angel Zagan'el revealed to Moses the son of Amram, when the living God revealed himself to him in the burning bush. Whoever knows it and makes mention of it in purity will never suffer injury." The author gives us, first, a long list of divine names; then, a much shorter list of angels, among them the "Gallisur" whom we remember from *Pesiqta* and its parallels. (He also appears in ms New York's text of *Hekhalot Zuṭarti*; above, section B1b.)

Without any further introduction, the author then (#515) quotes three Biblical passages: (1) Genesis 7:11, describing the outbreak of the great flood; (2) the words *wayyehi bayyom hashshelishi*, "on the third day," presumably from Exodus 19:16[50]; (3) Ezekiel 1:1. He adds: "Purify yourself and pronounce these names, these angels, and these two [!] verses, eighteen times."

Why does it occur to him to combine Genesis 7:11, Exodus 19:16, and Ezekiel 1:1? The first passage describes how "all the fountains of the great deep were split open, and the windows of heaven were opened [*'arubbot hashshamayim niftaḥu*]." These last words obviously suggest Ezekiel's *the heavens were opened.* Further, I suspect that the writer is following a tradition that read *meᶜonot* ("dwellings") for *maᶜyenot* ("fountains"). He thus understands Genesis 7:11, without concern for its context, to mean that God opened both the heavens and the subterranean realms – to Noah, to Ezekiel, or (as the allusion to Exodus 19:16 suggests) to the Israelites at Sinai. The *Visions of Ezekiel* (ID, F–G) tells us the same about Ezekiel; Lieberman's *Deuteronomy Rabbah*, about the Israelites (above, chapter VIII, section B4a).

The author evidently draws on one feature of the Shabuᶜot cycle; which, as we saw, could be shifted within that cycle from one context to another. With his three Biblical citations, he points to three of its possible contexts. Significantly, he begins with a revelation made to Moses.

We recall that a hymn in *Hekhalot Rabbati* takes language drawn from the synagogue exegesis of Ezekiel 1:24–25 and uses it in a context that evidently speaks of the Sinai revelation, with an explicit reference to Moses and an implicit reference to the burning bush (above, section B3c). This

---

50 In theory, the quote could also be from Genesis 34:25, 40:20, II Samuel 1:2, I Kings 3:18, or Esther 5:1. But I cannot conceive how any of these passages could be relevant to the author's purpose.

passage, too, reflects an understanding that Sinai and the *merkabah* belong together.

These materials remind us that we must confront the question of the relation of the *Hekhalot* to the Shabu^cot cycle.

If the arguments I have offered in section B are valid, we must regard the *Hekhalot* as having some at least of its roots in the synagogue tradition of *merkabah* exegesis. The Shabu^cot cycle is that tradition's most remarkable creation. We have seen evidence linking the Shabu^cot cycle to the figure of Joshua b. Levi; and, through Origen, to early third-century Caesarea. *Hekhalot* passages, which we have seen reason to trace back to the same city in the early fourth century, develop an exegetical tradition on Ezekiel 1:28 which is associated with the name of the same rabbi (above, chapter VII, section 2c).

The Shabu^cot cycle seems at times to be straining to cross the border into the *Hekhalot*. Between the ascension of Moses and the "descent to the *merkabah*" there is no enormous gulf. The man who believes he has made this "descent" steps into a role not far different from that of the preachers whom I have detected behind the figure of Ezekiel in the *Visions* (above, chapter VIII, section A5c).

The border, however, never vanishes. The *Hekhalot*, and the literature representing the Shabu^cot cycle, are distinct bodies of material which could hardly be mistaken for each other. The *Hekhalot* seldom take on the midrashic and homiletic qualities of the Shabu^cot materials. The Shabu^cot materials never offer themselves as manuals of practical instruction.

If I am to propose, as I did at the end of section A, that the essential logic of the *Hekhalot* is an extension of that of the Shabu^cot cycle, I cannot evade the task of examining more closely the features that the two corpora have in common. What exactly are those features? What do they tell us about the relationships between the materials that contain them?

2. The *Visions of Ezekiel*

a) The "prince" passage. The *Visions of Ezekiel*'s clearest links with the *Hekhalot* are concentrated in one single passage. This is section IID1—2, which discusses the "prince" in the third heaven.

R. Levi quoted R. Hama b. ^cUqba, quoting R. Johanan: The prince [*šar*] dwells only in *Zebul* [the third heaven], and it is he who constitutes the fullness of *Zebul*. Thousands of thousands and myriads of myriads are in his presence, serving him. ... [Citation of Daniel 7:9–10.] What is his name? *Qimos* is his name. R. Isaac says: *Me^cattah* is his name. R. ^cAnayni b. Sasson says: *Bizebul* is his name. R. Tanhum the elder says: *'ṭṭyh* is his name. Eleazar of Nadwad says: Metatron, like the name of the Power. Those who make use of the name say: *slns* is his name, *qs bs bs qbs* is his name, like the name of the creator of the world.

This passage, particularly in its latter part, is in its style and concerns so untypical of the *Visions* as to seem a foreign body incorporated into the text (above, chapter VIII, section A3a). Its contacts with the *Hekhalot* lie precisely in its idiosyncrasies.

Here, and nowhere else in the *Visions,* we have a series of sacred names, which in their strangeness yield nothing to the names found throughout the *Hekhalot*. In the phrase "those who make use of the name" (*meshammeshin beshum*), we have a fairly clear allusion to magical manipulation of these names. This activity, the very heart and soul of the *Hekhalot*, makes no other appearance in the *Visions*.

Most important, we have here a mysterious "prince," whom the author seems to conceive as a semi-divine being. He thus identifies him with the deity described in Daniel 7:9–10, and twice tells us that his name is like God's. One of ms New York's accounts of the "youth" represents him as a "prince" very much like this one (Schäfer, ##396–399; see Appendix III). Here as well as there (#397), Metatron is one of the names of the "prince," but not his single outstanding name.

With our passage's use of Daniel 7:9–10, we may compare a *Hekhalot* fragment found in the New York and Oxford manuscripts:

> Elisha b. Abuyah said: When I ascended to *pardes*, I saw Akhtariel Yah, God of Israel, Yahweh of hosts, sitting at the entrance of *pardes* with one hundred twenty myriads of angels around him. So it is written: *Thousands of thousands served him, and myriads of myriads stood before him* [Daniel 7:10]. When I saw them, I was appalled. I recoiled, then forced my way in before God. "Master of the world," I said to him, "it is written in your Torah: *The heavens and the heavens of heavens belong to the Lord your God* [Deuteronomy 10:14]. It is also written: *The firmament declares his handiwork* [Psalm 19:2]. [This implies] only one [God]!"
>
> "Elisha my son," he said to me, "did you come here to find fault with me? Haven't you heard the proverb ...?[51]"

We do not, unhappily, learn what proverb God has in mind, for the text breaks off at this point. ("I could not find the proverb," the copyist of ms New York complains.) But what we have learned is interesting enough. Some at least of the *Hekhalot* writers applied Daniel's description of the "ancient of days" to a godlike being who indeed bears some of God's titles, but who is distinct from the supreme God. This is what we find in the "prince" passage of the *Visions*.

The style of this passage, which stands out sharply from that of the rest of the *Visions*, finds a close parallel in *Hekhalot Zutarti* (Schäfer, #357; Elior, lines 134–142). I translate ms New York:

> Blessed be his great, terrible, mighty name. We put our hope in him, and adjure by his name. I adjure you ... [there follows a string of unintelligible words, *hayyata* (=*hayyot*?) among them].

---

51 Schäfer, #597. Scholem quotes and partly translates the passage, in the course of his discussion of "Akhtariel" (or, as he prefers to vocalize the name, "Akatriel") [598].

Balaam said: *ṭwṭypwm p'mwn* is his name, *ṭwpy ṭwpy pwsy pyymwn* is his name. Moses said: *sṭ šyyš* is his name. So said the angel of death [!]: *sṭ šyyš* is his name. David said: *'nqwlytwm 'nqlwwty mwn* is his name. Solomon said: *'nqwlwtwt 'nqlywtym 'nqlwwtymwn ḥsdsyhw yhwts* is his name.

I cannot hope to elucidate the details of this weird text. What concerns me is the pattern in which it is laid out: *A* said, *X* is his name; *B* said, *Y* is his name (*A 'amar X shemo, B 'amar Y shemo*). This is almost the same as the pattern that the *Visions* uses: *A 'omer X shemo, B 'omer Y shemo.*

Similarly, a passage in *Hekhalot Rabbati* (Schäfer, #277; Wertheimer, 28:2) lists eight names of Metatron in the pattern, *X* is his name, *Y* is his name, *Z* is his name, and so forth (*X shemo, Y shemo, Z shemo*).

What of the "prince's" names themselves? Metatron is by now familiar, although we have yet to be formally introduced. *'ṭṭyh*, however it is to be vocalized, occurs in a list of Metatron's names in a passage, which we will presently examine more closely, found in some manuscripts at the end of *3 Enoch* (Schäfer, #76; Odeberg, ch. 48D) [598]. It also crops up in an adjuration of the "prince of the presence" (#501); and perhaps, in the corrupted form *ᶜṭhyh*, in one version of a *Shiᶜur Qomah* text (#949, from ms Munich 40).

Meᶜattah, Bizebul, slns, and *qs bs bs qbs* do not appear, as far as I know, anywhere else. We would perhaps not expect to find the first two. *Bizebul* means simply "in *Zebul*," and may have coined within its present context. *Meᶜattah,* if I have vocalized it correctly, sounds suspiciously like the word meaning "as a consequence." It is as if *meᶜattah shemo* were once the beginning of a sentence, "his name consequently is ..."

As for *Qimos,* Gruenwald plausibly suggests that the name is derived from Latin *comes,* "court attendant" [229][52]. We might, then, perhaps hope to find it among the Greek and Latin titles that I have detected behind some of the epithets given to the "prince" in Schäfer, #397 (above, chapter VII, section 2c). And, indeed, one of these epithets is *qyṭws* (spelled *qyṭwm* in one manuscript), which could easily be a corruption of *qymws.* If so, this would strengthen the link we have already detected between this *Hekhalot* passage and the "prince" passage in the *Visions.*

b) Other. Outside this "prince" passage, however, clear and specific contacts between the *Visions* and the *Hekhalot* are few and far between.

The most striking parallel is with a passage in *3 Enoch* which lists the different kinds of God's chariots (Schäfer, #37; Odeberg, ch. 24). "How many chariots [*markabot*] does God have?" says Metatron to Ishmael.

---

52 The word develops into a title in late Latin, and is the ancestor of our words "count" and "countess."

"He has chariots of cherubim; as it is written, *He rode on a cherub, and flew* [Psalm 18:11]. He has chariots of wind; as it is written, *He soared on the wings of wind* [ibid.]. He has chariots of fast cloud [ᶜab qal]; as it is written, *The Lord rides on a fast cloud* [Isaiah 19:1]." And so on, through twenty more types of chariot, each with its own proof text.

At first, these multiple *merkabahs* remind us strongly of the seven *merkabahs* in the seven heavens of the *Visions*, each of which has its own name ("horses," "cherub," "cloud," and the like) and proof text. But the parallel becomes less impressive when we look at it more closely. What is distinctive about the *merkabahs* in the *Visions* is not that they are in the plural number, but that there are precisely seven of them. *3 Enoch*, by contrast, suggests numberless throngs. Moreover, few of the details overlap. The *Visions* names one of its *merkabahs* *Kerub* ("cherub") and another ᶜ*Ab* ("cloud"); and it invokes Psalm 18:11 and Isaiah 19:1, respectively, in support of these claims (IIF2, H2). This indeed resembles the beginning of the passage from *3 Enoch* (above). Both texts quote Psalm 68:18 — *3 Enoch* in connection with "chariots of 'two myriads,'" *Visions* in connection with the *merkabah* of *Melakhim* ("kings"; IIE2). *3 Enoch* speaks of "chariots of ᶜArabot," and ᶜArabot is the name of the sixth heaven in the *Visions* (and the seventh in most other systems). With these few resemblances, all of which could easily have arisen from independent contemplation of Biblical texts involving "riding" and "chariots," we have exhausted all that the *Visions'* seven *merkabahs* and *3 Enoch*'s twenty-three species of *merkabah* have in common.

We perhaps have a somewhat stronger parallel in a hymn quoted in ms Munich 40 (Schäfer, #966; Cohen translates an equivalent text as section N of his "*Shiᶜur Qomah*" [516]). This source speaks of God as dwelling in a sequence of seven heavens — *Shamayim, Sheme Shamayim, ᶜArafel, ᶜArabot, Zebul, Maᶜon,* and *Shehaqim* — and finally as "sitting on an exalted throne [*kisse' marom*] in the seventh [!] heaven." Six of the seven names (*Maᶜon* excepted) correspond to the first six heavens in the *Visions*; and *kisse' marom* reminds us of the *Visions'* seventh heaven, *Kisse' Kabod* ("throne of glory"). The sequence is not the same. It is striking, however, that both agree against nearly all the other lists of heavens in *not* making ᶜArabot the seventh.

The remaining points of contact can be summed up rapidly. A hymn in *Hekhalot Rabbati* says: "You ... make your creatures anew every day, servants from fire, to exalt the praises of your mysteries" (Schäfer, #269; Wertheimer, 26:3). This resembles *Visions*, IIC1. We have seen that one passage of ms New York (Schäfer, ##514−515) hints at an understanding of Ezekiel's *heavens were opened* akin to that of the *Visions*; while another passage of this manuscript (#343) draws, as does the *Visions*, on Targum Pseudo-Jonathan to Exodus 14:22 (above, sections B3c and C1; Appendix

IV). Most important, we have noted a resemblance between the function of Ezekiel in the *Visions* and the function of the visionary in *Hekhalot Rabbati* (above, chapter VIII, section A5c).

c) Conclusions. Not only is the *Visions of Ezekiel* not a *Hekhalot* text; it is, by and large, very unlike the *Hekhalot*. The *Hekhalot* have nothing like the sustained midrash that occupies the first half of the *Visions*. The *Visions*, outside the passage on the "prince," has nothing like the *Hekhalot*'s interminable hymns, strings of sacred names, and magical operations. As far as structure goes, the carefully organized *Visions* in no way resembles the sprawling and barely coherent *Hekhalot* writings.

If the *Visions* and the *Hekhalot* nevertheless have some points in common, we can explain these — with one exception — by supposing that both have roots in the Shabu\u1d9cot cycle. The author of the *Visions* drew extensively from the cycle's homiletic material, generally preserving its original content and purpose. The *Hekhalot* writers drew from it also, but turned what they borrowed into magic and magically induced experience.

Synagogue preachers, holding forth on Ezekiel's vision with all their passion and all their imagination, came to believe that they saw "with the understanding of the heart" what Ezekiel saw, and that it was their mission to evoke such "vision" in their hearers. Some of their hearers took them all too literally. Perhaps coveting the public authority of the preachers, they looked for ways to turn "the understanding of the heart" into the illusion of experience. Like the preachers, they made it their task to proclaim what they "saw" to others. One person's conviction thus became another's hallucination. I can easily imagine such a process lying behind the parallel between the role of "Ezekiel" in the *Visions,* and that of "you who descend to the *merkabah*" in *Hekhalot Rabbati*. It is harder for me to reverse the process, and conceive that the hallucination arose without the prior conviction.

The exception, which seems to baffle this explanation, is the "prince" passage. What is this one *Hekhalot*-like passage doing in a generally un-*Hekhalot*-like work?

The answer perhaps lies in its particular affinity with the passage of ms New York that describes the "youth" under his title "prince" (Schäfer, ##396–399). If I am right in connecting this latter passage with Joshua b. Levi on the one hand and with fourth-century Caesarea on the other (above, chapter VII, section 2c), we may guess that it comes from circles close to those that created and transmitted the materials of the Shabu\u1d9cot cycle. The cognate "prince" passage in the *Visions,* too, seems to be an early Palestinian source. The authentic-sounding attributions to third-century rabbis, which so impressed Scholem [599], suggest as much.

Both "prince" passages, I propose, are early "proto-*Hekhalot*" compositions, written by people who were in touch (or perhaps identical) with the transmitters of the Shabu^cot midrashim. One "prince" text thus became attached to these midrashim, and so made its way to the author of the *Visions*. Another found a home in the *Hekhalot*.

Significantly, the subject of both "proto-*Hekhalot*" compositions is the divinized being whom later writers will normally know as Metatron.

3. The Sinai-ascension materials

All told, the overlap between the *merkabah* traditions of the *Visions* and the conceptions of the *Hekhalot* is not very great. If we had only the *Visions* to represent the Shabu^cot homilies, we could hardly suppose that these homilies played any great role in the development of the *Hekhalot*.

The midrashim on the Sinai revelation and the ascension of Moses are another matter.

Ira Chernus has devoted considerable attention to the Sinai *haggadot*, and their *Hekhalot* parallels, in his *Mysticism in Rabbinic Judaism*. Although Chernus sometimes casts his net too wide, and records thematic resemblances that are too general to be useful, he also points out some extremely important parallels. When, for example, the angel Ozhayah warns the *merkabah* traveller to "stuff wool into your ears and nose and anus, so that your soul cannot escape before I can get there and revive you," we cannot doubt that this is somehow linked to the haggadah attributed to Joshua b. Levi in BT Shabb. 88b, in which the Israelites' souls leave them at each of God's utterances, and he must resurrect them each time (above, chapter VIII, section B3c; chapter IX, section A2b) [514].

As for the stories of Moses' ascension, their links to the *Hekhalot* have been clear and obvious to scholars at least since Zunz [363]. Both share an image of heaven as an often terrifying place. The angels are imposing figures with strange-sounding names, who menace any human who dares to set foot in their territory. The visitor normally survives by invoking a higher authority against the lower.

The parallels extend to details, as we will see.

a) The dangers of the ascent. When Moses meets Hadarniel, and again when he meets Sandalphon, he is so frightened that he wants to fall from his cloud[53]. This image of falling or being thrown from heaven recurs at

---

53 Full details of this and subsequent references to the ascension stories may be found in chapter VIII, section B2.

the beginning of *3 Enoch*. Ishmael, having reached the gate of the seventh palace, prays that "the merit of Aaron ... may protect me from the power of prince Qaspiel and the angels that are with him, that they may not throw me down from heaven" (Schäfer, #1; Odeberg, ch. 1).

Later in *3 Enoch*, Metatron tells Ishmael: "When the angels say *Holy [holy, holy is the Lord of hosts,* etc.], the pillars of the heavens and their bases are shaken, the gates of the palaces of ^cArabot Raqia^c quiver ... and all the stars and constellations are terrified, and the sun and the moon are so frightened that they run back twelve thousand parasangs out of their courses and try to throw themselves out of heaven" (Schäfer, #56; Odeberg, ch. 38).

Fear of falling is perhaps a natural enough sentiment in a human being who has just climbed to heaven. Yet Moses and the *merkabah* traveller have a particular reason to be worried about it, as we will later see.

In *Merkabah Rabbah*, Akiba warns Ishmael that, if he makes a mistake in using his method of learning Torah, certain beings — angels, evidently — "would then cause you harm" (*yifge^cu bakh*). Nehuniah b. ha-Qanah confirms this: "Were it not for the covenant made with Aaron, and the branch from which you spring, they would already have caused you harm and destroyed you utterly" (*pega^cukh we'ibbedukh min ha^colam*; Schäfer, #681). The language is reminiscent of Moses' encounters with the angels. Angel after angel "met" Moses (*paga^c bo*); this same verb *paga^c*, which normally has hostile overtones, I translate "cause harm" in *Merkabah Rabbah*. Of the first angel Moses meets, Kemuel, we read that "Moses struck him one blow and destroyed him utterly" (*'ibbedo min ha^colam*; so *Pesiqta Rabbati* and *Ma^cayan Hokhmah*). *Merkabah Rabbah*, as we saw, uses the same expression.

A hymn in *Ma^caseh Merkabah* declares: "Your power is over all the *merkabah*, your might over the holy *hayyot*. For you are a God living and enduring for ever; you are pure in all your world; your mercies are magnified over those who vanquish the *hayyot* [*menassehe hayyot*], for all eternity" (Schäfer, #592; Scholem, #32). Who are "those who vanquish the *hayyot*"? Altmann suggests, plausibly, that they are the people who ascend to heaven over the opposition of the *hayyot* and the other angelic guards [461]. Like Moses, they have defeated the heavenly powers.

b) A second area of contact between the *Hekhalot* and the Sinai-ascension *haggadot* is their concern with *the heavenly hymnody*. The *Hekhalot* writers devote a large proportion of their attention to this subject, which they develop in the most exuberant and fantastic ways. *Hekhalot Rabbati*'s description of the *hayyot* dancing around God (above, section B2) gives us some idea how far they were willing to go. The stories of Moses' ascension do not come near rivalling them. But their description of the liturgy, that accompanies the progress of Sandalphon's wreath toward God's head, points to a developing interest in this direction.

Here, too, we can supplement the general similarity with at least one detailed parallel. "When [the wreath] reaches [God's] throne," *Pesiqta* tells us, "the wheels of his throne rotate, the bases of the footstool are shaken, and trembling seizes all the heavens." Compare this with *3 Enoch*'s description, which I quoted in section 3a, of what happens when the angels recite the *Qedushshah.*

I must admit, however, that close parallels to the liturgy of the wreath itself are scarce. The most impressive ones occur at the conclusion of apocalyptic passages inserted into *Hekhalot Rabbati:* Schäfer, #126 (Wertheimer, 7:2) and #146 (not published elsewhere). We have somewhat more remote parallels in #296 (Wertheimer, 31:4; above, section B4), #744 (from *Seder Rabbah di-Bereshit*), and chapter 6 of *Massekhet Hekhalot.*

c) Who are *the beings who meet Moses* in the ascension stories? We read of Kemuel, Hadarniel, Sandalphon, the fiery river Rigyon, Gallisur, and, finally, "a troop of strong and mighty angels of destruction who surround the throne of glory." I have not been able to find Kemuel in the *Hekhalot* texts. But Hadarniel makes his appearance, albeit in disguise (below, section 4c). So, more openly, do Sandalphon, Rigyon, and Gallisur[54]. This last figure is particularly useful in linking the ascension stories to the *Hekhalot.*

In *Pesiqta* and its parallels, Gallisur gets his name because he reveals God's decrees to the world (*megalleh ṭa^came ṣur*). *3 Enoch* calls him "revealer of secrets" (*megalleh raz*; Schäfer, #25) or "revealer of all the secrets of the Torah" (*hammegalleh kol raze hattorah*; so the text in Odeberg, ch. 18, and cf. Schäfer, #861). In a passage in ms New York's text of *Hekhalot Zuṭarti*, he is one of two angels who stand on God's left hand and carry out his decrees (Schäfer, #372; above, section B1b).

The ascension stories attribute to Gallisur one function that seems particularly odd. "He takes iron pokers that have coals from Rigyon upon them," says *Pesiqta*, "and sets them up opposite kings and princes, so that the fear of them may fall upon the world." *Pesiqta*'s parallels differ on the details — *Ma^cayan Ḥokhmah* speaks of an iron pan filled with coals, ms Oxford of iron ox-goads (?) — but make the same point.

---

54 Sandalphon appears in *Ma^ca͗seh Merkabah* (Schäfer, ##574, 582; Scholem, ##20, 23) and at the beginning of *Merkabah Rabbah* (Schäfer, ##655–656, 821–822 [585]). Ms Oxford entitles the passage on Akhtariel, translated in section 2a above, *razo shel sandalfon*, "secret of Sandalphon" [598]. — On Rigyon, see above, chapter VI, section 2a. — Gallisur appears, aside from the passages cited here, in a list of angel-names in #514 (above, section 1). Mentioned with him are Michael, Gabriel, Ra^cashiel, and Lahaqiel.

The *Hekhalot* do not attribute any such activity to Gallisur. But they share the conception that God bestows his authority on the rulers of the world. "God gives some of his splendor and glory to the Gentile kings," says ms New York's description of the "youth" (Schäfer, #385; above, section B4). A parallel account has either God or the "prince" give "some of his glory to the princes of the Gentiles, [but] the crown on his head is named 'Israel'" (Schäfer, #398; see Appendix III). In *3 Enoch*, Metatron is engaged in distributing "greatness and kingship, power and glory" to the angelic representatives of the Gentile kingdoms, when Elisha b. Abuyah sees him and mistakes him for a divinity (Schäfer, #20; Odeberg, ch. 16). "We do not raise a hand against kingship," says the angel ᶜAnafᵉel in one of Gruenwald's Genizah fragments, "on account of the honor that [God] allots to kings of flesh and blood" [471]. Similar ideas are reflected in another passage of *3 Enoch* (Schäfer, #47; Odeberg, ch. 30), and in chapters 2 and 3 of *Massekhet Hekhalot*.

With Gallisur's "iron pokers," compare the rod or rods of fire that *Pirqe de-Rabbi Eliezer* and *Hekhalot Zuṭarti* describe God as holding in his hand (Schäfer, #372; above, section B1b, and Appendix VI).

d) The Moses/Metatron text. The parallels we have examined so far argue that there are links between the *Hekhalot* and the stories of Moses' ascension. But they have so far told us little about the nature of these links. If one body of material influenced the other, what was the direction of the influence? If one developed out of the other, which was the parent and which the offspring?

We now come to a text which will help us resolve these questions.

It is not clear how we are to classify this text. Perhaps we should consider it a part of *3 Enoch*, on the strength of those manuscripts that treat it as the conclusion of this work (the Oxford manuscript used by Odeberg, who prints the passage as ch. 48D; ms Vatican 228, published by Schäfer). But it appears in ms Munich 22 (and in Wertheimer) as part of the "Alphabet of R. Akiba," a text of rather mysterious origin that includes some material related to the *Hekhalot* [496a,503a,566a]. Finally, the first two paragraphs (Schäfer, ##76–77) turn up in the middle of ms New York's account of the "youth," in a slightly different form (Schäfer, ##387–388; see Appendix III). I do not know any way to resolve the issue of its original home. Since nothing rides for us on this question, I will provisionally treat it as an independent "Moses/Metatron text."

"Metatron has seventy names," the passage begins. "God took them from his own name and gave them to Metatron, who is Enoch son of Jared" (#76)[55]. There follows a long string of names, which Joseph Dan has

---

55 On this identification, see below, section 4a.

briefly discussed [522], and which concerns us only in that it includes the names Yofiel and *'ttyh* (above, section 2a) — and in its conclusion:

> ... faithful youth[56]; lesser Yahweh, named after his Lord, as it is written, *My name is in him* [Exodus 23:21]; Rakhrakhiel; Na^camiel; Sagnasgiel, the prince of wisdom.
>
> [#77] Why is he called Sagnasgiel? Because all the treasuries of wisdom have been put under his authority. All of them were opened to Moses on Sinai, until he had learned [the following] in forty days, while standing on the mountain[aa]: Torah, in the seventy aspects of the seventy languages; *halakhot*, in the seventy aspects of the seventy languages; traditions, in the seventy aspects of the seventy languages; *haggadot*, in the seventy aspects of the seventy languages; Toseftas, in the seventy aspects of the seventy languages.
>
> When the forty days were over, he forgot it all at once. God called to Yefefiah the prince of Torah [*śarah shel torah*], and he gave it to Moses as a gift [*mattanah*]. So it is written: *The Lord gave them to me* [Deuteronomy 10:4][57]. After that, he was able to remember it. How do we know that he remembered it? It is written: *Remember the Torah of Moses my servant* [*which I commanded him at Horeb for all Israel, laws and judgments*; Malachi 3:22]. *The Torah of Moses* refers to the Torah, the Prophets, and the Writings. *Laws* refers to *halakhot* and traditions. *Judgments* refers to *haggadot* and Toseftas. All of them were given to Moses at Sinai.

After a brief discussion of Metatron's names — "of the sort of the ineffable name that is on the *merkabah*, which are engraved on the throne of glory, and which God took from his own ineffable name and gave to Metatron's name" (#78) — the text returns to Moses. Metatron himself, who now numbers "prince of Torah" (*śar hattorah*) among his titles, is the speaker:

> [#79] "The Lord God of Israel is my witness that, when I revealed this secret to Moses, all the celestial troops in each of the heavens were outraged at me. 'Why,' they said, 'do you reveal this secret to a human being, woman's offspring, of a species subject to gonorrhea, impurity, menstrual blood, seminal emissions? By this secret were created heaven and earth, sea and dry land ... [there follows a long list of the orders of creation] Torah and wisdom, knowledge and thought, the understanding of the celestial beings and the fear of heaven. Why do you reveal it to flesh and blood?'
>
> " 'Because God gave me permission,' I said to them. 'Not only that, but I received permission from the exalted throne, from which all the ineffable names go forth like fiery lightnings and flashes of splendor.'
>
> "But they were not satisfied until God grew angry at them and chased them away with a rebuke. 'It is I,' he said to them, 'who willed and desired and decreed, who transmitted [the names? the secret?] to my servant Metatron alone, for he is one among the heavenly beings. [#80] Metatron may bring them [the names?] out of my treasuries.' "
>
> So he gave them to Moses, and Moses [gave them] to Joshua, Joshua to the elders, the elders to the prophets, the prophets to the men of the great synagogue, the men of the great synagogue to Ezra the scribe, Ezra the scribe to Hillel the elder, Hillel the elder to R. Abbahu, R. Abbahu to R. Zera, R. Zera to the men of faith, the men of faith to the masters of faiths[58]. They were to keep them carefully, and to use them to heal all the diseases that are rampant in the world. So it

---

56 *Na^car ne'eman.* In this passage, *na^car* could well mean "servant" rather than "youth." Cf. *^cebed ne'eman* ("faithful servant") in a passage from *Hekhalot Rabbati* (Schäfer, #96; Wertheimer, 3: 2). The importance of this point will become clear in section 4a, below.

57 The reference, in the Bible, is to the second set of tablets containing the ten commandments.

58 The Hebrew phrases are *'anshe 'amanah* and *ba^cale 'emunot*, respectively. I do not know what difference, if any, there is between them.

is written: *If you listen to the Lord your God and do what he thinks right, and you give ear to his commandments and keep his laws, then all the diseases that I gave the Egyptians I will not give you. I, the Lord, am he who heals you* [Exodus 15:26].

This text is obviously affiliated with the Sinai-ascension *haggadot*. Its resemblance to the end of *Maᶜayan Ḥokhmah* (above, chapter VIII, section B2f) is particularly striking. Both have Moses learn the Torah in forty days, forget it, and learn it again from "Yefefiah the prince of Torah." Both stress that Moses afterwards remembered what he learned. Both mention Metatron. *Maᶜayan Ḥokhmah*, however, leaves Metatron a subordinate figure, while our Moses/Metatron text makes him chief actor.

The Moses/Metatron text agrees with all versions of the ascension story that the angels do not want Moses to get his revelation. But here the differences between our text and the other stories are as important as the similarities. In *Pesiqta* and its parallels, it is the Torah that the angels want to keep for themselves. Here, it is a "secret" of some sort, which seems somehow linked with the names of Metatron. Metatron becomes an intermediary between God and Moses, and takes on features of both. Like God, he grants revelation to Moses. But, like Moses, he seems to need God to defend his right to be among the angels ("he is one among the heavenly beings"). This double role of Metatron is particularly important for us. We must return to it shortly.

Why do the angels object to revealing the secret to Moses? According to our text, they accuse him of being a creature of impurity. The ascension stories record a similar objection. "You come from a place of filth," Kemuel tells Moses. "What are you doing in a place of purity? You are the offspring of woman. What are you doing in a place of fire?" (*Pesiqta*). We will presently see that the angels object to Metatron's coming to heaven, for precisely the same reason.

One more parallel is worth noting. Certain "masters of faith," our text tells us, inherit Moses' secret, and they use it to heal diseases. We recognize in this a feature shared by *Pesiqta* and all its parallels, including BT Shabb. 89a: Moses receives not only the Torah, but also secrets of healing. Some of the versions (*Pesiqta, Maᶜayan Ḥokhmah, Pirqe de-Rabbi Eliezer*) suggest that the words *you took gifts for humanity* (Psalm 68:19) refer to these healing secrets.

When I first discussed the use of Psalm 68:19 in the Shabuᶜot cycle (chapter VIII, section B2e), I suggested that the *gifts* (*mattanot*) were originally understood as the Torah itself. When we find them reinterpreted to refer to miraculous healing, we may suppose that the "masters of faith," to whom we presumably owe our Moses/Metatron text, have left their fingerprints on the surviving versions of the story of Moses' ascent.

But, if the circles that produced the Moses/Metatron text have had their influence on the sources that now represent the Shabuᶜot cycle, this text betrays that it is itself rooted in the Shabu^cot cycle. Its author tells us that Yefefiah gave the Torah to Moses a second time "as a gift" (*mattanah*). Deuteronomy 10:4, which he then invokes in support of this claim, will hardly sustain it, for this verse never uses the noun *mattanah*. But Psalm 68:19 does; and Psalm 68:19 is, as we have seen, the germ of the ascension story in the Shabu^cot cycle. The Moses/Metatron text thus preserves a trace of a version of the ascension story, more original in this respect than *Pesiqta*'s, which explained *you took gifts for humanity* as meaning the Torah — called a "gift," in that Moses received it without effort. This original proof text dropped out of the story at some point. The author of the Moses/Metatron text tried to find a substitute for it in Deuteronomy 10:4, with very indifferent success.

Getting Torah without effort is, of course, what *Śar Torah* is all about. So is remembering it. ("I never again forgot anything," we recall R. Ishmael attesting, "of what I heard from my master and from my studies.") If the Moses/Metatron text is bound to the ascension stories, it is bound just as tightly to both the myth and the practice of *Śar Torah* (below, section D1). In this, we have a fresh clue to the mystery of the *Hekhalot*.

Before we can pursue it, however, we must turn our full attention at last to the figure of Metatron, and to Metatron's connection with Moses.

4. Metatron and Moses

a) Introduction. The problems associated with Metatron are among the most complicated in early Jewish angelology. We do not know where his name comes from or what it means [508,569,611,614a]; the classical Jewish sources give us little help in tracing his biography.

Metatron appears seldom in rabbinic literature, including three times in the Babylonian Talmud [492]. Two of these Talmudic references are particularly important. Sanh. 38b has a certain "Rab Idit" apply the name *Yahweh*, in Exodus 24:1, to "Metatron, whose name is like his master's." So, it appears from the sequel, Idit understands Exodus 23:20–21: *I am sending an angel before you. ... Beware of him, and pay attention to him. Do not rebel against him, for he will not pardon your sins. For my name is in him*[59]. To the reasonable-sounding proposal that we ought then to worship this angel, Idit responds with a midrash of the words *'al tamer bo* (*do not rebel against him*); which he interprets as *'al temireni bo*, "do not ex-

---

59 This exegesis of Exodus 23:21 obviously lies behind the passage in the Moses/Metatron text (Schäfer, #76) that calls Metatron "lesser Yahweh, named after his Lord, as it is written, *My name is in him*." See below, section 4c.

change me for him." It was into this error, according to Hag. 15a, that Elisha b. Abuyah fell. He saw Metatron seated in heaven, and drew from this the catastrophic deduction that Metatron is a second divinity (above, chapter I).

Reading the *Hekhalot* literature, which may indeed have been in the background of the Babylonian stories of the four rabbis' visit to *pardes*, one comes to sympathize with Elisha. Here Metatron indeed seems to be more than an angel, a second deity who is sometimes (as in the Moses/Metatron text) actually called "Lesser Yahweh" [446,598,611]. He appears in glory as the "youth" (*na^{c}ar*) or "prince" (*šar*) in an important text from ms New York (Appendix III; and below, section 4c), and in the "prince" passage of the *Visions of Ezekiel*. Although we are not told so explicitly, he is presumably the "youth" of the Ozhayah text, who is so like God that the traveller to the *merkabah* must be warned not to worship him.

Metatron has yet another extraordinary feature, apart from his near-divinity. He was once a human being. More exactly, he was the patriarch Enoch, whom God raised from the earth in the time before the Flood, transformed into a celestial being, set above the angels, and called "Lesser Yahweh." The early sections of *3 Enoch* describe this process in some detail (Schäfer, ##4–19; Odeberg, chs. 3–15). So, far more concisely, does a brief passage of uncertain context (Schäfer, ##295, 405; cf. Odeberg, ch. 48C):

> R. Akiba said: I heard a voice issuing from beneath the throne of glory. What did it say? "I made him great, I took him, I appointed him – that is, Enoch son of Jared, whose name is Metatron. I lifted him up from the human race and made for him a throne opposite mine, which measured four hundred million parasangs of fire. I put under his authority the seventy angels of the seventy nations. I set him in charge of all the heavenly retinue and all the earthly retinue. I arranged for him all the orders of creation. I gave him the name 'Lesser Lord,' the numerical value of which is seventy-one [60]. I gave him more wisdom and understanding than any of the angels, and made him greater than all of them."

The author of *3 Enoch* uses this tradition of Metatron's human origin to answer the puzzling question (which he puts into R. Ishmael's mouth) of how so august a being came to be called "youth." He is a Johnny-come-lately among the angels, "a youth among them in days and months and years, and that is why they call me 'youth'" (Schäfer, #6; Odeberg, ch. 4).

Scholem, followed by most recent scholars, has found this explanation forced and unconvincing. He rejects even its premise: the equation of Metatron with the exalted and transformed Enoch, he thinks, is a secondary development in the Metatron tradition. The word *na^{c}ar* originally did not mean "youth" at all, but "servant" (as in Exodus 33:11, where Joshua is

---

60 "Lesser Lord" = *'adonay haqqaṭan*; presumably a euphemism for "Lesser Yahweh" = *YHWH haqqaṭan*. Seventy-one is the combined value of the consonants in *'adonay*.

called Moses' *na^car*); that is, of the heavenly sanctuary. The custodians of the tradition later forgot the real meaning of this usage, and found themselves forced to devise explanations for it [506,532,569,598,611].

Scholem's explanation of *na^car* has some plausibility, and is supported not only by the evidence Scholem adduces (an Aramaic text which calls Metatron *shammasha rehima*, "beloved servant"), but also by the Moses/ Metatron text's reference to Metatron as "faithful *na^car*" (above). But it is not wholly satisfying. If the people who coined this term wanted to convey that Metatron was a servant, why did they not pick one of the familiar Hebrew words (like *^cebed* or *mesharet*) that would say this unambiguously? Why did they use *na^car*; which, though it can indeed mean "servant," is so much more commonly used for "youth" that it could hardly avoid conveying this meaning to anyone who heard it? We must suppose that Scholem's proposal contains a part, but only a part, of the truth. What the rest is, we will see at the end of this chapter.

We know too little about the development of the figure of Metatron to insist, against Scholem, that his identification with Enoch is primary and original. But there is no doubt that it is an important part of the image of Metatron as we have it in the *Hekhalot* literature. We must take it into account if we are to understand what Metatron meant to the authors and the audience of the *Hekhalot*.

It is particularly important to us. Metatron, in his role as an exalted and near-divinized human being, is more than a little reminiscent of the Moses of the Sinai-ascension *haggadot*. We must look more closely at how, and why, this is so.

b) Metatron as Moses. Let us begin our comparison with Moses' reception in heaven. In *Pesiqta* and its parallels, the angel Kemuel complains that he is "the offspring of a woman," who comes "from a place of filth." In the Moses/Metatron text, the angels call him "a human being, woman's offspring, of a species subject to gonorrhea, impurity, menstrual blood, seminal emissions."

Enoch-Metatron is challenged, in a similar way, by angels who do not like the way he smells. When he first ascends to heaven, as a human being, the *merkabah* creatures can smell him at a distance of 3,650,000,000 parasangs[61]. "Why," they demand of God, "should the smell of woman's offspring and the taste of a white drop come up to heaven to serve among beings carved out of fire?" (*3 Enoch*; Schäfer, #9; Odeberg, ch. 6).

---

61 I assume it is no coincidence that this figure is a multiple of Enoch's age at the time of his ascent (Genesis 5:23).

God, of course, intercedes on Enoch's behalf. We learn from the sequel, in *3 Enoch* and in the short account of Enoch's exaltation quoted above, that he receives a throne like God's and a status far above that of his critics. But we gather from another source that, even after his transformation into Metatron, traces of human smell continue to cling to him. A brief text, preserved in different contexts in mss New York and Vatican, describes how Metatron ascends into God's presence to speak on behalf of the exiled Israelites. "All the fiery, blazing beings trembled before him. When he ascended through eighty firmaments, the heavens were shaken, and the celestial holy ones said in unison: 'Why should the smell of woman's offspring come up to heaven?' " (Schäfer, ##149, 317). We recall from the Moses/Metatron text that, when Metatron is about to grant revelation to Moses, God must reaffirm that he (Metatron) belongs among the heavenly beings.

"I made him great, I took him, I appointed him," says God of Enoch in the passage quoted in section 4a. " ... I lifted him up from the human race and made for him a throne opposite mine, which measured four hundred million parasangs of fire." This claim suggests the detail in the ascension stories (BT Shabb. 88b–89a, as well as *Pesiqta* and its parallels) that Moses seized God's own throne.

In *3 Enoch*'s more detailed account of how Metatron got his throne, the resemblance is more striking (Schäfer, #13; Odeberg, ch. 10):

> R. Ishmael said: Metatron the angel, prince of the presence, said to me: "All this God made for me. [He made me] a throne like the throne of glory, and spread over me a curtain of splendor [*paraś ῾alay paraś shel ziw*], of radiance and glory and beauty and grace and favor. It was like the curtain [*paraś*] of the throne of glory, into which had been sewn all the kinds of splendor [*ziw*] of the world's luminaries.
>
> "He placed it at the gate of the seventh palace and seated me upon it. A herald went through all the heavens, proclaiming: 'I have made my servant Metatron prince and ruler over all the princes of my kingdom, and over all the heavenly beings, with the exception of eight particularly honored princes who are called Yahweh, by the name of their king[62]. If any angel or prince has a matter to bring before me, he should bring it to him. You must observe and do all that he enjoins upon you in my name. For I have assigned to him the prince of wisdom and the prince of understanding, to teach him the wisdom of the upper and lower realms, the wisdom of this world and of the world to come. I put him in charge of all the treasuries[63] of the palace of ῾Arabot, and of all the storehouses of life that I have in the high heavens.' "

The words "spread over me a curtain of splendor" (*paraś ῾alay paraś shel ziw*) plainly echo the midrash of Job 26:9 that underlies the ascension

---

62 I can offer no clarification of this reference, beyond what Odeberg gives in his note on the passage.

63 *Ginze*. This is perhaps related to the etymology of the name Sagnasgi'el in the Moses/Metatron text (Schäfer, #77; above).

stories' description of Moses at God's throne: *"When he seized the front of the throne,* [God] *spread over him the splendor of his cloud* [Job 26:9]. ... This teaches that the Almighty spread over him some of the splendor of his Shechinah and his cloud" (BT Shabb. 88b: *me'aḥez pene kisse' parshez ᶜalaw ᶜanano ... melammed sheppereś shadday mizziw shekhinato waᶜanano ᶜalaw*)^{bb)}. Only by supposing that this detail has been transferred from Moses to Metatron can we explain why the curtain is spread, incongruously, on top of him.

The conclusion of the passage, in which God assigns angelic teachers to Metatron, reminds us of "Yefefiah the prince of Torah" teaching Torah to Moses.

I add two more possible points of comparison.

Metatron relates in *3 Enoch* how, after God has crowned him, all the angels in heaven are afraid of him. "Even Sammael, prince of the accusers, who is greater than all the princes of the kingdoms in heaven, feared and trembled before me" (Schäfer, #17; Odeberg, ch. 13). The writer thus singles out one particularly dangerous character among the heavenly throng, and emphasizes that *even he* made his submission to Enoch/Metatron. The ascension stories, too, tell us that *not only* did the angels as a body become Moses' friends and teach him secrets, but "even the angel of death transmitted something to him" (BT Shabb. 89a).

A passage from ms Munich 22, speaking of the "youth," takes for granted that he has a pair of horns (Schäfer, #487; above, chapter VII, endnote *f*). A partial parallel in ms Munich 40 (Schäfer, #951) gives a similar description of God, and we cannot be sure to which of the two it originally applied. But, supposing that the horned being is properly the youth, and again supposing that the youth is to be equated with Metatron, we may find in his remarkable appurtenances a reflection of the horns of Moses (above, chapter VIII, sections B2, 6).

c) Again the "youth." This last observation brings us back to those passages in ms New York that describe the "youth," or the "prince" (see Appendix III). We have examined this material more than once. But we have not yet dealt with one particular aspect of it, which plays a large role in the second of ms New York's two recensions (Schäfer, ##395–400). The youth/prince is brought into some relation, the nature of which is not immediately clear, with Moses.

[#396] This youth is a prince^{cc)}, who is written with seven voices, with seven letters, with seventy names, with six by six⁶⁴. He is found among the innermost mysteries, innermost wonders, in-

---

64 I can do very little to explain the details of this sentence. The "seventy names" are plainly related

nermost rooms; and he serves in the presence of fire devouring fire. He was not given (*lo' nit-tan*)dd) to Adam, nor to Shem, nor to Abraham, nor to Isaac, nor to Jacob, but only to Moses.

Moses said to the Lord of all the worlds: "*If your presence* [literally, *face*] *does not go* [with us], *do not bring me* [read *us*, with MT?] *up from here* [Exodus 33:15]." So the Lord of all the worlds warned Moses that he should beware of that *face* of his. So it is written: *Beware of him* [literally, *of his face*; Exodus 23:21] 65.

This is he who is written with the one letter by which heaven and earth were created, and were sealed with the seal of *I am that I am* [Exodus 3:14]. This is the prince who is written with six and with seven and with twenty-two [??]. [#397] This is the prince who is called Yofiel Yahdariel. In the holy camps [of angels] ee) he is called Metatron; he is called Sasangiel.

There follows a string of mostly unintelligible words, most of which are evidently supposed to be names of the "prince." One of them is *lrp't*. I would read this word *lerappe'ot*, translate it "to heal," and understand it in connection with the Moses/Metatron text's concern with miraculous healing.

The text, when it again becomes comprehensible, speaks of "his great name, which was transmitted to Moses at Sinai from the faithful and suffering [?] God." From Moses the name was passed down to Hillel, then lost, then rediscovered by Abbahu (#397; above, chapter VII, section 2c). More strange words follow; then extravagant praise of the prince's supremacy in heaven; then a description of how the prince enters beneath God's throne (#398; above, chapter VII, section 2c).

This passage is clearly related to the Moses/Metatron text. Even if we disregard my speculation about *lrp't*, the two passages have in common the chain of transmission from Moses to Abbahu, the citation of Exodus 23: 21, and the claim that Metatron (or, the prince) has seventy names. A few individual names, apart from Metatron itself, crop up in both. Sasangiel is presumably a variant of Sagnasgielff). Yofiel is one of Metatron's names in the Moses/Metatron text. It is also a variant of Yefefiah, who gives Moses Torah in the Moses/Metatron text and in *Ma^cayan Ḥokhmah*; both names are from the root *yfh*, "to be beautiful66." Yahdariel, whose root *hdr* means much the same, is yet another expression of the same idea. This name is particularly important to us, for another reason: it is a slightly variant form of Hadarniel, familiar from the ascension stories in *Pesiqta* and its parallels.

---

to the seventy names of Metatron, in the Moses/Metatron text. Like the "seven voices," "seven letters," and "six by six," they appear in the parallel #389. The "seven voices" (which crop up again in #390) remind me vaguely of the "seven thunders" in Revelation 10:3–4. But I do not know what the significance of this resemblance, if there is any, might be.

65 The point of the citation is in the last words of verse 21: *For my name is in him*. See above, section 4a.

66 Significantly, the "Chapter of R. Nehuniah b. ha-Qanah" gives the name Yofiel to the "prince of Torah" (above, section A3b). We will presently return to this point.

The most important resemblance, of course, is that both texts bring the youth/prince/Metatron into a special revelatory relation with Moses[67]. Yet, precisely on this point, the two differ significantly.

What exactly does Moses receive from his celestial patron? In the Moses/Metatron text, he gets Torah. But the "prince" text does not mention Torah at all. Moses receives "his great name" — we cannot be sure whether it is God's name or the prince's, and the writer does not in any case sharply distinguish the two. More important, the prince himself seems to be "given" (*nittan*) to Moses. We cannot be sure exactly what this means. But the text gives the impression that Moses has received something of the prince's essence, binding him to the prince in a way that goes beyond anything that the patriarchs before him had known.

The evidence we have considered in section 4b, that Moses' experience and Metatron's mirror each other, provides the clue to the author's intention.

d) Conclusion. What I mean is this: As Metatron is a "lesser" Yahweh, so he is a "greater" Moses. More exactly, he is Moses gone a step farther.

Moses ascends to heaven; Metatron becomes ruler of heaven. Moses defeats the angels; Metatron dominates them. Moses grasps God's throne; Metatron sits on a throne identical to it. When Metatron grants revelation to Moses, he is giving a helping hand to his junior alter ego. When the author of the passage on the "prince" tells us that this being "was given" to Moses, what he is saying is that the ascending and conquering Moses shared in the essence of the exalted being whom most *Hekhalot* writers call Metatron.

These authors, I presume, saw the exalted Metatron as the primary figure, the ascending Moses as his junior replica. As historians of the tradition, however, we must reverse this relationship. First the Shabu^cot preachers had Moses invade heaven and lay hold of the throne. Then the authors of the *Hekhalot*, breaking the restraints of the older stories, let Metatron enjoy the fruits of conquest.

In section B4, I provisionally explained the youth, who "enters beneath the throne of glory" and takes precedence over the angels, as representative of the favored prayers of the Jewish people. I now extend this proposal, to

---

67 The only other *Hekhalot* text I know of that explicitly brings Moses and Metatron together is in ms New York of *Hekhalot Zuṭarti* (Schäfer, #341; Elior, lines 30–31). Several words seem to be missing before the beginning of the pertinent passage, which seems to start in the middle of a sentence: "... the fire which was in the bush. Metatron, great prince of Yahweh, prince of the host of Yehe, revealed himself to him and said, *Moses, Moses* [Exodus 3:4]." The writer plainly identifies Metatron as the God who appeared to Moses in the burning bush.

cover the additional evidence we have since examined. On a deeper level, the youth stands for a faith that a human being can gain divinity, and become master of those godlike beings who once lorded it over him.

The elements of the Shabu^cot cycle that told of the ascension of Moses inspired this faith in some of their hearers. Those who held this faith recorded it, usually in an oblique and distorted form, in the materials that we now know as the *Hekhalot*. They left a few marks of it in the texts that reflect the Shabu^cot cycle itself; hence, the *Visions of Ezekiel* describes the "prince" whom Daniel saw receiving the homage of thousands and of myriads. A few of them may have tried to actualize their faith by going into trances and convincing themselves that they, like Moses, had ascended to heaven in these trances.

Who were they? What led them to give their allegiance to these extravagant and barely intelligible fantasies?

These are the questions that we must now attack.

D. Śar Torah Revisited

1. Moses as hero of *Śar Torah*

Our pathway to the answers leads us again through the *Śar Torah*.

The Moses/Metatron text has already given us reason to believe that there is some connection between *Śar Torah* and the stories of Moses' ascension. Rooted in the latter, this text also has clear links with the former. Evidently drawing on Psalm 68:19, it claims that Yefefiah gave Moses Torah "as a gift" — presumably, without effort on Moses' part. Like *Ma^cayan Ḥokhmah*, it stresses that Moses did not again forget what he had learned. Effortless learning and secure memory are central concerns of *Śar Torah* [522a].

Moses, according to the Bible, neither ate nor drank during the forty days he spent on Sinai. He spent this time, according to *Ma^cayan Ḥokhmah* and the Moses/Metatron text, learning Torah. This is clearly the prototype of the forty-day fasts enjoined in *Hekhalot Zuṭarti* and the *Śar Torah* texts (above, sections A2c, 3b, c). The fasts are of course modified, since the average practitioner of *Śar Torah* will not be able to go for forty days without water.

One of Metatron's names in the Moses/Metatron text (and in ms New York, #397) is Yofiel. Its variant, Yefefiah, is the name of the angel who gives Moses Torah. In the "Chapter of R. Nehuniah b. ha-Qanah," one of the *Śar Torah* texts we examined early in this chapter (section A3b), Yofiel is the belligerent "prince of Torah" whom R. Ishmael conjures down.

Of these parallel details, the forty-day fast seems to have travelled from the haggadic context of the Shabuᶜot homilies to the magical context of Śar Torah. The name of the "prince of Torah" perhaps moved in the opposite direction. We do not yet have solid grounds for claiming overall priority either for the haggadah or for the magic. But we can say that the two are linked; and that the writers in the Śar Torah tradition came, by whatever paths, to consider Moses an exemplary hero, perhaps even founder.

It is no accident that the Karaite Salmon b. Yeruhim, retelling the foundation myth of Śar Torah (below), introduced into it language drawn from the Moses/Metatron text (Appendix VII; stanzas 10–11). He – or, more likely, his source – understood that these two narratives, despite the apparent difference in their settings, are cognate, and can be merged without violating the spirit of either.

Other evidence from the Hekhalot confirms these suggestions.

Near the beginning of Hekhalot Zuṭarti (Schäfer, #336; Elior, lines 9–14), we read: "When Moses ascended to God, he taught him as follows: If anyone finds that his mind is becoming confused [reading shogeh, not shoneh], recite over it the following names: In the name of ... let my mind grasp everything that I hear and learn, be it Bible, Mishnah, learning[68], halakhot, or haggadot. Let me never forget anything in this world or the next. Blessed be you, Lord; teach me your laws." Several lines afterward, ms New York adds a variant of this passage, which the other manuscripts omit (#340; Elior, lines 21–25).

Maᶜaśeh Merkabah begins with R. Ishmael asking R. Akiba to teach him a prayer which, if we are to follow ms New York, is to be used for ascending to the merkabah. The prayer concludes: "You revealed the deepest secrets and innermost arcana[gg)] to Moses. Moses [revealed them] to Israel, so that they could use them to perform the Torah and multiply learning [talmud]" (Schäfer, #544; Scholem, #1).

Later in Maᶜaśeh Merkabah, Ishmael asks Nehuniah about "the wisdom of the prince of Torah" (śar hattorah). Nehuniah responds with lists of magic words to be uttered, in imitation of the angels and the ḥayyot, at various points in the course of prayer. "Can anyone actually do this? There are, however, three letters which Moses wrote for Joshua on the inside of a cup, and then he drank [from it]. If you cannot do [the preceding ritual],

---

68 Talmud. It is of course possible that the writer has a fixed literary "Talmud" in mind. In this case, we could not date the passage any earlier than the fifth century, when PT (the earlier of the two Talmuds) was compiled. But, since we cannot be sure, I prefer to translate talmud as a common noun, to avoid prejudicing the issue.

inscribe them ...[69] and you will not suffer through the words of the mighty ones." Another string of magic words follows (Schäfer, #564; Scholem, #13).

It is not clear who the "mighty ones" (*gibborim*) are supposed to be. *Lev. R.* 31:5 (ed. 722–723 [191]) and its parallels [437] explain the *gibborim* of Proverbs 21:22 as angels, whose "city" Moses raids when he brings down the Torah. I think it very likely that the *Hekhalot* author is referring obliquely to Moses' exploit, which the magician can now imitate. But it seems possible, and will begin to seem probable as we go along, that the author is also hinting at human beings in a position of power, to whom his readers would prefer not to be subordinate.

A passage in ms New York's text of *Maʿaseh Merkabah* prescribes a series of rituals for "a student who wants to make use of this great secret" (Schäfer, ##572–578; Scholem, ##19–20). He must fast from the beginning of Sivan (the month in which Shabuʿot falls) until Shabuʿot itself. He must bathe repeatedly in the river (#572). In one ritual, he must invoke "those princes who split the firmament and gave the Torah to Moses, by the agency of Yahu Yahu Wahah. I adjure you, in the name of the great ... [70], that you preserve Torah in my heart" (#575). In another, he adjures "the great prince of Torah [*'isra rabba de'orayta*], you who were with Moses on Mount Sinai and preserved in his heart [read *uneṭarta belibbeh*] everything that he learned and heard, that you come to me [read *deteʿul weteti lewati*] and speedily remove the stone from my heart. Do not delay [read, with Scholem, *titʿakkeb*]" (#578).

Finally, we must recall a passage from *Merkabah Rabbah*, translated at the beginning of section A3c. God revealed his secrets to Moses, who transmitted them, through Joshua and the rest, "to all Israel. By means of them, the Israelites performed the Torah and multiplied learning [*talmud*] ... they performed and uttered and acted, were wise and made themselves wise" (Schäfer, #676). We now recognize in this an expanded form of a passage, quoted just above, from *Maʿaseh Merkabah* (Schäfer, #544).

2. The myth of Šar Torah

But all of these passages[hh)] pale in importance before a lengthy text, appended to *Hekhalot Rabbati*, which the copyist of ms Vatican entitles simply *Šar Torah* (Schäfer, ##281–306; Wertheimer, 28:5–32:3, 40:3–5). This text is nothing less than a legitimating myth for the whole conception

---

69 I do not know how to translate *bhwq*.
70 I do not know how to translate *ddryn*.

of *Śar Torah*. It mentions Moses and the Sinai revelation only in passing. It is set, instead, at the beginning of the Second Temple period. But it is plainly modelled after the stories of Moses' contest with the angels over the Torah, and sheds a brilliant light on how the people who cultivated *Śar Torah* understood that contest as applying to themselves.

The tenth-century Karaite writer Salmon b. Yeruhim devoted the final canto of his *Book of the Wars of the Lord* to an extended paraphrase of the *Śar Torah* myth, which I have fully translated in Appendix VII. Divergences between Salmon's paraphrase and our text of the myth suggest that he used a different recension as his source. His version seems to have been yet more strongly influenced than ours by the Sinai-ascension stories[71], and indeed to have conflated the *Śar Torah* myth with the Moses/Metatron text. It appears, too, to have had an anti-Christian thrust missing from our version, a point which we must take up later.

a) Text. As far as I know, no English translation of the *Śar Torah* myth has ever appeared[72]. I therefore translate it almost in full.

[#281] R. Ishmael quoted R. Akiba, in the name of R. Eliezer the Great: From the day that Torah was given to Israel until the time when the last temple [the Second Temple, presumably] was built, the Torah [itself] had been given. But its splendor, value, glory, greatness, magnificence, terror, fear, reverence, richness, loftiness, pride, trembling [?], resplendence, strength, power, dominion, and might were not given until the last temple was built, before the Shechinah had yet settled in it.

[#282] The Israelites arose to pour out their complaint before their father in heaven. "You have deluged us with hardships! Which are we to take hold of, which are we to leave alone? You have imposed on us great labor and a heavy burden. 'Build me a house,' you said to us. 'And, even though you are building, busy yourselves with Torah.'" (Thus far his children's speech.)

[#283] [God replied:] "You were entirely idle when you were in exile, and I had been eagerly looking forward to hearing my Torah from your lips. But, if you have not behaved well, I have not behaved well either. You did not behave well when you rebelled against me, so that I became angry with you and destroyed my city and my house and my children. But I did not behave well when I arose against you and sealed your doom. After all, a being [?] [ii)] that endures for ever and ever can hardly engage in struggle against a being [?] that lasts for perhaps a year, or two, or ten, or thirty, or by reason of strength a hundred, and then is finished. You did right to scold me. I accept your scolding.

[#284] "For the sound of Israel's groaning is sweet to me, and longing for Torah overwhelms me. Your words sound good to me, and I accept what you say. Go, busy yourselves with building my chosen house. The Torah nonetheless will not depart from your lips.

[#285] "For I am master of wonders, lord of asceticism [?]. Mighty deeds come to pass before me, miracles and wonders before my throne. Who has taken the initiative with me, without my rewarding him? Who has called on me, without my answering him at once? Tell me everything you want. Make your desires as many as you like.

---

71 Moshe Idel's observations on this point [566] have inspired much of my own perception of the *Śar Torah* myth.

72 Johann Maier has published a German translation [487]. Grodner's partial translation of *Hekhalot Rabbati* extends through #287 (Wertheimer, 29:5), but there breaks off — because, as Blumenthal explains in his footnote, the text "is no longer properly mystical" [463].

[#286] "Nothing is lacking from my storehouses and treasuries. Tell me what you want and you will get it. Your desires will at once be performed. For there is no time like now, no moment like the present. No time like now, since I have delayed [?] until I saw you. No moment like the present, when your love clings to my heart.

[#287] "I already know what you want, and I realize what you desire. You want much Torah, vast learning [*talmud*], multitudes of traditions. You look forward to investigating *halakhah*. You yearn for the multitudes of my secrets, to pile up testimony like mountains, wondrous wisdom like hills [?], to make learning great in the streets and dialectic in the lanes, to multiply *halakhot* like the sands of the sea and [make them?] as many as the dust of the earth. [#288] [You want] to establish academies[73] at the entrances of tents, there to distinguish the forbidden from the permitted, to decide what is impure and what is pure, what is fit and what is unfit; there to recognize the [signs of mentrual? or virginal?] blood, and to tell menstruating women what they must do. [You want] to bind garlands on your heads, royal crowns on your children's heads. [You want] to force kings to bow to you, princes to fall down before you. [You want] to spread your name beneath the sky, your reputation in the seacoast towns. [You want] your faces to shine like daybreak, [the place?] between your eyes like the planet Venus.

"If you are worthy of this seal, to make use of my crown, no uneducated person [*ᶜam ha'areṣ*] will be left in the world, and there will be no fool or stupid person among you.

[#289] "You are happy, but my servants are sad, that this secret — one of the secrets — is going forth from my treasuries. All of your academies will be like fatted calves. [They will learn Torah] without labor or struggle, by the name of this seal and the mention of this terrible crown. People will be astonished at you, sick [with envy] over you. Many will die groaning, and will expire when they hear of your glory.

[#290] "You will have great wealth and riches. The great ones of the world will adhere to you. The family that you marry into will gain status and power from all sides. He who blesses himself through you will be blessed; he who praises himself by you will be praised. You will be called *those who lead the many to righteousness* [Daniel 12:3] and 'those who justify humanity.' New moons will be fixed by your authority; intercalation of years, through the cunning of your wisdom.

[#291] "Patriarchs will be anointed by your agency, and court presidents will arise by your authority. You will establish exilarchs, and municipal magistrates will depend on your authority. The world's administration will be yours, and none will dispute it.

"My servants struggled fiercely with me. The angels made a powerful accusation." (Thus far [God's] speech.)

[#292] [The angels said:] "Do not let this secret go forth from your treasuries, this hidden cunning from your storehouses. Do not make flesh and blood equal to us; do not put human beings on our level. Let them labor in the Torah as they have for generations. Let them practice it with labor and struggle and great suffering [?]. It is to your honor and your glory that they forget [reading *meshakkeḥin,* with ms Vatican] and then study again. They call upon you with a perfect heart, beg for your favor with an eager spirit. [As for us,] let all that we have read remain ours, let all that we have studied stay in our minds. Let us absorb thoroughly all that we have heard, and let our minds grasp the learning [*talmud*] that we have heard from the teacher. [As for them,] let them honor one another. But, if you reveal this secret to your children, the small will be like the great, the fool like the wise man." (Thus far his servants' speech.)[74]

---

3 *Lehoshib yeshibot.* Here, as in ##289 and 298, I translate *yeshibah* in accord with the traditional understanding of this word. If David Goodblatt [401b,401c] is right, however, "to convene study sessions" might be a more appropriate translation. More on this, and on the "entrances of tents," below.

4 Significantly, the first words of the angels' speech recur, in a positive formulation, near the end of *Merkabah Rabbah.* They are part of a blessing which, to judge from its context, is supposed to help the speaker keep Torah in his memory: "Let this secret go forth from the treasuries of blessing, from your treasuries" (Schäfer, #707 [585]). In other words, the result that the prac-

[#293] [God replied:] "Please, my ministers! Please, my servants! Please don't bother me over this issue. This secret will go forth from my treasuries, this hidden cunning from my store-houses. I am revealing it to a beloved people, teaching it to a faithful seed. It was kept aside for them from all eternity, prepared for them since the time of creation. It did not occur to me to give it to any of the generations from Moses' time until now. It was reserved for this generation, so that they might make use of it until the end of all generations. *For they went forth from evil to evil, and they did not know me* [Jeremiah 9:2]. Their minds became stupid from exile, and the words of Torah became hard as bronze and iron in their ears. They may properly make use of [this secret] to bring Torah like water into their midst, like oil into their bones. For the Israelites have been in a sad state since I became angry at them *and struck them, and the mountains reeled, and their corpses were like excrement in the streets* [Isaiah 5:25].

[#294] "How can I appease them? How can I comfort them? What good and desirable thing do I have in heaven that I can bring forth and give them to make them happy? I looked and found that I have gold, but the world does too; I have silver, but the world does too; I have jewels and pearls, but the world does too; I have already put wheat and barley and honey and oil in the world. What does the world lack? This secret and this mystery, which is not in the world — an object of pride, for my children to take pride in."

[#297] [75] R. Ishmael said: Thus said R. Akiba, in the name of R. Eliezer the Great: Our fathers refused to set one stone on another in the Lord's temple, until they forced the king of the world and his servants to deal with them and to reveal to them the secret of Torah: how they were to do it, how they were to expound it, how they were to make use of it. Thereupon the holy spirit appeared from the third entrance of the house of the Lord[76]; for the Shechinah had not yet descended or settled in the holy of holies, on account of the decree. When our fathers saw the throne of glory hovering [?] between the porch and the altar ... [#298] ... [77] with the king of the world upon it, they fell on their faces.

Concerning that occasion, Scripture says: *The glory of this last house shall be greater than the first* [Haggai 2:9]. "For [said God] in the first temple only my voice was in attendance upon my children. This [temple] is for me [in person], for my throne, and for all my servants.

"Now, my children, why are you fallen on your faces? Rise, and sit before my throne the way you sit in the academy. Grasp the crown, receive the seal, and learn the order of the secret of Torah[78]. [Learn] how you are to perform it, how you are to expound it, how you are to make

---

titioner of *Śar Torah* wants to achieve is precisely the one that the angels want to prevent. — On the other hand, the practitioner can pray on his own behalf much as the angels do. So we find in ms Budapest, about a page after the end of the passage that I am translating here: "May we and our offspring, and the offspring of your people Israel, all know your name and learn your Torah for its own sake. Let all that we have read and will read remain ours. Let all that we have studied and will study stay in our minds. Let us absorb thoroughly all that we have heard and will hear. Let our minds grasp the learning of the Torah that you gave to your people Israel" (Schäfer, #330).

75 Despite the break in numbering, this is the immediate sequel of #294. Schäfer gives the numbers 295 and 296 to two passages, unrelated to the context, which ms Budapest inserts at this point.

76 *Mimmaboy hashshelishi 'asher bebet 'adonay.* We find an almost identical phrase in *Hekhalot Rabbati*'s account of Nehuniah b. ha-Qanah's lecture on the technique of "descending to the *mer-kabah*": "R. Ishmael said: Thereupon I arose and assembled all the Greater Sanhedrin and all the Lesser Sanhedrin to the third entrance of the house of the Lord" (Schäfer, #202; Wertheimer, 16:2). The common use of this apparently stereotypic detail is a new addition to the evidence, which we began to collect in section A3, arguing against there being any essential division be-tween the trance-journey materials of the *Hekhalot* and their *Śar Torah* traditions. The collection will continue to grow as we proceed.

77 These ellipses represent a series of very difficult and possibly corrupt phrases, amounting to about thirty-five words. They seem to be parenthetical, and do not advance the narrative. I there-fore do not even try to translate them.

78 The manuscripts vary considerably at this point.

use of it, how you are to lift up the paths of your minds, how your minds can gaze into the Torah."

Thereupon Zerubbabel the son of Shealtiel responded, and stood before [God] as his spokesman, specifying the names of the princes of Torah, each one by his name, the name of the crown, and the name of the seal.

[#299] R. Ishmael quoted R. Akiba, in the name of R. Eliezer the Great: If anyone decides to make use of the prince of Torah[79], he should wash his clothing and make a complete immersion, on the chance that he has acquired some impurity. He should enter a room or an upper chamber and sit there for twelve days. He must not leave it. He may eat and drink only each evening. He must eat pure bread, [made with] his own hands [?], and drink pure water. He may not eat vegetables.

[#300] He should fix this midrash of the prince of Torah in his prayers three times a day, after the prayers he utters, from beginning to end. He should then sit and repeat it over and over [?], all twelve days of his fast, from morning to evening. He must not go to sleep. As soon as he finishes it, he should stand up and adjure the servants by their king, and call upon each prince twelve times. Afterwards, he should adjure each one by the seal.

[#301] These are their names: Prince Shaqadhoziai Yahweh, Prince Zehafnuriai Yahweh ... [and so forth]. [#302] Let him adjure all twelve of them in the name of Yofiel, who, by permission of his king, is the splendor of heaven[80]; in the name of Sarkhiel, one of the princes of the *merkabah*; in the name of Shahadriel, a beloved prince; and in the name of Hasdiel, who is called to the power [that is, God?] six hours each day[81]. Let him adjure these four princes, in their turn, by the great seal and the great oath: in the name of 'Azbogah, who is the great seal; and in the name of Surtaq, the holy name and the terrible crown.

[#303] When the twelve days are finished, let him go forth to any aspect of Torah that he likes, whether it be Scripture, Mishnah, Talmud, or looking at the *merkabah* [*şefiyyat hammerkabah*]. For he goes forth with a pure character [?], from his great pains and his asceticism. This is a teaching [*talmud*] in our possession, an ordinance of our predecessors and a tradition of the ancients, which they wrote down and bequeathed to succeeding generations, so that humble folk [*şenuᶜim*] might make use of it. Whoever is worthy is answered when he does this.

Three of Schäfer's seven manuscripts (Budapest, Vatican, Munich 22) add further testimonials, as if to reinforce the promise of the last sentence:

[#304] R. Ishmael said: Thus said R. Akiba, in the name of R. Eliezer the Great: Happy is the man whose fathers' merit aids him, whose ancestors' righteousness stands him in good stead! He will make use of the crown and of this seal, they [the angels, presumably] will attend to him, and he will be exalted in the Torah's exaltation.

[#305] R. Ishmael said: R. Eliezer used this method and he was answered, but he [still] did not believe in it. I used it and I was answered, but I did not believe in it until I brought a certain

---

79 So all manuscripts except Budapest, which has "this secret of Torah" (*sod torah* for *śar torah*).

80 *Hadar marom*. The title is evidently a variant of the names Yahdariel and Hadarniel. See above, section C4c.

81 *Niqra' laggeburah shesh shaᶜot bekhol yom*. The expression recurs in *Hekhalot Rabbati*, in a cryptic dialogue between God and some unnamed being: " 'Why are you frightened, faithful servant [ᶜebed ne'eman]? Why do you recoil, servant, beloved one?' 'I say to you, Zoharariel Yahweh, God of Israel, that if I am not frightened, who should be frightened? If I do not recoil, who should recoil? I am called to the power six hours each day. They drag me a thousand times on my knees until I reach the throne of glory' " (Schäfer, #96; Wertheimer, 3:2). It is not at all clear whom God is addressing. The parallel of the next-to-last sentence with *Śar Torah* suggests he is an angel; the parallel of the last sentence with the reference to Ben Zoma in the Ozhayah text (above, section A2b) suggests he is a human being travelling to the *merkabah*; while the phrase ᶜebed ne'eman points to Moses (Numbers 12:7). Whichever solution we choose, we have here yet another link between *Śar Torah* and the trance-journey materials.

stupid fellow and he became just like me. Shepherds used it, and they became like me. By the authority of the court, R. Akiba was sent outside Palestine. He stayed there until the multitudes, who had never studied Bible or Mishnah, used it and became like scholars [*talmide ḥakhamim*].

He returned and gave testimony in the patriarch's court: "This method was used even outside Palestine, and it worked." R. Eliezer the Great and the scholars had suspected that it might have been the merit of Palestine that enabled us [to use the method], and they were skeptical – until they sent R. Akiba to Babylonia and he used it successfully, and testified to it. We then heard and rejoiced.

At last comes a hymn, shared by all seven of Schäfer's manuscripts, which describes the terror that seizes the angels as they utter God's name. One must open with this hymn, R. Ishmael says, "before he prays this *Śar Torah*" (#306).

With the hymn, our *Śar Torah* text concludes.

b) Analysis. The text falls into three main sections. The first is the *Śar Torah* myth proper (##281–298). The second is the ritual supposedly founded on this myth (##299–303). The third is the concluding testimonials (##304–305), which are not found in all the manuscripts and which may be a later addition.

The ritual, with its fasts, ablutions, and incantations, is obviously of a piece with the *Śar Torah* rituals we examined in section A3. Only one point deserves our special attention. #303 suggests that the *Śar Torah* ritual prepares one for "looking at the *merkabah*." This confirms my suspicion that there is some close relationship between magical methods for learning Torah and the "descent to the *merkabah*," and that the apparently purposeless ecstasy of the trance-journey may be bound up with more mundane objectives. The relationship is, to be sure, the reverse of what I have posited: *Śar Torah* magic is preliminary to viewing the *merkabah*, not the other way round. Yet it is significant that the connection is made.

The testimonials insist that the *Śar Torah* method is foolproof. It will work for anyone in any place, regardless of his intelligence, occupation, or intellectual background. These confident claims are very reminiscent of the conclusion of the Ozhayah text (above, section A2b). There, the object of the guarantee is the angel Ozhayah's method for descending to the *merkabah*. R. Ishmael uses it successfully, "but I still could not believe, until the least of the students in our college also did it. He descended ... and said to me: 'Go up and bear witness in the college[82].' " The implications of this parallel will concern us below.

---

82 If we had the missing words that once came after "descended" (*yarad*), we might conceivably find that this sentence does not refer to a descent to the *merkabah*; but, as in #305 (which uses *horidu*, from the same root, for the "sending" of Akiba), to Babylonia.

The *Šar Torah* testimonials presuppose an audience that is at least partly Babylonian. Otherwise, they would hardly have needed to make such a great point of the magic's usefulness even outside Palestine. Given that the testimonials may be an addition to the text, we cannot be sure that the same holds true for its other sections. But, even in the myth, there are indications of a Babylonian origin.

The most obvious is the reference to the Babylonian office of "exilarchs" (*rashe galiyyot*) in #291. This point, however, is less impressive than it seems at first. The preceding sentence speaks of the Palestinian "patriarchs" (*neśi'im*) and "court presidents" (*'abot bet din* [425a]); and, while it is perhaps more likely that a Babylonian writer would make rhetorical reference to Palestinian authorities than the other way round, the reverse is also conceivable.

It is more important that the myth's use of the word *yeshibah* (##288, 289, 298) seems to agree with that of the Babylonian Talmud, against that of the Palestinian rabbinic sources. We need not take sides in the recent controversy over whether BT uses this word to mean "academy" (so the older consensus, defended by Isaiah Gafni), or whether it means an informal "study session" (so David Goodblatt) [388a,388b,401b,401c]. The *Šar Torah* myth's references are, in this respect, as ambiguous as the Talmud's. But Gafni and Goodblatt agree that, when Palestinian sources speak of a *yeshibah*, they mean a court, and not a gathering (institutionalized or otherwise) for purposes of learning. Here the *Šar Torah* myth and BT are aligned. It is perhaps significant that three passages in BT, like #288, use the phrase *lehoshib yeshibah* (ᶜErubin 26a, Ketubbot 103a–b, Baba Qamma 16b–17a); and that BT Baba Mesiᶜa 86a depicts the "heavenly *yeshibah*" as being concerned, like the *yeshibot* in #288, to distinguish pure from impure.

We must, however, look more closely at the *yeshibot* of #288. BT's usage does nothing to explain why they should be located "at the entrances of tents" (*beshaᶜare 'ohalim*). This detail seems to rest on a midrash of Genesis 25:27. The Biblical text speaks of Jacob as *a quiet man, dwelling in tents* (*yosheb 'ohalim*); the midrash is unwilling to take the *tents* literally, and, on the strength of the verb *yosheb*, understands them to be *yeshibot*.

Thus, *Sifre Numb.* #52 (ed. 54 [221]), followed by *Numb. R.* 13:15–16, attributes to "Abba Hanin in the name of R. Eliezer" the claim that "Jashub" in Numbers 26:24 refers to the courts (*batte dinin*) of the tribe of Issachar. In support, the midrash cites the occurrences of the root *yšb* in Ezekiel 33:31 and Genesis 25:27. *Gen. R.* 63:10 (ed. 693 [188]) understands Jacob's *tents* as the "schools" (*bet midrash*) of Shem and Eber. Tanh. Buber *Wa-Yishlaḥ* #9 (ed. 84a [222]) adds the "school" of Abraham. Tanh. *Shemot* #1, followed by *Ex. R.* 1:1, explains the verse to mean that Jacob learned Torah in Isaac's "house of learning" (*bet talmud*). Significantly, the Targums to Genesis 25:27 all reflect this tradition. Onkelos renders *dwelling in tents* as "serving in the house of instruction" (*bet 'ulpana*); Pseudo-Jonathan, "serving in the school [*bet midrasha*] of Shem and in the school of Eber, seeking instruction from God"; Neofiti, "dwelling in houses of study" [223a,224,226]. It crops up again in Pseudo-Jonathan to Numbers 24:5 (*how good are your tents, O Jacob!*). There is an echo of it in *Pirqe de-Rabbi Eliezer*, chapter 32: "Jacob our father walked in the path of life, *dwelling in tents* and studying Torah all his daysjj)."

We do not have to work out the implications of this exegesis for the murky issue of what the rabbis meant when they used the word *yeshibah*. It is enough for us to observe that the *Śar Torah* myth, of uncertain date and probably Babylonian origin, has here drawn upon a bit of old Palestinian midrash, which we know to have been transmitted through the Targumic tradition. Once again, we find the *Hekhalot* and the Targums linked.

Have we any clues to the date of the myth? The witness of Salmon b. Yeruhim insures that it cannot be later than the beginning of the tenth century. But this is not very helpful; and the internal evidence of the text does not get us much farther.

If we could take #291's allusion to patriarchs (*nesi'im*) at face value, it would guarantee a date before 425 A.D.; for the Palestinian patriarchate did not exist after that year. But can we? It could easily be a bit of historical coloring, suitable for a narrative supposedly spoken by R. Eliezer at the end of the first century. On the other hand, it is strange that it refers to patriarchs' being "anointed" (*mitmashshehim*). I do not know of any rabbinic passage that speaks explicitly of the anointing of patriarchs. Yet such a practice would well suit the royal ideology of the patriarchate [425b]; and an anecdote in the Palestinian Talmud applies the phrase from Lamentations 4:20, "the anointed of the Lord," to Rabbi Judah the Patriarch (PT Shabb. 16:1, 15c; parallels in *Lev. R.* 15:4, ed. 328–330 [191], *Lam. R.* 4:20, ed. 77a [190]). Perhaps this is an authentic contemporary reference, after all.

One thing is clear. There are no good grounds for segregating the *Śar Torah* myth and rituals from the trance-journey materials in the *Hekhalot*, or for supposing that they are a later development of *Hekhalot* mysticism[83]. Parallels of language and content bind the two together. Most recently, we

---

83 Joseph Dan, making the case for such a separation, remarks that the *Śar Torah* myth looks to R. Eliezer the Great as its authority, while the "descent to the *merkabah*" traditions focus instead on Nehuniah b. ha-Qanah, Ishmael, and Akiba [518,522a]. But the *Śar Torah* materials we considered in section A3 have Ishmael and Nehuniah as their main characters; the *Merkabah Rabbah* passage assigns a key role also to Akiba. We will presently consider how Eliezer might have come to be a hero of *Śar Torah*.

have seen how the *Sar Torah* testimonials resemble that of the Ozhayah text; I have noted other points of contact, in section A3 and in my footnotes to ##297 and 302 (above). If the *Sar Torah* myth shows signs of coming from Babylonia, so do the trance-journey materials. This is, as we saw in section A2b, most obviously true of the Ozhayah text. But it holds for *Hekhalot Rabbati* as well. Ithamar Gruenwald has pointed out that this text presupposes a daily recitation of the *Qedushshah,* and thereby aligns itself with the Babylonian liturgical practice against the Palestinian [550]. True, Gruenwald recoils from the conclusion that *Hekhalot Rabbati* is, at least in its present form, Babylonian. Yet it is this conclusion that most naturally suggests itself.

On the contrary: trance-journey and *Sar Torah* are two aspects of the same activity. And the legitimating myth for *Sar Torah* vividly illuminates the purpose of that activity.

c) Implications: angels and ^cam ha'areṣ. Were there ever angels who wore their motives on their sleeves more patently than the ones of this text? Their slogan is inequality. Their demand is that inequality be perpetuated. "Do not make flesh and blood equal to us; do not put human beings on our level. ... If you reveal this secret to your children, the small will be like the great, the fool like the wise man" (#292).

This last sentence suggests that the real issue is not between humans and angels, but between different groups of humans[84]. This is how we must understand the words that come right before it, "let them honor one another": let people of inferior status honor their betters.

The angels, then, appear as spokesmen for a privileged group whose claim to privilege rests on mastery of the Torah. Who are the "Israelites" whom God favors against them? They are "humble folk" (#303), people who are too busy doing manual labor to have time for the Torah (##282, 284). It is they who demand and receive the promise that "the Torah nonetheless will not depart from your lips" (#284), that they can learn it "without labor or struggle" (#289).

Do we know any Jewish group during the rabbinic period that would fit this description? We do. #288 refers to them explicitly. They are the ^cam ha'areṣ, literally "people of the land." These appear in rabbinic sources as folk without the rabbis' expertise in Torah, refinement of manners, or

---

84 Professor Herbert W. Basser has pointed out to me that my interpretation of the *Sar Torah* myth, which I set forth in the coming pages, is in many ways parallel to a hypothesis recently advanced by Elaine Pagels. Gnostic mythology about the creator-God (demiurge) and his archons, Pagels suggests, is at least partly a reflection of Gnostic attitudes toward the authorities of the earthly church [724,725].

scrupulousness of ritual observance; Jews whom the rabbis often despised and loathed, and who often responded by hating the rabbis.

It is not easy to define the *ʿam ha'areṣ* historically or sociologically. Efforts to explain them in geographic terms (they were the population of Galilee, as opposed to Judea) or occupational ones (they were the farmers of Palestine) have not been very successful. Aharon Oppenheimer's recent re-examination of the problem, learned and meticulous as it is, has convinced me of little beyond that we are still very far from a solution [430]. But, if we cannot as yet give any very useful account of the *ʿam ha'areṣ*, we cannot deny either their existence or their antagonism to the rabbis without rejecting a considerable part of the rabbinic data.

A few of the rabbis' comments on the *ʿam ha'areṣ*, collected in BT Pes. 49a–b, will give some idea of the tension between the two groups.

> R. Meir used to say: Anyone who marries his daughter to an *ʿam ha'areṣ* might as well have tied her up and laid her before a lion. Just as a lion tramples and eats without a bit of shame, so an *ʿam ha'areṣ* beats and copulates without a bit of shame. [Pes. 49b]

> Our rabbis taught: A person ought to sell everything he has [for dowry] and marry the daughter of a scholar. If he cannot find the daughter of a scholar, let him marry a daughter of the generation's distinguished men. If he cannot find a daughter of the generation's distinguished men, let him marry the daughter of a synagogue president. If he cannot find the daughter of a synagogue president, let him marry the daughter of a charity collector. If he cannot find the daughter of a charity collector, let him marry the daughter of a schoolteacher. But he should under no circumstances marry the daughter of an *ʿam ha'areṣ*; for they are loathsome, their wives are reptiles, and Scripture says of their daughters: *Cursed be he who lies with any kind of beast* [Deuteronomy 27:21]. [49b]

Against the background of this brutal contempt, *Sar Torah*'s fantasy that "the family that you marry into will gain status and power from all sides" (#290) becomes particularly and pathetically intelligible. So does a remark attributed to the angels in Salmon b. Yeruhim's version of the *Sar Torah* myth, which declares the "small" and the foolish to be "comparable to beasts" (stanza 14; below, Appendix VII).

The *ʿam ha'areṣ* reciprocated the rabbis' hatred:

> R. Eliezer says: If they did not need our business, they would kill us. [Pes. 49b]

> R. Akiba said: "When I was an *ʿam ha'areṣ*, I used to say, 'If I could only get my hands on a scholar, I would bite him like an ass.'"
> His disciples said to him: "Rabbi, say 'like a dog.'"
> He replied: "[An ass] bites and breaks the bone; [a dog] bites but does not break the bone." [49b]

Akiba's remark dates from his uneducated youth, when he had not yet made his way into the company of the sages and adopted their viewpoint. Reading it, we are disposed to cheer. The rabbis' contempt for the *ʿam ha'areṣ* is irritating to us, and must have been a constant source of fury to the people at whom it was directed. But, much as they may have detested the rabbis, it is hard to imagine the *ʿam ha'areṣ* doing without them, and not only because they needed their business. As far as I know, there is no evidence that the *^cam ha'areṣ* ever evolved religious institutions independent of the rabbis, or had any cultural self-definition other than that which the rabbis provided for them. They could not remain forever with the young Akiba's hatred. Either they must break free of rabbinic leadership, or accept the rabbis' view of reality. And if they did the latter — which they indeed seem to have done — where did that leave them?

At least in the imaginations of the rabbis, an *^cam ha'areṣ* could occasionally demand respect from a rabbi, on the rabbi's own terms. Thus, *Lev. R.* 9:3 (ed. 176—179 [191]) tells how R. Yannai met a well-dressed stranger on the road and, assuming him to be educated[85], invited him home to dinner. He then discovered that the man was not only uneducated, but did not even know how to say grace. Yannai made him repeat grace after him, ending with the words, "A dog has eaten the bread of Yannai."

> He stood up and grabbed him. "You make use of my inheritance," he said, "and yet you humiliate me?"
>
> "How am I making use of your inheritance?" said [Yannai].
>
> "It's as the children say," he replied. "*The Torah that Moses commanded us is the inheritance of* — not *the congregation of Yannai* — but *the congregation of Jacob* [Deuteronomy 33:4]."
>
> Once they had made up, [Yannai] said to him: "How did you merit eating at my table?"
>
> He answered: "If I am insulted, I do not respond in kind; and I have never seen two people fighting without making peace between them."
>
> "Such a gentleman you are," he said, "and I called you a dog[86]!"

But suppose the *^cam ha'areṣ* could not reclaim from the rabbinic intelligentsia the Torah that was their inheritance, and could not get any acknowledgment of their claim to it beyond occasional bits of patronizing politeness? What choice did they have but to take it by force, as Moses did? And what force did they have at their disposal but magic?

3. Conclusion: toward a solution of the problem of the *Hekhalot*

We now can begin to understand the profound excitement that the Shabu^cot homilies must have stirred up among some at least of their hearers. We can also begin to grasp what the idea of heavenly ascent meant to them.

In part, the ascent was a means to an end. Israel would not have Torah if Moses had not fought his way through the angels to heaven. Israel could

---

85 An assumption which, incidentally, tells us something about the relative economic status of rabbis and *^cam ha'areṣ*.

86 The story is more subtle than it seems at first sight. Yannai, although not quite as obnoxious after the stranger's rebuke as he was at first, is still sufficiently self-important. The stranger then chides him more subtly. For it was the stranger who did not respond in kind to Yannai's insult; the stranger who made it possible for the two of them to make peace at least for the duration of the meal; and the stranger, not Yannai, who is the gentleman.

not learn Torah if Akiba had not fought his way through the angels to the *merkabah* (above, section A3c).

But it was also an image for the achievement of this end. He who masters Torah has climbed to the center of power. He is at the throne of God. From there he can, like Metatron, bully and intimidate the people who once bullied and intimidated him. Well might he crow, turning Lucifer/Nebuchadnezzar's threat into the past tense: *I have climbed to heaven, I have lifted my throne above the stars of God ... I have climbed upon the backs of the clouds, I have become like the Most High* [87].

In truth, the fantasies of *Śar Torah* are not very gentle or spiritual. What do the "Israelites" want? They want authority (#288), money (#290), power (#291). They want "to bind garlands on your heads, royal crowns on your children's heads; to force kings to bow to you, princes to fall down before you; to spread your name beneath the sky, your reputation in the seacoast towns" (#288). They want people — understand, the rabbis — to die of envy at the thought of them (#289). They want, as the concluding testimonials put it, to "be exalted in the Torah's exaltation" (#304)[88].

It is precisely this sort of megalomanic fantasy that we find in the enumeration, at the beginning of *Hekhalot Rabbati*, of the powers enjoyed by the man who descends to the *merkabah*, who stands "to the right of the throne of glory ... to see everything that is done before the throne of glory, to know everything that is going to happen in the world" (Schäfer, #81; Wertheimer, 1:2). Only here the images of power and revenge are yet wilder. The passage is too long for me to translate in its entirety. I give a few samples:

> Greater than all of them: If anyone lifts up his hand against him and strikes him, they clothe [that person] with plague and cover him with leprosy and crown him with leprous spots.
>
> Greater than all of them: If anyone slanders him, they cast upon [that person] all plagues of ulcers, dreadful wounds and sores dripping pus.
>
> Greater than all of them: He is different from everyone, and terrifying [? the Hebrew would normally mean "terrified"] in every way. He is respected among heavenly and earthly beings. If anyone becomes involved [in a struggle] with him, dreadful calamities fall upon [that person] from heaven. If anyone contemptuously raises a hand against him, the heavenly court will raise its hand against [that person]. ...

---

87 From Isaiah 14:13–14. See above, chapter VIII, section B6.

88 Ephraim E. Urbach has pointed out that the dialogues in the *Śar Torah* myth are directed against the rabbinic intelligentsia, and that their viewpoint is that of the social underdog. His observations have inspired much of my own argument. But he mistakenly supposes that ##287–288, 290–291 are addressed to the rabbis, and excoriate their alleged lust for money and status [617]. The lust, as the context shows, is that of the author, who does not see a thing wrong with being after money and status as long as the right people get them. — Joseph Dan's recent speculations on the social milieu of *Śar Torah* [522a] are parallel to mine.

R. Ishmael said: They taught concerning the vision of the *merkabah*: One who is sensitive to the *merkabah*[89] may rise before another person in only three circumstances — before the king, before the high priest, and before the Sanhedrin. The last applies only when the patriarch is present in the Sanhedrin. But, if the patriarch is not present, he should not rise even before the Sanhedrin. If he rose, he is considered mortally guilty; because, by rising before him, he lessens his days and shortens his years. [Schäfer, ##84–85, 93; Wertheimer, 1:4–5, 2:4]

The last sentence seems to mean: If I am one of those "sensitive to the *merkabah*," I am so important that it is positively wrong for me to show deference to anyone. Anyone to whom I do show deference will pay for it, and his suffering will then be my fault. The passage expresses a fantasy of near-omnipotence on earth. Metatron's near-deification in heaven is a mirror of this fantasy.

Heavenly ascension, then, is both a precondition and a metaphor for the acquisition of Torah, and with it the status and power that the believer craves. It can also help him get status in ways that are more modest and realistic. If he has somehow managed to convince himself that he has himself made the ascension, he can step into the role that the preachers fashioned for Ezekiel. This gives him the privilege — the solemn duty, rather — of bearing witness to the people of what he has seen at the *merkabah*. All eyes in the congregation will be upon him, as they were upon the preacher at Shabu^{c}ot, when he describes to them how God kisses Jacob's face at the moment they recite the *Qedushshah* (above, chapter VIII, section A5c).

But this practical benefit of ascension seems to have been fairly unimportant, to judge from how rarely the *Hekhalot* hint at it. More commonly, the idea of ascension gave the believer satisfactions that did not depend on his having personally executed it. He could share vicariously in the victory, and in the spoils, of Moses or Enoch-Metatron or Akiba.

Did some of the *Hekhalot's* writers or readers believe themselves to have travelled to the *merkabah*? The weight of the evidence seems to suggest that at least a few did. We have, at any rate, seen reason to believe that the *Hekhalot* sometimes reflect hallucinatory experiences (above, section B2). But it also seems to me that this question, interesting as it is, is not overwhelmingly important. However we answer it, we must say much the same about the heavenly ascension. It was a fantasy which the believer in the *Hekhalot* took for reality, which he contemplated with pleasure and excitement, and to which he attributed profound consequences for his own standing in earthly society. By enjoying or expecting to enjoy these consequences, he partook of the ascension. It is not crucial for us to decide how likely he was to turn his fantasies into hallucinations.

---

89 *Hahoshesh bammerkabah*. I have seen this expression only in this passage and the one right before it (Schäfer, #92), and am not at all sure what it means.

The hypothesis that I have set forth in the past few pages fits in well with what we discovered, in section A, about the people for whom the *Hekhalot* were written. How shall we tie it to the outcome of sections B and C, that the *Hekhalot* draw upon the *merkabah* exegesis of the synagogue, and are inspired above all by the ascension *haggadot* of the Shabuᶜot cycle?

We can deal with this question at the same time that we take up an objection which may by now have occurred to the reader. If, as I have supposed, the *Hekhalot* are the work of people who had every reason to detest the rabbis, and indeed are directed in large measure against the rabbis' status, how are we to explain their apparent reverence for the rabbis Ishmael and Akiba, Nehuniah b. ha-Qanah and "Eliezer the Great"?

The ᶜam ha'areṣ, much as they may have hated the rabbis, seem never to have created religious institutions or chosen religious authorities independent of the rabbis. The result — or perhaps cause — of this situation must have been a considerable ambivalence of people's feelings toward the rabbis. On the one hand, they are arrogant tyrants who have usurped the inheritance of the congregation of Jacob. On the other, they are the expert administrators of this inheritance, without whom the congregation would have no share in it at all. The *Hekhalot* reflect this ambivalence. The author of the *Šar Torah* myth may bitterly resent the rabbis-angels, but it does not occur to him to deny that they possess the secrets of Torah (#292). Far less does it dawn on any of the authors of the *Hekhalot* to raise any fundamental question about the rabbinic value system itself, to ask whether mastery of the Torah ought to give an intellectual elite the right to lord it over the rest of the Jewish people. The ᶜam ha'areṣ had well learned the lessons that the rabbinic preachers had taught them. When they stormed heaven in rebellion against the rabbis, they did it on the rabbis' own terms, inspired by rabbinic *haggadot*.

Seen in this way, it becomes clear why the authors of the *Hekhalot* should have adulated certain rabbis of the more or less remote past, who, they believed, had been willing to reveal to all Israel the secrets of the rabbinic clique. Significantly, one of their heroes was Akiba, whom tradition represented as an ᶜam ha'areṣ who had raised himself to the elite (BT Pes. 49b, quoted above) [383]. Another (admittedly far less important to them) was Eliezer b. Hyrcanus, "the Great," reputedly a farmer's son who did not begin to study Torah until his twenties [428]. Where tradition failed them, imagination took over. It showed them the young Ishmael, also outside the charmed circle, able to learn Torah only with the aid of magic[90].

---

90 Beneath the *Šar Torah* writer's loud adulation of Nehuniah and Ishmael, we can hear a whisper of contempt. These "great" rabbis, he tells his readers, were in fact no better or more clever

We now can understand why the *Hekhalot* writers took their inspiration from rabbinic lore, as transmitted by the synagogue preachers. Only in the synagogue could they gain the knowledge that would give shape to their longings, context and purpose to their magic formulae and rituals[91]. We can also see that the Shabu°ot sermons, with their vivid and impressive depictions of Ezekiel's *merkabah* and Moses' ascension, would have excited them above all else.

This was not, presumably, the excitement that the synagogue preachers themselves wanted to inspire. We saw in chapter VIII that their central purpose was to comfort the Jewish people, and to encourage them to keep faith in God and his Torah. We also saw that this encouragement was to some extent directed against the seduction, and later the intimidation, of the Christian church.

We cannot say that the preachers' eloquence had none of its intended effect on those among their hearers with whom we are now concerned. I suggested in chapter VIII (section C6) that at least one of the functions of the grandiose heavenly structures in the *Hekhalot* may have been to provide a Jewish answer — entirely imaginary, unfortunately — to the splendid religious buildings erected by the Christian Roman emperors as advertisements for their faith. We may also suppose that the *Hekhalot* authors' resentment of the rabbis was at times compounded with resentment of the Gentile overlords of Palestine. This would explain why *Hekhalot Rabbati* contains a crude but graphic fantasy about how R. Hananiah b. Teradyon, whom the Romans had planned to execute, took on the shape of the Roman emperor and so tyrannized over Rome itself (Schäfer, ##112–121; Wertheimer, 7:4–8:5). It might also explain a puzzling passage in Salmon b. Yeruhim's version of the *Sar Torah* myth (stanza 4; below, Appendix VII), which seems to represent the angels as proposing a crucified savior as a sort of opiate for humanity, a poor substitute for the revelation of their precious secret. To his attack on the rabbis, the author adds a jab at Christianity.

By and large, however, the *Hekhalot* writers transformed the ascension stories into a revolutionary manifesto. Their energies, which the preachers had used to defend the community as a whole, were now directed against privileged elements within the community. The *Hekhalot*, it seems, radically altered the significance of the ascension traditions that nurtured them.

---

than you or I. They got their "wisdom" only through certain magical techniques, which you too are now about to learn.

91 I leave untouched the difficult and important problem of where and how these writers learned their magic.

Or did they?

We noticed in chapter VIII (section B6) a strange ambiguity about the ascension tradition. Moses, in his capacity as invader of heaven, bears a disquieting resemblance to the rebellious star-god of Isaiah 14:12—15. The author of the Isaiah passage itself had assimilated the mythological "Morning-star, son of the Dawn," to a historical "king of Babylon," whom the rabbis naturally identified as Nebuchadnezzar. But the Christian tradition, perhaps penetrating the Biblical text more deeply, equated "Lucifer" (the Vulgate's rendering of "Morning-star") with the devil.

At the two ends of this chain, a horned Moses and a horned devil face each other, both ready to carry their assault into heaven and shake the power of the celestial beings. The main difference between them is that Moses wins and Lucifer loses. Moses successfully battles the angels and grasps the throne of God. Lucifer is *thrown down to She'ol, to the depths of the pit.* (We recall that this image of falling or being thrown from heaven crops up in the *Hekhalot* and in the stories of Moses' ascension; above, section C3a.) Metatron[92], on the other hand, carries Moses' success to a degree that matches Lucifer's wildest fantasy: *I will lift up my throne above the stars of God ... I will be like the Most High.*

The success or failure of the rebel depends on whether or not the story-teller sympathizes with him. Thus, the story of Moses' ascension is the story of Lucifer, told from the devil's point of view. The horned Moses and the horned Lucifer are mirror images, and we do not know who is inside and who outside the mirror.

More important, the two are inseparable. It is not easy, as Milton showed, to tell the story of Lucifer's rebellion without some sympathy for him. The reverse, I suspect, is also true. One cannot hear of the ascension of Moses without some awareness, however obscure, of the demonic shadow that clings to it.

The shadow points to revolution, and to overthrow of the powers that be. I suggested in chapter VIII (section C3d, end) that this is the basic meaning of the ascension theme. In both Origen and *Pesiqta Rabbati,* the ascent of the hero seems to have as its consequence the descent of the angels. Certain apocalyptic texts share this pattern (above, chapter III). The Apocalypse of Abraham in particular — which, as we saw, projects upon Abraham themes that originally belong to Moses and Sinai — stresses that the rise of the human means the fall of the angel. All this hints that in the ascension stories, as in the *Śar Torah,* the struggle over the Torah masks a struggle over the power and status that Torah confers and symbolizes.

---

92 Also horned, according to some sources; above, chapter VII, endnote *f.*

In short, the writers of the *Hekhalot* knew what they were doing when they chose the heavenly ascension as their paradigm.

We now are able to understand the connection between the ascensions of the apocalypses, the Moses *haggadot*, and the *Hekhalot*. The line that holds them together is not some practice of ecstatic mysticism, handed down from generation to generation. Rather, it is an ancient but endlessly self-renewing theme of conflict in which the lower rises against the upper.

The same theme, with its values and outcome reversed, appears in the myths (mainly Christian) of Lucifer's rebellion at the beginning of time, Antichrist's rebellion at the end [88]. So much is at stake in the battle that the storytellers of each side see their opponents as figures of terror. Hence the shuddery horror that surrounds Satan and the Antichrist. Hence the monstrosity and savagery of the guardians of the heavenly palaces. Hence their hostility to the heavenly traveller, and their intense concern to keep him from making his ascent.

But where did the theme itself come from, and why was it so powerful and durable? The answer that suggests itself is that it is rooted in an endlessly repeated experience of real human life. This is the conflict that ensues when a child begins to reach maturity, is about to finish his climb from the ground to the heights of the adult world, grasps at the power (sexual and other) that once belonged to the parent alone. Both sides of this generational conflict, generation after generation, projected their cravings and fears into the heavens.

Pure hypothesis? Perhaps. But the hypothesis accords well with Erik H. Erikson's observation that pre-adolescent boys tend to express concern with their maturation, sexual and otherwise, by making high towers of building blocks, then representing the towers collapsing or boys falling from them [832,833]. It runs parallel to Philip Slater's interpretation of the themes of flight and falling in Greek mythology, as expressions of the son's competition with his father and his fear of being destroyed in this competition [855]. Most important, it explains features of the *Hekhalot* that have until now baffled us.

We now at last understand why the *Hekhalot* writers represent the denizens of the heavenly realms as gigantic: to a child, the adult world is peopled by giants[93]. We understand these beings' overwhelming and terrible

---

93 Bruno Bettelheim describes a five-year-old boy's response to the story of Jack and the Beanstalk: "There aren't any such things as giants, are there? ... But there are such things as grownups, and they're like giants" [827]. Bettelheim, like Philip Slater, uses this principle to make sense of the fairy tale [828,854]. Freud used the same principle to interpret dreams: "A woman patient told me a dream in which *all the people were especially big*. 'That means,' she went on, 'that the

sexuality (above, section B2). We can perhaps also understand along these lines the bizarre multiplication of their organs, which has puzzled us since we first encountered it in the Targum to Ezekiel 1:6. It reflects, perhaps, the child's perception of the bewildering complexity of the grownup world. Generation after generation filled this reservoir of desire and terror. The authors of the *Hekhalot* drew upon it for their own ends. Using the mythic form with which the synagogue tradition had already clothes it, they expressed and legitimized their hunger for status in Jewish society, as well as the magical techniques by which they tried to achieve this status. With extraordinary perceptivity, they gave a name to their triumphant ascending hero, which accurately reflects who he originally was. They called him *na⁣ᶜar*, the youth.

dream must be to do with events in my early childhood, for at that time, of course, all grown-up people seemed to me enormously big' " [836].

Conclusion

It happens in many analyses that as one approaches their end new recollections emerge which have hitherto been kept carefully concealed. Or it may be that on one occasion some unpretentious remark is thrown out in an indifferent tone of voice as though it were superfluous; that then, on another occasion, something further is added, which begins to make the physician prick his ears; and that at last he comes to recognize this despised fragment of a memory as the key to the weightiest secrets that the patient's neurosis has screened.

Early in the analysis my patient had told me of a memory of the period in which his naughtiness had been in the habit of suddenly turning into anxiety. He was chasing a beautiful big butterfly with yellow stripes and large wings which ended in pointed projections — a swallow-tail, in fact. Suddenly, when the butterfly had settled on a flower, he was seized with a dreadful fear of the creature, and ran away screaming.

This memory recurred occasionally during the analysis, and required an explanation; but for a long time none was to be found. Nevertheless it was to be assumed as a matter of course that a detail like this had not kept its place in his recollection on its own account, but that it was a screen-memory, representing something of more importance with which it was in some way connected. ...

— Freud, "From the History of an Infantile Neurosis" [837b]

There is often a passage in even the most thoroughly interpreted dream which has to be left obscure; this is because we become aware during the work of interpretation that at that point there is a tangle of dream-thoughts which cannot be unravelled and which moreover adds nothing to our knowledge of the content of the dream. This is the dream's navel, the spot where it reaches down into the unknown. ... The dream-thoughts to which we are led by interpretation cannot, from the nature of things, have any definite endings; they are bound to branch out in every direction into the intricate network of our world of thought. It is at some point where this meshwork is particularly close that the dream-wish grows up, like a mushroom out of its mycelium.

— Freud, *The Interpretation of Dreams* [837]

I offer the following as the main results of our study:

1. One of the earliest and best-attested features of the Jewish *merkabah* tradition is its coupling of the vision of Ezekiel 1 with the Book of Exodus's account of the Sinai revelation. The synagogue practice, of reading the two passages together on the festival of Shabuᶜot, expressed and institutionalized the perception that they belong together, and that each must be read in the light of the other.

We first find this perception reflected in the Septuagint's rendering of Ezekiel 43:2. It is again presupposed, a few centuries later, in the *Apocalypse of Abraham* and in the rabbinic traditions of the *merkabah* expositions of R. Johanan b. Zakkai's disciples. It reaches its fullest development in a cycle of third-century rabbinic homilies for Shabu^cot, in whose composition R. Joshua b. Levi seems to have played a leading role.

The point at issue was the context in which the *merkabah* vision is to be understood. Ancient Jewish expositors were no less interested than modern commentators in interpreting any given Biblical passage in its proper context. But their ways of discovering the proper context were rather different from ours. In this case, they used Psalm 68:18's combination of *chariotry* with *Sinai* to bring the *merkabah* and the Sinai revelation into the same framework. (At the same time, the opening of Psalm 68:19 added to this picture the element of heavenly ascension.) They could thus discard the context which the Book of Ezekiel provided for the *merkabah* vision, and offer a new one in its place.

What advantages did the expositors gain from reading Exodus 19 and Ezekiel 1 as two segments of the same context? First, Ezekiel's vivid description of the *merkabah* gave people a starting point for visualizing, "with the eyes of the heart," the full glory of the Sinai revelation. (This is the conception that underlies the miraculous events in the Johanan b. Zakkai stories.) This taught them the splendor and power of the authority that stood behind the Torah. Second, the stories of Moses' struggle with the angels over the Torah (which found their way into the Shabu^cot homilies through Psalm 68:19) taught them how precious the Torah was, and how precious they were to God that he chose them to receive it.

All of this served to dramatize and strengthen the Jews' faith, particularly against the challenge of aggressive Christianity. But the combat element in the ascension stories had another effect, unlooked-for and important. Certain Jews, who felt a frustrated longing to rise in their social world, saw the heavenly ascension as a paradigm for their own struggle against the forces that held them down. These forces were the rabbis.

2. If the Sinai-*merkabah* link was one key element of the *merkabah* traditions of the synagogue, another was the conception of Ezekiel's *hayyot* and *'ofannim* as timeless heavenly beings devoted to the unending praise of God. This conception was rooted in a different context, which the earliest expositors had created for Ezekiel 1. The *merkabah* vision here stood in the company of Isaiah's Temple vision, and of Jacob's meeting with "camps" of angels (Isaiah 6:1–3, Genesis 32:1–2).

We must ask, again, what the advantages were of reading Ezekiel 1 in this way. Remote and ethereal speculations about the angelic hymnody would hardly have stirred those who heard them, if they had not seemed to have more or less concrete and immediate implications.

One answer to this question seems to lie in the emphasis, in the Targum and the rabbinic midrashim, on the interruption of the *hayyot*'s normally ceaseless song (Ezekiel 1:24—25). Angelic hymns take second place to God's interactions with his people. The *merkabah* vision, so interpreted, thus reinforces the synagogue worshipper's sense that he and the act he is engaged in are of cosmic importance.

The vision hints, as well, that gigantic and friendly beings stand beside the worshipper, bridging the terrible gulf between him and God. So the synagogue expositors read the "wheel" of Ezekiel 1:15, and the "rainbow" of Ezekiel 1:28.

3. We have so far considered the attractive features of the *merkabah* vision, seen from the viewpoint of preachers eager to catch their audiences' attention and evoke their faith and loyalty. Yet these attractions cast dark and forbidding shadows. Veneration of the rainbow, as bridge between earth and heaven, could be a door to nature-worship. God's adoring *hayyot* had certain disturbing traits, which one did not like to imagine in God's neighborhood. Their name was ambiguous; it could mean "beasts," with a full range of sinister connotations, as well as "living creatures." Apocalyptic writers noted their bestial violence (Revelation, Apocalypse of Abraham), or hinted that they were hostile forces which God had brought into grudging submission (Daniel). Comparison of *Gen. R.* 65:21 with its parallels suggests that some Jews, perhaps without being fully aware of it, perceived them as demons.

4. We can develop this last observation. As I have remarked, the *merkabah*-Sinai link permitted Jewish interpreters vividly to expound the glory of God's self-revelation at Sinai. But it also opened the door to disquieting speculations about the consequences of that self-revelation. The presence of an ox's face and a calf's foot in the divine vehicle (Ezekiel 1:7, 10) suggested that the Israelites promptly turned to worshipping a molten calf, not in spite of what God had shown them of himself, but because of it. What was worse, these passages of Ezekiel reinforced the suggestion of Exodus 32:24, that the calf had some eerie and compelling power of its own; and they gave the bold expositor the clue he needed to trace this power straight back to the divinity. The calf *was* divinity, split off and become demonic. God himself prepared the most damnable and traumatic apostasy of Jewish history. He, and the idolatry he condemns, are at bottom the same.

We find this understanding of the *merkabah* and the calf mostly in late midrashim. But much earlier sources, perhaps going back to the interpolated Ezekiel 10:14 and the Septuagint translation of Ezekiel 1:7, presuppose it in that they try to repress it. It is, in fact, our clearest case of the repression of a specific interpretation of Ezekiel's vision. The Biblical text seemed to have opened the window on a troubling ambiguity in the being of the Jewish God. The text's transmitters and interpreters fought a losing battle to force the window shut.

5. Similar ambiguities clung to the "terrible ice" of Ezekiel 1:22. Apocalyptic sources associated this feature of the vision with the heavenly waters, with the Red Sea, with the primordial monster-begetting waters, or with some combination of the three. (So, most significantly, the Book of Revelation.) The Babylonian rabbinic tradition echoed these conceptions in its warning against saying "water, water" in God's vicinity. Behind all these images lay the ancient idea of water as an embodiment of chaos, which engulfs God even as he masters it.

The *merkabah*-water theme runs parallel to the *merkabah*-calf theme. Some midrashic sources aptly underline this parallelism by rooting the Israelites' calf-worship in their experience of God at the Red Sea. The *Hekhalot*, too, imply that anyone who perceives water in God's presence must be descended from those who worshipped the calf.

6. Certain rabbis, then, caught glimpses of frightening ambiguities in the divine, amid the fantastic swirl of Ezekiel's images. These glimpses were what led them to try to bridle the synagogue preachers' enthusiasm for the *merkabah*. But perhaps they also helped generate this enthusiasm. People may have sensed that, in hearing and pondering the *merkabah* vision, they were wandering close to the forbidden. This may well have added to the vision's excitement, and given its faith-affirming aspects all the more power.

7. However this may be, it is clear that the aspect of the synagogue *merkabah* tradition that most caught its audiences' imagination was the tales of Moses' ascent to heaven and struggle with the angels over the Torah. These stories inspired a body of literature which we may regard as an offshoot of the synagogue *merkabah* exegesis: the *Hekhalot*.

Thus, we find the ascension of Moses transformed in the *Hekhalot* into the ascension materials. His seizure of the Torah is transformed into the *Sar Torah* materials. And, faithful to another portion of the synagogue tradition's agenda, the *Hekhalot* authors elaborate on the details of the heavenly hymnody.

8. The authors of the *Hekhalot* did more than borrow the ascension theme from the synagogue tradition. They made it into a paradigm of their own struggle with the rabbinic elite for a place of honor within Jewish society — an unequal and frustrating struggle which they waged with magic as their chief weapon. In doing so, however, they were not entirely innovative. Rather, they brought out certain aspects of the ascension theme which had always been there, in potential.

For the ascension myth is inherently and essentially revolutionary. It is very nearly a mirror image of the ancient myth of Lucifer, the rebellious deity who tries to set his throne above the stars and is therefore hurled down to hell. More exactly, it is the Lucifer myth told from the rebel's point of view, with the rebel victorious. Both, I suspect, are rooted in the psychological reality of the younger generation challenging the old. The difference lies in the sympathies of the narrator.

9. Centuries before the *Hekhalot*, certain apocalyptic writers described the heavenly ascensions of individual visionaries. They occasionally hinted at a link between the exaltation of the human being and the degradation of the heavenly beings (I Enoch, Apocalypse of Abraham). This is the core of the revolutionary significance of the ascension myth, which underlies the *Hekhalot*. If I am right in suggesting that this myth and its significance are rooted in the endlessly repeated conflict of generations, this will go a long way toward explaining why parallel ascensions appear in literatures separated from each other by hundreds of years.

Other factors, to be sure, may also have played a role. The Sinai-*merkabah* link may have suggested to the apocalyptic writers, as it later suggested to the authors of the Shabuᶜot homilies, that heavenly ascension is part of the package of ideas that contains the *merkabah*. Direct tradition, which we can demonstrate to some extent by comparing the pre-Christian Enoch materials (in I Enoch) with the "*3 Enoch*" of the *Hekhalot*, may also have played a part. But we no longer need to put the weight of our explanation on a continuous "ascension tradition" linking apocalypses and *Hekhalot*, and therefore need not be troubled by apparent gaps in the tradition — such as the Palestinian rabbinic literature, which gives no hint that *merkabah* or *maᶜaseh merkabah* have anything to do with heavenly journeys.

10. If we no longer need to postulate a continuous tradition of belief in heavenly ascensions, we have far less need to suppose a continuous tradition of ecstatic mystical practice. The question of whether people "really" engaged in heavenly journeys loses much of its importance. Talk of "real mystical experiences" was always misleading anyway, since what the mystics supposedly experienced was in no event real. The question was only whether people who believed in ascensions left their expectations at the level of conscious fantasy, or whether they converted them into bona fide hallucinations. I am inclined to suppose that the latter was very probably true for some at least of the *Hekhalot* authors, the former for the apocalyptic writers. But, whatever the answer, the issue is not crucial. What *is* crucial is what belief in ascension meant to the people who held it.

11. Of the ambiguities suggested by Ezekiel's *merkabah* and the traditions founded on it, the ascension myth has within it the most devastating. The ambiguity this time is not of God, but of the human quest for God. The *merkabah* traveller draws "nearer, my God, to thee" — in order to seize

God's throne and, by implication, to supplant him. His paradigmatic hero is Lucifer at the same time that it is Moses. (Naturally enough, the two figures start to blend. Both, for example, acquire a pair of horns.)

To the extent that the rabbis were aware of this development of the synagogue *merkabah* tradition, it must have been for them among the most horrific of all the lines of thought that led from Ezekiel's vision. It was obviously subversive of their own leadership. More profoundly, it plunged into ambiguity the essential nature of the hero who brought Torah for Israel; and, beyond that, the whole enterprise of seeking God.

It is not hard to imagine that other Jews might have found this development exciting and liberating, for exactly the same reasons.

Like the "Wolf Man's" butterfly, Ezekiel's *merkabah* became the nexus of these thrills and terrors in the mental world of rabbinic Judaism. The rabbis therefore chased it, and ran screaming from it.

The terrors, like the thrills, were their own creation. I see no evidence that any of the alarming developments of *merkabah* exegesis, sketched above, represent alien conceptions which assaulted rabbinic Judaism from the outside. It was the rabbis, or Jews in the rabbinic sphere, who conceived and elaborated them. But it was the rabbis, too, who saw them as threats to the collective sanity of their religious culture, and responded with suppression and dread.

It did not have to be this way. There are religions outside the Judaic sphere, particularly in the East, which seem perfectly comfortable with a monistic conception of God as source of both good and evil. Their adherents, we may imagine, would regard the "dangerous" ideas we have examined in these pages as self-evident and humdrum. That the rabbis did not, that they saw these ideas as dangerous and repudiated them in horror, is a fact of crucial importance in characterizing rabbinic religion.

The accomplishments of our study, therefore, are not limited to our having laid bare what the rabbis regarded as the secrets of the *merkabah*, elucidated a cluster of obscure passages in the rabbinic literature, explained the origin and function of the ascension materials in the apocalypses and more particularly in the *Hekhalot*. None of these achievements seems to me trivial, in and of itself. But we may subsume all of them in a greater one, of tracing out a set of ideas which the rabbinic system was on the one hand capable of evolving, and which on the other hand it rejected as utterly incompatible with its essential values. If, as I think, we can come to know an individual both through the nature of his repressed impulses and through the obligation he feels to repress them, it seems reasonable that we can approach a religious culture in the same way. We have therefore made a fresh contribution to the task of defining and describing what was basic about rabbinic Judaism.

Can we extend this achievement to other religions of the ancient Mediter-ranean, or to religion in general? I have chosen here to limit myself as much as possible to Judaism, and have made only the most sparing use of com-parisons across religious lines. I have indeed concerned myself with Origen, but only as an indirect source for Jewish exegetical traditions; I have made only occasional tentative forays into Origen's own faith.

I believe, nevertheless, that much of the work I have done here (partic-ularly in chapter IX) can serve as a starting point for future comparative studies. Origen's Christian mythology offers a particularly rich field for such investigations. Several passages of his *Homilies* on Numbers and Joshua, for example, seem to interpret Joshua's wars against the Canaanites as shadowy reflections of greater celestial struggles, in which humans chal-lenge and expel hostile powers entrenched in the heavens[1]. He invokes in this connection a passage which appears to have been one of his favorite. Scriptural quotations [800]; namely, Ephesians 6:12: "For we are not con-tending against flesh and blood, but against the principalities, against the powers, against the world rulers of this present darkness, against the spiri-tual hosts of wickedness in the heavenly places."

This conception is obviously parallel to the Jewish myth, underlying the *Hekhalot*, of the human invasion of heaven. But how are we to explain the connection? This parallel, unlike the ones analyzed in chapter VIII, is not so easily explained as a case of Jewish influence on Origen; his speculations seem too well integrated into his patterns of thought to be regarded as alien elements grafted on to them. I am therefore disposed to imagine a parallel development in Judaism and Christianity, conditioned by factors which remain to be clarified.

The same cluster of ideas may somehow be linked with the growth of the Arian "heresy" in the early fourth century. Conventionally, scholars have regarded the central issue between the Arians and their "orthodox" opponents as the relationship among the persons of the Trinity. Was the Son equal to the Father (as the "orthodox" claimed) or subordinate to him? But a recent study, by Robert C. Gregg and Dennis E. Groh, has argued for a shift of emphasis. The essential claim of Arianism, they pro-pose, was that Christ was a creature of God's whom God promoted to divinity, and that humans may strive for a comparable promotion [672b]. If Gregg and Groh are right — and I am hardly competent to judge this issue — the Arian Christ turns out to resemble the Metatron of the *Hekhalot*. Here again, I am not proposing Jewish influence on Arianism. I am suggest-

---

1 *Homilies on Numbers*, VII, 5–6; XVI, 6; cf. XXVIII, 1–3. *Homilies on Joshua*, I, 5–6; XII, 1–2; cf. XXIII, 4; XXV, 4. Annie Jaubert briefly discusses the role of these passages in Origen's angelology [630a]. The fact that "Jesus" is the Greek form of the name "Joshua" naturally encouraged this interpretation of Joshua's conquests.

ing, rather, that there may have been something in the intellectual atmosphere of the fourth-century Mediterranean world that made divinization an attractive and plausible fantasy. What this was, I do not attempt to speculate.

What of Gnosticism? Despite Scholem's controversial description of the faith of the *Hekhalot* as "Jewish Gnosticism" [589], scholars have so far not agreed on whether there can have been any such thing as a "Jewish Gnosticism," or, if there was, whether the *Hekhalot* represent it [548]. The theme that occupies the *Hekhalot*, of humans struggling upward against a hostile celestial hierarchy, is certainly redolent of Gnosticism. But the strong anti-Jewish thrust of most ancient Gnostic systems makes it hard for us simply to identify the *Hekhalot* as Gnostic. It does not get us very far to suggest that Gnosticism influenced the writers of the *Hekhalot*, since this does nothing to explain why these Jewish authors should so passionately have embraced alien conceptions. The reverse hypothesis, that the *Hekhalot* influenced Gnosticism, suffers from a similar liability, plus the chronological difficulty that the Gnostic texts seem to be older than the *Hekhalot* [504a].

The issue is important, and must be resolved sooner or later. I have not tried to deal with it here, because I could not see how it would contribute to solving the problems to which this book is devoted. On the contrary: only when we have understood what belief in heavenly ascension meant to the *Hekhalot* authors, in their own context, will we be able to make significant comparisons between ascensions in the *Hekhalot* and in Gnosticism. The current investigation is thus an essential preliminary to comparative analysis, and not the other way round.

I will not try to anticipate the results of such comparative study. Whatever they are, they will have to explain the specific parallels between midrashic and *Hekhalot* sources on the one hand and Gnostic writings on the other, which Ithamar Gruenwald has observed [548] and which I have discussed in Appendix VI. They will also, I think, have to take into account the parallel conclusions that Elaine Pagels and I reached, independently of each other, on how the social worlds of the Gnostic and the *Hekhalot* writers influenced their mythologies (above, page 437).

There is another way in which the implications of this book range beyond the study of Judaism. From time to time, I have made use of certain of the grand constructions of twentieth-century psychology, in order to make sense of the data before us. In chapter V, I invoked Jung's quaternities; in chapter IX, the views of Freud and his followers on the male terror of the vagina (section B2).

I came to the data without prior allegiance to either Freud or Jung, and have therefore had no qualms about using their ideas in an eclectic and piecemeal fashion. In doing so, I have provided what may be at least partial confirmation of one or both. If it is the case that Freud or Jung has permitted me to explain the otherwise inexplicable, it will follow that the theories of one or both must contain, even if neither represents, truth.

Whatever progress I have made in clearing up the riddles of the *merkabah* and its meaning for the rabbis, I do not sense that its mystery is entirely dispelled. A numinous mystery continues to cling to, if not to obscure, Ezekiel's strangest vision and the marks that it made on the thought of early Judaism.

Freud, often stereotyped as a reductionist, knew better than to box the world into a system. His favorite quotation was Hamlet's "There are more things in heaven and earth than are dreamed of in your philosophy" [837c]. He was aware that reality has its unruly threads which cannot be trimmed away, which lead off into unexplored darkness.

The dream, said Freud, has its "navel, the spot where it reaches down into the unknown" [837]. So, perhaps, do the communal dreams that lie at the heart of our religions.

For the rabbis, Ezekiel's *merkabah* was such a navel. Through it, their dreaming was nourished.

The manner of nourishment is what this book is about.

Appendix I

Orientation to Rabbinic Sources

In this appendix, I give the briefest possible sketch of the ancient documents that make up the rabbinic literature, and explain a few key terms used in discussing this literature and its creators. I intend to give the non-specialist reader just enough orientation to allow him to follow the arguments in the text.

I do not offer this appendix as a serious introduction to rabbinics. The reader who wishes such an introduction will profit from John Bowker's *The Targums and Rabbinic Literature,* Jacob Neusner's *Invitation to the Talmud,* and — allowing for its traditionalist bias and completely uncritical approach — Adin Steinsaltz's *The Essential Talmud.* Hermann L. Strack's *Introduction to the Talmud and Midrash* is the classic, but it is about as readable as a telephone directory, and is out of date besides. (Günter Stemberger's new edition of Strack, completely rewritten and brought up to date, is so far available only in German.) Recent articles by Neusner's students, compiled and published as *The Study of Ancient Judaism,* give introductions and bibliographies to Mishnah, Talmud, and midrash [256a, 336b,336e,340a,342,345a].

1. The *Mishnah* is the fundamental document of rabbinic Judaism. It is a compilation, arranged in a roughly topical manner, of Jewish common law (*halakhah,* in Hebrew) as it was known in Palestine early in the third century A.D. R. Judah the Patriarch, the leader of the rabbinic movement at the beginning of the third century, seems to have dominated the editorial process. But the details of this process, and particularly the principles by which material was included or rejected, remain entirely obscure [286a, 336c,336d,423a].

The Mishnah contains sixty-three "tractates," subdivided into chapters and again into *mishnayot* (Hebrew plural of *mishnah*)[1], and grouped according to their topic under six main headings (called "orders"). Citing the

---

1 The word *mishnah* designates a traditional teaching, handed down orally. It can therefore be used collectively for the entire corpus of rabbinic "teachings," as well as for each of its components.

Mishnah, one gives the name of the tractate and the number of the chapter and of the *mishnah* in question. Thus, "M. Abot 5:22" is shorthand for "Mishnah, tractate *Abot,* chapter 5, *mishnah* 22."

The Mishnah is not, as one sometimes hears said, a commentary on the Bible. Indeed, the genre *mishnah* (traditional teaching containing its own authority, without any recourse to Scripture) stands over against the other rabbinic genre of *midrash,* Scripture exposition [419a]. Nevertheless, bits of *midrash* are scattered here and there in Judah the Patriarch's Mishnah. Similarly, although it is mainly devoted to *halakhah,* the Mishnah contains bits of non-legal material as well. We call this non-legal material *haggadah.* It is not easy to define the word *haggadah,* except by saying that it is whatever is not *halakhah.* But the category includes, among other things, ethical teaching, historical or (more usually) pseudo-historical anecdotes, and whatever *midrash* is not directed toward legal ends.

The standard English translation of the Mishnah is Herbert Danby's. Eugene J. Lipman has prepared an extremely lucid translation of selected passages from the Mishnah, with equally lucid explanatory notes, which gives a good picture of the scope and concerns of this work. There are several English translations of the beautiful tractate *Abot,* or *Pirqe Abot* — the only tractate of the Mishnah wholly given over to *haggadah.* Of these, Judah Goldin's is the the most elegant and pleasant to read. (I give full bibliographical information on the cited translations in section 6 of my Reference List, under "Mishnah.")

2. We use the term *Tannaim* (singular *Tanna*) to designate those rabbis, almost all of them Palestinians, who lived and worked up to and during the time the Mishnah was compiled. We call their successors the *Amoraim* (singular *Amora*). These were the rabbis who expounded and developed Tannaitic *halakhah* in the major rabbinic centers of Palestine and Babylonia, during the third, fourth, and fifth centuries A.D.

3. Amoraic discussions of the Mishnah and of other Tannaitic sources (on which see below) were twice compiled into massive works called *Gemarot* (singular *Gemara*), which took the form of commentaries on the Mishnah. One *Gemara* was compiled in Palestine early in the fifth century, the other in Babylonia during the course of the sixth. The Mishnah, with its Palestinian Gemara, is called the *Palestinian Talmud*; with its Babylonian Gemara, the *Babylonian Talmud.* We know practically nothing of the process by which these documents came into existence and took on their present form [286a,336a].

Writing English, we can relieve this somewhat confusing ambiguity by capitalizing "Mishnah" when we intend the first meaning, leaving the "m" small when we intend the second.

Being commentaries on the Mishnah, both Talmuds are organized into tractates which follow those of the Mishnah[2]. One cites the Palestinian Gemara by giving the name of the tractate and the number of the chapter and of the *halakhah*. (These numbers are theoretically the same as those of the Mishnah-text being commented on; but, because of inconsistencies among the medieval manuscripts that lie behind our standard editions of the Mishnah and of the Palestinian Talmud, there is often some divergence.) One then adds the page and the column from the original edition of the Palestinian Talmud, published in Venice in 1523–24 and often reprinted since. Thus, "PT Hagigah 2:1 (77a)" means: "Palestinian Talmud, tractate *Hagigah*, chapter 2, *halakhah* 1 (that is, the Gemara to M. Hagigah 2:1), page 77 of the Venice edition, column *a*." The Babylonian Talmud is always cited by the tractate and by the page number of the Hebrew text, which has been the same in all editions from 1520 on. "BT Hagigah 13a" means "Babylonian Talmud, tractate *Hagigah*, page 13a[3]."

During the Middle Ages, Jews came to regard the Babylonian Talmud as the more authoritative of the two. When a modern writer refers to "the Talmud," without qualification, he means the Babylonian.

The Babylonian Talmud is available in an excellent English translation, thirty-five volumes long, usually referred to as the "Soncino Talmud" (after its publisher). An English translation of the Palestinian Talmud, by Jacob Neusner, has recently begun to appear. The late Saul Lieberman's criticism, however, suggests that the reader must use this translation with caution [329a]. German translations of several tractates, by Charles Horowitz and the late Gerd A. Wewers, are available. The older French translation by Moise Schwab is in generally bad odor. But I have made very little use of it myself, and cannot verify the disparaging comments about it that I have read and heard. (Unless stated otherwise, all translations of rabbinic sources in this book are my own.)

4. Only a fraction of the extant utterances of the Tannaim are contained in the Mishnah. Others have survived as "external teachings," *baraitot* (singular *baraita*). Many of these *baraitot* are preserved as quotations in the

---

2 Neither Gemara, however, has all the Mishnah's sixty-three tractates. For reasons that are not clear, the Babylonian Talmud has no Gemara for more than a third of the tractates; while the Palestinian Talmud omits the entire fifth order of the Mishnah and almost all of the sixth.

3 The numeral actually designates the *sheet*, which is printed on both sides (*a* and *b*). In the Venice edition of the Palestinian Talmud, there are four columns to a sheet, two on each side; the sheet numbered 77 therefore contains the four columns 77a, 77b, 77c, 77d. – In Hebrew, the Palestinian Talmud is usually called *Talmud Yerushalmi*, "Jerusalem Talmud." The title is inaccurate but is widely used even in English, and abbreviated "yer.," "jer.," "y.," "j.," "TJ." The reader will often encounter these abbreviations, or "TP," in place of my preferred "PT"; and he will often see the Babylonian Talmud cited as "TB" or "b."

Palestinian and Babylonian *Gemarot,* where they are normally set off from their context by distinctive formulae of introduction. Others make up the "Tannaitic midrashim" to the last four books of the Pentateuch, about which we will have more to say presently. Still others are collected in a mysterious anthology of *baraitot* called the *Tosefta,* which is organized along the same lines as the Mishnah. Who compiled the Tosefta; when, why, and how he or they compiled it; what principles he/they used in selecting its materials; and what relation it has to Judah the Patriarch's Mishnah — all of these are unsolved problems.

One cites the Tosefta by tractate (its tractates usually correspond to those of the Mishnah), and by number of chapter and *halakhah.* Different editions of the Tosefta, following different manuscripts, do not always number their chapters in the same way. Where divergent numberings exist, scholars cite both. Hence, "T. Megillah 3(4):28" means: "Tosefta; tractate *Megillah*; chapter 3 or chapter 4, depending on which edition one uses; *halakhah* 28."

Two modern editions of the Tosefta are widely used. Saul Lieberman's is the better, and is accompanied by an exhaustive commentary [324], but covers only the first half of the Tosefta. For the rest, we normally use the older edition of M. S. Zuckermandel. (See Reference List, section 5a, under "Tosefta.")

Jacob Neusner's English translation of the Tosefta began to appear in 1977, and is now complete.

5. We may conceive the Mishnah and its associated texts (the two Talmuds; the Tosefta) as one of the two great libraries of rabbinic literature. The second consists of the *midrashim* — texts devoted wholly or almost wholly to rabbinic expositions of Scripture. The Talmuds, the Tosefta, and even the Mishnah indeed contain materials of the genre *midrash*, but subordinate these materials to the very different agenda set by the Mishnah. Thus, for example, the Talmud may discuss and interpret a passage from the Bible that speaks of the Sabbath, but not as an end in itself; rather, because it seemed somehow to contribute to the interpretation or justification of the Sabbath law of the Mishnah. By contrast, the texts we are about to consider have their agenda set from beginning to end by the Scripture and by the need for interpreting it. Not surprisingly, these midrashic works usually (not always) follow the arrangement of the Biblical books that their materials expound[4].

---

4 The word *midrash* is ambiguous. It can refer to the genre of Scriptural exposition; to a single unit of Scripture exposition (a midrash on Deuteronomy 4:32, for example); or to one of the extended literary texts made up of many such units. A *midrash* (in the second sense) may occur

The midrashim are bewilderingly numerous, and it is hard to devise sub-categories that include them all. Several groups, however, do stand out.

First, there are the *"Tannaitic midrashim,"* a group of five midrashim to the last four books of the Pentateuch. The *Mekhilta of R. Ishmael* (often called simply *Mekhilta*, without qualification) and the *Mekhilta of R. Simeon b. Yohai* expound the Book of Exodus; *Sifra* expounds Leviticus; *Sifre* expounds Numbers; and another, independent midrash, also called *Sifre*, expounds Deuteronomy. As far as we can tell, these midrashim contain only Tannaitic material; at least, they do not invoke the names of post-Tannaitic authorities. Most scholars therefore assume that they were edited not long after the close of the Tannaitic period, at some time in the third century.

The *Mekhilta of R. Simeon b. Yohai* was lost for centuries, and even today we do not have the full text. In 1905, David Hoffmann published a not very successful attempt at reconstructing it, mainly on the basis of what he supposed were quotations from it in the fourteenth-century Yemenite *Midrash ha-Gadol*. But, even as Hoffmann wrote, substantial chunks of the lost midrash were coming to light among the manuscripts of the Cairo Genizah[5]. By 1955, Jacob Epstein and Ezra Z. Melamed were able to publish a fairly reliable reconstruction, based mainly on the Genizah texts and supplemented from the *Midrash ha-Gadol* and other sources. One cites the *Mekhilta of R. Simeon* by the page number of the Epstein-Melamed edition.

We normally cite the other four Tannaitic midrashim by the traditional divisions of the text, supplemented by the page numbers of the standard editions. *Mekhilta* is divided into "tractates" (which have nothing to do with the tractates of the Mishnah) and subdivided into chapters. *Sifre to Numbers* and *Sifre to Deuteronomy* are divided into major sections, corresponding to the traditional divisions of the Biblical text on which they comment, and into short, numbered sections. The traditional divisions of *Sifra*

---

in Mishnah, Tosefta, or Talmud, as well as in a *midrash* (in the third sense). For the rest of this appendix, I will consistently use *midrash* in its last meaning; that is, of a midrashic *text*. – The modern use of *midrash* (in English) to mean "legend" is careless and inappropriate. Writers who use the word in this sense would often be better served by *haggadah*.

5 *Genizah* is the Hebrew word for a synagogue storeroom, used to house worn-out copies of sacred books until they can be taken out and given an appropriate burial. For reasons we do not understand and can only be grateful for, the custodians of the medieval Ezra Synagogue in Cairo never got around to cleaning out their *genizah*. The result was that tens of thousands of pages of Hebrew and Judeo-Arabic manuscripts accumulated there, to be discovered by European scholars late in the nineteenth century. Their contents range from portions of the original Hebrew of the Apocryphal *Wisdom of Ben Sira*, to business letters written in Arabic by the Jewish merchants of medieval Cairo [301]. They include much midrashic material, some of it otherwise unknown. The *Visions of Ezekiel*, for example, which plays a key role in my argument in chapter VIII, survives only in two fragments from the Genizah.

are particularly irrational and confusing. It is divided into major sections, which are subdivided into chapters; some of the chapters are called *peraqim*, others *parashot*; *peraqim* and *parashot* are mixed together in the text, but are numbered in independent sequences.

Given the complexity and inconsistency of these divisions, it is easy to see why most scholars would rather depend on citing edition and page number. Unfortunately, there is so far no critical edition[6] of *Sifra*; for want of anything better, many scholars treat Hirsch's 1862 edition as standard. But H. S. Horovitz has published a critical edition of *Sifre to Numbers,* and Louis Finkelstein has done the same for *Sifre to Deuteronomy.* For the *Mekhilta of R. Ishmael,* there are two critical editions, one prepared by H. S. Horovitz and I. A. Rabin, the other by Jacob Z. Lauterbach. I cannot judge the relative merits of these two editions, but have preferred to cite Lauterbach's, because of its one great advantage: a good English translation, printed with the Hebrew on facing pages. (English translations of the other Tannaitic midrashim have only now begun to appear: portions of *Sifra,* by Jacob Neusner and Roger Brooks; *Sifre to Numbers*, by Neusner; *Sifre to Deuteronomy*, by Reuven Hammer.)

Hoffmann has published a reconstruction of what he thinks is a lost Tannaitic midrash to Deuteronomy, which he calls *Midrash Tannaim.*

6. If the Tannaitic midrashim are the oldest surviving midrashim — at least, in terms of the dates they were edited — the next oldest are those we call the "*classical Palestinian midrashim.*" This term designates a group of four texts which, in their contents, style, and linguistic features, are closely bound to each other and to the Palestinian Talmud. Most scholars date them, like the Palestinian Talmud itself, to the early fifth century, or perhaps a little later.

Three of these texts are midrashim to the Books of Genesis, Leviticus, and Lamentations. During the Middle Ages, they were incorporated into the *Midrash Rabbah* series (see below), and were given the titles *Genesis Rabbah, Leviticus Rabbah,* and *Lamentations Rabbah.* The fourth is a midrash, not to any one Biblical book, but to a sequence of Biblical passages read in the synagogue on festivals and certain special Sabbaths. It is called *Pesiqta de-Rab Kahana.*

---

6 By "critical edition," I mean an edition that is based on systematic examination and evaluation of the extant manuscripts, and which lays the results of this examination before the reader in a reasonably complete and intelligible way. A critical edition will normally print a "base text," which represents the manuscript that the editor judges to be the best; or, perhaps (if the editor subscribes to a different view of proper procedure), his own synthesis of the readings of several good manuscripts. A "critical apparatus," usually printed on the page beneath the base text, will record all significant manuscript variations.

Julius Theodor and Chanoch Albeck have published a critical edition of *Genesis Rabbah*, Mordecai Margulies has done the same for *Leviticus Rabbah*, and Bernard Mandelbaum the same for *Pesiqta de-Rab Kahana*. Solomon Buber has published a semi-critical edition of *Lamentations Rabbah*. But here there is an added complication; for the manuscript that Buber followed represents a different text-tradition, sometimes amounting to a different recension, from the version printed in the standard editions of *Midrash Rabbah*. The English translation of *Lamentations Rabbah* that appears in the "Soncino Midrash" (below) renders the *Midrash Rabbah* version, not Buber's.

Like the rest of the *Midrash Rabbah* series, the midrashim to Genesis, Leviticus, and Lamentations are divided into chapters and subdivided into sections. I cite them by these divisions, as well as by the page number of the critical edition. Thus, for example: *Gen. R.* 20:4, ed. 185–186 [188].

Pesiqta de-Rab Kahana is not divided into chapters, but into *pisqa'ot* (singular *pisqa*), corresponding to the individual Scripture lections to which the midrash is attached. Each *pisqa* has a title, and each is divided into numbered subsections. I cite passages from *Pesiqta de-Rab Kahana* by the title of the *pisqa*, the number of the subsection, and the page of Mandelbaum's edition (for example: *Pesiqta de-Rab Kahana, Ba-Ḥodesh* #22, ed. 219–221 [206]).

William G. Braude and Israel J. Kapstein have translated *Pesiqta de-Rab Kahana*, rather freely, into English. For translations of the other three classical Palestinian midrashim, the reader must turn to the "Soncino Midrash," where he can locate any passage by its chapter and section number.

7. At some point in the Middle Ages, Jews put together a series of midrashim covering the ten most widely-known books of the Hebrew Bible: the five books of the Pentateuch, and the "Five Scrolls" read on holidays (Song of Songs, Ruth, Lamentations, Ecclesiastes, Esther). The series eventually came to be known as *Midrash Rabbah*, "the great midrash"; and each of its component midrashim received the word *Rabbah* as part of its title (*Genesis Rabbah, Exodus Rabbah*, and so forth). The series was printed again and again in large folio volumes, with clusters of traditional commentaries. Soncino Press has published a ten-volume English translation, commonly referred to as the "Soncino Midrash."

The title *Midrash Rabbah* obscures the fact that we are not dealing with a single midrash in ten parts, but with a motley collection of midrashim placed side by side, as it were, on the same shelf. This assembly of texts contains sources that are relatively early, and others that are extremely late. We have seen that *Genesis Rabbah, Leviticus Rabbah,* and *Lamentations Rabbah* (in its two recensions) belong to the category of fifth-century Palestinian midrashim. *Deuteronomy Rabbah* belongs to a later cluster of midrashim, the *"Tanḥuma"* group (see below). So do the second part of *Exodus Rabbah* (from chapter 15 to its end) and the second part of *Numbers Rabbah* (again, from chapter 15 to its end). *Exodus Rabbah* and *Numbers Rabbah* are both composite, their first halves considerably later than their second halves; chapters 1–14 of both midrashim may perhaps be as recent as the twelfth century. We do not have any clear idea of the dates of the midrashim to Song of Songs, Ruth, Ecclesiastes, and Esther. We need not assume that they have any inherent connection with each other, or with any of the other midrashim of the *Rabbah* series.

As I have remarked, the *Midrash Rabbah* midrashim are divided into chapters and then into sections, and one normally uses the numbers of these divisions in citing them. Apart from *Genesis Rabbah, Leviticus Rabbah*, and *Lamentations Rabbah* (above)[7], none of them has appeared in anything like a critical edition. Myron Bialik Lerner has prepared a critical edition of *Ruth Rabbah*, which he submitted as his Ph.D. dissertation to the Hebrew University, and which has circulated in a mimeographed form. (He was kind enough to send me a copy.) But I am not aware that it has ever been published.

8. I discuss the *"Tanḥuma midrashim"* in chapter IV, section 5a. I add here only a few details to help the reader decipher my citations of them, and locate the few translations that we have.

The "printed *Tanḥuma*," and the distinct *Tanḥuma* recension that Solomon Buber published in 1885, both cover the entire Pentateuch. They are divided into titled sections corresponding to the lectionary divisions of the Pentateuch, which are in turn divided into numbered subsections. *"Tanḥuma, Terumah* #11," for example, refers to subsection 11 of that section of the printed *Tanḥuma* that covers Exodus 25:1–27:19 (= the synagogue reading called *Terumah*). I cite Buber's *Tanḥuma* in the same way, adding the page number of Buber's edition.

As far as I know, the "printed *Tanḥuma*" has never been translated into English. An English translation of Buber's *Tanḥuma*, by John T. Townsend, is forthcoming.

Deuteronomy Rabbah, and the second parts of *Exodus Rabbah* and *Numbers Rabbah*, belong to the *Midrash Rabbah* series and have been translated with it into English (above). The very different recension of *Deuteronomy Rabbah* published by Saul Lieberman has never been translated, and is best cited by the page number of Lieberman's edition. The midrashic material of the *"Tanḥuma"* genre that has been incorporated into *Pesiqta*

---

7 And now the first part of *Exodus Rabbah*: Avigdor Shinan, *Midrash Shemot Rabbah Chapters I–XIV: A Critical Edition* ... (Jerusalem: Dvir, 1984).

Rabbati is, of course, to be found in Braude's translation of that midrash
(below).

9. Outside the midrashic groups I have discussed so far, there is a large
and ill-bounded mass of midrashim which scholars generally suppose to be
late. "Late" is of course a vague term; and, apart from *Pirqe de-Rabbi
Eliezer* (below), these texts offer few clues that would help us date them
any more precisely. Where, however, we compare their versions of any
given haggadah with parallels in Tosefta, either Talmud, or the midrashim
discussed above, their versions normally seem to be derivative. We therefore
assume, without trying to be more exact about it, that these texts were
compiled in the centuries that followed the completion of the Babylonian
Talmud.

There would be no point in my trying to catalogue these midrashim. I
note only those few that play some significant role in this book.

The *Midrash on Psalms* is divided into chapters (which correspond to the
psalms being expounded) and sub-divided into sections (which have nothing
to do with the verses of these psalms). Solomon Buber published the text;
William G. Braude translated it into English. I cite it by chapter, section,
and page number of Buber's edition.

Pesiqta Rabbati is, like the much older *Pesiqta de-Rab Kahana,* a midrash
to a series of Scriptural texts read in synagogue on festivals and special
Sabbaths. It is obviously composite, however; and we do better to speak of
it as a collection of midrashic homilies on the individual lections, which
the editor strung together without unifying. He drew his homilies from several sources, including *Pesiqta de-Rab Kahana* itself, an otherwise unknown
midrash of the "*Tanhuma*" genre, and a rather peculiar Messianic tract
which Bamberger [255] has supposed to reflect the political situation at
the beginning of the Muslim conquests[8].

Pesiqta's homilies are numbered sequentially, and are divided into sections. I cite this midrash by homily, section, and page number of Meir
Friedmann's edition. Braude has published an English translation.

Abot de-Rabbi Natan is normally classified as a midrash, on account of
its contents. But, in its form, it is a Gemara to the Mishnah tractate *Pirqe
Abot,* which has no Gemara in either the Palestinian or the Babylonian Talmud. Its date is very uncertain, and not all agree that it is late.

The text has come down to us in two recensions, which Solomon Schechter published in parallel columns. Both versions are divided into chapters;
I use these chapters, with Schechter's page numbers, in my citations. Judah

---

8 In chapter VIII, section B1, I touch on the issue of *Pesiqta*'s sources in connection with homily
20's story of the ascension of Moses.

Goldin has translated Version A into English; Anthony J. Saldarini, Version B.

Pirqe de-Rabbi Eliezer, too, has a form very different from that of the standard midrash. It is a retelling of Biblical history from the creation down to the Israelites' wandering in the wilderness, interrupted by repeated digressions. The text represents itself as a discourse of R. Eliezer b. Hyrcanus (ca. 100 A.D.), but this does not prevent the writer from invoking the names of many rabbis who lived long after Eliezer. As far as we can tell, few of these citations are of any value in tracing the writer's actual sources. He himself seems to have lived in the eighth or early ninth century, as we may gather from his "prophecies" of Muslim rule in Palestine — which he represents as taking place "in the end of days," that is, in his own time (chapter 30).

To my knowledge, no critical edition of *Pirqe de-Rabbi Eliezer* has appeared. Gerald Friedlander has translated it into English, from a manuscript. I cite it by the chapters into which it is divided.

Finally, there is the mysterious *Seder Eliyahu Rabbah,* and its companion *Seder Eliyahu Zuta.* The form and contents of these documents are baffling, their dates unknown[9]. Braude, who has recently translated them into English, has suggested (how seriously, I cannot tell) that there is something supernatural about them [248]. Braude's translation seems to me to give the illusion that they are far more intelligible than they in fact are.

I cite *Seder Eliyahu Rabbah* and *Zuta* by chapter, and by the page numbers of Meir Friedmann's edition. Helpfully, Braude marks these page numbers in the margins of his translation.

10. The *Yalquṭim* are not midrashim in the usual sense of the word, but midrashic scrapbooks. Their compilers, who lived in the later Middle Ages, copied out extracts from the midrashim and arranged them so as to serve as running commentaries on books of the Bible. As compositions, the *Yalquṭim* do not have the slightest originality; they have never been translated, because there is no reason why anyone but a specialist would want to read them. Their value lies in their preservation of otherwise lost midrashic materials (above, chapter VI, section 8b), and of important textual variants in extant sources (above, chapter VIII, section B2d).

The earliest and most important of these works is the thirteenth-century *Yalquṭ Shimᶜoni,* often referred to simply as *Yalquṭ,* which covers the entire Hebrew Bible. It is divided into relatively short sections; those attached

---

9 I have made a few observations in this book which may someday contribute to clearing up these questions: chapter VI, endnote *w*; chapter VIII, sections A3b, C8.

to the Pentateuch are numbered consecutively in one series, those covering the Prophets and Writings in a second series. One cites a passage of *Yalquṭ* by its section number and by the book of the Bible to which it is attached.

In this book, I have made very little use of the other *Yalquṭim*: the fourteenth-century *Yalquṭ Makhiri*, the seventeenth-century *Yalquṭ Re'ubeni*.

Appendix II

Islamic Reflections of Merkabah Traditions

It has long been a commonplace among critical scholars that many of the practices and teachings of early Islam, particularly the stories about the long chain of prophets who preceded Muhammad and prepared the way for his revelations, have their origins in Judaism. This is true not only of the Koran, which God supposedly revealed directly to Muhammad, but also of the mass of traditional commentary (*tafsir*) that grew up around the Koran in the first centuries of Islam [757,764], and of the oral traditions (*hadith*) that early Muslims repeated in Muhammad's name [769][1].

This issue is obviously important for the history of Islam and of its haggadic tradition. It is important, too, for the history of Jewish haggadah. The Jewish sources that influenced Muslim commentators and storytellers do not always seem to have been those that Judaism itself preserved. Behind the Muslim texts we can occasionally detect variant forms of Judaism [773]; or, at least, important and otherwise unknown variants of Jewish traditions. We cannot, therefore, leave our study of the *merkabah* without raising the question of what traces, if any, the *merkabah* traditions have left in Islamic literature.

We have several reasons to expect some positive answer. The Koran attributes to "the Jews" — presumably, those Arabian Jews with whom Muhammad was acquainted — the claim that "Allah's hand is fettered" (Surah 5:64)[2]. *Lamentations Rabbah* to 2:3 (ed. 55b—56a [190]), which

---

1 I cannot attempt even a basic bibliography of the relevant literature. Abraham Geiger's classic study, and the more recent discussions by Charles Cutler Torrey, S. D. Goitein, and Abraham Katsh, are perhaps the best places to start [766,794,767,778]. Rudi Paret's German commentary on the Koran is a fund of references to the scholarly literature [789]. M. J. Kister has published a particularly valuable study of early Muslim attitudes toward the use of Jewish and Christian materials [780]. — For all that has been written on the issue of Islam's Jewish roots, we are still very far from having exhausted the evidence or its implications, particularly as concerns the post-Koranic sources. My friend and colleague Gordon D. Newby (who helped me greatly with the research for this appendix) has done much fresh and exciting research on the subject, and more lies ahead [782,783,784,785,786,787].

2 I use Pickthall's translation [790] for all my quotations of the Koran.

interprets the Biblical verse to mean that God subjected his right hand to enslavement (*yemini meshu^cbedet*) when the Temple was destroyed, may perhaps be at the root of this statement. Yet a passage in *3 Enoch,* already noted by Tor Andrae [756a], sets forth the image far more vividly: R. Ishmael sees God's right hand fixed behind him, on account of the destruction of the Temple, and its five fingers weeping five rivers of tears (Schäfer, ##68–70, cf. #63; Odeberg, ch. 48A, cf. 44). This suggests that some at least of the *Hekhalot* traditions were known to Jews in seventh-century Arabia.

One in particular of Muhammad's Jewish acquaintances, the young Medinese Ibn Sayyad, seems to have cultivated a practice akin to the trance-journeys of the *Hekhalot*, with visions of the throne and the *hayyot* (above, chapter VI, section 8c). The Muslim sources claim that "Ibn Sayyad was approaching puberty" [771]. This fits in well with what we have seen of *Sar Torah*'s appeal for adolescent boys, and with the importance of the adolescent in the concluding material of *Hekhalot Zutarti* (above, chapter IX, section A2c).

Finally, early Muslim traditions credit Muhammad with a heavenly ascension (*mi^craj*), loosely connected with an aerial journey from Mecca to Jerusalem [768a,794a]. Specific resemblances between the details of the *mi^craj* and the ascension materials in the *Hekhalot* are, admittedly, few. But the very fact that such a feat is attributed to Muhammad may reflect a value placed on ascension in the milieu of early Islam.

These observations, however, do little more than raise possibilities. To explore these possibilities in any systematic way would require a separate study, which I hope some day to undertake — but not now. My present aim is a far more modest one, to call attention to a few clusters of data from Koran, *hadith,* and *tafsir,* bearing on the Islamic afterlife of the *merkabah* traditions.

I therefore present, without any claim to being exhaustive, Muslim descriptions of the carriers of God's throne (*hamalat al-^carsh,* in Arabic), which are obviously modelled after Ezekiel's *hayyot.* I also present *tafsir* material on the "Samiri" and the making of the calf, which I drew upon for my argument in chapter V (section 5d); and certain claims about Moses which bear on the Sinai-ascension traditions analyzed in chapter VIII. Finally, I quote the Koran's account of how Solomon tested the queen of Sheba, with a few pertinent *tafsir*s. These data seem to have some bearing on the question of "water, water" (above, chapter VI), although it is hard to see what that bearing might be.

I omit, with regret, any treatment of the tangled problems of the *mi^craj,* which seem connected on the one hand to the *haggadot* surrounding Jacob's ladder, and on the other to the Muslim traditions about the sanctity of Jerusalem. Gordon D. Newby and I have begun to explore these questions in two papers, so far unpublished [774,788]. We intend to resume our investigations in the near future.

1. The throne-bearers

The Muslim traditions about the *hamalat al-ʿarsh* have tended to cluster around two Koranic passages. "Those who bear the Throne [*yahmiluna al-ʿarsh*], and all who are round about it, hymn the praises of their Lord and believe in Him and ask forgiveness for those who believe ..." (Surah 40: 7). "And the angels will be on the sides thereof [of heaven], and eight will uphold the Throne of thy Lord [*yahmilu ʿarsh rabbika*] that day, above them" (Surah 69:17).

Neither of these passages shows any knowledge of the *merkabah* traditions; and the second contradicts them, by making the throne-bearers eight instead of four (see below). Later Muslim writers, as we will see, describe the throne-bearers along the lines laid down by Ezekiel. But they did not learn this from their holy book.

a) The "Umayyah" fragment. The tenth-century cosmologist and historian Maqdisi quotes two lines from the early seventh-century poet Umayyah b. Abi 'l-Salt, their subject apparently the deployment of angelic beings beneath God's throne:

> Israfil confined [*habasa*] the pure ones under it; there was no weak or base one among them.
> A man and an ox were under its right leg; an eagle at the other, and a lion set on guard. [Ed. 1:168; tr. 1:155 [747]]

A *hadith* attributed to Ibn ʿAbbas reports Muhammad as having given his approval to the second of these lines, as well as two lines, dealing with the rising sun, whose context is not clear but which seem to have no relevance to our subject (Ibn Hanbal, ed. 1:256 [741]; Ibn Kathir, ed. 4:71 [742]; Maybudi, ed. 8:451, 10:211 [748]).

While the poet's description obviously goes back ultimately to Ezekiel, he does not seem to have been directly familiar with the Biblical text. Unlike Ezekiel, he seems to envision one wholly human form and three wholly animal forms. We must assume some intermediate stage, akin to what we find in Revelation 4:6–8. I see no reason to believe that the poet was familiar with Surah 40:7 or 69:17.

If the poems attributed to Umayyah are to be considered genuine, these lines will have been written during Muhammad's lifetime. But even the skeptical Tor Andrae grants that "Umayyah's" poems are old, emanating from the early school of popular Koran interpreters whose productions are associated with the names of Ibn ʿAbbas and his disciples. He believes he has found a reference to them in a remark attributed to Hajjaj (died

714) [756]. Thus, genuine or not, these lines are among the earliest relevant material at our disposal.

We will see how later Islamic tradition brought "Umayyah's" image into conformity with Ezekiel's. We will also have something to say about Israfil.

b) "Eight mountain goats." Tirmidhi (ed. 9:59–60 [754]), Ibn Majah (ed. 1:69 [743]), Abu Da'ud (ed. 2:533 [737]), and Ibn Kathir (ed. 4:72 [742]) quote a *hadith* which represents Muhammad as describing the distance from earth to God's throne. From earth to heaven is a journey of "seventy-one, seventy-two, or seventy-three years." There are seven heavens, with equivalent distances between them. "Above the seventh heaven is an ocean [*bahr*], from top to bottom equivalent to the distance between heavens. Above that are eight mountain goats [*aw^{c}al*], from their hooves to their knees equivalent to the distance between heavens. On their backs is the throne, from top to bottom equivalent to the distance between heavens. God is above that."

The *hadith*'s cosmography is obviously akin to that of BT Hagigah 13a and the Targumic Tosefta to Ezekiel 1:1 (above, chapter VIII, section A4a –b). But it does not correspond exactly to either passage, or to their less developed parallels in the Palestinian Talmud and the midrashim (PT Berakhot 1:1, 2c; 9:1, 13a; *Gen. R.* 6:6, ed. 45–46 [188]; Tanh. *Terumah* #9; Tanh. Buber *Terumah* #8, ed. 47a [222]; *Midr. Psalms* 4:3, ed. 22a [199]). In at least one respect, the *hadith* agrees with PT Berakhot 9:1 and the passages from *Tanhuma* and *Midr. Psalms*, against the other rabbinic sources: it speaks explicitly of the "hooves" of the throne-bearers (Arabic *azlafihinna*; Hebrew *talfe hahayyot*). Perhaps it is this detail, perhaps the "horns of the *hayyot*" of BT Hagigah 13a, that suggested to the Muslim narrator that the throne-bearers have the shape of mountain goats. He presumably fixed their number at eight in conformity with the Koran, Surah 69:17.

None of the rabbinic sources suggest any explanation for the *hadith*'s uncertainty about the precise distance from earth to heaven, or for the origin of the figures that it gives. Later Muslim scholars, who apparently had fresh access to Jewish materials, "corrected" the *hadith*'s numbers to the common rabbinic measurement (found in all the sources cited above) of a five hundred years' journey. (So Maybudi, ed. 10:210–211 [748]; Suyuti, tr. 138–39 [775].)

As far as I know, no surviving Jewish source locates the celestial ocean above the seventh heaven, immediately beneath the throne and its carriers. Yet the *hadith*'s picture is oddly similar to that of Revelation 4:6–8, and to the midrash describing how the primordial waters "rose until they reached the throne of glory" (*Midr. Psalms* 93:5, ed. 207b [199]; translated above, chapter VI, section 7). Perhaps the *hadith* preserves an authentically

Jewish variant of the haggadah, which the editors of the rabbinic texts were unwilling to pass on. We saw in chapter VI why they might have wanted it suppressed.

c) The number of the throne-bearers. We saw that "Umayyah," following the *merkabah* tradition, lists four carriers of the throne; while the Koran and the "mountain-goat" *hadith* declare their number to be eight.

Several commentators claim Muhammad's authority for a reconciliation of the two numbers: the throne-bearers are now four, but will, as Surah 69: 17 suggests, be increased to eight on the day of resurrection. So Tabari (ed. 29:58–59 [752]), Maybudi (ed. 10:210 [748]), Zamakhshari (ed. 4: 152 [755]), and Baydawi (ed. 353 [738]). Ibn Kathir, however, seems to offer this as his own deduction, without prophetic authority (ed. 4:71–72 [742]). Maqdisi (ed. 1:167, tr. 1:155 [747]), Kisa'i (ed. 7, tr. 6 [744, 745]), and Maybudi himself (ed. 8:451 [748]) give it without any source or argumentation.

Tabari brings forward yet another explanation of the "eight" of Surah 69:17, on the authority of Ibn ᶜAbbas: they are eight *ranks* of angels, their actual number known only to God (ed. 29:58 [752]). This view would seem to exclude, or at least declare irrelevant to the Koranic text, both "Umayyah" and the "mountain-goat" *hadith.*

d) Man, ox, eagle, lion. Immediately before quoting "Umayyah's" lines, Maqdisi gives his own description of the throne-bearers: "They are now four: one has a face like that of a eagle, the second has a face like that of a lion, the third has a face like that of an ox, and the fourth has a face like that of a man." This is similar to "Umayyah's" description, yet not quite the same: the animal features are restricted to the throne-bearers' faces. Unless this detail actually occurred somewhere else in the poem, we must suppose that Maqdisi had some other source of information on the *hayyot,* beyond what he could glean from "Umayyah."

The twelfth-century Koran commentator Maybudi gives two independent descriptions of the throne-bearers. The first, anonymous, calls them "four angels: an angel in human form [*malak fi ṣurat rajul*], who asks sustenance [*yastarziqu*] for the children of Adam"; and so on, through ox, lion, and eagle, each "angel" asking sustenance for the type of animal he represents. Apart from the throne-bearers' intercessory activity, about which we will have to say more, this is essentially the picture given by "Umayyah." But Maybudi goes on to quote a second account, which he attributes to an early eighth-century authority, Wahb b. Munabbih, who may possibly have been of Jewish origin. "The throne-bearers are now four, each angel of them having four faces and four wings: a face like that of a man, a face like that of a lion," and so forth (ed. 8:451−452, 10:211 [748]). This second description is, of course, Ezekiel's.

The eleventh- or twelfth-century *Tales of the Prophets* of Kisa'i (ed. 7, tr. 6−7 [744,745]) seems to conflate the two accounts used by Maybudi. Kisa'i gives each of the throne-bearers four "forms" (ṣuwar). After listing the "forms," he adds that each intercedes[3] on behalf of the species it represents, that it may receive sustenance. The twelfth-century commentator Zamakhshari, on the other hand, seems to have regarded the notion that each throne-bearer has four faces as a novelty of suspicious origin − if, indeed, he was aware of it at all. His own description is essentially "Umayyah's." "It is said that one of them is in the form of a man, one in the form of a lion," and so forth (ed. 4:152 [755]).

Surah 40:7 may well have encouraged the belief that each "throne-bearer" intercedes for its own species. But I suspect that the roots of the belief go back to Christian exegesis of Revelation 4:6−8, which represents each "living creature" as having the form of a different animal. This is suggested by an Amharic (Ethiopian) commentary on the Book of Revelation, which comments as follows on 4:7: "The first resembled a lion, because he (the cherub) lives praying for the beasts and guarding the beasts. ... And the second resembled a cow, because he lives praying for the beasts and guarding the beasts. ... And the third resembled a man, because he lives praying for man and guarding man. ... The fourth resembled an eagle, because he prays for the birds and guards the birds" [108a].

Muslim scholars, we might conjecture, got their original impression of the throne-bearers from Christianity, through the mediation of "Umayyah's" poems. Later, perhaps as late as the twelfth century, some of them amended this picture in accord with Jewish tradition, attributed to Wahb b. Munabbih. We have already seen how Maybudi, and later Suyuti, brought a *hadith*'s cosmic measurements into agreement with the Jewish reckoning. We will presently see another example of the influence of Christian exegesis on the Islamic "throne-bearer" lore.

e) The detail of *the four wings* occurs only in the account of the throne-bearers that Maybudi attributes to Wahb. "Each angel of them has ... four wings. ... With two his face is covered, lest it be smitten by the light of the throne. With two he flies" (ed. 10:211, cf. 8:452 [748]).

Like "Wahb's" description of the four faces, this feature is plainly drawn from the *merkabah* tradition. It is particularly suggestive of BT Hagigah 13b, which harmonizes Isaiah's six-winged seraphim with Ezekiel's four-

---

3 *Yashfaᶜu*. The verb is in the wrong gender, an irregularity which seems to come from Kisa'i's combination of his sources.

winged *hayyot* by supposing that two wings were removed between Isaiah's time and Ezekiel's (above, chapter IV, section 3b end). "Which of them were removed? ... The rabbis say: Those with which they covered their feet." This leaves the *hayyot* with the four wings "Wahb" describes.

f) Earth to heaven. The early tenth-century commentator Tabari, who habitually makes exhaustive use of traditional material in interpreting the text of the Koran, quotes a *hadith* which describes the throne-bearers as having their feet on the seventh, lowest earth. Their shoulders, which bear the throne, emerge from the heavens. A variant adds: "Their feet are at the limits" (ed. 29:59 [752]; Mahmoud M. Ayoub quotes a similar passage [760]).

Statements in Maybudi and Zamakhshari illuminate this last, cryptic remark. "Their feet are at the limits of the earths, and the earths and the heavens are at their sides" (Maybudi, ed. 8:452 [748]). "The feet of the eight [!] angels are at the limits of the seventh earth, and the throne is above their heads" (Zamakhshari, ed. 4:152 [755]). "Their feet are on the lowest earth, and their heads surpass the throne" (Zamakhshari, ed. 3:415 [755]). "Their feet penetrated to the seventh earth, upon the surface of the ground, and became established" (Maybudi, ed. 8:453 [748]).

A particularly interesting passage seems to restrict this description to *one* of the throne-bearers:

[It is transmitted] from the Prophet: Do not contemplate the greatness of your Lord. Rather, contemplate the angels that God has created. There is an angelic creature called Israfil: one of the corners of the throne is upon his shoulders; his feet are on the lowest earth; his head has passed through seven heavens. Yet he is as tiny as a little bird in comparison to the greatness of God. [Zamakhshari, ed. 3:415 [755], cf. Gätje's translation [765]; briefer version in Maybudi, ed. 8:453 [748].]

Maybudi identifies the throne-bearer in human form (as opposed to the ox, lion, and eagle) with Israfil (ed. 8:451 [748]). We recall that "Umayyah" has Israfil confine the throne-bearers under the throne.

The "Israfil" of Zamakhshari's *hadith* is plainly modelled after the Talmudic Sandalphon; who, according to two manuscripts of BT Hagigah 13b, "stands on the lowest earth and whose head reaches to between the *hayyot*" (above, chapter IV, endnote *i*). Originally, it appears, Israfil was (like Sandalphon) associated with the throne-bearers, but distinct from them. So "Umayyah." At some point — whether before or after "Umayyah" we cannot tell — he was credited with Sandalphon's gigantic stature. Once he had been identified with the human-like throne-bearer, it was natural enough that all the throne-bearers be given this stature.

This last development, already presupposed in Tabari's sources, has its parallel in the medieval *Midrash Konen*: "The feet of the Shechinah are upon their heads [of the *hayyot*] in ᶜArabot, and their feet are in the lowest earth" (above, chapter VI, section 8a). Shall we infer a fresh infusion of Jewish ideas? Or was it, in this instance, the Islamic cosmographers who influenced the Jewish ones? I see no way to decide.

g) The four elements. Tabari quotes another *hadith*, which describes God's instructions to the throne-bearers. He tells the four that he has created them to carry his throne, and offers them whatever they will of strength. The first asks for the strength of water, since the throne has hitherto rested on water. The second asks for the strength of the heavens, the third for the strength of the earth, and the fourth for the strength of the winds. God grants each his request. They take the throne on their backs and carry it (ed. 29:59 [752]).

Three of these four "powers" correspond to the classical elements water, earth, and air. Granting that the equation is not complete ("the heavens" takes the place of fire), it is hard to avoid the impression that a connection of the four throne-bearers with the four elements underlies this narrative.

Maqdisi confirms this (ed. 1:168, tr. 1:155—156 [747]). He inveighs against certain "deviators" (*ashab al-zaygh, za'ighin*), who try to allegorize supernatural realities as symbols of philosophical conceptions. Among other things, they equate the throne-bearers with the four elements (*al-arkan al-arba^c*). Tabari's *hadith* surely represents this identification, in popular dress.

We may perhaps have here, as in the case of the throne-bearers' intercessions, an echo of Christian exegesis. Commenting on Ezekiel 1:6, Jerome discusses the interpretations of the four faces made by those who "follow the foolish wisdom of the philosophers." One of these identifies Ezekiel's *hayyot* with the four elements (*Commentary on Ezekiel*, ed. 11—13 [622]).

h) The serpent. Kisa'i (ed. 8, tr. 7 [744,745]) speaks of a gigantic serpent that encircles the throne. Its head is of pearl, its body of gold, its eyes rubies. It has forty thousand wings made of precious stones. On each feather stands an angel, praising God.

This serpent (*hayyah*, in Arabic) may conceivably be a distorted reflection of the *hayyot*, who are also around the throne — although, of course, in a different sense. The details would presumably be inner-Islamic developments. But one item suggests a Jewish origin. "If this serpent," says Kisa'i, "were not moderated in its praising [God], all creatures would be thunderstruck [*su^{c}iqat*] by the might of its voice." In BT Sanhedrin 95b, Sennacherib's soldiers perish when they are enabled to hear the singing of the *hayyot*.

The idea of being "thunderstruck," and the Arabic root expressing it (*s^{c}q*), will presently occupy us in a different context.

i) Miscellaneous. I note a few stray associations of Islamic throne-bearer lore with Jewish sources:

Some Muslim sources, like Ezekiel, designate the throne-bearers as cherubim (Arabic *karubiyyun*). So Maybudi (ed. 8:451, 10:211 [748]), Baydawi (ed. 206 [738]), and Ibn Kathir (ed. 4:71, 414 [742]). Other writers (Jahiz in the ninth century, Qazwini in the thirteenth) treat throne-bearers and cherubim as distinct categories of angels [793]. Baydawi (ed. 206 [738]) speaks of the cherubim as "the highest of the angels in rank, and the first of them to exist." Ibn Kathir (ed. 4:414 [742]) claims, on the authority of Ibn ᶜAbbas, that there are eight divisions of cherubim, each of them as numerous as men, jinn, devils, and angels put together.

Kisa'i (ed. 7–8, tr. 7 [744,745]) quotes Wahb b. Munabbih as saying that the throne-bearers "genuflect on their knees, and are erect on their feet" (*jathiya ᶜala rukabihim wa-qiyam ᶜala aqdamihim*). Whatever the first part of this statement may mean, the second is very suggestive of Ezekiel 1:7. See above, chapter IV, section 6.

Maqdisi, discussing the relationship between the terms *ᶜarsh* and *kursi* (two Koranic words for "throne"), cites the opinion of the "traditionists" (*ashab al-hadith*) that the *kursi* is God's footstool, the *ᶜarsh* presumably being the throne proper (ed. 1:167, tr. 1:155 [747]). Similarly, BT Hagigah 14a identifies the "thrones" of Daniel 7:9 as God's seat and his footstool.

Zamakhshari (ed. 3:415 [755]) and Kisa'i (ed. 7, tr. 6 [744,745]) describe the throne as made of a green jewel (*jawharah khadra'*; similarly Suyuti, ed. 3, tr. 132 [775]). This perhaps suggests the sapphire throne of Ezekiel 1:26.

God, unlike most builders, fashioned the roof of his structure (that is, the throne) first, and only afterwards laid the foundations (that is, the heavens and the earths). So Kisa'i (ed. 7, tr. 6 [744,745]), on the authority of Ibn ᶜAbbas. The image, though not its application, suggests BT Hagigah 12a: "The school of Hillel said to the school of Shammai [who claimed that God created the heavens before he created the earth]: According to you, a man first builds the upper story, and afterwards the house!"

j) The merkabah-ox and the calf. I have kept for last a particularly important passage, which Mahmoud M. Ayoub translates from the Shiᶜite Koran commentator Tabarsi[4]. It is represented as an utterance of Ali, Muhammad's son-in-law, to whom Shiᶜite Muslims assign overwhelming religious importance.

---

4 Not, of course, to be confused with Tabari.

"The heavens and earth and all the creatures therein are contained in the *kursi*. Four angels bear it by God's leave. The first angel has a human image; it is the noblest image before God. He invokes God continuously and intercedes for human beings, praying for their sustenance. The second angel is in the image of a bull who invokes God continuously, interceding for all domestic animals and praying for their sustenance. The third angel is in the image of an eagle which is the lord of all birds. He invokes God and intercedes for all birds and prays for their sustenance. The fourth is in the image of a lion which is the king of beasts. In his devotion to God he intercedes and prays for the sustenance of all wild beasts. The most beautiful of all these was the image of the bull; it was of the best stature. When, however, the people of the Children of Israel took the calf for a god which they worshipped with devotion instead of God, the angel ... bowed his head in shame before God because man had worshipped something resembling him. He feared lest he be afflicted with punishment." [761]

The conclusion of this passage, which links the "bull" of the *merkabah* to the calf of the desert idolatry, will serve as bridge to our next topic.

2. The calf and the "Samaritan"

"And the folk of Moses, after (he had left them), chose a calf (for worship), (made) out of their ornaments, of saffron hue[5], which gave a lowing sound. Saw they not that it spake not unto them nor guided them to any way? They chose it, and became wrong-doers" (Surah 7:148).

So runs one of several Koranic allusions to the Israelites' worship of the calf (2:51–54, 92, 4:153, 7:148–153, 20:80–97). The last of these passages gives the fullest details:

83. And (it was said): What hath made thee hasten from thy folk, O Moses?

84. He said: They are close upon my track. I hastened unto Thee, my Lord, that Thou mightest be well pleased.

85. He said: Lo! We have tried thy folk in thine absence, and As-Sâmiri hath misled them.

86. Then Moses went back to his folk, angry and sad. He said: O my people! Hath not your Lord promised you a fair promise? Did the time appointed then appear too long for you, or did ye wish that wrath from your Lord should come upon you, that ye broke tryst with me?

87. They said: We broke not tryst with thee of our own will, but we were laden with burdens of ornaments of the folk, then cast them (in the fire), for thus As-Sâmiri proposed.

88. Then he produced for them a calf, of saffron hue, which gave forth a lowing sound. And they cried: This is your god and the god of Moses, but he hath forgotten.

89. See they not, then, that it returneth no saying unto them and possesseth for them neither hurt nor use?

90. And Aaron indeed had told them beforehand: O my people! Ye are but being seduced therewith, for lo! your Lord is the Beneficent, so follow me and obey my order.

91. They said: We shall by no means cease to be its votaries till Moses return unto us.

92. He (Moses) said: O Aaron! What held thee back when thou didst see them gone astray,

93. That thou followedst me not? Hast thou then disobeyed my order?

---

5 The Arabic word *jasad*^{an}, here and in Surah 20:88, would more naturally mean "possessing a body." But, Pickthall notes, since this "body" would have to be "of flesh and blood, the meaning 'saffron-coloured' better fits the context" [790]. We will presently see that matters are not quite so simple.

94. He said: O son of my mother! Clutch not my beard nor my head! I feared lest thou shouldst say: Thou hast caused division among the Children of Israel, and hast not waited for my word.

95. (Moses) said: And what hast thou to say, O Sâmiri?

96. He said: I perceived what they perceive not, so I seized a handful from the footsteps of the messenger, and then threw it in. Thus my soul commended to me.

97. (Moses) said: Then go! And lo! in this life it is for thee to say: Touch me not! and lo! there is for thee a tryst thou canst not break. Now look upon thy god of which thou hast remained a votary. Verily we will burn it and will scatter its dust over the sea.

This perplexing narrative stirred the curiosity of medieval Muslim commentators, as well as that of modern Orientalists [763,768,776,789, 792b,795]. What the commentators say about it often appears to be their own inferences from the Koranic text. But sometimes they seem to draw on independent traditions, which illuminate the background of the Koranic story and the Jewish haggadah from which it came[6].

a) Who was al-Samiri? Surah 20, as we saw, introduces al-Samiri as the maker of the calf, but makes no effort to explain who he was. The other Koranic passages on the calf do not mention him at all.

Muslim commentators try to fill the gap.

Tabari (ed. 16:206 [752]) attributes the following identification to Qatadah: "By God, the Samiri was one of the great ones of the children of Israel, from a tribe called Samirah. But the enemy of God became a hypocrite after he divided the sea with the children of Israel ... and their remnants today say, 'Do not touch' " (referring to Surah 20:97).

Zamakhshari (ed. 2:549 [755]) offers several alternatives, the first of which clearly ties al-Samiri to the Samaritans. He "is connected with a tribe of the children of Israel called al-Samirah. Al-Samirah is said to be a people of the Jews, differing from them in part of their religion. It is also said that he was of the people of Bajarma. It is also said that he was an infidel [ʿilj] of Kirman, his name Musa [= Moses] b. Zafar." He was of a cattle-worshipping people, Zamakhshari continues; and he hypocritically pretended to be a Muslim.

The twelfth-century commentator Razi (ed. 22:101 [751]) slightly varies Zamakhshari's report. "Ibn ʿAbbas said, in the narrative of Saʿid b. Jubayr: Samiri was an infidel of the people of Kirman who had come to Egypt; he was of a people who worshipped cattle. But most people hold that he was of the nobles of the Israelites, from a tribe called al-Samirah. Zajjaj and ʿAta quoted Ibn ʿAbbas: He was an Egyptian, a client [jar] of Moses, and he had believed in him."

---

6 Several of the items cited below also occur in the *tafsirs* to Surah 2:51, whose contents Mahmoud M. Ayoub has recently summarized in English [757].

Maybudi (ed. 6:162 [748]) reports: "Al-Samiri was from a cattle-worshipping people, the first known hypocrite of the sons of Adam. He was from the town of Bajarwan. It is said, too, that he was an infidel of Kirman. But the dominant interpretation is that he was one of the nobles of the children of Israel, from a tribe called Samirah. It is said that he and Moses were related; that he was not named Samiri but was from a town named Samirah, his name being Musa b. Zafar."

Maqdisi, too, knows this last proposal: "Samiri was Moses' cousin, his name Musa b. Tufayr. It is said he was of the people of Bajarma" (ed. 3:91, tr. 3:93 [747]).

Baydawi (ed. 603 [738]) abbreviates the suggestions of the earlier commentators. "Al-Samiri was connected with an Israelite tribe called Samirah. It is also said that he was an infidel from Kirman, or of Bajarma, named Musa b. Zafar. He was a hypocrite."

Apart from Maqdisi, all the writers I have cited at least entertain the possibility that al-Ṣamiri was so called because he was associated with a people claiming Israelite descent; that is, the Samaritans. Zamakhshari seems the best informed on who the Samaritans are. The claim that he was one of the Israelite nobles is perhaps linked to Exodus 24:11. The traditions that connect him with Bajarma (= Bajarwan?)[7] or Kirman are less easy to explain, and demand investigation. But the most interesting claim of all is that he was related to Moses (Maqdisi, Maybudi), was otherwise closely affiliated with him (Razi), or shared his name (Maqdisi, Zamakhshari, Maybudi, Baydawi). The Muslim tradition perhaps sensed that the maker of the calf was a mirror image, or a dark shadow, of Moses.

b) "The footsteps of the messenger." The commentators regularly understand "a handful from the footsteps of the messenger" (20:96) as dust from the footprint of the angel Gabriel's horse. Thus, Tabari quotes certain scholars (*ahl al-ᶜilm ... baᶜduhum*) as saying that Samiri fashioned the calf, "then threw some of the dust from Gabriel's horse's hoof into its mouth, and it lowed." He quotes Qatadah: Samiri "had bound up in his turban or his clothing a handful [of dust] from the footprint of Gabriel's horse, and he threw it with the jewellery and the form [?], and *he produced for them a calf, of saffron hue, which gave forth a lowing sound,* and it began to low like a cow. He said: *This is your god and the god of Moses*" (ed. 16:200 [752]). In a comment which Tabari attributes to Ibn ᶜAbbas, however, the dust seems to be from the footprint of Gabriel himself (ed. 16:201 [752]).

Zamakhshari has Samiri take dust from the footprint of "Ḥizum, the horse of Gabriel" (ed. 2:550 [755]). Satan had revealed to him that, when

---

7 A village near Raqqa, in Mesopotamia, according to Huart's note on his translation of Maqdisi.

this dust is mixed with an inanimate object, it will become animate. Later, Zamakhshari reports a variant reading of the text of 20:96, which he attributes to the early Koran transmitter Ibn Mas^cud: not *athar al-rasul* ("the footsteps of the messenger"), but *athar faras al-rasul* ("the footsteps of the messenger's horse"). He comments:

> You may ask why the text calls him *al-rasul*, and not Gabriel or the Holy Spirit. I reply: When the time came for [Moses] to go to the mountain, God sent [*arsala*] to Moses Gabriel, riding on Ḥizum, the horse of life [*faras al-ḥayah*], that he might transport him. When Samiri saw it, he said, "There's something important about that!", and took a handful of the dust of its footprint. When Moses asked him for his story, he said: "I took from the footprint of the horse of the one who was sent [*al-mursal*] to you, on the day of the appointed time." Perhaps he did not know it was Gabriel. [Ed. 2:551 [755]]

Baydawi (ed. 604 [738]) seems to condense Zamakhshari's comments. Paraphrasing Surah 20:96, he has Samiri tell Moses: "I saw what they did not see; that is, that Gabriel came to you on the horse of life [*faras al-ḥayah*]." (He does not use the name Ḥizum.) Why did Samiri refer to Gabriel as "the messenger"? "Perhaps he did not know he was Gabriel. Or, he wanted to make reference to the time when he was sent to him [*ursila ilayhi*; that is, to Moses] to carry him to the mountain."

Zamakhshari's exegesis seems to echo the "Sinai" version of the calf-*merkabah* tradition (above, chapter V, section 5f), in that it connects the fatal appearance of the divine being with the revelation at Sinai. Gabriel's horse has completely obscured Ezekiel's *ḥayyot*. But perhaps a trace of the original survives in the odd phrase "horse of life," *faras al-ḥayah*. This may be a distorted reflection of Hebrew *parsat ha-ḥayyah*, "the hoof of the ḥayyah"; cf. Targ. Ezekiel 1:7.

I cannot explain the name Ḥizum. The great medieval Arabic lexical compilation *Taj al-^cArus* (*s.v.* ḥzm [821]) records this as the name of the horse that Gabriel rode when he came to transport Moses, and notes that it is sometimes written with a final *nun* in place of *mim*. Could we perhaps read the resulting consonants *ḥayyazun*, and understand the word as a conflation of Hebrew *ḥayyah* with Greek *zōon*, both of them terms for the beings that Ezekiel saw? This suggestion is, I realize, very farfetched. Yet it perhaps draws some slight support from Zamakhshari's qualification of Ḥizum as *faras al-ḥayah*, which hints that his name is somehow connected with the root *ḥyy*.

c) The revelation at the sea. Beside the "Sinai" tradition, the commentators preserve traces of a variant tradition which connected the appearance of Gabriel on his horse with the crossing of the Red Sea. We recall the claim, which Tabari attributes to Qatadah, that Samiri "became a hypocrite after he divided the sea with the children of Israel" (ed. 16:206 [752]). Commenting on Surah 7:142, Tabari asserts, in the name of Abu Bakr b. ^cAbd Allah al-Hudhayli, that Samiri took a handful of dust from the foot-

print of Gabriel's horse, "when he saw him in the sea" (ed. 9:49 [752]).
We will presently note another passage of Tabari bearing on this issue.

Razi (ed. 22:101 [751]) seems to hint that the calf episode took place
by the sea, when he speaks of the people staying with Aaron on the seashore (*ᶜala sahil al-bahr*; cf. Exodus 14:30). He quotes, without giving a
source, the following story (ed. 22:105): "Some of the Jews said to Ali:
'You had not buried your prophet before you fell into dissension.' He replied: 'We differed from him, but not about him[8]. But as for you, your feet
had not dried from the water of the sea before you said to your prophet:
"Make for us a god, just as they have gods" ' " (cf. Exodus 32:1). Admittedly, this dialogue does not mention Samiri or Gabriel's horse. But it implies that the apostasy took place immediately after the crossing of the Red
Sea, and perhaps had some connection with it.

Maybudi, however, is the most explicit. He paraphrases Surah 20:96: "I
knew what the children of Israel did not know; that is, on the day they
entered the sea [*yawm dukhul al-bahr*]" (ed. 6:166 [748]).

Perhaps Baydawi also hints at this connection, when he suggests that the
Israelites took possession of the Egyptians' jewellery when "the sea threw
it upon the shore, after they were drowned" (ed. 603 [738]).

d) The jewellery of the Egyptians plays an important role in the commentators' explanations of how Samiri managed to seduce the Israelites
into worshipping the calf.

In Surah 20:87, the Israelites tell Moses that *we were laden with burdens
of ornaments of the folk.* Tabari quotes Mujahid as explaining that this was
"the jewellery that they had borrowed from Pharaoh's people" (cf. Exodus
12:35–36). The Arabic word *awzar*, "burdens," can also mean "sins" (cf.
Baydawi on this verse). This perhaps explains why, according to Tabari, Ibn
ᶜAbbas represents the people as saying: "We sinned through that which we
acquired of our enemies' jewellery" (Tabari, ed. 16:199 [752]).

Qatadah (as quoted by Tabari, ed. 16:200 [752]) has Samiri play on the
people's sense of guilt. "God had appointed thirty nights for Moses [to be
with him], then added ten more. When the thirty days had elapsed, God's
enemy Samiri said: 'That which happened to you [namely, that Moses had
not yet come back] happened as punishment for the jewellery that was
with you. Come on!' This was the jewellery they had borrowed from Pharaoh's people, which was with them when they travelled. They threw it
[?] to him, and he fashioned it into the shape of an ox [*baqarah*]." We
have already seen Qatadah's account of how Samiri brought this form to
life (above, section b).

---

8 *Innama ikhtalafna ᶜanhu wa-ma ikhtalafna fihi.* The remark is odd, and would make better sense
if reversed.

Al-Suddi (as quoted by Tabari, ed. 16:200 [752]) relates as follows: Samiri took "some of the dust of the footprint, the footprint of Gabriel's horse." When Moses went off, he left Aaron behind as his deputy, saying he would return after thirty days. When he stayed forty, Aaron blamed this on the fact that the Israelites had no right to the Egyptians' jewellery. They must dig a pit and bury it there. So far so good. But then (says Suddi) Samiri threw the handful of dust into the pit, and "God brought forth from the jewellery *a calf, of saffron hue, which gave forth a lowing sound* [Surah 20:88]." (There follows a claim, which contradicts what has preceded, that Moses indeed said he would return after forty days; but the Israelites counted a night and a day as two days, and therefore waited only twenty days. Both these explanations of the Israelites' despairing impatience recur in the commentaries.)

Tabari's sources, as we see, are not quite sure whether it was Samiri who raised the objection to the Israelites' keeping the Egyptians' jewellery, or whether Aaron originated this objection and Samiri then took advantage of it. A story (*khabar*) quoted by Razi perhaps reflects this uncertainty: "Aaron said: 'It [the jewellery] is impure; purify yourselves of it.' Samiri said: 'Moses has been detained on account of the jewellery' " (ed. 22:103 [751]).

Baydawi, who similarly portrays Samiri as manipulating the people's guilt, explains that the *ornaments of the folk* (Surah 20:87) are "the jewellery of the Egyptians, which we [Israelites] borrowed from them when we were plotting to leave Egypt, on the pretext of a wedding [*bismi 'l-ʿurs*][9]. Some say that they borrowed it for a festival [*ʿid*] of theirs, and then did not return it when they left because they were afraid [their departure] would become known." As we have seen, Baydawi offers a third alternative: the sea cast up the Egyptians' jewellery after it drowned them (ed. 603 [738]). The reference to a "festival" is presumably based on Exodus 5:1; while the "wedding" perhaps reflects the rabbinic conception of Sinai as a wedding between God and Israel.

In chapter V, section 5d, I have tried to show that these traditions linking the calf with the "borrowed" jewellery provide the key to the problem of how the Micah of the midrash, and hence the Koran's Samiri, came to be in the calf story in the first place.

e) The animation of the calf. Some of the commentators touch on the question of how — or even whether — Samiri was able to bring the calf to life.

---

9 So also the *Tafsir al-Jalilayn* to Surah 20:87 [746].

We saw that Tabari quotes al-Suddi to the effect that it was indeed Samiri who threw the dust into the pit filled with jewellery, but it was God who brought forth the animate calf. Zamakhshari (ed. 2:550 [755]) develops this idea in a particularly ingenious way. Gabriel, he explains, is equivalent to the Holy Spirit (*ruḥ al-quds*). God gave the Spirit the power that, when the dust touched by its horse's hoof comes into contact with an inanimate object, God will give it life. In a similar way, Jesus Christ was born of a virgin.

Tabari (ed. 16:205 [752]) quotes Ibn Abi Jurayj as making the now-familiar claim that Samiri got his *handful* "from beneath the hoof of Gabriel's horse," and that he "threw it upon the Israelites' [!] jewellery." But he adds that the calf "lowed" because the wind blew through it. This is evidently an effort to rationalize the story, by reducing the calf's animation to a piece of trickery by Samiri.

Razi also mentions the theory that the calf's voice was an illusion caused when the wind blew through holes, but seems to reject it. He invokes an explanation which supposedly originated with Ibn ʿAbbas: Samiri tricked Aaron into praying that God might give him whatever he requested; and, since Aaron was a prophet, God naturally answered his prayer. Samiri then requested that the calf be made to low (ed. 22:103–104 [751]).

I noted at the beginning of this section that the word *jasad^{an}* in 7:148 and 20:88, which Pickthall translates "of saffron hue," would more naturally mean "possessing a body." And this is how some of the commentators seem to have taken it. *Tafsir al-Jalilayn* glosses, "flesh and blood." Some such belief in the calf's transformation perhaps underlies a comment on 20:97 which Tabari (ed. 16:208 [752]) attributes to al-Suddi: Moses "seized it [the calf] and slaughtered it [*fa-dhabaḥahu*], then filed it down with a file and scattered it in the sea. There was no sea that day into which a bit of it did not fall."

f) "I perceived what they perceive not." Interpreting these words of Surah 20:96, Tabari discusses the suggestion that Samiri's "perception" was intellectual. In support of this view, he quotes a tradition in the name of Ibn Jurayj: "When Pharaoh killed the children, Samiri's mother said, 'If only I had removed him from me, that I might not see him, and not know of his death.' She put him in a cave [*ghar*]. Gabriel came, put his hand into [Samiri's] mouth [*fa-jaʿala kaff nafsihi fi fihi*], and began nursing him with honey and milk. He did not stop nursing him until he recognized him [that is, until Samiri was old enough to recognize him]. Thus it was that he recognized him, when he said, *I seized a handful from the footsteps of the messenger*" (ed. 16:204–205 [752]).

Ayoub translates a variant of this story, attributed to Ibn ʿAbbas, from Tabari's commentary on Surah 2:51. Samiri "was hidden in a cave at birth by his mother for fear of being slain. Gabriel used to come and nurse him by placing his fingers in his mouth to suck; in some there was honey, in others milk, and still others ghee for the infant's nourishment. This went on until the boy grew up. Thus he recognized Gabriel when he saw him at the seashore" [758]. Note that this version supposes that the revelation took place at the Red Sea (above).

Baydawi draws on this tradition when he remarks, on Surah 20:96: "It is said that the reason he recognized him was that his mother abandoned him, for fear of Pharaoh, after his birth, and Gabriel nourished him until he could take care of himself" (ed. 604 [738]). There is some tension between the tradition and the claim of the commentators – including Baydawi himself – that Samiri did *not* recognize Gabriel, and therefore called him just "the messenger" (above, section b).

The Muslim story is obviously derived from the rabbinic haggadah that has God appear, in the form of a handsome young man, to nourish the Israelite babies abandoned in the open field. Thus it was that these babies, grown, could recognize him at the Red Sea and say, *This is my God* (Exodus 15:2)[10]. The Muslim storytellers have transferred to Gabriel rabbinic accounts of the appearance of God, and to Samiri the experiences and actions of the whole Israelite people. This process helps explain how they transformed the *merkabah* into the horse of Gabriel.

3. Death and resurrection at Sinai

Several passages of the Koran make use of derivatives of the Arabic root *ṣ*^{c}*q*, "to be thunder-struck, stupefied." In Surah 2:19, the plural noun *ṣawā*^{c}*iq* fairly clearly means "thunder-claps" (Pickthall). Just as clearly, *ṣawā*^{c}*iq* means "thunderbolts" in 13:13. In 41:13—18, God sends the *ṣā*^{c}*iqah* (singular of *ṣawā*^{c}*iq*) to punish the unbelieving tribes of ^{c}Ad and Thamud. Here, too, Pickthall's "bolt" and "thunderbolt" are reasonable translations.

Surah 52:45—47 advises Muhammad to let the unbelievers alone "till they meet their day, in which they will be thunder-stricken [*yuṣ*^{c}*aquna*], a day in which their guile will naught avail them, nor will they be helped. And verily, for those who do wrong, there is a punishment beyond that." Surah 39:68, a passage to which we must later refer, describes the day of resurrection: "And the trumpet is blown, and all who are in the heavens

---

10 *Ex. R.* 23:8; above, chapter VI, section 5c. The midrash most strikingly resembles the Islamic story in its detail of how God nourished the babies: "He would put two pieces of flint in his hand. One of them would suckle [the baby] with oil, the other with honey. So it is written: *He suckled him with honey from the rock, [with oil from the flinty rock*; Deuteronomy 32:13]."

and all who are in the earth swoon away [*sa^ciqa*], save him whom Allah willeth. Then it is blown a second time, and behold them standing waiting!"

Three passages use this root to describe events at Mount Sinai. " ... ye said: O Moses! We will not believe in thee till we see Allah plainly; and even while ye gazed the lightning seized you [*akhadhatkumu 'l-sa^ciqah*]. Then We revived you after your extinction [*mawtikum*], that ye might give thanks" (2:55—56). Here and in the parallel 4:153 (which, however, does not mention the resurrection) we obviously have an echo of the rabbinic *haggadot* on the Israelites' death and resurrection at Sinai (above, chapter VIII, section B2f, 3c) [779]; and Pickthall's renderings "lightning" and "storm of lightning" (4:153) no longer seem quite adequate. Finally, Surah 7:143 has Moses alone experience the *sa^ciqah*:

> And when Moses came to Our appointed tryst and his Lord had spoken unto him, he said: My Lord! Show me (Thy Self), that I may gaze upon Thee. He said: Thou wilt not see Me, but gaze upon the mountain! If it stand still in its place, then thou wilt see Me. And when his Lord revealed (His) glory to the mountain he sent it crashing down. And Moses fell down senseless [*kharra musa sa^ciq^{an}*]. And when he woke he said: Glory unto Thee! I turn unto Thee repentant, and I am the first of (true) believers.

A little further on, the Koran speaks of a mysterious "trembling" (*rajfah*) that seized seventy men whom Moses had chosen for God's "appointed tryst" (7:155; cf. Exodus 24:9—11). The Muslim exegetical tradition seems to have interpreted this passage in the light of Surah 2:55—56, and to have conflated the two narratives. The commentators thus connect the *sa^ciqah* with the *rajfah*, and suppose that Moses' seventy companions were its victims [759,779]. Maqdisi lists, among the miracles of the wilderness period, "the seizure of the seventy men by the *sa^ciqah*, and their resurrection" (ed. 3:94, tr. 3:96 [747]).

Ayoub sums up what the commentators on 2:55—56 have to say about the *sa^ciqah*:

> Tabari interprets the word *sa^ciqah* as follows. "It is a dreadful portent or event which causes the person experiencing it to die of fear. It may also cause a person to lose his mind or another of his senses. It matters not whether the *sa^ciqah* is fire or earthquake. Death does not necessarily follow, as God says of Moses, '*Kharra sa^ciqan*' [he fell, stunned], [Q. 7:143]; that is, he swooned" (Tabari, II, p. 83; see also Qurtubi, I, pp. 403—404; Zamakhshari, I, p. 282). Most early traditionists, however, asserted that the men actually died and were later brought back to life. ᶜUrwah ibn Ruwaym, wishing to retain the literal meaning of the verse, said, "Some of them were killed by the *sa^ciqah*, while the others looked on; then they were revived, and the others killed" (Ibn Kathir, I, p. 162). [759]

Tabari, we see, understands Surah 7:143 to mean only that Moses swooned. Yet, in his commentary on this verse (ed. 9:50—52 [752]), he quotes a long story whose climax implies that Moses died and was brought back to life. He attributes the story to Ibn Ishaq, who supposedly had it from "a certain expert in the traditions of the people of Scripture" (*ba^cd ahl al-^cilm al-awwal bi'ahadith ahl al-kitab*). Its attribution alone is enough to commend it to our attention.

Moses, the story runs, prayed to be granted a direct vision of God. God warned him that "none can see me and live" (cf. Exodus 33:20), but finally agreed to grant him a vision. At God's command, Moses sat in an appointed spot at the top of the mountain, while God paraded his hosts before him. One after another, the troops of the seven heavens showed themselves to the increasingly frightened Moses. When God's glory itself descended on the mountain, Moses expired in terror. He thus learned, at first hand, that no one can see God and live.

Colette Sirat, who has translated the entire passage into French[11], perhaps exaggerates in calling it "a Jewish midrash in Muslim garb" [791]. But several of its details, at least, plainly derive from the *merkabah* tradition. Thus, some angels look like lions and some like eagles, while others have four faces. (Still others are fire and snow combined. Cf. *Pesiqta de-Rab Kahana, Wa-Yehi be-Yom Kallot Mosheh* #3, ed. 5–6 [206], and its parallels; and above, chapter III, section 3d.) Their praises sound "like the tumult of a mighty army" (*ka-lajab al-jaysh al-ʿazim*; cf. Ezekiel 1:24), or "like the sound of great thunder" (*ka-ṣawt al-raʿd al-shadid*; cf. Ezekiel 3: 12–13). At one point, we read that God has placed the distance of a five hundred years' journey between himself and his angels; and we recognize in this a staple of rabbinic cosmography.

The account of Moses' death and resurrection is particularly striking. God had told Moses, at the beginning of the revelation, to "look at the great rock at the top of the mountain. Behind and beneath it, there is a narrow spot, just wide enough for you to sit in." From that spot, Moses witnessed the terrifying spectacle. At its climax, "Moses son of Amram fell thunder-struck [*kharra ... ṣaʿiq^{an}*, the expression used in Surah 7:143] on his face, his spirit no longer with him. In his mercy, God sent life. In his mercy, he covered him. He inverted the rock that was over him [or, "that he was upon"], making it like a stomach [*maʿidah*], in the shape of a dome, that he might not be burned up. The spirit raised him up, like a mother raising up her fetus [*janin*] when it is thrown down."

Not all of these details are clear. But it is plain enough that the storyteller has turned the rock on the mountain into a womb from which Moses, having died, is born again. The theme of rebirth — latent, as Ira Chernus has shown [512], in the rabbinic accounts of the Israelites' death and resurrection at Sinai (above, chapter VIII, section C2c) — is here made explicit.

The Arabic story has Moses fall *on his face*, and implies that he is in danger of being burned up. Both details are reminiscent of a passage in the Ozhayah text, which Chernus has aptly compared to the stories of the Is-

---

11 Gordon D. Newby has prepared an English version, as part of his so far unpublished reconstruction and translation of Ibn Ishaq's lost *Book of Creation* [783].

raelites' death and resurrection. The *merkabah* traveller must not be frightened of the fires he sees spurting from the seventh palace into the sixth, but must lie *on his face* and stuff wool into all his apertures, "so that your soul cannot escape before I can get there and revive you" (above, chapter IX, section A2b).

Tirmidhi quotes a *hadith*, according to which one of Muhammad's companions struck a certain Jew who had implied, speaking in the market place of Medinah, that Moses was superior to Muhammad. The Prophet, it seems, disapproved. He quoted Surah 39:68: "*And the trumpet is blown, and all who are in the heavens and all who are in the earth swoon away* [*ṣaᶜiqa*], *save him whom Allah willeth. Then it is blown a second time, and behold them standing waiting!* I will be the first to raise my head, and I will see Moses holding on to one of the pillars of God's throne. I will not know whether he raised his head before me, or whether God spared him altogether." He added, rather cryptically: "If anyone says, 'I am greater than Jonah son of Amittai,' he is a liar" (Tirmidhi, ed. 8:370−371 [754]).

This *hadith* appears also in other collections: Ibn Hanbal, ed. 2:264, 451, 3:33, 40−41 [741]; Bukhari, ed. 2:354, 359, 360−361, 3:243, 322 [739]. Three of Bukhari's versions (ed. 2:354, 360−361, 3:243) suggest that Moses may perhaps be spared this eschatological *ṣaᶜiqah* because he had already experienced a *ṣaᶜiqah* at Mount Sinai. Many of the parallels either omit or transmit independently the concluding reference to Jonah. This remark does not seem to follow very well from what precedes, and I can only account for it by supposing it has something to do with Christian use of Jonah as a symbol of the resurrection.

Maqdisi quotes several interpretations of the Koran's words, *save him whom Allah willeth*. The exception perhaps applies to the martyrs around the throne; or to the houris; or to "Moses, since he had already been thunder-struck [*ṣaᶜiqa*] once[12]"; or to Gabriel, Michael, Israfil, the angel of death, and the throne-bearers (ed. 2:223, tr. 2:188 [747]).

We can hardly doubt that the *hadith* echoes that detail of the Jewish ascension stories according to which Moses laid hold of God's throne (above, chapter VIII, section B2d). Certain of its versions, supported by Maqdisi's comment on Surah 39:68, imply a connection between that act and the death and resurrection at Sinai. Some such linkage may underlie the story in *Pesiqta Rabbati* 20.

Tabari's citation of "the traditions of the people of Scripture," and the setting of the *hadith* − conflict between a Muslim and a Jew − help con-

---

12 Reading *li-'annahu ṣaᶜiqa marratan*. Huart, reading *la* for *li-'annahu*, translates misleadingly: "Moïse, qui n'est jamais mort."

firm that the material we have considered in this section is rooted in Judaism. More specifically, I believe, it derives from the traditions of the Shabuᶜot cycle. Future research must clarify the details of its development.

4. Solomon, the queen of Sheba, and the "water test"

David Brady has noticed that there is a curious resemblance between the "sea of glass" of Revelation 4:6, 15:2, and an episode of the Koran's story of Solomon's meeting with the queen of Sheba [762]. C. C. Rowland has made the same comparison, and extended it to the Talmudic warning against saying "water, water" [159].

The Koranic context runs as follows: King Solomon, who knows the language of the birds, has massed "his armies of the jinn and humankind, and of the birds" (Surah 27:17). The hoopoe, originally missing from the assembly, shows up at last with a report from the land of Sheba. "Lo! I found a woman ruling over them, and she hath been given (abundance) of all things, and hers is a mighty throne. I found her and her people worshipping the sun instead of Allah; and Satan maketh their works fairseeming unto them, and debarreth them from the way (of Truth), so that they go not aright; [s]o that they worship not Allah, Who bringeth forth the hidden in the heavens and the earth, and knoweth what ye hide and what ye proclaim, Allah; there is no God save Him, the Lord of the Tremendous Throne" (27:23–26). Pickthall's translation disguises the fact, which was to strike Tabari (ed. 19:151 [752]), that the Koran uses the same expression for the queen's "mighty throne" and for God's "Tremendous Throne": (al-)ᶜarsh (al-)ᶜaẓim.

Solomon summons the queen to surrender (or, to Islam; the Arabic could mean either), and scorns her efforts to buy him off (27:27–37). Then:

> 38. He said: O chiefs! Which of you will bring me her throne before they come unto me, surrendering[13]?
> 39. A stalwart of the jinn said: I will bring it thee before thou canst rise from thy place. Lo! I verily am strong and trusty for such work.
> 40. One with whom was knowledge of the Scripture said: I will bring it thee before thy gaze returneth unto thee. And when he saw it set in his presence, (Solomon) said: This is of the bounty of my Lord ...
> 41. He said: Disguise her throne for her that we may see whether she will go aright or be of those not rightly guided.

---

13 Or, "as Muslims." Tabari, taking the word in the latter sense, explains that once the queen of Sheba had become a Muslim Solomon would no longer have a right to seize her property. He was therefore anxious to get hold of her throne before she converted (ed. 19:160 [752]).

42. So, when she came, it was said (unto her): Is thy throne like this? She said: (It is) as though it were the very one. And (Solomon said): We were given the knowledge before her and we had surrendered (to Allah).

43. And (all) that she was wont to worship instead of Allah hindered her, for she came of disbelieving folk.

44. It was said unto her: Enter the hall. And when she saw it she deemed it a pool and bared her legs. (Solomon) said: Lo! it is a hall, made smooth, of glass. She said: My Lord! Lo! I have wronged myself, and I surrender with Solomon unto Allah, the Lord of the Worlds.

The Koran does not say explicitly that Solomon built the glass hall to test the queen. Her reaction to her mistake, however, suggests that she sees herself as having been tested and having somehow failed. We can hardly avoid thinking of those unworthy *merkabah* travellers who allow themselves to be fooled by the illusion of water, and thereby betray their unworthiness (*Hekhalot Rabbati* and *Zuṭarti*; above, chapter VI).

What was the point of the test? Thaᶜlabi, who included Solomon legends in the "tales of the prophets" that he compiled around the beginning of the eleventh century, explains that the demons were afraid Solomon would marry the queen and thus join forces with her to keep them enslaved. They therefore spread rumors about her: "There is something [wrong] with her mind ... she has a donkey's foot; she has hairy calves, because her mother was a jinniyyah." Solomon therefore had to find a way to get a look at her feet. As it turned out, when she bared her feet to wade in Solomon's supposed pool, "she had the prettiest calves and feet in the world, but her calves were hairy. When Solomon saw this, he looked away, and called out to her: '*It is a hall, made smooth, of glass*, not water'" (ed. 285 [753]). Tabari's comments presuppose the same story (ed. 19:166, 168−169 [752]).

Speyer quotes a parallel from the "Second Targum" to the Book of Esther (1:3), whose account of Solomon and the queen of Sheba throughout resembles that of the Ḳoran [792c]. "When [Solomon] heard that the queen of Sheba had arrived, he sat upon his throne in the hall of glass. The queen, assuming that Solomon's throne stood in the middle of the wateı, lifted her clothes to keep them from getting wet. The king thus saw that her legs were hairy. The king said: 'You are beautiful, like a woman; but your hair is like a man's. Such [hair] is beautiful upon a man, hateful upon a woman.'" This parallel, however, does not do much to illuminate the Muslim sources, since it does not explain why Solomon chooses to sit in his hall of glass, or why the queen's hairy legs are relevant to the story. On the contrary, the Targum's account itself only becomes intelligible when we assume that its background is a story like Thaᶜlabi's.

Will Thaᶜlabi's story explain Surah 27:44? Not quite. We still do not understand why, having mistaken glass for water, the queen concludes that *I have wronged myself, and I surrender with Solomon unto Allah, the Lord of the Worlds.* Thaᶜlabi, indeed, interposes a fresh episode between the two parts of the verse. The queen asks Solomon a riddle; which, with coaching from the demons, he successfully answers. God's intervention spares him from having to answer a more difficult question about "the being of your Lord" (*kawn rabbika*). Only then does he call the queen to Islam, and she accept (ed. 285–286 [753]). In the "Second Targum," too, the queen responds to Solomon's not very gallant remarks about her hairy legs with a series of riddles. When he answers correctly, she exclaims that the reports of his great wisdom were not half of the truth (cf. I Kings 10:6–7). To make sense of Surah 27:44 along Tha᷄labi's lines, we must suppose that the original story described some interaction of this sort, which Muhammad left out. If so, its parallel with the *Hekhalot*'s water test – in which the traveller's failure is the direct result of his having been tricked by the mirage – is presumably coincidental.

I am reluctant to draw this conclusion. The queen's "mighty throne" plays an important if obscure role in the Koranic story; the "Second Targum" to Esther offers no parallel to this detail. Tabari plausibly suggests, on the strength of the expression used in both verse 23 and verse 26, that the queen's "mighty throne" is a counterpart to God's "Tremendous Throne" (above). Tabari also quotes a story, which he traces back through Ibn Ishaq to Wahb b. Munabbih, that the queen placed her throne "inside seven houses [*abyat*], one inside the other, and locked the houses" (ed. 19: 160 [752]). Tha᷄labi, repeating this story, makes an obscure remark which I understand to mean that the throne, and the "houses" containing it, were "in the uttermost [= innermost?] of her palaces[14]." All of this suggests the divine throne surrounded by seven *Hekhalot*, and hints that there is indeed some link between the queen's "water test" and that of the *merkabah* traveller.

Solomon also has a throne, which plays a role in one strange account of the episode in the glass hall. Tabari quotes this story (ed. 19:168 [752]); deriving it, like his description of the "seven houses," from Wahb b. Munabbih by way of Ibn Ishaq:

> At Solomon's command, the demons built the hall out of glass, as white [that is, clear] as if it were water. He ran water beneath it, placed his throne [*sarir*] in it, and sat down upon it. The birds, jinn, and humans stood in attendance upon him.
>
> Then he said [to the queen], "Enter the hall"; for he intended to show her a kingdom stronger than her kingdom, a dominion mightier than her dominion. *And when she saw it she deemed it a pool and bared her legs*, not doubting that it was water through which she must wade. *It was said unto her: Enter. It is a hall, made smooth, of glass.*

---

14 Ed. 283 [753]: *thumma inna bilqis* [that is, the queen] *amarat bi᷄arshiha fa-ju᷄ila fi sab᷄at abyat ba᷄duha dakhil ba᷄d fi akhir qaṣr min quṣuriha.* – Zamakhshari (ed. 3:144 [755]) and Maybudi (ed. 7:207 [748]) also allude to this story.

When she stood before Solomon, he called her to the worship of God, and condemned her for worshipping the sun instead of God. She then uttered a heresy [*qawl al-zanadiqah*]; at which Solomon fell prostrating himself and magnifying [God], on account of what she had said. Everyone prostrated themselves with him. She was at her wits' end when she saw Solomon doing what he did.

When Solomon raised his head, he said: "What was it you said, damn you?"

"I've been made to forget it," she said.

Then she said: "*My Lord! Lo! I have wronged myself, and I surrender with Solomon unto Allah, the Lord of the Worlds.*" She became a good Muslim.

I cannot resolve the difficulties of this story. In particular, I cannot answer the question that is bound to occur to the reader, of what the queen's heretical utterance is supposed to have been. (Tha°labi's version, that she asked Solomon about "the being of your Lord," seems pale and inadequate.) But, obscure as it is, the account seems to reflect different aspects of the materials we examined in chapter VI. Like King Hiram in the rabbinic legend (chapter VI, section 8b), Solomon runs water beneath his structure. Like God, he sits on his throne amid the waters, his attendants hovering around him. The queen of Sheba, expecting to be blocked by waters where there are none, utters some sort of challenge to the faith. In this last respect, she is perhaps similar to the *merkabah* traveller who fails the water test: "He is descended from those who kissed the calf, and is not worthy to see the king and his throne" (*Hekhalot Rabbati*; above, chapter VI, section 2a).

Appendix III

The "Youth" Passages in Ms New York

In chapter VII (section 2c), and again in chapter IX (sections B4, C4c), I have drawn heavily on material in ms New York (Jewish Theological Seminary, 8128) that describes the activities of a "youth" (*na^{c}ar*), who is often referred to as the "prince" (*šar*) and identified with Metatron. This material occurs, in two different recensions, in folios 20a—22b of the manuscript. Schäfer publishes it as ##384—400 of his *Synopse* [495]. Parallels to it are scattered through the *Synopse*, in a bewildering variety of contexts. One of these parallels is contained in the material that Martin Samuel Cohen has translated into English, as *Shi^{c}ur Qomah* [516][1].

My piecemeal quotations from the text are likely to have left the reader bewildered as to its overall structure. Hence this appendix. I do not think it profitable to give here a full translation, which would needlessly repeat the material I have quoted in chapters VII and IX, and would force me to make judgments about issues that have no effect on my argument. I therefore restrict myself to a summary overview. Where appropriate, I make reference to my translations or discussions of the material, and to Cohen's translation of parallel materials.

As I have said, ##384—400 contains two parallel recensions of the same material. Unfortunately, the two recensions do not follow the same order. If we consider ##384—394 as recension A, and ##395—400 as recension B, we may express their correspondence as follows:

---

1 It appears in Cohen's sections J_X, K, L, L_X, as follows:
J_X = ##384—386, 389a = ##398a, 396a, c
K =   #396b
L = ##389b—390   = ##398b—399
L_X = ##391—392
##387—388, 393—395, 397, and 400 are not in the text Cohen translated.

The material of Cohen's sections J_X, K, and L appears in chapter 9 of the *Shi^{c}ur Qomah* translation published by Meltzer [488].

A	B	
	#395	
#384		
#385	#398a	
#386		
#387 ⎫		⎧The "Moses/Meta-
⎬	#397	⎨tron text" (##76–
#388 ⎭		⎩80); see below
#389a	#396a–c	
#389b	#398b	
#390	#399	
##391–394		
	#400	

#384: God is eternal. He is surrounded by wrathful troops, by darkness and fog and mud (?? *ṭiṭ hayyawen*). The space before him is like a field sown with stars. Also in his vicinity are lightnings, the arches of the rainbow, rope ladders (? I read *sullam* for *ḥotam*) which one can use to ascend and descend. There are the four faces of the *ḥayyot*. God's hand rests on the head of the youth, who is named Metatron (the parallels omit this surely secondary identification). Angels attend the youth. The youth prostrates himself before God and blesses God for having revealed his mysteries to Israel. The angels respond. (Cohen, section J_x. Partly summarized above, chapter IX, section B4.)

#385: The youth enters beneath the throne of glory, attended on his right and his left. God embraces him. Angels praise God. God distributes glory to the Gentile kings. The youth's stature fills the world. God calls him "youth." (Cohen, section J_x. Most of #398a is parallel. All but the beginning of #385 is translated above, chapter IX, section B4; noted in chapter VII, section 2c.)

#386: The youth is Metatron, prince (*śar*) of the presence. (Cohen, section J_x.)

#387: His seventy names. The list concludes with "*sgnzg'l*, prince of wisdom." (This passage, and the next, are not in Cohen's *Shiᶜur Qomah* text. They correspond to ##76–77, the opening of the "Moses/Metatron text"; see above, chapter IX, section C3d. #397 is very roughly parallel; see below.)

#388: He is called *sgnzg'l* because he has all the treasuries (*ginze*) of wisdom. He opened all these treasuries to Moses, who forgot what he learned until "Yephephiah prince of Torah" (*śar hattorah*) gave him this learning as a gift. It then stayed with him.

#389a: The youth is prince (*śar*) of the presence, of the Torah, of wisdom, and the like. He is greater than the angels. He is Metatron, prince of the presence. He is written with one letter by which heaven and earth were created, sealed with the seal of *I am that I am*. He is written with six, seven, and twenty-two letters; with seventy names and seven sanctifications and seven voices; other attributes of this sort, which I do not very well understand. He is kept in innermost chambers. (Cohen, section J_x. #396 contains parallel material, though not in the same order.)

#389b: His angels surround the throne on one side, the *hayyot* on the other. (Cohen, section L. Translated above, chapter IX, section B4. #398b is parallel.)

#390: A *hayyah* rises above the seraphim and descends on the youth's dwelling. The angels are silenced, and the youth puts the fire of deafness in the ears of the *hayyot*, so they cannot hear God's speech. The youth invokes the mighty name; which is then set forth, at some length. (Cohen, section L. Translated, except for the concluding incantation, in chapter IX, section B4. #399 is parallel.)

##391–392: A long and repetitious hymn, its relation to the context unclear. (Cohen, section L_x.)

#393: The speaker prays to be protected while he uses God's great name; long series of names.

#394: Long, disjointed string of syllables, names, and phrases.

#395: More syllables, names, and phrases, including the name "Yophiel" and the Aramaic phrase, "They call him *ssngy'l*" (cf. ##387–388, 397). A short Aramaic passage describes God as dwelling in a palace of fire and ice, having fixed his throne in fire and water.

#396a: This youth is the prince (*śar*) who is written with seven voices, seven letters, seventy names. He is kept in innermost chambers, and serves before the fire devouring fire. (Cohen, section J_x. #389a contains parallel material. All of #396 is translated above, chapter IX, section C4c.)

#396b: He was given only to Moses. Exodus 33:15 and 23:21 (*my name is in him*) are applied to him. (Cohen, section K. No parallel in ##384–390).

#396c: He is written with one letter by which heaven and earth are created, sealed with the seal of *I am that I am*. He is the prince written with six, seven, twenty-two. (Cohen, section J_x. #389a contains parallel material.)

#397: He is the prince whose names include Yophiel, Yahdariel, Metatron, *ssngy'l*. String of syllables, words, names. His name was revealed to Moses at Sinai, transmitted to Hillel, rediscovered by R. Abbahu. More syllables, names, phrases, some of which seem to conceal Greek and Latin words. He is the prince of the presence, greatest of the angelic princes, serving the greatest of the gods. (Parts of this passage are translated and discussed in chapter VII, section 2c, and chapter IX, section C4c. It is not part of Cohen's *Shiᶜur Qomah* text, and it has no exact parallel in ##384–390. But the names Yophiel and *ssngy'l* are reminiscent of ##387–388 [= ##76

—77, from the "Moses/Metatron text"]; the chain of transmission is parallel to #80, again from the "Moses/Metatron text"; and the word *lrp't*, used in #397, suggests the claims for magical healing made in #80.)

#398a: This is the prince written with seven sanctifications, sealed in seventy languages (cf. #389a). He returns under the throne, attended on his right and his left. When he enters under the throne, God is praised three times a day. He distributes some of his glory to Gentile princes. His crown is named "Israel." His body is like the rainbow, which is like fire (Ezekiel 1:27). (Cohen, section J$_x$. All but the opening is translated and discussed above, chapter VII, section 2c. #385 is parallel.)

#398b: Six men of his (? cf. Ezekiel 9:2) surround the throne of glory on one side, the *hayyot* on the other. (Cohen, section L. #389b is parallel.)

#399: A *hayyah* rises above the seraphim and descends on the youth's dwelling. The angels are silenced, and the youth puts the fire of deafness in the ears of the *hayyot*, so they cannot hear God's speech. The youth invokes the mighty name; which is then set forth, at some length. (Cohen, section L. #390 is parallel.)

#400: He calls the youth (a string of names). They are alike from the waist down, but not from the waist up (cf. Ezekiel 1:27); citation of Deuteronomy 33:2. Blessing on him who is "careful" with this material. Quotation of Abot 1:13. Syllables, names (including *^{c}np'l*) and phrases (including "servant who is named after his master"). Briefly discussed above, chapter IX, section B4.

Appendix IV

Additional Notes to "The Visions of Ezekiel"

1. "The primordial waters ... bound ... in layers" (section IE)

Sections ID–F of the *Visions* seems to assume, as we saw in chapter VI, that the primordial waters flow through the river Chebar, and that the *merkabah* and its attendants can be seen in them.

The image of the primordial waters as a river is not entirely unique. T. Sukk. 3:3–10 expounds Ezekiel's vision of a life-bearing river bubbling forth from the threshold of the temple (47:1–12), and concludes, apparently in reference to this river, that "all the primordial waters[1] are going to flow forth as if from the mouth of a flask." Ezekiel 47:12's description of the trees growing on either side of the river is reminiscent of the account of the trees of Eden in Genesis 2:9 and 3:6, and this resemblance doubtless encouraged certain haggadists to connect Ezekiel's river with the rivers of Genesis 2:10[2]. PT Ber. 1:1 (2c) [284] presumably refers to these rivers when it says, in the name of Judah b. Ilai, that "every division of the primordial waters" originates beneath the tree of life. (*Gen. R.* 15:6, ed. 138 [188], quotes a similar statement; other parallels are cited in the editor's notes to that passage.)

But the description of these waters in section•IE of the *Visions* remains outstandingly difficult. The oddest of its details, the "mountain underneath the river," will occupy us presently. For now, we must focus on the hardly less peculiar claim that the primordial waters "are bound up in the great sea and in layers" (*nidbakhin*).

The author quotes Job 38:16 in support of his assertion. He has evidently understood the puzzling phrase *nibekhe yam*, which RSV translates "the springs of the sea," as if it were *nidbekhe yam*, "the layers of the sea." But

---

1 *Meme bereshit*. Section IE of the *Visions* uses the same phrase.

2 Professor Moshe Goshen-Gottstein (Hebrew University) has pointed out to me that two of the translators of Genesis 3:6 into Aramaic seem to have made a similar connection; for they claim, evidently on the basis of Ezekiel 47:12, that the tree of knowledge was good for *healing* the eyes (Onkelos, Pseudo-Jonathan).

he seems also to have in mind another passage from Job: *mibbekhi neharot hibbesh* (28:11), which RSV doubtfully translates as "he binds up the streams so that they do not trickle." Like some more recent scholars [30a], the author apparently reads *mibbekhi* as *nibekhe*; and, as in 38:16, interprets it as *nidbekhe*: "he [God] bound up the layers of the rivers." There seems no question that he uses the root *ḥbš* ("bind") in this passage because he found it in Job 28:11[3].

But how did the writer envision this "binding," and what did he mean by "layers"?

The former image reminds me of those Syriac sources in which God's hosts are "held fast" (*'aḥidin*) by his word or his seal, until the time comes for them to be loosed on the world (II Baruch 51:11; Odes of Solomon, 4:7—8)[4]. Here, it is perhaps meant to convey that God has forced his ancient enemy, the waters, into his service[5].

To understand the "layers," we must look to the Targums to Exodus 14:22. The Hebrew text of this verse describes the waters of the Red Sea as a "wall" (*ḥomah*), to the Israelites' right and to their left. Targum Onkelos translates "walls" (*shurin*); Neofiti I, "walls of water" (*shurin demayin*); while Pseudo-Jonathan explains that "the waters were congealed like walls three hundred miles high" (*umayya qarshun he keshurin remin telat me'ah milin*). Now, the Aramaic word *shura*, "wall" (plural *shurin*), is very much like the Hebrew word *shurah* (plural *shurot*), which means "line" or "row." The author of the *Visions* evidently was familiar with the Targumic rendering[6], and misconstrued it to mean that God had turned the waters of the Red Sea into "rows" of building materials; that is, "layers" (*nidbakhin*, which rabbinic Hebrew normally uses for the courses of stones in a building).

---

3 I have assumed Gruenwald's emendation of החביש to החבושין. But perhaps we can keep the text as it stands, reading the word as *heḥebishan* (Hiph⁏il with suffix): "God showed Ezekiel the primordial waters, which he had bound up ...." The Syntax, admittedly, is a little awkward, and, although Jastrow [808] records a Hiph⁏il of *ḥbš* in rabbinic Hebrew, he does not attribute to it the simple meaning of the root, "to bind."

4 Above, chapter III, section 4f, and endnote *f*. *Hekhalot* and Arabic sources use *ḥbš*, and its Arabic cognate *ḥbs*, to describe the "binding" of the *merkabah* beings beneath God's throne (chapter IX, endnote *x*; Appendix II, section 1a).

5 It is perhaps significant that the haggadah quoted in Tanh. *Hayye Sarah* #3 and *Ex. R.* 15:22 applies Job 38:16 to God's primeval victory over the waters. It derives *nibekhe* from the root *bky*, "to weep," and understands it as referring to the weeping of the waters. *Gen. R.* 5:4 (ed. 34—35 [188]) treats *mibbekhi* (Job 28:11) in a similar way.

6 An Aramaic passage near the beginning of ms New York's text of *Hekhalot Zuṭarti* (Schäfer, #343) also shows a trace of Pseudo-Jonathan's influence, when it relates that Moses at the Red Sea "made the water into lofty walls" (*ᶜabad mayya shurin remin*). See above, chapter IX, section B3e.

I suggested in chapter VI that certain rabbis expressed God's subjection of the primordial waters by imagining that God turned them solid and used them to build his heavenly temple. The author of the *Visions* seems to imply this image, adding a hint that Ezekiel saw the structure not only in the water, but as part of the water. Significantly, he draws part of his allusion from the Targums' description of the Red Sea, and thus confirms the suspicion that occurred to us in chapter VI: that some at least of the *merkabah* expositors merged God's prehistoric victory over the waters and his deed at the Red Sea into one.

2. "A mountain underneath the river" (section IE)

The same paragraph refers also to "a mountain underneath the river [*har mittahtaw shel nahar*], by means of which the temple vessels are to return." Earlier scholars have explained the passage by altering it. Thus, Gruenwald emends to *nahar mittahtaw shel har*, "a river at the base of the mountain." He supposes that the mountain is the temple mount, and that the river is the one Ezekiel sees flowing from the temple (47:1–12). Saul Lieberman proposes the reading *nahar mittahtaw shel nahar* ("a river underneath the river") and explains our text by combining it with two passages from late midrashic sources: a river will flow from the temple, mingle with the Euphrates, and bring to light the temple vessels sunk at its bottom [329].

But I do not think that we need to change the text. The Muslim collections of traditions (*hadith*), attributed to the prophet Muhammad, contain several slightly different versions of a prediction that "the last hour will not come before the Euphrates reveals [by the falling of its waters] a mountain of gold. People will fight over it, and ninety-nine out of every hundred will be killed[7]." Some variants speak of a "treasure of gold" instead of a mountain; but since the amount of treasure involved must be enormous, this does not much alter the image.

Now, some Jewish sources identify the Euphrates with Ezekiel's river Chebar. *Gen. R.* 16:3 (ed. 145–146 [188]) quotes the fourth-century

---

7 Muslim, *Sahih*, ed 4:2219–2220 [749] (cf. tr. 4:1500 [750]); several variants follow. We find parallels in Ibn Hanbal, *Musnad*, ed. 2:161, 306, 332, 346, 415, 5:139–140 [741]; Bukhari, *Sahih*, ed. 4:380 [739]; Abu Da'ud, *Sunan*, ed. 4:155 [737]; Ibn Majah, *Sunan*, ed. 2:1343 [743]; Tirmidhi, *Sunan*, ed. 7:244–245 [754]. The tenth-century Muslim writer Maqdisi relates, in his *Book of Creation*, a strange story which may be somehow relevant: "It is reported that the level of the Euphrates fell in the time of Mu^cawiyah [caliph from 661 to 680] and deposited on its bank a pomegranate the size of a full-grown camel. Ka^cb [al-Ahbar, the famous Jewish scholar converted to Islam] said that it came from paradise" (ed. 2:44–45, tr. 2:42 [747]).

Palestinian Amora Judan as saying that the two are the same. Kimhi, in his comment on Ezekiel 1:1, quotes a Targumic variant which renders "Chebar" as "Euphrates" [224]. Given this equation, I am inclined to suppose that the mountain that Ezekiel sees beneath the river is the same as the one described in the Muslim traditions, and that the temple vessels are among its golden treasures.

Are we then to suppose that the *Visions of Ezekiel* draws on Islamic legend? If so, this would guarantee a late date for it. But there is another possibility. As scholars have long recognized, the pious storytellers of early Islam borrowed heavily from Judaism. Among their borrowings may have been the belief that, in the end of days, the Euphrates would dwindle to reveal a mound of treasures, the long-lost temple vessels among them. It seems possible that some such belief may underlie the explanation, which *Gen. R.* 16:3 attributes to Judan, that the Euphrates is called "Chebar" because "its waters disappear." The *Visions of Ezekiel* and the Muslim *hadith* may independently reflect this Jewish tradition.

Gruenwald observes that the implication of section IE, that the temple vessels are hidden beneath the waters, seems to contradict what IIF1 says about their being in the fifth heaven. Perhaps this apparent contradiction is another example of the blurring of the distinction between the heavens and the waters.

3. "God ... descended to the Red Sea/to the lower regions" (section IIF2)

The end of the third sentence in section IIF2 (from the British Museum fragment) is blurred, and very difficult to read. Marmorstein read it as *lattahtonim*, and thus had God descend on the *merkabah* of *Kerub* "to the lower regions"; that is, to the earth. Mann, followed by Wertheimer, preferred *leyam suf*, "to the Red Sea." Gruenwald found that what remained of the letters favored Marmorstein's reading.

Two considerations seem to me to argue for the Red Sea. First, the use of the perfect tense ("when he descended") suggests that we are dealing with a specific historical event — like God's descent to Sinai (E2), and corresponding to his future descent for judgment (J2) — and not with his habitual visits to earth. Second, rabbinic midrash often applies Psalm 18:11 and the surrounding verses to God's presence at the Red Sea: *Mekhilta, Be-Shallah* chapter 3 (ed./tr. 1:212–213 [195]; cf. PT Sot. 8:3, 22b), *Shirah* chapter 4 (ed./tr. 2:30); *Song R.* to 1:9; *'Abot de-Rabbi Natan,* Version A, chapters 27, 33, 34 (ed. 42a, 48a–b, 51b [183])); *Midr. Psalms* 18:14 (ed. 72a–b [199])); see above, chapter VI, section 5.

A few passages, however, apply Psalm 18:10 to the Sinai event: *Mekhilta, Ba-Hodesh* chapter 9 (ed./tr. 2:276 [195]); *Lev. R.* 19:4 (ed. 424–425

[191]); *Eccl. R.* 10:18. It seems just possible that the author of the *Visions* wrote *lattaḥtonim*, intending a second reference to Sinai.

When the newly discovered leaf of the Cambridge manuscript is published, it will of course render this whole discussion obsolete.

4. The seven heavens

The *Visions of Ezekiel* significantly contradicts itself in regard to its multiple heavens. Section IG declares them to be seven, and then names them: *Shamayim, Sheme Shamayim, Zebul, ᶜArafel, Sheḥaqim, ᶜArabot,* and *Kisse' Kabod.* But the full description of the heavens in section II contradicts this list in two respects. It inserts an eighth heaven, *Makhon,* between *Sheḥaqim* and *ᶜArabot* (IIG). It does not call the first heaven *Shamayim* (which means simply "heaven"), but refers to it as "the firmament," *raqiaᶜ,* which may or may not be understood as a proper name.

On both of these points, the brief list in IG seems to me the more original.

Let us take the second issue first. The second heaven is called *Sheme (ha-)Shamayim,* "the heaven of heavens," in both of the main sections of the *Visions* (IG, IICl, Dl). The name is presumably derived from Deuteronomy 10:14, which BT Ḥag. 12b invokes to prove that there are two heavens: *The heavens (hashshamayim) and the heaven of heavens (sheme hashshamayim) belong to the Lord your God.* The second heaven's being called *Sheme (ha-)Shamayim* therefore implies that the first heaven is called *Shamayim.* Section IIB may also imply the use of this name when it identifies the celestial waters with the *heavens (shamayim)* of Genesis 1:8, and quotes in reference to them Isaiah 40:22, which also speaks of *shamayim.* Someone evidently substituted "firmament" for "heaven" in IIA1, doubtless under the influence of BT Ḥag. 13a and its Palestinian parallels: "From earth to the firmament is a journey of five hundred years, and the thickness of the firmament is a journey of five hundred years ...[8]."

As for the heaven *Makhon,* we have reason to believe that the passage describing it is an insertion into the text. It is the only one of the heavens of the *Visions of Ezekiel* that does not contain its own *merkabah.* It also seems completely needless, since almost all of its contents turn up again in the next heaven, *ᶜArabot.*

---

8 *Halo' min ha'areṣ ᶜad laraqiaᶜ mahalakh ḥamesh me'ot shanah weᶜobyo shel raqiaᶜ mahalakh ḥamesh me'ot shanah.* The Palestinian parallels are in PT Ber. 1:1 (2c), 9:1 (13a), *Gen. R.* 6:6 (ed. 45–46 [188]); in the later midrashim, Tanh. *Terumah* #9 (= Tanh. Buber *Terumah* #8, ed. 47a [222]), #11, *Midr. Psalms* 4:3 (ed. 22a [199]).

To explain its presence, we must start with the observation that almost all lists of the heavens in rabbinic literature, whatever their differences, agree that *cArabot* is the name of the seventh and highest heaven [232, 391]. The *Visions* stands alone in placing it in the sixth position[9]. Some transmitter of the text, disturbed by this unusual feature, tried to eliminate it by treating *Kisse' Kabod* as if it were not the name of a heaven, but were instead what its name means: the "throne of glory," which rests above all the heavens (cf. BT Hag. 13a). He then needed to add a new heaven which would make *cArabot* the seventh. He chose for this purpose *Makhon,* which is the sixth heaven in BT Hag. 12b, containing (among other things) "treasuries of snow and treasuries of hail." He copied its contents from the following description of *cArabot*, adding "hail" in accord with the Talmud.

This suggestion also explains the incongruous reference to *cArabot* in the middle of the description of *Kisse' Kabod* (IIJ1). If, as the reviser supposed, *Kisse' Kabod* is not a heaven, it makes no sense to ask the standard question "What is in it?" This question, which was plainly part of the text that lay before the reviser, was therefore referred back to the last-mentioned heaven.

From what I have said so far, it will be clear that we cannot use the contradictions between IG and section II to argue that the two main divisions of the *Visions of Ezekiel* are two originally independent sources which an editor taped together. They have too much in common for that: their lists of the heavens are basically in harmony, and they share the remarkable notion – which we find nowhere outside the *Visions of Ezekiel* – that there is a *merkabah* in each of the seven heavens. We see in chapter VIII, section A5b, that the *Visions*, for all the diversity of its contents and the different traditions on which it seems to draw, develops a single theme from beginning to end; and that we have every reason to suppose that its author wrote it as a unified work. After the text was finished, someone revised a few elements of the enumeration of heavens that occupies its second half, but neglected to make parallel corrections in the brief list in section IG.

5. The seven *merkabah*s

At the end of chapter VIII, I offer my explanation of what led the author of the *Visions* to suppose the existence of not one but seven *mer-*

---

9 It is perhaps significant that the passage quoted from *Hekhalot Rabbati* in chapter VI, section 2a, connects *cArabot Raqiac* with the goings-on at the gate of the *sixth* palace. I have argued, however (at the end of section 2c), that this location is not an original part of the text. Moreover, the parallel passage from *Hekhalot Zuṭarti* (also quoted in section 2a) does not mention *cArabot Raqiac* at all, introducing "the seventh palace" in its place.

*kabah*s, one in each of the heavens. I do not need here to add to these remarks. But the names the author assigns to his *merkabah*s, and the Biblical proof texts he invokes for them, raise a number of problems which demand our attention.

The first two *merkabah*s do not present any particular difficulty. It is clear enough from Micah 1:13, which links the word *merkabah* to the rare poetic *rekhesh*, how the author deduced that the latter is a name for one of the seven *merkabah*s. We can explain the origin of the name *Susim* as easily, if we suppose that the Biblical text that gave rise to this name was not in fact Zechariah 1:8 (which the *Visions* quotes), but a similar passage from the same book — 6:1—7, where four *merkabah*s are connected to horses *(susim)* of different colors [229]. In connection with the name of the heaven that contains *Susim*, it is perhaps significant that Zechariah 6:5 identifies the four *merkabah*s with the four winds of the heaven *(shamayim)*.

Similarly, we have no real trouble with the last two *merkabah*s. One of them bears the name *cAb*, because Isaiah 19:1 has God *riding (rokheb,* from the same root as *merkabah)* on a *cloud (cab)*. The author has perhaps located it in *cArabot* on the strength of the resemblance of Isaiah's language to that of Psalm 68:5, which calls God *the rider (rokheb) in cArabot*[10]. The derivation of the name of the *merkabah* in *Kisse' Kabod*, from Isaiah 66:15, is likewise clear. The author places it in the highest heaven because the verse from Isaiah gives his composition the eschatological climax he wants. He substitutes "storm" *(secarah)* for Isaiah's *whirlwind (sufah)*, in order to link this climax to the beginning of Ezekiel's vision (Ezekiel 1:4 describes "a storm wind," *ruah secarah,* which comes with "fire," *'esh)*.

The intervening *merkabah*s are more problematic. The name of the *merkabah* in *Zebul* (IID3) has, to my knowledge, so far resisted explanation [229,540]. While the meaning of *Melakhim* (IIE2) is clear enough, it is far from obvious what "kings" have to do with the proof text invoked for this *merkabah*[11].

We can best resolve these problems if we assume that the links between the middle three heavens, the names of their *merkabah*s, and the proof texts offered for them, have gotten mixed up. (I will presently try to explain how this dislocation took place.) As they now stand, they are:

Zebul (heaven) — *ha-Lewiyyah (merkabah)* — Psalm 68:34 (D)
cArafel (heaven) — *Melakhim (merkabah)* — Psalm 68:18 (E)
Shehaqim (heaven) — *Kerub (merkabah)* — Psalm 18:11 (F)

---

10 BT Hag. 12b invokes the latter verse to prove the existence of a heaven named *cArabot*.
11 Gruenwald [229] writes that Mann's emendation of *melakhim* to *mal'akhim* ("angels") is unnecessary, but offers no explanation of the significance of the "kings."

But let us suppose that *Melakhim* was originally the *merkabah* in *Sheḥa-qim*, and that the proof text for it was a combination of the passages quoted in D3 and F1, extending from Psalm 68:33 through verse 36:

> [33]O kingdoms [*mamlekhot*] of the earth, sing to God, hymn the Lord. Selah. [34][Sing praises] to him who rides the heavens, the ancient heavens [*rokheb bisheme sheme qedem*]. He utters his voice, a mighty voice.
> [35]Ascribe strength to God. His pride is over Israel, and his strength is in the clouds [*sheḥa-qim*]. [36]Terrible is God from your sanctuaries. He is the God of Israel, giving strength and power to his people.

We can imagine how an expositor might have deduced from this passage not only that God rides a *merkabah* in *Sheḥaqim*, but that that *merkabah* is named after the rulers of the "kingdoms" called upon to hymn its rider.

Now let us make a second assumption: that, just as the proof text for *Melakhim* has been mistakenly attached to *ha-Lewiyyah*, the reverse has also happened, and that the verse associated with *ha-Lewiyyah* was once Psalm 68:18.

With this assumption, we have the key to the meaning of the name. It is an allusion to a midrash on Psalm 68:18, which several *Tanḥuma* sources attribute to R. Berechiah:

> The divine chariotry is two myriads, thousands of shin'an. ... R. Berechiah ha-Kohen be-Rabbi said: [Their number] corresponded to the camp of the Levites [*maḥaneh hallewiyyim*], for God foresaw that none would stand faithful [?] except for the Levites. Therefore twenty-two thousand [chariots] descended, corresponding to the Levitic camp [*maḥaneh lewiyyah*]. [*Pesiqta de-Rab Kahana, Ba-Ḥodesh* #22 (ed. 219–221 [206]); see above, chapter IV, section 5.]

In the last sentence, the expositor may perhaps have intended a play on *lewiyyah* and *lewayah*, "escort" (that is, the angelic escort that accompanied God to Sinai). I am therefore not sure whether, in the *Visions*, we are to read the name of the *merkabah* as *ha-Lewiyyah* ("the *merkabah* of the Levites") or as *ha-Lewayah* ("the *merkabah* of the escort"). Either way, it seems fairly clear that the name refers back to the midrash attributed to Berechiah, and that this *merkabah* is the one "in which God descended to Sinai."

Does *ha-Lewiyyah* belong in *Zebul* or in *ᶜArafel*? Section E1's quotation of Exodus 20:18, which ties the name *ᶜArafel* to the Sinai revelation, points to the second alternative. But here we meet a difficulty. The *merkabah* called *Kerub* (F2) has an excellent claim of its own to residence in *ᶜArafel* — as well as in *Sheḥaqim*, where it is now located, but where, according to our rearrangements, it cannot originally have belonged. Psalm 18:11, which obviously was the original proof text for *Kerub*, comes immediately after a passage that mentions *ᶜArafel* (verse 10: *he bent the heavens and descended, thick cloud [ᶜarafel] beneath his feet*). It comes immediately before a passage that mentions *Sheḥaqim* (verse 12: *he made darkness his covering around him, his canopy thick clouds [sheḥaqim] dark with water* [RSV]). *Kerub* and *ha-Lewiyyah* cannot both have been in *ʿArafel.*

This difficulty, however, turns out to be to our advantage, in that it helps us explain how the dislocations we have posited came about in the first place.

We must assume that the author of the *Visions* drew upon material which included a number of variant combinations of heavens, *merkabah*s, and proof texts. Among them were the combinations we have reconstructed:

Shehaqim (heaven) — *Melakhim* (*merkabah*) — Psalm 68:33—36
ʿArafel (heaven) — *ha-Lewiyyah* (*merkabah*) — Psalm 68:18

But they also included:

Shehaqim (heaven) — *Kerub* (*merkabah*) — Psalm 18:11—12

And perhaps also:

ʿArafel (heaven) — *Kerub* (*merkabah*) — Psalm 18:10—11

The author wanted to use the third of these combinations. He therefore had to find a new home for *Melakhim*, which *Kerub* had displaced from *Shehaqim*; he moved it down one heaven, to *ʿArafel*. This forced a similar move for *ha-Lewiyyah*, from *ʿArafel* to *Zebul*. (We do not know what it displaced from *Zebul*.) In the course of rearranging his material, the author accidentally exchanged the proof texts for *ha-Lewiyyah* and *Melakhim*.

6. The seven *merkabah*s: an alternative hypothesis

The phrase *sheme sheme qedem* ("the heavens, the ancient heavens"), used in Psalm 68:34, is very reminiscent of the name of the second heaven, *Sheme (ha-)Shamayim*. This resemblance suggests an alternative way of rearranging the combinations of heavens, *merkabah*s, and proof texts, which in some ways is more attractive than the one I have just proposed.

According to this alternative hypothesis, Psalm 68:33—34 was not read together with verses 35—36, and thus applied to *Shehaqim*. Rather, the former verses were read as a separate unit, and understood to describe *Melakhim*, the *merkabah* of *Sheme Shamayim*. *Susim*, which now appears as the *merkabah* of *Sheme Shamayim*, was originally connected with *Shamayim*, as Zechariah 6:5 perhaps suggests.

The upshot of this proposal would be that we are to leave the last three heavens as they stand, but rearrange the first four. In the text as we now have it, they are:

Raqia^c (orig. *Shamayim*; heaven) — *Rekhesh* (*merkabah*) — Micah 1:
   13 (A)

Sheme Shamayim (heaven) — *Susim* (*merkabah*) — Zechariah 1:8 (orig.
   6:1–7) (C)

Zebul (heaven) — *ha-Lewiyyah* (*merkabah*) — Psalm 68:34 (D)

^cArafel (heaven) — *Melakhim* (*merkabah*) — Psalm 68:18 (E)

According to our alternative hypothesis, this would once have been:

Shamayim (heaven) — *Susim* (*merkabah*) — Zechariah 6:1–7

Sheme Shamayim (heaven) — *Melakhim* (*merkabah*) — Psalm 68:33–34

Zebul (heaven) — ? — ?

^cArafel (heaven) — *ha-Lewiyyah* (*merkabah*) — Psalm 68:18

? — *Rekhesh* (*merkabah*) — Micah 1:13

My real problem with this reconstruction is that I cannot think of an explanation of how we got here from there, how the heavens and the *merkabah*s came to be rearranged in the way we now have them. For this
reason, I offer it only as a conceivable alternative.

Appendix V

Index to the Merkabah Exegesis of the Hekhalot

The following pages contain an index to those *Hekhalot* passages that quote or seem to allude to texts from the *merkabah* visions of the Book of Ezekiel. I have separated the quotations and the allusions into two distinct lists, and arranged each according to the sequence of the Biblical verses quoted or referred to.

I intend this index to be as complete as possible. I have included in it all the material published in Schäfer's *Synopse zur Hekhalot-Literatur* (including those materials, such as *Seder Rabbah di-Bereshit*, whose affiliation with the *Hekhalot* is doubtful), plus Wertheimer's edition of *Massekhet Hekhalot* and Gruenwald's publication of Genizah *Hekhalot* fragments [495,499,466]. Where I am uncertain whether a passage deserves to be included, I include it. I do not, however, list all occurrences of words like *merkabah, hayyot, 'ofannim,* and *hashmal*; or of the phrase *barukh kebod YHWH mimmeqomo,* which, although originally drawn from Ezekiel 3:12, had long been at least as accessible in its secondary context in the *Qedushshah* prayer.

About three-quarters of the passages listed below are quoted, or at least mentioned, in the body of this book. For such passages, I have given only the reference to Schäfer (or Wertheimer or Gruenwald), and to the section of this book in which I treat the passage. The remaining passages, which I have not dealt with so far, I quote or summarize. Where appropriate, I cite not only Schäfer but also the older publications containing them: Wertheimer's *Hekhalot Rabbati*, Elior's *Hekhalot Zutarti*, Odeberg's *3 Enoch*, Scholem's *Maʿaseh Merkabah*, Séd's *Seder Rabbah di-Bereshit*, and Schäfer's own *Sar ha-Panim* [500,464,490,603,213,493].

1. Quotations

Ezekiel 1:1:
  Schäfer, #515; above, chapter IX, section C1.

Ezekiel 1:4:
  Schäfer, #371; above, chapter IX, section B1b.

Massekhet Hekhalot, ch. 3 (ed. 56–57 [499]): The throne of glory beneath God is made of sapphire stone (*'eben sappir*, Ezekiel 1:26). It is
established beneath the feet of the Shechinah (inferred from Exodus 24:
10). It is high and exalted (Isaiah 6:1). "Its appearance is *like the color of
hashmal*. So it is written: *From its midst came something like the color of
hashmal, from the midst of the fire* [Ezekiel 1:4]. What does 'hashmal'
mean? That three hundred and seventy-eight kinds of the most splendid
luminaries, the least of which is like the sun, are embedded in it [the
throne]; for the numerical value of *hashmal* is three hundred and seventy-
eight." A matchless garment of splendor is spread over the throne, so that
even the holy *hayyot*, the cherubim, and the *'ofannim* cannot look at it.
— We may assume that the writer erred when he quoted 1:4. Rather, the
tradition on which he drew probably originally expounded the reference to
hashmal in 1:27; which, like verse 26, describes the throne and the one sitting on it. I know no parallel to the interpretation of *hashmal* by the numerical value of its letters. The collocation of Ezekiel 1:26 and Exodus 24:10,
however, is reminiscent of BT Sotah 17a and its parallels (above, chapter
VI, section 4).

Ezekiel 1:8:
   Schäfer, #273; above, chapter IX, section B3d.

Ezekiel 1:11:
   Schäfer, #596; above, chapter IX, section B3c.

Ezekiel 1:12:
   Schäfer, #370; above, chapter IX, section B1b.

Ezekiel 1:13:
   Schäfer, #373; above, chapter IX, section B1b.

Ezekiel 1:14:
   Schäfer, #37; above, chapter IX, section B3a.
   Schäfer, #353; above, chapter IX, section B1a.
   See also below, under Ezekiel 3:12.

Ezekiel 1:15:
   Schäfer, #745, above, chapter VI, section 8a.

Ezekiel 1:21:
   Schäfer, ##628–633; from the text that Schäfer earlier published under
the title "Adjuration of the *Śar ha-Panim*" [493], lines 80–141: Of the
fourteen names of the prince of the presence (*śar ha-panim*; ##628–629),
four are inscribed on the heads of the *hayyot* (#630), four on the four
sides of the throne (#631). "Four are engraved on the four crowns of the
'ofannim, who stand opposite the *hayyot*. So it is written: *When* [the
hayyot] *went, so did* [the *'ofannim*]; *when these stood still, so did those*
[Ezekiel 1:21]" (#632). The remaining two are on God's crown (#633).

Ezekiel 1:22:

Schäfer, #520; from *Seder Rabbah di-Bereshit*: In the course of a vertical survey of the structures of the celestial realms, we find the *firmament the color of the terrible ice* placed upon the horns of the *ḥayyot*. The author quotes Ezekiel 1:22 in its entirety to support this claim. (The parallels #464 and #472 include "the firmament of terrible ice" in the same series of heavenly structures, but leave out the proof text. So Séd, pages 88–89.)

Massekhet Hekhalot, ch. 7 (Wertheimer's text, page 61, is very difficult here, and must be read with Jellinek's [479]): Above the *ḥayyot* is a dwelling (? *me*^c*onah*), in the likeness of a firmament the color of the terrible ice, on the heads of the *ḥayyot* (Ezekiel 1:22; word order rearranged). It is splendid and glorious (Psalm 96:5 invoked), established with a·multitude of appearances of fire and flame. *And there was a likeness on the heads of the ḥayyot, a firmament* (Ezekiel 1:22). Amazing wonders are established there: the wheels (*galgalle*) of the *merkabah* on which the throne rests, wheel opposite wheel, radiance of splendor of wheel opposite radiance of splendor of wheel, wondrous work of wheel opposite wondrous work of wheel.

Ezekiel 1:24:

Schäfer, #370; above, chapter IX, section B1b.

Schäfer, #596; above, chapter IX, section B3c. (The word order of the quotation, *beqol (!) mayim rabbim qol kanfehem,* is different from MT's.)

Ezekiel 1:25:

Schäfer, ##96–97; from *Hekhalot Rabbati* (Wertheimer, 3:2): Ezekiel 1:25 is quoted in the context of a cryptic dialogue between God and some unnamed being. "'Why are you frightened, faithful servant? Why do you recoil, servant, beloved one?' 'I say to you, Zoharariel Yahweh, God of Israel, that if I am not frightened, who should be frightened? If I do not recoil, who should recoil? I am called to the power six hours each day. They drag me a thousand times on my knees until I reach the throne of glory.' Then the voice would reply to him; as it is written, *And there was a voice from above the firmament that was over their heads. When they stood, they let down their wings* [Ezekiel 1:25]. 'There is no way to disparage the words or to contradict the speech of those who do these things to you. They are called ministers to his glory.'" If we had a clearer idea of who it is that God is addressing, we might have a clue to the author's understanding of the Biblical verse. See my note on Schäfer, #302, in chapter IX, section D2a.

Ezekiel 1:26:

Schäfer, #250; above, chapter IX, section B2.

Gruenwald [466], page 370: A fragmentary passage has someone (R. Ishmael, presumably) quote the "prince" *Sgnsg'l*: "At the entrance to the terrible palace, the palace of the firmament that is above [   ] in the words of *merkabah*; as it is written, *And above the firmament that was upon their heads* [   ] of the world is the glory of the king of the world, and it is the air of [   ] and breaks forth in the seven firmaments and illuminates [   ] for if it were not for its luminescence the firmament Vilon would be abandoned [?] [   ] what is in his hand. R. Ishmael said: I bore witness [   ] the gates of *the firmament that is on the heads of the cherubim* ... " At this point, the text becomes too difficult for me to translate. – The first quotation is from Ezekiel 1:26, the second (not quite exact) from 10:1. Gruenwald plausibly inserts "the seven firmaments" at the beginning of the first lacuna.

See also above, under Ezekiel 1:4.

Ezekiel 1:27:

Schäfer, ##258–259; above, chapter VI, section 2; chapter IX, section B2.

Schäfer, #372; above, chapter IX, section B1b. (The Hebrew has *hahashmal* instead of *hashmal*, and is therefore, strictly speaking, taken from 1:4 rather than 1:27. But the context of the *Hekhalot* passage suggests that the author intended to quote 1:27.)

Schäfer, #398; above, chapter VII, section 2c; chapter IX, section B4; Appendix III. (On the parallels in #367 and #487, see chapter VII, endnote *f*.)

Schäfer, ##407–410; above, chapter VI, section 2; chapter IX, section B2.

See also above, under Ezekiel 1:4.

Ezekiel 3:12:

Schäfer, #352; from *Hekhalot Zutarti* (Elior, lines 94–99): A series of opinions, evidently on the manner of seeing God. The holy celestial beings say: We see *like the appearance of bazaq* (Ezekiel 1:14). The prophets say: We see in a dream-vision. The kings of the earth utter a few unintelligible words. Rabbi (? or R. Akiba) says: He can hardly be like us; but he is greater than all things, and his glory is that he is hidden from us. Moses says: "Do not adhere to any of these opinions. Rather, he is in his place. That is why it is written: *Blessed be the glory of the Lord from his place* [Ezekiel 3:12]."

Schäfer, ##538, 714, 818; from *Seder Rabbah di-Bereshit* (Jellinek published a parallel passage as a separate text [482]): The *hayyot* beneath the throne of glory respond to the angels' *Holy holy holy* with *Blessed be the glory of the Lord from his place*. A midrash follows: "Why do they not say, *in his place* [*bimeqomo*, instead of *mimmeqomo*]? Because the Shechinah is everywhere. In the future, when the Shechinah returns to its place in the holy of holies, they will say, *Blessed be the glory of the Lord from his place*" (#714; the other versions differ slightly). The midrash would make a

good deal more sense if it had *in his place* at the end, but no version actually reads this way. Perhaps the habit of writing the familiar liturgical phrase
proved too strong for the scribes. – Two parallel passages (Schäfer, ##188,
798) omit the midrash, while including the preceding description of the
angelic hymnody.

Ezekiel 10:1:
  See above, under Ezekiel 1:26.

2. Allusions

Ezekiel 1:5:
  Schäfer, #371; above, chapter IX, section B1b.

Ezekiel 1:6:
  Schäfer, #354; above, chapter IX, section B1a.
  Schäfer, #368; above, chapter IX, section B1b.
  Schäfer, #371; above, chapter IX, section B1b.

Ezekiel 1:8:
  Schäfer, #34; from *3 Enoch* (Odeberg, ch. 22): A long description of the
cherubim includes the detail that "their hands are under their wings and
their feet are covered by their wings" (ms Munich 40: *widehem tahat kanfehem weraglehem mekhussot bekhanfehem*). The first part of this statement comes from Ezekiel 1:8, the second from Isaiah 6:2. – Another part
of this passage speaks of the cherubim singing with their wings; above,
chapter IX, section B3c.
  Schäfer, #384; above, chapter IX, section B4.

Ezekiel 1:10:
  Schäfer, #273; above, chapter IX, section B3d.
  Schäfer, ##368–369; above, chapter IX, section B1b.

Ezekiel 1:11 (or 1:23):
  Schäfer, #355; above, chapter IX, section B1a.
  Schäfer, #370; above, chapter IX, section B1b.

Ezekiel 1:13:
  Schäfer, #247; above, chapter IX, section B2.

Ezekiel 1:14:
  Schäfer, #52; above, chapter IX, section B3a.

Ezekiel 1:16:
  Schäfer, #371; above, chapter IX, section B1b.
  Gruenwald [466], page 362: The Ozhayah text's account of the visitor's
welcome to the seventh palace (above, chapter IX, section A2b) includes
the detail: "A double wheel flies about like a bird" (*we'ofan kaful*

me[*ᶜofef*] *keᶜof*). The "double wheel" evidently refers to the *wheel within a wheel* of Ezekiel 1:16. It again appears in *Hekhalot Zuṭarti*'s description of the welcome (Schäfer, #411; Elior, line 323; above, chapter IX, beginning of section A2c), where a "double wheel" proclaims: "Whoever is worthy to see the king in his beauty, come and look!"

Ezekiel 1:23:
    See above, under Ezekiel 1:11.

Ezekiel 1:24:
    Schäfer, #189; above, chapter IX, section B3c.
    (##34 and 593 should perhaps also be listed here, in that they deal with singing wings; above, chapter IX, section B3c.)
    Schäfer, #355; above, chapter IX, section B1a.

Ezekiel 1:26:
    Schäfer, #371; above, chapter IX, section B1b.
    Schäfer, ##521–522; from *Seder Rabbah di-Bereshit*: A step up in the celestial structures from "the firmament of terrible ice" (above, "Quotations," Ezekiel 1:22), we find "like the appearance of splendor" (*kemar'eh hannogah*; cf. Ezekiel 1:28); and, a step up from that, the "throne of sapphire stone" (*kisse' 'eben sappir*; cf. Ezekiel 1:26). Similar phrases occur in the parallel ##465–467, 725–727; but, in #727, *kemar'eh 'eben sappir* takes the place of *kisse' 'eben sappir*. Cf. Séd, pages 88–91.

Ezekiel 1:27:
    Schäfer, #376; above, chapter IX, section B5.
    Schäfer, #400; above, chapter IX, section B4; Appendix III.

Ezekiel 1:28:
    Schäfer, #353; above, chapter IX, section B1a.
    Schäfer, #371; above, chapter IX, section B1b.
    Schäfer, #398; above, chapter VII, section 2c; chapter IX, section B4; Appendix III. (On the parallels in #367 and #487, see chapter VII, endnote *f*.)

Ezekiel 3:12:
    Schäfer, #553; above, chapter IX, section B3b.

Appendix VI

Pirqe de-Rabbi Eliezer, the Hekhalot, and the Nag Hammadi Texts

1. In the fourth chapter of *Pirqe de-Rabbi Eliezer,* the author of the midrash undertakes to describe what God did on the second day of Creation. He uses this as an opportunity to give a detailed description, much of it drawn from Ezekiel's *merkabah,* of God's throne and the surrounding entities. The passage is too long to quote in full here. I give those parts of it that are particularly important for us, in connection with the passage we have examined from ms New York of *Hekhalot Zuṭarti* (chapter IX, section B1b).

> On the second day, God created the firmament, the angels, ordinary fire, and hellfire. ... What firmament did he create on the second day? R. Eliezer says: The firmament that is on the heads of the four *ḥayyot.* So it is written: *On the heads of the ḥayyot was the likeness of a firmament, like the color of the terrible ice* [Ezekiel 1:22].
>
> What is meant by *like the color of the terrible ice*? Like jewels and pearls. It shines on the entire heaven, like a lamp in a house, like the sun shining at its full strength at noonday. ... Were it not for that firmament, the world would be swallowed up by the waters above it and below it. ...
>
> Four groups of ministering angels sing God's praises. The first camp, Michael's, is on God's right. The second, Gabriel's, is on his left. The third, Uriel's, is in front of him. The fourth, Raphael's, is behind him.
>
> God's Shechinah is in the middle. He sits on a lofty and exalted throne, suspended high in the air. The appearances of his glory are *like the color of ḥashmal;* as it is written, *I saw like the color of ḥashmal* [literally, *like the eye of ḥashmal, ke͑en ḥashmal*; Ezekiel 1:27]. He has a crown on his head, the wreath of the ineffable name on his forehead. His eyes travel about through all the earth [cf. Zechariah 4:10][1]. Half of it is fire and half of it is ice. On his right hand is life; on his left, death. He holds a fiery rod in his hand. A curtain is spread before him, and the seven angels who were created first serve him inside the curtain. ...

---

1 To judge from Friedlander's translation and notes, this sentence is absent from the manuscripts at this point, and was added to the text in the Venice edition of 1544; it belongs later on, after the words "a curtain is spread before him." It does seem to break up the context here, for the following sentence should refer back to God's crown. Still, we may well wonder how these words came to be inserted here. I suspect that they are connected with a literal exegesis of *ke͑en ḥashmal* to mean *like the eye of ḥashmal. Hekhalot Rabbati* and *Zuṭarti,* as we have seen, understand Ezekiel 1:27 to describe this critical and scrutinizing *eye of ḥashmal* (chapter VI, section 2; chapter IX, section B2).

His throne is the color of sapphire. It has four legs, with the four *hayyot* fixed at each leg. Each of them has four faces and each has four wings; as it is written, *Each had four faces*, and so forth [Ezekiel 1:6]. They are identical with the cherubim. ...

Over against them are the Ophannim and the wheels of the *merkabah* [*galgalle merkabah*]. ... Two seraphim are standing, one on God's right, one on his left. Each has six wings. *With two he covers his face*, in order not to gaze upon the Shechinah. With two they cover their feet, that they be not exposed to the Shechinah, so that the standing of the *calf's foot* [Ezekiel 1:7] may be forgotten. With two they fly, exalting and sanctifying his great name [cf. Isaiah 6:2].

One [seraph] calls out and the other responds: *Holy holy holy is the Lord of hosts, the whole earth is full of his glory* [Isaiah 6:3]. The *hayyot* stand by his glory, yet do not know the place of his glory. They respond: Wherever his glory may be, *blessed be the glory of the Lord from its place* [Ezekiel 3:12]. Then responds Israel, a unique nation that unifies his name every day. *Hear O Israel*, they say, *the Lord is our God, the Lord is one* [Deuteronomy 6:4]. He then answers his people Israel: *I am the Lord your God* [Numbers 15:41], who saves you from all troubles[2].

The author of *Massekhet Hekhalot* incorporates extracts from this chapter into his own account of the heavenly realms, at the beginning of chapter 6 and the end of chapter 7. He elaborates upon them in a characteristically extravagant fashion, sometimes combining them with other sources. Thus, at the end of chapter 7, he supplements *Pirqe de-Rabbi Eliezer*'s "seven angels who were created first" with the "seven overseers" of *Sefer ha-Razim* ("First Heaven"; ed. 67 [216]). The dependence is clear, and shows nothing more than that *Massekhet Hekhalot* is later than *Pirqe de-Rabbi Eliezer*, and that its author found this midrash a useful source.

The relationship of this midrashic passage to *Hekhalot Zuṭarti*, ms New York (Schäfer, ##368–373), is entirely different. The two are obviously connected. The fourth paragraph of the quotation given above has point after point in common with Schäfer, #372: God is in the middle; his glory is *like the color of ḥashmal*; he wears a crown and the wreath of the ineffable name; life is on his right hand, death on his left; he holds a rod or rods of fire; a curtain is spread before him; seven special angels serve him inside that curtain. In the next paragraph, *Pirqe de-Rabbi Eliezer* describes the *ḥayyot* as fixed (*qebuᶜot*) at the four legs of the throne. This is only a step from ms New York's claim that they *are* these legs[3].

The similarities between the two sources extend to their language. Yet there are obvious differences between them, and it would be very hard to argue for literary dependence of one upon the other. Rather – and we shall soon see this judgment confirmed – we are to look for a common tradition.

---

2 Deuteronomy 6:4 opens the *Shemaᶜ*; Numbers 15:41 concludes it.

3 A well-known passage in the late *Midrash on Proverbs*, enumerating the sciences associated with "the viewing of the *merkabah*," perhaps presupposes this identification when it speaks of the question of "how my throne of glory stands, what function its first leg serves, what functions its second, its third, and its fourth" (chapter 10; ed. 33b–34a; partially translated by Scholem and Cohen [611a,516a]).

In what setting might this tradition have been cultiviated? We have seen that the *merkabah* exegesis of the *Hekhalot* passage is linked to that of the synagogue (chapter IX, section B1b). Chapter 4 of *Pirqe de-Rabbi Eliezer* points in the same direction. The chapter's exegesis of the three segments of Isaiah 6:3 follows the lines laid down by the synagogue *merkabah* tradition (chapter V, section 2). Its conclusion elaborates on the heavenly liturgy and the Jewish people's central role in it, an issue which we have seen to be specially important to the synagogue tradition (chapter IV, section 4) and to play a role in the *Hekhalot* as well (chapter IX, section B3c). We may recall, in this connection, *Pirqe de-Rabbi Eliezer*'s evident ties to the Palestinian Targumim [410].

2. A passage in the *Midrash on Psalms*, 90:12 (ed. 196a–b), echoes a claim shared by *Pirqe de-Rabbi Eliezer* and *Hekhalot Zuṭarti*: that God has life on his right hand, death on his left.

> R. Abbahu b. Ze^cera said: ... Seven things were in existence two thousand years before the world was created: the Torah, the throne of glory, paradise, hell, repentance, the heavenly temple, and the name of the Messiah. Where was the Torah written? In black fire on white fire, laid on God's knees. God sat on the throne of glory; and the throne of glory was established by God's grace on the firmament on the heads of the *ḥayyot*, even though the *ḥayyot* did not yet exist. Paradise was on God's right, hell on his left, the temple established before him, and the name of the Messiah inscribed on a jewel on the altar. [As for repentance,] a heavenly voice would proclaim, *Return, children of men* [Psalm 90:3].
>
> It was then God's power that supported all this. But when God created his world, and created the holy *ḥayyot*, he fixed the firmament carrying it all on the horns of the *ḥayyot*. So it is written: *On the heads of the ḥayyot was the likeness of a firmament* [Ezekiel 1:22].

The author of this midrash did not invent his enumeration of primordial entities; similar lists of seven (or six) such entities appear in older rabbinic sources (*Gen. R.* 1:4, ed. 6, and parallels [188]). Nor did he invent its attribution to "Abbahu b. Ze^cera"; the name is obviously a corruption of the "R. Ahabah b. R. Ze^cera" quoted in *Gen. R.* 1:4. We shall therefore be inclined to suppose that even the features of this midrash that seem unique – notably, its effort to locate the primordial entities in space – are not original with its author, but rest on traditions that do not survive anywhere else.

One such feature is particularly striking: the statement that "paradise was on God's right, hell on his left." This is obviously a variant of *Pirqe de-Rabbi Eliezer*'s claim that life is on God's right hand, death on his left. The parallel is all the more significant in that the two passages do not show the slightest trace of a literary relationship, and in fact contradict each other. For *Midr. Psalms* 90:12 assumes that the "firmament" of Ezekiel 1:22 was in existence long before the creation, even though the *ḥayyot* that carry it were not; while *Pirqe de-Rabbi Eliezer* identifies it with the firmament that God created on the second day (Genesis 1:6–8). In placing life/paradise on God's right and death/hell on his left, both midrashim seem to draw on a common tradition, which the authors of both take for granted.

3. We now find this speculation confirmed from an unexpected source: a Coptic Gnostic text discovered at Nag Hammadi in Egypt, entitled *The Hypostasis of the Archons*[4]. Scholars date the manuscript containing this document to the fourth century A.D. The document itself, which seems to have been translated into Coptic from Greek, may be considerably older.

The text describes, in conventional Gnostic fashion, the criminal arrogance of the monster-god Yaldabaoth, fashioner of the dark and evil Matter; and his consequent punishment at the hands of Sophia ("Wisdom") and her daughter Zoe ("Life"). But unconventionally, it adds a new character to the drama, a repentant son of Yaldabaoth's:

> "Now when his offspring Sabaoth saw the force of that angel, he repented and condemned his father and his mother Matter.
>
> "He loathed her, but he sang songs of praise up to Sophia and her daughter Zoe. And Sophia and Zoe caught him up and gave him charge of the seventh heaven, below the veil between Above and Below. And he is called 'God of the Forces, Sabaoth,' since he is up above the Forces of Chaos, for Sophia established him.
>
> "Now when these (events) had come to pass, he made himself a huge four-faced chariot of cherubim[5], and infinitely many angels to act as ministers, and also harps and lyres.
>
> "And Sophia took her daughter Zoe and had her sit upon his right to teach him about the things that exist in the Eighth (Heaven); and the Angel [of] Wrath she placed upon his left. [Since] that day, [his right] has been called Life; and the left has come to represent the unrighteousness of the realm of absolute power above. ..." [Tr. 158–159 [729]]

"Sabaoth" is certainly the Jewish God. His name is the Hebrew *seba'ot,* "hosts," and is drawn from the common Biblical title of God as "Lord of hosts." (Similarly, the Latin *Sanctus* hymn, based on Isaiah 6:3, turns "the Lord of hosts" into *Dominus Deus Sabaoth.*) But, while the Gnostics normally cast the creator of the material world and author of the Old Testament in a purely villainous role, our text seems bent on at least partially rehabilitating him [709]. It therefore allows him a glory which is, if derivative, at least real and legitimate.

The author plainly draws his account of this glory from what the Jews themselves said about it. That is, he repeats a description which only makes complete sense if we understand it as applying to the one supreme God, and not to the low-level functionary of the *Hypostasis of the Archons*. In the present context of the description, we can understand well enough why "Life" (Zoe) should sit at Sabaoth's right, to teach him wisdom. But why should he have the Angel of Wrath on his left? This detail is intelligible only in a monotheistic scheme which has the Lord Sabaoth at its center, the life

---

4 Nicolas Séd, and more particularly Ithamar Gruenwald, anticipate several of the observations I make in this and the next section [731,548].

5 The Coptic translator uses the Greek words *harma* ("chariot") and *cheroubin*, which presumably stood in the original. They perhaps hark back to the Greek text of I Chronicles 28:18 (*tou harmatos tōn cheroubin*) or Sira 49:8 (*harmatos cheroubin*).

he grants and the punishment he inflicts on either side of him. This picture, which we have already seen in *Hekhalot Zuṭarti, Pirqe de-Rabbi Eliezer*, and *Midr. Psalms* 90:12, was known to a Gnostic writer who cannot have lived after the fourth century.

Gruenwald seems to be right in inferring, not that the Jewish sources are in some way Gnostic, but that certain Gnostics were familiar with Jewish *merkabah* lore [548]. This lore must have circulated fairly widely within Judaism, in order to have percolated outside. Our observations on *Pirqe de-Rabbi Eliezer* suggest what we might in any case have guessed, that the synagogue provided the channels in which it circulated.

4. The plot thickens when we turn to a second Nag Hammadi text, untitled, which modern scholars have dubbed *On the Origin of the World*. Here we have a far more elaborate version of the same story, of Sabaoth's repentance and exaltation; and several of the new details that enrich it seem to be fresh imports from Judaism.

> But when Sabaoth, the son of Yaldabaoth, heard the voice of Pistis[6], he worshipped [her] ... she sent seven archangels from her light to Sabaoth. They snatched him away up to the seventh heaven. They took their stand before him as servants. Furthermore, she sent him three other archangels. She established the kingdom for him above every one so that he might come to be above the twelve gods of Chaos.
> But when Sabaoth received the place of repose because of his repentance, Pistis moreover gave him her daughter Zoe, with a great authority so that she might inform him about everything that exists in the eighth (heaven). And since he had an authority, he first created a dwelling place for himself. It is a large place which is very excellent, sevenfold (greater) than all those which exist [in the] seven heavens.
> Then in front of his dwelling place he created a great throne on a four-faced chariot called "Cherubin." And the Cherubin has eight forms for each of the four corners – lion forms, and bull forms, and human forms, and eagle forms – so that all of the forms total sixty-four forms. And seven archangels stand before him. He is the eighth, having authority. All of the forms total seventy-two. For from this chariot the seventy-two gods receive a pattern; and they receive a pattern so that they might rule over the seventy-two languages of the nations. And on that throne he created some other dragon-shaped angels called "Seraphin," who glorify him continually.
> Afterward he created an angelic church – thousands and myriads, without number, (belong to her) – being like the church which is in the eighth. And a first-born called "Israel," i.e., "the man who sees god[7]," and (also) having another name, "Jesus the Christ," who is like the Savior who is above the eighth, sits at his right upon an excellent throne. But on his left the virgin of the holy spirit sits upon a throne praising him. And the seven virgins stand before her while thirty (other virgins) (with) lyres and harps [and] trumpets in their hands glorify him. And all of the armies of angels glorify him and praise him. But he sits on a throne concealed by a great light-cloud. And there was no one with him in the cloud except Sophia Pistis, teaching him about all those which exist in the eighth so that the likeness of those might be created, in order that the kingdom might continue for him until the consummation of the heavens of Chaos and their powers.

---

6 "Faith," often combined with Sophia into Pistis-Sophia, "Faith-Wisdom."

7 A standard Hellenistic Jewish etymology for "Israel," which we have already met in Origen's ninth homily on Joshua (chapter VIII, section C3b).

Now Pistis Sophia separated him from the darkness. She summoned him to her right. But she left the First Father on her left. Since that day right has been called "justice," but left has been called "injustice." Moreover, because of this they all received an order of the assembly of justice; and the injustice stands above all ⟨their⟩ creations. [Tr. 165–166 [729]]

"All of the forms total sixty-four forms" seems almost a quotation from the Targum to Ezekiel 1:6: "The total number of faces of the four creatures was sixty-four." The seven archangels who "took their stand before him as servants" appear in *Pirqe de-Rabbi Eliezer* and *Hekhalot Zutarti* as the seven angels who serve inside the curtain. The "twelve gods of Chaos" whom Sabaoth rules are reminiscent of the twelve angels who surround the throne in *Hekhalot Zutarti*[8]. The exaltation of the personified Israel suggests similar developments in the Jewish sources. *Pirqe de-Rabbi Eliezer* gives "Israel" the key role in the heavenly liturgy; the *Hekhalot* have the Jewish people represented in the heavenly worship by "a *hayyah* whose name is Israel," or by the exalted "youth" Metatron, who also sits by God on an excellent throne (chapter IX, section B4). (The identification of this "Israel" with Jesus Christ sounds like an afterthought of a Christian Gnostic writer or editor.) One *Hekhalot* passage has God "give some of his splendor and glory to the Gentile kings," in connection with the youth's appearance beneath his throne (#385; chapter IX, section B4); and a parallel passage has the "prince" himself "give some of his glory to the princes of the Gentiles; [while] the crown on his head is named 'Israel'" (#398; chapter VII, section 2c). We hear an echo of these claims in *On the Origin of the World*: "For from this chariot the seventy-two gods receive a pattern; and they receive a pattern so that they might rule over the seventy-two languages of the nations."

The Nag Hammadi document's parallels, I suspect, are less with the *Hekhalot* themselves than with the synagogue *merkabah* exegesis from which they spring. That is why it announces a grand total of "sixty-four forms," agreeing with the Targum to Ezekiel 1:6, against the *Hekhalot* passages that develop the Targum's computations (chapter IX, section B1). When the Gnostic author wanted to learn more about the enthroned Sabaoth than *The Hypostasis of the Archons* could tell him, he turned, as his predecessor had done, to the lore of the synagogue sermons.

5. The last paragraph of my quotation from *On the Origin of the World*, however, raises the possibility that the flow of information may not always have been in the same direction.

---

8 Schäfer, #372. Their names, which I omitted from the translation of this passage that I gave in the text, are "*kwbky'l pdy'l myk'l* on the right, *ᶜzry'l zkry'l šmᶜ'l* on the left, *gbry'l rp'l 'hzy'l* behind him, *rgᶜy'l dnn'l 'wry'l* in front of him." The third, seventh, eighth, and twelfth of these names are the familiar Michael, Gabriel, Raphael, and Uriel.

The Hypostasis of the Archons, we recall, had Sabaoth sit in the middle, with Life on his right and the Angel of Wrath on his left; and we saw that this detail must have come directly from a Jewish source. *On the Origin of the World*, however, puts Pistis Sophia in the middle, with Sabaoth on her right and the "First Father" (the Coptic text uses the Greek word *archigenetōr*) on her left. The sequel, which speaks of Sabaoth as the son of "the First Father of Chaos," shows that the "First Father" must be Yaldabaoth.

In other words, Sophia has replaced Zoe as the female figure on the tableau; she and Sabaoth have switched places; and Yaldabaoth has replaced the Angel of Wrath on the left. The first two of these changes do not concern us. But when we consider the third, and recall that Yaldabaoth often figures as the Gnostic world-creator ("demiurge"), we can hardly avoid linking this passage with the peculiar name *Hekhalot Zutarti* gives one of the two "mighty ones" on God's left: *habbore'*, "the creator" (Schäfer, #372).

This detail, unlike most we have examined so far, seems more at home in Gnosticism than in Judaism. *Hekhalot Zutarti* thus shows here a trace of direct Gnostic influence. Through what channels this influence operated, and how it was related to the more obvious Jewish influence on the two Gnostic texts we have considered, are questions I must leave for a later investigation. In chapter VIII, section C5d, I pointed to evidence for a reciprocal influence between the Greek Shabuᶜot homilies and contemporary Christian exegesis. Perhaps these two cases of reciprocal influence, when we finally clear them up, will turn out to be parallel.

Appendix VII

Salmon b. Yeruhim's Version of the Sar Torah Myth

Early in the tenth century A.D., the Karaite Salmon b. Yeruhim composed a bitter attack on Saadiah Gaon, and on the rabbinic Judaism that Saadiah represented. He wrote his polemic in rhymed Hebrew verse, and called it, in imitation of Numbers 21:14, *Sefer Milḥamot 'Adonay*, "The Book of the Wars of the Lord[1]."

Salmon devoted the early part of his work to abuse of rabbinic *halakhah*; then, in the last four cantos (14–17), turned to haggadic teachings which he thought absurd or blasphemous. He laid particular weight on the "Book of Secrets" (*Sefer ha-Razim*), on the *Hekhalot* in general, and on the *Shiʿur Qomah* in particular. He believed, or affected to believe, that *Shiʿur Qomah* was in fact the work of Ishmael and Akiba. He could therefore hold rabbinic Judaism, and hence Saadiah, responsible for it:

> You [Saadiah] say: "The Karaites are innovators, while our ancient rabbis are holy." Well, if the authors of abominations of this sort are holy saints, then Sisera, Haman, and their ilk must be at rest in Paradise! [Canto 14, stanza 21]

The final canto of the *Book of the Wars of the Lord* is devoted entirely to a version of the *Sar Torah* myth, clearly related to the text I translated in chapter IX (section D2a), but differing from it in certain details. Not all of these divergences, to be sure, indicate that Salmon's source was different from our text. At times, Salmon seems to have misunderstood his source (stanzas 16–17). At other times, he deliberately tampered with its wording or its arrangement, to suit his rhyme and his acrostic scheme. (Thus, stanzas 20–22 are clearly out of their proper sequence, while the progress of the dialogue in stanzas 12–14 makes little sense.) But there are other divergences which cannot be explained so simply, and which do nothing to advance Salmon's own polemical ends. We must suppose that they go back to a variant tradition of *Sar Torah*.

---

1 The reader can find more about Salmon, and about the anti-rabbinic Karaite movement in early medieval Judaism, in Leon Nemoy's *Karaite Anthology* [250a]. Nemoy translates the first three cantos from the *Book of the Wars of the Lord*.

These significant variations include a polemic against Christianity (stanza 4); borrowings from the Moses/Metatron text (stanzas 10, 11); allusions to and borrowings from the *haggadot* on Moses' struggle for the Torah, absent from our text of the *Śar Torah* myth (stanzas 4, 8, 12, 13); and the angels' (understand, rabbis') comparison of humans (understand, *cam ha'areṣ*) to animals (stanza 14). They also include a curious and important tradition, which I have not seen anywhere else, that Enoch-Metatron originally opposed God's revelation of his "secret" to humans, and only came to collaborate in it under pressure from God.

Long before Israel Davidson published the full text of the *Book of the Wars of the Lord* in 1934 [244], Heinrich Grätz made use of canto 17 in a classic article on the *Hekhalot* and *Shicur Qomah* [528]. More recent scholars have largely ignored it. To my knowledge, only Moshe Idel has given it its just due, stressing the resemblance of Salmon's narrative to the rabbinic stories of Moses' capture of the Torah [566]. Idel's remarks have inspired much of my own perception of the *Śar Torah* myth.

I here offer a full translation of canto 17, from Davidson's edition. I translate each stanza as a prose paragraph, and make no effort to convey the poetic structure of the original. Nor do I try to distinguish actual quotation of the source from Salmon's paraphrase. I do, however, mark in italics the derogatory comments that Salmon inserts from time to time.

In the right-hand margin, I note the corresponding paragraphs (from Schäfer) of our version of the *Śar Torah* myth.

1. *Then, after these measurements*[2], *the unbelieving men say as follows*: When God desired to reveal this secret — *that is, these loathsome things* — the celestial princes took it hard, and were grieved.

2. God's youth [*naCar*], his beloved Enoch son of Jared, came before him. Thus he admonished him: "Do not let this secret go forth from your treasuries, to be written down. Do not let the great secret out of your storehouses, to be put to use.   #292
"
"

3. "You should loathe flesh and blood, not exalt him to our level. Do not liken "
him ... [three words which I do not know how to translate]. Hear our outcry, re- "
ceive our admonition. Leave man to labor in the Torah, and let him not become "
like us. "

4. "Let his Torah be his lot, sufficient for him. If you want to justify him, give him in addition a crucified man, to torment him[3]. But do not reveal the measure [*shiCur*], on account of his impurity[4]."

---

2 That is, *ShiCur Qomah*, which has absorbed Salmon's indignant attention through cantos 15 and 16. We may perhaps infer that Salmon's source represented the *Śar Torah* myth as part of, or as an appendix to, *ShiCur Qomah*.

3 *We'im roṣeh 'attah lezakkoto / hosef lo muṣlab leCannoto*. Grätz, evidently understanding *muṣlab* to mean "crucifixion," takes this as a reference to R. Ishmael's martyrdom at the hands of the Romans, which is indeed mentioned in stanza 7 [528a]. There are several objections to this inter-

5. The Rock [God] answered him: "I hear your convern. But please, my be-
loved, don't let it disturb you. Do not take it ill, nor raise your voice [to complain]   Cf. #293
that I am taking this secret away from you.

6. "I am bringing this secret out of my treasures. It did not occur to me to give   "   "
it to my camps, my angels, or all my hosts. It is only for my son Ishmael, who keeps   "   "
my qualities [? *shomer middotay*] [5].

7. "He is a descendant of Aaron[6], offspring of noble families. He has taken upon
himself to die at the hands of pagans. Through him do I reveal it, that the Israelites
may be justified by means of it. Do not be angry, for he is greater than my great
servants [the angels].

8. "Consider the descendants of my lover [Abraham] [7]. I did not create for my
servants [the angels] the good or the evil inclination. There is no conflict among
them, no stealing or robbery. But for Ishmael I created all these[8]."

9. *He is pure, and his servants are pure. He is chosen, and they are chosen likewise. He is upright, and they are upright like him. He is greater than all* [angelic]
holy ones and watchers[9].

10. The beloved youth Enoch advised the angels that they should speak no more,
nor raise their voices against God. He received permission from the king of the world,
and he alone sheltered R. Ishmael against their outcry[10].

---

pretation. First, it is more plausible to translate the participle *muṣlab* as "crucified man" than as
"crucifixion." Second, the natural antecedent of the masculine pronouns is "man" (*'adam*, stanza
3), not Ishmael, who has not yet been mentioned. Third, the martyr-legends have Ishmael skin-
ned alive, not crucified [479b,486a]. I prefer to take this sentence as a polemical reference to
Christianity, which the author represents as a second-rate substitute for the secret of Torah, proposed for humanity by humanity's jealous rivals. – Salmon b. Yeruhim was, to be sure, no ad-
mirer of Christianity. (Canto 15, stanza 2: "If the misguided Christian lunatics had not lifted up
their images on spear-tips to outrage [God], their Lord's disgrace would [never] have become
public knowledge.") But, seen as his insertion, this passage makes no sense. We must suppose that
it comes from his source, and reflects the anti-Christian animus of the circles that created the
Śar Torah myth. – It is not clear whether the object of the tormenting is the "crucified man,"
or "man" in general.

4 This argument is reminiscent of the charges the angels bring against Moses in *Pesiqta* and its parallels, and in the Moses/Metatron text (Schäfer, #79). We will meet it again in stanza 13.

5 This peculiar expression is perhaps somehow connected with the use of the word *shamur* (which
I translate "reserved") in #293.

6 *Zera[c] 'aharon*. Cf. *zera[c] ne'eman*, "faithful seed," in #293.

7 *Zera[c] 'ohabi*. This is the usage of *Hekhalot Rabbati*, which calls the Jews "descendants of [God's]
lover Abraham" (#218, *zera[c] 'abraham 'ohabo*; above, chapter VIII, section A5c). But it also suggests the "beloved people" (*[c]am 'ahub*) of #293.

8 Ishmael's virtue therefore proves him to be greater than the angels. – These remarks on the inherent sinlessness of angels are, as Idel points out [566], very reminiscent of Moses' argument in
the ascension stories that the Torah is appropriate for humans and not for angels (above, chapter
VIII, section B2d). Of the several parallel versions [293a], BT Shabbat 89a is the closest to Salmon's text: "*You shall not murder, you shall not commit adultery, you shall not steal. Is there
jealousy among you* [angels]? *The evil inclination?*"

9 I take this stanza to be Salmon's insertion, its point that God and his angels are too lofty for the
squalid parleying that the *Śar Torah* myth attributes to them. (Salmon makes a very similar point
in canto 15, stanza 9.) If we regard it rather as part of Salmon's source, we must suppose that it
continues the theme of Ishmael's superiority over the angels. But then who are Ishmael's "servants" (*mesharetaw*)? – The designation "holy ones and watchers" (*qaddishin we[c]irin*) for angels
is drawn from Daniel 4:10, 14, 20.

10 The first part of this sentence is, as Davidson observed in his note on the passage [244], drawn
from what I have called the Moses/Metatron text (Schäfer, #79). I have commented on the sig-

11. Fiercely did the angels argue against their Rock over the revelation and ex- Cf. #291, end
planation of the measurements, until the Rock cried out and loudly rebuked them[11]:

12. "Wasn't it enough that you sided against me and disputed with me over the
Torah that I gave to my people, until I killed some of you in my anger? Now keep
quiet and leave me alone! If you don't, I will rise up and wipe you out[12]."

13. When they saw him so angry, they said to each other: "What shall we do?"
They placated him, and said: "Don't do it. Don't reveal this secret to a being filthy Cf. #292, end
in all that he does[13].   "   "

14. "We are very much afraid that the small will become like the great in wisdom, #292, end
the fool like the wise man in knowledge and intelligence. They are comparable to   "   "
beasts[14]!" So answered his servants, in terror.   "   "

15. The Rock set himself to comfort them. "Please, my ministers and servants, #293
don't keep on complaining. I am not going to reveal this secret to my people until   "
they become enlightened. From Moses' time until now I have not transmitted it to   "
any creature. That is why the words of my Torah were like brass and iron in their   "
ears, and they did not practice my religion.   "

16. "I struck them, and the mountains reeled. Their corpses were like excrement   "
before all passers-by. Now how shall I comfort and placate them, setting crowns on #294
their heads? I see that my people has immeasurable amounts of silver in this world.   " (cf. #288)

17. "I look about and see that my people has gold. Indeed, my world is full of   "
gold[15]. My people has pearls and jewels, to give honor to my name.   "

18. "I see that the world has wheat and honey, wine and oil, and all sorts of deli-   "
cacies. What, then, does the world lack? Only this secret, which is hidden from all.   "
I will reveal it to my children, and spread out their banner."   "

19. The angels then accepted his answer, and each went off to his work. God sits
with the youth Enoch, in his love. *God forbid we should say things like this*[16]!

20. Israel and their Rock had many quarrels – *so they say* – until their Rock Cf. #282
replied to them: "You have not behaved well" – *so they conclude* – "and I have not #283

---

nificance of this borrowing in chapter IX, section D1. – My translation of the rest of the sentence, *wenimsa' yekhapper lebaddo rabbi yishmaᶜ'el behillulam*, is guesswork. Hebrew *hillul*
means "singing praises," while its Aramaic cognate *hillula* takes on the additional meanings of
"wedding" or "celebration." None of these meanings would suit a hostile outcry. Perhaps Arabic
istahalla, "to talk loudly; raise one's voice" [801a], influenced Salmon's usage.

11 Similarly, in the Moses/Metatron text, the angels "were not satisfied until God grew angry at
them and chased them away with a rebuke" (Schäfer, #79). Admittedly, the Hebrew words for
"rebuke" are different in the two sources (*gaᶜar, nezifah*).

12 God's rebuke not only alludes to the angels' resistance to the revelation of Torah, but seems modelled after a scolding he gives them in *Pesiqta Rabbati* and its parallels: "You always were an argu-
mentative lot! When I wanted to create Adam, you started complaining, *Why should you keep
humans in mind* [Psalm 8:5], and you did not leave me alone until I burned up group after group
of you. And now you are struggling to keep me from giving Torah to Israel." (See above, chapter
VIII, section B2c, on Hadarniel; parallels in Grözinger [292a].)

13 *Metunnaf bekhol maᶜaś*. The accusation suggests Kemuel's rebuke of Moses: "You come from a
place of filth [*meqom tinofet*]. What are you doing in a place of purity?" (*Pesiqta Rabbati* and
ms Oxford; above, chapter VIII, section B2b).

14 This last sentence is missing from our text of the *Śar Torah* myth. Yet we have no reason to
doubt that Salmon found it in his source. I discuss its significance in chapter IX, section D2c.

15 *Paniti wehinneh zahab leᶜammi / wegam zahab male' ᶜolami*. Our text of the *Śar Torah* myth
has: *safiti wera'iti zahab ᶜimmi zahab baᶜolam*, "I looked and found that I have gold, but the
world does too" (and so for silver, jewels, and pearls). It seems that Salmon found the same or
nearly the same reading in his source, but misread ᶜ*immi* ("with me") as ᶜ*ammi* ("my people").
The ensuing misunderstanding dominates stanza 17 and the last sentence of 16.

behaved well" – *so they assert.* "Remember and understand that you profaned me
and treated me lightly.

21. "I turned on you in my wrath. But now I accept your scolding, for you have #283
many more claims [?] upon me. I am giving you your reward: my hidden secret, as #285, 286
much as you please.   „   „

22. "Now be you joyful, while my servants groan in sorrow. For this secret is #289
one of the mighty [?] secrets. The world's great ones will split open and die when ##289–290
they see that you have it."

---

16 Salmon evidently imagines – without, as far as I can see, any justification – that the *Hekhalot*
   represent God as having a homosexual attachment to his "youth." He then recoils in horror before the blasphemy that he has himself invented.

Endnotes

Chapter I

a) Tanh. *Toledot* #7 explains R. Judah's explanation: The man born blind "seems like a bearer of false witness when he says, 'blessed be the fashioner of the luminaries,' without ever having seen luminaries."

b) The sentence that follows, "R. Joshua began to expound *maʿaśeh merkabah*," is omitted by one manuscript, found only in the margin in a second, and misplaced in the text in a third. I suspect it is an interpolation, its purpose to magnify the role of R. Joshua [559].

c) So the weight of the manuscript evidence. The printed editions, followed by the Soncino translation, have "Hananiah b. Hezekiah," as in the preceding story [458, 552].

d) Several minor but suggestive features link the traditions about the Book of Ezekiel with those about the Book of Ecclesiastes. (1) BT's account of the attempt to "conceal" Ecclesiastes (Shabb. 30b) resembles the traditions about Ezekiel in BT Hag. 13a and parallels, both in language and in attribution ("Rab Judah, son of Rab Samuel b. Shilat, in the name of Rab"). (2) Other traditions about Ecclesiastes credit King Hezekiah and his "men" (Proverbs 25:1) with rescuing the book from "concealment" (*'Abot de-Rabbi Natan*, ch. 1) [403]. In one of the Ezekiel traditions, the book's savior is Hananiah b. *Hezekiah*. (3) The story in *'Abot de-Rabbi Natan*, in which a book's being "written" is the opposite of its being "concealed," yields the key to the BT passage that says that Hezekiah and his "company" (*siʿato*) "wrote" the Solomonic books; what they did was save them from "concealment" (B.B. 14b–15a). Now, *'Abot de-Rabbi Natan* seems to equate, in a very obscure way, the "men of Hezekiah king of Judah" with the "men of the Great Synagogue"; and a passage from B.B. 14b–15a that has long puzzled scholars [15,17, 30] says that "the men of the Great Synagogue wrote Ezekiel." Can the author of B.B. 14b–15a have regarded Hezekiah's men and the "men of the Great Synagogue" as two closely related bodies, one of which rescued Ecclesiastes from suppression, the other of which saved Ezekiel? (4) Hananiah b. Hezekiah's resemblance to King Hezekiah is not limited to his name. King Hezekiah is the only character who, in the Babylonian Talmud, appears regularly with a "company" (*siʿah*) [811]; in BT Shabb. 13b, "Hananiah b. Hezekiah and his company" (*siʿato*) are said to have written the Scroll of Fasting. (5) BT Shabb. 13b makes this last statement in answer to the question, "Who wrote [*mi katab*] the Scroll of Fasting?" BT B.B. 14b–15a opens with a similar question about the books of the Bible – "who wrote them?" (*umi ketaban*) – and answers, in part, that Hezekiah and his "company" wrote Ecclesiastes, the men of the Great Synagogue wrote Ezekiel. The role of Hananiah b. Hezekiah and his "company" is thus parallel to that of King Hezekiah and his "company."

Chapter II

a) Cf. Ezekiel 1:9, *hoberot 'ishshah 'el 'aḥotah*, with Exodus 26:3; cf. Ezekiel 1:11, *kanfehem perudot millemaʿlah*, with Exodus 25:20, *poreśe khenafayim lemaʿlah*. Cf. Ezekiel 1:15–21 with I Kings 7:30–33; and especially Ezekiel 1:16, *mar'eh ha'ofannim umaʿaśehem*, with I Kings 7:33, *umaʿaśeh ha'ofannim kemaʿaśeh 'ofan hammerkabah*.

b) We will see a few examples from the apocalyptic literature in the next chapter. Both Talmuds preserve a fantastic story of how a high priest, who performed the incense offering of the Day of Atonement in the way prescribed by the Sadducees, was fatally kicked in the Holy of Holies by one of the *ḥayyot* (PT Yoma 1:5, 39a; BT Yoma 19b) [419]. The story assumes that the *ḥayyot*, being cherubim, are at home in the Holy of Holies; they are, as it were, the spirits of the gold-plated cherubim who once reposed there. We may assume that the story is Pharisee propaganda dating from a time before the destruction of the Temple, when the Yom Kippur incense offering was a live issue. The *ḥayyot* = cherubim theme, weak enough even before the destruction, fades away almost totally afterward.

c) Schiffman gives many examples. I note here one that I find particularly striking. The second fragment of the Angelic Liturgy uses the phrases *beriqmat kabod* and *memullaḥ ṭohar* in parallelism, both of them employed rather oddly (line 6 of Strugnell's text; lines 12–13 of my translation, below). A passage conventionally attributed to *Hekhalot Rabbati* lists *memullaḥ* (after *roqeaḥ*; cf. Exodus 30:35) in a long series of virtues attributed to God; and, shortly afterward, declares him *melekh ... mehuddar beruqme shir* (Schäfer, ##251–252; Wertheimer, 25:1 [495,500]).

d) The Hebrew text is as follows:

1 וב[ר]כו בהרומם   2
קול דממת אלוהים
[   ] והמון רנה ברים כנפיהם   3
קול [דממ]ת אלוהים
5 תבנית כסא מרכבה מברכים
ממעל לרקיע הכרובים   4
[והו]ד רקיע האור ירננו
((מ))מתחת מושב כבודו
ובלכת האופנים ישובו מלאכי קודש
10 יצא(ו) (ו)מבין[/ג]לגלי כבודו כמראי אש רוחו"ת" קודש קדשים   5
סביב מראי שבולי אש בדמות חשמל
ומעשי / [נ]וגה בריקמת כבוד   6
צבעי פלא ממולח טוה(ר)
רוחות [א]לוהים חיים מתהלכים תמיד עם כבוד
מרכבות/ [ה]פלא   7
15 וקול דממת ברכ בהמון לכתם
והללו קודש בהשיב דרכיהם
בהרומם ירוממו פלא
ובשובן / [יעמ]ודו   8
קול גילות רנה השקיט
20 ודממ[ת] ברך [א]לוהים
בכול מחני אלוהים

The numbers in the left-hand margin indicate the lines of the original text. In discussing the passage, I use the line numbers of my arrangement (marked in the right-hand margin).

Schiffman's reading of the text differs from Strugnell's in only three places, all of them involving decisions between the letters *waw* and *yod*, which look practically the same in Qumran script. In line 3, Strugnell reads *berim*, Schiffman *berum*; in line 11, Strugnell reads *shibbole*, Schiffman *shebile*; in line 12, Strugnell reads *beruqmat*, Schiffman *beriqmat*. I follow Strugnell in the first two cases, Schiffman in the third. In line 18, I read *beshuban* for *beshokhen*; see below.

Notes on the text and translation: (1) Ezekiel 10:17, *uberomam yerommu*, has probably influenced *beheromam* in line 1; it has certainly influenced *beheromam yeromemu* in line 17. (2) I see no need to assume, as do Strugnell and Schiffman, that the lacuna at the beginning of line 3 contained *lemaᶜlah*. (3) *Hamon rinnah* (line 3) also occurs in a broken line in fragment 23 of the *Hodayot*. The use of *hamon*, here and in line 16, has probably been influenced by Daniel 10:6, *weqol debaraw keqol hamon*. Qumran texts sometimes use *hamon* to indicate the roaring of the sea, usually with a sinister connotation (1QH ii, 16, 27, iii, 12–16; cf. iii, 32). (4) I read, with Strugnell, Hiphᶜil *barim* (< *beharim*) *kanfehem* in line 3. Cf. Ezekiel 10:16, *ubiś'et ... 'et kanfehem larum meᶜal ha'areṣ*. (5) Lines 5–6 are drawn from Ezekiel 1:26: *mimmaᶜal lireqiaᶜ hakkerubim* (vocalizing with Schiffman) from *mimmaᶜal laraqiaᶜ 'asher ᶜal rosham*; *tabnit kisse' merkabah* from *demut kisse'*. The use of *tabnit* may reflect I Chronicles 28:18. (6) The parallelism of *qodesh* and *qodesh qodashim* (lines 9–10) inclines me to translate *qodesh* as "holy place" (here and in line 16) rather than "holiness." This usage is rare at Qumran but there are a few examples in the recently published "Temple Scroll" (xvii, 9, xxxii, 12, cf. xlvi, 10; ed. 2:55, 99, 139 [82]). 1QS viii, 5–6, and ix, 6, use *qodesh* and *qodesh qodashim* together, both times in connection with Aaron. (7) *Ubelekhet ha'ofannim* (line 9) seems to reflect Ezekiel 1:17, 19–21, 10: 11, 16. The emergence of fiery entities *mibben galgalle kebodo* (line 10) reflects Ezekiel 10:6. (8) In line 11, *shibbole 'esh* could mean "rivers of fire" (Strugnell), and *shebile 'esh* could mean "paths of fire" (Schiffman). Both translations are plausible. But if, as I suspect, line 11 is an anticipatory description of the "spirits of the living God" (line 14), neither is quite appropriate. I suggest that line 11 describes God's throngs of spirit servitors as looking like a field filled with ears of grain – only, of fire. Perhaps this image, and the preceding *sabib*, is linked to the circular procession of sheaves of grain in Genesis 37:7, *tesubbenah 'alummotekhem*. Cf. 1QM v 11, *mar'e shibbolet*. (9) The parallelism of *mar'e* and *ma‡ase* in lines 11–12 reflects Ezekiel 1:16, *mar'eh ha'ofannim uma‡asehem*. (10) My translation of *memullah* as "mixed" is based on the Targums of Exodus 30:35, which render *memullah* by *me‡arab* (Onkelos, Pseudo-Jonathan) or *memazzag* (Neofiti). Cf. endnote *c*. (11) Both Strugnell and Schiffman read *beshokhen* in line 18. I read *beshuban*, "when they return." Lines 17–18, *beheromam yeromemu pele' ubeshuban ya‡amodu*, are modeled after Ezekiel 10:17, *be‡omdam ya‡amodu uberomam yerommu*; except that *beshuban* replaces Ezekiel's *be‡omdam*, in parallelism with *behashib darkhehem* (line 16). This suggestion is open to a very serious objection: the use of *nun* for third person masculine plural suffix, common in rabbinic Hebrew, is to my knowledge unheard of at Qumran. But, as Schiffman observes, we need a suffix for this word, and it is easier to suppose that a vulgar usage influenced the scribe than it is to emend to *beshokhnam*.

e) The LXX *Vorlage* omitted this word, which, as I have said above, I consider an exegetical gloss. The Qumran *merkabah* fragment agrees in another respect with MT against the LXX *Vorlage*: it speaks of *hayyot kegahale 'esh*, which agrees with MT's comparison of the *hayyot* to "coals of fire," against LXX's claim that something looking like coals of fire was in the midst of the *hayyot* (Ezekiel 1:13). William H. Brownlee has observed that, unlike some other books of the Bible [62], Ezekiel seems to have been known at Qumran only in its Masoretic text form [56].

f) There are several other points in the Greek translations of the *merkabah* passages (LXX, Aquila, Symmachus, Theodotion, *Hebraios*) which do not advance our argument, but which deserve to be noted.

LXX: (1) The neuter pronouns used in Ezekiel 1:17–18, 10:11, suggest that the translator applied these verses (and presumably also 10:12) to the *hayyot* (*ta zōa*) rather than to the *'ofannim* (*hoi trochoi*). It is thus the *hayyot* who are "covered with eyes." This tradition is shared by Symmachus (below), by Revelation 4:6, and by a paraphrase of Ezekiel 1:18 and 10:12 quoted in Pseudo-Makarios' homily on the chariot: "The living creatures were very lofty, covered with eyes, and no one had the ability to discover the number of the eyes" [625]. (2) LXX consistently translates *baddim* in chapter 9 with *podērē* (verses 2, 3, 11), but with *tēn stolēn tēn hagian* in chapter 10 (verses 6–7; cf. verse 2). Both renderings have strong hieratic connections in LXX Greek; the latter is particularly suggestive of LXX Leviticus 16:32, and may indicate that the translator is interpreting Ezekiel 10:2, 6–7 as an instance of the high-priestly purification rite of Leviticus 16 (cf. Ezekiel 10:2 with Leviticus 16:12). This may perhaps explain why LXX Ezekiel 43:3 translates *lemishhat* (*tou chrisai*) in place of MT *leshahet*. The reading of *naos* for *lithos* in one manuscript of Ezekiel 10:1 [51a], although presumably based on a misreading in the uncial manuscript from which the scribe copied ⟨ΝΑΟΣ for ΛΙΘΟΣ⟩, was perhaps influenced by the priestly atmosphere of LXX Ezekiel 10. (3) The insertion of *hē nephelē* in Ezekiel 1:20 is surely an inner-Greek error based on the preceding *ēn*. I assume it was influenced by Ezekiel 1:4, 28, 10:3–4; by the cloud that marked the divine presence during the Israelites' wanderings in the desert (Exodus 40:34–38); and by such New Testament passages as Matthew 17:5 and parallels, Acts 1:9, Revelation 11:12.

Aquila: (1) He renders *‡egel* with *strongylon* in Ezekiel 1:7 (below). (2) He translates the *hapax habbazaq* in 1:14 with *aporroias*: "flowing off, stream; emanation, efflux" [3]. I do not know what he or his Tannaitic mentors may have had in mind. The word *aporroia* is used for a divine emanation in Wisdom of Solomon 7:25, which becomes a key text for Origen's Christology (*De Principiis* I.ii.5, 9–13; tr. 18, 22–28 [636]). As a loan-word into Coptic, *aporroia* is used in the Gnostic "Odes of Solomon" for a stream that "spread over the surface of all the earth/And it filled everything" (cf. Ezekiel 47:1–12), and in the "Pistis Sophia" for "light stream" [103]. I have no idea what of this may underlie Aquila's translation. (3) He translates *wegabbehen* at the beginning of 1:18 with *auchenes*, "necks," the word used by some LXX manuscripts to translate *wegabbehem* in I Kings 7:33 (LXX 7:19), the description of the wheels of Solomon's laver-stands. (4) He translates *tarshish* in Ezekiel 1:16, 10:9, Daniel 10:6, with *chrysolithou* (so LXX Exodus 28:20, 36:20); against the tendency of other translations and the rabbinic tradition to attribute to *tarshish* a blue color, usually associated with the sea (LXX Daniel 10:6, Symmachus to Ezekiel 1:16, 10:9, Targ. Exodus 28:20, 39:13, Vulg. Ezekiel 1:16, BT Hull. 91b, *Mek. Simeon* to Exodus 24:10 (ed. 221 [196]).

Symmachus: (1) He translates *le'arba^cat panaw* in Ezekiel 1:15 with *tetraprōsopos*, referring to the *trochos*. I have argued that this translation attests the same exegesis of *le'arba^cat panaw* as does Ezekiel 10:14 [9]. (2) He explicitly applies 1:18 to the *hayyot*: *kai anastēma ēn tois zōois kai hypsē*. (3) He suggests a causal relationship between the two parts of 1:25: when there is a voice above the firmament, the *hayyot* stand and their wings become slack. We will see that Targum states explicitly the image that underlies this translation. In all three cases, Symmachus' translation has influenced Jerome's Vulgate.

Theodotion translates *qol hamullah* in 1:24 as if it were *qol hammillah*: *phōnē tou logou*. As we will see, Targum shares this understanding.

Hebraios: Field's Hexapla [644] lists 28 renderings in Ezekiel attributed to this mysterious entity, including simple transliterations (2:4, 8:14, 10:9, 27:12, 39:16; cf. 46:5, 47:19) as well as translations very literal (43:2, 3) and very free (13:18, 16:6, 32:23). Other *Hebraios* passages: 1:4, 7:17, 9:2, 7, 16:7–8 (three times), 21:3, 26, 22:28, 23:20, 24:16, 29:3, 44:20, 25, 47:3, 8. Two of the *Hebraios* translations are relevant to our study: (1) In 1:4, he translates (from *wenogah lo sabib* onward): "For there was light in the midst of it like the appearance of a rainbow [*iridos*], and this [the rainbow?] was discernible [? *dieidēs*] in the midst of them." "Light" apparently translates *nogah*, and the "rainbow" seems to correspond to *hashmal*; the translation is surely influenced by Ezekiel 1:27–28. Revelation 4:3 also uses *iris* for "rainbow," against the *toxos* of LXX Ezekiel 1:28. (2) He translates the end of Ezekiel 21:3 (from *weniṣrebu*): "And every face among them shall be scorched by the fire coming from the north." The reference must be to the fire of Ezekiel 1:4, which is perceived as an agent of eschatological catastrophe; cf. the Qumran hymn 1QH iii 29–30, based on Ezekiel 21:3.

Chapter III

a) There is the "river of fire," which seems to be a heavenly projection of the river that Ezekiel sees flowing from the eschatological Temple in 47:1–12 (below). And there are faint but suggestive resemblances between the language of Daniel 7:9–18 and that of a Qumran fragment evidently belonging to a "Description of the New Jerusalem" (2Q24, fragment 4 [52]): *wahazet ^cad di* (line 11), *haze hawet ^cad di yehib* (line 17), *^cad ^ciddan di yetibu* (line 19, cf. Daniel 7:9), *letinyanah di qa'em* (line 16, cf. Daniel 7:10, 16). The action of the fragment takes place in a "temple" (*hekhla*, line 3).

b) *Lev. R.* 21:12 (ed. 492–493 [191]) attributes this midrash to R. Abbahu himself. *Pes. R.* 47:3 (ed. 190a [209]) leaves it anonymous, and weaves it into a much longer midrash.

c) The ellipsis corresponds to a corrupt interpolation based on PT Ber. 9:1 (13a, misnumbered 12a), conflated with PT Ber. 1:1 (2c).

d) To Frederic Mann's list of studies dealing with the liturgical associations of the Book of Revelation [135], we should perhaps add a 1976 dissertation of C. W. Fishbarne [118], which I have not seen.

e) I think of the depiction of the near-sacrifice of Isaac in the much later (sixth century) mosaic floor of the synagogue at Bet Alpha: God's hand emerges from a cloud which seems to be dark, but also seems to emit rays of light [713].

f) The twin apocalypses II Baruch and IV Ezra contain a number of liturgical pieces of this sort: II Baruch 21:4–8, 48:2–10, 51:7–14, 54:1–5; IV Ezra 6:1–5, 8:20–23. (The last piece is closely parallel to II Baruch 21:4–8. All but II Baruch 54:1–5 contain some reference to angels.) Their rhythmic and repetitive structure sets them off from their context, and gives the impression that they are traditional material that the apocalyptic writers drew upon rather than their own free creations. This material may be related to the Qumran *Hodayot* ("Thanksgiving Hymns"); II Baruch 51:10–11, at any rate, resembles 1QH iii, 19–23, tr. 158 [77] (cf. Syriac *bameromohi ger dehaw* ^c*alma* with Hebrew *lerum* ^c*olam, petayohi dafardaysa* with *bemishor le'en heqer* [71]). We may also compare the use of *'ahidin* in II Baruch 51:11 with that of the Syriac Christian "Odes of Solomon," 4:7–8 (ed./tr. 21–22 [102]), which may be nearly as early [106a]: "Because Thy seal is known;/And Thy creatures are known to it./And Thy hosts possess it,/And the elect archangels are clothed with it." The third line reads in Syriac, *wahaylawatakh 'ahidin leh*, and should perhaps be translated, "Thy hosts are held fast to it." The function of the "seal" would then presumably be to hold God's unruly forces in check, as in II Baruch.

g) This assumption, that the author of the "Apocalypse of Moses" is drawing upon Psalm 96, may provide an unexpected solution to a problem that has long puzzled patrologists. Justin Martyr (mid-second century A.D.) quotes, as the supposedly original and authentic text of Psalm 96:10: "The Lord hath reigned from the tree" (*Dialogue with Trypho*, 73:1, tr. 264 [624]). The Jews, he charges, have suppressed the words *from the tree*, which he naturally supposes to refer to Jesus' cross. Tertullian and a long series of Latin Christian writers follow Justin [623]. There is no evidence whatever that *from the tree* was ever an authentic part of the Biblical text, and it is natural to assume tampering by some Christian (hardly Justin himself). But this is not entirely satisfactory; for why should this Christian interpolator have restrained himself from explicitly saying that *the Lord hath reigned from the cross*? Perhaps *from the tree* is a Jewish midrashic gloss which originally referred, as in the "Apocalypse of Moses," to God's establishing his judgment seat in the tree of life. Similarly, the *Hekhalot* text conventionally called *3 Enoch* relates, "from the time that God expelled Adam from the garden of Eden, the Shechinah was dwelling on a cherub under the tree of life" (Schäfer, #7; Odeberg, ch. 5 [495,490]). – There is perhaps some link between this problem and that of the variant *triumphing in the tree* (*thriambeusas en tō xylō*), which Origen quotes as from Colossians 2:15 (below, chapter VIII, section C3d).

Chapter IV

a) The *haftarah* manuscripts I have examined in the Institute of Microfilm Hebrew Manuscripts, National and University Library, Jerusalem, represent the Shabu^cot *haftarah* as follows:

Ezekiel 1:1–2:2, 3:12 – Sassoon 332; British Museum Or. 1470; Budapest-Kaufman 10; British Museum Add. 9403 (in the last, however, a later hand has added 2:1–2, 3:12).
1:1–28, 3:12 – Cincinnati 4.3; Sassoon 282.
1:1–14, 27–28, 3:12 – British Museum Harl. 5706.
1:1–13, 27–28, 3:12 – Cincinnati 1.3, 9.
1:1–13, 3:12 – British Museum Add. 15,282.
1:1–17, 27–28 – Cincinnati 3.
1:1–17, 27–28 – British Museum Add. 11,639.

b) *Hezu yeqar shekhinta da'adonay*. Targum Neofiti to Exodus 24:10, and Pseudo-Jonathan to 24: 11, translate "they saw the God of Israel" with *hamun yat 'iqar shekhintah da'adonay. Midrash ha-Gadol* to Exodus 24:10 (ed. 555 [198a]) preserves what appears to be an early tradition, attributed to R. Eliezer, which condemns as a blasphemer anyone who translates this verse *wahazu yat yeqar shekhinat 'elaha deyiśra'el*, "for he creates a trinity of *yeqar. shekhinah*. and *el*." (T. Meg. 3[4]:41 and BT Qidd. 49a attribute the beginning of this utterance to R. Eliezer's disciple Judah b. Ilai. R. Hananel's comment on Qidd. 49a, quoted in Tosafot *ad loc.* [243,809], seems to be based on the full utterance.) It thus appears that Targ. Ezekiel 1:1 employs a highly controversial locution, which was nevertheless widely used in the Palestinian synagogues.

c) I translate *ke'anafa* ^c*ena lemihze* on the assumption that *'anafa* is an Aph^cel nominal form from the root *nwf*, "to swing, wave" (Targ. Isaiah 13:2, Fragment Targum to Leviticus 7:30); I understand it to mean that the creatures move as rapidly as the eye can trace their motion. (I vocalize *k'np'* on the basis of the Yemenite manuscripts used by Sperber and Silbermann [226,225]; the reading *knp'* in mss British Museum Add. 9403, Harl. 5706, suggests a weak vowel under the *aleph*.) Cf. *Gen. R.* 50:1 (ed. 515–516 [188]), which quotes an interpretation of *bazaq* as *keziqa le^cena*. – I am guessing at the meaning of *biryat hada*, literally "creature of one." The reading of the editions, *biryata kahada*, makes excellent sense, but is without manuscript support (Sperber), and seems like an "improvement" of a difficult text.

d) Onkelos and Jonathan regularly translate *mittahat* with *milra^c l-*: Genesis 35:8, Exodus 20:4, 30:4, 37:27, Deuteronomy 4:18, 39, 5:8, Jeremiah 38:12, Ezekiel 46:23. I do not know a precise parallel to *rum shemayya*. Onkelos translates *qomah* with *ruma* in Genesis 6:15, Exodus 25:10; cf. Numbers 23:22, 24:8, Deuteronomy 33:17. Jonathan uses *ruma* for *shamayim* in Isaiah 14:12–13, *gobah* in Ezekiel 41:8, and *marom* in Isaiah 22:16, Obadiah 3 (cf. Targ. Psalm 73:8, Job 5:11). On *rum ^calma* (Targ. Jeremiah 31:14) = *rum ^colam*, see below, chapter VI, section 5b (and chapter III, endnote *f*).

e) It is particularly hard to pinpoint the precise nuance of the preposition *leqabbala*. In Onkelos (which I cite, rather than Jonathan, because a concordance to it has been published [810a]), *leqobel* translates *le^cummat, liqrat, neged, mul, 'el mul, nokhah, lenokhah, 'el nokhah, 'el,* and *'et.* In Genesis 41:3, *leqiblehon* translates *'esel.*

f) Targumic Tosefta *daman kerum 'ar^ca lerum shemayya,* from 1:15, *mishtewe kemilra^c lerum shemayya.* Targumic Tosefta [*daman ...*] *ukheqobel shib^ca reqi^cin ukhesumkewatehon,* from 1:18, *shewan leqabbala reqi^ca.*

g) *Hayyah* applied to Gentile powers: Targ. Isaiah 35:9, 43:20, 56:9, Jeremiah 12:9 (which perhaps influenced Targ. II Samuel 23:13), Ezekiel 31:6, 34:5, 8, 28. Translation of a word by its cognate: *'esh - 'ishshata* (Ezekiel 1:4, 13, 27), *ke^cen - ke^cen* (verses 4, 7, 16, 22, 27), *gewiyyotehenah (-hem) - giwyatehon* (verses 11, 23), *bo^carot - ba^caran* (verse 13), *raqia^c - reqi^ca* (verses 22, 25, 26), *safon - sippuna* (verse 4).

Onkelos does not use *biryeta* at all (but does have *beri'ah* in Numbers 16:30). Jonathan uses *biryeta* for *yeser* in Isaiah 29:16 and Amos 7:1 (where MT has *yoser*). Pseudo-Jonathan translates *hayyah* with *biryata* twice in Genesis 1:24, but elsewhere in Genesis 1:20–31 translates it with its Aramaic cognate; it uses *biryata* for "living creatures" in general in Genesis 1:5 and Deuteronomy 28:15, where there is no Hebrew equivalent. Targ. Job 5:2 uses *buryeta* for "people," without Hebrew equivalent. (Since I did not use a concordance for any Targum but Onkelos – E.G. Clarke's concordance to Pseudo-Jonathan, like Bernard Grossfeld's to the First Targum to Esther, appeared too late for me to use – this is far from being a systematic survey.)

h) I list, for the sake of completeness, a few other features of Targum's translation. Targum adds, after *wa'er'eh* (1:1), the phrase *behezu nebu'ah disherat ^calay.* In 1:4, *umittokhah* is rendered *umiggo ^canana umiggo ^cal^cula.* In 1:13, *hi' mithallekhet* is translated *'ishshata mishtalheba*; this same phrase renders *'esh mitlaqqahat* in 1:4. Both *'eben sappir* (1:26, 10:1) and (*'eben*) *tarshish* (1:16, 10:9) are translated *'eben taba,* with no attempt at precise definition (so Targ. Exodus 24:10, Isaiah 54:11); while the translator simply Aramaicizes *hashmal* into *hashmela,* suggesting that he does not think it another type of gem but is unable or unwilling to say what it is.

1:22 translates *haqqerah hannora'* with *gelid hasin,* "powerful ice"; I do not know what this is supposed to convey. (*Nora'* is translated *hasin* in Targ. Deuteronomy 10:21, cf. Isaiah 21:1; *dehil* in Targ. Deuteronomy 7:21, 10:17, 28:58; cf. Ezekiel 1:18, *dehilin 'innun.*) 1:7 translates *nehoshet qalal* with *nehash mesalhab,* the adjective presumably referring to its golden color; cf. Pseudo-Jonathan to Leviticus 13:30, 32, 36. *Haruah* is translated *ra^cawa* in 1:12, 20; while, in 1:20–21 (cf. 10:17), *ki ruah hahayyah ba'ofannim* becomes *'are keruah biryata begalgallayya. Makhwenan* translates both *hoberot* (1:9, 11) and *yesharot* (1:23).

Targumic Toseftas: Kimhi (to 1:1 [224]) quotes a Targumic variant that identifies Chebar with Euphrates (*nehar perat*); so *Gen. R.* 16:3 (ed. 145–146 [188]; see Appendix IV, section 2). – Kimhi (to 1:3) and *^cArukh* (to *bz* II [813]) quote *targum yerushalmi* as identifying Ezekiel's father with Jeremiah, and explain that he was called Buzi, *^cal shehayu mebazzin 'oto. Yalqut Shim^coni* to Ezekiel (#336) makes a similar remark. I know of no parallel in an early source. *Pesiqta de-Rab Kahana* (*Dibre Yirmeyahu* #12, ed. 236–237 [206]), however, says that the Jews despised (*mezalzelin*) both Jeremiah and Ezekiel because they were descended from Rahab the harlot (cf. *Dibre Yirmeyahu* #4–5, ed. 227–229 [206]; *Ruth R.* 2:1; *Midr. Shemuel* 9:6, ed. 38a [199a]). – *Mahzor Vitry* [216e] contains a Targumic Tosefta to Ezekiel 1:12, which summarizes Ezekiel's vision and compares it to Isaiah's. I suspect that the compilers of the

Maḥzor themselves composed this note, and that it tells us nothing about *merkabah* exegesis in antiquity.

i) I have used the standard printed text of the Talmud as the basis for my translation, but have also consulted facsimile editions of mss Munich 95 and Vatican 134, as well as the textual notes in Rabbinowicz's *Diqduqe Soferim* [184,185,819]. When I was in Israel in 1975, I copied the text of paragraphs D–D3 from mss Vatican 171, London 400, Oxford 366, and Göttingen 3 (available in the Institute of Microfilm Hebrew Manuscripts, National and University Library, Jerusalem). I did not have further access to these four manuscripts while writing this book.

I note where I have translated a manuscript reading rather than that of the printed editions, as well as all textual variations that have a bearing on our study: – A1: Both Munich and Vatican 134 read "R. Jose b. Hanina" in place of "Rab Judah." – D1: All mss but London read *yesh* after *'eḥad*; London and the printed edition omit it, doubtless on account of haplography with the first letter of *shehu'*. I translate the text of the mss. – Munich reads the end of the sentence: "whose head reaches to beside the heads of the *ḥayyot*." Vatican 171: "who stands from earth to heaven and whose head reaches to between the feet of the *ḥayyot*." London and Oxford (supported by *'Aggadot ha-Talmud* [819]): "who stands on the lowest earth and whose head reaches to between the *ḥayyot*." The last reading has been influenced by medieval cosmography: below, chapter VI, section 8a; Islamic parallels in Appendix II. – D2: I translate plural "companions" (*ḥaberaw*) with all mss except London; London and the printed edition read singular *ḥabero*. – D3: I translate the reading of all mss, *bedukhteh*, "in its place," instead of the edition's *beresheh*, "on his head." The laconic language of the concluding sentence invited scribal revision and expansion, as the mss show. – F: I translate the reading of the mss. The printed editions quote Exodus 15:1 in place of verse 21 (the two are nearly identical); they read *shirah* (from *'ashirah*?) instead of *shiru* at the beginning of the next sentence, introduce "the lion is king of beasts ..." with the words *da'amar mar*, and add "and over all the world" to the end of the last sentence. Munich reads *we'adam bekhullan* in place of *we'adam mitga'eh ᶜalehen*. – G: I translate the mss' *pene shor*, "ox's face" (after the quotation of 10:14); editions omit *pene*. – The readings of Munich (*wekhi qategor naᶜaseh sinegor*) and the witnesses that Rabbinowicz [819] cites (*'en qategor naᶜaseh sinegor*), although probably secondary, support my decision to translate *qategor yeᶜaseh sinegor* as a rhetorical question rather than as a wish ("let the prosecuting attorney become an advocate!"); so do the parallels in PT R.H. 3:2 (58d), BT Ber. 59a, R.H. 26a, Qidd. 5a. – Paragraphs H-H1 are quoted in BT Sukk. 5b, in what seems a secondary and late context. The compiler in *Sukkah* seems to understand "large faces, small faces" as do R. Hananel and Rashi.

j) *Song R.* attributes the midrash to "R. Berechiah quoting R. Bun, quoting R. Abbahu." The origin of this chain is clear from *Midr. Psalms* 103:16, where some mss give "R. Berechiah quoting R. Abbahu," others "R. Berechiah quoting R. Abin" (Buber's note, p. 219a). "Abbahu" is obviously based on a misreading of the abbreviation *'b*, for "Abin." These two variants must have lain before the author of the *Song R.* passage, who conflated them (Bun = Abin).

k) I translate the Theodor-Albeck text, with the following exceptions: – A: Although Theodor keeps the reading of the London manuscript that he used as his base text, "R. Phinehas quoted R. Abin," he acknowledges in a footnote that "R. Reuben" (used in the other manuscripts, Tanh. *Qedoshim* #6, Tanh. Buber *Qedoshim* #6) is preferable. R. Phinehas regularly transmits R. Reuben's statements [343]. – A2: The last word of the quotation from Daniel 7:16 is spelled *q'my'* (*qa'amayya*) in MT. Most manuscripts of *Gen. R.* spell *qmy'* (*qamayya*), and add, apparently in explanation, the form *qyymyh* (*qayemayya*). (So the parallel in PT Ber. 1:1, 2c; see below.) The addition probably has no exegetical significance, but, like the Qere to Daniel 3:3, explains the obsolete Biblical form by adding the form current in Palestinian Aramaic. I see no need to reproduce the point in translation. – A4: The best manuscripts of *Gen. R.* (London, Vatican 30 and 60 [187]) repeat *beᶜomdam* after *we'aḥar kakh*. But I do not see what the word can mean in this position, and see no alternative to excising it (with the printed editions, the Yemen and Stuttgart manuscripts, and the *Yalquṭ*). – B: The text of this paragraph is often awkward, and I have translated rather freely, sometimes preferring the readings in the apparatus over those in the text.

l) Tanh. *Qedoshim* #6; Tanh. Buber *Be-Shallaḥ* #13, *Qedoshim* #6 (ed. 31a, 37b [222]); *Deut. R.*

Lieberman (ed. 68–69 [186]): *Ex. R.* 43:4 (cf. Tanh. *Bereshit* #5); *Midr. Psalms* 1:2 (ed. 1a–2a [199]).

m) The parallel in *Sifre Deut.*, which seems at first sight to confirm BT's claim that the exegesis of Job 38:7 is Tannaitic, appears in fact to be dependent on BT. *Sifre's* insertion of *wahadar* between the two parts of the verse betrays this dependence; while its use of the phrase *mazkirin shemo*, and its pointless citation of the *Shema^c*, are intelligible only when seen against the full context of BT Hull. 91a. This passage, which is only very loosely attached to its present context, may possibly be a late addition to *Sifre*, from BT. – The apparent parallel in *Midrash Tanna'im* (ed. 71 [201]) seems to be dependent on both BT Hull. 91a and *Gen. R.* 65:21, as the superfluous *we'ahar kakh* in its quotation of Job 38:7 shows. – There is an obvious literary connection between *Deut. R.* Lieberman, ed. 69 [186], and BT Hull. 91a, but I cannot define its direction.

n) "Chariots of angels" (*markabot shel mal'akhe hashsharet*) in Tanh. Buber *Yitro* #14, Tanh. *Wa-Yishlah* #2, Tanh. *Be-Midbar* #14, Tanh. Buber *Be-Midbar* #15, *Midr. Psalms* 68:18. But *Pesiqta* ms Oxford, *Deut. R.* Lieberman ed. 68 [186], and *Pesiqta Rabbati* 21:8 all omit *markabot*; they leave *shel* standing, awkwardly, right after the numeral. *Ex. R.* 29:2, the context of which shows that it understands the number to refer to angels, clearly presupposes the latter reading. The evidence of the other parallels helps us trace the process by which *markabot* dropped out. *Numb. R.* 2:3, *ribebot shel mal'akhim*, suggests that מרכבות was corrupted to רבבות, which in turn was read as רבוא כתות (so *Pesiqta* ms Safed: *ribbo' kittot shel mal'akhe hashsharet*). The resulting "twenty-two thousand myriad [=220,000,000] bands of angels" seemed far out of line with the Biblical text, and was "corrected" by the deletion of *ribbo' kittot*. We will presently see that the copyists had a particular motive for wanting to get rid of the *markabot*: as long as they remain, there is no evident difference between paragraph B and the "other explanation" in paragraph D.

o) Mandelbaum's edition, following the Oxford manuscript, needlessly repeats the first part of Psalm 68:18 after paragraph C. The Safed manuscript, to judge from Buber's edition [205], omits these words.

p) *'Im ken*. Without the following words (beginning *me^cattah*), this opening is left dangling. *Pesiqta Rabbati's 'im ken me^cattah* (ed. 102b [209]) is plainly a corruption of *'im ken me^cattah*.

q) *Pesiqta de-Rab Kahana's* version of the Elijah Recension contains the following: "Another explanation: *The divine chariotry is two myriads*, and so forth. R. Eleazar b. Pedath says: Wherever there are throngs there is bound to be pressure. But when God came to Sinai, thousands and myriads descended with him ... and they nonetheless had plenty of room. ... R. Eleazar b. Azariah and R. Eliezer of Modin [commented on this point]. One said: Could the mountain hold them [*umahaziq hayah hahar*]? God said to it: Extend and broaden yourself, and receive your Lord's children [*ha'arekh weharheb weqabbel bene 'adonekha*]. The other said: When God returns to Jerusalem, he will bring all the exiles back into it. So it is written: *They shall come from far, from north and west*, and so forth [Isaiah 49:12]. Will it be able to hold them? God will say to it: *Broaden the place of your tent*, and so forth [Isaiah 54:2]." – Compare this with the context of the Yannai Recension (following the printed *Tanhuma*): Just as God can gather more than a million Israelites at the entrance of the tent of meeting (Leviticus 8:3), "so I will accomplish at Zion in future time. Where are all the throngs from Adam to the resurrection supposed to find room to stand? They will say: *The place is too narrow for me; make room for me to dwell in* [Isaiah 49:20, RSV]. Thereupon I will broaden it for them. So it is written: *Broaden the place of your tent* [Isaiah 54:2]." (Cf. Chernus's translation [514a].) The author clinches this by pointing out that the same thing happened at Sinai. He invokes the Yannai Recension, as I have translated it in the text, and then concludes: "Could it hold them [*umahaziq hayah*]? It was a miracle. God said to the mountain: Broaden and extend yourself, and receive your faithful ones [*harheb weha'arekh weqabbel bene 'emunekha*; the last word is plainly a variant of *'adonekha*]." – The midrash that encases the Yannai Recension thus seems to be derivative: its author took the remarks attributed in the Elijah Recension to Eleazar b. Azariah and Eliezer of Modin, reversed their order, and expanded them to make a framework for the Yannai Recension.

r) *Lev. R.* inserts, between the final sentence and what precedes it, a brief midrash on the words *its timber and its stones*, which it attributes to Abba b. Kahana. (PT places this midrash, abbrevi-

ated and without an attribution, immediately after the end of "Samuel b. Nahman's" midrash.)
Several witnesses to the text of *Lev. R.* restore, in one form or another, the conclusion of "Samuel b. Nahman's" midrash to its proper place (Margulies' apparatus *ad loc.*); so does *Pesiqta Rabbati*, ed. 114a [209].

s) The two versions of this complex, in PT and *Lev. R.*, are so different that we can only explain their relationship by saying that they are separate literary crystallizations of the same body of oral materials. *Pesiqta Rabbati* 22:6 (ed. 113b–114b [209]) seems to derive from *Lev. R.* [252].

Chapter V

a) *Shello' yire'u pene shekhinah.* Moshe Greenberg pointed out to me that *ra'ah pene* means "be exposed to" in BT B.B. 82a (*ro'eh pene hammah*). The copyist of the Oxford manuscript of *Pesiqta* that Mandelbaum used as the basis of his edition evidently found the expression troublesome and vocalized Niph^{c}al *yera'u*, perhaps with his eye on Exodus 23:15, 34:20. The copyists of *Lev. R.* also had a hard time with the phrase, to judge from the alterations that Margulies records in his apparatus.

b) *Gewiyyateh* would normally mean "his body." I prefer here the secondary meaning "genitals" (Jastrow [808]); for it is hard to understand why the Aramaic translator chose *gewiyyateh* to render *raglaw* ("his feet"), unless we assume that he took the Hebrew word as a euphemism and translated it with an Aramaic euphemism.

c) Literally, "an ox of the days of the year"; *Mekhilta of R. Simeon,* "an ox on the rest of the days of the year." I follow Lauterbach, who uses the reading of the Oxford and Munich manuscripts. Horovitz's edition (p. 113) keeps the apparently corrupt reading of the printed texts: "Concerning the terrestrial ox; one might imagine ..." (*beshor shel maṭṭah yakhol ...*). There are several reasons to prefer the reading of the manuscript. It is clearer than that of the printed texts; *Mekhilta of R. Simeon* supports it; it does not switch from "I might think" (*shomea^c 'ani*) in paragraph D1 to "one might imagine" (*yakhol*) in D2, but uses *shomea^c 'ani* consistently. Horovitz himself, in a footnote, recognizes its superiority.

d) M. Sheq. 4:7, Naz. 3:2, ^{c}Ed. 7:5–7, Tem. 3:1; also T. Sanh. 2:13, BT Bes. 29b, Sanh. 94a; *Mekhilta,* ^{c}*Amaleq* chapter 3 (ed./tr. 2:175 [195]).

e) Later midrashic writers did not understand the expression *hayyot hannisse'ot* and therefore "corrected" it. *Numb. R.* 14:22, which otherwise quotes the *Sifra* passage almost verbatim, makes it into *hayyot hannose'ot 'et hakkisse',* "the *hayyot* who carry the throne" (so *Ex. R.* 23:15). The printed editions of *Sifra* [218,219] carry the correction still further: "the *hayyot haqqodesh* who carry the throne of glory." Similarly, with *te^{c}unot* for *nose'ot, Midr. Psalms* 103:5 (ed. 217a [199]).

f) Preserved in the thirteenth-century *Midrash ha-Gadol,* to Exodus 20:4 (ed. 405 [198a]).

g) Cf. *'Abot de-Rabbi Natan,* Version A, chapter 27 (ed. 42a [183]); *Numb. R.* 8:3; *Pirqe de-Rabbi Eliezer,* chapter 42. *Ex. R.* 23:14 once contained a midrash that ran closely parallel to *Song R.* to 1:9, until a medieval scribe decided to save himself the trouble of copying it by the expedient of copying the beginning and referring the reader to *Song R.* for the rest. We will return to these sources in chapter VI, section 5.

h) *Gen. R.* 21:1 (ed. 198 [188]); *Ex. R.* 32:1 (parallels in *Numb. R.* 16:24, Tanh. Buber *Shelah* #2, ed. 39a [222]); *Eccl. R.* 7:29; cf. *Deut. R.* 9:8.

i) The exegeses that he favored did not fare nearly so well. *Ruth R.* 7:11 reproduces the "approved" interpretation of Psalm 106:20, as a parenthetical aside: "There is nothing more disgusting than an ox when it is eating grass" (following M. B. Lerner's edition of the text [210]). But, apart from this, we find the exegeses attributed to Akiba only in passages that are actually dependent on *Mekhilta*'s dialogues: *Song R.* to 1:9 (all four dialogues; but, as we have seen, the author tinkers with *Mekhilta*'s attributions); *Gen. R.* 21:5, ed. 200–201 [188] (the dialogue on Genesis 3:22); *Midr. Psalms* 106:6, ed. 228a–b [199] (the dialogue on Psalm 106:20; translated above). Several sources develop the dialogue on Job 23:13, either by itself (*Ex. R.* 4:3, where we must certainly read "Pappus" or "Papias" for "Phinehas"), or combined with a cluster of midrashim focusing on I Kings 22:19, which occur by themselves in PT Sanh. 1:1, 18a (Tanh. *Shemot* #18;

Tanh. Buber *Shemot* #14, ed. 4b–5a [222]; *Wa-Yera'* #21, ed. 49a [222]; *Midr. Psalms* 119: 35, ed. 249a–b [199]).

j) I restore these last words on the basis of a quotation by Nachmanides (*Commentary* to Exodus 32:1 [224,251]). The awkward repetition of "they will anger me with it" after the quotation of Ezekiel 1:10 in IIB5 (deleted from IIIB5) suggests that the author of text II found these words in his source after Ezekiel 1:10. Cf. the following discussion of the relationship of texts I, II, and III.

k) I read *mitbonenin bo*, with ms Oxford 153, fol. 89b (consulted in the Institute of Microfilm Hebrew Manuscripts, National and University Library, Jerusalem). The printed edition of *Tanhuma* has *mitkawwenim bo*, "concentrate on it." (So *Ex. R.* 43:8, according to ms Paris 187/15, fol. 288a–b.)

l) BT Hag. 13b, paragraph F, and parallels (above, chapter IV, section 3d). – I follow Ginzberg's emendation of the text's *mal'akhe*, "angels," to *malkhe*, "rulers." – The Hebrew word for "carried" is singular, despite its plural subject; the writer was doubtless thinking of singular *merkabah*. Similarly, the writer uses the feminine rather than the masculine form of the word "four," perhaps because he is thinking of feminine *hayyot* rather than masculine *malkhe*.

m) Found in several late midrashim: *Pesiqta Rabbati* 46:3 (ed. 188a–b [209]); *Pirqe de-Rabbi Eliezer*, chapter 3; end of *Midrash Konen* (ed. 38–39 [478]).

n) The quotation of Jeremiah 49:24 that follows is probably a lexical gloss (Einhorn [200]). One manuscript (Munich 50) reads "Johanan" for "Judan"; another (Oxford-Neubauer 164) calls him "Judan b. Neriah" (?).

o) *Pirqe de-Rabbi Eliezer*'s invocation of "R. Judah" seems itself to go back to *Pesiqta de-Rab Kahana, Shor 'o Keśeb* #8 (ed. 157 [206]), and its parallels, which combine a midrash concerning the calf with a distinct midrash of Isaiah 1:3, attributed to "R. Judah b. R. Simon."

p) For the sake of completeness, I quote a variant of the Sinai version from the medieval midrashic compilation *Leqah Tob* (ca. 1100; quoted in Kasher's *Torah Shelemah* [810]): "He [Aaron?] cast the gold into the furnace, and fashioned it in the image of an ox. Why? Because the Israelites said: '[We want an image] like the image we saw on the day the Torah was given.' It is written, *Under his feet was what seemed like a construction of sapphire brick* [Exodus 24:10]. This teaches that they saw the angels, *the soles of* whose *feet were like the sole of a calf's foot* [Ezekiel 1:7]. That was why they asked for the image of a calf."

q) He may not have been the only person to notice the resemblance of the Biblical to the rabbinic story. Several manuscripts of BT Hag. 14b say, at the beginning of the story of Johanan and Eleazar, that Johanan "was going forth from Jerusalem" [558]. Perhaps the copyists unconsciously altered their text in accord with I Kings 11:29, *Jeroboam had gone forth from Jerusalem.*

Chapter VI

a) A passage conventionally associated with *Hekhalot Zutarti*, which Schäfer [495] has published for the first time (#424), regulates how the "mystic" (perhaps "magician" would be a better word) may test another person to whom he intends to reveal his formulae: "If he wants to test him, let him test him once, but not twice. Let him be very careful with him when he tests him, so that he may not make a mistake and destroy God's world." But we are given no details of these tests, and have no reason to believe that they have anything to do with the tests that the angels impose, in the passages we are now examining.

b) Two passages relate Elisha b. Abuyah's encounter with Metatron, described in BT Hag. 15a (above, chapter I, section 7). One of them, found in Odeberg's *3 Enoch*, tells the story from Metatron's viewpoint (Schäfer, #20; Odeberg, ch. 16). In the other, which I translate in chapter IX (section C2a), Elisha is the speaker, and the being he encounters is called "Akhtariel Yah, God of Israel, Yahweh of hosts" (Schäfer, #597 [598]). Both passages are perhaps dependent on BT. – A Genizah fragment that Gruenwald published [468a] has the angel Ozhayah describe Ben Zoma's fate: "They dragged Ben Zoma a hundred times through the first palace ... two hundred times through the second, four hundred times through the third," and so forth (fuller translation in chapter IX, section A2b). The sequel to this passage, describing the hordes of angels that burst forth upon the traveller from the gate of the sixth palace, faintly resembles *Hekhalot Zuṭarti*'s account of the water test; I will deal with it later in this section. – *3 Enoch* describes one angel as "appointed to record the merits of Israel," and another as "striking the *ḥayyot* with fiery lashes" (Schäfer, ##26, 31; Odeberg, chs. 18:17, 20). Both phrases seem to be reminiscences of the Elisha-Metatron story in BT Hag. 15a. – *Hekhalot Rabbati* puts "pure marble" (*shayish ṭahor*) at the end of a series of six heavenly gems, the first five of which are drawn from Exodus 28:17–18, 39:10–11 (or, perhaps, Ezekiel 28:13); it has Nehuniah b. ha-Qanah sit on a "stool of pure marble" while lecturing on the journey to the *merkabah* (Schäfer, ##166, 202; Wertheimer, 11:4, 16:2). – *Hekhalot Rabbati* speaks of "descending safely" (*yoredin beshalom*) from the *merkabah* (Schäfer, #216; Wertheimer, 18:3; translated below, chapter VIII, section A5c). A broken passage in one of Gruenwald's fragments [473a] contains the words: "Everyone who enters, enters by their authority; everyone who goes out, goes out by their authority" (*nikhnas kol hannikhnas weyoṣe' kol hayyoṣe'*). Both of these expressions suggest the language of the *pardes* story.

c) In this and the next sentence, read *mizzarᶜan* (with ms Vatican) for the ungrammatical *mizzarᶜo*. – Ms New York adds "in his beauty" (*beyofyo*) at the end of the sentence, in accord with text II.

d) *Soḥaṭin 'oto*, "they squeeze him" (like someone squeezing the juice out of a fruit), in mss Oxford and Munich 22. Ms New York reads *shoḥaṭin 'oto*, "they slaughter him." Mss Dropsie and Munich 40 (which often go together in this passage) read *doḥafin 'oto*, "they push him."

e) First sentence: I read *kemi*, "like someone," which I assume to underlie both *bemi* (mss Oxford, Munich 22) and *kewan* (ms New York). Mss Dropsie and Munich 40 read *lemi*, "to someone"; the scribes apparently felt, reasonably enough, that *mi* ought to refer to an observer. We will presently try to make some sense of this very strange sentence. – Hai Gaon [241], who quotes the first two sentences of section B in a text differing significantly from that of the manuscripts, reads: "like someone [*kemi*] in whom [!] there are thousands and myriads of waves of water." – Second sentence: I read *me'or ziw*, "the light of the splendor," with ms New York. All the other manuscripts have *me'awir ziw*, "from the air of the splendor," which seems to me meaningless. This latter reading gave rise to *'awir ziw*, "the air of the splendor" (Hai Gaon); as well as to the expression *ziw 'awir*, used by the individual(s) who added IIC and D (see below). – "Built into the palace" is my guess at the meaning of the odd expression *selulot bahekhal*. Hai Gaon reads *selulot kahekhal*, "clear as the palace," which is just as strange (*salul* is normally used for liquids). R. Hananel, quoting the passage in his comment on Hag. 14b [242], reads (according to some witnesses) *kelulot bahekhal*, "part of the palace." – *Ziw nora' mimmayim*, "a splendor more terrible than water," perhaps draws upon MT Ezekiel 1:22 (*haqqeraḥ hannora'*, "the terrible crystal"), and suits the idea I have been developing of the sinister implications of the waters. But I am very tempted to emend (without manuscript support) to *ziw nir'eh kemayim*, "a splendor resembling water." – Fourth sentence: Mss Dropsie and Munich 40 read *'im tomeru*, "if you [plural] say." The scribes were obviously influenced by Akiba's utterance in BT Hag. 14b (*'al tomeru*); see below. – Seventh sentence: Ms Oxford accidentally omits "goes forth" after "heavenly voice." I restore on the basis of the other manuscripts. – Ms Oxford shares the reading "before you [singular]" (*lefanekha*) with ms Munich 22 (*millefanekha*); mss Dropsie and New York read "before him" (*lefanaw*); ms Munich 40 omits the entire sentence. It is hard to believe that any scribe would arbitrarily have introduced the bizarre second-person reading. Perhaps it is a fossil of a stage of the tradition in which it was used for the instruction of a would-be traveller. See below, section 2c.

f) I read *'eno mash'ilan* ("does not ask them") for ms Oxford's *'eno mesha'alin*, which seems meaningless; cf. mss New York (*'eno mash'ilin*) and Munich 22 (*'eno sho'alan*). For reasons I do not understand, mss Dropsie and Munich 40 treat the angels as the subject of the verb (*'enam meshu'alin*, or *mush'alin*), and omit *'eno ra'uy* ("if he is not worthy") from the beginning of the sentence. They also read *ziw 'awir* in place of *'awir ziw*.

g) "Ben Azzai" only in ms New York; the other manuscripts read *peloni 'almoni*, "so-and-so." This reading leaves the anecdote completely pointless, and is best explained as an alteration by scribes who did not want to attribute to the saintly Ben Azzai a fate normally reserved for the descendants of calf-worshippers.

h) The author substitutes "behind the celestial curtain" (*le'aḥore happargod*) for "at the celestial curtain" (*lappargod* or *'el happargod*), probably under the influence of Hag. 15a and 16a, "from behind the celestial curtain" (*me'aḥore happargod*). He replaces "to injure me" (*leḥabbeleni*) with "and tried to drive me away" (*ubiqqeshu ᶜalay ledoḥafeni*), in accord with Hag. 15b, "tried to drive him away" (*biqqeshu ... ledoḥafo*). He adds the quotation of Song 1:4, with its incongruous third-person opening (*ᶜalaw*), from Hag. 15b.

i) Hai Gaon's testimony perhaps supports my analysis of text II. In his responsum [241], Hai quotes the beginning of IIB in order to account for Akiba's warning. But he goes on to explain that Ben Azzai died because "his time had come to depart this world," and that Ben Zoma "went mad from the terrifying sights, which his mind could not bear." Hai was clearly not familiar with text VII, and we might also infer that he did not know IID. It is also possible, however, that Hai knew a text of IID that had "so-and-so" in place of "Ben Azzai" (above, endnote *g*), and that it did not occur to him to connect the anecdote with Ben Azzai's death.

j) Gruenwald's text: *shehayah petaḥ hekhal sheni* (read *shishshi*) *dohef weṭored umoṣi' rebabot rebabot umaḥanot umaḥanot ufamali'ot pamali'ot beshaᶜah 'aḥat*. Ms Oxford: *hekhal hashshishshi hayah nir'eh bemi* (read *kemi*) *sheṭṭoredin bo me'ah 'alfe 'alafim weribe rebabot galle yam*. Ms Munich 22 and Hai Gaon's quotation have *petaḥ* at the beginning of the sentence, before *hekhal*. With *dohef* in Gruenwald's fragment, cf. the variant *doḥafin 'oto* for *soḥaṭin 'oto*, in IIA3 (above, endnote *d*).

k) The only other reference I know of occurs in a passage found only in ms New York (Schäfer, #369; Elior's *Hekhalot Zuṭarti*, lines 251–252), and in its parallel in ms Munich 40 (#955): "When the Israelites sinned by making the calf, the ox's face [of the *ḥayyot*] was concealed, and a cherub put in its place" (full translation below, chapter IX, section B1b). The preceding paragraph in ms New York (Schäfer, #368; Elior, lines 239–243; found also in mss Oxford, Dropsie, Munich 22 and 40) gives the name of the first of the *ḥayyot* as ᶜAglay or ᶜAgloy; this is perhaps related to ᶜegel, "calf." – Near the beginning of the *Hekhalot* text that Odeberg published under the title of *3 Enoch*, Enoch is carried to heaven and there accused by the angels of being "one of the offspring of those who perished in the flood" (Schäfer, #6; Odeberg, ch. 4). This anachronistic accusation is perhaps modelled on the notion that some people are unworthy to travel to the *merkabah* because they are descended from those who worshipped the calf.

l) He glosses "pure marble" with the words "shining like clear water" (*mayim ṣelulin*). The adjective *ṣelulin* occurs, in its feminine form (*ṣelulot*), in Hai Gaon's quotation of text IIB (above, endnote *e*), where it is inappropriately applied to the marble stones themselves. The reading of the manuscripts, *ṣelulot* ("built into"?) is also difficult. Perhaps Rashi draws his *mayim ṣelulin* from a *Hekhalot* source describing the "water" test, which survives, in somewhat corrupted form, in our witnesses to the text of IIB.

m) Lauterbach chose to print the reading of the editions (and of a fragment of *Yalquṭ Makhiri* [235]): " ... what Isaiah, Ezekiel, and the rest of the prophets did not." But the shorter reading seems better attested, and we can explain the addition of "the rest of the prophets" as an attempt to conform the midrash to the language of Hosea 12:11. We will soon see that there is reason to believe that, in its oldest form, the midrash mentioned only Ezekiel.

n) I emend the difficult *lo' nir'eti lakhem ḥazon ḥezyonot harbeh* (which Braude translates, "Did I not multiply for your sakes your seeing of many visions?" [245]) by inserting *'ella* after *ḥazon*.

o) Following the text of a Genizah fragment published by Ginzberg [204].

p) Buber, supposing that the reference to the sea was omitted by a copyist's error, inserts the "missing" words in brackets. He tells us in a footnote that the older editions of the printed *Tanḥuma* also omitted the sea; its appearance in the more recent editions of Tanh. *Shelaḥ* #15 is due to a "correction" by the copy editors. Both Buber and his predecessors were, I believe, mistaken. The three-link chain does not, as we will see, reflect the earliest form of Meir's haggadah. But it does represent *Tanḥuma*'s version of it.

q) The triple comparison of God to heaven, sea, and cloud suggests *Midr. Psalms* 24:12. Can we suppose that the author of the Greek incantation (which Deissmann dates to about 300 A.D. [707]) was familiar with this version of Meir's haggadah? We could only answer this question in the course of a more general investigation of the haggadah presupposed in magical texts, and its relation to rabbinic traditions. Cf. above, chapter II, section 3c.

r) Ms Oxford (Neubauer 164; consulted in the Hebrew University's Institute of Microfilm Hebrew Manuscripts) reads *werabbi ḥelbo* after *rabbi berekhyah*. The other two manuscripts I have checked (Munich 50,2, Vatican 76,3), like the printed editions, omit these words. But I believe they are original. It is easier to imagine a scribe leaving them out than arbitrarily inserting them; and the chain Berechiah – Helbo – Samuel b. Nahman is an extremely plausible one [344].

s) Ms Paris 187/15 is abridged in precisely the same way as the printed editions. I do not know of any unmutilated text.

t) Reading, with ms Paris 187/15, (*miyyad*) *hittishan ... wehetisan* (*ᶜal hayyam*), for the printed edition's *hesitan ... wehesitan*.

u) The words *rimmah bayyam*, "he has tricked [you] in the sea," occur in the Pesaro edition of 1519 [338] and in two of the three manuscripts I have consulted (Munich 50,2, Vatican 76,3). The more recent editions omit them by haplography (after *ramah bayyam*). Ms Oxford-Neubauer 164 omits *rimmah*, with the result that *bayyam* is meaninglessly repeated. – The plural *re'u mah*, attested by the Pesaro edition and all three manuscripts, accords with plural "you" (*lakhem*) in the following sentence. The later editions give singular *re'eh mah*, as in *Ex. R.* (below). – The spelling, in Hebrew letters, of Greek *epithesis* varies slightly among the manuscripts and editions. The preceding midrash of *ramah* ("he has hurled") as *rimmah* ("he has tricked") practically insures that this word is indeed *epithesis*, which combines the meanings "attack" and "trick." Perles, Brüll (cited by Rosenthal), Moussafia, Krauss, and Levy [338,812,815,818], championed this identification, but without knowing of the reading *rimmah*. Other proposals include: *hypodysis*, "escape, refuge" (Kohut); *hippothoros*, "a tune played to mares upon being covered" (Jastrow); *hypsistos*, "the most high" (Löw); *hyptiōsis*, "throwing on one's back" (Rosenthal) [812,808,815,338].

v) Lieberman's *Deut. R.* (ed. 14–15 [186]) attributes a somewhat more developed variant of this story to "R. Hiyya the Great." The editor certainly intends Hiyya I, a Tanna of the early third century; but we may suspect that, at an earlier stage, the tradition bore the name of the Amora Hiyya II. Hiyya II often appears in rabbinic literature as transmitting Johanan's utterances; perhaps, if *Deut. R.*'s attribution is accurate, he is here elaborating his master's teaching. – BT Sot. 11b attributes to one "Rab Awira" a version of this haggadah, presumably Babylonian, with its anthropomorphism toned down considerably. *Ex. R.* 1:12 takes this version from BT, but attributes it to R. Akiba, probably through misunderstanding an abbreviation for "Rab Awira" (*r"ᶜ*). Cf. *Yalquṭ Exodus*, ##164, 245; *Ezekiel*, #354. – *Pesiqta Rabbati* 47:2 (ed. 189a–b [209]) briefly takes up this haggadah. Heinemann points out that certain of its features, evidently drawn from Jewish sources, occur in the Samaritan *Memar Marqah* [409,844].

w) The late *Seder 'Eliyahu Rabbah* (chapter 1; ed. 3 [211]) preserves this exposition in something like its original form. "*He drove the man out*: teaching that God divorced him like a wife. *He settled the cherubim, more ancient than the garden of Eden*: teaching that the cherubim are older than creation. *The fiery sword that turned every which way*: meaning hell. *To guard the way*: meaning good manners [literally, "the way of the world"], and teaching that good manners came before everything. *The tree of life* must be the Torah, as it is written, *It is a tree of life to those who hold fast to it* [Proverbs 3:18]." William G. Braude, who has translated *Seder 'Eliyahu* into English, seems to me completely to have misunderstood this passage [249,257]. – The Palestinian Targums of Genesis 3:24 (Pseudo-Jonathan, "Fragment Targum," Neofiti I) take this exposition as their starting point, but construct elaborate sermons to weave its diverse images into a coherent whole. – We find parallels to individual interpretations in *Gen. R.* 19:9 (ed. 178 –179 [188]), *Lev. R.* 9:3, 35:6 (ed. 179, 824 [191]).

x) Reading, with *Midrash ha-Gadol*, *'arbaᶜah ᶜammudim shel barzel 'arukkim*, for *Yalquṭ*'s obviously corrupt *'arbaᶜim ᶜammudim shel barzel merubbaᶜim 'arukkim*. *'Arbaᶜim* is plainly an error for *'arbaᶜah*, *merubbaᶜim* a dittograph of *'arbaᶜim*.

y) *Yalquṭ* has *barzel* ("iron") both here and in the third sentence of the paragraph; but this is hardly possible, for the second firmament was of iron. I read *bedil*, "tin," as in *Midrash ha-Gadol*. – The text printed by Jellinek has the third firmament of "lead" (*ᶜoferet*), the fourth of an unspecified "metal" (*mattekhet*). This vague designation seems unlikely to be original. It is, however, rather reminiscent of the fifth metal on Celsus's list (below).

z) Beside the sources that I cited earlier in this section, we find allusions to Hiram, his longevity, and his self-deification in Tanh. *Wa-Yeḥi* #3 (=Tanh. Buber *Wa-Yeḥi* #5, ed. 107a [222]), Tanh.

Buber *Wa-Yesheb* #13 (ed. 92b [222]), *Ex. R.* 1:26. Tanh. *Wa-'Era'* #9 (=Tanh. Buber *Wa-'Era'* #8, ed. 12a–b [222]) lists Hiram as one of four men who claimed to be gods and were sexually violated like women (the others were Nebuchadnezzar, Joash, and Pharaoh). This haggadah, which *Midrash ha-Gadol* uses as framework for the story of Hiram's palace, occurs in a bowdlerized version in *Ex. R.* 8:3. *Mekhilta, Shirah* chapter 2, ed./tr. 2:18–19 [195] (=*Mek. Simeon*, ed. 75 [196]; taken up in Tanh. *Be-Shallaḥ* #12) speaks of the arrogance of the "prince of Tyre," but does not identify him with Hiram.

Chapter VII

a) The version in *Pesiqta de-Rab Kahana, Parah 'Adummah* #4 (ed. 65–66 [206]), seems to be adapted from *Gen. R.* 27:1. The midrash recurs in later sources: *Eccl. R.* to 2:21 and 8:1, Tanh. *Ḥuqqat* #6 (*Numb. R.* 19:4), *Pesiqta Rabbati* 14:10 (ed. 61b [209]). We find elements of it in Tanh. Buber *Bereshit* #34 (ed. 12b [222]), *Midr. Psalms* 1:4 (ed. 3a [199]).

b) I give the Hebrew text of the five versions of this passage. (The text quoted before A1 is that material, found with considerable variation in our printed Talmud texts, that immediately precedes the addition.)

Munich 95	Cambridge	Vatican 134
אמ' רבא	ראבה]א'	א' רבא
זה המסתכל בקשת	זה המסתכל] בקשת	זה המסתכל בקשת
רב יוסף אמ' זה	רב יוסף א' זה	רב יוסף א' זה
העובר עבירה אחת	ה]עובר] עברה ב. תר	העובר עבי' בסתר
בסתר דכל	דא' ר' יוחנן כל	דא"ר יוחנ' כל
העובר עבירה בסתר	העובר ע]ברה בסתר]	העובר עבירה בסתר
הקב"ה מגלה עליו בגלוי	הק מגלה עליו בגלוי	הק' מגל ה עליו בגלוי
רבה אמ'	ראבה א	רבה א'
זה המסתכל בקש'	]זה המסתכל בק]שת	זה המסתכל בקשת
דכתי' כמראה הקשת	שנ' כמראה הקש]ת	דכת' כמראה הקשת
אשר יהיה בענן	אשר יהיה בענן] וגו'	אשר יהיה בענן
ביום הגשם כן מראה		ביום הגשם כן מראה
הנוגה סביב הוא		הנוגה סביב היא
מראה דמות כבוד יי		מראה דמות כבוד יי
		וארא ה ואפול על פני

A1

A2

	לאטי עלה במערבה	לייטי עלה במערבא
	משום דמחזי	משום מיתחזי
	כמינות]	כמינות

A3

| לימ' | אל]א נימא | אלא א' |
| ברוך זוכר הברית | ב' זוכר הבר' | ברוך זוכר הברי' |

^cEn Ya^caqob	Oxford 366

רבי אבא אמר
זה המסתכל בקשת
דכתיב כמראה הקשת
אשר יהיה בענן וגו׳
רב יוסף אמר זה
העובר עבירה בסתר
דאמר מר כל העובר
עבירה בסתר הקב״ה
מגלה עליו בגלוי

           והא דלא מצי כאיף
           ליה ליצריה

רבא אמר   אמ׳ רבא A1
כל המסתכל בקשת   כל המסתכל בקשת
צריך שיפול על פניו   צריך שיפול על פניו
דכתיב כמראה הקשת   דכתי׳ כמראה הקשת
אשר יהיה בענן   אשר יהיה בענן וגו׳
ביום הגשם כן מראה
הנוגה סביב הוא
מראה דמות כבוד ה׳
וארא ה ואפול על פני
ואשמע קול מדבר

לייטי עלה במערבא   לייטי במערבא A2
משום דמיחזי   משום דמיתחזי
כמינות   כמאן דפלח ליה

אלא לימא   A3
ברוך זוכר הברית

	Munich 95	Cambridge	Vatican 134
B1			
B2	ר' ישמעאל בנו של	ר ישמעאל בנו	ר' ישמעא' בנו של
	ר' יוחנן בן ברוקה	שלר' יוחנן בן ברוקא ר' יוחנן בן ברוקה	ר' יוחנ' בן ברוקה
	אמ'	או'	או'
	ברוך זוכר הברית	[זו]כר הב[ו]רית	ברוך זוכר הברית
	ונאמן בבריתו	ונאמן בבריתו	ונאמן בבריתו
	וקיים במאמרו	ומקיים במאמרו	וקיים במאמרו
		ארב פפא	
		הולכך נימרינהו	
		לתרויהו	

Rabbinowicz [819] quotes the text of ms Oxford in a footnote to Hag. 16a. – Sirkes, *Haggahot ha-B"H* to Hag. 16a, quotes *ᶜEn Yaᶜaqob*'s text with a few very minor variations, attaching it to the words *rab yosef 'amar zeh haᶜober ᶜaberah beseter*. He claims to have found the passage in the margin of a Talmud manuscript. – Besides the divergences from ms Oxford that I mentioned in the text, *ᶜEn Yaᶜaqob* adds *may mebarekh* to B1 (doubtless influenced by Ber. 59a), and words B2 differently. The reading of ms Vatican is based on that found in *ᶜEn Yaᶜaqob*, but the scribe accidentally omitted A1 (his eye jumped from the first to the second occurrence of *wa'eppol ᶜal panay*), and deliberately omitted B1 because it seemed superfluous. The copyist of ms Munich had this truncated version before him; he abbreviated it further, omitting the now meaningless A2 and the opening *'ella* of A3. The Cambridge fragment, badly preserved as it is, clearly follows the reading of ms Vatican or a closely related text, but adds a conclusion from Ber. 59a. Where they do not abbreviate, mss Vatican, Munich, and Cambridge support *ᶜEn Yaᶜaqob* against ms Oxford.

c) Ms Munich 95 differs from the printed edition at four points. At all four, the edition's reading seems preferable: – A: Ms reads "R. Johanan" for "R. Joshua b. Levi." But "R. Johanan" cannot be original, for this passage owes its inclusion in the Gemara to its chain of transmission as the printed edition reports it: the preceding haggadah, which is linked directly to the mishnah under discussion (Ber. 9:2), is attributed to "R. Alexander quoting R. Joshua b. Levi"; it thus drew our passage into the Gemara after it. Further, the second-generation Palestinian Amora Alexander elsewhere transmits sayings of Joshua b. Levi; he is less likely to have transmitted the words of his contemporary Johanan, and Bacher records no case of such a transmission [797]. – A2: Ms adds that the object of the Palestinians' curse is "anyone who falls on his face," presumably to avoid implying that they curse Joshua b. Levi (or Johanan) himself. – B2, 3: Ms twice reads "oath" for "word," and changes the order of the clauses in B3. – It is worth noting that several of the variants Rabbinowicz cites in his notes to Ber. 59a [819] show traces of the influence of Hag. 16a+.

d) The parallel in *Pesiqta de-Rab Kahana* (*Wa-Yehi Be-Shallah* #15; ed. 190–191 [206]), which seems on other grounds to be secondary, attributes the story to "R. Hezekiah quoting R. Jeremiah" (both fourth-century Palestinians). This is probably a mistake, based on the context in which the anonymous story appears in *Gen. R.*: a series of statements in praise of Simeon b. Yohai, attributed to "R. Hezekiah quoting R. Jeremiah." (We also find this series, *without* the story, in PT Ber. 9:2, 13d.) Several later sources draw upon this legend: BT Ket. 77b, *Midr. Psalms* 36:8 (ed. 126b [199]), *Midrash ha-Gadol* to Genesis 9:14 (ed. 187 [198]), and the "Story of R. Joshua b. Levi" [479a].

e) The extant *Pesiqta* manuscripts are corrupt and unintelligible at this point. For *'amar rabbi shimᶜon ben yohay hu' simana deᶜalma*, read (with *Midrash ha-Gadol* to Genesis 9:14, ed. 187 [198]): *zeh rabbi shimᶜon ben yohay dehu' simaneh deᶜalma*.

ᶜEn Yaᶜaqob	Oxford 366	
הרואה את הקשת	הרואה את הקשת	B1
צריך לברך	צריך לברך	
מאי מברך		
ברוך זוכר הברית	ברוך זוכר הברית	
רבי ישמעאל בנו של	ר׳ ישמעאל בנו של	B2
רבי יוחנן בן ברוקא	ר׳ יוחנן בן ברוקא	
אומר	מסיים בה הכי	
ברוך זוכר הברית		
ונאמן בבריתו	נאמן בבריתו	
וקיים במאמרו	וקיים במאמרו	

f) I emend the unintelligible *lmr'h bytyh sbyb* to *lmr'h š byt lh sbyb*, in accord with the parallels in mss Oxford 1531 and Munich 40, and with Ezekiel 1:27. – Two parallel texts raise a series of difficult problems which I can only touch on here. The first is an earlier passage in ms New York, which includes the last sentence ("his body resembles the rainbow ...") in a form nearly identical to the one we have here, but in a very different and rather incongruous context; namely, a list of the names of certain of God's bodily organs and equipment (Schäfer, #367, immediately preceding the long passage translated and discussed in chapter IX, section B1b; parallel, from ms Munich 40, in #953; Martin Samuel Cohen translates equivalent material as sections H–I of "*Shiᶜur Qomah*" [516]). The relation of this sentence to the one that follows, which considerably resembles it in the original but which seems to speak of God's "bow" in a military sense (read Aramaic *qashta ruma*, with the other manuscripts of #367, in place of Hebrew *qashto domeh*), promises to be a horrendously complicated problem which we do best to avoid. – The second passage, from ms Munich 22 (Schäfer, #487), combines features of ms New York's two parallel versions of the youth/prince passage (see below, and more especially Appendix III). "This youth is the prince whose name is written with seven letters. ... His stature fills the world. ... The crown on his head measures five hundred by five hundred parasangs. Its name is 'Israel.' The stone between his horns [!] is named Shalish ᶜAmmiel. [We should probably split *šlyš* into two halves, take the second as an abbreviation for *yiśra'el*, and understand the name to mean: "Belonging to Israel, the people of God."] The crown resembles the rainbow, and the rainbow resembles all *the appearance of fire all around it* [reading *lh* for *lḥt lhb*]." A partial parallel in ms Munich 40 (Schäfer, #951; translation of equivalent material in Cohen, section F) attributes several of these features to God himself: a five-hundred-parasang crown named "Israel," horns (!), and a precious stone between them named "Israel is my people" (*yiśra'el ᶜammi li*). But it does not invoke Ezekiel 1:27 or the comparison with the rainbow. – The horns, attributed variously to God and to the "youth," are perhaps somehow related to the horns of Moses, which will claim our attention in chapters VIII and IX. The image of the gigantic being crowned with the rainbow is oddly reminiscent of Revelation 10:1–7; I do not know what significance, if any, there is in the parallel.

Chapter VIII

a) This use of the form *re'uyot* for "visions" is very odd; we would expect *re'iyyot*. But the reading of the manuscript is clear, and is supported by the spelling of the word in the Cambridge fragment (below).

b) The thirteenth-century Christian polemicist Raimundo Martini quotes the *Song. R.* passage in his *Pugio Fidei*, without *bammishnah*; this key word must have been missing from the manuscript Martini used. Ms Vatican 76,3 supports the reading of the printed edition (with *bammishnah*). Ms Munich 50,2 has the very different reading *kakh 'ameru baᶜale hammishnah* ("thus said the masters of the Mishnah"). – I translate the *Hekhalot* passages in chapter VI, section 2a, as texts III–VII. Text VI reads *bammishnah* in place of *bemishnatam*. Text V omits the word altogether.

c) Rimon Kasher lists mss Budapest-Kaufmann 570 and Sassoon 569 as sources for this Tosefta [308,312]. The Gaster Collection in Manchester, England, includes a typescript, evidently made from a manuscript, which contains this Tosefta (among other items). It is there entitled *casarta bihezqel*; that is, the *haftarah* reading for Shabu^cot, from Ezekiel (Institute of Microfilm Hebrew Manuscripts, National and University Library, Jerusalem, reel no. 16076). The Genizah collection of Dropsie University, Philadelphia, has a one-page fragment containing the second half of the Tosefta, which bears the title *targum wayyehi bisheloshim shanah*, "the Targum of *it came to pass in the thirtieth year.*" (Halper's catalog describes the fragment [802]. Professor Abraham Katsh kindly permitted me to examine it in 1974.) Moses Cordovero's commentary on the Zohar cites the text under the title *tosefta dinebu'at yehezqel*, "Tosefta of Ezekiel's prophecy" [820].

d) *Kol qobel shib^cah reqi^cin ukhesumkewatehon* (Tosefta); *keneged shib^cah reqi^cim weshib^cah ^cobyan* (*Visions*).

e) *Berukhim lashshamayim wela'areṣ yorede merkabah*. The expression is rather peculiar, and the text (which ms Oxford shares with ms New York) is perhaps corrupt. Mss Vatican and Budapest have *berukhim 'attem li shamayim we'areṣ weyorede merkabah*, "blessed are you to me, heaven, earth, and you who descend to the *merkabah*." (So ms Munich 22, with a very slight alteration. Mss Munich 40 and Dropsie omit *'attem*.) But this reading is even more troublesome, in that it seems to imply that heaven and earth, like "those who descend to the *merkabah*," are to act as God's messengers to his people.

f) I read *hebel hayyose' mippikhem*, with ms Budapest and the margin of ms Dropsie. Ms Oxford has *hakkol* for *hebel* (*kaph* written in place of *bet*); the other manuscripts "correct" to *haqqol*. *Haqqol hayyose' mippikhem*, "the sound that goes forth from your mouths," makes sense, but is not likely to be original. It does not explain the variants; and the comparison to the smell of sacrifice is less apt for "voice" than for "breath."

g) *Weyiddaresh weyimmase'*; literally, "that he may be sought and found." This is probably an allusion to Isaiah 55:6, *Seek the Lord when he may be found* (*direshu YHWH bihimmaṣe'o*).

h) Ms Oxford has *ba^cale* before *yorede hammerkabah*; I delete it, with the other manuscripts. I do not know how the word came to be in ms Oxford. Perhaps it is a trace of a variant *ba^cale hammerkabah*, "masters of the *merkabah*"?

i) Following the other manuscripts, I read *she'en ken bekhol hekhal*. Ms Oxford has *bo* for *ken*.

j) This is in the description of the angel Gallisur (see below), where the author of *Pesiqta* or his source seems to have twice misread *melakhah* ("function"; so the Oxford manuscript) as *mal'akh* ("angel"), and thus created three angels out of one [293]. – The independence of the *Pesiqta*-Oxford tradition from *Ma^cayan Hokhmah* is particularly clear in their treatment of Gallisur. *Pesiqta* and the Oxford text do not know *Ma^cayan Hokhmah*'s identification of Gallisur with Raziel, or its claim that this angel reveals God's decrees to Elijah, who transmits them to the world. On the other hand, *Pesiqta* and the Oxford text have a bit of information absent from *Ma^cayan Hokhmah*, that one of Gallisur's tasks is to proclaim: "This year barley and wheat will prosper, and wine will be cheap." (So Oxford; *Pesiqta* leaves out the barley. If the resemblance of this passage to Revelation 6:6 is more than a coincidence, we are dealing with a very old tradition indeed.) It is hard to see why the author of any of the sources would have suppressed any such information if he had known it. We therefore do best to suppose that we are dealing with independent recensions. – We will see that the ending of the story in *Ma^cayan Hokhmah* is entirely different from that of the other two sources. It is hard to imagine that, if the author of either version had known the other one's ending, he would not have kept some trace of it.

k) *Ma^cayan Hokhmah* begins the second sentence with the single word *miyyad*, "thereupon." In place of *miyyad*, ms Oxford has *ubesha^cah shettese' hakketer miyyado shel sandalfon*, "when the wreath leaves Sandalphon's hand." This makes good sense in context, but is perhaps an expansion of *miyyad*. *Pesiqta*'s *ubesha^cah shemmaggia^c keter lerosh 'adono shel ^colam*, "when the wreath reaches the head of the Lord of the world," certainly does not suit the context; the scribe perhaps repeated material, inappropriately, from the first sentence. – Ms Oxford has, at the end of the second sentence, *wehayyot romemot nohamot ka'ari*, which we must translate: "the exalted *hayyot* roar like a lion." Ms Parma of *Pesiqta* also reads *romemot*, according to Grözinger's apparatus. But ms Casanata and the printed edition give the absurd reading *wehayyot domemot wenohamot ka'ari*, "the *hayyot* are silent and roar like a lion." The author of *Ma^cayan Hokhmah* tries to make sense out of the statement by expanding it: *wehayyot haqqodesh dome-*

mot weśarfe haqqodesh nohamim ke'aryeh, "the holy *hayyot* are silent, and the holy seraphim roar like a lion."

l) See also endnote *j,* above; and below, chapter IX, section C3c. In translating the account of Gallisur's third function, Braude accepts – mistakenly, in my opinion [293] – the reading *keneged hammal'akhim weneged negidim* (which he renders "angels and kings") instead of *keneged melakhim weneged negidim* ("kings and princes").

m) It is particularly interesting, in connection with the question of how the date of a literary source relates to the date of its materials, that the form of this midrash that is closest to Origen's (and, it would appear from its contents, most original) occurs anonymously in Tanh. *Noah* #5. A somewhat more developed version appears in Tanh. Buber *Wa-Yesheb* #5 (ed. 90b [222]), attributed to "R. Levi quoting R. Johanan." *Gen. R.* 30:8 (ed. 274–275 [188]) quotes, in the name of "R. Levi" alone, a version that is later still.

n) A slightly different version of this midrash, perhaps influenced by the citation of *Lam. R.* in *Tosafot* to Sukk. 45a, has been inserted into one manuscript of *Pesiqta de-Rab Kahana* (*Dibre Yirmeyahu* #9, ed. 232 [206]).

o) Incidentally, the conclusion of the eighth homily on Judges (VIII, 5; ed. 7:515 [640]) suggests that Origen planned to expound the books of the Old Testament in the sequence Judges – Kings (that is, Samuel-Kings) – Isaiah – Jeremiah. In other words, Origen used the sequence of the Masoretic Text, not (as Nautin assumes) the Septuagint. The implications of this for the question of Origen's relations with Judaism are worth pondering.

p) I do not know how otherwise to understand the Latin text: " ... et Spiritum sanctum descendisse, ut, postquam Dominus *adscendisset in excelsum captivam ducens captivitatem,* tribueret nobis Spiritum, qui ad se venerat, quem quidem et dedit resurrectionis suae tempore dicens: *Accipite Spiritum sanctum,*" etc. If *quem quidem et dedit* is supposed to supplement the preceding *qui ad se venerat* ("which had come to him, and which he also gave"), it seems gratuitous after *ut ... tribueret nobis Spiritum.* – The textual witnesses invoked in Max Rauer's apparatus (ed. 9:171 [643]) differ on the placing of the crucial *et.* One manuscript puts it before *quem,* which considerably tones down the impression of a second gift of the spirit; while the printed edition, placing it before *resurrectionis,* greatly strengthens this impression.

q) Contrast the expression *noṣeṣe qelalim,* used in one *Hekhalot* text (*Massekhet Hekhalot,* ch. 6 [479,499]) for one of the many concentric circles that surround the feet of the *hayyot.* The derivation of this phrase from MT Ezekiel 1:7, *noṣeṣim ke͑en nehoshet qalal,* is obvious.

r) The details of this sentence, including the number of angels, are stereotypic, and occur elsewhere in *Seder 'Eliyahu Rabbah:* chapters 7(6), 17, 29(31) (ed. 32, 84, 156–157, 163 [211]). I do not know the source for the number of angels. Chapter 22 of *Seder 'Eliyahu Rabbah* (ed. 119) interprets Psalm 68:18 to mean that God was attended at Sinai by three groups of two hundred forty-eight angels (cf. *Seder 'Eliyahu Zuṭa,* chapter 12; ed. 193 [211]). With several zeroes added, this figure becomes precisely half of the one in our passage. I have no idea what this might signify.

Chapter IX

a) Schafer, #214 [495]. I do not know where Scholem gets the text of this passage that he quotes and translates [596]. It does not follow any of the manuscripts that Schäfer prints, or the editions of Jellinek or Wertheimer. The reading of ms New York 8128 is closest to Scholem's text: "The mouth of each horse is three times the size of the gate of Caesarea, and each manger is equivalent to three of the mangers of Caesarea." The other manuscripts omit, evidently by scribal error, several words of the New York reading.

b) Scholem and Ch. Wirszubski established a critical text of *Hekhalot Rabbati* [590,614]. But it was never published, and I do not know if the manuscript is still extant. Schäfer cites an unpublished Master's thesis by Carl S. Waldman, *Hekhalot Zutarti. A Critical Edition Based on a Geniza Manuscript,* submitted in 1978 to the Bernard Revel Graduate School (Yeshiva University, New York) [496].

c) Their number is variously given as ten and as four. – The links between this passage and the "Legend of the Ten Martyrs" (a story of ten second-century rabbis supposedly put to death by the Romans, best known to most Jews through a lachrymose rendition that has made its way into the liturgy for the afternoon of Yom Kippur [459,479b,486a]) deserve further investigation. Joseph Dan has led the way [521]. – Gottfried Reeg has now prepared a synoptic edition and translation of the several recensions of the "Legend," with a full introduction: *Die Geschichte von den Zehn Märtyrern*, J. C. B. Mohr (Paul Siebeck), Tübingen, 1985.

d) This is my guess at the meaning of *wehifsaqti 'otakh*. I assume that the author is using the root *psq* with its meaning "decide," "give judgment" (as in *pesaq-din, pesaq-halakhah*). But I cannot offer any parallel for the use of the Hiph^{c}il in this sense. Gruenwald's translation, "For I have interrupted you!", better suits the Hebrew, but seems absurd in context [546].

e) *Me'ah sehubot sehabuhu leben zoma*. On this "dragging," cf. the passage from *Hekhalot Rabbati* quoted below, footnote 81 (Schäfer, #96; Wertheimer, 3:2).

f) Reading *uferashti* for *uferushaw*.

g) I am very unsure how to translate these words. An alternative translation – "It is written four times: 'The testimony of the seal of the *merkabah* becomes visible ...'" – better suits the language, but makes poorer sense in context.

h) The language of #411 is reminiscent of that used in Gruenwald's fragments (pages 362, 370). Part of Gruenwald's *Sar Torah* text (pages 366–367, lines 37–49) is very closely parallel to ##420–421 (below). We are evidently dealing with two recensions of the same material.

i) Reading *yelaḥesh*, with mss New York and Oxford. Mss Dropsie, Munich 22 and 40 read *yaḥlosh*, "he will sink." But "whisper" makes more sense in context; and the fact that mss Dropsie and Munich 40 write *yaḥlosh* without the *waw* suggests that the reading originated from a reversal of the middle letters of *yelaḥesh*. Hai Gaon's *loḥesh la'areṣ* ("whispers to the earth") is plainly based on the New York-Oxford reading; see below.

j) Musajoff had earlier published this passage in *Merkabah Shelemah*, pages 4a–5a [489]. It corresponds to ##7–17 in Schäfer's German summary of *Merkabah Rabbah* [585].

k) This is not the only place in the *Hekhalot* where Ishmael's Aaronic descent protects him from harm. In *Ma^{c}aseh Merkabah*, Nehuniah is shocked to hear that Ishmael has uttered the names of all the angels in all the palaces. "The Torah that Aaron acquired," Nehuniah explains, "has protected you, so that you did not suffer on account of this secret. But [in the future] if you want to make use of this secret, strengthen yourself with five prayers" – which Nehuniah goes on to teach him (Schäfer, #586; Scholem, #26 [603]). At the beginning of *3 Enoch*, Ishmael goes up to heaven to see the *merkabah*, and passes through six of the palaces. At the gate of the seventh, he prays that "the merit of Aaron ... may protect me from the power of prince Qaspiel and the angels that are with him, that they may not throw me down from heaven" (Schäfer, #1; Odeberg, ch. 1). We may also compare a Messianic prophecy which the copyist of ms New York inserted into *Hekhalot Rabbati*, in which Metatron tells Ishmael that he is worthy of a vision of the Messiah because his honor is like Aaron's (Schäfer, #140; also published by Eben-Shemuel [237]).

l) It is curious, though, that the hymn to the divine throne, which R. Ishmael goes on (#687) to prescribe for "every student [*talmid ḥakham*] who knows this great secret," seems to be spoken by a convert. "You will be great among all the seed of Jacob," the speaker tells the throne, "and, when I came to take refuge in the shadow of your wings, [(God) rejoiced over you with a merry heart]." (I restore the missing words *beśimḥat lebab śamaḥ bakh* on the basis of the parallels in *Hekhalot Rabbati* – Schäfer, #94; Wertheimer, 2:5 – and Gruenwald's fragments [472]. The scribe's eye evidently jumped from *beśimḥat* to *ki śiḥatakh*, and he omitted the words in between.) He thus appears to contrast himself with "all the seed of Jacob"; and what he says about himself is apparently drawn from Ruth 2:12, which praises the convert Ruth for coming to take refuge beneath God's wings. – It seems barely possible that the reference in #676 to "God-fearers" (or, as ms New York has it, "heaven-fearers") is a nod to the semi-converts mentioned in rabbinic and Greek sources [422b,711a,732a,734a].

m) I translate an eclectic text, based mainly on mss New York and Munich 22. These two manuscripts are clearly superior in #353, where the other three (Oxford, Dropsie, Munich 40) omit the first two "if anyone ... " sentences, through either scribal error or scribal laziness. I mostly translate ms New York for #353, but turn to Munich 22 for a few passages where the New York text seems corrupt. I translate "like the splendor of clouds of glory" from ms Oxford, *kezohar ^{c}anane kabod*. All other manuscripts have either *kezoham ^{c}anane kabod*, "like the filth of clouds of glory," or a corruption thereof. (A Genizah fragment published by Elior [465], which differs considerably from the other manuscripts, reads *niḥamah*, "consolation," in place of *kabod*.) This is obviously the *lectio difficilior*, but is so *difficilis* as to be incomprehensible. I am not comfortable with "like the appearance of a bride" (Munich 22, *kehezu dekhalla*), but it is the best I can do with the text. – In #354, ms New York gives first the text of Targ. Ezekiel 1:6, then a text of *Hekhalot Zuṭarti* which consistently supports ms Munich 22. I translate Munich 22, which is slightly better. – For #355, I follow ms Munich 22, with a few emendations from ms New York.

n) Translating ms New York, *keṣurat neshamah*.

o) He replaces Targum's *mezi^can* with the more Hebraic *mera^cashan*, probably on the strength of Ezekiel 3:12–13, where Targum renders *qol ra^cash gadol* with *qal zeya^c saggi*. – I note two minor examples of our text's use of the Targum. "Like the appearance of the rainbow in the cloud" (*kehezu qashta ba^canana*) is nearly a quotation of Targ. Ezekiel 1:28 (*kehezu qashta dehawe ba^canana*). "The feet of the *ḥayyot*" (*parsot ragle hahayyot*) perhaps reflects Targ. Ezekiel 1:7 (*parsat raglehon*).

p) I restore "the likeness of an ox" on the basis of the "*Shi^cur Qomah*" version (#954, from ms Munich 40), and the parallel in #384 (below, section 4). The sequel shows that it must originally have been part of the text, and perhaps also suggests the reason why the copyist omitted it here. – I do not know what "sealed up" (*ḥatum*) means here. ##954 and 384 have in its place *satum*, whose meaning partly overlaps that of *ḥatum* but which has more the sense of "kept secret."

q) Three manuscripts (Dropsie, Oxford, Munich 40) read "wings" instead of "faces." I assume that this is a correction in accord with Targ. Ezekiel 1:6. The 512 eyes mentioned in the next paragraph imply 256 faces.

r) With mss Dropsie and Munich 40, I read *kol ṣurot panim*, and omit the second *panim* that immediately follows. I assume that *shellahem* is the first word of this sentence and not the last word of the preceding one. As I indicate below, I consider the entire sentence an interpolation.

s) *Pequ^cah keshi^cur kebarah gedolah shel ... .* The manuscripts disagree on the reading of the word that follows *shel*; none of the variants makes any sense to me. I conjecture that the original reading was *menappim*, "winnowers" [562a]. I do not know why Grodner [463] translates "sieve woven of branches."

t) So mss Oxford, Munich 40, Dropsie, and Vatican. Mss Munich 22 and Budapest supply (*'et*) *penehem* after *mefare^cot*, while ms New York reads the verb as *mitpare^cot*. But it is easier to understand a copyist's motive for inserting an object or for turning the verb into a reflexive than for proceeding in the opposite direction; and, as we will see, the original author had reason to be ambiguous about what it is that the *ḥayyot* uncover.

u) *Kikhebarah* is the reading of mss Budapest, Vatican, and New York (although Schäfer notes that the reading of the last is uncertain). Ms Oxford omits the word altogether; ms Munich 40 reads *bkbrh*; ms Dropsie has *bkbdh*, but notes the variant *kwkb d^ct* in the margin; ms Munich 22 reads *kwkb d^c'*. The variations attest that the scribes found the expression strange, and did not know quite what to do with it. – I read *mippene hadar ziw*, with mss Budapest, Munich 22, and the original text of Vatican. Mss Oxford, New York, and a correction in ms Vatican, insert *melekh* before *hadar*, presumably under the influence of *melekh hadur* at the beginning of the passage. Mss Dropsie and Munich 40 conflate the two readings: *mippene melekh mippene hadar ziw.*

v) Each of the four *ḥayyot* has four faces and wings, each wing big enough to cover the world. But they also have "faces amid faces ... wings amid wings," which give each of them a total of two hundred and forty-eight faces and three hundred and sixty-five wings. Each also has two thousand crowns, each of them like the rainbow, shining like the sun (Schäfer, #32; Odeberg, ch. 21). – Ofafanniel, the angel in charge of the *'ofannim*, has sixteen faces, four on each side, and one hundred wings on each side. He also has 8766 eyes, 2191 on each of his four sides, and two in his face (which one?). His charges, the *'ofannim*, are full not only of eyes (Ezekiel 1:18), but also of wings (Schäfer, ##39–40; Odeberg, ch. 25). – Each of the four seraphim has six wings, as Isaiah tells us (6:2). But he also has sixteen faces, four in each direction (Schäfer, #42; Odeberg, ch. 26). – When the angels sing the *Qedushshah*, the ineffable names inscribed on God's throne "fly like eagles with sixteen wings, and surround God on the four directions from the place of the glory of his Shechinah" (Schäfer, #57; Odeberg, ch. 39). The sixteen wings may perhaps echo Targ. Ezekiel 1:6. – *Massekhet Hekhalot* gives each of the *ḥayyot* twenty-four faces and twenty-four wings, "twenty faces amid four faces and twenty wings amid four wings" (Wertheimer, page 60). This reads like a sobered-up version of *3 Enoch*'s description of the *ḥayyot*.

w) Ms Budapest has best preserved what seems to be the original text: *'attah dar belabbat dinurin weshalhabiyyot.* The unfamiliar word *belabbat*, which confused many of the scribes, is a direct allusion to Exodus 3:2, where the angel of the Lord appears to Moses *belabbat 'esh mittokh hasseneh*, "in a flame of fire out of the midst of a bush" (RSV).

x) The idea of the *hayyot* as "bound" (*habushim*) occurs again a few lines later, where it is applied to the cherubim and *'ofannim* as well (Schäfer, #100; Wertheimer, 3:5). The image seems to have been an ancient and persistent one. It goes back at least to the first century, for II Baruch 51:11 suggests that the living creatures are "held fast" (Syriac *'ahidin*) beneath God's throne (above, chapter III, section 4f, and endnote *f*). It is reminiscent of *Pirqe de-Rabbi Eliezer*, chapter 4, which has the *hayyot* "fixed" (*qebu^cot*) at the four legs of the throne (see Appendix VI). It must have somehow percolated into seventh-century Arabia, for we find it mentioned in a poetic fragment attributed to Muhammad's contemporary Umayyah b. Abi 'l-Salt, which is obviously based on Jewish *merkabah* traditions: "[The angel] Israfil confined the pure ones under it [God's throne]; there was no weak or base one among them. A man and an ox were under its right leg; an eagle at the other, and a lion set on guard" (references in Appendix II, section 1a). The Arabic verb for "confined," *habasa*, is cognate to Hebrew *habushim*.

y) I emend *mehazzaqo berob panim* to *mehabbeqo be'or panim*. Cf. the parallel in Schäfer, #958.

z) I emend *'et harishit* to *'et 'esh haharishut* (this conjectural reading will explain the many variants found in the parallels, although it does not actually occur in any of them); and read, with the parallels, *dibbur* for *dober*.

aa) I translate "until ... mountain" from ms New York (Schäfer, #388).

bb) Following the midrash (which was, I assume, influenced by the *shin* of *parshez*), *3 Enoch* preserves the Biblical spelling of *paraś* with a *śin* rather than the more common rabbinic spelling with a *samekh*. — I have noted two other allusions to Job 26:9 in the *Hekhalot*, both of them in *Hekhalot Zuṭarti*. Schäfer, #356 (Elior, lines 122–123) numbers *me'ahez pene kisse'* and *parshez ^calaw ^canano* among the circles that surround the feet of the *hayyot*. #373 (Elior, line 284) asks about the name of God that even the angels do not know, and concludes its answer with the statement: *"Me'ahez pene kisse'* is his name."

cc) Schäfer mistakenly prints *wehanna^car* at the end of #395. It belongs, as the parallels show, with the first sentence of #396. — The parallels omit *śar*. But the sentence reads more easily with it, and it is safe to assume that it was accidentally left out before *shennikhtab*.

dd) I vocalize in accord with the parallels. Two parallel passages, more distant from #396 than the ones that Schäfer prints beside it, read *lo' natan haqqadosh barukh hu' reshut lehishtammesh bo*, "God did not give permission to make use of him" (that is, his name), for magical purposes (#487, from ms Munich 22; #960, from ms Munich 40). This strikes me as an explanatory expansion of the puzzling *lo' nittan* of #396. I will presently offer my own explanation of these words.

ee) With the parallels, I read *mahanot* for ms New York's *'otot*. On the camps of the angels, see above, chapter II.

ff) We have seen yet another variant of Sagnasgiel in the "Zagan'el" of Schäfer, #514 (above, section 1). A legend of the death of Moses, tacked on to *Deut. R.* 11:10 [455], claims that Moses learned the ineffable name from "Zagzag'el, master and scribe of the heavenly beings." Parallel texts spell the name *zgz'l* (*Yalquṭ Shim^coni* to Deuteronomy, #940), *zngzy'l* (Jellinek [477], page 120), *zgzy'l* (ibid., page 129).

gg) The unusual use of *kebashim* for "arcana" is presumably based on a midrash of Proverbs 27:26, attributed to R. Abbahu in BT Hag. 13a [552].

hh) I take this opportunity to list, for the sake of completeness, all other *Hekhalot* references to Moses that I have come across: Schäfer, ##68–69 (*3 Enoch*; Odeberg, ch. 48A), #352 (*Hekhalot Zuṭarti*; Elior, lines 94–99, see Appendix V, quotations of Ezekiel 3:12), #492, 498, 508 (not part of any of the conventional texts), #694 (*Merkabah Rabbah*). The magic text *Harba de-Mosheh*, which Schäfer includes in his *Synopse*, mentions Moses in ##598 and 606; in both passages, ms New York adds the claim that R. Ishmael also received the secrets revealed to Moses, when he ascended to the *merkabah*. #639 (adjuration of the prince of the presence, also published separately by Schäfer [494]) mentions the revelation at Sinai. Most manuscripts of #92 (*Hekhalot Rabbati*; Wertheimer, 2:3) speak of "the day that Torah was given to Israel, to the upright ones," and so forth (*miyyom shennittenah torah leyiśra'el layyesharim*). But ms Vatican gives what is probably the original reading: "the day that permission was given to upright ones" (*miyyom shennittenah reshut layyesharim*).

ii) The context seems to require this meaning for *middah*.

jj) The medieval Yemenite *Midrash ha-Gadol* (to Genesis 25:27; ed. 441 [198]) attributes the following to R. Hama b. Hanina: "*Dwelling in tents* means that he established [*yishsheb*] tents. The text does not say *tent*, but *tents*, meaning that he served in many schools [*batte midrashot*]: the school of Eber, the school of Shem, and the school of Abraham." This midrash seems to draw upon the Targumic tradition, as well as Tanh. *Shemot* #1. – *Pesiqta Rabbati* 5:8 (ed. 18b [209]) and *Seder Eliyahu Rabbah*, ch. 5(6) (ed. 29 [211]), reflect similar ideas.

Reference List

The following list of sources is divided into sixteen sections, according to topic:
1. Book of Ezekiel.
2. Hebrew Bible (aside from Ezekiel and Daniel); ancient Near East; Septuagint.
3. Qumran and New Testament (aside from Revelation).
4. Apocalyptic literature (including Daniel and Revelation).
5. Editions of rabbinic and related texts.
   a. Arranged alphabetically, by texts.
   b. Arranged alphabetically, by authors (medieval) or editors (modern).
6. Translations of rabbinic and related texts.
7. Rabbinic studies: sources and criticism.
8. Rabbinic studies: history and theology.
9. Editions and translations of *Hekhalot* texts.
10. Studies of the *Hekhalot*, and of "*merkabah* mysticism."
11. Editions and translations of patristic authors (arranged alphabetically, by author).
12. Patristic studies.
13. Religious trends in the Greco-Roman world (including Gnosticism and Hellenistic Judaism).
14. Islam.
   a. Editions and translations of *hadith, tafsir,* and "tales of the prophets."
   b. Other.
15. Dictionaries, concordances, other reference works.
16. Miscellaneous.

Within each section, I arrange the sources alphabetically − normally, by the author or editor's last name. In sections 11 and 14a, which list works by ancient and medieval authors, I alphabetize according to the name by which the author is most commonly known (for example: Jerome, Bukhari). In sections 5a and 6, where the sources are anonymous, I alphabetize according to their conventional titles (for example: Babylonian Talmud, Genesis Rabbah). In section 9, where the sources are not only anonymous but cannot well be classified under titles, I alphabetize according to the last name of the modern editor or translator.

In sections 9 and 10, I have tried to give reasonably complete bibliographies of editions and translations of the *Hekhalot*, and of studies relating to the *Hekhalot* and to the problem of "*merkabah* mysticism," whether or not I actually cite these materials in this book. In section 6, I have listed English translations for as many rabbinic texts as I could, even though I normally did not use these translations while preparing the book. (Nearly all the translations I quote are my own.) I did not try, however, to list all available translations of any given text; my purpose was not to be complete, but to enable the reader without Hebrew or Aramaic to consult as many as possible of my references in their original context.

Elsewhere, I have made no effort to construct full bibliographies, but only to list the sources that I cite. Very occasionally, I cite materials (usually Ph.D. dissertations) that I have not seen, whose titles have suggested to me that the reader will find them helpful in exploring one point or another. In these cases, I state in the reference list that I have not seen the work in question.

I have followed the format recommended in Mary-Claire van Leunen's *Handbook for Scholars* [860]. The numbers attached in the reference list to sources (or to pages or clusters of pages within a source) correspond to the numbers bracketed in the text (and in the preceding sentence). In citing journal articles, I record the title, volume, and number (where I know it) of the journal containing the article in question, the pages the article occupies, and the year of the volume. Thus, for example: *Vetus Testamentum* IV(3):225−245, 1954. Following van Leunen, I do not use abbreviations for journal titles, but write them out in full. In citing books, I normally do not give the city where a major American publishing house is located, since I assume that a reader who wants to obtain a copy of Scholem's *Major Trends in Jewish Mysticism* [604a] from Schocken Books will not be helped by the information that the firm is located in New York City. In this matter, too, I follow van Leunen.

Authors and editors of books and articles in Hebrew often attach to their work a second title, in English or some other European language. Where such a title exists, I use it to cite the work, and then note that the work is written in Hebrew. (I sometimes omit this notice where I think the use of Hebrew is self-evident, as in section 5a.) Otherwise, I transliterate the Hebrew title, and attach in parentheses my own translation of it.

I conclude this note with an expression of gratitude to my research assistant, Robert B. Spencer, upon whom I cast the detailed and often maddening work of preparing the materials for this reference list. He executed it painstakingly and masterfully.

1. Book of Ezekiel

1] George Albert Cooke. *A Critical and Exegetical Commentary on the Book of Ezekiel.* T. & T. Clark, Edinburgh, 1936. International Critical Commentary.

1a] G. R. Driver. Ezekiel's Inaugural Vision. *Vetus Testamentum* I(1):60–62, 1951.

2] G. R. Driver. Problems and Solutions, pages 239–240. *Vetus Testamentum* IV(3):225–245, 1954.

3] G. R. Driver. Ezekiel: Linguistic and Textual Problems, page 145. *Biblica* 35(2):145–159, and 35(3):299–312, 1954.

4] Lorenz Dürr. *Ezechiels Vision von der Erscheinung Gottes (Ez. ch. 1 u. 10) im Lichte der Vorderasiatischen Altertumskunde.* Aschendorff, Münster, 1917.

5] Eliezer of Beaugency. *Kommentar zu Ezechiel und den XII kleinen Propheten,* pages 7–8. Edited by S. Poznanski. Warsaw, 1913. In Hebrew.

6] Moshe Greenberg. *Ezekiel 1–20: A New Translation With Introduction and Commentary.* Doubleday, 1983. The Anchor Bible, volume 22.

    7] Pages 51–59.

8] Moshe Greenberg. The Vision of Jerusalem in Ezekiel 8–11. A Holistic Interpretation. In James L. Crenshaw and Samuel Sandmel, editors, *The Divine Helmsman: Studies on God's Control of Human Events, Presented to Lou H. Silbermann,* pages 143–164. Ktav, 1980.

9] David J. Halperin. The Exegetical Character of Ezek. x 9–17. *Vetus Testamentum* XXVI(2): 129–141, 1976.

10] Cornelius B. Houk. The Final Redaction of Ezekiel 10. *Journal of Biblical Literature* 90(1): 42–54, 1971.

11] Cornelius B. Houk. A Statistical Linguistic Study of Ezekiel 1 4 – 3 11. *Zeitschrift für die alttestamentliche Wissenschaft* 93(1):76–85, 1981.

12] Bernhard Lang. *Ezechiel, Der Prophet und das Buch.* Wissenschaftliche Buchgesellschaft, Darmstadt, 1981. Erträge der Forschung, volume 153.

    Tryggve N. D. Mettinger. *The Dethronement of Sabaoth: Studies in the Shem and Kabod Theologies.* Translated by Frederick H. Cryer. CWK Gleerup, 1982. Coniectanea Biblica, Old Testament Series 18. I owe this reference to my colleague, Professor John Van Seters.

    12a] Page 69.

    12b] Pages 97–111.

13] H. Van Dyke Parunak. The Literary Architecture of Ezekiel's *Mar'ot 'Elohim. Journal of Biblical Literature* 99(1):61–74, 1980.

14] H. H. Rowley. *Men of God: Studies in Old Testament History and Prophecy,* pages 169–210. Nelson, 1963.

    Shalom Spiegel. Toward Certainty in Ezekiel. *Journal of Biblical Literature* 54:145–171, 1935.

    15] Pages 159–163.

    16] Page 168.

17] Charles C. Torrey. *Pseudo-Ezekiel and the Original Prophecy.* Ktav, 1970. Originally published by Yale University Press, 1930. The Library of Biblical Studies.

18] Ernst Vogt. Die vier "Gesichter" (panim) der Keruben in Ez. *Biblica* 60(3):327–347, 1979.

19] Walther Zimmerli. *Ezekiel: A Commentary on The Book of the Prophet Ezekiel.* Two volumes. Volume 1 translated from the German by Ronald E. Clements; edited by Frank Moore Cross, Klaus Baltzer, and Leonard Jay Greenspoon. Volume 2 translated by James D. Martin; edited by Paul D. Hanson and Greenspoon. Fortress Press, 1979, 1983. The German original was published in 1969.

2. Hebrew Bible (aside from Ezekiel and Daniel); ancient Near East; Septuagint

20] W. F. Albright. What were the Cherubim? *Biblical Archaeologist* I(1):1–3, 1938. Reprinted in David Noel Freedman and G. Ernest Wright, editors, *The Biblical Archaeologist Reader*, pages 95–97. Doubleday, Anchor Books, 1961.

21] James Barr. *Comparative Philology and the Text of the Old Testament*, page 235. Clarendon Press, Oxford, 1968.

22] Dominique Barthélemy. *Les devanciers d'Aquila: permière publication intégrale du texte, des fragments du Dodécaprophéton trouvés dans le désert de Juda, précédée d'une étude sur les traductions et recensions grecques de la Bible réalisées au premier siècle de notre ère sous l'influence du rabbinat palestinien*. E. J. Brill, Leiden, 1963. Supplements to *Vetus Testamentum*, volume 10.
    23] Pages 144–157.

24] Bernard F. Batto. The Reed Sea: *Requiescat in Pace*. *Journal of Biblical Literature* 102(1):27–35, 1983.
    25] Page 33.

26] The Bible. Revised Standard Version. New Testament first published in 1946 (second edition, 1971), Old Testament in 1952, Apocrypha in 1957. Printed, with highly useful annotations, as the *Oxford Annotated Bible* and *Apocrypha*, by Oxford University Press, 1962 (Old and New Testaments), 1965 (Apocrypha), 1977 (expanded edition of Apocrypha, containing III and IV Maccabees and Psalm 151). The fullest and most recent edition is *The New Oxford Annotated Bible With the Apocrypha: Revised Standard Version*, edited by Herbert G. May and Bruce M. Metzger, Oxford University Press, 1977. I have regularly used the RSV for quotations from the New Testament; occasionally (only where designated) for quotations from the Hebrew Bible. I assume it is likely to be the translation that the reader has before him.

27] Umberto Cassuto. *The Goddess Anath. Canaanite Epics of The Patriarchal Age*. Translated by Israel Abrahams. Magnes, Jerusalem, 1971.
    28] Pages 33–34.

28a] Alan Cooper. Ps 24:7–10: Mythology and Exegesis. *Journal of Biblical Literature* 102(1):37–60, 1983. Cooper focuses on the passage's relevance to the myth of the descent to the netherworld; but touches (pages 57–58) on its application to the ascension.

28b] P. C. Craigie. Helel, Athtar, and Phaethon (Jes 14,12–15). *Zeitschrift für die alttestamentliche Wissenschaft* 85:223–225, 1973.

29] A. H. W. Curtis. The "Subjugation of the Waters" Motif in the Psalms; Imagery or Polemic? *Journal of Semitic Studies* XXIII(2):245–256, 1978.

30] Samuel Rolles Driver. *An Introduction to the Literature of the Old Testament*, pages vi–ix. Scribner, 1942.

30a] Samuel Rolles Driver and George Buchanan Gray. *A Critical and Exegetical Commentary on the Book of Job, Together With a New Translation*, page 195. T. & T. Clark, Edinburgh, 1921. International Critical Commentary.

31] Henri Frankfort. *Cylinder Seals: A Documentary Essay on the Art and Religion of the Ancient Near East*, pages 124–129. Macmillan, London, 1939. I owe this reference to Professor Thorkild Jacobsen.

32] T. H. Gaster. Angel. In *The Interpreter's Dictionary of the Bible: An Illustrated Encyclopedia*, volume I, pages 128–134. Abingdon, 1962.

32a] Christian D. Ginsburg. *Introduction to the Massoretico-Critical Edition of the Hebrew Bible*, pages 334–338. Originally published 1897. Reprinted, with a Prolegomenon by Harry M. Orlinsky, by Ktav, 1966.

33] Cyrus H. Gordon. The Wine-Dark Sea. *Journal of Near Eastern Studies* 37(1):51–52, 1978.

33a] P. Grelot. Isaïe XIV 12–15 et son arrière-plan mythologique. *Revue de l'Histoire des Religions* 149:18–48, 1956.

34] David J. Halperin. Merkabah Midrash in the Septuagint. *Journal of Biblical Literature* 101(3):351–363, 1982.

35] Alexander Heidel. *The Gilgamesh Epic and Old Testament Parallels*. University of Chicago Press, second edition, 1971.

36] *The Holy Scriptures according to the Masoretic text*. Jewish Publication Society of America, 1917.

37] Sidney Jellicoe. *The Septuagint and Modern Study*. Clarendon Press, Oxford, 1968.

38] Aarre Lauha. Das Schilfmeermotiv im Alten Testament. Suppl. to *Vetus Testamentum* IX:32–46, 1963. Congress Volume, Bonn, 1962.

Miriam Lichtheim. *Ancient Egyptian Literature: A Book of Readings.* Three volumes. University of California Press, 1973–1980. I owe this reference to Professor Edmund Meltzer.
  39] Volume III, pages 125–151.
  40] Volume III, page 129.

40a] J. W. McKay. Helel and the Dawn-Goddess: A re-examination of the myth in Isaiah XIV 12–15. *Vetus Testamentum* XX(4):451–464, 1970.

40b] George F. Moore. *A Critical and Exegetical Commentary on Judges,* pages 400–402. T. & T. Clark, Edinburgh, 1895. International Critical Commentary.

41] David Neiman. The Supercaelian Sea. *Journal of Near Eastern Studies* 28(4):243–249, 1969.

41a] Harry M. Orlinsky. Introductory Essay: On Anthropomorphisms and Anthropopathisms in the Septuagint and Targum. In Bernard M. Zlotowitz, *The Septuagint Translation of the Hebrew Terms in Relation to God in the Book of Jeremiah,* pages xv–xxiv. Ktav Publishing House, 1981.

42] Shalom M. Paul and Louis Isaac Rabinowitz. Cherub. In *Encyclopedia Judaica,* volume 5, columns 399–402. Macmillan, 1971.

43] Robert H. Pfeiffer. *Introduction to the Old Testament,* page 243. Harper and Brothers, revised edition, 1948.

44] James Bennett Pritchard, editor. *Ancient Near Eastern Texts Relating to the Old Testament.* pages 84–85. Princeton University Press, third edition, 1969.

45] Moses Hirsch Segal. *Sefer Ben Sira ha-Shalem* (The Complete Book of Ben Sira: Including all the Hebrew Fragments Discovered in the Genizah and a Reconstruction of the Missing Portions), pages 336–339. Bialik Institute, Jerusalem, second edition, 1958.

46] N. H. Snaith. The Sea of Reeds: The Red Sea. *Vetus Testamentum* XV(3):395–398, 1965.

47] H. St. John Thackeray. The Greek Translators of Ezekiel. *Journal of Theological Studies* IV: 398–411, 1903.

48] H. St. John Thackeray. *The Septuagint and Jewish Worship: A Study in Origins,* pages 49–51. H. Milford, London, 1921.

49] Nigel Turner. The Greek Translators of Ezekiel. *Journal of Theological Studies,* New Series, VII(1): 12–24, 1956.

49a] Mary K. Wakeman. *God's Battle With the Monster: A Study in Biblical Imagery.* E. J. Brill, Leiden, 1973.

49b] John William Wevers, editor. *Numeri.* Vandenhoeck & Ruprecht, Göttingen, 1982. Septuaginta ... Gottingensis, vol. III, 1.

50] Walter Wifall. The Sea of Reeds as Sheol. *Zeitschrift für die alttestamentliche Wissenschaft* 92(3):325–332, 1980.

51] Ronald J. Williams. Ancient Egyptian Folk Tales. *University of Toronto Quarterly* XXVII (3):256–272, 1957–58. I owe this reference to Edmund Meltzer.

51a] Nicolas Wyatt. ᶜAttar and the Devil. *Transactions of the Glasgow University Oriental Society* XXV:85–97, 1973–74. (Published in 1976.)

51b] Joseph Ziegler, editor. *Ezechiel.* Vandenhoeck & Ruprecht, second edition, Göttingen, 1977. Septuaginta ... Gottingensis, vol. XVI, 1.

3. Qumran and New Testament (aside from Revelation)

52] M. Baillet, J. T. Milik and R. de Vaux. *Les "petites grottes" de Qumran: exploration de la falaise. les grottes 2Q, 3Q, 5Q, 6Q, 7Q à 10Q, le rouleau de cuivre,* volume I, pages 86–87. Two volumes. Clarendon Press, Oxford, 1962. Discoveries in the Judaean Desert of Jordan, 3.

53] D. Barthélemy and J. T. Milik. *Qumran Cave I.* Clarendon Press, Oxford, 1955. Discoveries in the Judaean Desert, 1.

53a] J. M. Baumgarten. The Counting of the Sabbath in Ancient Sources. *Vetus Testamentum* XVI(3):277–286, 1966.

54] P. Benoit, J. T. Milik, and R. de Vaux. *Les grottes de Murabbaᶜat.* Two volumes. Clarendon Press, Oxford, 1961. Discoveries in the Judaean Desert, 2.

55] Matthew Black. *The Scrolls and Christian Origins: Studies in the Jewish Background of the New Testament,* page 109. Scribner, 1961. Cited in Barbara Thiering, The Biblical Source of Qumran Asceticism, page 442. *Journal of Biblical Literature* 93(3):429–444, 1974.

56] William H. Brownlee. The Scroll of Ezekiel from the Eleventh Qumran Cave. *Revue de Qumrân* 4(1):11–28, pl. 1–2, 1963–64.

57] Millar Burrows. *The Dead Sea Scrolls.* Viking, 1955.

58] Millar Burrows. *More Light on the Dead Sea Scrolls: New Scrolls and New Interpretations, with Translations of Important Recent Discoveries.* Viking, 1958.

59] Jean Carmignac. Règle des Chants pour l'Holocauste du Sabbat. Quelques détails du lecture. *Revue de Qumràn* 4(4):563–566, 1963–64.

60] Wesley Carr. *Angels and Principalities: The Background, Meaning and Development of the Pauline Phrase hai archai kai hai exousiai.* Cambridge University Press, 1981.

61] Frank Moore Cross, Jr. *The Ancient Library of Qumran and Modern Biblical Studies.* Doubleday, 1958.

62] Frank Moore Cross, Jr. The History of the Biblical Text in the Light of the Discoveries in the Judaean Desert. *Harvard Theological Review* 57(4):281–299, 1964.

63] A. Dupont-Sommer. *The Essene Writings From Qumran.* Translated by G. Vermes, from the second edition of the French (*Les Écrits esséniens découverts près de la mer Morte*). Basil Blackwell, Oxford, 1961.

64] Paul Feine and Johannes Behm. *Introductioh to the New Testament,* pages 325–326. Edited by Werner Georg Kümmel. Translated by A. J. Mattill, Jr. Abingdon Press, fourteenth edition, 1966.

65] Joseph A. Fitzmyer. *The Dead Sea Scrolls: Major Publications and Tools for Study.* Scholars Press for the Society of Biblical Literature, 1975.

66] Shozo Fujita. *The Temple Theology of the Qumran Sect and the Book of Ezekiel: Their Relationship to Jewish Literature of the Last Two Centuries B.C.* Three volumes. University Microfilms, 1973. Ph.D. dissertation, Princeton Theological Seminary, 1970.

   67] Pages 295–305.

68] Theodor H. Gaster. *The Dead Sea Scriptures: In English Translation.* Anchor Books, third edition, 1976.

69] H. Gressman. Vom reichen Mann und armen Lazarus. *Abhandlungen der Berliner Akademie der Wissenschaften,* philosophical-historical class, 7, 1918. Cited in Lichtheim [39], page 127.

70] Ernst Haenchen. *The Acts of the Apostles: A Commentary.* Translated by Bernard Noble, Gerald Shinn, Hugh Anderson, and R. McL. Wilson. Westminster Press, 1971.

71] Jacob Licht, editor. *The Thanksgiving Scroll: A Scroll from the Wilderness of Judea,* page 84. Bialik Institute, Jerusalem, 1957. In Hebrew.

71a] G. H. C. Macgregor. The Acts of the Apostles: Exegesis. In *The Interpreter's Bible,* volume IX, pages 72–73. Abingdon-Cokesbury, 1954.

71b] J. T. Milik. *Ten Years of Discovery in the Wilderness of Judaea,* pages 20–21. Translated by J. Strugnell. Alec R. Allenson, 635 East Ogden Avenue, Naperville, Illinois. 1959.

72] No reference.

73] Richard Rubinkiewicz. Ps LXVIII 19 (=Eph IV 8): Another Textual Tradition or Targum? *Novum Testamentum* XVII(3):219–224, 1975.

73a] Samuel Sandmel. *The Genius of Paul: A Study in History,* pages xi–xii. Fortress Press, third edition, 1979.

74] Lawrence H. Schiffman. Merkavah Speculation at Qumran: The 4Q *Serekh Shirot 'Olat ha-Shabbat.* In Jehuda Reinharz and Daniel Swetchinski, editors, *Mystics, Philosophers, and Politicians: Essays in Jewish Intellectual History in Honor of Alexander Altmann,* pages 15–47. Duke University Press, 1982.

75] John Strugnell. The Angelic Liturgy at Qumrân – 4Q Serek Šîrôt 'Ôlat Haššabbāt. *Vetus Testamentum,* Supplements VII: 318–345, 1960.

   76] Page 344.

77] Geza Vermes. *The Dead Sea Scrolls in English.* Penguin, second edition, 1975.

77a] Geza Vermes. *The Dead Sea Scrolls: Qumran in Perspective.* With the collaboration of Pamela Vermes. Fortress Press, revised edition, 1981.

78] Edmund Wilson. *The Dead Sea Scrolls 1947–1969.* Oxford University Press, 1969.

   79] Page 81.

80] Yigael Yadin. The Excavation of Masada – 1963/4. Preliminary Report, pages 81–82, 105–108. *Israel Exploration Journal* 15(1–2):1–120, 1965.

81] Yigael Yadin. *Masada: Herod's Fortress and the Zealots' Last Stand,* pages 173–174. Translated from the Hebrew by Moshe Pearlman. Weidenfeld and Nicolson, London, 1966.

82] Yigael Yadin, editor, *The Temple Scroll.* Three volumes. Israel Exploration Society, Jerusalem, 1977. In Hebrew. An English translation, also published by the Israel Exploration Society, has recently appeared.

4. Apocalyptic literature (including Daniel and Revelation)

83] No reference.

84] Joseph M. Baumgarten. The Duodecimal Courts of Qumran, Revelation and the Sanhedrin. *Journal of Biblical Literature* 95(1):59–78, 1976.

85] Elias Bickerman. *Four Strange Books of the Bible: Jonah, Daniel, Koheleth, Esther.* Schocken, 1968.

86] Matthew Black, editor. *Apocalypsis Henochi Graece.* E. J. Brill, Leiden, 1970. Pseudepigrapha Veteris Testamenti Graece, 3.

87] Matthew Black. The Throne-Theophany Prophetic Commission and the "Son of Man": A Study in Tradition History. In Robert Hamerton-Kelly and Robin Scroggs, editors, *Jews, Greeks and Christians: religious cultures in late antiquity. Essays in honor of William D. Davies*, pages 57–73. E. J. Brill, Leiden, 1976.

88] Wilhelm Bousset. *The Antichrist Legend: A Chapter in Christian and Jewish Folklore.* Translated from the German by A. H. Keane. Hutchinson and Company, London, 1896.

89] John Bowman. The Background of the Term "Son of Man." *Expository Times* LIX(11):283–288, 1948.

90] George Herbert Box, translator. *The Apocalypse of Abraham, Edited, with a Translation from the Slavonic Text and Notes.* Society for Promoting Christian Knowledge, London, and Macmillan, 1918.

    91] Pages xv–xvi.

92] Raymond R. Brewer. Revelation 4.6 and Translations Thereof. *Journal of Biblical Literature* LXXI(4): 227–231, 1952.

93] George B. Caird. *A Commentary on the Revelation of St. John the Divine.* A. and C. Black, London, 1966. Black's New Testament Commentaries.

    94] Pages 63–64.
    95] Pages 65–68.
    96] Pages 70–73.

96a] Maurice Casey. The Use of Term 'Son of Man' in the Similitudes of Enoch. *Journal for the Study of Judaism* VII(1):11–29, 1976.

97] Antonio Maria Ceriani, editor. Apocalypsis Moysi in Medio Mutila. In Stone and Schaefer [169], pages 14–19. Originally published in Ceriani, *Monumenta Sacra et Profana ex Codicibus Praesertim Bibliothecae Ambrosianae, Opera Collegii Doctorum Eiusdem*, volume V. (I do not know the date of this volume. According to the *National Union Catalog Pre-1956 Imprints*, the series to which it belongs, containing seven volumes in eight, began to appear in 1861.)

98] R. H. Charles, editor. *The Apocrypha and Pseudepigrapha of the Old Testament in English, with Introductions and Critical and Explanatory Notes to the Several Books.* Two volumes. Clarendon Press, Oxford, 1913.

98a] R. H. Charles, translator. *The Ascension of Isaiah.* Society for Promoting Christian Knowledge, London, 1919.

98b] R. H. Charles, translator. *The Book of Enoch, or I Enoch; translated from the editor's Ethiopic text and edited with the introduction notes and indexes of the first edition wholly recast enlarged and rewritten*, Appendix I. Reprint by Makor Publishing, Jerusalem, 1973, Originally published by Oxford, 1893.

99] R. H. Charles. *A Critical and Exegetical Commentary on the Revelation of St. John, with Introduction, Notes, and Indices, also the Greek Text and English Translation*, volume I, pages 267–268. Two volumes. T. and T. Clark, Edinburgh, 1920. International Critical Commentary.

    100] Volume I, pages cxlii–clii.
    101] Volume I, pages 223–224.

102] James Hamilton Charlesworth, editor and translator. *The Odes of Solomon: the Syriac Texts.* Scholars Press, revised edition, 1978. Originally published by Clarendon Press, Oxford, 1973.

    103] Pages 28–31.

104] James H. Charlesworth, editor. *The Old Testament Pseudepigrapha.* Volume I: *Apocalyptic Literature and Testaments.* Doubleday, 1983. Volume II: *Expansions of the "Old Testament" and Legends, Wisdom and Philosophical Literature, Prayers, Psalms, and Odes, Fragments of Lost Judeo-Hellenistic Works.* Doubleday, 1985. (I have not made use of the second volume.)

105] James H. Charlesworth. *The Pseudepigrapha and Modern Research, with a Supplement.*

Scholars Press for the Society of Biblical Literature, 1981. Originally published, without supplement, in 1976.

106] Pages 163–166.
106a] Pages 189–194.

107] Adela Yarbro Collins. *The Combat Myth in the Book of Revelation.* Scholars Press for Harvard Theological Review, 1976.

107a] Pages 22–26.

108] Fred C. Conybeare. On the Apocalypse of Moses. *Jewish Quarterly Review,* Old Series, VII:216–235, 1894–95.

108a] Roger W. Cowley. *The Traditional Interpretation of the Apocalypse of St John in the Ethiopian Orthodox Church,* page 219. Cambridge University Press, 1983.

109] M. Delcor. Les sources du chapitre VII de Daniel. *Vetus Testamentum* XVIII(3):290–312, 1968.

110] No reference.

111] Albert-Marie Denis. *Introduction aux Pseudépigraphes Grecs d'Ancien Testament.* E. J. Brill, Leiden, 1970.

112] Pages 3–14.
113] Page 79.
114] Pages 134–135.

115] Morton Scott Enslin. *Christian Beginnings,* pages 357–372. Harper and Brothers, 1938. Part III, containing pages 203–533, was published separately as *The Literature of the Christian Movement,* Harper & Row, 1956.

116] André Feuillet. Le Fils de l'homme de Daniel et la tradition biblique. *Revue biblique* LX (2): 170–202, and LX(3):321–346, 1953.

117] André Feuillet. Les vingt-quatre vieillards de l'Apocalypse. *Revue biblique* LXV(1):5–32, 1958.

118] C. W. Fishbarne. *Liturgical Patterns and Structures in the Johannine Apocalypse, Against the Background of Jewish and Early Christian Worship.* Ph.D. dissertation, Edinburgh, 1976. I have not seen this item.

118a] T. Francis Glasson. *Greek Influence in Jewish Eschatology: With Special Reference to the Apocalypses and Pseudepigraphs.* Society for Promoting Christian Knowledge, London, 1961.

119] T. Francis Glasson. The Son of Man Imagery: Enoch XIV and Daniel VII. *New Testament Studies* 23(1):82–90, 1976.

120] Jonas C. Greenfield and Michael E. Stone. The Enochic Pentateuch and the Date of the Similitudes. *Harvard Theological Review* 70(1–2):51–65, 1977.

121] Page 62.

122] Hermann Gunkel. *Schöpfung und Chaos in Urzeit und Endzeit: Eine religionsgeschichtliche Untersuchung über Gen I und Ap Joh 12.* Vanderhoeck and Ruprecht, Göttingen, 1895.

123] Pages 29–114.
124] Pages 31–32.

124a] John Gwynn. *The Apocalypse of St John In a Syriac Version Hitherto Unknown,* Part I, page xxxiii; Part II, page 51. Reprinted by APA-Philo Press, Amsterdam, 1981. Originally published 1897, by Dublin University Press.

125] Paul D. Hansen. Rebellion in Heaven, Azazel, and Euhemeristic Heroes in I Enoch 6–11. *Journal of Biblical Literature* 96(2):195–234, 1977.

126] Louis F. Hartman and Alexander A. DiLella. *The Book of Daniel: A New Translation with Notes and Commentary.* Doubleday, 1978. The Anchor Bible, 23.

127] Andrew K. Helmbold. Gnostic Elements in the 'Ascension of Isaiah.' *New Testament Studies* 18(2):222–227, 1972.

128] Ephraim Isaac. New Light Upon the Book of Enoch from Newly-Found Ethiopic MSS. *Journal of the American Oriental Society* 103(2):399–411, 1983.

128a] E[phraim] Isaac. 1 (Ethiopic Apocalypse of) Enoch: A New Translation and Introduction. In Charlesworth [104], volume I, pages 5–89.

129] Vatroslav Jagić, editor and translator. Die altkirchenslavischen Texte des Adambuches. In Stone and Schaefer [169], pages 44–66. Originally published in Vatroslav Jagić, Slavische Beiträge zu den biblischen Apocryphen, pages 18–40, in *Denkschriften der Wiener Akademie der Wissenschaften,* philosophical-historical class, volume 42, Vienna, 1893.

129a] H. C. Kee. Testaments of the Twelve Patriarchs: A New Translation and Introduction. In Charlesworth [104], volume I, pages 775–828. Includes a brief annotated bibliography.

129b] M[ichael] A. Knibb. The Date of the Parables of Enoch: A Critical Review. *New Testament Studies* 25(3):345–359, 1979.

130] Michael A. Knibb, editor and translator. *The Ethiopic Book of Enoch: A New Edition in Light of the Aramaic Dead Sea Fragments.* Two volumes. Clarendon Press, Oxford, and Oxford University Press, 1978. Revision of Ph.D. dissertation, University of London, 1974.

131] Anitra Bingham Kolenkow. The Genre Testament and Forecasts of the Future in the Hellenistic Jewish Milieu, pages 62–63. *Journal for the Study of Judaism* VI(1):57–71, 1975.

132] No reference.

133] Heinrich Kraft. *Die Offenbarung des Johannes,* page 201. Mohr, Tübingen, 1974. Handbuch zum Neuen Testament, 16a.

133a] R. A. Kraft, et al., editors. *The Testament of Job.* Society of Biblical Literature, 1974. Pseudepigrapha Series, 4.

133b] Barnabas Lindars. Re-enter the Apocalyptic Son of Man. *New Testament Studies* 22(1): 52–72, 1975.

134] J. Lust. The Order of the Final Events in Revelation and Ezekiel. In J. Lambrecht and G. R. Beasley-Murray, editors, *L'Apocalypse johannique et l'Apocalyptique dans le Nouveau Testament,* pages 179–183. Editions J. Duculot, Gembloux, Belgium, and Leuven University Press, Louvain, 1980.

135] Frédéric Manns. Traces d'une Haggadah chrétienne dans l'Apocalypse de Jean? *Antonianum* LVI(2–3):265–295, 1981.
    136] Pages 289–290.

136a] Christopher L. Mearns. Dating the Similitudes of Enoch. *New Testament Studies* 25(3):360 –369, 1979.

137] W. Meyer. Vita Adae et Evae. In Stone and Schaefer [169], pages 20–43. Originally published in *Abhandlungen der Bayrischen Akademie der Wissenschaften,* 14(3):221–244, 1878.

138] J. T. Milik and Matthew Black, editors. *The Books of Enoch: Aramaic Fragments of Qumrân Cave 4.* Clarendon Press, Oxford, 1976.
    139] Pages 89–98.
    140] Pages 107–116.
    141] Pages 172–174.
    142] Pages 198–200.
    143] Pages 231–236, 287–291.

144] J. H. Mozley. The 'Vita Adae.' *Journal of Theological Studies* XXX:121–149, 1929.

145] George W. E. Nickelsburg. Apocalyptic and Myth in I Enoch 6–11. *Journal of Biblical Literature* 96(3):383–406, 1977.

146] George W. E. Nickelsburg. Enoch, Levi, and Peter: Recipients of Revelation in Upper Galilee. *Journal of Biblical Literature* 100(4):575–600, 1981.
    147] Page 589.

    Pierre Prigent. *Apocalypse et Liturgie.* Delachaux et Neistlé, Neuchâtel, 1964. Cahiers Théologiques, new series, 52.
    148] Pages 46–76.
    149] Pages 47–49.

150] Christopher Rowland. *The Open Heaven: A Study of Apocalyptic in Judaism and Early Christianity.* Crossroad, 1982.
    151] Pages 61–70.
    152] Pages 78–94.
    153] Pages 94–113.
    154] Pages 178–189.
    155] Pages 214–247.
    156] Pages 255–258.
    157] Pages 403–413.

158] Christopher Rowland. The Vision of the Risen Christ in Revelation i.13ff.: The Debt of an Early Christology to an Aspect of Jewish Angelology. *Journal of Theological Studies,* New Series, XXXI(1):1–11, 1980.

159] Christopher Rowland. The Visions of God in Apocalyptic Literature. *Journal for the Study of Judaism* X(2):137–154, 1979.
    160] Pages 142–145.

160a] R. Rubinkiewicz. Apocalypse of Abraham: A New Translation and Introduction. Revised and notes added by H. G. Lunt. In Charlesworth [104], volume I, pages 681–705.

161] Arie Rubinstein. Hebraisms in the "Apocalypse of Abraham." *Journal of Jewish Studies* V(3):132–135, 1954.

162] Arie Rubinstein. Hebraisms in the Slavonic "Apocalypse of Abraham." *Journal of Jewish Studies* IV(3):108–115, 1953.

163] Arie Rubinstein. Observations in the Slavonic Book of Enoch. *Journal of Jewish Studies* XIII(1–4):1–21, 1962.

164] Arie Rubinstein. A Problematic Passage in the Apocalypse of Abraham. *Journal of Jewish Studies* VIII(1–2):45–50, 1957.

165] David Syme Russell. *The Method and Message of Jewish Apocalyptic, 200 B.C.–A.D. 100.* Westminster Press, 1964.
    166] Pages 158–173.

167] John Lawrence Sharpe. Prolegomena to the Establishment of the Critical Text of the Greek Apocalypse of Moses. Ph.D. dissertation, Duke University, 1969.

168] John L[awrence] Sharpe. The Second Adam in the Apocalypse of Moses. *Catholic Biblical Quarterly* 35(1):35–46, 1973.

168a] H. F. D. Sparks, editor. *The Apocryphal Old Testament.* Clarendon Press, Oxford, 1984.

169] M[ichael E.] Stone and A. Schaefer, editors. *Sifre Hayye 'Adam we-Hawwah; Sefer She'ar Dibre Barukh (Sefer Barukh D.) (The Books of the Life of Adam and Eve; the Book of the Rest of the Words of Baruch [IV Baruch]).* Hebrew University (Akademon), Jerusalem, 1973–1974. This booklet, edited as a sourcebook for a course Stone taught at the Hebrew University, includes the Greek, Latin, and Slavic versions (the last with German translation) of "The Life of Adam and Eve."

170] Michael E. Stone, translator. *The Testament of Abraham. The Greek Recensions.* Society of Biblical Literature, 1972.

171] David Suter. Fallen Angel, Fallen Priest: the Problem of Family Purity in I Enoch 6–16. *Hebrew Union College Annual* L:115–136, 1979.
    172] Page 134.

173] David Suter. *Tradition and Composition in the Parables of Enoch.* Scholars Press, 1979. Ph.D. dissertation, University of Chicago, 1976. Dissertation Series, no. 47.

174] Konstantin von Tischendorf, editor. Apocalypsis Mosis. In Stone and Schaefer [169], pages 2–13. Originally published as pages 1–23 of Tischendorf, *Apocalypses apocryphae Mosis, Esdrae, Pauli, Iohannis, item Marie dormitio, additis Evangeliorum et actuum Apocryphorum supplementis,* H. Mendelssohn, Leipzig, 1866; reprinted by G. Olms, Hildesheim, 1966.

174a] Charles C. Torrey. *The Apocalypse of John.* Yale University Press, 1958.

175] K. E. Tuck. *The Use of the Major Prophets and the Book of Daniel in the Book of Revelation.* Ph.D. dissertation, Melbourne, 1974. I have not seen this item, and cannot be sure it supports the assertion I make in the text. I include it in order to inform the reader that it exists.

176] Emile Turdeanu. L'*Apocalypse d'Abraham* en Slave. *Journal for the Study of Judaism* III (2):153–180, 1972.
    177] Page 160.

178] James C. VanderKam. Some Major Issues in the Contemporary Study of 1 Enoch: Reflections on J. T. Milik's *The Books of Enoch: Aramaic Fragments of Qumrân Cave 4. Maarav* 3(1):85–97, 1982.

179] Albert Vanhoye. L'Utilisation du Livre d'Ezechiel dans l'Apocalypse. *Biblica* 43(3):436–476, 1962.
    180] Pages 443–461.

181] No reference.

182] L. S. A. Wells. The Books of Adam and Eve. Introduction. In Charles [98], volume II, pages 123–133.

5. Editions of rabbinic and related texts

a) Arranged alphabetically, by texts
Abot de-Rabbi Natan:

    183] Solomon Schechter, editor. *Aboth de Rabbi Nathan.* Philipp Feldheim, third edition, 1967.

'Aggadat Bereshit:
183a] Salomon Buber, editor. *Agadath Bereshith: midraschische Auslegungen zum ersten Buche Mosis*. Fischer, Krakow, 1902.
Babylonian Talmud:
184] *Babylonian Talmud Codex Munich 95*. Facsimile edition. Three volumes. Sefer, Jerusalem, 1971.
185] *Manuscripts of the Babylonian Talmud from the Collection of the Vatican Library*. Facsimile edition. Six volumes. Makor, Jerusalem, 1972.
Book of Secrets, see *Sefer ha-Razim*.
Deuteronomy Rabbah:
186] Saul Liebermann, editor. *Midrash Debarim Rabbah. Edited for the First Time from the Oxford ms. No. 147 with an Introduction and Notes*. Wahrmann Books, Jerusalem, third edition, 1974. A very different version of *Deut. R.* appears in the standard edition of *Midrash Rabbah* [200].
Genesis Rabbah:
187] *Midrash Bereshit Rabbah, Codex Vatican 60*. Facsimile edition. Makor, Jerusalem, 1972.
188] Julius Theodor and Chanoch Albeck, editors. *Midrash Bereshit Rabbah: Critical Edition with Notes and Commentary*. Three volumes. Wahrmann Books, Jerusalem, second edition, 1965. Originally published by Itzkowski and Poppalauer, Berlin, 1903–1936. See also *Midrash Rabbah* [200].
    189] Page 200, footnote.
    189a] Introduction, pages 43–44 (in volume III, written by Albeck).

Lamentations Rabbah:
190] Salomon Buber, editor. *Midrasch Echa Rabbati: Sammlung agadischer Auslegungen der Klagelieder*. Tel Aviv, 1963–1964. Originally published by Romm, Vilna, 1899. A different recension of this text appears in the standard edition of *Midrash Rabbah* [200].
Leviticus Rabbah:
191] Mordecai Margulies, editor. *Midrash Wayyikra Rabbah: A Critical Edition based on Manuscripts and Genizah Fragments with Variants and Notes*. Three volumes. Wahrmann Books, Jerusalem, 1972. Originally published in Jerusalem, 1953–1960. See also *Midrash Rabbah* [200].
    192] Introduction, page XXII.
Mekhilta of R. Ishmael:
193] H. S. Horovitz and I. A. Rabin, editors. *Mechilta d'Rabbi Ismael*. Wahrmann Books, Jerusalem, 1970. Originally published by Kauffman, Frankfurt a.M., 1931.
    194] Pages 112–113, note.
195] Jacob Z. Lauterbach, editor and translator. *Mekhilta de-Rabbi Ishmael: A Critical Edition on the Basis of the Manuscripts and Early Editions*. Jewish Publication Society of America, 1933–1935, 1949. The Schiff Library of Jewish Classics. An independent critical edition of the Hebrew text, with English translation on facing pages.
Mekhilta of R. Simeon b. Yohai:
196] J. N. Epstein and E. Z. Melamed, editors. *Mekhilta d'Rabbi Šim'on b. Jochai*. Mekize Nirdamim, Jerusalem, 1955. Based mainly on Genizah fragments.
197] David Hoffman, editor. *Mechilta de-Rabbi Simon b. Jochai*. Kauffman, Frankfurt am Main, 1905. An early conjectural reconstruction, superseded by Epstein and Melamed [196].
Midrash ha-Gadol:
198] Mordecai Margulies, editor. *Midrash Haggadol on the Pentateuch: Genesis*. Mossad Harav Kook, Jerusalem, second printing, 1975. Originally published in 1947.
198a] Mordecai Margulies, editor. *Midrash Haggadol on the Pentateuch: Exodus*. Mossad Harav Kook, Jerusalem, third printing, 1976. Originally published in 1956.
Midrash on Proverbs:
198b] Salomon Buber, editor. *Midrash Mishle*. Originally published by Romm, Vilna, 1893. Reprinted in Jerusalem, 1965, and bound with *Midrash Shemu'el* [199a].
Midrash on Psalms:
199] Salomon Buber, editor. *Midrasch Tehillim (Schocher tob)*. Jerusalem, 1966. Originally published by Romm, Vilna, 1891.
Midrash on Samuel:
199a] Salomon Buber, editor. *Midrash Shemu'el*. Originally published by Joseph Fischer, Krakow, 1893. Reprinted in Jerusalem, 1965, and bound with *Midrash Mishle* [198b].
Midrash Rabbah:
200] *Sefer Midrash Rabbah*. Two volumes. Jerusalem, n.p., 1961. Originally published by Romm,

Vilna, 1878. (See also the editions of *Midrash Rabbah* on individual books [186,188,190, 191,210].) The midrashic text is accompanied by several commentaries, including those of David Luria (*RaDaL*) and Z. W. Einborn (*MaHRZU*).

"Midrash Tannaim":
201] David Hoffman, editor. *Midrasch Tannaim Zum Deuteronomium*. Itzkowski, Berlin, 1908– 1909. Conjectural reconstruction of a lost Tannaitic midrash on Deuteronomy.

Mishnah:
202] Chanoch Albeck, editor. *Shishah Sidre Mishnah* (The Six Orders of the Mishnah, with Commentary), volume II (*Mo^Ced*), pages 510–511. Six volumes. Bialik Institute and Dvir, Jerusalem, 1952–1959.

203] Joseph Rabbinowitz, editor and translator. *Mishnah Megillah, edited, with introduction, translation, commentary and critical notes*, page 134. Oxford University Press, H. Milford, 1931.

Palestinian Talmud:
204] Louis Ginzberg, editor. *Yerushalmi Fragments from the Genizah*, page 3. Jewish Theological Seminary of America, 1909.

Passover Haggadah:
204a] Nahum Norbert Glatzer, editor. *The Passover Haggadah*, pages 40–43. Based on commentaries of E. D. Goldschmidt. Haggadah text translated by Jacob Sloan. Schocken, third edition, 1979. Hebrew and English on facing pages.

Pesiqta de-Rab Kahana:
205] Salomon Buber, editor. *Pesikta, die älteste Hagada, redigirt in Palästina von Rab Kahana*. Silbermann, Lyck, 1868. Superseded by Mandelbaum [206].

206] Bernard Mandelbaum, editor. *Pesikta de Rav Kahana, according to an Oxford Manuscript with Variants from All Known Manuscripts and Genizoth Fragments and Parallel Passages with Commentary and Introduction*. Two volumes. Jewish Theological Seminary of America, 1962.
    207] Page 169, footnote.
    208] Page 213, footnote.

Pesiqta Rabbati:
209] Meir Friedmann, editor. *Pesikta Rabbati. Midrasch für den Fest-Cyclus und die ausgezeichneten Sabbathe*. Opst, Tel Aviv, 1963. Originally published privately in Vienna, 1880.

Pirqe de-Rabbi Eliezer:
209a] Pirqe Rabbi 'Eli^Cezer ... ^Cim Be'ur ha-Bayit ha-Gadol ... be-Seruf Nispahim: Ṣawwa'ot de-Rabbi 'Eli^Cezer ha-Gadol ... Midrash ^CAṡeret ha-Dibberot (*Pirqe Rabbi Eliezer* ... with the commentary *Bayit ha-Gadol* [by Abraham Aaron Braude] ... and two additional texts: *The Testaments of R. Eliezer the Great* and *The Midrash of the Ten Commandments*). Eshkol, Jerusalem, 1973. I use this edition because it is the one now available to me. I do not particularly recommend it.

Ruth Rabbah:
210] Myron Bialik Lerner. *The Book of Ruth in Aggadic Literature and Midrash Ruth Rabba*, volume II, page 190. Three volumes. Ph.D. dissertation, Hebrew University, 1971. Mimeographed. Critical edition of the midrash, which also appears in the standard edition of *Midrash Rabbah* [200]. I am grateful to Professor Lerner for sending me a copy.

Seder Eliyahu:
211] Meir Friedmann, editor. *Seder Eliahu Rabba und Seder Eliahu Zuta* (*Tanna d'be Eliahu*); *Pseudo-Seder Eliahu Zuta*. Wahrmann Books, Jerusalem, 1969. Originally published in Vienna, 1902–1904.
    212] Introduction, pages 59–60.

Seder Rabbah di-Bereshit:
213] Nicolas Séd, editor and translator. *Une Cosmologie Juive du Haut Moyen Age: La Běraytā Dī Ma^Caseh Běrēšīt*. *Revue des études juives* III(3–4):259–305, 1964, and IV(1–2):23– 123, 1965.
    214] Volume III, page 260.
    215] Volume III, pages 287, 289, 298–299; volume IV, page 70.
    See also Wertheimer [498,501].

Sefer ha-Razim:
216] Mordecai Margulies, editor. *Sefer ha-razim: A Newly Recovered Book of Magic from the Talmudic Period*. The Judah Leib and Minnie Epstein Foundation, the Academy for Judaic Studies in the United States, Jerusalem, 1966–1967.

Siddur:
216a] Philip Birnbaum, editor and translator. *Daily Prayer Book: Ha-Siddur ha-Shalem.* Hebrew Publishing Company, 1977. Hebrew and English on facing pages.

    216b] Pages 57–58.
    216c] Page 71.
    216d] Pages 71–74, 83–84, 341–344, 351–354.

216e] Simhah ben Samuel of Vitry (eleventh century). *Machsor Vitry, nach der Handschrift im British Museum (Cod. Add. No. 27200 u. 27201)*, pages 169–170. Edited by Simeon Hurwitz. Lyon Press, 1959–60. Originally published in Nuremberg, 1923.

Sifra:
217] Louis Finkelstein, editor. *Sifra or Torat Kohanim According to Codex Assemani LXVI*, pages 8–9. Facsimile edition, with introduction by the editor. Jewish Theological Seminary of America, 1956.

218] Schachne Koleditzky, editor. *Sifra, or Torat Kohanim, and Commentary by Rabbenu Hillel ben Eliakim.* Jerusalem, 1961.

219] Isaac Hirsch Weiss, editor. *Sifra. Commentar zu Leviticus aus dem Anfange des III Jahrhunderts. Nebst der Erlaüterung des R. Abraham ben David (RABeD).* Jacob Schlossberg, Vienna, 1862.

Sifre, Deuteronomy:
220] Louis Finkelstein, editor. *Sifre on Deuteronomy.* Jewish Theological Seminary of America, 1969. Originally published by Jüdischer Kulturbund, Berlin, 1939.

Sifre, Numbers:
221] H. S. Horovitz, editor. *Siphre d'Be Rab. Siphre ad Numeros Adjecto Siphre Zutta.* Wahrmann Books, Jerusalem, 1966. Originally published by G. Fock, Leipzig, 1917.

Tanḥuma:
222] Salomon Buber, editor. *Midrasch Tanchuma: Ein agadischer Commentar zum Pentateuch von Rabbi Tanchuma ben Rabbi Abba.* Books Export Enterprises Ltd., Israel. Originally published by Romm, Vilna, 1885. A different recension of *Tanḥuma* from the one that follows.

223] *Midrash Tanḥuma ᶜal Hamishshah Ḥumshe Torah.* Lewin-Epstein, Jerusalem, 1973. The standard "printed *Tanḥuma*," with the commentaries ᶜ*Eṣ Yosef* and ᶜ*Anaf Yosef.*

Targum:
223a] Alejandro Díez Macho, editor. *Neophyti 1: Targum Palestinense Ms de la Biblioteca Vaticana.* Six volumes. Consejo Superior de Investigaciones Cientificas, Madrid and Barcelona, 1968–79. Aramaic text, with translations into Spanish, English, and French.

224] *Miqra'ot Gedolot.* Five volumes. Etz-Hayyim, Jerusalem, 1974. Originally published in Vienna, 1859, and Warsaw, 1862–1866. Includes the Masoretic Text of the Bible; a not very reliable text of the Targums; and an assortment of medieval commentators, including Rashi, David Kimḥi , and Nachmanides.

225] Samuel Silbermann, editor. *Das Targum zu Ezechiel nach einer südarabischen Handschrift.* Strassburg, 1902.

226] Alexander Sperber, editor. *The Bible in Aramaic, based on Old Manuscripts and Printed Texts.* Four volumes in five. E. J. Brill, Leiden, 1959–73. The text of the Targum I have normally used.

Targumic Tosefta to Ezekiel:
227] Meir Zvi Weiss. Šeridim min ha-Genizah (Genizah fragments). *Ha-Ṣofeh le-Ḥokhmat Yiśra'el* 6:313–318, 1922.
See also Wertheimer [503].

Tosefta:
227a] Saul Lieberman. *The Tosefta: According to Codex Vienna, With Variants From Codex Erfurt, Genizah Mss. and Editio Princeps (Venice 1521). Together with References to Parallel Passages in Talmudic Literature and a Brief Commentary.* Four volumes, covering the orders *Zeraᶜim, Moᶜed,* and *Nashim.* Jewish Theological Seminary of America, 1955–73.

228] M. S. Zuckermandel. *Tosephta: Based on the Erfurt and Vienna Codices.* Wahrmann Books, Jerusalem, 1970. Reprint of the second edition published by Bamberger and Wahrmann, Jerusalem, 1937; containing Zuckermandel's edition of 1880, with supplements by Zuckermandel (1882, 1899), and a "Supplement to the Tosephta" by Saul Liebermann (so the name is spelled on the title page).

Visions of Ezekiel:
229] Ithamar Gruenwald. Re'uyot Yeḥezqel (The Visions of Ezekiel). In Israel Weinstock, editor,

Temirin: Texts and Studies in Kabbala and Hasidism, volume I, pages 101–139. Mossad Harav Kook, Jerusalem, 1972.
- 230] Pages 101–102.
- 231] Pages 112–114.
- 232] Pages 115–119.

233] Jacob Mann. Pereq Re'iyyot Yeḥezqel (The Chapter of the Visions of Ezekiel). *Ha-Ṣofeh le-Hokhmat Yiśra'el* 5:256–264, 1921.

234] Arthur Marmorstein. A Fragment of the Visions of Ezekiel. *Jewish Quarterly Review*, New Series, VIII:367–378, 1917–1918.
See also Wertheimer [502].

Yalquṭ Makhiri, Re'ubeni:

235] A. W. Greenup. Fragment of the Yalkut of R. Machir Bar Abba Mari on Hosea (I.9–XIV.1). Edited, for the First Time, from the Vatican MS No. 291 Heb, page 205. *Jewish Quarterly Review*, New Series, XV:141–212, 1924–1925.

236] *Yalquṭ Re'ubeni.* Jerusalem, 1962. Originally published in Warsaw, 1883–1884.

b) Arranged alphabetically, by authors (medieval) or editors (modern)

237] Yehudah Eben-Shemuel, editor. *Midreshe Ge'ullah* (Aspects of Jewish Apocalyptic, from The Completion of the Babylonian Talmud to the Beginning of the Sixth Millennium [that is, 1200 A.D.]), pages 326–327. Bialik Institute, Jerusalem-Tel Aviv, second edition, 1954.

Louis Ginzberg, editor. *Genizah Studies in Memory of Doctor Solomon Schechter.* Three volumes. Jewish Theological Seminary of America, 1969. Texts and Studies of the Jewish Theological Seminary of America, volumes 7–9. In Hebrew.
- 238] Volume 1, page 37.
- 239] Volume 1, pages 235–245.

240] Louis Ginzberg. Haggadot Qeṭuᶜot (Fragmentary Haggadot), pages 65–66. *Ha-Goren* 9, 1922.

240a] Jacob ben Solomon ibn Habib (d. 1515/16). *Sefer ᶜEn Yaᶜaqob.* (Title page adds, in Hebrew: *Collection of all the haggadot and midrashim scattered throughout the Babylonian Talmud, with haggadot from the Palestinian Talmud.*) Four volumes. Opst, Jerusalem, 1976. Originally published in Vilna, 1883.

Adolf Jellinek, *Bet ha-Midrasch*; see Jellinek [475] in section 9.

Benjamin M. Lewin. *Otzar ha-Geonim: Thesaurus of the Gaonic Responsa and Commentaries.* Volume IV: Tractate Jom-Tow, Chagiga and Maschkin. Hebrew University Press Association, Jerusalem, 1931.
- 241] Pages 13–15.
- 242] Page 61.

243] Bernhard Lewin. *Otzar ha-Geonim. Thesaurus of the Gaonic Responsa and Commentaries.* Volume IX: Tractate Qiddushin, part iii, page 34. Central Press, Jerusalem, 1939.

244] Salmon ben Yeruhim (tenth century). *The Book of the Wars of the Lord: Containing the Polemics of the Karaite Salmon ben Yeruhim Against Saadia Gaon.* Edited by Israel Davidson. Jewish Theological Seminary of America, 1934.

Solomon Wertheimer, *Batei Midrashot*; see Wertheimer [497] in section 9.

6. Translations of rabbinic and related texts

Abot de-Rabbi Natan:
Judah Goldin. *The Fathers According to Rabbi Nathan.* Yale University Press, 1955. Yale Judaica Series, volume 10.
Anthony J. Saldarini. *The Fathers According to Rabbi Nathan (Abot de Rabbi Nathan) Version B.* E. J. Brill, Leiden, 1975.

Babylonian Talmud:
I[sidore] Epstein, editor. *The Babylonian Talmud: Translated Into English With Notes, Glossary, and Indices.* Thirty-five volumes. Soncino Press, London, 1935–48.

Book of Secrets, see Sefer ha-Razim.

Deuteronomy Rabbah:
Lieberman's text [186] has not been translated. The version that appears in *Midrash Rabbah* [200] is available in English with the rest of this series. See *Midrash Rabbah,* below.

Genesis, Lamentations, Leviticus Rabbah:
See *Midrash Rabbah.*

Mekhilta of R. Ishmael:
> See Lauterbach [195].

Midrash on Psalms:
> William G. Braude. *The Midrash on Psalms.* Two volumes. Yale University Press, 1959. Yale Judaica Series, volume 13.

Midrash Rabbah:
> H. Freedman and M. Simon, editors. *Midrash Rabbah. Translated in English with Notes, Glossary and Indices.* Ten volumes. Soncino Press, London, 1961.

Mishnah:
> Herbert Danby. *The Mishnah: Translated From the Hebrew With Introduction and Brief Explanatory Notes.* Clarendon Press, Oxford, 1933.

244a] Judah Goldin. *The Living Talmud: The Wisdom of the Fathers and its Classical Commentaries.* University of Chicago Press and Mentor, 1957. Translation of tractate *Pirqe Abot.*

> Eugene J. Lipman. *The Mishnah: Oral Teachings of Judaism.* Schocken Books, 1974. Annotated selections from all tractates of the Mishn ah except *Pirqe Abot.* See also Rabbinowitz [203].

Palestinian Talmud:
> Jacob Neusner. *The Talmud of the Land of Israel: A Preliminary Translation and Explanation.* Thirty-five volumes projected. University of Chicago Press, 1982–. Neusner appears to be issuing the volumes in reverse order, starting with volume 34. The Foreword to volume 34 includes an outline of the entire project (pages viii–ix).

Passover Haggadah:
> See Glatzer [204a].

Pesiqta de-Rab Kahana:
> William G. Braude and Israel J. Kapstein. *Pesikta de-Rab Kahana: R. Kahana's Compilation of Discourses for Sabbaths and Festal Days.* Jewish Publication Society of America, 1975.

Pesiqta Rabbati:
245] William G. Braude. *Pesikta Rabbati: Discourses for Feasts, Fasts, and Special Sabbaths.* Two volumes. Yale University Press, 1968. Yale Judaica Series, volume 18.

> 246] Introduction, pages 20–26.
> 247] Page 406, footnote.

Pirqe de-Rabbi Eliezer:
> Gerald Friedlander. *Pirke de Rabbi Eliezer (The Chapters of Rabbi Eliezer the Great) According to the Text of the Manuscript Belonging to Abraham Epstein of Vienna.* Sepher-Hermon Press, fourth edition, 1981. Originally published in London, 1916.

Ruth Rabbah:
> See *Midrash Rabbah.*

Seder Eliyahu:
> William G. Braude and Israel J. Kapstein. *Tanna debe Eliyyahu = The Lore of the School of Elijah.* Jewish Publication Society of America, 1981.

> 248] Introduction, pages 3–12.
> 249] Pages 42–43.

Seder Rabbah di-Bereshit:
> See Séd [213] (in French).

Sefer ha-Razim:
249a] Michael A. Morgan. *Sepher ha-Razim = The Book of the Mysteries.* Scholars Press, 1983.

Siddur:
> See Birnbaum [216a].

Sifra:
> Jacob Neusner and Roger Brooks. *Sifra, The Rabbinic Commentary on Leviticus: An American Translation.* Scholars Press, 1985. Translates *Sifra* to Leviticus 13:1–14:57, 19:5–10.

Sifre, Deuteronomy:
> Reuven Hammer. *Sifre: A Tannaitic Commentary on the Book of Deuteronomy.* Yale University Press, 1986. Yale Judaica Series, volume 24.

Sifre, Numbers:
> Jacob Neusner. *Sifre to Numbers: An American Translation and Explanation.* Two volumes. Scholars Press, 1986. Covers slightly more than half of the text. A projected third volume, by William Green, is to complete the translation.

Targum:
> Moses Aberbach and Bernard Grossfeld. *Targum Onkelos to Genesis: A Critical Analysis*

Together With An English Translation of the Text (Based on A. Sperber's Edition). Ktav, 1982. Text and translation on facing pages.

Roger Le Déaut. *Targum du Pentateuque: Traduction des Deux Recensions Palestiniennes Complètes Avec Introduction. Parallèles. Notes Et Index.* Four volumes. Éditions du Cerf, Paris, 1978–80. Sources Chrétiennes, 245, 256, 261, 271. Translations, printed on facing pages, of Neofiti and Pseudo-Jonathan.

Díez Macho's edition of Neofiti [223a] includes translations into Spanish, English, and French. For Ezekiel 1, see Levey [302].

Tosefta:

Jacob Neusner. *The Tosefta.* Six volumes. Ktav, 1977–86. Neusner's students translated volume I.

Visions of Ezekiel:

250] Louis Jacobs, editor. *Jewish Mystical Testimonies,* pages 26–31. Schocken, 1977.

Other:

250a] Leon Nemoy. *Karaite Anthology: Excerpts from the Early Literature.* Yale University Press, 1952. Yale Judaica Series, Volume VII.

251] Ramban (Nachmanides). *Commentary on the Torah,* volume II, page 552. Five volumes. Translated and annotated by Charles B. Chavel. Shilo, 1971–1976.

7. Rabbinic studies: sources and criticism

252] Chanoch Albeck. Midrash Vayikra Rabba, page 41. In *Louis Ginzberg Jubilee Volume on The Occasion of His Seventieth Birthday,* pages 25–44, Hebrew section. American Academy for Jewish Research, 1945. In Hebrew.

253] P. S. Alexander. The Rabbinic Lists of Forbidden Targumim. *Journal of Jewish Studies* XXVII: 177–191, 1976.

254] Wilhelm Bacher. Kritische Untersuchungen Zum Prophetentargum. Nebst einem Anhange über das gegenseitige Verhältniss der pentateuchischen Targumim. *Zeitschrift der Deutschen Morgenländischen Gesellschaft* 28:1–72, 1894.

255] Bernard J. Bamberger. A Messianic Document of the Seventh Century. *Hebrew Union College Annual* XV:425–431, 1940.

256] Lewis M. Barth. The "Three of Rebuke and Seven of Consolation" Sermons in the Pesikta de Rav Kahana. In Vermes and Neusner [349], pages 503–515.

256a] John Bowker. *The Targums and Rabbinic Literature: An Introduction to Jewish Interpretations of Scripture.* Cambridge University Press, 1969.

257] William G. Braude. "Conjecture" and Interpolation in Translating Rabbinic Texts. Illustrated by a Chapter from Tanna Debe Eliyyahu. In Jacob Neusner, editor, *Christianity, Judaism and Other Greco-Roman Cults: Studies for Morton Smith at Sixty,* volume IV, pages 77–89. Four volumes. E. J. Brill, Leiden, 1975. Studies in Judaism in Late Antiquity, volume 12.

258] Marc Bregman. Review of Böhl: Aufbau und literarische Formen des aggadischen Teils im Jelamdenu-Midrasch. *Journal of the American Oriental Society* 100(2):169–170, 1980.

259] Marc Bregman. The Triennial Haftarot and the Perorations of the Midrashic Homilies. *Journal of Jewish Studies* XXXII(1):74–84, 1981.

260] Marc Bregman. Petihta'ot MaᶜAgaliyot u-Fetihta'ot 'Zo Hi She-Ne'emerah be-Ruah ha-Qodesh' (Circular Petihot, and Petihot of the "So It Was Spoken Through the Holy Spirit" Genre). In *Studies in Aggadah, Targum and Jewish Liturgy in Memory of Joseph Heinemann,* pages 39–51. Magnes Press, Jerusalem, 1981.

260a] Marc Bregman. An Early Fragment of *Avot Derabbi Natan* From a Scroll. *Tarbiz* LII(2): 201–222, 1982–83. In Hebrew.

261] W. H. Brownlee. The Habakkuk Midrash and Targum of Jonathan. *Journal of Jewish Studies* VII(3–4):169–186, 1956.

262] Adolf Büchler. Die Bedeutung von עֲרִירוּת in Chagiga III und Megilla IV, 10, pages 112–113. *Monatsschrift für Geschichte und Wissenschaft des Judenthums* 38(2):108–116, 145–151, 1894.

263] Adolf Büchler. The Reading of the Law and Prophets in a Triennial Cycle. *Jewish Quarterly Review,* Old Series, 5:420–468, April 1893, and 6:1–73, October 1893.

264] Page 462, footnote.

264a] Pinkhos Churgin. *Targum Jonathan to the Prophets,* Yale University Press, 1927. Reprinted, with an introduction and three additional studies by Leivy Smolar and Moshe Aberbach, by Ktav Publishing House and the Baltimore Hebrew College, 1983.

265] Pages 13–15.
266] Pages 20–21.
267] Pages 22–29.
268] Norman J. Cohen. Structure and Editing in the Homiletic Midrashim. *AJSreview* VI:1–20, 1981. Association for Jewish Studies, Cambridge, Massachusetts.
    269] Pages 1–2.
270] Norman J. Cohen. Leviticus Rabbah, Parashah 3: An Example of a Classic Rabbinic Homily. *Jewish Quarterly Review*, New Series, LXXII(1):18–31, 1981.
271] Alejandro Diez-Macho. Un segundo fragmento del Targum Palastinense a los Profetas. *Biblica* 39(2):198–205, 1958.
272] Alejandro Diez-Macho. Un nuevo Targum a los Profetas. *Estudios Biblicos*, second series, 15(2–3):287–295, 1956.
273] Alejandro Diez-Macho. Nuevos manuscritos importantes biblicos o litúrgicos, en hebreo o arameo. *Sefarad* XVI(1):3–22, 1956.
274] No reference.
275] A. Epstein. Me^{c}at Meqorot ha-Midrashim (A Few Sources of the Midrashim). In *Mi-Qadmoniyyot ha-Yehudim*, volume II, pages 54–75. Jerusalem, 1957.
    275a] Pages 61–63.
Jacob Nahum Halevi Epstein. *Mabo' le-Nusah ha-Mishnah* (Introduction to the Text of the Mishnah). Magnes Press, Jerusalem, and Dvir, Tel Aviv, second edition, 1964.
    276] Pages 753–762.
    277] Pages 762–767.
278] Jacob N[ahum Halevi] Epstein. *Introduction to Tannaitic Literature: Mishna, Tosephta and Halakhic Midrashim*, pages 67–69. Magnes Press, Jerusalem, and Dvir, Tel Aviv, 1957. In Hebrew.
279] Asher Feldman. *The Parables and Similes of the Rabbis, Agricultural and Pastoral*, pages 84–99. Folcroft Library Editions, Folcroft, Pennsylvania, and Norwood Editions, 1975, and R. West, 1976. Originally published by Cambridge University Press, second edition, 1927.
280] Ezra Fleischer. Towards a Clarification of the Expression 'Poreis 'Al Shema' '. *Tarbiz* XLI (2):133–144, 1971–72. In Hebrew.
281] J. Terence Forestell. *Targumic Traditions and the New Testament: an Annotated Bibliography with a New Testament Index*. Scholars Press, 1979. I have not seen this item.
282] Zechariah Frankel. *Mebo' ha-Yerushalmi* (Introduction to the Palestinian Talmud), page 60a–b. Jerusalem, 1967. Originally published by Schlätter, Breslau, 1870.
283] M. Ginsburger. Les Introductions Araméennes a la Lecture du Targoum, pages 15–16. *Revue des études juives* 73:14–26, 186–194, 1921.
283a] Louis Ginzberg. *A Commentary on the Palestinian Talmud*. Four volumes; first three reprinted by Ktav, 1971. Originally published by the Jewish Theological Seminary of America, 1941–1961. Texts and Studies, 10–12, 21. In Hebrew.
    284] Volume I, page 53.
    285] Volume I, pages 114–118.
    286] Volume I, pages 409–412.
286a] Louis Ginzberg. An Introduction to the Palestinian Talmud. In *On Jewish Law and Lore*, pages 3–57. Atheneum, 1970. Originally published as an introductory essay (in English) to volume I of Ginzberg's *Commentary* [283a].
287] Arnold Goldberg. Petiha und Hariza. *Journal for the Study of Judaism* X(2):213–218, 1979.
288] Karl-Erich Grözinger. *Ich bin der Herr, dein Gott! Eine rabbinische Homilie zum Ersten Gebot (PesR 20)*. Herbert Lang, Bern, and Peter Lang, Frankfurt am Main, 1976. Frankfurter judaistische Studien, 2.
    289] Pages 6–20.
    290] Pages 130–141.
    291] Page 142.
    292] Page 149.
    292a] Pages 150–158.
    293] Pages 173–176.
    293a] Pages 182–185.
    294] Pages 186–189.
    295] Pages 193–197.
    296] Pages 206–207.
    297] Pages 289–290.

298] Page 291.

299] Pages 296–301.

300] Bernard Grossfeld, editor. *A Bibliography of Targum Literature.* Two volumes. Hebrew Union College Press and Ktav, 1972, 1977.

301] Abraham Meir Habermann. Genizah. In *Encyclopedia Judaica*, volume 7, columns 404–407. Macmillan, 1971.

302] Joseph Heinemann. Birkat Kohanim ... Lo' Niqret welo' Mittargemet (The Blessing of the Priests ... Is Neither Read nor Translated). *Annual of Bar-Ilan University* VI:33–41, 1968.

303] Joseph Heinemann. The Proem in the Aggadic Midrashim: A Form-Critical Study. In Joseph Heinemann and Dov Noy, editors, *Studies in Aggada and Folk-Literature*, pages 100–122. Magnes Press, Jerusalem, 1971. Scripta Hierosolymitana, volume 22.

    303a] Pages 103–104.

304] Joseph Heinemann. Śeridim Mi-yeṣiratam ha-Piyyuṭit shel ha-Meturgemanim ha-Qedumim (Remains of the Piyyutic Creativity of the Early Aramaic Translators). *Sifrut* 4:362–375, 1973.

    305] Pages 363–365.

    305a] Page 374.

306] Joseph Heinemann. The Triennial Lectionary Cycle. *Journal of Jewish Studies* 19(1–4):41–48, 1968.

307] Rimmon Kasher. Ha-Tosefta ha-Targumit la-Nebi'im (The Targumic Tosefta to the Prophets). M.A. Thesis, Bar-Ilan University, 1973.

    308] Page 6.

    309] Pages 18ff, 70–72, 98ff.

310] Rim[m]on Kasher. The Targumic Additions to the *Haphtara* for the Sabbath of Hannuka. *Tarbiz* XLV(1–2):27–45, 1975–76. In Hebrew.

    311] Pages 29–32.

    312] Page 31, footnote.

313] Michael J. Klein. Four Notes on the Triennial Lectionary Cycle. *Journal of Jewish Studies* XXXII(1):65–73, 1981.

314] Klaus Koch. Messias und Sündenvergebung in Jesaja 53-Targum. *Journal for the Study of Judaism* III(2):117–148, 1972.

315] Yehuda Komlosh. *The Bible in the Light of the Aramaic Translations.* Bar-Ilan University, Ramat-Gan, 1973. In Hebrew.

    316] Pages 57–65.

317] Roger LeDeaut. The Current State of Targumic Studies. *Biblical Theology Bulletin* 4(1):3–32, 1974.

    318] Page 17.

319] Samson H. Levey. The Date of Targum Jonathan to the Prophets. *Vetus Testamentum* XXI (2):186–196, 1971.

320] Samson H. Levey. The Targum to Ezekiel. *Hebrew Union College Annual* XLVI:139–158, 1975.

321] Saul Lieberman. *The Talmud of Caesarea. Jerushalmi Tractate Nezikin*, pages 16–17. Jerusalem, 1931. In Hebrew.

    Saul Lieberman. *Yemenite Midrashim: A Lecture on the Yemenite Midrashim, their Character and Value.* Wahrmann Books, Jerusalem, second edition, 1970. In Hebrew.

    322] Pages 13–17.

    323] Pages 17–18.

324] Saul Lieberman. *Tosefta ki-fshuta: A Comprehensive Commentary on the Tosefta.* Eight volumes. Jewish Theological Seminary of America, 1955–1973. In Hebrew.

    325] Volume 1, pages 108–109.

    326] Volume 5, pages 1218–1219.

    327] Volume 5, page 1289.

    328] Volume 8, page 661.

    329] Volume 8, page 733.

329a] Saul Lieberman. A Tragedy or a Comedy? *Journal of the American Oriental Society* 104(2):315–319, 1984.

    Martin McNamara. *The New Testament and the Palestinian Targum to the Pentateuch.* Pontifical Biblical Institute, Rome, 1966. Analecta Biblica, 27.

    330] Pages 82–86.

    331] Pages 97–125, 189–237.

332] Pages 192–199.
333] Pages 200–204.
334] No reference.
335] Martin McNamara. *Targum and Testament: Aramaic Paraphrases of the Hebrew Bible; a Light on the New Testament*. Irish University Press, Shannon, Ireland, 1972.
    335a] Page 208.
336] Jacob Mann. *The Bible as Read and Preached in the Old Synagogue: A Study in the Cycles of the Readings from Torah and Prophets, as well as from Psalms and in the Structure of the Midrashic Homilies*. Prolegomenon by Ben Zion Wacholder. Volume I, Ktav, 1971; Volume II, Mann-Sonne Publication Committee, Hebrew Union College, Jewish Institute of Religion, 1966. Volume I originally published by Mann-Sonne, 1940.
336a] Jacob Neusner, editor. *The Formation of the Babylonian Talmud: Studies in the achievements of late nineteenth and twentieth century historical and literary-critical research*. Brill, Leiden, 1970.
336b] Jacob Neusner. *Invitation to the Talmud: A Teaching Book*. Harper & Row, 1973.
336c] Jacob Neusner. *Judaism: The Evidence of the Mishnah*. University of Chicago Press, 1981.
336d] Jacob Neusner, editor. *The Modern Study of the Mishnah*. Brill, Leiden, 1973.
336e] Jacob Neusner, editor. *The Study of Ancient Judaism*. Two volumes. Ktav, 1981.
337] A. Rosenthal. Ha-Piyyuṭim ha-'Aramiyyim le-Shabu[c]ot (The Aramaic Piyyutim for Shabu[c]ot), page 86. M.A. thesis, Hebrew University of Jerusalem, 1966.
338] Eliezer Shimshon Rosenthal. A Contribution to the Talmudic Lexicon – Elucidation of Words Based on Textual Variants, pages 178–182. *Tarbiz* XL(2):178–200, 1970–71. In Hebrew.
338a] Shmuel Safrai. Midrashic Fragments From the Cairo Geniza. *Immanuel* 8:69–71, 1978.
339] Richard S. Sarason. The Petihtot in Leviticus Rabba: "Oral Homilies" or Redactional Constructions? In Vermes and Neusner [349], pages 557–567.
339a] Leivy Smolar and Moses Aberbach. Introduction to the Ktav edition of Churgin [264a].
340] Michael Sokoloff. Ha-[c]Ibrit shel Bereshit Rabbah le-Fi Ketab-Yad Vatican 30 (The Hebrew of *Genesis Rabbah* according to Ms. Vatican 30), page 277. *Leshonenu* 33:25ff., 135ff., 270ff., 1969.
340a] Adin Steinsaltz. *The Essential Talmud*. Translated from the Hebrew by Chaya Galai. Bantam Books, 1976.
341] Günter Stemberger. Die Datierung der Mekhilta. *Kairos* XXI(2–3):81–118, 1979.
342] Hermann L. Strack. *Introduction to the Talmud and Midrash*. Meridian Books, 1959. Originally published by the Jewish Publication Society of America, 1931.
    343] Page 123.
    344] Pages 128–129.
    345] Pages 204–205, 210–216.
345a] Hermann L. Strack and Günter Stemberger. *Einleitung in Talmud und Midrasch*. C. H. Beck, Munich, seventh edition, 1982.
346] A. Tal. *The Language of the Targum of the Former Prophets and its Position within the Aramaic Dialects*. Ph.D. dissertation, Jerusalem, 1971. Cited in LeDeaut [317], page 16.
347] Julius Theodor. Die neue Ausgabe des Seder Eliahu rabba und suta, page 79. *Monatsschrift für Geschichte und Wissenschaft des Judenthums* 47:70–79, 1903.
348] Ephraim E. Urbach. Li-She'elat Leshono u-Meqorotaw shel Sefer Seder 'Eliyahu (On the Question of the Language and Sources of the *Seder 'Eliyahu*). *Leshonenu* 21:183–197, 1957.
349] Geza Vermes and Jacob Neusner, editors. *Essays in Honour of Yigael Yadin*. Allenheld, Osmun, 1983. Represents *Journal of Jewish Studies* XXXIII (1982).
350] Ben Zion Wacholder. The Date of the Mekilta de-Rabbi Ishmael. *Hebrew Union College Annual* XXXIX:117–144, 1968.
351] Ben Zion Wacholder. Prolegomenon to Mann [336].
352] Asher Weiser. "Ilmalle' Hu' Nignaz Sefer Yeḥezqel" (If Not for Him, The Book of Ezekiel Would Have Been Concealed). *Sinai* 51:37–45, 1962.
353] Abraham Weiss. *Studies in the Literature of the Amoraim*, pages 260–261. Yeshiva University, 1962. In Hebrew.
354] N. Weider. The Habakkuk Scroll and the Targum. *Journal of Jewish Studies* IV(1):14–18, 1953.
354a] Anthony D. York. The Dating of Targumic Literature. *Journal for the Study of Judaism* V(1):49–62, 1974.
355] Anthony D. York. The Targum in the Synagogue and in the School. *Journal for the Study of Judaism* X(1):74–86, 1979.

356] Ignaz Ziegler. *Die Königsgleichnisse des Midrasch, beleuchtet durch die römische Kaiserzeit.* S. Schottlaender, Breslau, 1903.

357] Moses Zucker. *Rav Saadya Gaon's Translation of the Torah: Exegesis, Halakha, and Polemics in R. Saadya's Translation of the Pentateuch,* pages 117–127, 203–219. Feldheim, 1959. In Hebrew. I owe this reference to Professor Baruch Bokser.

Leopold Zunz and Chanoch Albeck. *Ha-Derashot be-Yiśra'el* (Jewish Synagogue Expositions). Translated into Hebrew from Zunz's *Die gottesdienstlichen Vorträge der Juden historisch entwickelt,* second edition, 1892; brought up to date with expansions and annotations by Albeck. Bialik Institute, Jerusalem, 1947.

    358] Pages 39–40, 263–264.
    359] Page 51.
    360] Pages 53–57.
    361] Pages 115, 119–121.
    362] Pages 124–125.
    363] Page 379, note 16.

8. Rabbinic studies: history and theology

364] Gedaliahu Alon. Ha-Shiṭah ha-Soṣiyologit be-Ḥeqer ha-Halakhah (The Sociological Approach to the Study of the Halakhah), page 197. In *Studies in Jewish History in the Times of the Second Temple, the Mishna and the Talmud,* volume II, pages 181–227. Hakibutz Hameuchad, Tel Aviv, 1976. Review of Louis Finkelstein [383].

365] Avigdor Aptowitzer. The Heavenly Temple in the Agada. *Tarbiz* 2(2):137–153, January 1931, and 2(3):257–287, April 1931. In Hebrew.

    366] Pages 150–151.

Michael Avi-Yonah. *The Jew of Palestine; A Political History from the Bar Kokhba War to the Arab Conquest.* B. Blackwell, Oxford, 1976.

    367] Chapters IV–V, VII, IX.
    368] Pages 161–166, 223–225.

Wilhelm Bacher. *Die agada der palästinenischen amoräer.* Three volumes. G. Olm, Hildesheim, 1965. Originally published by K. J. Trübner, Strassburg, 1892–1899.

    369] Volume 1, page 127.
    370] Volume 1, pages 187–194.
    371] Volume 3, pages 547, 674.
    372] Volume 3, pages 643–644.

373] Jacob Bamberger. *Die Litteratur der Adambücher und die haggadische Elemente in der syrischen Schatzhöhle,* pages 47–49, C. Krebs, Aschaffenburg, 1901.

374] Hans Bietenhard. *Die himmlische Welt im Urchristentum und Spätjudentum.* J. C. B. Mohr, Tübingen, 1951. Wissenschaftliche Untersuchungen zum Neuen Testament, 2.

    375] Page 63.

376] Ben Zion Bokser. The Thread of Blue. *Proceedings of the American Academy of Jewish Research* XXXI:1–32, 1963.

    377] Page 5.

378] Jacob Cohn. Mystic Experience and Elijah-Revelations in Talmudic Times. In Judah Rosenthal, editor, *Meyer Waxman Jubilee Volume, On the Occasion of His Seventy-Fifth Birthday,* English section, pages 34–44. College of Jewish Studies Press, and Mordecai Newman Publishing House, Jerusalem-Tel Aviv, 1966.

379] William D. Davies. *The Gospel and the Land: Early Christianity and Jewish Territorial Doctrine,* pages 142–154. University of California, 1974.

380] Ismar Elbogen. *Der jüdische Gottesdienst in seiner geschichtlichen Entwicklung,* pages 22, 26. Frankfurt am Main, 1931.

381] Ismar Elbogen. *Der jüdische Gottesdienst in seiner geschichtlichen Entwicklung,* page 66. Translated into Hebrew by Yehoshua Amir. Edited and supplemented by Joseph Heinemann, Israel Adler, Avraham Negev, Jacob Petuchowsky, and Hayyim Schirmann. Dvir, Tel Aviv, 1972.

382] *Encyclopedia Judaica,* Macmillan, 1971. Pappus ben Judah, volume 13, columns 69–70.

383] Louis Finkelstein. *Akiba, Scholar, Saint and Martyr.* Athenaeum, 1970. Originally published in 1936.

    384] Pages 195–198.

385] Louis Finkelstein. *The Pharisees, the Sociological Background of their Faith*, page 185 and page 675, note 38. Two volumes. Jewish Publication Society of America, 1940.

386] Henry A. Fischel. *Rabbinic Literature and Greco-Roman Philosophy: A Study of Epicurea and Rhetorica in Early Midrashic Writings*, pages 78–89. E. J. Brill, Leiden, 1973.

387] David Flusser. Sanktus und Gloria, page 139. In Otto Betz, Martin Hengel, and Peter Schmidt, editors, *Abraham Unser Vater: Juden und Christen im Gespräch über die Bibel. Festschrift für Otto Michel zum 60*, pages 129–152. E. J. Brill, Leiden, 1963. Arbeiten zur Geschichte des Spätjudentums und Urchristentums, 5.

388] Jonah Fraenkel. The Character of Rabbi Jehoshua ben Levi in the Stories of the Babylonian Talmud. In *The Proceedings of the Sixth World Congress of Jewish Studies*, pages 403–417. Jerusalem, 1973. In Hebrew.

388a] I[saiah] Gafni. Concerning D. Goodblatt's Article. *Zion* XLVI(1):52–56, 1981. In Hebrew.

388b] Isaiah Gafni. Yeshiva and Metivta. *Zion* XLIII(1–2):12–37, 1978. In Hebrew.

Abraham Geiger. *Urschrift und Übersetzungen der Bibel in ihrer Abhängigkeit von der innern Entwicklung des Judentums*. Verlag Madda, Frankfurt am Main, 1928.

389] Page 343.

390] Pages 367–370.

Louis Ginzberg. *Legends of the Jews*. Seven volumes. Translated by Henrietta Szold and Paul Radin. Jewish Publication Society of America, 1942–1947.

391] Volume 1, pages 9–11; volume 5, pages 9–12.

392] Volume 2, pages 181–182.

393] Volume 3, pages 9–13, 26.

394] Volume 3, page 97; volume 6, page 39.

395] Volume 4, pages 49–50; volume 6, pages 13, 209–210.

396] Volume 5, page 19.

397] Volume 5, page 290.

398] Volume 5, page 307.

398a] Volume 6, page 52, note 267.

399] Volume 6, pages 127, 328–329.

400] Volume 6, pages 424–426.

401] Volume 6, pages 466–473.

401a] Arnold Goldberg. Service of the Heart: Liturgical Aspects of Synagogue Worship, pages 204–206. Translated from the German. In Asher Finkel and Lawrence Frizzell, editors, *Standing Before God: Studies on Prayer in Scriptures and in Tradition with Essays In Honor of John M. Oesterreicher*, pages 194–211. Ktav, 1981.

401b] D[avid M.] Goodblatt. New Developments in the Study of the Babylonian *Yeshivot*. *Zion* XLVI(1):14–38, 1981. In Hebrew.

401c] David M. Goodblatt. *Rabbinic Instruction in Sasanian Babylonia*, pages 63–92. E. J. Brill, Leiden, 1975.

402] H. Grätz. Hillel, der Patriarchensohn. *Monatsschrift für Geschichte und Wissenschaft des Judenthums* 30:433–443, 1881.

403] David J. Halperin. The *Book of Remedies*, the Canonization of the Solomonic Writings, and the Riddle of Pseudo-Eusebius. *Jewish Quarterly Review* LXXII(4):269–292, 1982.

404] M. Haran. Problems of the Canonization of Scripture. *Tarbiz* XXV(3):245–271, 1955–56. In Hebrew.

405] Isaak Heinemann. Darkhe Ha-agadah (The Ways of the Aggadah), pages 29–30, 192. Magnes Press and Masada, Jerusalem, 1970. In Hebrew.

Joseph Heinemann. *Aggadah and Its Development*. Keter, Jerusalem, 1974. In Hebrew.

406] Pages 17–26.

406a] Page 27.

407] Pages 49–63.

408] Pages 78–84.

409] Page 92.

410] Pages 197–199.

410a] Joseph Heinemann. *Prayer in the Period of the Tanna'im and the Amora'im: Its Nature and its Patterns*. Perry Foundation for Biblical Research Publications, Hebrew University, Jerusalem, 1964. In Hebrew.

411] Pages 84–87.

412] Pages 145–147.

413] Pages 174–175.

414] R. Travers Herford. *Christianity in Talmud and Midrash*. Williams and Norgate, London, 1903.

Abraham Zebi Idelsohn. *Jewish Liturgy and Its Development*. H. Holt, and Sacred Music Press, 1932.
　　415] Page 82.
　　416] Pages 94–99.

417] Irving Jacobs. Elements of Near-Eastern Mythology in Rabbinic Aggadah. *Journal of Jewish Studies* XXVIII(1):1–11, 1977.

418] Jacob Z. Lauterbach. *Rabbinic Essays*. Hebrew Union College Press, 1951.
　　419] Pages 64–72.
　　419a] Pages 163–256.

420] Sid Z. Leiman. *The Canonization of Hebrew Scripture: The Talmudic and Midrashic Evidence*. Archon Books, 1976.

421] Lee I. Levine. *Caesarea Under Roman Rule*. E. J. Brill, Leiden, 1975. Studies in Judaism in Late Antiquity, volume 7.
　　422] Pages 70–71.

422a] Saul Lieberman. *Greek in Jewish Palestine: Studies in the Life and Manners of Jewish Palestine in the II–IV Centuries C.E.* Jewish Theological Seminary of America, 1942.
　　422b] Pages 68–90.

423] Saul Lieberman. *Hellenism in Jewish Palestine: Studies in the Literary Transmission, Beliefs and Manners of Palestine in the I Century B.C.E.–IV Century C.E.* Jewish Theological Seminary of America, 1950.
　　423a] Pages 83–99.

424] Saul Lieberman. How Much Greek in Jewish Palestine? In Alexander Altmann, editor, *Biblical and Other Studies*, pages 123–141. Harvard University Press, 1963.

425] Johann Maier. *Jesus von Nazareth in der Talmudischen Überlieferung*. Wissenschaftliche Buchgesellschaft, Darmstadt, 1978. Erträge der Forschung, volume 82.
Hugo Mantel. *Studies in the History of the Sanhedrin*. Harvard University Press, 1965.
　　425a] Pages 102–139.
　　425b] Pages 242–244.

426] Reuben Margulies. *Mal'akhe ᶜElyon* (Angels on High; mentioned in the Babylonian and Palestinian Talmuds, all the Midrashim, the Zohar and Tiqqunim, Targumim and Yalqutim, with references to the holy books of Kabbalah), pages 175, 285. Mossad Harav Kook, Jerusalem, 1945.

427] Jacob Neusner. *The Rabbinic Traditions About the Pharisees Before 70*. Three volumes. E. J. Brill, Leiden, 1971.

428] Jacob Neusner. *Eliezer ben Hyrcanus: The Tradition and the Man*, volume I, pages 437–446. Two volumes. E. J. Brill, Leiden, 1973. Studies in Judaism in Late Antiquity, volumes 3, 4.

429] Jacob Neusner. *A History of the Jews in Babylonia*, volume 4, pages 406–417. Five volumes. E. J. Brill, Leiden, second edition, 1965–1970.

430] Aharon Oppenheimer. *The ᶜAm Ha-aretz: A Study in the Social History of the Jewish People in the Hellenistic-Roman Period*. Translated from the Hebrew by I. H. Levine. E. J. Brill, Leiden, 1977. Arbeiten zur Literatur und Geschichte des Hellenistischen Judentums, 8.

431] Charles Perrot. *La Lecture de la Bible dans la Synagogue: les anciennes lectures palestiniennes du Shabbat et des fêtes*. Gerstenberg, Hildesheim, 1973. Collection Massorah. Series 1. Études Classiques et textes, no. 1.

432] Poppelauer. *Literaturblatt des Orients*, col. 618, 1851. (I have not had access to this source since I originally made a note on it in Jerusalem in 1975, and can supply no more information about it.)

433] Jean Potin. *La fête juive de la Pentecôte: Étude des textes liturgiques*. Two volumes. Editions du Cerf, Paris, 1971. Lectio Divina 65, a–b.
　　434] Pages 183–192.

434a] S[hmuel] Safrai. Kiddush Ha-Shem in the Teachings of the Tannaim, pages 32–38. *Zion* XLIV:28–42, 1979. In Hebrew.

435] Peter Schäfer. *Rivalität zwischen Engeln und Menschen: Untersuchungen zur rabbinischen Engelvorstellung*. W. de Gruyter, Berlin and New York, 1975.
　　436] Pages 119–139.
　　437] Pages 126–127, 138.
　　438] Page 129.
　　439] Pages 140–142.

440] Joseph P. Schultz. Angelic Opposition to the Ascension of Moses and the Revelation of the Law. *Jewish Quarterly Review*, New Series, LXI(4):282–307, 1971.

441] Pages 289–290.

442] Emil Schürer. *The History of the Jewish People in the Age of Jesus Christ (175 B.C.– A.D. 135)*, volume I, pages 556–557. Edited by Geza Vermes, Pamela Vermes, Fergus Millar, and Matthew Black. T. and T. Clark, Edinburgh, revised edition, 1973.

443] Emil Schürer. *The Literature of the Jewish People in the Time of Jesus*, pages 168–172. Edited by Nahum N. Glatzer. Schocken, 1972.

444] Moise Schwab. *Vocabulaire de l'angélologie, d'après les manuscrits hébreux de la Bibliothèque nationale*, page 201. C. Klincksieck, Paris, 1897.

445] Alan Segal. *Two Powers in Heaven: Early Rabbinic Reports about Christianity and Gnosticism*. E. J. Brill, Leiden, 1977. Studies in Judaism in Late Antiquity, vol. 25.
    446] Pages 60–73.

447] Leivy Smolar and Moshe Aberbach. The Golden Calf Episode in Postbiblical Literature. *Hebrew Union College Annual* XXXIX:91–116, 1968.

Hermann L. Strack and Paul Billerbeck. *Kommentar zum Neuen Testament aus Talmud und Midrasch*. Six volumes. Beck, Munich, 1922–1961.
    448] Volume 1, page 977.
    449] Volume 2, pages 604–605.

450] No reference.

451] Gedaliahu G. Stroumsa. Aher: A Gnostic. In Bentley Layton, editor, *The Rediscovery of Gnosticism: Proceedings of the International Conference on Gnosticism at Yale, New Haven, Connecticut, March 28–31, 1978*, volume II, pages 808–818. Two volumes. E. J. Brill, Leiden, 1980–1981. Studies in the History of Religions: Supplements to Numen, 41.

452] Ephraim E. Urbach. *Mishmarot* and *Ma^{c}amadot*. *Tarbiz* XLII(3–4):304–327, 1972–73. In Hebrew.

Ephraim E. Urbach. *The Sages: Their Concepts and Beliefs*. Two volumes. Translated from the Hebrew by Israel Abrahams. Magnes Press, Jerusalem, 1975.
    453] Volume I, pages 80–96.
    454] Volume I, pages 147–148.
    455] Volume I, pages 172–177.

456] Ephraim E. Urbach. Yerushalayim shel Maṭṭah Wirushalayim shel Ma^{c}lah (Heavenly and Earthly Jerusalem). In *Jerusalem Through the Ages*, pages 156–171. Israel Exploration Society, Jerusalem, 1968.

456a] Yigael Yadin. *Bar-Kokhba: The rediscovery of the legendary hero of the Second Jewish Revolt against Rome*, pages 17–27, 255–259. Random House, 1971.

457] Solomon Zeitlin. An Historical Study of the Canonization of the Hebrew Scripture. *Proceedings of the American Academy of Jewish Research* 3:121–158, 1931–1932.
    458] Page 127.

459] Solomon Zeitlin. The Legend of the Ten Martyrs and Its Apocalyptic Origins. In *Studies in the Early History of Judaism*, volume II, pages 165–180. Four volumes. Ktav, 1974. Originally published in *Jewish Quarterly Review*, New Series, 36:1–16, 1945–46.

9. Editions and translations of *Hekhalot* texts

459a] P. Alexander. 3 (Hebrew Apocalypse of) Enoch: A New Translation and Introduction. In Charlesworth [104], pages 223–315.

Alexander Altmann. Shire Qedushshah be-Sifrut ha-Hekhalot ha-Qedumah (Liturgical Poetry in the Early Hekhalot Literature). *Melilah* 2:1–24, 1946. Quotes and annotates nearly half the material that Scholem published under the title *Ma^{c}aśeh Merkabah* [603]. *Ma^{c}aśeh Merkabah* [603].
    460] Pages 6–8.
    461] Pages 14–16.
    462] Pages 16–18.

463] David R. Blumenthal, editor. *Understanding Jewish Mysticism: A Source Reader: The Merkabah Tradition and the Zoharic Tradition*. Ktav, 1978. The Library of Judaic Learning, volume 2. Includes a partial translation of *Hekhalot Rabbati* (titled, confusingly, "*Pirkei Heikhalot*"), prepared by Lauren Grodner. Must be used with caution.

464] Rachel Elior. *Hekhalot Zutarti*. Magnes Press, Hebrew University, Jerusalem, 1982. Jerusalem Studies in Jewish Thought, Supplement I. In Hebrew. The only full publication of this text, outside Schäfer [495]. Marc Bregman called my attention to it.

465]   Pages 38–41.
466]   Ithamar Gruenwald. New Passages from *Hekhalot* Literature. *Tarbiz* XXXVIII(4):354–372, 1968–69. In Hebrew.
467]   Page 357.
468]   Pages 358–364.
468a] Page 359.
469]   Page 362.
470]   Pages 363–364.
471]   Page 367.
472]   Page 369.
473]   Page 370.
473a] Page 371.
474]   Ithamar Gruenwald. Remarks on the Article "New Passages from *Hekhalot* Literature." *Tarbiz* XXXIX(2):216–217, 1969–70. In Hebrew.
475]   Adolf Jellinek. *Bet ha-Midrasch: Sammlung Kleiner Midraschim und vermischter Abhandlungen aus der ältern jüdischen Literatur.* Six volumes in two. Wahrmann Books, Jerusalem, third edition, 1967. Originally published by Nies, 1853, and Vollrath, 1855–1857, Leipzig, and Winter Brothers, Vienna, 1873–1877. In Hebrew, with introductory material in German.
476]   Volume I, pages 58–61: *Ma^{c}ayan Hokhmah.*
477]   Volume I, pages 115–129: *Midrash Peṭirat Mosheh Rabbenu* ("midrash on the death of Moses our teacher").
478]   Volume II, pages 23–39: *Midrash Konen.*
479]   Volume II, pages 40–47: *Massekhet Hekhalot.*
479a] Volume II, pages 48–51: *Ma^{c}aśeh de-Rabbi Yehoshua^c ben Lewi* ("the story of R. Joshua b. Levi").
479b] Volume II, pages 64–72: *Midrash 'Elleh 'Ezkerah* (legend of the ten martyrs).
480]   Volume II, pages 114–117: *Sefer Hanokh* ("the book of Enoch"; corresponds to Odeberg [490], ch. 48B–D, Schäfer [495], ##71–80).
481]   Volume III, pages 83–108: *Hekhalot Rabbati.*
482]   Volume III, pages 161–163: *Pereq mi-Pirqe Hekhalot* ("a chapter of the *Hekhalot*"; corresponds to Schäfer, ##173–174, 178–188).
483]   Volume V, pages 111–112: *^{c}Inyan Ḥiram Melekh Ṣor* ("the story of Hiram king of Tyre").
484]   Volume V, pages 165–166: *Haggadat Shema^c Yiśra'el.*
485]   Volume V, pages 167–169: "additions to *Hekhalot Rabbati,* chs. 4 and 5" (corresponds to Schäfer, ##107–109, 122–126, 111, 119, 202–203).
486]   Volume V, pages 170–190: *Sefer Hekhalot* (=Odeberg's *3 Enoch* [490]).
486a] Volume VI, pages 19–35: *Ma^{c}aśeh ^{c}Aśarah Haruge Malkhut* (legend of the ten martyrs), versions B and C.
487]   Johann Maier. "Gesetz" und "Gnade" im Wandel des Gesetzesverständnisses der nachtalmudischen Zeit, pages 105–109. *Judaica* 25(1–2):64–176, 1969. Translation of the *Śar Torah* myth.
488]   David Meltzer, editor. *The Secret Garden: An Anthology in the Kabbalah,* pages 23–37. Seabury Press, 1976. Includes a translation, which must be used with some caution, of *Shi^{c}ur Qomah* materials.
489]   Shlomo Musajoff, editor. *Merkabah Shelemah.* Jerusalem, 1921. A grossly unscientific publication of important and (until Schäfer) otherwise inaccessible *Hekhalot* material, including portions of *Merkabah Rabbah* and a few bits of *Hekhalot Zuṭarti.*
490]   Hugo Odeberg. *3 Enoch, or the Hebrew Book of Enoch.* Ktav, 1973. Originally published by Cambridge University Press, 1928. Hebrew text; with English translation, introduction, and commentary.
491]   Introduction, pages 23–43.
492]   Introduction, pages 90–96.
492a] Pages 113–114 (note to chapter 33).
493]   Peter Schäfer. Die Beschwörung des Sar Ha-Panim. *Frankfurter Judaistische Beiträge* 6:107–145, 1978. Hebrew text, with German translation.
494]   Page 145.
494a] Peter Schäfer, editor. *Geniza-Fragmente zur Hekhalot-Literatur.* J. C. B. Mohr (Paul Siebeck), Tübingen, 1984. Texte und Studien zum Antiken Judentum, vol. 6.
495]   Peter Schäfer, editor. *Synopse zur Hekhalot-Literatur.* J. C. B. Mohr (Paul Siebeck), Tübin-

gen, 1981. Texte und Studien zum Antiken Judentum, vol. 2. Synoptic publication of the major *Hekhalot* manuscripts. This is the single most important publication ever to appear in the field of *Hekhalot* research.

496] Introduction, pages VI–VIII.
496a] Introduction, page IX.

497] ̇Solomon Wertheimer. *Batei Midrashot: Twenty-Five Midrashim Published for the First Time from Manuscripts Discovered in the Genizoth of Jerusalem and Egypt, with Introductions and Annotations.* Two volumes. Ktab Wasepher, second edition, 1968. Second edition originally published by Mosad Harav Kook, Jerusalem, 1950–1953. In Hebrew.

498] Volume I, pages 3–48: *Seder Rabbah di-Bereshit.*
498a] Volume I, pages 45–47.
499] Volume I, pages 49–62: *Ma^{c}aśeh Merkabah* (=Jellinek's *Massekhet Hekhalot* [479]: it has no connection to the text Scholem published as *Ma^{c}aśeh Merkabah* [603]).
500] Volume I, pages 63–136: *Pirqe Hekhalot Rabbati.*
501] Volume I, pages 355–369: *Siddur Rabba di-Bereshit Rabba* (a variant text of *Seder Rabbah di-Bereshit*, added to the second edition by Abraham Joseph Wertheimer).
502] Volume II, pages 125–134: *Pereq Re'iyyot Yehezqel* (the "Visions of Ezekiel"; now superseded by Gruenwald's edition [229]).
503] Volume II, pages 135–140: *Tosefta be-Targum Resh Sefer Yehezqel* (Targumic Tosefta to Ezekiel 1:1).
503a] Volume II, pages 333–418: *Midrash 'Otiyot de-Rabbi ^{c}Aqiba ha-Shalem* ("Alphabet of R. Akiba," in two versions). Pages 350–355 (Version A, end of "Aleph") correspond to Schäfer, ##71–80, and to Jellinek [480].

504] August Wünsche. *Aus Israels Lehrhallen: Kleine Midraschim zur späteren legendarischen Literatur des Alten Testaments*, volume III, pages 33–47. Five volumes in two. Eduard Pfeiffer, Leipzig, 1907–10. German translation of *Massekhet Hekhalot*; known to me only from Scholem's citation [590]).

10. Studies of the *Hekhalot*, and of "*merkabah* mysticism"

504a] P. S. Alexander. Comparing Merkavah Mysticism and Gnosticism: An Essay in Method. *Journal of Jewish Studies* XXXV(1):1–18, 1984.
505] P. S. Alexander. The Historical Setting of the Hebrew Book of Enoch. *Journal of Jewish Studies* XXVIII(2):156–180, 1977.
506] Pages 156–167.

Hanoch Avenary. Der Einfluss der jüdischen Mystik auf den Synagogengesang. *Kairos* XVI (1): 79–87, 1974. Only pages 79–80 touch on the *Hekhalot*.

H. W. Basser. The rabbinic attempt to democratize salvation and revelation. *Sciences Religieuses/Studies in Religion* 12(1):27–33, 1983.

Joseph M. Baumgarten. *Perek Shirah*, an Early Response to Psalm 151. *Revue de Qumrân* 9 (4):575–578, 1977–78.

507] Avram Biram. Ma^{c}aseh Bereshit; Ma^{c}aseh Merkabah, volume 8, pages 235–236. In Isidore Singer, editor, *The Jewish Encyclopedia*. Funk and Wagnalls, 1907.
508] M. Black. The Origin of the Name Metatron. *Vetus Testamentum* I(3):217–219, 1951.
509] Philipp Bloch. Die מרכבה יורדי, die Mystiker der Gaonenzeit, und ihr Einfluss auf die Liturgie. *Monatsschrift für Geschichte und Wissenschaft des Judenthums* 37:18–25, 69–74, 257–266, 305–311, 1893.
510] Ira Chernus. Individual and Community in the Redaction of the Hekhalot Literature. *Hebrew Union College Annual* LII:253–274, 1981.
511] Page 272.
512] Ira Chernus. *Mysticism in Rabbinic Judaism: Studies in the History of Midrash.* W. de Gruyter, Berlin and New York, 1982.
512a] Page 2.
512b] Page 10.
513] Pages 27–30.
514] Pages 38–39.
514a] Pages 95–96.
515] Ira Chernus. Visions of God in Merkabah Mysticism. *Journal for the Study of Judaism* XIII (1–2):123–146, 1982.

570   *Reference List*

516]   Martin Samuel Cohen. *The Shi^cur Qomah: Liturgy and Theurgy in Pre-Kabbalistic Jewish Mysticism.* University Press of America, 1983.
      516a]   Pages 57–58.
      516b]   Page 242.

517]   Joseph Dan. Anafiel, Metatron, and the Creator. *Tarbiz* LII(3):447–457, 1982–83. In Hebrew.

518]   Joseph Dan. Book Review: I. Gruenwald, *Apocalyptic and Merkavah Mysticism*, 1981. *Tarbiz* LI(4):685–691, 1981–82. In Hebrew.

519]   Joseph Dan. The Chambers of the Chariot. *Tarbiz* XLVII(1–2):49–55, 1977–78. In Hebrew.

520]   Joseph Dan. Mysticism in Jewish History, Religion and Literature. In Dan and Talmage [523], pages 1–14.

521]   Joseph Dan. Pirqe Hekhalot Rabbati u-Ma^ca´seh ^cA´seret Haruge Malkhut (Hekhalot Rabbati and the Legend of the Ten Martyrs). In Reuben Bonfil, Jacob Blidstein, Yosef Salmon and Avigdor Shinan, editors, *'Eshel Be'ersheba^c* (The Tamarisk of Beersheba: Studies in the History of Jewish Thought), pages 63–80. Department of Jewish Thought, Ben-Gurion University in the Negev, Beersheva, 1980.

522]   Joseph Dan. The Seventy Names of Metatron. In *Proceedings of the Eighth World Congress of Jewish Studies,* Division C, pages 19–23. Jerusalem, 1982.

522a]   Joseph Dan. *Three Types of Ancient Jewish Mysticism* (Seventh Annual Rabbi Louis Feinberg Memorial Lecture in Judaic Studies, Judaic Studies Program, University of Cincinnati, April 26, 1984), pages 24–31. Printed by the Judaic Studies Program, n.d.

523]   Joseph Dan and Frank Talmage, editors. *Studies in Jewish Mysticism: Proceedings of Regional Conferences Held at the University of California, Los Angeles and McGill University in April, 1978.* Association for Jewish Studies, Cambridge, Massachusetts, 1982.
      David Flusser. Scholem's recent book on Merkabah Literature. *Journal of Jewish Studies* XI(1–2):59–68, 1960. Review article of Scholem [589].

524]   Arnold Goldberg. Einige Bemerkungen zu den Quellen und den redaktionellen Einheiten der Grossen Hekhalot. *Frankfurter Judaistische Beiträge* 1:1–49, 1973.
      524a]   Pages 19–28.

525]   Arnold Goldberg. Rabban Yohanans Traum: Der Sinai in der frühen Merkavamystik. *Frankfurter Judaistische Beiträge* 3:1–27, 1975.

526]   Arnold Goldberg. Der verkannte Gott: Prüfung und Scheitern der Adepten in der Merkawamystik. *Zeitschrift für Religions- und Geistesgeschichte* 26(1):17–29, 1974.

527]   Arnold Goldberg. Der Vortrag des Ma'ase Merkawa: Eine Vermutung zur fruehen Merkawamystik, pages 15–16. *Judaica* 29(1):4–23, 1973.

528]   [Heinrich] Grätz. Die mystische Literatur in der gaonischen Epoche. *Monatsschrift für Geschichte und Wissenschaft des Judenthums* 8:67–78, 103–118, 140–153, 1859.
      528a]   Pages 72–73.

529]   Jonas C. Greenfield. Prolegomenon. In Odeberg [490].
      530]   Page XVIII.
      531]   Pages XXVII–XXX.
      532]   Pages XXX–XXXII.

533]   Karl Erich Grözinger. *Musik und Gesang in der Theologie der frühen jüdischen Literatur: Talmud Midrasch Mystik.* Mohr, Tübingen, 1982.
      533a]   Pages 321–322.
      533b]   Pages 326–329.

534]   Karl-Erich Grözinger. Singen und ekstatische Sprache in der frühen jüdischen Mystik. *Journal for the Study of Judaism* XI(1):66–77, 1980.
      534a]   Pages 76–77.

535]   Ithamar Gruenwald. *Apocalyptic and Merkavah Mysticism.* E. J. Brill, Leiden, 1980. Arbeiten zur Geschichte des antiken Judentums und des Urchristentums, volume 14.
      536]   Pages 3–28.
      537]   Pages 29–72.
      538]   Pages 99–101.
      539]   Page 122.
      540]   Pages 134–141.
      541]   Page 134.
      542]   Page 142.
      543]   Pages 143, 171.
      544]   Page 157.

545] Pages 174–180.
546] Pages 188–190.
547] Ithamar Gruenwald. Ha-'Ispeqlariyah we-ha-Ṭekhniqah shel ha-Ḥazon ha-Nebu'i we-ha-'Apoqalipṭi (Mirrors and the Technique of Prophetic and Apocalyptic Vision). *Beth Mikra* 40:95–97, 1970.
　Ithamar Gruenwald. The Jewish Esoteric Literature in the Time of the Mishnah and Talmud. *Immanuel* 4:37–46, 1974.
548] Ithamar Gruenwald. Jewish Merkavah Mysticism and Gnosticism. In Dan and Talmage [523], pages 41–55.
549] Ithamar Gruenwald. Knowledge and Vision: Towards a Clarification of Two "Gnostic" Concepts in the Light of their Alleged Origins, page 97, footnote. *Israel Oriental Studies* 3:63–107, 1973.
550] Ithamar Gruenwald. Shirat ha-Mal'akhim, ha-"Qedushshah" u-Beᶜayat Ḥibburah shel Sifrut ha-Hekhalot (The Song of the Angels, the *Qedushshah*, and the Problem of the Composition of the *Hekhalot* Literature). In *Peraqim be-Toledot Yerushalayim Bime Bayit Sheni (Studies in the History of Jerusalem in the Second Temple Period)*, pages 459–481. Yitzhak Ben-Zvi Foundation, Jerusalem, 1981.
551] Ithamar Greenwald (sic). Yannai and Hekhaloth Literature. *Tarbiz* XXXVI(3):257–277, 1966–67. In Hebrew. Rabinowitz [578] vigorously responds to Gruenwald's claims.
　551a] Page 272.
552] David J. Halperin. *The Merkabah in Rabbinic Literature*. American Oriental Society, 1980. American Oriental Series, 62.
　553] Page 9, footnote.
　554] Pages 21–22.
　555] Pages 37–39.
　556] Pages 53–54.
　557] Pages 87–88.
　558] Page 110, footnote.
　559] Page 134.
　560] Pages 157–158.
　561] Pages 158–162.
562] David J. Halperin. A New Edition of the Hekhalot Literature. *Journal of the American Oriental Society* 104(3):543–552, 1984. Review article of Schäfer [495], with extended comments on Elior [464].
562a] David J. Halperin. A Sexual Image in Hekhalot Rabbati, and Its Implications. In Joseph Dan, editor, *Proceedings of the First International Conference on the History of Jewish Mysticism: Early Jewish Mysticism*, English section, pages 117–132. Hebrew University, Jerusalem, 1987.
　Lawrence A. Hoffman. Censoring In and Censoring Out: A Function of Liturgical Language. In Joseph Gutmann, editor, *Ancient Synagogues: The State of Research*, pages 19–37. Scholars Press, 1981. On the relation of certain portions of the Jewish liturgy to the hymns of the "*merkavah*" tradition." (I owe this reference to Professor Baruch M. Bokser.)
563] Moshe Idel. The Evil Thought of the Deity. *Tarbiz* XLIX(3–4):356–364, 1979–80. In Hebrew.
564] Moshe Idel. Le-Gilgulleha shel Ṭekhniqah Qedumah shel Ḥazon Nebu'i Bime ha-Benayim (On the Medieval Development of an Ancient Technique for Prophetic Vision). *Sinai* 86(1–2):1–7, 1979–80.
565] Moshe Idel. On the History of the Interdiction against the Study of Kabbalah before the Age of Forty. *AJSreview* V:1–20, Hebrew Section, 1980. Association for Jewish Studies, Cambridge, Massachusetts.
566] Moshe Idel. Tefisat ha-Torah be-Sifrut ha-Hekhalot we-Gilgulleha ba-Qabbalah (The Concept of Torah in *Hekhalot* Literature, and Its Development in Kabbalah), pages 23–33. In *Meḥqere Yerushalayim be-Maḥshebet Yiśra'el (Jerusalem Studies in Jewish Thought)*, pages 23–84. Magnes Press, Hebrew University, Jerusalem, 1981.
566a] Kaufman Kohler. Akiba ben Joseph, Alphabet of, volume 1, pages 310–311. In Isadore Singer, editor, *The Jewish Encyclopedia*. Funk and Wagnalls, 1907. Kohler's "Version A" corresponds to Wertheimer's [503a] "Version B," and vice versa.
　S. T. Lachs. Midrash Hallel and Merkabah Mysticism. In Isidore David Passow and Samuel Tobias Lachs, editors, *Gratz College Anniversary Volume*, pages 193–203. Gratz College, Philadelphia, 1971. I owe this reference to Marc Bregman.

567] Johanan [Hans] Levy. Remainders of Greek Phrases and Nouns in "Hechaloth Rabathi," pages 264–265. In *Studies in Jewish Hellenism*, pages 259–265. Bialik Institute, Jerusalem, 1969. Originally appeared in *Tarbiz* XII(2):163–167, 1940–41. In Hebrew.

568] Saul Lieberman. The Knowledge of *Halakha* by the Author (or Authors) of the *Heikhaloth*. Appendix 2 to Gruenwald [535], pages 241–244.

569] Saul Lieberman. Metatron, the Meaning of His Name and His Functions. Appendix 1 to Gruenwald [535], pages 235–241.

570] Saul Lieberman. Mishnat Shir ha-Shirim (The Tannaitic Oral Teaching Concerning the Song of Songs). Appendix D to Scholem [589], pages 118–126.

    571] Page 122.

572] Raphael Loewe. The Divine Garment and Shi'ur Qomah. *Harvard Theological Review* 57 (1):153–160, 1965.

573] Samuel Loewenstamm. On an Alleged Gnostic Element in Mishna Hagiga ii, 1. In Menahem Haran, editor, *Yehezkel Kaufmann Jubilee Volume: Studies in Bible and Jewish Religion*, pages 112–121. Magnes Press, Jerusalem, 1960. In Hebrew.

574] Johann Maier. Das Gefährdungsmotiv bei der Himmelsreise in der jüdischen Apokalyptik und "Gnosis." *Kairos* 5(1):18–40, 1963.

    575] Page 23.

576] J[ohann] Maier. Hekhalot Rabbati XXVII, 2–5: גאה בבריות אדם. *Judaica* 22(4): 209–217, 1966.

577] André Neher. Le voyage mystique des quatre. *Revue de l'Histoire des Religions* CXL:59–82, 1951.

    Jacob Neusner. The Development of the *Merkavah* Tradition. *Journal for the Study of Judaism* II(2):149–160, 1971. On the stories of the *merkabah* expositions of Johanan b. Zakkai's disciples.

578] Z. M. Rabinowitz. On the Relationship of Yannai, the Payyetan, to the Literature of the Merkavah Mysticists. *Tarbiz* XXXVI(4):402–405, 1966–67. In Hebrew.

579] Peter Schäfer. Aufbau und redaktionelle Identität der Hekalot Zutarti. In Vermes and Neusner [349], pages 569–582.

580] Peter Schäfer. Engel und Menschen in der Hekhalot-Literatur. *Kairos* XXII(3–4):201–225, 1980.

    581] Pages 202–203, 208–215.

    582] Pages 215–218.

582a] Peter Schäfer. Handschriften zur Hekhalot-Literatur. *Frankfurter Judaistische Beiträge* 11: 113–193, 1983.

583] Peter Schäfer. New Testament and Hekhalot Literature: The Journey into Heaven in Paul and in Merkavah Mysticism. *Journal of Jewish Studies* XXXV(1):19–35, 1984. Critical of Scholem's position [593].

584] Peter Schäfer. Prolegomena zu Einer Kritischen Edition und Analyse der Merkava Rabba. *Frankfurter Judaistische Beiträge* 5:65–99, 1977.

    585] Pages 75–82.

586] Peter Schäfer. Tradition and Redaction in Hekhalot Literature. *Journal for the Study of Judaism* XIV(2):172–181, 1983.

587] Lawrence H. Schiffman. The Recall of Rabbi Nehuniah Ben Ha-Qanah from Ecstasy in the *Hekhalot Rabbati*. *AJSreview* I:269–281, 1976. Association for Jewish Studies, Cambridge, Massachusetts.

588] Margarete Schlüter. Die Erzählung von der Rückholung des R. Nehunya ben Haqana aus der *Merkava*-Schau in ihrem redaktionellen Rahmen. *Frankfurter Judaistische Beiträge* 10: 65–109, 1982.

589] Gershom G. Scholem. *Jewish Gnosticism, Merkabah Mysticism, and Talmudic Tradition*. Jewish Theological Seminary of America, 1960.

    590] Pages 5–7.

    591] Pages 9–13.

    592] Page 12.

    593] Pages 14–19.

    594] Page 20.

    595] Pages 20–35.

    596] Page 32.

    597] Pages 36–42.

    598] Pages 43–55.

    599] Pages 44–45.

    600] Page 57.

601] Page 63.
602] Pages 77–78.
603] Pages 101–117 (=Appendix C, Scholem's edition of the text he calls *Ma*ᶜ*aśeh Merkabah*).
    Pages 118–126 (=Appendix D; see Lieberman [570]).
604] Page 128.
604a] Gershom G. Scholem. *Major Trends in Jewish Mysticism*. Schocken, third edition, 1954.
605] Pages 40–79.
606] Pages 42–43.
607] Pages 43–44.
608] Pages 46–47.
609] Pages 52–53.
610] Page 61.
611] Pages 67–70.
611a] Page 71.
612] Gershom G. Scholem. Sandalfon. In *Encyclopedia Judaica*, volume XIV, columns 827–828. Macmillan, 1971.
613] Gershom G. Scholem. *Ursprung und Anfänge der Kabbala*, pages 15–20. W. de Gruyter, Berlin, 1962. Studia Judaica: Forschungen zur Wissenschaft des Judentums, vol. 3.
    Nicolas Séd. Les traditions secrètes et les disciples de Rabban Yohanan ben Zakkai. *Revue de l'Histoire des Religions* CLXXXIV(1):49–66, 1973.
614] Morton Smith. Observations on Hekhalot Rabbati. In Alexander Altmann, editor, *Biblical and Other Studies*, pages 142–160. Harvard University Press, 1963. Studies and Texts, volume I.
614a] Gedaliahu G. Stroumsa. Form(s) of God: Some Notes on Metatron and Christ. *Harvard Theological Review* 76(3):269–288, 1983.
    Ephraim E. Urbach. The Traditions about Merkabah Mysticism in the Tannaitic Period. In Ephraim E. Urbach, R. J. Zvi Werblowsky and Ch. Wirszubski, editors, *Studies in Mysticism and Religion Presented to Gershom G. Scholem on His Seventieth Birthday by Pupils, Colleagues and Friends*, pages 1–28, Hebrew section. Magnes Press, Jerusalem, 1967. In Hebrew.
615] Pages 2–11.
616] Pages 12–17.
617] Pages 23–25.
    Georges Vajda. Recherches récentes sur l'ésotérisme juif. (Troisième série, années 1963–1975). *Revue de l'Histoire des Religions* CXCII(1):31–55, July 1977; CXCII(2):165–197, October, 1977. Pages 32–47 deal with mysticism before the thirteenth century.

11. Editions and translations of patristic authors
(arranged alphabetically, by author)

618] Augustine. *Concerning the City of God against the Pagans*, page 664. Translated by Henry Bettenson. Penguin, 1972.
619] Ephraem the Syrian. *Sancti Patris Nostri Ephraem Syri Opera Omnia, Syriace et Latine*, volume II. Edited by Joseph Simon Assemani. Rome, 1740. Syriac text, with Latin translation.
620] Eusebius. *The History of the Church from Christ to Constantine*. Translated by G. A. Williamson. Penguin Books, 1965.
621] Jerome. *Sancti Eusebii Hieronymi Epistulae*. In Isidor Hilberg, editor, *Corpus Scriptorum Ecclesiasticorum Latinorum*, volume I, LIV. F. Tempsky, Vienna, and G. Freytag, Leipzig, 1910–1918. Latin text.
622] Jerome. *S. Hieronymi Presbyteri Opera, Pars I: Opera Exegetica, 4: Commentarium in Hiezechielem libri XIV*. Franciscus Glorie, editor. Typographi Brepols, Turnhout, 1964. Corpus Christianorum Series Latina, 75. Latin text.
622a] Page 5.
622b] Page 125.
622c] Jerome. *S. Hieronymi Presbyteri Opera, Pars I: Opera Exegetica, 6: Commentarii in Prophetas Minores*. M. Adriaen, editor. Typographi Brepols, Turnhout, 1969. Corpus Christianorum Series Latina, 76. Latin text.
623] Justin Martyr. *Dialogue avec Tryphon: Texte grec, Traduction Francaise, Introduction,*

Notes et Index, volume I, page 351. Two volumes. Edited and translated by Georges Archambault. A. Picard, Paris, 1901. Textes et documents pour l'etude historique du christianisme, 8, 11.

624] Justin Martyr. *The First Apology, the Second Apology, Dialogue with Trypho, Exhortation to the Greeks, Discourse to the Greeks, the Monarchy; or, the Rule of God.* Translated by Thomas B. Falls. Christian Heritage, 1949.

625] Makarios the Egyptian. *Sanctorum Patrum Macarii Aegyptii, Macarii Alexandrini, Opera Quae Supersunt Omnia*, column 452C. In J.-P. Migne, editor, *Patrologiae Cursus Completus, Series Graeca*, volume XXXIV(1). Garnier Fratres, Paris, 1903. Greek text, with Latin translation.

626] Novatian. *Opera, quae supersunt nunc primum in unum collecta ad fidem codicum, qui adhuc extant, necnon adhibitis editionibus veteribus.* Edited by G. F. Diercks. Typographi Brepols, Turnhout, 1972. Corpus Christianorum Series Latina, 4. Latin text.

627] Origen. *Contra Celsum.* Translated into English by Henry Chadwick. Cambridge University Press, 1965.

628] Origen. *An Exhortation to Martyrdom, Prayer. First Principles: Book IV. Prologue to the Commentary on the Song of Songs. Homily XXVII on Numbers.* Translated by Rowan A. Greer. Paulist Press, 1979. The Classics of Western Spirituality.

629] Origen. *Commentaire sur saint Jean.* Four volumes. Edited by Cécile Blanc. Editions du Cerf, 1966–82. Sources chrétiennes, nos. 120, 157, 222, 290. Greek text, with French translation.

630] Origen. *Homélies sur Josué: Texte Latin, Introduction, Traduction et Notes.* Edited and translated by Annie Jaubert. Editions du Cerf, Paris, 1960. Sources Chrétiennes, 71.
      630a]   Pages 63–67.
        631]   Pages 68–82.

632] Origen. *Homélies sur la Genèse.* Latin text edited and translated by Louis Doutreleau. Editions du Cerf, Paris, 1943.

633] Origen. *Homélies sur les Nombres.* Translated by André Méhat. Editions du Cerf, Paris, 1951. Sources chrétiennes, 29.

634] Origen. *Homélies sur S. Luc. Texte Latin et Fragments Grecs.* Translated by Henri Crouzel, Francois Fournier, and Pierre Périchon. Editions du Cerf, Paris, 1962.

635] Origen. A Letter from Origen to Africanus. In Alexander Roberts and James Donaldson, editors, *Ante-Nicene Christian Library: Translations of the Writings of the Fathers Down to A.D. 325.* Volume X, *The Writings of Origen*, section I, pages 371–387. Translated by Frederick Crombie. T. and T. Clark, Edinburgh, 1869.

635a] Origen. *Opera Omnia*, volume 2, column 1056. Edited by Charles and Charles Vincent Delarue. In J.-P. Migne, editor, *Patrologiae Cursus Completus, Series Graeca Prior*, volume XII. J.-P. Migne, Paris, 1862. Greek text, with Latin translation.

636] Origen. *Origen on First Principles, being Koetschau's Text of the De Principiis Translated into English, Together with an Introduction and Notes.* Translated by G. W. Butterworth. Society for Promoting Christian Knowledge, 1936.
      637]   Pages lxii–lxiv, 155–156.

638] Origen. *Origenes Werke.* Volume IV: *Der Johanneskommentar.* Edited by Erwin Preuschen. Hinrichs, Leipzig, 1903. Griechischen Christlichen Schriftsteller (GCS), 10.

639] Origen. *Origenes Werke.* Volume VI: *Homilien zum Hexateuch in Rufins Übersetzung ... zu Genesis, Exodus, und Leviticus.* Edited by W. A. Baehrens. Hinrichs, Leipzig, 1920. GCS, 29.

640] Origen. *Origenes Werke.* Volume VII: *Homilien zum Hexateuch in Rufins Übersetzung ... zu Numeri, Josua und Judices.* Edited by W. A. Baehrens. Hinrichs, Leipzig, 1921. GCS, 30.

641] Origen. *Origenes Werke.* Volume VIII: *Homilien zu Samuel I, zum Hohelied und zu den Propheten; Kommentar zum Hohelied; in Rufins und Hieronymus' Übersetzungen.* Edited by W. A. Baehrens. Hinrichs, Leipzig, 1925. GCS, 33. Contains the Latin text of the *Homilies on Ezekiel*, with Greek fragments.
      642]   Page 330.

643] Origen. *Origenes Werke.* Volume IX: *Die Homilien zu Lukas in der Übersetzung des Hieronymus und die griechischen Reste der Homilien und des Lukas-Kommentars.* Edited by Max Rauer. Hinrichs, Leipzig, 1930. GCS, 35.

644] Origen. *Origenis Hexaplorum quae supersunt; sive veterum interpretum graecorum in totum Vetus Testamentum Fragmenta.* Edited by Frederick Field. Two volumes. Clarendon, 1875. Greek fragments collected or reconstructed.

645] Origen. *The Song of Songs: Commentary and Homilies.* Translated by R. P. Lawson. Newman Press, and Longmans, Green, London, 1957. Ancient Christian Writers: The Works of the Fathers in Translation, 26.

646] Theodoret of Cyrus. *Opera Omnia.* Edited by Joan Ludov Schulze. In J.-P. Migne, editor, *Patrologiae Cursus Completus, Series Graeca Prior,* volume LXXXI. J.-P. Migne, Paris, 1864. Greek text, with Latin translation.

Anonymous texts:

647] Edgar Hennecke and Wilhelm Schneemelcher, editors. *New Testament Apocrypha.* Two volumes. Translated from the German by A. J. B. Higgins and others, edited by R. McL. Wilson. Westminster Press, 1963, 1966.

    648] Volume II, pages 425–531: *Acts of Thomas.*

    649] Volume II, pages 642–663: *Ascension of Isaiah.*

650] Paul Anton de Lagarde. *Onomastica Sacra,* page 89. Adalberti Rente, Göttingen, 1870.

651] Franz Xaver Wutz. *Onomastica Sacra: Untersuchungen zum Liber Interpretationis Nominum Hebraicorum des Hl. Hieronymus.* Hinrichs, Leipzig, 1914. Texte und Untersuchungen zur Geschichte der Altchristlichen Literatur, vol. 41.

12. Patristic studies

652] Wilhelm Bacher. The Church Father, Origen, and Rabbi Hoshaya. *Jewish Quarterly Review,* Old Series, III:357–360, 1890–91.

653] Gustave Bardy. Les traditions juives dans l'oeuvre d'Origène, page 227. *Revue biblique* 34 (2):217–252, 1925.

654] Gustave Bardy. Saint Jérôme et ses Maîtres Hébreux, *Revue Bénédictine* XLVI(4):145–164, 1934.

655] James Barr. St. Jerome's Appreciation of Hebrew. *Bulletin of the John Rylands Library* 49(2):281–302, 1967.

656] Dominique Barthélemy. Est-ce Hoshaya Rabba qui censura le "Commentaire Allegorique"? A partir des retouches faites aux citations bibliques, étude sur la tradition textuelle du Commentaire Allegorique de Philon. In *Etudes D'Histoire du Texte de l'Ancien Testament,* pages 140–173. Editions Universitaires, Fribourg; and Vandenhoeck and Ruprecht, Göttingen, 1978. Originally published in *Philon d'Alexandrie, Lyon, 11–15 septembre 1966,* pages 45–78. Éditions du Centre National de la Recherche Scientifique, 1967.

657] Walther Bauer. *Orthodoxy and Heresy in Earliest Christianity.* Edited by Robert A. Kraft and Gerhard Krodel; translated from the German by a team from the Philadelphia Seminar on Christian Origins. Fortress Press, 1971.

658] Hans Bietenhard. *Caesarea, Origenes, und die Juden.* W. Kohlhammer, Stuttgart, 1974.

659] Jay Braverman. *Jerome's Commentary on Daniel: A Study of Comparative Jewish and Christian Interpretations of the Hebrew Bible.* Catholic Biblical Association of America, 1978. Catholic Biblical Quarterly, Monograph Series, 7.

660] Roberta C. Chesnut. *Three Monophysite Christologies: Severus of Antioch, Philoxenus of Mabbug and Jacob of Sarug.* Oxford University Press, 1976.

661] Henri Crouzel. *Bibligraphie Critique d'Origène.* Nijhoff, La Haye, 1971.

662] Jean Daniélou. *The Angels and their Mission; according to the fathers of the church.* Translated from the French by David Heimann. Newman Press, 1957.

    663] Pages 37–40.

664] Nicholas Robert Michael DeLange. *Origen and the Jews: Studies in Jewish-Christian Relations in Third Century Palestine.* Cambridge University Press, 1976.

    665] Pages 21–27.

    666] Pages 41–43.

    667] Pages 63–73.

    668] Pages 86–87.

    668a] Page 111.

669] H. Dörries. Makarius, volume 4, section 619. In *Die Religion in Geschichte und Gegenwart: Handwörterbuch für Theologie und Religionswissenschaft,* J. C. B. Mohr, Tübingen, 1960.

670] Carl Martin Edsman. *Le Baptême de Feu.* A. Lorentz, Leipzig, and Ludequistska, Uppsala, 1940. Acta Seminarii Neotestamentici Upsaliensis, IX.

671] Louis Ginzberg. Die Haggada bei den Kirchenvätern und in der apokryphischen Literatur.

Monatsschrift für Geschichte und Wissenschaft des Judenthums 43:17–22, 61–75, 117 –125, 149–159, 217–231, 293–303, 409–415, 461–470, 485–504, 529–547, 1899.

672]   H. Grätz. Hagadische Elemente bei den Kirchenvätern. *Monatsschrift für Geschichte und Wissenschaft des Judenthums* 3:311–319, 352–355, 381–387, 428–431, 1854.

672a] Robert M. Grant. Review of N. R. M. de Lange, *Origen and the Jews* [664]. *History of Religions* 18(1):95–98, 1978.

672b] Robert C. Gregg and Dennis E. Groh. *Early Arianism – A View of Salvation.* Fortress Press, 1981.

673]   David J. Halperin. Origen, Ezekiel's Merkabah, and the Ascension of Moses. *Church History* 50(3):261–275, 1981.

674]   Richard Patrick Crosland Hanson. *Allegory and Event: A Study of the Sources and Significance of Origen's Interpretation of Scripture.* John Knox Press, 1959.
        675] Pages 335–341.
        Adolf von Harnack. *Der Kirchengeschichtliche Ertrag der Exegetischen Arbeiten des Origenes.* Two volumes, J. C. Hinrichs, Leipzig, 1918–1919. Texte und Untersuchungen zur Geschichte der altchristlichen Literatur.
        676] Volume I, pages 68–69.
        677] Volume II, page 54.
        678] Volume II, page 67.

679]   Reuven Kimelman. Rabbi Yohanan and Origen on the Song of Songs: A Third-Century Jewish-Christian Disputation. *Harvard Theological Review* 73(3–4):567–595, 1980.

680]   K. Kohler. The Origin and Composition of the Eighteen Benedictions with a Translation of the Corresponding Essene Prayers in the Apostolic Constitutions, pages 415–416. *Hebrew Union College Annual* 1:387–426, 1924.

681]   Heinrich Kraft, editor. *Kirchenväter Lexikon*, pages 389–391. Kösel, Munich, 1966. Texte der Kirchenväter, volume 5.
        S. Krauss. The Jews in the Works of the Church Fathers. *Jewish Quarterly Review,* Old Series, V:122–157, 1892–93.
        682] Pages 151–152.
        683] Pages 156–157.

684]   Georg Kretschmar. Himmelfahrt und Pfingsten. *Zeitschrift für Kirchengeschichte* LXVI (III):209–253, 1954–1955.

685]   Jules Lebreton and Jacques Zeiller. *The Triumph of Christianity*, page 49. Translated from the French by Ernest C. Messenger. Collier Books, 1962. A History of the Early Church, IV. Originally published as part of *The History of the Primitive Church*, Macmillan, 1946–1947. The translation of the eulogy, quoted on this page, is Metcalfe's.

686]   Pierre Nautin. *Origène: sa vie et son oeuvre.* Beauchesne, Paris, 1977. Christianisme antique, I.
        687] Pages 184–197.
        688] Pages 254–255.
        689] Pages 275–279.
        690] Pages 303–361.
        691] Pages 377–380.
        692] Pages 380–384.
        693] Pages 389–409.
        694] Page 417.

695]   Wilhelm Neuss. *Das Buch Ezechiel in Theologie und Kunst bis zum Ende des XII. Jahrhunderts, mit besonderer Berücksichtigung der Gemälde in der Kirche zu Schwarzrheindorf: Ein Beitrag zur Entwicklungsgeschichte der Typologie der christlichen Kunst, vornehmlich in den Benediktinerklöstern.* Aschendorff, Münster, 1912. Beiträge zur Geschichte des altern Mönchtums und des Benediktinerordens, vol. 1–2.
        696] Pages 48–50.
        697] Pages 137–138.

698]   Moritz Rahmer. *Die hebräischen Traditionen in den Werken des Hieronymus: Durch eine Vergleichung mit den jüdischen Quellen, kritisch beleuchtet.* Volume I: Schletter, Breslau, 1861. Volume II appeared serially in *Monatsschrift für Geschichte und Wissenschaft des Judenthums*, volumes XIV, XVI, XVII, XLVI, XLVII.

698a] A. Rose. "Attollite Portas, Principes, Vestras ...": Aperçus sur la Lecture Chrétienne du Ps. 24 (23) B. In *Miscellanea Liturgica in Onore di sua Eminenza il Cardinale Giacomo Lercaro*, volume I, pages 453–478. Desclée, Rome, 1966. I owe this reference to Professor Daniel Sheerin.

699] Joseph W[ilson] Trigg. The Charismatic Intellectual: Origen's Understanding of Religious Leadership. *Church History* 50(1):5–19, 1981.

700] Joseph Wilson Trigg. *Origen: The Bible and Philosophy in the Third-Century Church*. John Knox, 1983.

701] Ephraim E. Urbach. The Homiletical Interpretations of the Sages and the Expositions of Origen on Canticles, and the Jewish-Christian Disputation. *Scripta Hierosolymitana* 22: 247–275, 1971. Studies in Aggadah and Folk-Literature. This article is an English version of the following:

702] Ephraim E. Urbach. Rabbinic Exegesis and Origenes' Commentaries on the Song of Songs and Jewish-Christian Polemics. *Tarbiz* XXX(2):148–170, 1960–61. In Hebrew.

703] Abraham Wasserstein. A Rabbinic Midrash as a Source of Origen's Homily on Ezekiel. *Tarbiz* XLVI(3–4):317–318. 1976–77. In Hebrew. Deals with *Homilies on Ezekiel*, IV, 8.

13. Religious trends in the Greco-Roman world
(including Gnosticism and Hellenistic Judaism)

704] Wilhelm Bousset. Die Himmelsreise der Seele, pages 234–249. *Archiv für Religionswissenschaft* 4:136–169, 229–273, 1901.

705] Roger Aubrey Bullard, editor and translator. *The Hypostasis of the Archons: The Coptic Text with Translation and Commentary*, pages 55–58. W. de Gruyter, Berlin, 1970. Ph.D. dissertation, Vanderbilt University, 1965.

706] Gustav Adolf Deissman. *Light from the Ancient East: The New Testament Illustrated by Recently Discovered Texts of the Greco-Roman World*. Translated from the German by Lionel R. M. Strachan. George H. Doran Company, 1927. Originally published by Hodder and Stoughton, London, 1910.

    707] Pages 257, 262.

708] Eric Robertson Dodds. *Pagan and Christian in an Age of Anxiety: Some Aspects of Religious Experience from Marcus Aurelius to Constantine*, pages 127–132. Cambridge University Press, 1965.

709] Francis T. Fallon. *The Enthronement of Sabaoth: Jewish Elements in Gnostic Creation Myths*. E. J. Brill, Leiden, 1978.

    710] Page 46.

711] Louis H. Feldman. Prolegomenon, pages xxviii–xxxi. In Pseudo-Philo [726].

711a] Thomas M. Finn. The God-fearers Reconsidered. *Catholic Biblical Quarterly* 47(1):75–84, 1985. Professor John H. Schütz called my attention to this paper.

712] John G. Gager, Jr. *Moses in Greco-Roman Paganism*, pages 137–140. Abingdon Press, 1972. Erwin R. Goodenough. *Jewish Symbols in the Greco-Roman Period*. Thirteen volumes. Pantheon Books, 1953–1968. Bollingen Series XXXVII.

    713] Volume 1, pages 246–248.

    714] Volume 5, pages 105–110.

    715] Volume 10, pages 46–49.

716] John M. Hull. *Hellenistic Magic and the Synoptic Tradition*, pages 21–24. A. R. Allenson, Naperville, Illinois, and SCM Press, London, 1974. Studies in Biblical Theology, second series, 28.

716a] Howard Jacobson. *The Exagoge of Ezekiel*, pages 55, 89–97. Cambridge University Press, 1983.

717] Manuel Joël. *Blicke in die Religionsgeschichte, zu Anfang des zweiten Christlichen Jahrhunderts*, volume 1, pages 157–159. Two volumes, S. Schottlaender, Breslau, 1880–1883.
Hans Jonas. *The Gnostic Religion: The Message of the Alien God and the Beginnings of Christianity*. Beacon Press, second edition, 1963.

    718] Pages 137–146.

    719] Pages 162–163.

719a] Jean-Georges Kahn. Did Philo Know Hebrew? The Testimony of the "Etymologies," pages 342–343. *Tarbiz* XXXIV(4):337–345, 1964–65. In Hebrew.

719b] Jean-Georges Kahn (Cohen-Yashar). Israel – *Videns Deum*. *Tarbiz* XL(3):285–292, 1970–71. In Hebrew.

720] Bentley Layton. The Hypostasis of the Archons, or *The Reality of the Rulers*. A Gnostic Story of the Creation, Fall, and Ultimate Salvation of Man, and the Origin and Reality of His Enemies, sections 4–5. *Harvard Theological Review* 67(4): 351–425, 1974.

721] Lucretius. *On the Nature of the Universe*, page 58. Translated by R. E. Latham. Penguin, 1951.

722] Wayne A. Meeks. *The Prophet-King: Moses Traditions and the Johannine Christology*, pages 147–149. E. J. Brill, Leiden, 1967. Supplements to *Novum Testamentum*, 14. Ph.D. dissertation, Yale, 1965.

723] Martin Ninck. *Die Bedeutung des Wassers im Kult und Leben der Alten: Eine Symbolgeschichtliche Untersuchung*, pages 47–99. Wissenschaftliche Buchgesellschaft, Darmstadt, second edition, 1960. Originally published by Dieterich'sche Verlagsbuchhandlung m.b.h., 1921. Philologus: Supplements XIV, II.

724] Elaine Pagels. "The Demiurge and His Archons" – a Gnostic View of the Bishop and Presbyters? *Harvard Theological Review* 69(3–4):301–324, 1976.

725] Elaine Pagels. *The Gnostic Gospels*, pages 28–47. Random House, 1979. A popularly written summary of Pagels' argument [724].

726] "Philo." *The Biblical Antiquities*. Translated from Latin by Montague Rhodes James. Ktav, 1971 (with a Prolegomenon by Louis H. Feldman). Originally published by Society for Promoting Christian Knowedge, London, 1917. We know little about the author of this work (Feldman, Zeron [736]), except that he was *not* the Jewish Alexandrian philosopher Philo (next entry). We normally refer to him as "Pseudo-Philo."

727] Philo. *Philo, with an English Translation*, volume 9, page 167. Ten volumes. Translated by F. H. Colson and G. H. Whitaker. Putnam, 1929–1962. Loeb Classical Library, Greek authors.

728] Richard Reitzenstein. *Hellenistische Wundererzählungen*, pages 115–116. B. G. Teubner, Leipzig, 1906, 1922.

729] James M. Robinson, editor. *The Nag Hammadi Library: In English*. Harper & Row, 1977.

729a] Samuel Sandmel. *The First Christian Century in Judaism and Christianity: Certainties and Uncertainties*. Oxford University Press, 1969.

    729b] Pages 16–21.
    729c] Pages 28–33, 68–69.
    729d] Pages 107–142.

730] Daniel Schwartz. Priesthood and Priestly Descent: Josephus, *Antiquities* 10.80. *Journal of Theological Studies* XXXII(1):129–135, 1981.

731] Nicolas Séd. Les douze hebdomades, le char de Sabaoth, et les soixante-douze langues, pages 160–162. *Novum Testamentum* XXXI(2):156–184, 1979.

732] Alan F. Segal. Heavenly Ascent in Hellenistic Judaism, Early Christianity and their Environment. In Wolfgang Haase, editor, *Aufstieg und Niedergang der Römischen Welt*, volume II.23.2, pages 1333–1394. Walter de Gruyter, Berlin and New York, 1980.

732a] Folker Siegert. Gottesfürchtige und Sympathisanten. *Journal for the Study of Judaism* IV(2):109–164, 1973.

733] Jonathan Z. Smith. The Prayer of Joseph, pages 259–271. In Jacob Neusner, editor, *Religions of Antiquity: Essays in Memory of Erwin Ramsdell Goodenough*, pages 253–294. E. J. Brill, Leiden, 1968. Studies in the History of Religions, 14.

734] Morton Smith. The Image of God: Notes on the Hellenization of Judaism, with Especial Reference to Goodenough's Work on Jewish Symbols, page 497. *Bulletin of the John Rylands Library* 40(2):473–512, 1958.

734a] Menahem Stern. *Greek and Latin Authors on Jews and Judaism*. Volume Two: *From Tacitus to Simplicius*, pages 102–107. Israel Academy of Sciences and Humanities, Jerusalem, 1980.

735] Pieter W. van der Horst. Moses' Throne Vision in Ezekiel the Dramatist. *Journal of Jewish Studies* XXXIV(1):21–29, 1983.

736] A. Zeron. Erwägungen zu Pseudo-Philos Quellen und Zeit. *Journal for the Study of Judaism* XI(1):38–52, 1980.

14. Islam

a) Editions and translations of hadith, tafsir, and "tales of the prophets"

737] Abu Da'ud (full name: A. D. Sulayman b. al-Ash^Cath b. Ishaq al-Azdi al-Sijistani; d. 889). *Sunan Abi Da'ud*. Two volumes. Mustafa al-Babi al-Halabi, Cairo, 1952.

738] Baydawi (full name: ^CAbd Allah b. ^CUmar al-B.; d. 1286). *Beidhawii Commentarius in Coranum. ex codd. parisiensibus. dresdensibus et lipsiensibus ....* Edited by H. O. Fleischer. Two volumes. F. C. W. Vogel, Leipzig, 1846–48.

739] Bukhari (full name: Abu ᶜAbd Allah Muhammad b. Ismaᶜil al-B.; d. 870). *Le recueil des traditions mahométanes par Abou Abdallah Mohammed ibn Ismail el-Bokhâri.* Edited by Ludolf Krehl and Th. W. Juynboll. Four volumes. E. J. Brill, Leiden, 1862–1908.

740] Bukhari. *Les traditions islamiques traduites de l'arabe avec notes et index.* Translated by O. Houdas and W. Marçais. Four volumes. Imprimerie nationale, Paris, 1903–14. Publications de "École des langues orientales vivantes," IV ser., t. III–VI.

741] Ibn Hanbal (full name: Abu ᶜAbd Allah Ahmad b. Muhammad b. H.; d. 855). *Musnad al-Imam Aḥmad bn Ḥanbal.* Six volumes. Al-Maimaniyyah Press, Cairo, 1895.

742] Ibn Kathir (full name: Abu 'l-Fida' Ismaᶜil b. ᶜUmar b. K. al-Qurshi al-Dimashqi; d. 1373). *Tafsir al-Qur'an al-ᶜAzim.* Four volumes. Dar Ihya' al-Turath al-ᶜArabi, Beirut, 1969.

743] Ibn Majah (full name: Abu ᶜAbd Allah Muhammad b. Yazid b. M. al-Qazwini; d. 887). *Sunan Abi ᶜAbd Allah Muhammad bn Yazid al-Qazwini ibn Majah.* Edited by Muhammad Fu'ad ᶜAbd al-Baqi. Two volumes. ᶜIsa al-Babi al-Halabi, Cairo, 1952–54.

744] Kisa'i (full name: Muhammad b. ᶜAbd Allah al-K.; date uncertain). *Vita prophetarum, auctore Muhammed ben ᶜAbdallah al-Kisa'i, ex codicibus qui in Monaco, Bonna, Lugd. Batav., Lipsia et Gothana asservaṅtur.* Edited by Isaac Eisenberg. Two volumes. E. J. Brill, Leiden, 1922–23.

745] Kisa'i. *The Tales of the Prophets of al-Kisa'i.* Translated by W. M. Thackston, Jr. Twayne Publishers, 1978.

746] Mahalli (full name: Jalal al-Din Muhammad b. Ahmad al-M.; d. 1459); and Jalal al-Din al-Suyuti (d. 1505). *Qur'an Karim ... bi-Hamish Tafsir al-Imamayn al-Jalilayn.* Edited by ᶜAbd al-ᶜAziz Sayyid al-Ahl (?). Al-Mushahhid al-Husayni Press and Bookseller, Cairo, n.d.

747] Maqdisi (full name: Mutahhar b. Tahir al-M.; fl. 966). *Le livre de la création et de l'histoire de Motahhar ben Tâhir el-Maqdisi. Attribué a Abou-Zéid Ahmed ben Sahl el-Balkhi.* Edited and translated from the Arabic by Cl. Huart. Six volumes. E. Laroux, Paris, 1899–1919. Publications de l'École des langues orientales vivantes, IVe série, vol. XVI–XVIII, XXI–XXIII.

748] Maybudi (full name: Rashid al-Din Ahmad b. Muhammad al-M.; fl. 1126). *Kashf al-Asrar wa-ᶜUddat al-Abrar.* Ten volumes. Teheran, 1952/53–1960/61.

749] Muslim (full name: M. b. al-Hajjaj al-Qushayri; d. 875). *Ṣahih Muslim.* Five volumes. Dar Ihya' al-Kutub al-ᶜArabiyyah, Cairo, 1955–56.

750] Muslim. *Ṣaḥiḥ Muslim: being a translation of the sayings and doings of the prophet Muhammad as narrated by his companions and compiled under the title al-Jamiᶜ-us-ṣaḥiḥ, by Imām Muslim.* Translated by ᶜAbdul Hamid Siddiqi. Four volumes. Sh. Muhammad Ashraf, Lahore, 1971–75.

751] Razi (full name: Fakhr al-Din Muhammad b. ᶜUmar al-R.; d. 1210). *Al-Tafsir al-Kabir.* Thirty-two volumes. Al-Bahiyyah al-Misriyyah, Cairo, 1934–62.
Suyuti (full name: Jalal al-Din ᶜAbd al-Rahman b. Abi Bakr al-S.; d. 1505). See Mahalli [746], Heinen [775].

752] Tabari (full name: Abu Jaᶜfar Muhammad b. Jarir al-T.; d. 923). *Jamiᶜ al-Bayan ᶜan Ta'wil Ay al-Qur'an.* Thirty volumes in twelve. Mustafa al-Babi al-Halabi, Cairo, second edition, 1954.

753] Thaᶜlabi (full name: Ahmad b. Muhammad al-T.; d. 1035). *Qiṣaṣ al-Anbiya'.* 1970.

754] Tirmidhi (full name: Muhammad b. ᶜIsa al-T.; d. 892). *Sunan al-Tirmidhi.* Edited by ᶜIzzat ᶜUbayd al-Daᶜas. Ten volumes in five. Dar al-Daᶜwah, Homs, 1965–69.

755] Zamakhshari (full name: Abu 'l-Qasim Mahmud b. ᶜUmar al-Z.; d. 1144). *Al-Kashshaf ᶜan Haqa'iq al-Tanzil wa-ᶜUyun al-Aqawil Fi Wujuh al-Ta'wil.* Four volumes. Mustafa al-Babi al-Halabi, Cairo, 1966–68.

b) Other

Tor Andrae. *Der Ursprung des Islams und das Christentum.* The volume gives neither publisher nor date. According to the card catalog of the Duke Divinity Library, it is taken from *Kyrkohistorisk arsskrift*, 1923–25. It is paginated 149–292, 45–112.
756] Pages 196–204.
756a] Page 252, footnote.

757] Mahmoud Ayoub. *The Qur'an and Its Interpreters.* Volume I of a projected series. State University of New York Press, 1984.
758] Page 100.
759] Pages 103–105.
760] Page 215.
761] Page 250.

762] David Brady. The Book of Revelation and the Qur'an: Is There a Possible Literary Relationship? page 222. *Journal of Semitic Studies* XXIII(2):216–225, 1978.

763] Siegmund Fraenkel. Miscellen zum Koran. *Zeitschrift der Deutschen Morgenländischen Gesellschaft* 56:71–73, 1902.

764] Helmut Gätje. *The Qur'an and its Exegesis: Selected Texts with Classical and Modern Muslim Interpretations.* Translated from the German and edited by Alford T. Welch. University of California Press, 1976.

765] Page 164.

766] Abraham Geiger. *Judaism and Islam.* Translated from the German by F. M. Young; republished with a prolegomenon by Moshe Pearlman. Ktav Publishing House, 1970. Originally published in 1833, under the title *Was hat Mohammed aus dem Judenthume aufgenommen?*

767] S. D. Goitein. *Jews and Arabs: Their Contacts Through the Ages,* pages 46–61. Schocken Books, third edition, 1974.

768] I. Goldziher. La Misasa. *Revue Africaine* 52:23–28, 1908.

768a] A[lfred] Guillaume. *The Life of Muhammad: A Translation of* [Ibn] *Ishāq's Sīrat Rasūl Allāh,* pages 181–187. Oxford University Press, 1955. Reprinted in Karachi, Pakistan, 1967.

769] Alfred Guillaume. *The Traditions of Islam: An Introduction to the study of the Hadith Literature.* Clarendon Press, Oxford, 1924.

770] David J. Halperin. The Ibn Ṣayyād Traditions and the Legend of al-Dajjāl, pages 213–215. *Journal of the American Oriental Society* 96(2):213–225, 1976.

771] Page 214.

772] Page 217.

773] David J. Halperin and Gordon D. Newby. Two Castrated Bulls: A Study in the Haggadah of Ka'b al-Ahbar. *Journal of the American Oriental Society* 102(4):631–638, 1982.

774] David J. Halperin and Gordon D. Newby. Two Observations on the Cult of the Sakhrah. Paper delivered before the American Oriental Society, Boston, 1981.

775] Anton M. Heinen. *Islamic Cosmology: A study of as-Suyuti's al-Hay'a as-saniya fi l-hay'a as-sunniya, with critical edition, translation, and commentary.* Franz Steiner Verlag, Wiesbaden, 1982. Beiruter Texte und Studien, 27.

776] Josef Horovitz. *Koranische Untersuchungen,* pages 114–115. W. de Gruyter, Berlin and Leipzig, 1926.

777] Arthur Jeffery, editor. *A Reader on Islam: Passages from Standard Arabic Writings Illustrative of the Beliefs and Practices of Muslims,* pages 167–168. Mouton and Company, The Hague, 1962. Columbia University, Publications in Near and Middle East Studies, series A2.

778] Abraham I. Katsh. *Judaism in Islam: Biblical and Talmudic Backgrounds of the Koran and Its Commentaries.* Bloch Publishing Company, 1954.

779] Pages 53–56.

780] M. J. Kister. Haddithū ᶜan banī isrā'īla wa-lā haraja: A Study of an early tradition. *Israel Oriental Studies* II:215–239, 1972.

781] Guy Le Strange. *Palestine Under the Moslems: A Description of Syria and the Holy Land from A.D. 650 to 1500,* page 339. Houghton, Mifflin, 1890.

782] Gordon D. Newby. Abraha and Sennacherib: A Talmudic Parallel to the *Tafsir* on *Surat al-Fil. Journal of the American Oriental Society* 94(4):431–437, 1974.

783] Gordon D. Newby. *The Book of Beginnings: The Reception of Biblical Materials in Early Islam As Seen in the Earliest Biography of Muhammad.* Manuscript.

784] Gordon D. Newby. The Drowned Son: Midrash and Midrash Making in the Qur'an and *Tafsir.* In William M. Brinner and Stephen D. Ricks, editors, *Studies in Islamic and Judaic Traditions,* pages 19–32. Scholars Press, 1986.

785] Gordon D. Newby. Observations About an Early Judaeo-Arabic. *Jewish Quarterly Review* LXI(3):212–221, 1970–71.

786] Gordon D. Newby. The *Sīrah* as a source for Arabian Jewish history: problems and perspectives. *Jerusalem Studies in Arabic and Islam* 7:121–138, 1986.

787] Gordon D. Newby. *Tafsir Isra'iliyat*: The Development of Qur'an Commentary in Early Islam in its Relationship to Judaeo-Christian Traditions of Scriptural Commentary. *Journal of the American Academy of Religion Thematic Issue: Studies in Qur'an and Tafsir* XLVII(4):685–697, 1979.

788] Gordon D. Newby and David J. Halperin. A Ladder to Heaven: Ascension Isomorphs in Rabbinic and Early Islamic Literature. Paper delivered before the American Oriental Society, St. Louis, 1979.

789] Rudi Paret. *Der Koran: Kommentar und Konkordanz.* Kohlhammer, Stuttgart, 1971.

790] Mohammed Marmaduke Pickthall, translator. *The Meaning of the Glorious Koran: An Explanatory Translation.* New American Library, 1953.

791] Colette Sirat. Un midraš juif en habit musulman: la vision de Moïse sur le mont Sinai. *Revue de l'Histoire des Religions* 168:15–28, 1965.

792] Heinrich Speyer. *Die Biblischen Erzählungen im Qoran.* Georg Olms, Hildesheim, third edition, 1971.
    792a] Pages 54–58.
    792b] Pages 323–333.
    792c] Pages 396–398.

793] S. M. Stern. *Studies in Early Ismaᶜilism*, pages 26–29. Magnes Press, Hebrew University, Jerusalem, 1983.

794] Charles Cutler Torrey. *The Jewish Foundation of Islam.* Ktav Publishing House, 1967. With an introduction by Franz Rosenthal. (Originally published, without the introduction, in 1933.)

794a] Geo Widengren. *Muhammad, the Apostle of God, and His Ascension (King and Savior V)*, pages 96–114. Uppsala Universitets Arsskrift 1955:1. Almqvist & Wiksells, Boktryckeri Aktiebolag, Uppsala, 1955. Earlier literature cited in a footnote to page 96.

795] A. S. Yahuda. A Contribution to Qur'ān and Ḥadith Interpretation. In Samuel Löwinger and Joseph Somogyi, editors, *Ignace Goldziher Memorial Volume*, volume I, pages 280–308. Budapest, n.p., 1948.

15. Dictionaries, concordances, other reference works

796] Wilhelm Bacher. *Die Exegetische Terminologie der Jüdischen Traditionsliteratur.* Two volumes. Hinrichs, Leipzig, 1899, 1905.

797] Wilhelm Bacher. *Tradition und Tradenten in der Schulen Palästinas und Babyloniens. Studien und Materialien zur Entstehungsgeschichte des Talmuds.* Edited by L. Blau. W. de Gruyter, Berlin, 1966. Originally published by G. Fock, Leipzig, 1914.
    798] Page 158.

799] Elieser Ben Yehudah, editor. *Thesaurus totius hebraitatis et veteris et recentioris*, volume 8, page 3775. Sixteen volumes. Langenscheidt, Berlin, and Hemda and Benyehuda, Jerusalem, 1908–1959. In Hebrew.

800] André Benoit and others, editors. *Biblia Patristica: Index des Citations et Allusions Bibliques Dans La Littérature Patristique.* Three volumes have so far appeared. Éditions du Centre National de la Recherche Scientifique, Paris, 1975–80.

801] Francis Brown, S. R. Driver, and Charles A. Briggs, editors. *A Hebrew and English Lexicon of the Old Testament, with an Appendix Containing the Biblical Aramaic.* Clarendon, Oxford, 1952. Originally published by Houghton Mifflin, 1891–1906.

801a] Elias A. Elias and Ed. E. Elias. *Elias' Modern Dictionary: Arabic-English.* Elias' Modern Press, Cairo, ninth edition, 1962.

802] N. Halper. *Descriptive Catalogue of Genizah Fragments in Philadelphia*, page 37. Dropsie College, Philadelphia, 1924.

803] Edwin Hatch and Henry A. Redpath, editors. *A Concordance to the Septuagint and the Other Greek Versions of the Old Testament (Including the Apocryphal Books).* Two volumes. Akademische Druck- u. Verlagsanstalt, Graz, Austria, 1954. Originally published by Clarendon Press, Oxford, 1895–1898.

804] Aaron Hyman, editor. *Torah Hakethubah Vehamessurah. A Reference Book of the Scriptural Passages Quoted in Talmudic, Midrashic and Early Rabbinic Literature.* Three volumes. Second edition, revised by Arthur B. Hyman. Dvir, Tel-Aviv, 1979. In Hebrew.

805] Aaron Hyman. *Toldoth Tannaim ve'Amoraim: Comprising the Biographies of All the Rabbis and Other Persons Mentioned in Rabbinic Literature.* Three volumes. Boys Town Jerusalem Publishers, 1964. Originally published in London, 1910. In Hebrew.
    806] Volume I, pages 60–61.
    807] Volume III, page 1146.

808] Marcus Jastrow, editor. *A Dictionary of the Targumim, the Talmud Babli and Yerushalmi, and the Midrashic Literature; with an Index of Scriptural Quotations.* Two volumes. Pardes, 1950. Originally published by G. P. Putnam, and Trübner, London, 1886–1890.

Menachem M. Kasher. *Torah Shelemah: Talmudic-Midrashic Encyclopedia on the Pentateuch; Text with Commentary, "Torah sheb'alpeh."* Twenty-three volumes. Volumes 1 through 7, Jerusalem, 1927–1938. Volumes 8 through 23, American Biblical Encyclopedia Society, 1944–1961. In Hebrew.

809] Volume 19, page 268, note 84.

810] Volume 21, page 90.

810a] Chaim Joshua Kasowski, editor. *'Oṣar ha-Targum: Qonqordanṣiyah le-Targum 'Onqelos* (Concordance to Targum Onkelos). Mosad Harav Kook, Jerusalem, 1940.

811] Chaim Joshua Kasowski, editor. *Thesaurus Talmudis: Concordantiae Verborum, quae in Talmude Babilonica reperiuntur.* Forty-one volumes. Ministry of Education and Culture, Government of Israel, and the Jewish Theological Seminary of America, 1954–82. In Hebrew.

812] Alexander Kohut, editor. *Aruch completum; sive Lexicon vocabula et res, quae in libris Targumicis, Talmudicis et Midraschicis continentur, explicans auctore Nathane filio Jechielis.* Eight volumes. G. Brög, A. Fanto, Vienna, 1878–1892. In Hebrew. Original text by Nathan b. Jehiel of Rome (eleventh century); additional notes by Benjamin Moussafia (seventeenth century) and by Kohut himself.

813] Volume 2, page 29.

814] Biniamin Kosowsky, editor. *Thesaurus Nominum Quae in Talmude Babylonico Reperiuntur.* Five volumes. Ministry of Education and Culture, Government of Israel, and the Jewish Theological Seminary of America, 1976–1983. In Hebrew.

Samuel Krauss. *Griechische und Lateinische Lehnwörter in Talmud, Midrasch und Targum.* Two volumes, S. Calvary and Co., Berlin, 1891–1899. Contains additional notes by Immanuel Löw.

815] Volume II, page 117.

816] Volume II, pages 260, 564–565.

817] Jacob Levy, editor. *Chaldäisches Wörterbuch über die Targumim und einer grossen Theil des Rabbinischen Schrifthums.* J. Melzer, Cologne, 1959. Originally published by G. Engel, Leipzig, 1866.

818] Jacob Levy, editor. *Wörterbuch über die Talmudim und Midraschim.* Wissenschaftliche Buchgesellschaft, Darmstadt, 1963. Originally published by F. A. Brockhaus, Leipzig, 1876–1889.

818a] Otto Michel. οἰκονομος, οἰκονομια. In Gerhard Kittel and Gerhard Friedrich, editors, *Theological Dictionary of the New Testament*, volume V, pages 149–153. Ten volumes. Translated from the German and edited by Geoffrey W. Bromiley. Wm B. Eerdmans, 1964–76.

819] Raphael Rabbinowicz. *Diqduqe Soferim: Variae Lectiones in Mischnam et in Talmud Babylonicum.* Two volumes. M. P. Press, New York, 1976. Originally published in fifteen volumes in Munich, 1868–1886. In Hebrew.

820] Gershom G. Scholem. *Kitve Yad ha-ᶜIbriyyim, ha-Nimṣa'im be-Bet ha-Sefarim ha-Le'umi we-ha-Universiṭa'i birushalayim* (The Hebrew Manuscripts in the National and University Library, Jerusalem, volume I, page 95). Assisted by Issachar Joel. Hebrew University, Jerusalem, 1930. Special supplement to *Kiryat-Sefer*, 7.

821] *Sharḥ al-Qamus al-Musamma Taj al-ᶜArus min Jawahir al-Qamus.* Ten volumes. Al-Maṭbaᶜah al-Khayriyyah, Cairo, 1888–90.

Stith Thompson. *Motif Index of Folk-Literature: A Classification of Narrative Elements in Folk-Tales, Ballads, Myths, Fables, Mediaeval Romances, Exempla, Jest-Books, and Local Legends.* Six volumes. Indiana University Studies XIX–XXIII (96, 97, 100, 101, 105, 106, 108–112), June 1932–June 1936, and *FF Communications*, 106–109, 116, 117, 1932–1936.

822] Sections B120–B169 (esp. B133.1, B141.4), B733, E421.1.

823] Section J1791.

824] Yosef Umanski. *Ḥakhame ha-Talmud* (The Sages of the Talmud: a List of all the Tannaim and Amoraim Mentioned in the Palestinian Talmud, in Alphabetical Order, with a Listing of All the Places Where Their Names Appear). Mossad Harav Kook, Jerusalem, 1952.

16. Miscellaneous

825] Gray Barker. *They Knew Too Much About Flying Saucers*, pages 160–165. University Books, 1956. A modern variant of the belief in spirit-sighted animals (Krappe [843]).

826] Bruno Bettelheim. *The Uses of Enchantment: The Meaning and Importance of Fairy Tales.* Random House, 1977.

827] Page 27.

       828] Pages 183–194.

829] David Biale. *Gershom Scholem: Kabbalah and counter-history*. Harvard University Press, second edition, 1982.

830] Mary Ellen Chase. *A Goodly Heritage*, pages 140–141. H. Holt, 1932.

831] Avis M. Dry. *The Psychology of Jung: A Critical Interpretation*, pages 203–208. Wiley, and Methuen, London, 1961.

832] Erik H. Erikson. *Childhood and Society*, pages 97–108. W. W. Norton, second edition, 1963.

833] Erik H. Erikson. Sex Differences in the Play Configurations of American Adolescents. In Margaret Mead and Martha Wolfenstein, editors, *Childhood in Contemporary Cultures*, pages 324–341. University of Chicago Press, 1955.

834] Sigmund Freud. *The Interpretation of Dreams*. Translated from the German and edited by James Strachey. Avon Books, 1965.

       835] Pages 234–235.
       836] Page 443.
       837] Page 564.

837a] Sigmund Freud. Medusa's Head. In volume XVIII of James Strachey, editor, *The Standard Edition of the Complete Psychological Works of Sigmund Freud*, pages 273–274. Hogarth Press, London, 1955.

837b] Sigmund Freud. *Three Case Histories*, pages 281–282. Translated from the German. Edited by Philip Rieff. Collier Books, 1963.

837c] Ernest Jones. *The Life and Work of Sigmund Freud*. Volume 3: *The Last Phase: 1919–1939*, page 381. Basic Books, 1957.

838] Carl Gustav Jung. *The Collected Works*. Nineteen volumes + index volume. Edited by Herbert Read and others. Translated by R. F. C. Hull and others. Pantheon Books, 1953–1967. Princeton University Press, 1967–1978. Bollingen Series, XX.

839] Carl Gustav Jung. *Jung and Religious Belief*, paragraphs 1599–1618. Translated by R. F. C. Hull. In *The Collected Works* [838], volume XVIII: *The Symbolic Life; Miscellaneous Writings*, paragraphs 1584–1690.

840] Carl Gustav Jung. *A Psychological Approach to the Dogma of the Trinity*, paragraphs 243–285 (=chapter 5). Translated by R. F. C. Hull. In *The Collected Works* [838], volume XI: *Psychology and Religion, West and East*, paragraphs 169–295.

841] Carl Gustav Jung. *Psychology and Religion*, paragraphs 103–107 (=end of chapter 2). In *The Collected Works* [838], volume XI, paragraphs 1–168. Originally written in English, and published, as The Terry Lectures of 1937, by Yale University Press and Oxford University Press, 1938.

842] G. Kauffman. Antipodes, volume I, pages 2531–2533. In Georg Wissowa, editor, *Paulys Real-Encyclopädie der Classischen Altertumswissenschaft*. J. B. Metzlerscher Verlag, Stuttgart, 1894–.

843] Alexander H. Krappe. Spirit-Sighted Animals. *Folk-Lore* LIV(4):391–401, 1943.

844] John McDonald, editor and translator. *Memar Marqah – The Teaching of Marqah*, volume 1, pages 103–104, volume 2, pages 172–173. Two volumes. A. Töpelmann, Berlin, 1963. Beihefte zur Zeitschrift für die alttestamentliche Wissenschaft, 84.

845] Ruth Mellinkoff. *The Horned Moses in Medieval Art and Thought*. University of California Press, 1970.

846] Donald H. Menzel. *Flying Saucers*. Harvard University Press, 1953. The author, an astrophysicist, conjectures that Ezekiel saw an atmospheric phenomenon called "sundogs."

847] Flannery O'Connor. *Three: Wise Blood, A Good Man is Hard to Find, The Violent Bear It Away*, page 314. New American Library, 1964.

848] Arthur W. Orton. The Four-Faced Visitors of Ezekiel. *Analog Science Fact-Fiction* LXVII (1):99–115, March 1961. A methodical and ingenious argument that Ezekiel 1 "is the account of an actual happening; the landing of extraterrestrial beings, reported by a careful, truthful and self-possessed observer" (page 100).

848a] George Orwell. *A Clergyman's Daughter*, chapter IV, section VI. Avon Books, n.d. Originally published 1935.

849] Rudolf Otto. *The Idea of the Holy: An Inquiry into the non-rational factor in the idea of the divine and its relation to the rational*. Translated from the German by John W. Harvey. Oxford University Press, second edition, 1950.

       850] Page 106, footnote.

851] Carl Sagan. *The Cosmic Connection: An Extraterrestrial Perspective*, pages 92–93. Produced by Jerome Agel. Anchor Press, 1973.

852]   Leo W. Schwarz, editor. *The Jewish Caravan: Great stories of twenty-five centuries*, pages 320–321. Farrar and Rinehart, 1935.

852a] Irwin and Fred Silber, compilers. *Folksinger's Workbook: Words to Over 1,000 Songs*, page 357. Oak Publications, 1973.

853]   Philip E. Slater. *The Glory of Hera: Greek Mythology and the Greek Family*. Beacon Press, 1968.

      854]   Pages 316–318.

      855]   Pages 395–396.

856]   Melford E. Spiro. *Oedipus in the Trobriands*, pages 113–140. University of Chicago Press, 1982.

857]   Alfred Stapleton. *All About the Merry Tales of Gotham*, pages 32–33, 176. Norwood editions, 1976. Originally published by R. N. Pearson, Nottingham, 1900.

858]   Milton Steinberg. *As a Driven Leaf*. Bobbs-Merrill and Behrman House, 1939.

859]   Ronald Story. *The space-gods revealed: a close look at the theories of Erich von Däniken*. Harper & Row, 1976.

859a] R. Campbell Thompson. *Semitic Magic: Its Origins and Development*. Reprinted by Ktav Publishing House, 1971. Originally published 1908. See the index, under "Dust."

860]   Mary-Claire van Leunen. *A Handbook for Scholars*. Alfred A. Knopf, 1978.

861]   Heinz Westman. *The Springs of Creativity*. Atheneum, and Routledge and Paul, London, 1961.

Indexes

I. Citations

A. Bible (including LXX, Targums, Targumic Tosefta)

B. Apocrypha and Pseudepigrapha

C. New Testament

D. Mishnah

E. Tosefta

Sukkah
3:3–10	197, 495
3:11	395

Megillah
3(4):1–9	18, 24
3(4):28	12–13, 19, 36
3(4):31–38	20, 22, 184
3(4):36	21
3(4):37	22
3(4):41	527

Ḥagigah
2:1	13–19, 188
2:2	29

2:3–4	29, 31–32, 36, 204
2:5	29
2:6	29, 236
2:7	30

Soṭah
3:19	320
5:9	165

Baba Qamma
7:9	157

Hullin
2:23	33

F. Palestinian Talmud

Berakhot
1:1 (2c)	133, 150–151, 155, 266, 271, 470, 495, 499, 526
1:2 (3c)	217
2:9 (5d)	166
5:1 (9a)	345
9:1 (13a)	133, 271, 470, 499, 526
9:2 (13d)	254, 256
9:5 (14b)	34

Shabbat
16:1 (15c)	310–311, 436

Yoma
1:5 (39a)	82, 524
5:2 (42c)	82

Sukkah
4:6 (54d)	82

Rosh Hashanah
2:4 (58a)	84
3:2 (58d)	161, 529

Ta‘anit
4:8 (68d)	197

Megillah
4:5 (75b)	149
4:11 (75c)	21

Ḥagigah
2:1 (77a–b)	29
(77a)	4, 13–19, 149, 257
(77b–c)	31
(77b)	17, 30–32, 35, 194, 202–205
2:2 (78a)	236

Soṭah
1:7 (17a)	165
7:1 (21b)	346
8:3 (22b)	498

Qiddushin
4:4 (65d)	166

Baba Batra
5:1 (15a)	166

Sanhedrin
6:6 (23c)	236

Shebu‘ot
6:5 (37a)	151, 152, 155

G. Babylonian Talmud

Berakhot
6b	223
10b	130, 150
59a	130, 253, 255, 529
61b	33, 166

Shabbat
13b	27, 523
30b	523

88a	143, 157, 321
88b–89a	298–312, 316
88b	17, 317, 333, 414, 424
89a	419, 424, 520
89b	157

‘Erubin
19a	236
26a	435

H. Tannaitic Midrashim

I. Midrash Rabbah

J. Other Midrashim (arranged alphabetically)

See also Index VI: *Leqaḥ Ṭob; Midrash Konen; Yalquṭ*

K. Origen

L. Hekhalot

Passages are listed according to the paragraphs of Schäfer's *Synopse.* Corresponding chapter numbers of Odeberg's *3 Enoch* and Wertheimer's *Hekhalot Rabbati,* and paragraph numbers of Scholem's *Ma^{c}aséh Merkabah,* are given in parentheses.

M. Islamic Sources

II. Foreign Words

Hebrew verbs are alphabetized according to the consonants of the root. The Hebrew definite article (*ha-*) is not considered in the alphabetizing of nouns.

III. Modern Authors

IV. Tannaim and Amoraim

V. Divine Names, Angels, Demons

VI. General